TExES Science 7 -
236 Teacher Certification Exam

By: Sharon Wynne, M.S.

XAMonline, INC.

Boston

XAMonline, Inc.
21 Orient Avenue
Melrose, MA 02176
Toll Free 1-800-301-4647
Email: info@xamonline.com
Web www.xamonline.com
Fax: 1-617-583-5552

Library of Congress Cataloging-in-Publication Data

Wynne, Sharon A.
    Science 7-12 236: Teacher Certification / Sharon A. Wynne.
    ISBN 978-1-60787-375-4
    1. Science 7-12 236.   2. Study Guides.   3. TExES
    4. Teachers' Certification & Licensure.   5. Careers

Disclaimer:
The opinions expressed in this publication are the sole works of XAMonline and were created independently from the National Education Association, Educational Testing Service, or any State Department of Education, National Evaluation Systems or other testing affiliates.

Between the time of publication and printing, state specific standards as well as testing formats and website information may change that is not included in part or in whole within this product. Sample test questions are developed by XAMonline and reflect similar content as on real tests; however, they are not former tests. XAMonline assembles content that aligns with state standards but makes no claims nor guarantees teacher candidates a passing score. Numerical scores are determined by testing companies such as NES or ETS and then are compared with individual state standards. A passing score varies from state to state.

Printed in the United States of America

TExES Science 7-12 236
ISBN: 978-1-60787-375-4

Table of Contents

<u>DOMAIN I.</u>   <u>SCIENTIFIC INQUIRY AND PROCESSES</u>

Competency 0001   **The teacher understands how to collect and manage learning activities to ensure the safety of all students and the correct use and care of organisms, natural resources, materials, equipment, and technologies.**

DOMAIN IV.   CELL STRUCTURE AND PROCESSES

Competency 0021   **The teacher understands the structure and function of biomolecules.**

Competency 0022   **The teacher understands that cells are the basic structures of living things and have specialized parts that perform specific functions.**

DOMAIN V.   HEREDITY AND EVOLUTION OF LIFE

Competency 0025   **The teacher understands the structures and functions of nucleic acids in the mechanisms of genetics.**

Competency 0026   **The teacher understands the continuity and variations of traits from one generation to the next.**

DOMAIN VI.   DIVERSITY OF LIFE

Competency 0032   **The teacher understands the relationship between biology and behavior.**

DOMAIN VII.   **LIFE AND ENVIRONMENTAL SYSTEMS**

Competency 0033   **The teacher understands the relationships between abiotic and biotic factors of terrestrial and aquatic ecosystems, habitats, and biomes, including the flow of matter and energy.**

Competency 0043   **The teacher understands the role of the sun in the solar system and the characteristics of planets and other objects that orbit the sun.**

Competency 0044   **The teacher understands composition, history, and properties of the universe.**

Competency 0045   The teacher understands the history and methods of astronomy.

DOMAIN X.   **SCIENCE LEARNING, INSTRUCTION, AND ASSESSMENT**

Great Study and Testing Tips!

What to study in order to prepare for the subject assessments is the focus of this study guide but equally important is *how* you study.

You can increase your chances of truly mastering the information by taking some simple, but effective steps.

Study Tips:

1. Some foods aid the learning process. Foods such as milk, nuts, seeds, rice, and oats help your study efforts by releasing natural memory enhancers called CCKs (*cholecystokinin*) composed of *tryptophan*, *choline*, and *phenylalanine*. All of these chemicals enhance the neurotransmitters associated with memory. Before studying, try a light, protein-rich meal of eggs, turkey, and fish. All of these foods release the memory enhancing chemicals. The better the connections, the more you comprehend.

Likewise, before you take a test, stick to a light snack of energy boosting and relaxing foods. A glass of milk, a piece of fruit, or some peanuts all release various memory-boosting chemicals and help you to relax and focus on the subject at hand.

2. Learn to take great notes. A by-product of our modern culture is that we have grown accustomed to getting our information in short doses (i.e. TV news sound bites or USA Today style newspaper articles.)

Consequently, we've subconsciously trained ourselves to assimilate information better in neat little packages. If your notes are scrawled all over the paper, it fragments the flow of the information. Strive for clarity. Newspapers use a standard format to achieve clarity. Your notes can be much clearer through use of proper formatting. A very effective format is called the *"Cornell Method."*

> Take a sheet of loose-leaf lined notebook paper and draw a line all the way down the paper about 1-2" from the left-hand edge.

> Draw another line across the width of the paper about 1-2" up from the bottom. Repeat this process on the reverse side of the page.

Look at the highly effective result. You have ample room for notes, a left hand margin for special emphasis items or inserting supplementary data from the textbook, a large area at the bottom for a brief summary, and a little rectangular space for just about anything you want.

3. Get the concept then the details. Too often we focus on the details and don't gather an understanding of the concept. However, if you simply memorize only dates, places, or names, you may well miss the whole point of the subject.

A key way to understand things is to put them in your own words. If you are working from a textbook, automatically summarize each paragraph in your mind. If you are outlining text, don't simply copy the author's words.

Rephrase them in your own words. You remember your own thoughts and words much better than someone else's, and subconsciously tend to associate the important details to the core concepts.

4. Ask Why? Pull apart written material paragraph by paragraph and don't forget the captions under the illustrations.

Example: If the heading is "Stream Erosion", flip it around to read "Why do streams erode?" Then answer the questions.

If you train your mind to think in a series of questions and answers, not only will you learn more, but it also helps to lessen the test anxiety because you are used to answering questions.

5. Read for reinforcement and future needs. Even if you only have 10 minutes, put your notes or a book in your hand. Your mind is similar to a computer; you have to input data in order to have it processed. *By reading, you are creating the neural connections for future retrieval.* The more times you read something, the more you reinforce the learning of ideas.

Even if you don't fully understand something on the first pass, *your mind stores much of the material for later recall.*

6. Relax to learn so go into exile. Our bodies respond to an inner clock called biorhythms. Burning the midnight oil works well for some people, but not everyone.

If possible, set aside a particular place to study that is free of distractions. Shut off the television, cell phone, and pager and exile your friends and family during your study period.

If you really are bothered by silence, try background music. Light classical music at a low volume has been shown to aid in concentration over other types. Music that evokes pleasant emotions without lyrics is highly suggested. Try just about anything by Mozart. It relaxes you.

7. **Use arrows not highlighters.** At best, it's difficult to read a page full of yellow, pink, blue, and green streaks. Try staring at a neon sign for a while and you'll soon see that the horde of colors obscure the message.

A quick note, a brief dash of color, an underline, and an arrow pointing to a particular passage is much clearer than a horde of highlighted words.

8. **Budget your study time.** Although you shouldn't ignore any of the material, *allocate your available study time in the same ratio that topics may appear on the test.*

Testing Tips:

1. Get smart, play dumb. Don't read anything into the question. Don't make an assumption that the test writer is looking for something else than what is asked. Stick to the question as written and don't read extra things into it.

2. Read the question and all the choices *twice* before answering the question. You may miss something by not carefully reading, and then re-reading both the question and the answers.

If you really don't have a clue as to the right answer, leave it blank on the first time through. Go on to the other questions, as they may provide a clue as to how to answer the skipped questions.

If later on, you still can't answer the skipped ones . . . *Guess.* The only penalty for guessing is that you *might* get it wrong. Only one thing is certain; if you don't put anything down, you will get it wrong!

3. Turn the question into a statement. Look at the way the questions are worded. The syntax of the question usually provides a clue. Does it seem more familiar as a statement rather than as a question? Does it sound strange?

By turning a question into a statement, you may be able to spot if an answer sounds right, and it may also trigger memories of material you have read.

4. Look for hidden clues. It's actually very difficult to compose multiple-foil (choice) questions without giving away part of the answer in the options presented.

In most multiple-choice questions you can often readily eliminate one or two of the potential answers. This leaves you with only two real possibilities and automatically your odds go to Fifty-Fifty for very little work.

5. Trust your instincts. For every fact that you have read, you subconsciously retain something of that knowledge. On questions that you aren't really certain about, go with your basic instincts. **Your first impression on how to answer a question is usually correct.**

6. Mark your answers directly on the test booklet. Don't bother trying to fill in the optical scan sheet on the first pass through the test.

Just be very careful not to miss-mark your answers when you eventually transcribe them to the scan sheet.

7. Watch the clock! You have a set amount of time to answer the questions. Don't get bogged down trying to answer a single question at the expense of 10 questions you can more readily answer.

DOMAIN I.	SCIENTIFIC INQUIRY AND PROCESSES

Competency 0001   **The teacher understands how to collect and manage learning activities to ensure the safety of all students and the correct use and care of organisms, natural resources, materials, equipment, and technologies.**

Skill 1.1   **The beginning teacher uses current sources of information about laboratory safety, including safety regulations and guidelines for the use of science facilities.**

All science labs should contain the following items of safety equipment. The following are requirements by law.

- Fire blanket which is visible and accessible
- Ground Fault Circuit Interrupters (GFCI) within two feet of water supplies
- Emergency shower capable of providing a continuous flow of water
- Signs designating room exits
- Emergency eye wash station which can be activated by the foot or forearm
- Eye protection for every student and a means of sanitizing equipment
- Emergency exhaust fans providing ventilation to the outside of the building
- Master cut-off switches for gas, electric, and compressed air. Switches must have permanently attached handles. Cut-off switches must be clearly labeled.
- An ABC fire extinguisher
- Storage cabinets for flammable materials

Also recommended, but not required by law:

- Chemical spill control kit
- Fume hood with a motor which is spark proof
- Protective laboratory aprons made of flame retardant material
- Signs which will alert people to potential hazardous conditions
- Containers for broken glassware, flammables, corrosives, and waste.
- Containers should be labeled.

It is the responsibility of teachers to provide a safe environment for their students. Proper supervision greatly reduces the risk of injury and a teacher should never leave a class for any reason without providing alternate supervision. After an accident, two factors are considered; foreseeability and negligence.

Foreseeability is the anticipation that an event may occur under certain circumstances. **Negligence** is the failure to exercise ordinary or reasonable care. It is best for a teacher to meet all special requirements for disabled students, and to be good at supervising large groups. However, if a teacher can prove that s/he has done a reasonable job to ensure a safe and effective learning environment, then it is unlikely that she/he would be found negligent. Safety procedures should be a part of the science curriculum and a well managed classroom is important to avoid potential lawsuits

The **"Right to Know Law" statutes** cover science teachers who work with potentially hazardous chemicals. Briefly, the law states that employees must be informed of potentially toxic chemicals. An inventory must be made available if requested. The inventory must contain information about the hazards and properties of the chemicals. Training must be provided in the safe handling and interpretation of the Material Safety Data Sheet.

Skill 1.2   **The beginning teacher recognizes potential safety hazards in the laboratory and in the field and knows how to apply procedures, including basic first aid, for responding to accidents.**

Safety in the science classroom and laboratory is of paramount importance to the science educator. The following is a general summary of the types of safety equipment that should be made available within a given school system as well as general locations where the protective equipment or devices should be maintained and used. Please note that this is only a partial list and that your school system should be reviewed for unique hazards and site-specific hazards at each facility.

The key to maintaining a safe learning environment is through proactive training and regular in-service updates for all staff and students who utilize the science laboratory. Proactive training should include how to **identify potential hazards**, **evaluate potential hazards**, and **how to prevent or respond to hazards**.

The following types of training should be considered:

a) Right to Know, OSHA, properly recognizing and safely working with hazardous materials, chemical hygiene, and MSDS trainings
b) Instruction in how to use a fire extinguisher
c) Instruction in how to use a chemical fume hood
d) General guidance in when and how to use personal protective equipment (e.g. safety glasses or gloves)
e) Instruction in how to monitor activities for potential impacts on indoor air quality.

It is also important for the instructor to utilize **Material Data Safety Sheets**. Maintain a copy of the material safety data sheet for every item in your chemical inventory. This information will assist you in determining how to store and handle your materials by outlining the health and safety hazards posed by the substance. In most cases the manufacturer will provide recommendations with regard to protective equipment, ventilation and storage practices. This information should be your first guide when considering the use of a new material.

Frequent monitoring and in-service training on all equipment, materials, and procedures will help to ensure a safe and orderly laboratory environment. It will also provide everyone who uses the laboratory the safety fundamentals necessary to discern a safety hazard and to respond appropriately.

Skill 1.3   The beginning teacher employs safe practices in planning and implementing all instructional activities and designs, and implements rules and procedures to maintain a safe learning environment.

With appropriate planning and training, the maintenance of safe practices and procedures in areas of science instruction becomes integrated with the procedures for instruction and laboratory investigation. Safety procedures should be taught early and emphasized often to maintain a high level of safety awareness.

Safety Equipment

- Keep appropriate safety equipment on hand, including an emergency shower, eye-wash station, fume hood, fire blankets, and fire extinguisher. All students and teacher(s) should have and wear safety goggles and protective aprons when working in the lab.

- Ensure proper eye protection devices are worn by everyone engaged in supervising, observing, or conducting science activities involving potential hazards to the eye.

- Provide protective rubber or latex gloves for students when they dissect laboratory specimens.

- Use heat-safety items such as safety tongs, mittens, and aprons when handling either cold or hot materials.

- Use safety shields or screens whenever there is potential danger that an explosion or implosion might occur. Keep a bucket of 90 percent sand and 10 percent vermicullite or kitty litter (dried bentonite particles) in all rooms in which chemicals are handled or stored. The bucket must be properly labeled and have a lid that prevents other debris from contaminating the contents.

Teaching Procedures

- Set a good example when demonstrating experiments by modeling safety techniques such as wearing aprons and goggles.

- Help students develop a positive attitude toward safety. Students should not fear doing experiments or using reagents or equipment, but they should respect them for potential hazards.

- Always demonstrate procedures before allowing students to begin the activity. Look for possible hazards and alert students to potential dangers.

- Explain and post safety instructions each time you do an experiment.

- Maintain constant supervision of student activities. Never allow students to perform unauthorized experiments or conduct experiments in the laboratory alone.

- Protect all laboratory animals and ensure that they are treated humanely.

- Remind students that many plants have poisonous parts and should be handled with care.

- For safety, consider the National Science Teachers Association's recommendation to limit science classes to 24 or fewer students.

Student Safety Tips

- Read lab materials in advance. Note all cautions (written and oral).

- Never assume an experiment is safe just because it is in print.

- Do not eat or drink in the laboratory.

- Keep personal items off the lab tables.

- Restrain long hair and loose clothing. Wear laboratory aprons when appropriate.

- Avoid all rough play and mischief in science classrooms or labs.

- Wear closed-toed shoes when conducting experiments with liquids or with heated or heavy items.

- Never use mouth suction when filling pipettes with chemical reagents.

- Never force glass tubing into rubber stoppers.

- Avoid transferring chemicals to your face, hands, or other areas of exposed skin.

- Thoroughly clean all work surfaces and equipment after each use.

- Make certain all hot plates and burners are turned off before leaving the laboratory.

Lab Environment

- Place smoke, carbon monoxide, and heat detectors in laboratories and storerooms.

- Ensure that all new laboratories have two unobstructed exits. Consider adding additional exits to rooms with only one door.

- Frequently inspect a laboratory's electrical, gas, and water systems.

- Install ground fault circuit interrupters at all electrical outlets in science laboratories.

- Install a single central shut-off for gas, electricity, and water for all the laboratories in the school, especially if your school is in an earthquake zone.

- Maintain Material Safety Data Sheets (MSDS) on all school chemicals and an inventory of all science equipment.

- Conduct frequent laboratory inspections and an annual, verified safety check of each laboratory.

Skill 1.4 **The beginning teacher understands procedures for selecting, maintaining, and safely using chemicals, tools, technologies, materials, specimens, and equipment, including procedures for the recycling, reuse, and conservation of laboratory resources and for the safe handling and ethical treatment of organisms.**

Safety goggles are the single most important piece of safety equipment in the laboratory, and should be used any time a scientist is using glassware, heat, or chemicals. Other equipment (e.g. tongs, gloves, or even a buret stand) has its place for various applications. However, the most important is safety goggles.

All laboratory solutions should be prepared as directed in the lab manual. Care should be taken to avoid contamination. All glassware should be rinsed thoroughly with distilled water before using, and cleaned well after use. Safety goggles should be worn while working with glassware in case of an accident. All solutions should be made with distilled water as tap water contains dissolved particles which may affect the results of an experiment. Chemical storage should be located in a secured, dry area. Chemicals should be stored in accordance with reactability. Acids are to be locked in a separate area. Used solutions should be disposed of according to local disposal procedures. Any questions regarding safe disposal or chemical safety may be directed to the local fire department.

The following chemicals are potential carcinogens and are not allowed in school facilities:

Acrylonitriel, Arsenic compounds, Asbestos, Bensidine, Benzene, Cadmium compounds, Chloroform, Chromium compounds, Ethylene oxide, Ortho-toluidine, Nickel powder, Mercury.

Dissections - Animals which are not obtained from recognized sources should not be used. Decaying animals or those of unknown origin may harbor pathogens and/or parasites. Specimens should be rinsed before handling. Latex gloves are desirable. If gloves are not available, students with sores or scratches should be excused from the activity. Formaldehyde is a carcinogen and should be avoided or disposed of according to district regulations. Students objecting to dissections for moral reasons should be given an alternative assignment.

Live specimens - No dissections may be performed on living mammalian vertebrates or birds. Lower order life and invertebrates may be used. Biological experiments may be done with all animals except mammalian vertebrates or birds. No physiological harm may result to the animal. All animals housed and cared for in the school must be handled in a safe and humane manner. Animals are not to remain on school premises during extended vacations unless adequate care is provided. Many state laws stipulate that any instructor who intentionally refuses to comply with the laws may be suspended or dismissed.

Microbiology - Pathogenic organisms must never be used for experimentation. Students should adhere to the following rules at all times when working with microorganisms to avoid accidental contamination:

1. Treat all microorganisms as if they were pathogenic.
2. Maintain sterile conditions at all times

Skill 1.5 **The beginning teacher knows how to use appropriate equipment and technology (e.g., Internet, spreadsheet, calculator) for gathering, organizing, displaying, and communicating data in a variety of ways (e.g., charts, tables, graphs, diagrams, written reports, oral presentations).**

Scientists use a variety of tools and technologies to perform tests, collect and display data, and analyze relationships. Examples of commonly used tools include computer-linked probes, spreadsheets, and graphing calculators.

Scientists use computer-linked probes to measure various environmental factors including temperature, dissolved oxygen, pH, ionic concentration, and pressure. The advantage of computer-linked probes, as compared to more traditional observational tools, is that the probes automatically gather data and present it in an accessible format. This property of computer-linked probes eliminates the need for constant human observation and manipulation.

Scientists use spreadsheets to organize, analyze, and display data. For example, conservation ecologists use spreadsheets to model population growth and development, apply sampling techniques, and create statistical distributions to analyze relationships. Spreadsheet use simplifies data collection and manipulation and allows the presentation of data in a logical and understandable format.

Graphing calculators are another technology with many applications to biology. For example, biologists use algebraic functions to analyze growth, development and other natural processes. Graphing calculators can manipulate algebraic data and create graphs for analysis and observation. In addition, biologists use the matrix function of graphing calculators to model problems in genetics. The use of graphing calculators simplifies the creation of graphical displays including histograms, scatter plots, and line graphs. Biologists can also transfer data and displays to computers for further analysis. Scientists connect computer-linked probes, used to collect data, to graphing calculators to ease the collection, transmission, and analysis of data.

Classifying is grouping items according to their similarities. It is important for students to realize relationships and similarity as well as differences to reach a reasonable conclusion in a lab experience.

Graphing is an important skill to visually display collected data for analysis. The two types of graphs most commonly used are the **line graph** and the **bar graph** (histogram). Line graphs are set up to show two variables represented by one point on the graph. The X axis is the horizontal axis and represents the dependent variable. Dependent variables are those that would be present independently of the experiment. A common example of a dependent variable is time. Time proceeds regardless of anything else occurring. The Y axis is the vertical axis and represents the independent variable. Independent variables are manipulated by the experiment, such as the amount of light, or the height of a plant. Graphs should be calibrated at equal intervals. If one space represents one day, the next space may not represent ten days. A "best fit" line is drawn to join the points and may not include all the points in the data. Axes must always be labeled, for the graph to be meaningful. A good title will describe both the dependent and the independent variable. Bar graphs are set up similarly in regards to axes, but points are not plotted. Instead, the dependent variable is set up as a bar where the X axis intersects with the Y axis. Each bar is a separate item of data and is not joined by a continuous line.

Normally, knowledge is integrated in the form of a **lab report**. A report has many sections. It should include a specific **title** and tell exactly what is being studied. The **abstract** is a summary of the report written at the beginning of the paper. The **purpose** should always be defined and will state the problem. The purpose should include the **hypothesis** (educated guess) of what is expected from the outcome of the experiment. The entire experiment should relate to this problem. It is important to describe exactly what was done to prove or disprove a hypothesis. A **control** is necessary to prove that the results occurred from the changed conditions and would not have happened normally. Only one variable should be manipulated at a time. **Observations** and **results** of the experiment should be recorded including all results from data. Drawings, graphs and illustrations should be included to support information. Observations are objective, whereas analysis and interpretation is subjective. A **conclusion** should explain why the results of the experiment either proved or disproved the hypothesis.

Skill 1.6   The beginning teacher understands how to use a variety of tools, techniques, and technology to gather, organize, and analyze data and how to apply appropriate methods of statistical measures and analysis.

Scientists use a variety of tools and technologies to perform tests, collect and display data, and analyze relationships. Examples of commonly used tools include computer-linked probes, spreadsheets, and graphing calculators.

Scientists use computer-linked probes to measure various environmental factors including temperature, dissolved oxygen, pH, ionic concentration, and pressure. The advantage of computer-linked probes, as compared to more traditional observational tools, is that the probes automatically gather data and present it in an accessible format. This property of computer-linked probes eliminates the need for constant human observation and manipulation.

Scientists use spreadsheets to organize, analyze, and display data. For example, conservation ecologists use spreadsheets to model population growth and development, apply sampling techniques, and create statistical distributions to analyze relationships. Spreadsheet use simplifies data collection and manipulation and allows the presentation of data in a logical and understandable format.

Graphing calculators are another technology with many applications to science. For example, scientists use algebraic functions to analyze growth, development and other natural processes. Graphing calculators can manipulate algebraic data and create graphs for analysis and observation. In addition, biologists use the matrix function of graphing calculators to model problems in genetics. The use of graphing calculators simplifies the creation of graphical displays including histograms, scatter plots, and line graphs. Scientists can also transfer data and displays to computers for further analysis. Finally, scientists connect computer-linked probes, used to collect data, to graphing calculators to ease the collection, transmission, and analysis of data.

Graphical models combine probability theory and graph theory to provide a natural tool for dealing with uncertainty and complexity, two major issues in applied mathematics and science. This type of model may provide the user with a visual representation of dependencies and correlations among random variables, or a computer generated and easily manipulated representation of a system to be studied. A computer aided design (CAD) system can be used to generate graphical models of 2- or 3-dimensional objects. These programs are designed to allow variable input dimensions, enabling graphic models to represent moving parts, to portray various scenarios and to provide the option of interaction between operator and model. Quantitative data, such as geometry and dimension observations, are entered into such programs by the operator through standard input means including keyboards, graphic tablets, etc. Following data entry, models and drawings are plotted according to the CAD's particular analysis method and purpose.

Care of microscopes

Light microscopes are commonly used in high school laboratory experiments. Total magnification is determined by multiplying the ocular (usually 10X) and the objective (usually 10X on low, 40X on high) lenses. A few steps should be followed to properly care for this equipment.

- Clean all lenses with lens paper only.
- Carry microscopes with two hands, one on the arm and one on the base.
- Always begin focusing on low power, then switch to high power.
- Store microscopes with the low power objective down.
- Always use a cover slip when viewing wet mount slides.
- Bring the objective down to its lowest position then focus moving up to avoid the slide from breaking or scratching.

Preparation of laboratory solutions

This is a critical skill needed for any experimental success. The procedure for making solutions must be followed to get maximum accuracy.

i)   weigh out the required amount of each solute
ii)   dissolve the solute in less than the total desired volume (about 75%)
iii)   add enough solvent to get the desired volume

1. Weight/volume:
Usually expressed as mg/ml for small amounts of chemicals and other specialized biological solutions. e.g. 100 mg/ml ampicillin = 100 mg. of ampicillin dissolved in 1 ml of water.

2. Molarity: moles of solute dissolved/ liter of solution

Mole = 6.02 times 10^{23} atoms = Avagadro's number
Mole = gram formula weight (FW) or gram molecular weight (MW)
* These values are usually found on the labels or in Periodic Table.

Example: Na_2SO4

2 sodium atoms - 2 times 22.99g = 45.98 g
1 sulfur atom   - 1 times 32.06g = 32.06 g
4 oxygen atoms – 4 times16.00g = 64.00 g
  Total   = 142.04g

1M = 1 mole/liter, 1 mM = 1 millimole/liter, 1 uM = 1 umole/liter

Question: How much sodium is needed to make 1L of 1M solution?

Formula weight of sodium sulfate = 142.04g
Dissolve 142.04g of sodium sulfate in about 750mL of water, dissolve sodium sulfate thoroughly and make up the volume to 1 liter (L)

Skill 1.7 **The beginning teacher knows how to apply techniques to calibrate measuring devices and understands concepts of precision, accuracy, and error with regard to reading and recording numerical data from scientific instruments.**

Statistical variability is the deviation of an individual in a population from the mean of the population. Variability is inherent in biology because living things are innately unique. For example, the individual weights of humans vary greatly from the mean weight of the population. Thus, when conducting experiments involving the study of living things, we must control for innate variability. Control groups are identical to the experimental group in every way with the exception of the variable being studied. Comparing the experimental group to the control group allows us to determine the effects of the manipulated variable in relation to statistical variability.

Accuracy is the degree of conformity of a measured, calculated quantity to its actual (true) value. Precision also called reproducibility or repeatability and is the degree to which further measurements or calculations will show the same or similar results.

Accuracy is the degree of veracity while precision is the degree of reproducibility. The best analogy to explain accuracy and precision is the target comparison.

Repeated measurements are compared to arrows that are fired at a target. Accuracy describes the closeness of arrows to the bull's eye at the target center. Arrows that strike closer to the bull's eye are considered more accurate.

Unavoidable experimental error is the random error inherent in scientific experiments regardless of the methods used. One source of unavoidable error is measurement and the use of measurement devices. Using measurement devices is an imprecise process because it is often impossible to accurately read measurements. For example, when using a ruler to measure the length of an object, if the length falls between markings on the ruler, we must estimate the true value. Another source of unavoidable error is the randomness of population sampling and the behavior of any random variable. For example, when sampling a population we cannot guarantee that our sample is completely representative of the larger population. In addition, because we cannot constantly monitor the behavior of a random variable, any observations necessarily contain some level of unavoidable error.

Skill 1.8 **The beginning teacher uses the International System of Units (i.e., metric system) and performs unit conversions within and across measurement systems.**

Science may be defined as a body of knowledge that is systematically derived from study, observations and experimentation. Its goal is to identify and establish principles and theories that may be applied to solve problems. Pseudoscience, on the other hand, is a belief that is not warranted. There is no scientific methodology or application.

Science uses the metric system as it is accepted worldwide and allows easier comparison among experiments done by scientists around the world. Learn the following basic units and prefixes:

> **meter** - measure of length
> **liter** - measure of volume
> **gram** - measure of mass

deca- (meter, liter, gram) = 10X the base unit   **deci** = 1/10 the base unit
hecto- (meter, liter, gram) = 100X the base unit   **centi** = 1/100 the base unit
kilo-   (meter, liter, gram) = 1000X the base unit   **milli** = 1/1000 the base unit

Competency 0002   **The teacher understands the nature of science, the process of scientific inquiry, and the unifying concepts that are common to all sciences.**

Skill 2.1   **The beginning teacher understands the nature of science, the relationship between science and technology, the predictive power of science, and limitations to the scope of science (i.e., the types of questions that science can and cannot answer).**

Science and technology, while distinct concepts, are closely related. Science attempts to investigate and explain the natural world, while technology attempts to solve human adaptation problems. Technology often results from the application of scientific discoveries, and advances in technology can increase the impact of scientific discoveries. For example, Watson and Crick used science to discover the structure of DNA and their discovery led to many biotechnological advances in the manipulation of DNA. These technological advances greatly influenced the medical and pharmaceutical fields. The success of Watson and Crick's experiments, however, was dependent on the technology available. Without the necessary technology, the experiments would have failed.

Science can play many important roles in helping resolve personal, societal, and global challenges. Scientific research and advances in technology help solve many problems and predict future needs. On a personal level, science can help individuals with medical issues, nutrition, and general health. On the societal level, science can help resolve problems of waste disposal, disease prevention, security, and environmental protection. Finally, on the global level, science can help address the challenges of resource allocation, energy production, food production, and global security.

Only certain types of questions can truly be answered by science because the scientific method relies on observable phenomenon. That is, only hypotheses that can be *tested* are valid. Often this means that we can control the variables in a system to an extent that allows us to truly determine their effects. If we don't have full control over the variables, for instance, in environmental biology, we can study several different naturally occurring systems in which the desired variable is different. Also, the fewer variables manipulated in the experiment, the more clear the correlation between variable and result will be.

The scientific method is particularly useful for determining 'cause and effect' type relationships. Thus appropriate hypotheses are often of this nature. The hypothesis is simply a prediction about a certain behavior that occurs in a system. Then variables are changed to determine whether the hypothesis is correct. For instance, let's consider several identical potted African violets and suppose we have lights of different color, fertilizer, water and a variety of common household items. Below are some possible questions, phrased as hypotheses, and a bit about why they are or are not valid.

1. African violets will grow taller in blue light than they will in red light.
   This hypothesis is valid because it could easily be tested by growing one violet in blue light and another in red. The results are easily observed by measuring the height of the violets.

2. Invisible microbes cause the leaves of African violets to turn yellow.
   This hypothesis is not valid because we cannot know whether a given violet is infected with the microbe. This hypothesis could be tested if we had appropriate technology to detect the presence of the microbe.

3. Lack of water will stop the growth of African violets.
   This hypothesis is also valid because it could be tested by denying water to one violet while continuing to water another. The hypothesis may need to be refined to more specifically define how growth will be measured, but presumably this could be easily done.

4. African violets will not grow well in swamps.
   This hypothesis is not valid in our specific situation because we have only potted plants. It could be tested by actually attempting to grow African violets in a swamp, but that is not within this scenario.

Skill 2.2   The beginning teacher knows the characteristics of various types of scientific investigations (e.g., descriptive studies, controlled experiments, comparative data analysis) and how and why scientists use different types of scientific investigations.

Most research in the scientific field is conducted using the scientific method to discover the answer to a scientific problem. The scientific method is the process of thinking through possible solutions to a problem and testing each possibility to find the best solution. The scientific method generally involves the following steps: forming a hypothesis, choosing a method and design, conducting experimentation (collecting data), analyzing data, drawing a conclusion, and reporting the findings. Depending on the hypothesis and data to be collected and analyzed, different types of scientific investigation may be used.

Descriptive studies are often the first form of investigation used in new areas of scientific inquiry. The most important element in descriptive reporting is a specific, clear, and measurable definition of the disease, condition, or factor in question. Descriptive studies always address the five W's: who, what, when, where, and why. They also add an additional "so what?" Descriptive studies include case reports, case-series reports, cross-sectional students, surveillance studies with individuals, and correlational studies with populations. Descriptive studies are used primarily for trend analysis, health-care planning, and hypothesis generation.

A **controlled experiment** is a form of scientific investigation in which one variable, the independent or control variable, is manipulated to reveal the effect on another variable, the dependent (experimental) variable, while are other variables in the system remain fixed. The control group is virtually identical to the dependent variable except for the one aspect whose effect is being tested. Testing the effects of bleach water on a growing plant, the plant receiving bleach water would be the dependent group, while the plant receiving plain water would be the control group. It is good practice to have several replicate samples for the experiment being performed, which allows for results to be averaged or obvious discrepancies to be discarded.

Comparative data analysis is a statistical form of investigation that allows the researcher to gain new or unexpected insight into data based primarily on graphic representation. Comparative data analysis, whether within the research of an individual project or a meta-analysis, allows the researcher to maximize the understanding of the particular data set, uncover underlying structural similarities between research, extract important variables, test underlying assumptions, and detect outliers and anomalies. Most comparative data analysis techniques are graphical in nature with a few quantitative techniques. The use of graphics to compare data allows the researcher to explore the data open-mindedly.

Skill 2.3   **The beginning teacher understands principles and procedures for designing and conducting a variety of scientific investigations, with emphasis on inquiry-based investigations, and how to communicate and defend scientific results.**

A central concept in science is that all evidence is empirical. This means that all evidence must be is observed by the five senses. The phenomenon must be both observable and measurable, with reproducible results.

The question stage of scientific inquiry involves repetition. By repeating the experiment you can discover whether or not you have reproducibility. If results are reproducible, the hypothesis is valid. If the results are not reproducible, one has more questions to ask. It is also important to recognize that one experiment is often a stepping-stone for another. It is possible that data will be re-tested (by the same scientist or by another), and that a different conclusion may be found. In this way, scientific competition acts as a system of checks and balances.

An experiment is proposed and performed with the sole objective of testing a hypothesis. When evaluating an experiment, it is important to first look at the question it was supposed to answer. How logically did the experiment flow from there? How many variables existed? It is best to only test one variable at a time. You discover a scientist conducting an experiment with the following characteristics. He has two rows each set up with four stations. The first row has a piece of tile as the base at each station. The second row has a piece of linoleum as the base at each station. The scientist has eight eggs and is prepared to drop one over each station. What is he testing? He is trying to answer whether or not the egg is more likely to break when dropped over one material as opposed to the other. His hypothesis might have been: The egg will be less likely to break when dropped on linoleum. This is a simple experiment. If the experiment was more complicated, or for example, conducted on a microscopic level, one might want to examine the appropriateness of the instruments utilized and their calibration.

Conclusions must be communicated by clearly describing the information using accurate data, visual presentation and other appropriate media such as a power point presentation. Examples of visual presentations are graphs (bar/line/pie), tables/charts, diagrams, and artwork. Modern technology must be used whenever necessary. The method of communication must be suitable to the audience. Written communication is as important as oral communication. The scientist's strongest ally is a solid set of reproducible data.

Skill 2.4 The beginning teacher understands how logical reasoning, verifiable observational and experimental evidence, and peer review are used in the process of generating and evaluating scientific knowledge.

Armed with knowledge of the subject matter, students can effectively conduct investigations. They need to learn to think critically and logically to connect evidence with explanations. This includes deciding what evidence should be used and accounting for unusual data. Based upon data collected during experimentation, basic statistical analysis, and measures of probability can be used to make predictions and develop interpretations.

Students should be able to review the data, summarize, and form a logical argument about the cause-and-effect relationships. It is important to differentiate between causes and effects and determine when causality is uncertain.

When developing proposed explanations, the students should be able to express their level of confidence in the proposed explanations and point out possible sources of uncertainty and error. When formulating explanations, it is important to distinguish between error and unanticipated results. Possible sources of error would include assumptions of models and measuring techniques or devices.

With confidence in the proposed explanations, the students need to identify what would be required to reject the proposed explanations. Based upon their experience, they should develop new questions to promote further inquiry.

Most scientific studies are ultimately presented in technical journals (some well known examples include *Nature*, *Science*, and the *Journal of the American Medical Association*). Scientists prepare manuscripts detailing the conditions of their experiments and the results they obtained. They will typically also include their interpretation of those results and their impact on current theories in the field. These manuscripts are not wholly unlike lab reports, though they are considerably more polished, of course. Manuscripts are then submitted to appropriate technical journals.

All reputable scientific journals use peer review to assess the quality of research submitted for publication. Peer review is the process by which scientific results produced by one group are subjected to the analysis of other experts in the field. Reviewers of scientific work are typically experts in the field, but it is important that they be objective in their evaluations. Peer review is typically done anonymously so that the identity of the review remains unknown by the scientists submitting work for review. The goal of peer review is to "weed out" any science not performed by appropriate standards. Reviewers will determine whether proper controls were in place, enough replicates were performed, and that the experiments clearly address the presented hypothesis. The reviewer will scrutinize the interpretations and how they fit into what is already known in the field. Often reviewers will suggest that additional experiments be done to further corroborate presented conclusions. If the reviews are satisfied with the quality of the work it will be published and made available to the entire scientific community.

Skill 2.5   The beginning teacher understands how to identify potential sources of error in an investigation, evaluate the validity of scientific data, and develop and analyze different explanations for a given scientific result.

Because people often attempt to use scientific evidence in support of political or personal agendas, the ability to evaluate the credibility of scientific claims is a necessary skill in today's society. In evaluating scientific claims made in the media, public debates, and advertising, one should follow several guidelines.

First, scientific, peer-reviewed journals are the most accepted source for information on scientific experiments and studies. One should carefully scrutinize any claim that does not reference peer-reviewed literature.

Second, the media and those with an agenda to advance (advertisers, debaters, etc.) often overemphasize the certainty and importance of experimental results. One should question any scientific claim that sounds fantastical or overly certain.

Finally, knowledge of experimental design and the scientific method is important in evaluating the credibility of studies. For example, one should look for the inclusion of control groups and the presence of data to support the given conclusions.

Skill 2.6   The beginning teacher knows the characteristics and general features of systems; how properties and patterns of systems can be described in terms of space, time, energy, and matter; and how system components and different systems interact.

Students identify and analyze systems and the ways their components work together or affect each other. Topics can range from a variety of scientific concepts directly into environmental and community related concepts. Some examples could include the following:

Multicultural, Politics, Computers, Cities, Government, Transportation, Manufacturing, Communication, Climate, Stock Market, Agriculture, Machines, Conservation

Any of these examples can be put into clearer context as follows:
Biological (e.g., ecosystems)
Physical (e.g., electrical)
Social (e.g., manufacturing)

Students in the Elementary areas should adequately demonstrate the following concepts between systems and subsystems.

Recognize things that work together.
Identify components of a system.
Communicate functions of a system.
Classify systems based on functions or properties.
Distinguish between systems and subsystems and describe interactions between them.
Analyze how the properties of the components of a system affect their function.
Investigate system feedback and self-regulation.
Create a system.

Students in the Middle School areas should also demonstrate the following concepts:

Investigate and illustrate a system; identify its components and interrelationships with other systems.
Demonstrate how a single system can have multiple functions and applications.
Investigate the role of energy flow in systems.
Evaluate the effects of subsystems and their components on a system.
Design a new system or modify an existing one.

Skill 2.7 **The beginning teacher knows how to apply and analyze the systems model (e.g., interacting parts, boundaries, input, output, feedback, subsystems) across the science disciplines.**

All of science and technology may be thought of in terms of a system. A systems model is a representation of how different elements are involved in and interact as a system. In the case of science, this model illustrates how there are common themes among the sciences and technology that interact as a system. Since most real-world situations do not represent a science in isolation, students should be taught to see the skills and themes common to all sciences and technology in a systematic manner rather than learning in a haphazard way.

A systems model may be used to demonstrate how the parts of each science and technology interact and yet have boundaries and how one science receives input from the other sciences and technology and in turn gives output or feedback to those sciences and technology (a give-and-take relationship). If we think of science and technology as a parent model or system, then physical science may be a subsystem within the larger system.

Speaking generally, physical science is made up of physics and chemistry. Common themes to remember among physical science and the other disciplines are:

- Matter – everything in the universe, living or non-living, is composed of matter
- Energy – both living and non-living things produce and consume energy
- Motion – motion is studied in both living and non-living things
- Forces – forces act upon living and non-living things
- Physical environment – affects living and non-living things

Skill 2.8   **The beginning teacher understands how shared themes and concepts (e.g., systems, order, and organization; evidence, models, and explanation; change, constancy, and measurements; evolution and equilibrium; and form and function) provide a unifying framework in science.**

The following are the concepts and processes generally recognized as common to all scientific disciplines.

Systems, order, and organization
Evidence, models, and explanation
Constancy, change, and measurement
Evolution and equilibrium
Form and function

Systems, order, and organization

Because the natural world is so complex, the study of science involves the organization of items into smaller groups based on interaction or interdependence. These groups are called systems. Examples of organization are the periodic table of elements and the five-kingdom classification scheme for living organisms. Examples of systems are the solar system, cardiovascular system, Newton's laws of force and motion, and the laws of conservation.

Order refers to the behavior and measurability of organisms and events in nature. The arrangement of planets in the solar system and the life cycle of bacterial cells are examples of order.

Evidence, models, and explanations

Scientists use evidence and models to form explanations of natural events. Models are miniaturized representations of a larger event or system. Evidence is anything that furnishes proof.

Constancy, change, and measurement

Constancy and change describe the observable properties of natural organisms and events. Scientists use different systems of measurement to observe change and constancy. For example, the freezing and melting points of given substances and the speed of sound are constant under constant conditions. Growth, decay, and erosion are all examples of natural change.

Evolution and equilibrium

Evolution is the process of change over a long period of time. While biological evolution is the most common example, one can also classify technological advancement, changes in the universe, and changes in the environment as evolution.

Equilibrium is the state of balance between opposing forces of change. Homeostasis and ecological balance are examples of equilibrium.

Form and function

Form and function are properties of organisms and systems that are closely related. The function of an object usually dictates its form and the form of an object usually facilitates its function. For example, the form of the heart (e.g. muscle, valves) allows it to perform its function of circulating blood through the body.

Skill 2.9 **The beginning teacher understands how models are used to represent the natural world and how to evaluate the strengths and limitations of a variety of scientific models (e.g., physical, conceptual, mathematical).**

The model is a basic element of the scientific method. Many things in science are studied with models. A model is any simplification or substitute for what we are actually studying, understanding or predicting. A model is a substitute, but it is similar to what it represents. We encounter models at every step of our daily living. The Periodic Table of the elements is a model chemists use for predicting the properties of the elements. Physicists use Newton's laws to predict how objects will interact, such as planets and spaceships. In geology, the continental drift model predicts the past positions of continents. Sample, ideas, and methods are all examples of models. At every step of scientific study models are extensively use. The primary activity of the hundreds of thousands of US scientists is to produce new models, resulting in tens of thousands of scientific papers published per year.

Types of models

1. Scale models: some models are basically downsized or enlarged copies of their target systems like the models of protein, DNA etc.
2. Idealized models: An idealization is a deliberate simplification of something complicated with the objective of making it easier to understand. Some examples are frictionless planes, point masses, isolated systems etc.
3. Analogical models: standard examples of analogical models are the billiard model of a gas, the computer model of the mind, or the liquid drop model of the nucleus.
4. Phenomenological models: These are usually defined as models that are independent of theories.
5. Data models: It s a corrected, rectified, regimented, and in many instances, idealized version of the data we gain from immediate observation (raw data).
6. Theory models: Any structure is a model if it represents an idea (theory). An example of this is a flow chart, which summarizes a set of ideas.

Uses of models

1. Models are crucial for understanding the structure and function of processes in science.
2. Models help us to visualize the organs/systems they represent just like putting a face to person.
3. Models are very useful to predict and foresee future events like hurricanes etc.

Limitations

1. Though models are every useful to us, they can never replace the real thing.
2. Models are not exactly like the real item they represent.
3. Caution must be exercised before presenting the models to the class, as they may not be accurate.
4. It is the responsibility of the educator to analyze the model critically for the proportions, content value, and other important data.
5. One must be careful about the representation style. This style differs from person to person.

Competency 0003   The teacher understands the history of science, how science impacts the daily lives of students, and how science interacts with and influences personal and societal decisions.

Skill 3.1   The beginning teacher understands the historical development of science, key events in the history of science, and the contributions that diverse cultures and individuals of both genders have made to scientific knowledge.

The history of biology traces mans' understanding of the living world from the earliest recorded history to modern times. Though the concept of biology as a field of science arose only in the 19th century, the origin of biological sciences could be traced back to ancient Greeks (Galen and Aristotle).

During the Renaissance and Age of Discovery, renewed interest in the rapidly increasing number of known organisms generated lot of interest in biology.

Andreas Vesalius (1514-1564), a Belgian anatomist and physician whose dissections of human body and descriptions of his findings helped to correct the misconceptions of science. The books Vesalius wrote on anatomy were the most accurate and comprehensive anatomical texts to date.

Anton van Leeuwenhoek is known as the father of microscopy. In the 1650s, Leeuwenhoek began making tiny lenses that gave magnifications up to 300x. He was the first to see and describe bacteria, yeast plants, and the microscopic life found in water.   Over the years, light microscopes have advanced to produce greater clarity and magnification. The scanning electron microscope (SEM) was developed in the 1950s. Instead of light, a beam of electrons passes through the specimen. Scanning electron microscopes have a resolution about one thousand times greater than light microscopes. The disadvantage of the SEM is that the chemical and physical methods used to prepare the sample result in the death of the specimen.

Robert Hooke (1635-1703) was a renowned inventor, a natural philosopher, astronomer, experimenter and a cell biologist. He deserves more recognition than he had, but he is remembered mainly for his law, the Hooke's law an equation describing elasticity that is still used today. He was the type of scientist that was then called a "virtuoso"- able to contribute findings of major importance in any field of science. Hooke published *Micrographia* in 1665. Hooke devised the compound microscope and illumination system, one of the best such microscopes of his time, and used it in his demonstrations at the Royal Society's meetings. With it he observed organisms as diverse as insects, sponges, bryozoans, foraminifera, and bird feathers. Micrographia is an accurate and detailed record of his observations, illustrated with magnificent drawings.

Carl Von Linnaeus (1707-1778), a Swedish botanist, physician and zoologist is well known for his contributions in ecology and taxonomy. Linnaeus is famous for his binomial system of nomenclature in which each living organism has two names, a genus and a species name. He is considered as the father of modern ecology and taxonomy.

In the late 1800s, Pasteur discovered the role of microorganisms in the cause of disease, pasteurization, and the rabies vaccine. Koch took this observations one step further by formulating that specific diseases were caused by specific pathogens. Koch's postulates are still used as guidelines in the field of microbiology. They state that the same pathogen must be found in every diseased person, the pathogen must be isolated and grown in culture, the disease is induced in experimental animals from the culture, and the same pathogen must be isolated from the experimental animal.

Mattias Schleiden, a German botanist is famous for his cell theory. He observed plant cells microscopically and concluded that cell is the common structural unit of plants. He proposed the cell theory along with Schwann, a zoologist, who observed cells in animals.

In the 18th century, many fields of science like botany, zoology and geology began to evolve as scientific disciplines in the modern sense.

In the 20th century, the rediscovery of Mendel's work led to the rapid development of genetics by Thomas Hunt Morgan and his students.

DNA structure was another key event in biological study. In the 1950s, James Watson and Francis Crick discovered the structure of a DNA molecule as that of a double helix. This structure made it possible to explain DNA's ability to replicate and to control the synthesis of proteins.

Francois Jacob and Jacques Monod contributed greatly to the field of lysogeny and bacterial reproduction by conjugation and both of them won Nobel Prize for their contributions.

Following the cracking of the genetic code biology has largely split between organismal biology consisting of ecology, ethology, systematics, paleontology, and evolutionary biology, developmental biology, and other disciplines that deal with whole organisms or group of organisms and the disciplines related to molecular biology - including cell biology, biophysics, biochemistry, neuroscience, immunology, and many other overlapping subjects.

The use of animals in biological research has expedited many scientific discoveries. Animal research has allowed scientists to learn more about animal biological systems, including the circulatory and reproductive systems. One significant use of animals is for the testing of drugs, vaccines, and other products (such as perfumes and shampoos) before use or consumption by humans. Along with the pros of animal research, the cons are also very significant. The debate about the ethical treatment of animals has been ongoing since the introduction of animals in research. Many people believe the use of animals in research is cruel and unnecessary. Animal use is federally and locally regulated. The purpose of the Institutional Animal Care and Use Committee (IACUC) is to oversee and evaluate all aspects of an institution's animal care and use program.

Skill 3.2   The beginning teacher knows how to use examples from the history of science to demonstrate the changing nature of scientific theories and knowledge (i.e., that scientific theories and knowledge are always subject to revision in light of new evidence).

Observations, however general they may seem, lead scientists to create a viable question and an educated guess (hypothesis) about what to expect. While scientists often have laboratories set up to study a specific thing, it is likely that along the way they will find an unexpected result. It is important to be open-minded and to look at all of the information. An open-minded approach to science provides room for more questioning, and, hence, more learning. A central concept in science is that all evidence is empirical. This means that all evidence must be is observed by the five senses. The phenomenon must be both observable and measurable, with reproducible results.

The question stage of scientific inquiry involves repetition. By repeating the experiment you can discover whether or not you have reproducibility. If results are reproducible, the hypothesis is valid. If the results are not reproducible, one has more questions to ask. It is also important to recognize that one experiment is often a stepping stone for another. It is possible that data will be re-tested by the same scientist or by another, and that a different conclusion may be found. In this way, scientific competition acts as a system of checks and balances.

A great example of the evolution of a scientific theory is that of the model of the universe. The universe was originally thought to be geocentric. Over time, and amid much disagreement from state and church authorities, it was established that the universe is heliocentric. This took many years of research and dischord on the behalf of multiple scholars, but it is now common place knowledge.

Skill 3.3 **The beginning teacher knows that science is a human endeavor influenced by societal, cultural, and personal views of the world, and that decisions about the use and direction of science are based on factors such as ethical standards, economics, and personal and societal biases and needs.**

Society as a whole impacts biological research. The pressure from the majority of society has led to bans and restrictions on research. Human cloning has been restricted in the United States and many other countries. The U.S. legislature has banned the use of federal funds for the development of human cloning techniques. Some individual states have banned human cloning regardless of where the funds originate.

The demand for genetically modified crops by society and industry has steadily increased over the years. Genetic engineering in the agricultural field has led to improved crops for human use and consumption. Crops are genetically modified for increased growth and insect resistance because of the demand for larger and greater quantities of produce.

With advances in biotechnology come those in society who oppose it. Ethical questions arise when discussing animal and human research. Does it need to be done? What are the effects on humans and animals? There are no right or wrong answers to these questions. There are governmental agencies in place to regulate the use of humans and animals for research.

Science and technology are often referred to as a "double-edged sword." Although advances in medicine have greatly improved the quality and length of life, certain moral and ethical controversies have arisen. Unforeseen environmental problems may result from technological advances. Advances in science have led to an improved economy through biotechnology as applied to agriculture, yet it has put our health care system at risk and has caused the cost of medical care to increase substantially. Society depends on science, yet it is necessary that the public be scientifically literate and informed in order to prevent potentially unethical procedures from occurring. Especially vulnerable are the areas of genetic research and fertility. It is important for science teachers to stay aware of current research and to involve students in critical thinking and ethics whenever possible.

It is easy to say one is for or against something. Biotechnological advances are reaching new heights. This is both exciting and yet it may create anxiety. We are stretching our boundaries and rethinking old standards. Things we never thought possible, such as the human genome project, now seem ordinary, and cloning, once in the realm of science fiction, is now available. These revelations force us to rethink our stance on issues. It is normal to reevaluate one's beliefs. Reevaluation requires truly thinking about a topic, which in turn allows for recommitment to a topic or, possibly, a new, well thought out, position.

It is important to realize that many of the most complex scientific questions have been answered in a collaborative form. The human genome project is a great example of research conducted and shared by multiple countries world wide. It is also interesting to note that because of differing cultural beliefs, some cultures may be more likely to allow areas of research that other cultures may be unlikely to examine.

Skill 3.4   The beginning teacher understands the application of scientific ethics to the conducting, analyzing, and publishing of scientific investigations.

To understand scientific ethics, we need to have a clear understanding of ethics. Ethics is defined as a system of public, general rules for guiding human conduct (Gert, 1988). The rules are general in that they are supposed to all people at all times and they are public in that they are not secret codes or practices.

Scientists are expected to show good conduct in their scientific pursuits. Conduct here refers to all aspects of scientific activity including experimentation, testing, education, data evaluation, data analysis, data storing, peer review, government funding, the staff, etc.

The following are some of the guiding principles of scientific ethics:

1. Scientific Honesty: not to fraud, fabricate or misinterpret data for personal gain
2. Caution: to avoid errors and sloppiness in all scientific experimentation
3. Credit: give credit where credit is due and not to copy
4. Responsibility: only to report reliable information to public and not to mislead in the name of science
5. Freedom: freedom to criticize old ideas, question new research and freedom to research

Many more principles could be added to this list. Though these principles seem straightforward and clear it is very difficult to put them into practice since they could be interpreted in more ways than one. Nevertheless, it is not an excuse for scientists to overlook these guiding principles of scientific ethics.

To discuss scientific ethics, we can look at natural phenomena like rain. Rain in the normal sense is extremely useful to us and it is absolutely important that there is water cycle. When rain gets polluted with acid, it becomes acid rain. Here lies the ethical issue of releasing all these pollutants into the atmosphere. Should the scientists communicate the whole truth about acid rain or withhold some information because it may alarm the public. There are many issues like this. Scientists are expected to be honest and forthright with the public.

Skill 3.5 **The beginning teacher applies scientific principles to analyze factors (e.g., diet, exercise, personal behavior) that influence personal and societal choices concerning fitness and health (e.g., physiological and psychological effects and risks associated with the use of substances and substance abuse).**

Because biology is the study of living things, we can easily apply the knowledge of biology to daily life and personal decision-making. For example, biology greatly influences the health decisions humans make everyday. What foods to eat, when and how to exercise, and how often to bathe are just three of the many decisions we make everyday that are based on our knowledge of biology. Other areas of daily life where biology affects decision-making are parenting, interpersonal relationships, family planning, and consumer spending.

While genetics plays an important role in health, human behaviors can greatly affect short- and long-term health both positively and negatively. Behaviors that negatively affect health include smoking, excessive alcohol consumption, substance abuse, and poor eating habits. Behaviors that positively affect health include good nutrition and regular exercise.

Smoking negatively affects health in many ways. First, smoking decreases lung capacity, causes persistent coughing, and limits the ability to engage in strenuous physical activity. In addition, the long-term affects are even more damaging. Long-term smoking can cause lung cancer, heart disease, and emphysema (a lung disease).

Alcohol is the most abused legal drug. Excessive alcohol consumption has both short- and long-term negative effects. Drunkenness can lead to reckless behavior and distorted judgment that can cause injury or death. In addition, extreme alcohol abuse can cause alcohol poisoning that can result in immediate death. Long-term alcohol abuse is also extremely hazardous. The potential effects of long-term alcohol abuse include liver cirrhosis, heart problems, high blood pressure, stomach ulcers, and cancer.

The abuse of illegal substances can also negatively affect health. Commonly abused drugs include cocaine, heroin, opiates, methamphetamines, and marijuana. Drug abuse can cause immediate death or injury and, if used for a long time, can cause many physical and psychological health problems.

A healthy diet and regular exercise are the cornerstones of a healthy lifestyle. A diet rich in whole grains, fruits, vegetables, polyunsaturated fats, and lean protein and low in saturated fat and sugar, can positively affect overall health. Such diets can reduce cholesterol levels, lower blood pressure, and help manage body weight. Conversely, diets high in saturated fat and sugar can contribute to weight gain, heart disease, strokes, and cancer.

Finally, regular exercise has both short- and long-term health benefits. Exercise increases physical fitness, improving energy levels, overall body function, and mental well-being. Long-term, exercise helps protect against chronic diseases, maintains healthy bones and muscles, helps maintain a healthy body weight, and strengthens the body's immune system.

Skill 3.6   The beginning teacher applies scientific principles, the theory of probability, and risk/benefit analysis to analyze the advantages of, disadvantages of, or alternatives to a given decision or course of action.

While technology and technological design can provide solutions to problems faced by humans, technology must exist within nature and cannot contradict physical or biological principles. In addition, technological solutions are temporary and new technologies typically provide better solutions in the future. Monetary costs, available materials, time, and available tools also limit the scope of scientific and technological design and solutions. Finally, solutions must have intended benefits and no expected consequences. Scientists must attempt to predict the unintended consequences and minimize any negative impact on nature or society.

The problems and needs, ranging from very simple to highly complex, that technological design can solve are nearly limitless. Disposal of toxic waste, routing of rainwater, crop irrigation, and energy creation are but a few examples of real-world problems that scientists address or attempt to address with technology.

The technological design process consists of identifying a problem, proposing designs and choosing between alternative solutions, implementing the proposed solution, evaluating the solution and its consequences, and reporting the results

After the identification of a problem, the scientist must propose several designs and choose between the alternatives. In evaluating and choosing between potential solutions to a design problem, scientists utilize modeling, simulation, and experimentation techniques. Small-scale modeling and simulation help test the effectiveness and unexpected consequences of proposed solutions while limiting the initial costs. Modeling and simulation may also reveal potential problems that scientists can address prior to full-scale implementation of the solution. Experimentation allows for evaluation of proposed solutions in a controlled environment where scientists can manipulate and test specific variables.

Implementation of the chosen solution involves the use of various tools depending on the problem, solution, and technology. Scientists may use both physical tools and objects and computer software. After implementation of the solution, scientists evaluate the success or failure of the solution against pre-determined criteria. In evaluating the solution, scientists must consider the negative consequences as well as the planned benefits.

Finally, scientists must communicate results in different ways – orally, written, models, diagrams, and demonstrations.

Skill 3.7   The beginning teacher understands the role science can play in helping resolve personal, societal, and global issues (e.g., population growth, disease prevention, resource use).

Science can play many important roles in helping resolve personal, societal, and global challenges. Scientific research and advances in technology help solve many problems. In this section, we will discuss just a few of the many roles of science. On a personal level, science can help individuals with medical issues, nutrition, and general health. On the societal level, science can help resolve problems of waste disposal, disease prevention, security, and environmental protection. Finally, on the global level, science can help address the challenges of resource allocation, energy production, food production, and global security.

Science greatly affects our personal lives, improving our quality of life and increasing longevity. Advances in medicine have lessened the impact of many diseases and medical conditions and increased the average life expectancy. Scientific research has helped establish lifestyle guidelines for diet and exercise that increase awareness of fitness and the health-related benefits of regular exercise and proper nutrition.

On the societal level, science helps solve many logistical problems related to the management of a large number of people in a limited space. Science tells us how development will affect the natural environment and helps us build and develop in an environmentally friendly manner. Science can also help develop strategies and technologies for efficient waste disposal and disease prevention. Finally, many products and technologies related to security and defense derive from scientific research.

Science is, and will continue to be, a very important factor in the security and continued viability of the planet. On the global level, science must attempt to resolve the challenges related to natural resource allocation, energy production, and food production. These challenges have an obvious affect on the ecological viability of the planet; however, they also have a pronounced affect on global security. Availability and use of resources, food production, global health, and the economic impact of these factors lays the foundation for global conflict and terrorism. Third World poverty and resource deficiencies create global unrest and an unstable global environment. Scientific and technological advances have the potential to alleviate these problems and increase global security and stability.

DOMAIN II.   PHYSICS

Competency 0004   **The teacher understands the description of motion in one and two dimensions.**

Skill 4.1   **The beginning teacher analyzes and interprets graphs describing the motion of a particle.**

The relationship between time, position or distance, velocity and acceleration can be understood conceptually by looking at a graphical representation of each as a function of time. Simply, the velocity is the slope of the position vs. time graph and the acceleration is the slope of the velocity vs. time graph.

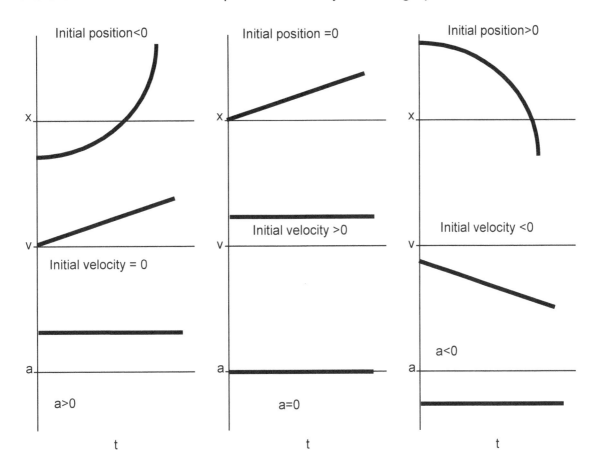

There are three things to notice:

1. In each case acceleration is constant. This isn't always the case, but a simplification for this illustration.
2. A non-zero acceleration produces a position curve that is a parabola.
3. In each case the initial velocity and position are specified separately. The acceleration curve gives the shape of the velocity curve, but not the initial value and the velocity curve gives the shape of the position curve but not the initial position.

Skill 4.2   The beginning teacher applies vector concepts to displacement, velocity, and acceleration in order to analyze and describe the motion of a particle.

The science of describing the motion of bodies is known as **kinematics**. The motion of bodies is described using words, diagrams, numbers, graphs, and equations.

The following words are used to describe motion: distance, displacement, speed, velocity, and acceleration.

Distance is a scalar quantity that refers to how much ground an object has covered while moving. **Displacement** is a vector quantity that refers to the object's change in position.

Example:

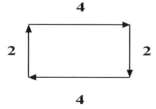

Jamie walked 2 miles north, 4 miles east, 2 miles south, and then 4 miles west. In terms of distance, she walked 12 miles. However, there is no displacement because the directions cancelled each other out, and she returned to her starting position.

Speed is a scalar quantity that refers to how fast an object is moving (ex. the car was traveling 60 mi./hr). **Velocity** is a vector quantity that refers to the rate at which an object changes its position. In other words, velocity is speed with direction (ex. the car was traveling 60 mi./hr east).

Skill 4.3   **The beginning teacher solves problems involving uniform and accelerated motion using scalar and vector quantities.**

Speed is a scalar quantity that refers to how fast an object is moving (ex. the car was traveling 60 mi./hr). **Velocity** is a vector quantity that refers to the rate at which an object changes its position. In other words, velocity is speed with direction (ex. the car was traveling 60 mi./hr east).

$$\text{Average Speed} = \frac{\text{Distance traveled}}{\text{time of travel}}$$

$$V = \frac{d}{t}$$

$$\text{Average Velocity} = \frac{\Delta \text{position}}{\text{time}} = \frac{\text{displacement}}{\text{time}}$$

Instantaneous Speed - speed at any given instant in time.

Average Speed - average of all instantaneous speeds, found simply by a distance/time ratio.

Acceleration is a vector quantity defined as the rate at which an object changes its velocity.

$$a = \frac{\Delta \text{velocity}}{\text{time}} = \frac{v_f - v_i}{t}$$

where *f* represents the final velocity and *i* represents the initial velocity

Since acceleration is a vector quantity, it always has a direction associated with it. The direction of the acceleration vector depends on

1. whether the object is speeding up or slowing down
2. whether the object is moving in the positive or negative direction.

Skill 4.4   **The beginning teacher analyzes and solves problems involving projectile motion.**

By definition, a **projectile** only has one force acting upon it – the force of gravity.

Gravity influences the vertical motion of the projectile, causing vertical acceleration. The horizontal motion of the projectile is the result of the tendency of any object in motion to remain in motion at constant velocity. (Remember, there are no horizontal forces acting upon the projectile. By definition, gravity is the only force acting upon the projectile.)

Projectiles travel with a parabolic trajectory due to the fact that the downward force of gravity accelerates them downward from their otherwise straight-line trajectory. Gravity affects the vertical motion, not the horizontal motion, of the projectile. Gravity causes a downward displacement from the position that the object would be in if there were no gravity.

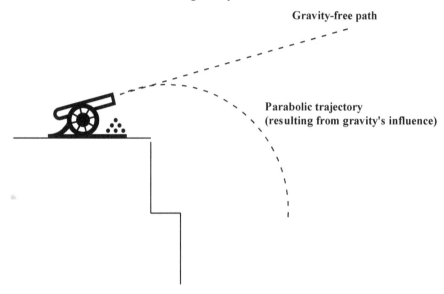

Gravity-free path

Parabolic trajectory
(resulting from gravity's influence)

Skill 4.5   The beginning teacher analyzes and solves problems involving uniform circular and rotary motion.

Straight-line motion

To make an object move, initially a force has to be applied, since force has the capacity to move an object. We also need to take into account friction, which makes moving objects slow down. This characteristic was noticed for the first time by Galileo. This is Newton's first law of motion, which states that an object at rest remains at rest unless acted upon by force. Force can cause a lot of things to moving objects - make them move, slow down, stop them, increase their speed, decrease their speed etc.

A moving object has speed, velocity and acceleration. To summarize, when force is applied to an object it moves in a straight line (Newton's first law) and adding force can make it go faster or slow it down.

Circular motion

Circular motion is defined as rotation along a circle: a circular path or a circular orbit. The rotation around a fixed axis of a three-dimensional body involves circular motion of its parts. Circular motion involves acceleration of the moving object by a centripetal force that pulls the moving object towards the center of the circular orbit. Without this acceleration, the object would move slowly in a straight line, according to Newton's first law of motion. Circular motion is accelerated even though the speed is constant, because the object's velocity is constantly changing direction.

A special kind of circular motion is when an object rotates around its own center of mass. This can be called a spinning (or rotational) motion.

Examples of circular motion are: an artificial satellite orbiting the earth in a geosynchronous orbit, a stone which is tied to a rope and is being swung in circles, a race car turning through a curve in a racetrack, an electron moving perpendicular to a uniform magnetic field, and a gear turning inside a mechanism.

Periodic motion

Periodic motion is when an object moves back and forth in regular motion. Some examples of this periodic motion are: weight on a string swinging back and forth (pendulum) and a ball bouncing up and down. Periodic motion is characterized by three things.

1. Velocity - they all have velocity, the bouncing ball, weight on a pendulum etc.
2. Period - the period is the time the object takes to go back and forth. You can measure the time the ball takes to bounce back. Sometimes, the word period is being replaced by the word frequency. Frequency is the reciprocal of period.
3. Amplitude - the amplitude is half the distance the object goes from one side of the period to the other. For an object in rotation, the amplitude is the radius of the circle (1/2 the diameter).

There are many devices that use the characteristics of periodic motion. A clock is the most common device. Another use of periodic motion is in the study of wave motion, including light, sound and music.

Skill 4.6   The beginning teacher understands motion of fluids.

The weight of a column of fluid creates hydrostatic pressure. Common situations in which we might analyze hydrostatic pressure include tanks of fluid, a swimming pool, or the ocean. Also, atmospheric pressure is an example of hydrostatic pressure.

Because hydrostatic pressure results from the force of gravity interacting with the mass of the fluid or gas, for an incompressible fluid it is governed by the following equation:

$$P = \rho g h$$

where P=hydrostatic pressure
p=density of the fluid
g=acceleration of gravity
h=height of the fluid column

According to **Pascal's principle**, when pressure is applied to an enclosed fluid, it is transmitted undiminished to all parts of the fluid. For instance, if an additional pressure P_0 is applied to the top surface of a column of liquid of height h as described above, the pressure at the bottom of the liquid will increase by P_0 and will be given by $P = P_0 + \rho g h$. This principle is used in devices such as a **hydraulic lift** (shown below) which consists of two fluid-filled cylinders, one narrow and one wide, connected at the bottom. Pressure P (force = P X A1) applied on the surface of the fluid in the narrow cylinder is transmitted undiminished to the wider cylinder resulting in a larger net force (P X A2) transmitted through its surface. Thus a relatively small force is used to lift a heavy object. This does not violate the conservation of energy since the small force has to be applied through a large distance to move the heavy object a small distance.

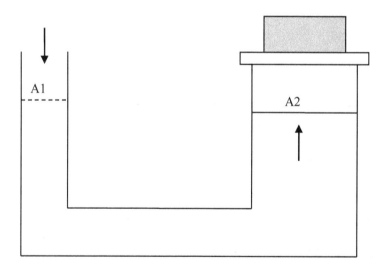

Archimedes' Principle states that, for an object in a fluid, "the upthrust is equal to the weight of the displaced fluid" and the weight of displaced fluid is directly proportional to the volume of displaced fluid. The second part of his discovery is useful when we want to determine the volume of an oddly shaped object. We determine its volume by immersing it in a graduated cylinder and measuring how much fluid is displaced. We explore his first observation in more depth below.

Today, we call Archimedes' "upthrust" **buoyancy**. Buoyancy is the force produced by a fluid on a fully or partially immersed object. The buoyant force ($F_{buoyant}$) is found using the following equation:

$$F_{bouyant} = \rho V g$$

where p=density of the fluid
V=volume of fluid displaced by the submerged object
g=the acceleration of gravity

Notice that the buoyant force opposes the force of gravity. For an immersed object, a gravitational force (equal to the object's mass times the acceleration of gravity) pulls it downward, while a buoyant force (equal to the weight of the displaced fluid) pushes it upward.

Also note that, from this principle, we can predict *whether* an object will sink or float in a given liquid. We can simply compare the density of the material from which the object is made to that of the liquid. If the material has a lower density, it will float; if it has a higher density it will sink. Finally, if an object has a density equal to that of the liquid, it will neither sink nor float.

Skill 4.7   The beginning teacher understands motion in terms of frames of reference and relativity concepts.

When we analyze a situation using the laws of physics, we must first consider the perspective from which it is viewed. This is known as the frame of reference. The principles which describe the relationships between different frames of reference are known as relativities. The type of relativity discussed below is known as Galilean or Newtonian relativity and is valid for physical situations in which velocities are relatively low. When velocities approach the speed of light, we must use Einstein's special relativity.

There are two general types of reference frames: inertial and non-inertial

Inertial: These frames translate at a constant vector velocity, meaning the velocity does not change direction or magnitude (i.e., travel in a straight line without acceleration).

Non-inertial: These frames include all other situations in which there is non-constant velocity, such as acceleration or rotation. Galilean relativity does not apply to non-inertial frames, as explained below.

Galilean relativity states that the laws of physics are the same in all inertial frames. That is, these same laws would apply to an experiment performed on the surface of the Earth and an experiment performed in a reference frame moving at constant velocity with respect to the earth. For instance, two baseball players can have the same game of catch either standing on the ground or in a moving bus (so long as the bus's motion has constant direction and magnitude).

It is true, however, that phenomenon will have different appearance depending on our frame of reference. Relative velocity is a useful concept to help us analyze such cases. We can understand relative velocity by again considering the game of catch being played on a bus:

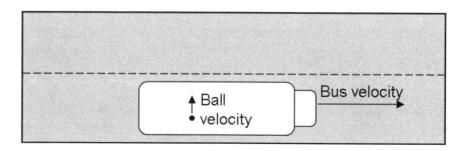

Inside the frame of reference of the bus, the ball travels at the velocity with which it was thrown and straight across the bus (shown by the ball velocity vector above). However, if we use stationary earth as our frame of reference, then the ball is not only moving across the bus, but down the road at the velocity with which the bus is driven. To determine the ball's velocity relative to the earth, then, we must add the ball's velocity relative to the bus and the bus's velocity relative to the earth. This can be performed with simple vector addition.

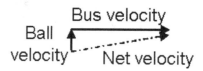

Competency 0005   **The teacher understands the laws of motion.**

Skill 5.1   **The beginning teacher identifies and analyzes the forces acting in a given situation and constructs a free-body diagram.**

Mechanics can be defined as the branch of physics concerned with the action of forces on matter or material systems, and the behavior of the receiving body. As such, mechanics is a tangible subject easily related to common occurrences. Mechanics encompasses the movement of all matter under the influence of the four fundamental forces, which are gravity, the strong and weak interactions, and electromagnetic interaction. Mechanics is also at the heart of technology, which is the application of physical knowledge for human purposes (ie. engineering). Classical mechanics has often been viewed as an exact science. It requires the exacting use of mathematics and theories, as well as experimentation.

Quantum mechanics is the study of mechanics on a subatomic level. For the purposes of this essay we will refer to the more commonly referred to mechanics (classical) and review its necessary principles.

Newton's Laws of Motion are the three physical laws that provide relationships between the forces acting on a body and the motion of that body. His laws form the basis of classical mechanics. They can be used to explain the motion of physical objects.

First Law: A body at rest remains at rest, and a body in motion continues to move in a straight line with a constant speed unless and until an external unbalanced force acts upon it.

Second Law: The rate of change of momentum of a body is directly proportional to the impressed force and takes place in the direction in which the force acts.

Third Law: To every action (force applied) there is an equal and opposite reaction (equal force in the opposite direction).

It is important to note that these three laws along with his law of gravitation provide an explanation of motion of everyday macroscopic objects under everyday conditions. These same laws are NOT valid when applied to high speeds or microscopic objects (those conditions are better explained by Einstein's laws of quantum physics).

A **free-body diagram** is a diagram that shows the direction and relative magnitude of forces acting upon an object in a given situation. It is a special example of a vector diagram. The direction of the arrow indicates the direction in which the force is acting, and the size of the arrow indicates the magnitude of the force. Each arrow is labeled to represent the exact type of force. A box is used to represent the object and the force arrows are drawn outward from the center of the box in the directions they are acting.

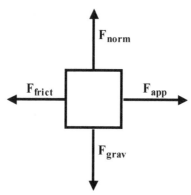

In this example, the object has four forces acting upon it, which is not always the case. Sometimes, there could be one, two, or three forces. The only rule is that all forces acting upon the object in that given situation should be depicted. Therefore, it is important that you be familiar with the various types of forces and be able to identify which forces are present in the situation.

Skill 5.2   The beginning teacher solves problems involving the vector nature of force (e.g., resolving forces into components, analyzing static or dynamic equilibrium of a particle).

An object is said to be in a state of equilibrium when the forces exerted upon it are balanced. That is to say, forces to the left balance the forces exerted to the right, and upward forces are balanced by downward forces. The net force acting on the object is zero and the acceleration is 0 meters per second squared. This does not necessarily mean that the object is at rest. According to Newton's first law of motion, an object at equilibrium is either at rest and remaining at rest (**static equilibrium**), or in motion and continuing in motion with the same speed and direction (**dynamic equilibrium**).

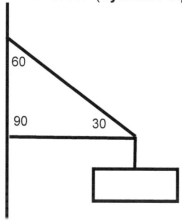

Equilibrium of forces is often used to analyze situations where objects are in static equilibrium. One can determine the weight of an object in static equilibrium or the forces necessary to hold an object at equilibrium. The following are examples of each type of problem.

<u>Problem</u>: A sign hangs outside a building supported as shown in the diagram. The sign has a mass of 50 kg. Calculate the tension in the cable.

<u>Solution</u>: Since there is only one upward pulling cable it must balance the weight. The sign exerts a downward force of 490 N. Therefore, the cable pulls upwards with a force of 490 N. It does so at an angle of 30 degrees. To find the total tension in the cable:

$$F_{total} = 490 \text{ N} / \sin 30°$$
$$F_{total} = 980 \text{ N}$$

Skill 5.3   **The beginning teacher identifies and applies Newton's laws to analyze and solve a variety of practical problems (e.g., properties of frictional forces, acceleration of a particle on an inclined plane, displacement of a mass on a spring, forces on a pendulum).**

Newton's first law of motion: "An object at rest tends to stay at rest and an object in motion tends to stay in motion with the same speed and in the same direction unless acted upon by an unbalanced force". This tendency of an object to continue in its state of rest or motion is known as **inertia**. Note that, at any point in time, most objects have multiple forces acting on them. If the vector addition of all the forces on an object results in a zero net force, then the forces on the object are said to be **balanced**. If the net force on an object is non-zero, an **unbalanced** force is acting on the object.

Prior to Newton's formulation of this law, being at rest was considered the natural state of all objects because at the earth's surface we have the force of gravity working at all times which causes nearly any object put into motion to eventually come to rest. Newton's brilliant leap was to recognize that an unbalanced force changes the motion of a body, whether that body begins at rest or at some non-zero speed.

We experience the consequences of this law everyday. For instance, the first law is why seat belts are necessary to prevent injuries. When a car stops suddenly, say by hitting a road barrier, the driver continues on forward due to inertia until acted upon by a force. The seat belt provides that force and distributes the load across the whole body rather than allowing the driver to fly forward and experience the force against the steering wheel.

Newton's second law of motion: "The acceleration of an object as produced by a net force is directly proportional to the magnitude of the net force, in the same direction as the net force, and inversely proportional to the mass of the object". In the equation form, it is stated as $F = ma$, force equals mass times acceleration. It is important, again, to remember that this is the net force and that forces are vector quantities. Thus if an object is acted upon by 12 forces that sum to zero, there is no acceleration. Also, this law embodies the idea of inertia as a consequence of mass. For a given force, the resulting acceleration is proportionally smaller for a more massive object because the larger object has more inertia.

The first two laws are generally applied together via the equation **F=ma.** The first law is largely the conceptual foundation for the more specific and quantitative second law. Newton's first law and second law are valid only in **inertial reference frames** (described in previous section).

The **weight** of an object is the result of the gravitational force of the earth acting on its mass. The acceleration due to Earth's gravity on an object is 9.81 m/s². Since force equals mass * acceleration, the magnitude of the gravitational force created by the earth on an object is

$$F_{Gravity} = m_{object} \cdot 9.81 \, m/s^2$$

Example: For the arrangement shown, find the force necessary to overcome the 500 N force pushing to the left and move the truck to the right with an acceleration of 5 m/s².

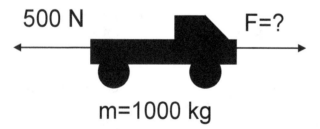

Solution: Since we know the acceleration and mass, we can calculate the net force necessary to move the truck with this acceleration. Assuming that to the right is the positive direction we sum the forces and get
F-500N = 1000kg x 5 m/s². Solving for F, we get 5500 N.

Newton's third law of motion: "For every action, there is an equal and opposite reaction". This statement means that, in every interaction, there is a pair of forces acting on the two interacting objects. The size of the force on the first object equals the size of the force on the second object. The direction of the force on the first object is opposite to the direction of the force on the second object.

1. **The propulsion/movement of fish through water:** A fish uses its fins to push water backwards. The water pushes back on the fish. Because the force on the fish is unbalanced the fish moves forward.
2. **The motion of car:** A car's wheels push against the road and the road pushes back. Since the force of the road on the car is unbalanced the car moves forward.
3. **Walking:** When one pushes backwards on the foot with the muscles of the leg, the floor pushes back on the foot. If the forces of the leg on the foot and the floor on the foot are balanced, the foot will not move and the muscles of the body can move the other leg forward.

In the real world, whenever an object moves its motion is opposed by a force known as friction. How strong the frictional force is depends on numerous factors such as the roughness of the surfaces (for two objects sliding against each other) or the viscosity of the liquid an object is moving through. Most problems involving the effect of friction on motion deal with sliding friction. This is the type of friction that makes it harder to push a box across cement than across a marble floor. When you try and push an object from rest, you must overcome the maximum **static friction** force to get it to move. Once the object is in motion, you are working against **kinetic friction,** which is smaller than the static friction force previously mentioned. Sliding friction is primarily dependent on two things, the **coefficient of friction (μ)** which is dependent on the roughness of the surfaces involved and the amount of force pushing the two surfaces together. This force is also known as the **normal force (F_n)**, the perpendicular force between two surfaces. When an object is resting on a flat surface, the normal force is pushing opposite to the gravitational force – straight up. When the object is resting on an incline, the normal force is less (because it is only opposing that portion of the gravitational force acting perpendicularly to the object) and its direction is perpendicular to the surface of incline but at an angle from the ground. Therefore, for an object experiencing no external action, the magnitude of the normal force is either equal to or less than the magnitude of the gravitational force **(F_g)** acting on it. The frictional force **(F_f)** acts perpendicularly to the normal force, opposing the direction of the object's motion.

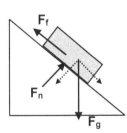

The frictional force is normally directly proportional to the normal force and, unless you are told otherwise, can be calculated as $F_f = \mu \; F_n$ where μ is either the coefficient of static friction or kinetic friction depending on whether the object starts at rest or in motion. In the first case, the problem is often stated as "how much force does it take to start an object moving" and the frictional force is given by $F_f > \mu_s F_n$ where μ_s is the coefficient of static friction. When questions are of the form "what is the magnitude of the frictional force opposing the motion of this object," the frictional force is given by **$F_f = \mu_k F_n$** where μ_k is the coefficient of kinetic friction.

A static frictional force is needed in order to start a ball or a wheel rolling; without this force the object would just slide or spin. **Rolling friction** is the force that resists the rolling motion of an object such as a wheel once it is already in motion. Rolling friction arises from the roughness of the surfaces in contact and from the deformation of the rolling object or surface on which it is rolling. Rolling resistance $Ff = \mu r\ Fn$ where μr is the coefficient of rolling friction.

There are several important things to remember when solving problems about friction.

1. The frictional force acts in opposition to the direction of motion.
2. The frictional force is proportional to, and acts perpendicular to, the normal force.
3. The normal force is perpendicular to the surface the object is lying on. If there is a force pushing the object against the surface, it will increase the normal force.

Problem:

A woman is pushing an 800N box across the floor. She pushes with a force of 1000 N in the direction indicated in the diagram below. The coefficient of kinetic friction is 0.50. If the box is already moving, what is the force of friction acting on the box?

Solution:

First it is necessary to solve for the normal force.

Fn= 800N + 1000N (sin 30°) = 1300N

Then, since **Ff = μ Fn** = 0.5*1300=650N

Competency 0006   **The teacher understands the concepts of gravitational and electromagnetic forces in nature.**

Skill 6.1   **The beginning teacher applies the Law of Universal Gravitation to solve a variety of problems (e.g., determining the gravitational fields of the planets, analyzing properties of satellite orbits).**

Newton's universal law of gravitation states that any two objects experience a force between them as the result of their masses. Specifically, the force between two masses m_1 and m_2 can be summarized as

$$F = G \frac{m_1 m_2}{r^2}$$

where G is the gravitational constant ($G = 6.672 \times 10^{-11}\, Nm^2/kg^2$), and r is the distance between the two objects.

Important things to remember:

1. The gravitational force is proportional to the masses of the two objects, but *inversely* proportional to the *square of the distance* between the two objects.
2. When calculating the effects of the acceleration due to gravity for an object above the earth's surface, the distance above the surface is ignored because it is inconsequential compared to the radius of the earth. The constant figure of 9.81 m/s² is used instead.

Problem: Two identical 4 kg balls are floating in space, 2 meters apart. What is the magnitude of the gravitational force they exert on each other?

Solution:

$$F = G \frac{m_1 m_2}{r^2} = G \frac{4 \times 4}{2^2} = 4G = 2.67 \times 10^{-10}\, N$$

For a satellite of mass *m* in orbit around the earth (mass *M*), the gravitational attraction of the earth provides the centripetal force that keeps the satellite in motion:

$$\frac{GMm}{r^2} = \frac{mv^2}{r} = mr\omega^2 = mr\left(\frac{2\pi}{T}\right)^2$$

Thus, the period *T* of rotation of the satellite may be obtained from the equation:

$$\frac{T^2}{r^3} = \frac{4\pi^2}{GM}.$$

Johannes Kepler was a German mathematician who studied the astronomical observations made by Tyco Brahe. He derived the following three laws of planetary motion. Kepler's laws also predict the motion of comets.

First law

This law describes the shape of planetary orbits. Specifically, the orbit of a planet is an ellipse that has the sun at one of the foci. Such an orbit looks like this:

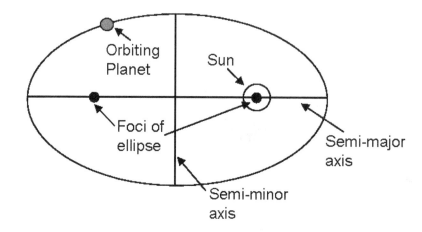

To analyze this situation mathematically, remember that the semi-major axis is denoted a, the semi-minor axis denoted b, and the general equation for an ellipse in polar coordinates is:

$$r = \frac{l}{1 + e\cos\theta}$$

Where r=radial coordinate
θ=angular coordinate
l= semi-latus rectum (l=b^2/a)

e=eccentricity (for an ellipse, e=$\sqrt{1 - \dfrac{b^2}{a^2}}$

Thus, we can also determine the planet's maximum and minimum distance from the Sun.

The point at which the planet is closest to the Sun is known as the perihelion and occurs when θ=0:

$$r_{min} = \frac{l}{1+e}$$

The point at which the planet is farthest from the Sun is known as the aphelion and occurs when θ=180°:

$$r_{max} = \frac{l}{1-e}$$

Second Law

The second law pertains to the relative speed of a planet as it orbits. This law says that a line joining the planet and the Sun sweeps out equal areas in equal intervals of time. In the diagram below, the two shaded areas demonstrate equal areas.

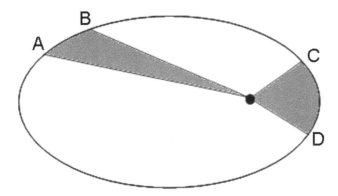

By Kepler's second law, we know that the planet will take the same amount of time to move between points A and B and between points C and D. Note that this means that the speed of the planet is inversely proportional to its distance from the sun (i.e., the plant moves fastest when it is closest to the Sun).

Kepler was only able to demonstrate the existence of this phenomenon but we now know that it is an effect of the Sun's gravity. The gravity of the Sun pulls the planet toward it thereby accelerating the planet as it nears. Using the first two laws together, Kepler was able to calculate a planet's position from the time elapsed since the perihelion.

Third law

The third law is also known as the harmonic law and it relates the size of a planet's orbital to the time needed to complete it. It states that the square of a planet's period is proportional to the cube of its mean distances from the Sun (this mean distance can be shown to be equal to the semi-major axis). So, we can state the third law as:

$$P^2 \propto a^3$$

where P=planet's orbital period (length of time needed to complete one orbit)
a=semi-major axis of orbit

Furthermore, for two planets A and B:

$$P_A^2 / P_B^2 = a_A^3 / a_B^3$$

The units for period and semi-major axis have been defined such that $P^2a^{-3}=1$ for all planets in our solar system. These units are sidereal years (yr) and astronomical units (AU). Sample values are given in the table below. Note that in each case $P^2 \sim a^3$

Planet	P (yr)	a (AU)	P^2	a^3
Venus	0.62	0.72	0.39	0.37
Earth	1.0	1.0	1.0	1.0
Jupiter	11.9	5.20	142	141

Skill 6.2   The beginning teacher calculates electrostatic forces, fields, and potentials.

Any point charge may experience force resulting from attraction to or repulsion from another charged object. The easiest way to begin analyzing this phenomenon and calculating this force is by considering two point charges. Let us say that the charge on the first point is Q_1, the charge on the second point is Q_2, and the distance between them is *r*. Their interaction is governed by **Coulomb's Law,** which gives the formula for the force F as:

$$F = k \frac{Q_1 Q_2}{r^2}$$

where $k = 9.0 \times 10^9 \dfrac{N \cdot m^2}{C^2}$ (known as Coulomb's constant)

The charge is a scalar quantity, however, the force has direction. For two point charges, the direction of the force is along a line joining the two charges. Note that the force will be repulsive if the two charges are both positive or both negative and attractive if one charge is positive and the other negative. Thus, a negative force indicates an attractive force.

When more than one point charge is exerting force on a point charge, we simply apply Coulomb's Law multiple times and then combine the forces as we would in any statics problem. Let's examine the process in the following example problem.

Problem: Three point charges are located at the vertices of a right triangle as shown below. Charges, angles, and distances are provided (drawing not to scale). Find the force exerted on the point charge A.

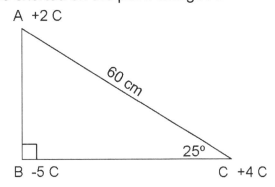

Solution: First we find the individual forces exerted on A by point B and point C. We have the information we need to find the magnitude of the force exerted on A by C.

$$F_{AC} = k\frac{Q_1Q_2}{r^2} = 9\times10^9 \frac{N\cdot m^2}{C^2}\left(\frac{4C\times2C}{(0.6m)^2}\right) = 2\times10^{11}N$$

To determine the magnitude of the force exerted on A by B, we must first determine the distance between them.

$$\sin 25° = \frac{r_{AB}}{60cm}$$
$$r_{AB} = 60cm\times\sin 25° = 25cm$$

Now we can determine the force.

$$F_{AB} = k\frac{Q_1Q_2}{r^2} = 9\times10^9 \frac{N\cdot m^2}{C^2}\left(\frac{-5C\times2C}{(0.25m)^2}\right) = -1.4\times10^{12}N$$

We can see that there is an attraction in the direction of B (negative force) and repulsion in the direction of C (positive force). To find the net force, we must consider the direction of these forces (along the line connecting any two point charges). We add them together using the law of cosines.

$$F_A^2 = F_{AB}^2 + F_{AC}^2 - 2F_{AB}F_{AC}\cos 75°$$
$$F_A^2 = (-1.4 \times 10^{12}\,N)^2 + (2 \times 10^{11}\,N)^2 - 2(-1.4 \times 10^{12}\,N)(2 \times 10^{11}\,N)^2 \cos 75°$$
$$F_A = 1.5 \times 10^{12}\,N$$

This gives us the magnitude of the net force, now we will find its direction using the law of sines.

$$\frac{\sin\theta}{F_{AC}} = \frac{\sin 75°}{F_A}$$
$$\sin\theta = F_{AC}\frac{\sin 75°}{F_A} = 2 \times 10^{11}\,N \frac{\sin 75°}{1.5 \times 10^{12}\,N}$$
$$\theta = 7.3°$$

Thus, the net force on A is 7.3° west of south and has magnitude 1.5 x 10^{12}N. Looking back at our diagram, this makes sense, because A should be attracted to B (pulled straight south) but the repulsion away from C "pushes" this force in a westward direction.

An **electric field** exists in the space surrounding a charge. Electric fields have both direction and magnitude determined by the strength and direction in which they exhibit force on a test charge. The units used to measure electric fields are newtons per coulomb (N/C). **Electric potential** is simply the **potential energy** per unit of charge. Given this definition, it is clear that electric potential must be measured in joules per coulomb and this unit is known as a volt (J/C=V).

Within an electric field there are typically differences in potential energy. This **potential difference** may be referred to as **voltage**. The difference in electrical potential between two points is the amount of work needed to move a unit charge from the first point to the second point. Stated mathematically, this is:

$$V = \frac{W}{Q}$$

where V= the potential difference
W= the work done to move the charge
Q= the charge

We know from mechanics, however, that work is simply force applied over a certain distance. We can combine this with Coulomb's law to find the work done between two charges distance r apart.

$$W = F.r = k\frac{Q_1 Q_2}{r^2}.r = k\frac{Q_1 Q_2}{r}$$

Now we can simply substitute this back into the equation above for electric potential:

$$V_2 = \frac{W}{Q_2} = \frac{k\dfrac{Q_1 Q_2}{r}}{Q_2} = k\frac{Q_1}{r}$$

Let's examine a sample problem involving electrical potential.

Problem: What is the electric potential at point A due to the 2 shown charges? If a charge of +2.0 C were infinitely far away, how much work would be required to bring it to point A?

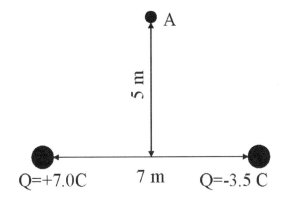

Solution: To determine the electric potential at point A, we simple find and add the potential from the two charges (this is the principle of superposition). From the diagram, we can assume that A is equidistant from each charge. Using the Pythagorean theorem, we determine this distance to be 6.1 m.

$$V = \frac{kq}{r} = k\left(\frac{7.0C}{6.1m} + \frac{-3.5C}{6.1m}\right) = 9 \times 10^9 \frac{N.m^2}{C^2}\left(0.57\frac{C}{m}\right) = 5.13 \times 10^9 V$$

Now, let's consider bringing the charged particle to point A. We assume that electric potential of these particle is initially zero because it is infinitely far away. Since now know the potential at point A, we can calculate the work necessary to bring the particle from V=0, i.e. the potential energy of the charge in the electrical field:

$$W = VQ = (5.13 \times 10^9) \times 2J = 10.26 \times 10^9 J$$

The large results for potential and work make it apparent how large the unit coulomb is. For this reason, most problems deal in microcoulombs (μ C).

Skill 6.3   The beginning teacher understands the properties of magnetic materials and the molecular theory of magnetism.

Magnetism is a phenomenon in which certain materials, known as magnetic materials, attract or repel each other. A magnet has two poles, a south pole and a north pole. Like poles repel while unlike poles attract. Magnetic poles always occur in pairs known as **magnetic dipoles**. One cannot isolate a single magnetic pole. If a magnet is broken in half, opposite poles appear at both sides of the break point so that one now has two magnets each with a south pole and a north pole. No matter how small the pieces a magnet is broken into, the smallest unit at the atomic level is still a dipole.

A large magnet can be thought of as one with many small dipoles that are aligned in such a way that apart from the pole areas, the internal south and north poles cancel each other out. Destroying this long range order within a magnet by heating or hammering can demagnetize it. The dipoles in a **non-magnetic** material are randomly aligned while they are perfectly aligned in a preferred direction in **permanent** magnets. In a **ferromagnet**, there are domains where the magnetic dipoles are aligned, however, the domains themselves are randomly oriented. A ferromagnet can be magnetized by placing it in an external magnetic field that exerts a force to line up the domains.

Weber's theory of molecular magnetism assumes that all magnetic substances are made up of tiny molecular magnets. An unmagnetized material has no magnetic effect because adjacent molecular magnets neutralize the magnetic forces of its molecular magnets.

Most of the molecular magnets of a magnetized material line up so that each molecule's north pole points in one direction, and the south pole points in the opposite direction. When the molecules are aligned in this manner, the material has one effective north pole and one effective south pole.

The retention of magnetism in the fragments of a broken magnet suggests the existence of molecular magnets. Regardless of how many times you break a magnet, each fragment is still a magnet. Each fragment has a pole at the breaking point that is equally strong as, but opposite to, the pole at the breaking point of the other fragment. Reconstructing the magnet in the order in which it was broken restores its original properties. This suggests that the molecules of a magnet are magnets themselves.

Skill 6.4 **The beginning teacher identifies the source of the magnetic field and calculates the magnetic field for various simple current distributions.**

A magnet produces a magnetic field that exerts a force on any other magnet or current-carrying conductor placed in the field. Magnetic field lines are a good way to visualize a magnetic field. The distance between magnetic fields lines indicates the strength of the magnetic field such that the lines are closer together near the poles of the magnets where the magnetic field is the strongest. The lines spread out above and below the middle of the magnet, as the field is weakest at those points furthest from the two poles. The SI unit for magnetic field known as magnetic induction is Tesla(T) given by $1T = 1\ N.s/(C.m) = 1\ N/(A.m)$. Magnetic fields are often expressed in the smaller unit Gauss (G) (1 T = 10,000 G). Magnetic field lines always point from the north pole of a magnet to the south pole.

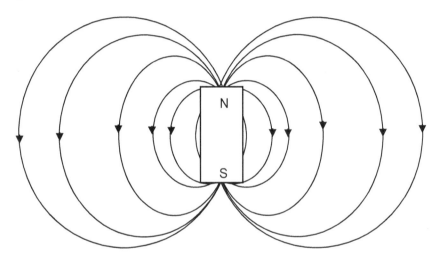

Magnetic field lines can be plotted with a magnetized needle that is free to turn in 3 dimensions. Usually a compass needle is used in demonstrations. The direction tangent to the magnetic field line is the direction the compass needle will point in a magnetic field. Iron filings spread on a flat surface or magnetic field viewing film which contains a slurry of iron filings are another way to see magnetic field lines.

The magnetic force exerted on a charge moving in a magnetic field depends on the size and velocity of the charge as well as the magnitude of the magnetic field. One important fact to remember is that only the velocity of the charge in a direction perpendicular to the magnetic field will affect the force exerted. Therefore, a charge moving parallel to the magnetic field will have no force acting upon it whereas a charge will feel the greatest force when moving perpendicular to the magnetic field.

Conductors through which electrical currents travel will produce magnetic fields. The magnetic field *dB* induced at a distance *r* by an element of current *Idl* flowing through a wire element of length *dl* is given by the **Biot-Savart** law

$$dB = \frac{\mu_0}{4\pi} \frac{Idl \times \hat{r}}{r^2}$$

where μ_0 is a constant known as the permeability of free space and $\hat{r}$ is the unit vector pointing from the current element to the point where the magnetic field is calculated.

An alternate statement of this law is **Ampere's law** according to which the line integral of *B.dl* around any closed path enclosing a steady current *I* is given by

$$\oint_C B \cdot dl = \mu_0 I$$

The basis of this phenomenon is the same no matter what the shape of the conductor, but we will consider three common situations:

Straight Wire

Around a current-carrying straight wire, the magnetic field lines form concentric circles around the wire. The direction of the magnetic field is given by the right-hand rule: When the thumb of the right hand points in the direction of the current, the fingers curl around the wire in the direction of the magnetic field. Note the direction of the current and magnetic field in the diagram.

To find the magnetic field of an infinitely long (allowing us to disregarding end effects) we apply Ampere's Law to a circular path at a distance r around the wire:

$$B = \frac{\mu_0 I}{2\pi r}$$

where μ_0=the permeability of free space (4π x 10-7 T·m/A)
I=current
r=distance from the wire

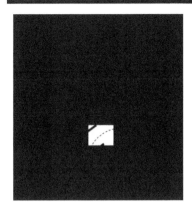

Loops

Like the straight wire from which it's been made, a looped wire has magnetic field lines that form concentric circles with direction following the right-hand rule. However, the field are additive in the center of the loop creating a field like the one shown. The magnetic field of a loop is found similarly to that for a straight wire.

In the center of the loop, the magnetic field is:

$$B = \frac{\mu_0 I}{2r}$$

Solenoids

A solenoid is essentially a coil of conduction wire wrapped around a central object. This means it is a series of loops and the magnetic field is similarly a sum of the fields that would form around several loops, as shown.

The magnetic field of a solenoid can be found as with the following equation:

$$B = \mu_0 nI$$

In this equation, n is turn density, which is simply the number of turns divided by the length of the solenoid.

Displacement current

While Ampere's law works perfectly for a steady current, for a situation where the current varies and a charge builds up (e.g. charging of a capacitor) it does not hold. Maxwell amended Ampere's law to include an additional term that includes the displacement current. This is not a true current but actually refers to changes in the electric field and is given by

$$I_d = \varepsilon_0 \frac{d\varphi_e}{dt}$$

where φ_e is the flux of the electric field. Including the displacement current, Ampere's law is given by

$$\oint \boldsymbol{B}.d\boldsymbol{l} = \mu_0 I + \mu_0 \varepsilon_0 \frac{d\varphi_e}{dt}$$

The displacement current essentially indicates that changing electric flux produces a magnetic field.

Skill 6.5 **The beginning teacher analyzes the magnetic force on charged particles and current-carrying conductors.**

The direction of the magnetic force, or the magnetic component of the **Lorenz force** (force on a charged particle in an electrical and magnetic field), is always at a right angle to the plane formed by the velocity vector v and the magnetic field B and is given by applying the right hand rule - if the fingers of the right hand are curled in a way that seems to rotate the v vector into the B vector, the thumb points in the direction of the force. The magnitude of the force is equal to the cross product of the velocity of the charge with the magnetic field multiplied by the magnitude of the charge.

$$F=q \ (\mathbf{v} \ X \ \mathbf{B}) \ \text{or} \ F=q \ v \ B\sin(\theta)$$

Where θ is the angle formed between the vectors of velocity of the charge and direction of magnetic field.

Problem: Assuming we have a particle of 1 x 10⁻⁶ kg that has a charge of -8 coulombs that is moving perpendicular to a magnetic field in a clockwise direction on a circular path with a radius of 2 m and a speed of 2000 m/s, let's determine the magnitude and direction of the magnetic field acting upon it.

Solution: We know the mass, charge, speed, and path radius of the charged particle. Combining the equation above with the equation for centripetal force we get

$$qvB = \frac{mv^2}{r} \quad \text{or} \quad B = \frac{mv}{qr}$$

Thus B= (1 x 10⁻⁶ kg) (2000m/s) / (-8 C)(2 m) = 1.25 x 10⁻⁴ Tesla

Since the particle is moving in a clockwise direction, we use the right hand rule and point our fingers clockwise along a circular path in the plane of the paper while pointing the thumb towards the center in the direction of the centripetal force. This requires the fingers to curl in a way that indicates that the magnetic field is pointing out of the page. However, since the particle has a negative charge we must reverse the final direction of the magnetic field into the page.

A **mass spectrometer** measures the mass to charge ratio of ions using a setup similar to the one described above. m/q is determined by measuring the path radius of particles of known velocity moving in a known magnetic field.

A **cyclotron**, a type of particle accelerator, also uses a perpendicular magnetic field to keep particles on a circular path. After each half circle, the particles are accelerated by an electric field and the path radius is increased. Thus the beam of particles moves faster and faster in a growing spiral within the confines of the cyclotron until they exit at a high speed near the outer edge. Its compactness is one of the advantages a cyclotron has over linear accelerators.

The **force on a current-carrying conductor** in a magnetic field is the sum of the forces on the moving charged particles that create the current. For a current I flowing in a straight wire segment of length l in a magnetic field B, this force is given by

$$F = Il \times B$$

where l is a vector of magnitude l and direction in the direction of the current.

When a current-carrying loop is placed in a magnetic field, the net force on it is zero since the forces on the different parts of the loop act in different directions and cancel each other out. There is, however, a net torque on the loop that tends to rotate it so that the area of the loop is perpendicular to the magnetic field. For a current I flowing in a loop of area A, this torque is given by

$$\tau = IA\hat{n} \times B$$

where $\hat{n}$ is the unit vector perpendicular to the plane of the loop.

Magnetic flux (Gauss's law of magnetism)

Carl Friedrich Gauss developed laws that related electric or gravitational flux to electrical charge or mass, respectively. Gauss's law, along with others, was eventually generalized by James Clerk Maxwell to explain the relationships between electromagnetic phenomena (Maxwell's Equations).

To understand Gauss's law for magnetism, we must first define magnetic flux. Magnetic flux is the magnetic field that passes through a given area. It is given by the following equation:

$$\Phi = B(\cos\phi)A$$

where Φ=flux
B=the magnetic field
A=area
ϕ= the angle between the electric field and a vector normal to the surface A

Thus, if a plane is parallel to a magnetic field, no magnetic field lines will pass through that plane and the flux will be zero. If a plane is perpendicular to a magnetic field, the flux will be maximal.

Now we can state Gauss's law of magnetism: the net magnetic flux out of any closed surface is zero. Mathematically, this may be stated as:

$$\vec{\nabla} \cdot \vec{B} = 0$$

where $\vec{\nabla}$ = the del operator
$\vec{B}$ = magnetic field

One of the most important implications of this law is that there are no magnetic monopoles (that is, magnets always have a positive and negative pole). This is because a magnetic monopole source would give a non-zero product in the equation above. For a magnetic dipole with closed surface, of course, the net flux will always be zero. This is because the magnetic flux directed inward toward the south pole is always equal to the magnetic flux outward from the north pole.

Skill 6.6 **The beginning teacher understands induced electric and magnetic fields and analyzes the relationship between electricity and magnetism.**

When the magnetic flux through a coil is changed, a voltage is produced which is known as induced electromagnetic force. Magnetic flux is a term used to describe the number of magnetic fields lines that pass through an area and is described by the equation:

$\Phi = B\, A \cos\theta$
Where Φ is the angle between the magnetic field B, and the normal to the plane of the coil of area A

By changing any of these three inputs, magnetic field, area of coil, or angle between field and coil, the flux will change and an EMF can be induced. The speed at which these changes occur also affects the magnitude of the EMF, as a more rapid transition generates more EMF than a gradual one. This is described by **Faraday's law** of induction:

$\varepsilon = -N\, \Delta\Phi\, /\, \Delta t$
where ε is emf induced, N is the number of loops in a coil, t is time, and Φ is magnetic flux

The negative sign signifies **Lenz's law,** which states that induced emf in a coil acts to oppose any change in magnetic flux. Thus the current flows in a way that creates a magnetic field in the direction opposing the change in flux. The right hand rule for this is that if your fingers curl in the direction of the induced current, your thumb points in the direction of the magnetic field it produces through the loop.

To determine the direction the current flows in the coil we need to apply the right hand rule and Lenz's law. The magnetic flux is being increased out of the page, with your thumb pointing up the fingers are coiling counterclockwise. However, Lenz's law tells us the current will oppose the change in flux so the current in the coil will be flowing clockwise.

Skill 6.7 The beginning teacher understands the electromagnetic spectrum and the production of electromagnetic waves.

The electromagnetic spectrum is measured using frequency (f) in hertz or wavelength (λ) in meters. The frequency times the wavelength of every electromagnetic wave equals the speed of light (3.0×10^8 meters/second).

Roughly, the range of wavelengths of the electromagnetic spectrum is:

	f	λ
Radio waves	$10^{5} - 10^{-1}$ hertz	$10^{3} - 10^{9}$ meters
Microwaves	$3 \times 10^{9} - 3 \times 10^{11}$ hertz	$10^{-3} - 10^{-1}$ meters
Infrared radiation	$3 \times 10^{11} - 4 \times 10^{14}$ hertz	$7 \times 10^{-7} - 10^{-3}$ meters
Visible light	$4 \times 10^{14} - 7.5 \times 10^{14}$ hertz	$4 \times 10^{-7} - 7 \times 10^{-7}$ meters
Ultraviolet radiation	$7.5 \times 10^{14} - 3 \times 10^{16}$ hertz	$10^{-8} - 4 \times 10^{-7}$ meters
X-Rays	$3 \times 10^{16} - 3 \times 10^{19}$ hertz	$10^{-11} - 10^{-8}$ meters
Gamma Rays	$> 3 \times 10^{19}$ hertz	$< 10^{-11}$ meters

Radio waves are used for transmitting data. Common examples are television, cell phones, and wireless computer networks. Microwaves are used to heat food and deliver Wi-Fi service. Infrared waves are utilized in night vision goggles. Visible light we are all familiar with as the human eye is most sensitive to this wavelength range. Light of different colors have different wavelengths. In the visible range, red light has the largest wavelength while violet light has the smallest. UV light causes sunburns and would be even more harmful if most of it were not captured in the Earth's ozone layer. X-rays aid us in the medical field and gamma rays are most useful in the field of astronomy.

A changing electric field produces a magnetic field, and a changing magnetic field produces an electric field. Electromagnetic waves are produced when an electric field connects with a magnetic field. The waves are produced by the motion of electrically charged particles. The electric and magnetic fields are perpendicular to each other and to the direction of the wave.

Radio waves are produced by antennae whose dimensions must be comparable to the wavelength in order for the antennae to work efficiently and by cosmic phenomena in deep space. Microwaves are produced by vacuum-based devices such as the magnetron, klystron, traveling wave tube, and gyrotron. Anything with a temperature greater than about 10 kelvin produces terahertz radiation; however, the emissions are very weak. The only effective sources of stronger terahertz radiation are the gyrotron, far infrared laser, quantum cascade laser, synchrotron light sources, the backward wave oscillator, the free electron laser, and single-cycle sources used in Terahertz time domain spectroscopy. Infrared radiation comes from the sun and from visible light that is absorbed and then re-radiated at longer wavelengths. Ultraviolet radiation is naturally transmitted by the sun. Artificial UV radiation is created in the form of vacuum UV and extreme UV. X-rays are produced by accelerating electrons in order to collide with a metal target. Gamma rays are produced by sub-atomic particle interaction, such as radioactive decay, but most are created by nuclear reactions in space.

Competency 0007   **The teacher understands applications of electricity and magnetism.**

Skill 7.1   **The beginning teacher analyzes common examples of electrostatics (e.g., a charged balloon attached to a wall, behavior of an electroscope, charging by induction).**

Electrical current requires the free flow of electrons. Various materials allow different degrees of electron movement and are classified as conductors, insulators, or semiconductors (in certain, typically man-made environments, superconductors also exist). When charge is transferred to a mass of material, the response is highly dependent on whether that material is a conductor or insulator.

Conductors: Those materials that allow for free and easy movement of electrons are called conductors. Some of the best conductors are metal, especially copper and silver. This is because these materials are held together with metallic bonds, which involve de-localized electrons shared by atoms in a lattice. If a charge is transferred to a conductor, the electrons will flow freely and the charge will quickly distribute itself across the material in a manner dictated by the conductor's shape.

Insulators: Materials that do not allow conduction are call insulators. Good insulators include, glass, rubber, and wood. These materials have chemical structures in which the electrons are closely localized to the individual atoms. In contrast to a conductor, a charge transferred to an insulator will remain localized at the point where it was introduced. This is because the movement of electrons will be highly impeded.

Semiconductors: Materials with intermediate conduction properties are known as semiconductors. Their properties are similar to insulators in that they have few free electrons to carry the charge. However, these electrons can be thermally excited into higher energy states that allow them sufficient freedom to transmit electrical charge. The electrical properties of a semiconductor are often improved by introducing impurities, a procedure known as doping. Doping introduces extra electrons or extra electron acceptors to facilitate the movement of charge. *Temporary* changes in electrical properties can be induced by applying an electrical field.

Charge can be transferred to materials in a few different ways.

Conduction: In the most general sense, electrical conduction is the movement of charged particles (electrons) through a medium. As explained above, in conducting materials, electrons loosely attached to atoms are capable of carrying an electrical current. This requires that the atoms of the conducting material be brought into physical contact with the charge source. For example, if a conductor is brought in contact with another charged conductor or a current source (such as a battery), the charge will be transferred to that conductor.

Friction: When two materials are brought into contact (or rubbed against each other), electrons may be transferred between them. If the materials are then separated, one will be left with a negative charge and the other will have a positive charge. This phenomenon is known as the triboelectric effect. Both the polarity and strength of the resultant charge depends upon the materials, surface roughness, temperature, and strain. Some common examples of combinations that produce significant charges are glass with silk and rubber with fur.

Induction: Electromagnetic induction is the production of voltage that occurs when a conductor interacts with a magnetic field. A conductor can be charged either by moving it through a static electric field or by placing it in a changing magnetic field. Induction was discovered by Michael Faraday and Faraday's Law governs this phenomenon.

Skill 7.2 The beginning teacher understands electric current, resistance and resistivity, potential difference, capacitance, and electromotive force in conductors and circuits.

Semiconductors, conductors and superconductors are differentiated by how "easily" current can flow in the presence of an applied electric field. Dielectrics (insulators) conduct little or no current in the presence of an applied electric field, as the charged components of the material (for example, atoms and their associated electrons) are tightly bound and are not free to move within the material. In the case of materials with some amount of conductivity, so-called valence (higher energy level) electrons are only loosely bound and may move among positive charge centers (i.e., atoms or ions).

Conductors, such as metals like aluminum and iron, have numerous valence electrons distributed among the atoms that compose the material. These electrons can move freely, especially under the influence of an applied electric field. In the absence of any applied field, these electrons move randomly, resulting in no net current. If a static electric field is applied, the mobile electrons reorient themselves to minimize the energy of the system and create an equipotential on the surface of the metal (in the ideal case of infinite conductivity). The highly mobile charge carriers do not allow a net field inside the metal; thus conductors can "shield" electromagnetic fields.

Semiconductors, such as silicon and germanium, are materials that can neither be described as conductors, nor as insulators. A certain number of charge carriers are mobile in the semiconductor, but this number is nowhere near the free charge populations of conductors such as metals. "Doping" of a semiconductor by adding so-called donor atoms or acceptor atoms to the intrinsic (or pure) semiconductor can increase the conductivity of the material.

Furthermore, combination of a number of differently doped semiconductors (such as donor-doped silicon and acceptor-doped silicon) can produce a device with beneficial electrical characteristics (such as the diode). The conductivity of such devices can be controlled by applying voltages across specific portions of the device.

A useful way to visualize the relationship of conductors and semiconductors is by way of energy band diagrams. For purposes of comparison, an example of an insulator is included here as well.

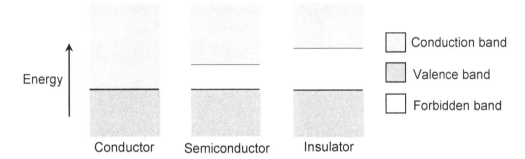

Prior to the 1960s most electronic apparatuses relied on either vacuum tubes or mechanical devices, typically relays. As semiconductors became increasingly available, however, vacuum tubes were replaced with solid state devices. Vacuum tubes conduct electrons through a heated vacuum but semiconductors allow electrons to flow through them while still solid. Solid state has come to mean any circuit that does not contain the aforementioned vacuum tubes and, in short, operates with "no moving parts". The lack of these elements make solid state devices more resistant to physical stressors, such as vibration, and more durable in general, since they are less susceptible to wear. A familiar example of this are the solid state "flash cards" that are popular for data storage. Previously, hard disk players were primarily used for a similar function but their moving parts make them of limited durability and less practical to transport.

Semiconductors are extremely useful because their conductive properties can be controlled. This is done by "doping" or introducing impurities. The impurity or dopant is used to introduce extra electrons or extra free orbital space that can be filled with electrons. This allows much freer movement of electrons and, therefore, flows of current through the material. Semiconductors doped to contain extra electrons are known as N-type, while those doped to contain extra "holes" are known a P-type. Typically, either type of semiconductor can be made from the same base material. For instance, silicon can be doped with boron to create a P-type semiconductor or with phosphorus to create an N-type semiconductor. Two of the most common and important semiconductor devices today are diodes and transistors.

Transistors: Just like the vacuum tubes they replaced, transistors control current flow. They serve a variety of functions in circuits and can act as amplifiers, switches, voltage regulators, signal modulators, or oscillators. They are perhaps the most important building block of modern circuitry and electronics. As in solid state diodes, the properties of semiconductors are exploited in transistors to control the flow of current. However, where the diode is analogous to a check valve, a transistor function more like a tap on a sink and is able to control the rate of current flow or eliminate it all together. Today, most transistors are either bipolar junction transistors (BJT) or field effect transistors (FET).

Ohm's Law is the most important tool we posses to analyze electrical circuits. Ohm's Law states that the current passing through a conductor is directly proportional to the voltage drop and inversely proportional to the resistance of the conductor. Stated mathematically, this is:

$$V = IR$$

Problem:
The circuit diagram at right shows three resistors connected to a battery in series. A current of 1.0A flows through the circuit in the direction shown. It is known that the equivalent resistance of this circuit is 25 Ω. What is the total voltage supplied by the battery?

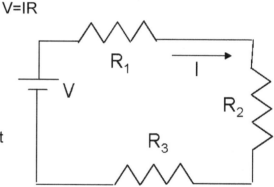

Solution:
To determine the battery's voltage, we simply apply Ohm's Law:

$$V = IR = 1.0A \times 25\Omega = 25V$$

Conductors are those materials that allow for the free passage of electrical current. However, all materials exhibit a certain opposition to the movement of electrons. This opposition is known as **resistivity** (ρ). Resistivity is determined experimentally by measuring the resistance of a uniformly shaped sample of the material and applying the following equation:

$$\rho = R\frac{A}{l}$$

where ρ = static resistivity of the material
R = electrical resistance of the material sample
A = cross-sectional area of the material sample
L = length of the material sample

The temperature at which these measurements are taken is important as it has been shown that resistivity is a function of temperature. For conductors, resistivity increases with increasing temperature and decreases with decreasing temperature. At extremely low temperatures resistivity assumes a low and constant value known as residual resistivity (ρ_0). Residual resistivity is a function of the type and purity of the conductor.

Capacitance (C) is a measure of the stored electric charge per unit electric potential. The mathematical definition is:

$$C = \frac{Q}{V}$$

It follows from the definition above that the units of capacitance are coulombs per volt, a unit known as a farad ($F = C/V$). In circuits, devices called parallel plate capacitors are formed by two closely spaced conductors. The function of capacitors is to store electrical energy. When a voltage is applied, electrical charges build up in both the conductors (typically referred to as plates). These charges on the two plates have equal magnitude but opposite sign.

In summary, a capacitor is "charged" as electrical energy is delivered to it and opposite charges accumulate on the two plates. The two plates generate electric fields and a voltage develops across the dielectric. The energy stored in the capacitor, then, is equal to the amount of work necessary to create this voltage.

Skill 7.3   The beginning teacher analyzes series and parallel DC circuits in terms of current, resistance, voltage, and power.

Often resistors and capacitors are used together in series or parallel. Two components are in series if one end of the first element is connected to one end of the second component. The components are in parallel if both ends of one element are connected to the corresponding ends of another. A series circuit has a single path for current flow through all of its elements. A parallel circuit is one that requires more than one path for current flow in order to reach all of the circuit elements. Below is a diagram demonstrating a simple circuit with resistors in parallel (on right) and in series (on left). Note the symbols used for a battery (noted V) and the resistors (noted R).

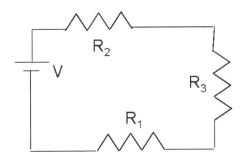
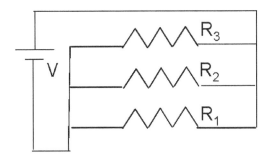

Thus, when the resistors are placed in series, the current through each one will be the same. When they are placed in parallel, the voltage through each one will be the same. To understand basic circuitry, it is important to master the rules by which the equivalent resistance (R_{eq}) or capacitance (C_{eq}) can be calculated from a number of resistors or capacitors as follows.

Resistors in parallel:
$$\frac{1}{R_{eq}} = \frac{1}{R_1} + \frac{1}{R_2} + \cdots + \frac{1}{R_n}$$

Resistors in series:
$$R_{eq} = R_1 + R_2 + \cdots + R_n$$

Capacitors in parallel:
$$C_{eq} = C_1 + C_2 + \cdots + C_n$$

Capacitors in series:
$$\frac{1}{C_{eq}} = \frac{1}{C_1} + \frac{1}{C_2} + \cdots + \frac{1}{C_n}$$

Skill 7.4   The beginning teacher identifies basic components and characteristics of AC circuits.

Alternating current (AC) is a type of electrical current with cyclically varying magnitude and direction. This is differentiated from direct current (DC), which has constant direction. AC is the type of current delivered to businesses and residences.

Though other waveforms are sometimes used, the vast majority of AC current is sinusoidal. Thus we can use wave terminology to help us describe AC current. Since AC current is a function of time, we can express it mathematically as:

$$v(t) = V_{peak} \cdot \sin(\omega t)$$

where V_{peak}= the peak voltage; the maximum value of the voltage
ω=angular frequency; a measure of rotation rate
t=time

The instantaneous power or energy transmission per unit time is given by $I^2_{peak} R \sin^2(\omega t)$, a value that varies over time. In order to asses the overall rate of energy transmission, however, we need some kind of average value. The **root mean square value (V_{rms}, I_{rms})** is useful because an AC current will deliver the same power as a DC current if its $V_{rms}=V_{DC}$, i.e. average power or average energy transmission per unit time is given by $P_{av} = V_{rms} I_{rms}$.

Skill 7.5 The beginning teacher understands the operation of an electromagnet.

The movement of electric charges (i.e., a current density **J**) results in a magnetic field **H**, as described by the Maxwell equation based on Ampere's law:

$$\nabla \times \mathbf{H}(r,t) = \frac{\partial \mathbf{D}(r,t)}{\partial t} + \mathbf{J}(r,t)$$

For the case where the time derivative of the electric flux density **D** is zero, this reduces to the simpler Ampere's law:

$$\nabla \times \mathbf{H}(r,t) = \mathbf{J}(r,t)$$

Electromagnets take advantage of this relationship between the current and the magnetic field by, for example, coiling a current-carrying wire (a solenoid), sometimes around a ferromagnetic or paramagnetic material. This creates a magnetic dipole with a strength that varies depending on a number of factors.

The direction of the dipole relative to the direction of current flow is determined by the right hand rule: the fingers curl in the direction of the current, and the thumb points in the (north) direction of the dipole.

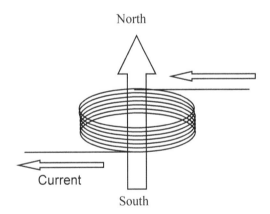

The strength of the electromagnet (i.e., the induced magnetic dipole) can be increased by adding to the number of turns (or loops) of current-carrying wire. The principle of superposition applies here and the induced magnetic field varies proportionally according to the number of turns. Also, by varying the current, the strength of the electromagnet can be increased or decreased. Imperfections in the solenoid, such as imperfectly packed wire loops, which can cause magnetic flux leakage, can adversely affect the strength of the electromagnet. Also, the spatial extent of the solenoid (or other form of electromagnet, such as a toroid) must be considered if exact numerical calculations are pursued.

Another critical factor that affects the electromagnet is the material used inside the coil; specifically, the magnetic properties of the material. Magnetizable materials with permeabilities (μ) greater than unity can be used to increase the magnitude of the induced magnetic dipole. Ferromagnetic materials, for example, can have very large permeabilities. One such example is iron. A ferromagnetic core is magnetized when the magnetic field induced by the current-carrying wire is applied resulting in a stronger magnetic dipole than would have been produced if a non-magnetic material (such as air) had been used. The ability of a magnetic material core to increase the strength of the electromagnet is limited, however. In the case of a ferromagnetic material, once all the magnetic domains have been aligned with the magnetic field of the electromagnet, saturation has been reached and the material cannot be magnetized further.

Skill 7.6 The beginning teacher understands the operation of electric meters, motors, generators, and transformers.

Ammeter: An ammeter placed in series in a circuit measures the current through the circuit. An ammeter typically has a very small resistance so that the current in the circuit is not changed too much by insertion of the ammeter.

Voltmeter: A voltmeter is used to measure potential difference. The potential difference across a resistor is measured by a voltmeter placed in parallel across it. An ideal voltmeter has very high resistance so that it does not appreciably alter circuit resistance and therefore the voltage drop it is measuring.

Galvanometer: A galvanometer is a device that measures current and is a component of an ammeter or a voltmeter. A typical galvanometer consists of a coil of wire, an indicator and a scale that is designed to be proportional to the current in the galvanometer. The principle that a current-carrying wire experiences a force in a magnetic field is used in the construction of a galvanometer. In order to create a voltmeter from a galvanometer, resistors are added in series to it. To build an ammeter using a galvanometer, a small resistance known as a shunt resistor is placed in parallel with it.

Potentiometer: A potentiometer is a variable resistance device in which the user can vary the resistance to control the current and voltage applied to a circuit. Since the potentiometer can be used to control what fraction of the emf of a battery is applied to a circuit, it is also known as a voltage divider. It can be used to measure an unknown voltage by comparing it with a known value.

Multimeter: A common electrical meter, typically known as a multimeter, is capable of measuring voltage, resistance, and current. Many of these devices can also measure capacitance (farads), frequency (hertz), duty cycle (a percentage), temperature (degrees), conductance (siemens), and inductance (henrys).

Electric motors are found in many common appliances such as fans and washing machines. The operation of a motor is based on the principle that a magnetic field exerts a force on a current carrying conductor. This force is essentially due to the fact that the current carrying conductor itself generates a magnetic field; the basic principle that governs the behavior of an electromagnet. In a motor, this idea is used to convert electrical energy into mechanical energy, most commonly rotational energy. Thus the components of the simplest motors must include a strong magnet and a current-carrying coil placed in the magnetic field in such a way that the force on it causes it to rotate.

Motors may be run using DC or AC current and may be designed in a number of ways with varying levels of complexity. A very basic DC motor consists of the following components:

- A **field magnet**
- An **armature** with a coil around it that rotates between the poles of the field magnet
- A **power supply** that supplies current to the armature
- An **axle** that transfers the rotational energy of the armature to the working parts of the motor
- A set of **commutators** and **brushes** that reverse the direction of power flow every half rotation so that the armature continues to rotate

Generators are devices that are the opposite of motors in that they convert **mechanical energy into electrical energy**. The mechanical energy can come from a variety of sources; combustion engines, blowing wind, falling water, or even a hand crank or bicycle wheel. Most generators rely upon electromagnetic induction to create an electrical current. These generators basically consist of magnets and a coil. The magnets create a magnetic field and the coil is located within this field. Mechanical energy, from whatever source, is used to spin the coil within this field. As stated by Faraday's Law, this produces a voltage.

Electromagnetic induction is used in a **transformer**, a device that magnetically couples two circuits together to allow the transfer of energy between the two circuits without requiring motion. Typically, a transformer consists of a couple of coils and a magnetic core. A changing voltage applied to one coil (the primary) creates a flux in the magnetic core, which induces voltage in the other coil (the secondary). All transformers operate on this simple principle though they range in size and function from those in tiny microphones to those that connect the components of the United States power grid. One of the most important functions of transformers is that they allow us to "step-up" and "step-down" between vastly different voltages.

Competency 0008   **The teacher understands the conservation of energy and momentum.**

Skill 8.1   The beginning teacher understands the concept of work.

Energy: the ability to do work (to cause change).

Work: the energy expended when the position or speed of an object is moved against an opposing force. Measured in Joules, work is the product of the force on an object and the distance through which the object is moved.

Thermal Energy (heat): the energy of moving atoms and molecules.

Chemical Energy: the energy that bonds atoms and molecules together.

Nuclear Energy: the energy of moving the nucleus of an atom.

Mechanical Energy: the energy of moving objects.

Potential Energy: the energy stored in an object due to its position.

Elastic Potential Energy: the energy stored in elastic (stretchable) objects such as rubber bands or springs.

Gravitational Potential Energy: the energy an object has when it is in an elevated position.

Kinetic Energy: the energy an object has due to its mass and motion.

Energy is neither created nor destroyed. When something happens, energy is simply changing from one form to another.

Skill 8.2   The beginning teacher understands the relationships among work, energy and power.

Energy and Work

Whenever work is done upon an object by an external force, there will be a change in the total mechanical energy of the object. If only internal forces are doing work (no work done by external forces), there is no change in total mechanical energy, the total mechanical energy is "conserved." The quantitative relationship between work and mechanical energy is expressed by the following equation:

$$TME_i + W_{ext} = TME_f$$

The equation states that the initial amount of total mechanical energy (TME_i) plus the work done by external forces (W_{ext}) is equal to the final amount of total mechanical energy (TME_f).

Power

Power is the rate at which work is done. It is the work/time ration. The following equation is the formula used to compute power:

$$Power = \frac{Work}{Time}$$

The standard metric unit of power is the Watt. A unit of power is equivalent to a unit of work divided by a unit of time. Therefore, a Watt is equivalent to a Joule/second.

Mechanical Advantage

There are two types of mechanical advantage, ideal and actual. Ideal mechanical advantage is the mechanical advantage of an ideal machine. Because such a machine does not really exist, we use physics principals to "theoretically" solve such equations. The ideal mechanical advantage (IMA) is found using the following formula:

$$IMA = D_E / D_R$$

The effort distance over the resistance distance gives us the IMA.

Actual mechanical advantage it the mechanical advantage of a real machine and takes into consideration factors such as energy lost to friction. Actual mechanical advantage (AMA) is calculated using the following formula:

$$AMA = R / E_{actual}$$

Dividing the resistance force by the actual effort force we can determine the actual mechanical advantage of a machine.

Efficiency is the relationship between energy input and energy output. Efficiency is expressed as a percentage. The more efficient a system is, the less energy that is lost within that system. The percentage efficiency of any machine can be calculated as long as you know how much energy has to be put into the machine and how much useful energy comes out. The following equation is used:

% efficiency = useful energy produced x 100 / total energy used

Skill 8.3   The beginning teacher solves problems using the conservation of mechanical energy in a physical system (e.g., determining potential energy for conservative forces, analyzing the motion of a pendulum).

The principle of conservation states that certain measurable properties of an isolated system remain constant despite changes in the system. Two important principles of conservation are the conservation of mass and charge.

The principle of conservation of mass states that the total mass of a system is constant. Examples of conservation in mass in nature include the burning of wood, rusting of iron, and phase changes of matter. When wood burns, the total mass of the products, such as soot, ash, and gases, equals the mass of the wood and the oxygen that reacts with it. When iron reacts with oxygen, rust forms. The total mass of the iron-rust complex does not change. Finally, when matter changes phase, mass remains constant. Thus, when a glacier melts due to atmospheric warming, the mass of liquid water formed is equal to the mass of the glacier.

The principle of conservation of charge states that the total electrical charge of a closed system is constant. Thus, in chemical reactions and interactions of charged objects, the total charge does not change. Chemical reactions and the interaction of charged molecules are essential and common processes in living organisms and systems.

Interacting objects in the universe constantly exchange and transform energy. Total energy remains the same, but the form of the energy readily changes. Energy often changes from kinetic (motion) to potential (stored) or potential to kinetic. In reality, available energy, energy that is easily utilized, is rarely conserved in energy transformations. Heat energy is an example of relatively "useless" energy often generated during energy transformations. Exothermic reactions release heat and endothermic reactions require heat energy to proceed. For example, the human body is notoriously inefficient in converting chemical energy from food into mechanical energy. The digestion of food is exothermic and produces substantial heat energy.

Skill 8.4 **The beginning teacher applies the work-energy theorem to analyze and solve a variety of practical problems (e.g., finding the speed of an object given its potential energy, determining the work done by frictional forces on a decelerating car).**

The work-energy theorem states that the amount of work done on an object is equal to its change in mechanical energy (kinetic or potential energy). Specifically, in systems where multiple forces are at work, the energy change of the system is the work done by the *net* force on the object. Problems dealing with the work-energy theorem may look at changes in kinetic energy, changes in potential energy, or some combination of the two. It is also important to remember that only external forces can cause changes in an object's total amount of mechanical energy. Internal forces, such as spring force or gravity, only lead to conversions between kinetic and potential energy rather than changes in the total level of mechanical energy.

Examples:

1. A woman driving a 2000 kg car along a level road at 30 m/s takes her foot off the gas to see how far her car will roll before it slows to a stop. She discovers that it takes 150m. What is the average force of friction acting on the car?

According to the work-energy theorem, the amount of work done on the car is equal to the change in its mechanical energy, which in this case is its change in kinetic energy. Since the only force acting on the car is friction, all the work can be attributed to the frictional force.

$$W = \Delta KE$$

$$f \cdot s \cos \theta = \tfrac{1}{2} m v^2_{final} - \tfrac{1}{2} m v^2_{initial}$$

$$f \cdot 150 \cdot (-1) = \tfrac{1}{2} \cdot 2000 \cdot 0^2 - \tfrac{1}{2} \cdot 2000 \cdot 30^2$$

$$-150 f = -900000$$

$$f = 6000 N$$

It is important to realize, for this problem, that the force of friction is against the direction of motion, and thus $\cos \theta = -1$.

2. A 20kg child lifts his .5 kg ball off the floor to put it away on his bookshelf 1.5 meters above the ground. How much work has he done?

$$W = \Delta PE$$

$$W = mgh_{final} - mgh_{initial}$$

$$W = mg(h_{final} - h_{initial}) = .5 \cdot 9.8 \cdot 1.5 = 7.35 J$$

Skill 8.5 The beginning teacher understands linear and angular momentum.

Momentum is the amount of moving mass. Its SI unit is kg m/s because it is calculated as the mass multiplied by the velocity of an object. Momentum is the mathematical restatement of Newton's laws- it is the tendency of an object to continue to move in its direction of travel, unless acted on by a net external force. Momentum is 'conserved' (the total momentum of a closed system cannot be changed.

Linear motion is measured in rectangular coordinates. Rotational motion is measured differently, in terms of the angle of displacement. There are three common ways to measure rotational displacement; degrees, revolutions, and radians. Degrees and revolutions have an easy to understand relationship, one revolution is 360°. Radians are slightly less well known and are defined as

$$\frac{arc\ length}{radius}.$$ Therefore 360°=2π radians and 1 radian = 57.3°.

The major concepts of linear motion are duplicated in rotational motion with linear displacement replaced by **angular displacement**.

Angular velocity ω = rate of change of angular displacement.
Angular acceleration α = rate of change of angular velocity.

Also, the linear velocity v of a rolling object can be written as $v = r\omega$ and the linear acceleration as $a = r\alpha$.

One important difference in the equations relates to the use of mass in rotational systems. In rotational problems, not only is the mass of an object important but also its location. In order to include the spatial distribution of the mass of the object, a term called **moment of inertia** is used, $I = m_1 r_1^2 + m_2 r_2^2 + \cdots + m_n r_n^2$. The moment of inertia is always defined with respect to a particular axis of rotation.

Skill 8.6 The beginning teacher solves a variety of problems (e.g., collisions) using the conservation of linear and angular momentum.

A collision may be **elastic** or **inelastic**. In a totally elastic collision, the kinetic energy is conserved along with the momentum. In a totally inelastic collision, on the other hand, the kinetic energy associated with the center of mass remains unchanged but the kinetic energy relative to the center of mass is lost.

An example of a totally inelastic collision is one in which the bodies stick to each other and move together after the collision. Most collisions are neither perfectly elastic nor perfectly inelastic and only a portion of the kinetic energy relative to the center of mass is lost. Imagine two carts rolling towards each other as in the diagram below.

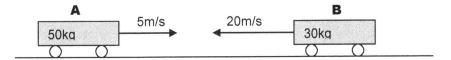

Before the collision, cart A has 250 kg m/s of momentum, and cart B has – 600 kg m/s of momentum. In other words, the system has a total momentum of –350 kg m/s of momentum.

After the inelastic collision, the two cards stick to each other, and continue moving. How do we determine how fast, and in what direction, they go?

We know that the new mass of the cart is 80kg, and that the total momentum of the system is –350 kg m/s. Therefore, the velocity of the two carts stuck together must be $\dfrac{-350}{80} = -4.375 \, m/s$

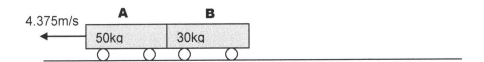

Conservation of momentum works the same way in two dimensions, the only change is that you need to use vector math to determine the total momentum and any changes, instead of simple addition.

Imagine a pool table like the one below. Both balls are 0.5 kg in mass.

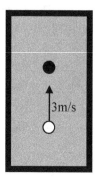

Before the collision, the white ball is moving with the velocity indicated by the solid line and the black ball is at rest.

After the collision the black ball is moving with the velocity indicated by the dashed line (a 135° angle from the direction of the white ball).

With what speed, and in what direction, is the white ball moving after the collision?

$$p_{white/before} = .5 \cdot (0,3) = (0,1.5) \quad p_{black/before} = 0 \quad p_{total/before} = (0,1.5)$$

$$p_{black/after} = .5 \cdot (2\cos 45, 2\sin 45) = (0.71, 0.71)$$

$$p_{white/after} = (-0.71, 0.79)$$

i.e. the white ball has a velocity of $v = \sqrt{(-.71)^2 + (0.79)^2} = 1.06 m/s$

and is moving at an angle of $\theta = \tan^{-1}\left(\dfrac{0.79}{-0.71}\right) = -48°$ from the horizontal.

Competency 0009   **The teacher understands the laws of thermodynamics.**

Skill 9.1   **The beginning teacher understands methods of heat transfer (i.e., convection, conduction, and radiation).**

Heat can be transferred through the processes of conduction, radiation, and convection. Conduction is the transmission of heat across something. Heat transfer always moves from a higher to a lower temperature. More dense substances usually conduct heat more readily than less dense matter. Radiation is the process of emitting energy. Energy is radiated in the form of waves or particles. Convection is the transfer of heat by currents within fluid form (liquids and gases only).

Skill 9.2   **The beginning teacher understands the molecular interpretation of temperature and heat.**

Heat: the total kinetic energy of the random motion of a substance's atoms and molecules.

Temperature: the measure of the average kinetic energy of the motion of atoms and molecules of a substance.

It's very important to understand that there is a major difference between heat and temperature.

Temperature is not a measure of how much heat a substance contains; instead, it is focused on the increase or decrease of the kinetic energy of the atoms and molecules of a substance.

Essentially, temperature is a measure of hotness, not heat. Although we use thermometers to measure temperature, we can't directly measure heat; it must be calculated.

Temperature Measurement Units

Temperature is measured on three scales. These are degrees Fahrenheit (F), degrees Celsius (C), and Kelvin units (K).
Note: Kelvin (K) is the measurement unit used in the System International (SI).

Celsius Scale: the temperature scale in general scientific use.
Example: Water freezes at 0° and boils at 100° on the Celsius scale.

Fahrenheit Scale: the non-SI technical scale still used in some countries.
Example: Water freezes at 32° and boils at 212° on the Fahrenheit scale.

Kelvin (K): the SI base unit of temperature, Kelvin is a unit on an absolute temperature scale.
Note: There is no degree symbol (°) written after a temperature expressed in Kelvin.

The point at which all motion ceases is called **Absolute Zero**.
0 Kelvin = -273 degrees Celsius = -459.4 degrees Fahrenheit.
Note: *Absolute Zero does not represent the temperature of freezing*
 32 degrees Fahrenheit = 0 degrees Celsius = 273 Kelvin.

Heat Measurement Units

The primary heat measurement units is Joules (J). However, depending on the situation, it is also commonly measured as Calories (cal). Yet another measurement scale is British Thermal Units (Btu).

Joule (J): the SI (System International) unit of measure for work and energy, the amount of work equal to the force of one Newton (1N) moving an object a distance of 1 meter (1 m).

Calorie (cal): the amount of heat energy required to change (raise or lower), the temperature of 1 gram of water, by 1 degree Celsius.

British Thermal Unit (Btu): the amount of heat energy required to change (raise or lower), the temperature of 1 pound (lb.) of water by 1 degree Fahrenheit. The Btu expresses heat unit in non-metric terms.
Note: Btu's and calories essentially express the same concept using different quantities and measurement units.

Equivalencies Between Heat Measurement Units:

1 Joule (J) = 0.2389 cal = 9.48 X 10-4 Btu.
1 Calories (cal) = 4.184 J = 3.087 ft/lb.
1 British Thermal Unit (Btu) = 1054 J = 252.0 cal.

Skill 9.3   The beginning teacher solves problems involving thermal expansion, heat capacity, and the relationship between heat and other forms of energy.

There are four states of matter: Liquid, Solid, Gas, and Plasma.
Note: *Plasma is essentially a superheated, molten gas, and not all physicists or textbooks agree that it is a separate state of matter.*

Matter can change state if the temperature of the substance is increased or lowered.

When we apply heat from a source to a substance, we are actually transferring energy from the heat source to the substance. The molecules absorb the energy and move faster. This causes the temperature of the substance to rise.

Latent Heat: the amount of heat energy required to change matter from one state to another. Example: The amount of temperature change needed to cause evaporation or condensation of water.

Heat Capacity: The ability of a substance to resist a change in temperature.

Example: Water has an extremely high heat capacity and is very resistant to a change in temperature. It takes a great deal of energy transfer to heat up water, but conversely, it also takes a great amount of energy loss to cool it down.

Specific Heat: The amount of heat required to raise or lower the temperature of 1 gram of a substance by 1 degree Celsius.
Note: This is virtually identical to the definition of a calorie or Btu. The distinction lies in the word water versus substance.

Heat of Vaporization: The amount of heat energy required to change 1 gram of water from a liquid to a vapor, or back.

The heat of vaporization is equal to 540 cal/gram.

Example: 1 gram of water at 99° C requires 1 cal of heat to raise the boiling point of water, temperature to 100° C.

However, the water will not turn into steam until an additional 540 cal is added. This is because of water's high heat capacity. The requirement for additional calories to force a change of state works in our favor because without the law of heat of vaporization, the oceans would totally vaporize.

The oceans remain as a liquid and absorb heat (energy) until the extra 546 calories have been absorbed (added), causing vaporization. Fortunately, this vaporization occurs only in very small amounts in relation to the mass (volume) of the oceans.

Rain represents the opposite pattern of the Heat of Vaporization. In rain, 540 calories have been removed, changing the state of water from a vapor (gas) to a liquid.

Heat of Fusion: the amount of heat energy expressed in calories required to change 1 gram of water from a solid to a liquid, or back.

The heat of fusion is equal to 80 cal/gram.

It takes more heat transfer to cause a change from a liquid to a vapor, or a vapor to a liquid (evaporation), than it does to change a solid to a liquid, or a liquid to a solid (fusion).

Glaciers, ice caps and the Polar Ice Packs are made possible by the heat of fusion. It takes much less energy to make ice than it does to melt it.

Skill 9.4   The beginning teacher applies the first law of thermodynamics to analyze energy transformations in a variety of everyday situations (e.g., electric light bulb, power generating plant).

The first law of thermodynamics is a restatement of conservation of energy, i.e. the principle that energy cannot be created or destroyed. It also governs the behavior of a system and its surroundings. The change in heat energy supplied to a system (Q) is equal to the sum of the change in the internal energy (U) and the change in the work (W) done by the system against internal forces.

The internal energy of a material is the sum of the total kinetic energy of its molecules and the potential energy of interactions between those molecules. Total kinetic energy includes the contributions from translational motion and other components of motion such as rotation. The potential energy includes energy stored in the form of resisting intermolecular attractions between molecules. Mathematically, we can express the relationship between the heat supplied to a system, its internal energy and work done by it as

$$\Delta Q = \Delta U + \Delta W$$

The first law of thermodynamics can be observed in an electric light bulb. Work is done on the system as an electric current is driven through the tungsten filament. The system becomes hotter and there is a positive change in energy. Once the filament becomes hot enough, it begins to glow. At that point, it does work. A fluorescent light bulb converts about 20% of the electric current into visible light energy, whereas an incandescent light bulb converts only about 5%. In both cases, the remaining current is converted to waste heat.

In an example of a power generating plant, the feed-pump works to supply water to a boiler. Heat is supplied to the system through the boiler and drives the steam turbine. The steam turbine produces work and heat. The heat is rejected from the system by the condenser. Overall, we have work and heat going in and work and heat going out.

Skill 9.5   The beginning teacher understands the concept of entropy and its relationship to the second law of thermodynamics.

To understand the second law of thermodynamics, we must first understand the concept of entropy. Entropy is the transformation of energy to a more disordered state and is the measure of how much energy or heat is available for work. The greater the entropy of a system, the less energy is available for work. The simplest statement of the second law of thermodynamics is that the entropy of an isolated system not in equilibrium tends to increase over time. The entropy approaches a maximum value at equilibrium. Below are several common examples in which we see the manifestation of the second law.

- The diffusion of molecules of perfume out of an open bottle
- Even the most carefully designed engine releases some heat and cannot convert all the chemical energy in the fuel into mechanical energy
- A block sliding on a rough surface slows down
- An ice cube sitting on a hot sidewalk melts into a little puddle; we must provide energy to a freezer to facilitate the creation of ice

When discussing the second law, scientists often refer to the "arrow of time". This is to help us conceptualize how the second law forces events to proceed in a certain direction. To understand the direction of the arrow of time, consider some of the examples above; we would never think of them as proceeding in reverse. That is, as time progresses, we would never see a puddle in the hot sun spontaneously freeze into an ice cube or the molecules of perfume dispersed in a room spontaneously re-concentrate themselves in the bottle. The above-mentioned examples are **spontaneous** as well as **irreversible**, both characteristic of increased entropy. Entropy change is zero for a **reversible process**, a process where infinitesimal quasi-static changes in the absence of dissipative forces can bring a system back to its original state without a net change to the system or its surroundings. All real processes are irreversible. The idea of a reversible process, however, is a useful abstraction that can be a good approximation in some cases.

The second law of thermodynamics may also be stated in the following ways:

1. No machine is 100% efficient.

2. Heat cannot spontaneously pass from a colder to a hotter object.

Competency 0010   **The teacher understands the characteristics and behavior of waves.**

Skill 10.1   **The beginning teacher understands interrelationships among wave characteristics such as velocity, frequency, wavelength, and amplitude and relates them to properties of sound and light (e.g., pitch, color).**

The **pitch** of a sound depends on the **frequency** that the ear receives. High-pitched sound waves have high frequencies. High notes are produced by an object that is vibrating at a greater number of times per second than one that produces a low note.

The intensity of a sound is the amount of energy that crosses a unit of area in a given unit of time. The loudness of the sound is subjective and depends upon the effect on the human ear. Two tones of the same intensity but different pitches may appear to have different loudness. The intensity level of sound is measured in decibels. Normal conversation is about 60 decibels. A power saw is about 110 decibels.

The **amplitude** of a sound wave determines its loudness. Loud sound waves have large amplitudes. The larger the sound wave, the more energy is needed to create the wave.

Wavelength

Light, microwaves, x-rays, and TV and radio transmissions are all kinds of electromagnetic waves. They are all a wavy disturbance that repeats itself over a distance called the wavelength. Electromagnetic waves come in varying sizes and properties, by which they are organized in the electromagnetic spectrum. The electromagnetic spectrum is measured in frequency (f) in hertz and wavelength (λ) in meters. The frequency times the wavelength of every electromagnetic wave equals the speed of light (3.0×10^9 meters/second).

Roughly, the range of wavelengths of the electromagnetic spectrum is:

	λ	f
Radio waves	$10^{5} - 10^{-1}$ meters	$10^{3} - 10^{9}$ hertz
Microwaves	$10^{-1} - 10^{-3}$ meters	$10^{9} - 10^{11}$ hertz
Infrared radiation	$10^{-3} - 10^{-6}$ meters	$10^{11.2} - 10^{14.3}$ hertz
Visible light	$10^{-6.2} - 10^{-6.9}$ meters	$10^{14.3} - 10^{15}$ hertz
Ultraviolet radiation	$10^{-7} - 10^{-9}$ meters	$10^{15} - 10^{17.2}$ hertz
X-Rays	$10^{-9} - 10^{-11}$ meters	$10^{17.2} - 10^{19}$ hertz
Gamma Rays	$10^{-11} - 10^{-15}$ meters	$10^{19} - 10^{23.25}$ hertz

Radio waves are used for transmitting data. Common examples are television, cell phones, and wireless computer networks. Microwaves are used to heat food and deliver Wi-Fi service. Infrared waves are utilized in night vision goggles. Visible light we are all familiar with as the human eye is most sensitive to this wavelength range. UV light causes sunburns and would be even more harmful if most of it were not captured in the Earth's ozone layer. X-rays aid us in the medical field and gamma rays are most useful in the field of astronomy.

Skill 10.2   The beginning teacher compares and contrasts transverse and longitudinal waves.

Transverse waves are characterized by the particle motion being perpendicular to the wave motion; **longitudinal waves** are characterized by the particle motion being parallel to the wave motion.

Transverse Wave

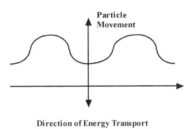

Longitudinal Wave

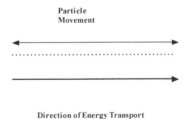

Transverse waves cannot spread in a gas or liquid. Sound waves are a good example of longitudinal waves.

Skill 10.3   The beginning teacher describes how various waves are propagated through different media.

Sound waves need a medium in which to spread; light waves do not. The speed of any wave depends upon the elastic and inertial properties of the medium through which it travels. The density of a medium is an example of an **inertial property**. Sound usually travels faster in denser material. A sound wave will travel nearly three times as fast through helium than through air. On the other hand, the speed of light is slower in denser materials. The speed of light is slower in glass than in air. (The standard for the speed of light, c, is actually the speed of light in a vacuum, such as empty space.)

Elastic properties are properties related to the tendency of a medium to maintain its shape when acted upon by force or stress. Sound waves travel faster in solids than they do in liquids, and faster in liquids than they do in gases. The inertial factor would seem to indicate otherwise. However, the elastic factor has a greater influence on the speed of the wave.

When a wave strikes an object, some of the wave energy is reflected off the object, some of the energy goes into and is absorbed by the object, and some of the energy goes through the object. For example, sound waves can penetrate walls. However, sound waves from the air cannot penetrate water, and sound waves from water cannot penetrate the air. Light passes through some materials such as glass but not many other materials.

Skill 10.4   The beginning teacher applies properties of reflection and refraction to analyze optical phenomena (e.g., mirrors, lenses, fiber-optic cable).

Shadows illustrate on of the basic properties of light. Light travels in a straight line. If you put your hand between a light source and a wall, you will interrupt the light and produce a shadow.

When light hits a surface, it is **reflected.** The angle of the incoming light - the angle of incidence - is the same as the angle of the reflected light - the angle of reflection. It is this reflected light that allows you to see objects. You see the objects when the reflected light reaches your eyes.

Different surfaces reflect light differently. Rough surfaces scatter light in many different directions. A smooth surface reflects the light in one direction. If it is smooth and shiny (like a mirror) reflection allows you to see your image in the surface.

When light enters a different medium, it bends. This bending, or change of speed, is called **refraction**.

Light can be **diffracted**, or bent around the edges of an object. Diffraction occurs when light goes through a narrow slit. As light passes through it, the light bends slightly around the edges of the slit. You can demonstrate this by pressing your thumb and forefinger together, making a very thin slit between them. Hold them about 8 cm from your eye and look at a distant source of light. The pattern you observe is caused by the diffraction of light.

Skill 10.5   The beginning teacher applies principles of wave interference to analyze wave phenomena, including acoustical (e.g., harmonics) and optical phenomena (e.g., patterns created by thin films and diffraction gratings).

Wave **interference** occurs when two waves meet while traveling along the same medium. The medium takes on a shape resulting from the net effect of the individual waves upon the particles of the medium. There are two types of interference: constructive and destructive.

Constructive interference occurs when two crests or two troughs of the same shape meet. The medium will take on the shape of a crest or a trough with twice the amplitude of the two interfering crests or troughs. If a trough and a crest of the same shape meet, the two pulses will cancel each other out, and the medium will assume the equilibrium position. This is called **destructive** interference.

Destructive interference in sound waves will reduce the loudness of the sound. This is a disadvantage in rooms, such as auditoriums, where sound needs to be at its optimum. However, it can be used as an advantage in noise reduction systems. When two sound waves differing slightly in frequency are superimposed, beats are created by the alternation of constructive and destructive interference. The frequency of the beats is equal to the difference between the frequencies of the interfering sound waves.

Wave interference occurs with light waves in much the same manner that it does with sound waves. If two light waves of the same color, frequency, and amplitude are combined, the interference shows up as fringes of alternating light and dark bands. In order for this to happen, the light waves must come from the same source.

Diffraction grating is a reflecting or transparent element whose optical properties are periodically modulated. In simple terms, diffraction gratings are fine parallel and equally spaced grooves or rulings on a material surface. When light is incident on a diffraction grating, light is reflected or transmitted in discrete directions, called diffraction orders. Because of their light dispersive properties, gratings are commonly used in monochromators and spectrophotometers. Gratings are usually designated by their groove density, expressed in grooves/millimeter. A fundamental property of gratings is that the angle of deviation of all but one of the diffracted beams depends on the wavelength of the incident light.

Skill 10.6   The beginning teacher identifies and interprets how wave characteristics and behaviors are used in medical, industrial, and other real-world applications.

Ultrasound waves are high frequency, longitudinal waves used in medical imaging. The waves penetrate the human body well and some of the waves reflect off tissue boundaries. The pulses sent back are used to create a picture of the inside of the body.

In echo–sounding or echolocation, a system called sonar transmits sound waves to detect and locate objects underwater or measure the distance to the floor of a body of water. The sound wave pulses are reflected off the object or floor, picked up and timed. Since their speed is known, the distance can be calculated. From the pulses, a picture can be built.

Patterns of seismic waves picked up by seismometers can be used to locate distant earthquakes and major explosions and to research the internal structure of the earth. For example, the "shadows" of S-waves prove that the core of the earth is molten.

Radar uses electromagnetic waves to identify the speed, altitude, and direction of both fixed objects and objects in motion. Radio waves are discharged by a transmitter. A receiver detects the waves reflected off the object. Even though the waves are usually very weak, they can be amplified, which makes them more useful than sound waves or visible light. Radar is used in meteorology to detect precipitation, in air traffic control to monitor the locations of planes, in police work to detect speeders, and in military operations.

X-rays are a form of electromagnetic radiation. They are produced by accelerating electrons in order to collide with a metal target. X-rays behave more like a particle than a wave because of their short wavelength. X-rays do not pass through dense materials such as bone but do pass through softer tissues. Where the X-rays pass through soft tissue and strike the photographic plate, the plate turns black, creating a contrast between those areas not penetrated by the X-rays and those that are. X-rays are used in diagnostic imaging for teeth, the skeletal system, and detection of lung cancer, pulmonary edema, and pneumonia, and certain abdominal disorders. X-rays are also used in microscopic analysis to produce images of very small objects and in art to examine the underlying layers of paintings.

Monochromators are optical devices that send a narrow band of wavelengths of light selected from a wider range of wavelengths. They are often used in absorption spectrophotometers to supply light to a sample. Absorption spectrophotometers are used to study enzymes, create optical thermometers, and measure the performance of sunglasses, laser protective glasses, and other optical filters, among other things.

Microwaves are used in microwave ovens to cook food by passing microwave radiation through the food. They are used in broadcasting and telecommunications transmissions because of their short wavelength. A typical example is transmitting television news from a specially equipped van at a remote location to a television station. Bluetooth technology, cable TV, and Internet access on co-ax cable use microwaves. A maser works in a manner similar to a laser but uses microwaves. Most radio astronomy uses microwaves.

Competency 0011   **The teacher understands the fundamental concepts of quantum physics.**

Skill 11.1   **The beginning teacher interprets wave-particle duality.**

Wave-particle duality is the exhibition of both wavelike and particle-like properties by a single entity. Wave-particle duality is usually a quantum phenomenon relating to photons, electrons, and protons. Quantum mechanics shows that such objects sometimes behave like particles, sometimes like waves, and sometimes both. All objects exhibit wave-particle duality to some extent, but the larger the object the harder it is to observe. Individual molecules are often too large to show their quantum mechanical behavior.

An everyday example of wave-particle duality is sunlight. When standing in the sun, the shadow your body makes suggests that the light travels straight from the sun and is blocked by your body. Here the light is behaving like a collection of particles sent from the sun. However, if you take two pieces of glass with a little water between them and hold them in the sun, you will see fringes; these are formed by the interference of waves.

Skill 11.2   **The beginning teacher identifies examples and consequences of the Uncertainty Principle.**

Heisenberg's uncertainty principle places a limit on the accuracy with which one can measure the properties of a physical system. This limit is not due to the imperfections of measuring instruments or experimental methods but arises from the fundamental wave-particle duality inherent in quantum systems.

One statement of the uncertainty principle is made in terms of the position and momentum of a particle. If Δx is the uncertainty in the position of a particle in one dimension and Δp the uncertainty in its momentum in that dimension, then according to the uncertainty principle

$$\Delta x \Delta p \geq \hbar / 2$$

where the reduced Planck's constant $\hbar = h / 2\pi = 1.05457168 \times 10^{-34} \, J.s$

Thus if we measure the position of a particle with greater and greater accuracy, at some point the accuracy in the measurement of its momentum will begin to fall. A simple way to understand this is by considering the wave nature of a subatomic particle. If the wave has a single wavelength, then the momentum of the particle is also exactly known using the DeBroglie momentum-wavelength relationship. The position of the wave, however, extends through all space. If waves of several different wavelengths are superposed, the position of the wave becomes increasingly localized as more wavelengths are added. The increased spread in wavelength, however, then results in an increased momentum spread.

An alternate statement of the uncertainty principle may be made in terms of energy and time.

$$\Delta E \Delta t \geq h / 2$$

Thus, for a particle that has a very short lifetime, the uncertainty in the determination of its energy will be large.

Problem: If a proton is confined to a nucleus that is approximately $10^{-15} m$ in diameter, estimate the minimum uncertainty in its momentum in any one dimension.

Solution: The uncertainty of the position of the proton in any dimension cannot be greater than $10^{-15} m$. Using the uncertainty principle we find that the approximate uncertainty in its momentum in any one dimension must be greater than

$$\Delta p = h / (2\Delta x) \approx 10^{-19} \, Kg.m/s$$

Skill 11.3   The beginning teacher understands the photoelectric effect.

The **photoelectric effect** occurs when **light shining on a clean metal surface causes the surface to emit electrons**. The energy of an absorbed photon is transferred to an electron as shown to the right. If this energy is greater than the binding energy holding the electron close to nearby nuclei then the electron will move. A high energy (high frequency, low wavelength) photon will not only dislodge an electron from the "electron sea"**Error! Bookmark not defined.** of a metal but it will also impart kinetic energy to the electron, making it move rapidly. These electrons in motion will produce an electric current if a circuit is present.

When the metal surface on which light is incident is a cathode with the anode held at a higher potential V, an electric current flows in the external circuit. It is observed that current flows only for light of higher frequencies. Also there is a threshold negative potential, the **stopping potential** V_0 below which no current will flow in the circuit.

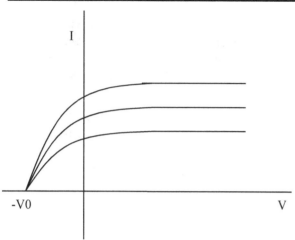

The figure previously displayed shows current flow vs. potential for three different intensities of light. It shows that the maximum current flow increases with increasing light intensity but the stopping potential remains the same.

All these observations are counter-intuitive if one considers light to be a wave but may be understood in terms of light particles or photons. According to this interpretation, each photon transfers its energy to a single electron in the metal. Since the energy of a photon depends on its frequency, only a photon of higher frequency can transfer enough energy to an electron to enable it to pass the stopping potential threshold.

When V is negative, only electrons with a kinetic energy greater than $|eV|$ can reach the anode. The maximum kinetic energy of the emitted electrons is given by eV_0. This is expressed by Einstein's photoelectric equation as

$$(\tfrac{1}{2}mv^2)_{max} = eV_0 = hf - \varphi$$

where the **work function** φ is the energy needed to release an electron from the metal and is characteristic of the metal.

Problem: The work function for potassium is 2.20eV. What is the stopping potential for light of wavelength 400nm?

Solution:
$$eV_0 = hf - \varphi = hc/\lambda - \varphi = 4.136\times 10^{-15} \times 3\times 10^8 / (400\times 10^{-9}) - 2.20 = 3.10 - 2.20 = 0.90eV$$

Thus stopping potential V_0 = 0.90V

Skill 11.4   The beginning teacher uses the quantum model of the atom to describe and analyze absorption and emission spectra (e.g., line spectra, blackbody radiation).

As quantum theory was developed and popularized, chemists and physicists began to consider how it might apply to atomic structure. Niels Bohr put forward a model of the atom in which electrons could only orbit the nucleus in circular orbitals with specific distances from the nucleus, energy levels, and angular momentums. In this model, electrons could only make instantaneous "quantum leaps" between the fixed energy levels of the various orbitals. The Bohr model of the atom was altered slightly by Arnold Sommerfeld in 1916 to reflect the fact that the orbitals were elliptical instead of round.

Though the Bohr model is still thought to be largely correct, it was discovered that electrons do not truly occupy neat, cleanly defined orbitals. Rather, they exist as more of an "electron cloud." An electron can actually be located at any distance from the nucleus. However, we can find the *probability* that the electrons exist at given energy levels as described in the Bohr model.

The quantum structure of the atom describes electrons in discrete energy levels surrounding the nucleus. When an electron moves from a high energy orbital to a lower energy orbital, a quantum of electromagnetic radiation is emitted, and for an electron to move from a low energy to a higher energy level, a quantum of radiation must be absorbed. The particle that carries this electromagnetic force is called a **photon**. The quantum structure of the atom predicts that only photons corresponding to certain wavelengths of light will be emitted or absorbed by atoms. These distinct wavelengths are measured by **atomic spectroscopy**.

In **atomic absorption spectroscopy**, a continuous spectrum (light consisting of all wavelengths) is passed through the element. The frequencies of absorbed photons are then determined as the electrons increase in energy. An **absorption spectrum** in the visible region usually appears as a rainbow of color stretching from red to violet interrupted by a few black lines corresponding to distinct wavelengths of absorption.

In **atomic emission spectroscopy**, the electrons of an element are excited by heating or by an electric discharge. The frequencies of emitted photons are then determined as the electrons release energy. An **emission spectrum** in the visible region typically consists of lines of light at certain colors corresponding to distinct wavelengths of emission. The bands of emitted or absorbed light at these wavelengths are called **spectral lines**. **Each element has a unique line spectrum**. Light from a star (including the sun) may be analyzed to determine what elements are present.

The constituents of an atom include **protons** that have a positive charge, **neutrons** that have no charge, and **electrons** that have a negative charge.

Atoms have no net charge and thus have an equal number of protons and electrons. Protons and neutrons are contained in a small volume at the center of the atom called the **nucleus**. Electrons move in the remaining space of the atom and have very little mass—about 1/1800 of the mass of a proton or neutron. Electrons are prevented from flying away from the nucleus by the attraction that exists between opposite electrical charges. This force is known as **electrostatic** or **coulomb** attraction. **Nuclear force**, which holds the nucleus together, is a byproduct of **strong interactions** and is clearly far stronger than electrostatic forces, which would otherwise cause the protons in the nucleus to repel one another.

Most lines in the hydrogen spectrum are not at visible wavelengths. Larger energy transitions produce ultraviolet radiation and smaller energy transitions produce infrared or longer wavelengths of radiation. **Blackbody radiation** is the characteristic radiation of an ideal blackbody, i.e. a body that absorbs all of the radiation incident upon it. Theoretical calculations of the frequency distribution of this radiation using classical physics showed that the energy density of this wave should increase as frequency increases. This result agreed with experiments at shorter wavelengths but failed at large wavelengths where experiment shows that that the energy density of the radiation actually falls back to zero.

In trying to resolve this impasse and derive the spectral distribution of blackbody radiation, Max Planck proposed that an atom can absorb or emit energy only in chunks known as quanta. The energy E contained in each quantum depends on the frequency of the radiation and is given by $E = hf$ where Planck's constant $h = 6.626 \times 10^{-34} \, J.s = 4.136 \times 10^{-15} eV.s$. Using this quantum hypothesis, Planck was able to provide an explanation for blackbody radiation that matched experiment.

Einstein extended Planck's idea further to suggest that quantization is a fundamental property of electromagnetic radiation which consists of quanta of energy known as **photons**. The energy of each photon is hf where h is Planck's constant.

Skill 11.5   The beginning teacher explores real-world applications of quantum phenomena (e.g., lasers, photoelectric sensors, semiconductors, superconductivity).

The names "laser" and "maser" are acronyms for "light amplification by stimulated emission of radiation" and "microwave amplification by stimulated emission of radiation." Thus, as is evident by their names, these two devices are based on the principle of stimulated emission.

According to quantum theory, an atom in an excited state has a certain probability in a given time frame for relaxing to a lower state through, for example, the emission of a photon of the same energy as the energy difference between the two states. Stimulated emission, however, may take place when the excited atom is perturbed by a passing photon of the same energy as the excitation. In such a case, the atom relaxes to a lower energy by emitting a new photon, resulting in a total of two photons of equal frequency (and, thus, energy) and equal phase. That is to say, the photons are coherent.

In order to produce a significant level of stimulated emission for application in typical lasers and masers, population inversion is required. Population inversion is a situation in which there are more atoms in a particular excited state than in a particular lower-energy state. In order to achieve this condition, the material must be "pumped," which can be performed using electromagnetic fields (light). Pumping to produce population inversion often requires three or more atomic energy levels. The energy difference between levels can be emitted in the form of a phonon (vibration mode in the material, or heat).

The abundance of excited atoms due to population inversion allow for a "chain reaction" to form when photons of the proper frequency (proportional by Planck's constant to the energy difference between the excited state and lower-energy state) are incident. This results in a cascading increase in photon intensity through stimulated emission, thus producing the coherent, high-power light that is used by the laser or maser. This process has its limits, of course, as determined by how quickly the atoms can be pumped in relation to the relaxation processes. A saturation level exists beyond which the rate of stimulated emission cannot be increased. Spontaneously emitted photons can start the cascading process of stimulated emission.

The main components of a laser are a gain medium, an energy source (pump) for the gain medium and a resonant optical cavity with a partial transparency in one mirror. The resonant cavity is tuned to a particular frequency such that the photons of the desired laser frequency are coherent and, largely, isolated within the cavity. A partially transparent mirror on one end of the cavity allows some of the light to exit, thus producing the laser beam.

Masers, which operate at lower frequencies than lasers, generally rely on the same principles as lasers, although the types of gain media and resonant cavities may differ.

According to the theory of energy bands, as derived from quantum mechanics, electrons in the ground state reside in the valence band and are bound to their associated atoms or molecules. If the electrons gain sufficient energy, such as through heat, they can jump across the forbidden band (in which no electrons may exist) to the conduction band, thus becoming free electrons that can form a current in the presence of an applied field. For conductors, the valence band and conduction band meet or overlap, allowing electrons to easily jump to unoccupied conduction states. Thus, conductors have an abundance of free electrons. It is noteworthy that only two bands are shown in the diagram above, but that an infinite number of bands may exist at higher energies. A more general statement of the difference in band structures is that, for insulators and semiconductors, the valence electrons fill up all the states in a particular band, leaving a gap between the highest energy valence electrons and the next available band. The difference between these two types of materials is simply a matter of the "size" of the forbidden band. For conductors, the band that contains the highest energy electrons has additional available states.

A nearly ideal conducting material is a **superconductor**. As a material increases in temperature, increased vibrational motion of the atoms or molecules leads to decreased charge carrier mobility and decreased conductivity. In the case of semiconductors, the increase in free carrier population outweighs the loss in mobility of the charge carriers, meaning that the semiconductor increases in conductivity as temperature increases. Superconductors, on the other hand, reach their peak conductivity at extremely low temperatures (although there are currently numerous efforts to achieve superconductivity at higher and higher temperatures, with room temperature or higher being the ultimate goal). The critical temperature of the material is the temperature at which superconducting properties emerge. At this temperature, the material has a nearly infinite conductivity and maintains an almost perfect equipotential across its surface when in the presence of a static electric field. Inside a superconductor, the electric field is virtually zero at all times. As a result, the time derivative of the electric flux density is zero, and, by Maxwell's equations, the magnetic flux density must likewise be zero. Since the electric field is also zero, the current density J inside the superconductor must also be zero (or very nearly so). This elimination of the magnetic flux density inside a superconductor is called the **Meissner effect**.

DOMAIN III.   **CHEMISTRY**

Competency 0012   **The teacher understands the characteristics of matter and atomic structure.**

Skill 12.1   **The beginning teacher differentiates between physical and chemical properties and changes of matter.**

Physical properties and chemical properties of matter describe the appearance or behavior of a substance. A **physical property** can be observed without changing the identity of a substance. For instance, you can describe the color, mass, shape, and volume of a book. **Chemical properties** describe the ability of a substance to be changed into new substances. Baking powder goes through a chemical change as it changes into carbon dioxide gas during the baking process.

Matter constantly changes. A **physical change** is a change that does not produce a new substance. The freezing and melting of water is an example of physical change. A **chemical change (or chemical reaction)** is any change of a substance into one or more other substances. Burning materials turn into smoke, a seltzer tablet fizzes into gas bubbles.

Skill 12.2   **The beginning teacher explains the structure and properties of solids, liquids, and gases.**

The **phase of matter** (solid, liquid, or gas) is identified by its shape and volume. A **solid** has a definite shape and volume. A **liquid** has a definite volume, but no shape. A **gas** has no shape or volume because it will spread out to occupy the entire space of whatever container it is in.

Energy is the ability to cause change in matter. Applying heat to a frozen liquid changes it from solid back to liquid. Continue heating it and it will boil and give off steam, a gas.

Evaporation is the change in phase from liquid to gas. **Condensation** is the change in phase from gas to liquid.

Skill 12.3   **The beginning teacher identifies and analyzes properties of substances (i.e., elements and compounds) and mixtures.**

An **element** is a substance that can not be broken down into other substances. Today, scientists have identified 109 elements: 89 are found in nature and 20 are synthetic.

An **atom** is the smallest particle of the element that has the properties of that element. All of the atoms of a particular element are the same. The atoms of each element are different from the atoms of the other elements.

Elements are assigned an identifying symbol of one or two letters. The symbol for oxygen is O and stands for one atom of oxygen. However, because oxygen atoms in nature are joined together is pairs, the symbol O_2 represents oxygen. This pair of oxygen molecules is a molecule. A **molecule** is the smallest particle of substance that can exist independently and has all of the properties of that substance. A molecule of most elements is made up of one atom. However, oxygen, hydrogen, nitrogen, and chlorine molecules are made of two atoms each.

A **compound** is made of two or more elements that have been chemically combined. Atoms join together when elements are chemically combined. The result is that the elements lose their individual identities when they are joined. The compound that they become has different properties.

We use a formula to show the elements of a chemical compound. A **chemical formula** is a shorthand way of showing what is in a compound by using symbols and subscripts. The letter symbols let us know what elements are involved and the number subscript tells how many atoms of each element are involved. No subscript is used if there is only one atom involved. For example, carbon dioxide is made up of one atom of carbon (C) and two atoms of oxygen (O_2), so the formula would be represented as CO_2.

Substances can combine without a chemical change. A **mixture** is any combination of two or more substances in which the substances keep their own properties. A fruit salad is a mixture. So is an ice cream sundae, although you might not recognize each part if it is stirred together. Colognes and perfumes are the other examples. You may not readily recognize the individual elements. However, they can be separated.

Compounds and **mixtures** are similar in that they are made up of two or more substances. However, they have the following opposite characteristics:

Compounds:

1. Made up of one kind of particle
2. Formed during a chemical change
3. Broken down only by chemical changes
4. Properties are different from its parts
5. Has a specific amount of each ingredient.

Mixtures:

1. Made up of two or more particles
2. Not formed by a chemical change
3. Can be separated by physical changes
4. Properties are the same as its parts.
5. Does not have a definite amount of each ingredient.

Common compounds are **acid, base, salt**, and **oxides** and are classified according to their characteristics.

Skill 12.4   The beginning teacher models the atom in terms of protons, neutrons, and electron clouds.

An **atom** is a nucleus surrounded by a cloud with moving electrons (**electron cloud**).

The **nucleus** is the center of the atom. The positive particles inside the nucleus are called **protons.** The mass of a proton is about 2,000 times that of the mass of an electron. The number of protons in the nucleus of an atom is called the **atomic number**. All atoms of the same element have the same atomic number.

Neutrons are another type of particle in the nucleus. Neutrons and protons have about the same mass, but neutrons have no charge. Neutrons were discovered because scientists observed that not all atoms in neon gas have the same mass. They had identified isotopes. **Isotopes** of an element have the same number of protons in the nucleus, but have different masses. Neutrons explain the difference in mass. They have mass but no charge.

Skill 12.5   The beginning teacher identifies elements and isotopes by atomic number and mass number.

The mass of matter is measured against a standard mass such as the gram. Scientists measure the mass of an atom by comparing it to that of a standard atom. The result is relative mass. The **relative mass** of an atom is its mass expressed in terms of the mass of the standard atom. The isotope of the element carbon is the standard atom. It has six (6) neutrons and is called carbon-12. It is assigned a mass of 12 atomic mass units (amu). Therefore, the **atomic mass unit (amu)** is the standard unit for measuring the mass of an atom. It is equal to the mass of a carbon atom.

The **mass number** of an atom is the sum of its protons and neutrons. In any element, there is a mixture of isotopes, some having slightly more or slightly fewer protons and neutrons. The **atomic mass** of an element is an average of the mass numbers of its atoms. The following table summarizes the terms used to describe atomic nuclei.

Term	Example	Meaning	Characteristic
Atomic Number	# protons (p)	same for all atoms of a given element	Carbon (C) atomic number = 6 (6p)
Mass number	# protons + # neutrons (p + n)	changes for different isotopes of an element	C-12 (6p + 6n) C-13 (6p + 7n)
Atomic mass	average mass of the atoms of the element	usually not a whole number	atomic mass of carbon equals 12.011

Skill 12.6 **The beginning teacher understands atomic orbitals and electron configurations and describes the relationship between electron energy levels and atomic structure.**

Each atom has an equal number of electrons (negative) and protons (positive). Therefore, atoms are neutral. Electrons orbiting the nucleus occupy energy levels that are arranged in order and the electrons tend to occupy the lowest energy level available. A **stable electron arrangement** is an atom that has all of its electrons in the lowest possible energy levels.

Each energy level holds a maximum number of electrons. However, an atom with more than one level does not hold more than 8 electrons in its outermost shell.

Level	Name	Max. # of Electrons
First	K shell	2
Second	L shell	8
Third	M shell	18
Fourth	N shell	32

This can help explain why chemical reactions occur. Atoms react with each other when their outer levels are unfilled. When atoms either exchange or share electrons with each other, these energy levels become filled and the atom becomes more stable.

As an electron gains energy, it moves from one energy level to a higher energy level. The electron can not leave one level until it has enough energy to reach the next level. **Excited electrons** are electrons that have absorbed energy and have moved farther from the nucleus.

Electrons can also lose energy. When they do, they fall to a lower level. However, they can only fall to the lowest level that has room for them. This explains why atoms do not collapse.

Skill 12.7   The beginning teacher understands the nature and historical significance of the periodic table.

The **periodic table of elements** is an arrangement of the elements in rows and columns so that it is easy to locate elements with similar properties. The elements of the modern periodic table are arranged in numerical order by atomic number.

The **periods** are the rows down the left side of the table. They are called first period, second period, etc. The columns of the periodic table are called **groups**, or **families.** Elements in a family have similar properties.

There are three types of elements that are grouped by color: metals, nonmetals, and metalloids.

Element Key
Atomic
Number

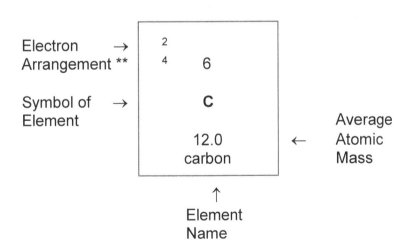

** Number of electrons on each level. Top number represents the innermost level.

Skill 12.8   The beginning teacher applies the concept of periodicity to predict the physical and chemical properties of an element.

The periodic table arranges metals into families with similar properties. The periodic table has its columns marked IA - VIIIA. These are the traditional group numbers. Arabic numbers 1 - 18 are also used, as suggested by the Union of Physicists and Chemists. The Arabic numerals will be used in this text.

Metals

With the exception of hydrogen, all elements in Group 1 are **alkali metals**. These metals are shiny, softer, and less dense, and the most chemically active.

Group 2 metals are the **alkaline earth metals.** They are harder, denser, have higher melting points, and are chemically active.

The **transition elements** can be found by finding the periods (rows) from 4 to 7 under the groups (columns) 3 - 12. They are metals that do not show a range of properties as you move across the chart. They are hard and have high melting points. Compounds of these elements are colorful, such as silver, gold, and mercury.

Elements can be combined to make metallic objects. An **alloy** is a mixture of two or more elements having properties of metals. The elements do not have to be all metals. For instance, steel is made up of the metal iron and the non-metal carbon.

Nonmetals

Nonmetals are not as easy to recognize as metals because they do not always share physical properties. However, in general the properties of nonmetals are the opposite of metals. They are not shiny, are brittle, and are not good conductors of heat and electricity.

Nonmetals are solids, gases, and one liquid (bromine).

Nonmetals have four to eight electrons in their outermost energy levels and tend to attract electrons to their outer energy levels. As a result, the outer levels usually are filled with eight electrons. This difference in the number of electrons is what caused the differences between metals and nonmetals. The outstanding chemical property of nonmetals is that react with metals.

The **halogens** can be found in Group 17. Halogens combine readily with metals to form salts. Table salt, fluoride toothpaste, and bleach all have an element from the halogen family.
The **Noble Gases** got their name from the fact that they did not react chemically with other elements, much like the nobility did not mix with the masses. These

gases (found in Group 18) will only combine with other elements under very specific conditions. They are **inert** (inactive).

In recent years, scientists have found this to be only generally true, since chemists have been able to prepare compounds of krypton and xenon.

Metalloids

Metalloids have properties in between metals and nonmetals. They can be found in Groups 13 - 16, but do not occupy the entire group. They are arranged in stair steps across the groups.

Physical Properties:
1. All are solids having the appearance of metals.
2. All are white or gray, but not shiny.
3. They will conduct electricity, but not as well as a metal.

Chemical Properties:
1. Have some characteristics of metals and nonmetals.
2. Properties do not follow patterns like metals and nonmetals. Each must be studied individually.

Boron is the first element in Group 13. It is a poor conductor of electricity at low temperatures. However, increase its temperature and it becomes a good conductor. By comparison, metals, which are good conductors, lose their ability as they are heated. It is because of this property that boron is so useful. Boron is a semiconductor. **Semiconductors** are used in electrical devices that have to function at temperatures too high for metals.

Silicon is the second element in Group 14. It is also a semiconductor and is found in great abundance in the earth's crust. Sand is made of a silicon compound, silicon dioxide. Silicon is also used in the manufacture of glass and cement.

Competency 0013   **The teacher understands the properties of gases.**

Skill 13.1   **The beginning teacher understands interrelationships among temperature, moles, pressure, and volume of gases contained within a closed system.**

The ideal gas law states that a gas sample is composed of molecules that are totally independent of each other and hence behave ideally. In reality, the ideal gas law is an equation:

$$PV = nRT$$

where R = universal gas constant
P = Pressure
V = Volume
n = number of moles
T = Temperature

Gas **pressure** results from molecular collisions with container walls. The **number of molecules** striking an **area** on the walls and the **average kinetic energy** per molecule are the only factors that contribute to pressure. A higher **temperature** increases speed and kinetic energy. There are more collisions at higher temperatures, but the average distance between molecules does not change, and thus density does not change in a sealed container.

Skill 13.2   **The beginning teacher analyzes data obtained from investigations with gases in a closed system and determines whether the data are consistent with the ideal gas law.**

A 'real gas' is a gas that deviates from ideal gas behavior. On the contrary, if a gas behaves exactly as the ideal gas laws would predict, then it is an ideal gas. Now, with this background, let us examine the effects of intermolecular forces on real gases:

1. Effect of pressure: Lowering of pressure allows gas molecules to spread out farther from one another. Because the molecules are far apart, there will be fewer intermolecular forces acting on them to the extent that the intermolecular forces are almost zero. At this juncture, the gas would behave as an ideal gas.

2. Effect of temperature: raising the temperature of gas would automatically increase the Average Kinetic Energy of the gas molecules and speed them up in their motion towards one another. This increase in speed will overcome any intermolecular forces acting between the molecules and the gas would behave almost as an ideal gas.

3. Volume of gas under laboratory conditions: This is very interesting because even if conditions in the lab were ideal, the volume of the gas would not be exactly the same as the volume of ideal gas. There is difference in the volumes of the 'real gas' and the theoretical volume calculations. This emphasizes the fact that the gas was real, not ideal. It deviated from the behavior of ideal gas.

Skill 13.3 **The beginning teacher applies the gas laws (e.g., Charles's law, Boyle's law, combined gas law) to predict gas behavior in a variety of situations.**

Charles's law states that the volume of a fixed amount of gas at constant pressure is directly proportional to absolute temperature, or:

$$V \propto T.$$

Boyle's law states that the volume of a fixed amount of gas at constant temperature is inversely proportional to the gas pressure, or:

$$V \propto \frac{1}{P}.$$

Gay-Lussac's law states that the pressure of a fixed amount of gas in a fixed volume is proportional to absolute temperature, or:

$$P \propto T.$$

The **combined gas law** uses the above laws to determine a proportionality expression that is used for a constant quantity of gas:

$$V \propto \frac{T}{P}.$$

The combined gas law is often expressed as an equality between identical amounts of an ideal gas at two different states ($n_1 = n_2$):

$$\frac{P_1 V_1}{T_1} = \frac{P_2 V_2}{T_2}.$$

Skill 13.4 **The beginning teacher applies Dalton's law of partial pressure in various situations (e.g., collecting a gas over water).**

For mixtures of gases in a container, each gas exerts a **partial pressure** that it would have if it were present in the container alone. **Dalton's law** of partial pressures states that the total pressure of a gas mixture is simply the sum of these partial pressures:

$$P_{total} = P_1 + P_2 + P_3 + \ldots$$

Dalton's law may be applied to the ideal gas law:

$$P_{total}V = (P_1 + P_2 + P_3 + \ldots \qquad \ldots \quad .$$

Skill 13.5 **The beginning teacher understands the relationship between Kinetic Molecular Theory and the ideal gas law.**

Kinetic molecular theory (KMT) explains how the pressure and temperature influences behavior of gases by making a few assumptions, namely:

1) The energies of intermolecular attractive and repulsive forces may be neglected.
2) The average kinetic energy of the molecules is proportional to absolute temperature.
3) Energy can be transferred between molecules during collisions and the collisions are elastic, so the average kinetic energy of the molecules doesn't change due to collisions.
4) The volume of all molecules in a gas is negligible compared to the total volume of the container.

Strictly speaking, molecules also contain some kinetic energy by rotating or experiencing other motions. The motion of a molecule from one place to another is called **translation**. Translational kinetic energy is the form that is transferred by collisions, and kinetic molecular theory ignores other forms of kinetic energy because they are not proportional to temperature.

Molecules have **kinetic energy** (they move around), and they also have **intermolecular attractive forces** (they stick to each other). The relationship between these two determines whether a collection of molecules will be a gas, liquid, or solid.

A **gas** has an indefinite shape and an indefinite volume. The kinetic model for a gas is a collection of widely separated molecules, each moving in a random and free fashion, with negligible attractive or repulsive forces between them. Gases will expand to occupy a larger container so there is more space between the molecules. Gases can also be compressed to fit into a small container so the molecules are less separated. **Diffusion** occurs when one material spreads into or through another. Gases diffuse rapidly and move from one place to another.

A **liquid** assumes the shape of the portion of any container that it occupies and has a specific volume. The kinetic model for a liquid is a collection of molecules attracted to each other with sufficient strength to keep them close to each other but with insufficient strength to prevent them from moving around randomly. Liquids have a higher density and are much less compressible than gases because the molecules in a liquid are closer together. Diffusion occurs more slowly in liquids than in gases because the molecules in a liquid stick to each other and are not completely free to move.

A **solid** has a definite volume and definite shape. The kinetic model for a solid is a collection of molecules attracted to each other with sufficient strength to essentially lock them in place. Each molecule may vibrate, but it has an average position relative to its neighbors. If these positions form an ordered pattern, the solid is called **crystalline**. Otherwise, it is called **amorphous**. Solids have a high density and are almost incompressible because the molecules are close together. Diffusion occurs extremely slowly because the molecules almost never alter their position.

In a solid, the energy of intermolecular attractive forces is much stronger than the kinetic energy of the molecules, so kinetic energy and kinetic molecular theory are not very important. As temperature increases in a solid, the vibrations of individual molecules grow more intense and the molecules spread slightly further apart, decreasing the density of the solid.

In a liquid, the energy of intermolecular attractive forces is about as strong as the kinetic energy of the molecules and both play a role in the properties of liquids.

In a gas, the energy of intermolecular forces is much weaker than the kinetic energy of the molecules. Kinetic molecular theory is usually applied for gases and is best applied by imagining ourselves shrinking down to become a molecule and picturing what happens when we bump into other molecules and into container walls.

Skill 13.6 **The beginning teacher knows how to apply the ideal gas law to analyze mass relationships between reactants and products in chemical reactions involving gases.**

The ideal gas law allows us to not only characterize gases at certain conditions, but to investigate reactions between gases. In problems such as these, **knowledge of both stoichiometry and the gas laws is needed**. This is most clearly demonstrated with the following example.

Example: Calculate the volume of gaseous NO_2 generated from the combustion of 100 grams of NH_3 when the following reaction occurs at STP:

$$4NH_3 \text{ (g)} + 7O_2 \text{ (g)} \rightarrow 4NO_2 \text{ (g)} + 6H_2O \text{ (l)}$$

Solution: First we must calculate how many moles of NH_3 are present in 100 g, knowing that the molecular weight is 17.034 g/mol:

$$100 \text{ g } NH_3 / (17.034 \text{ g/mol}) = 5.87 \text{ mol } NH_3$$

The molar ratio between NH_3 and NO_2 is 1:1. Therefore, 5.87 mol of NO_2 will be formed in this reaction. STP (standard temperature and pressure) occurs at 273.15 K and 1 atm. Rearranging the ideal gas law and using the appropriate units of $R = 0.08206$ L-atm/K-mol:

$$V = nRT/P$$

$V = (5.87 \text{ mol } NO_2 \times 0.08206 \text{ L-atm/K-mol} \times 273.15 \text{ K})/1 \text{ atm} = 132 \text{ L } NO_3$

The example above is a typical example of a gas stoichiometry problem. In other problems, the density of the gas will be included and a different version of the ideal gas law will be more helpful, as seen below:

$$d = \frac{nM}{V} = \frac{PM}{RT}$$

Competency 0014   **The teacher understands properties and characteristics of ionic and covalent bonds.**

Skill 14.1   The beginning teacher relates the electron configuration of an atom to its chemical reactivity.

Electrons in the **outermost shell** are called **valence shell electrons**. The **periodic table** may be used to write down the electron configuration of any element. The table may be divided up into **blocks corresponding to the subshell** designation of the most recent orbital to be filled by the building-up rule.

Elements in the s- and p-blocks are known as **main-group elements**. The d-block elements are called **transition metals.** The f-block elements are called **inner transition metals**.

The maximum number of electrons in each subshell (2, 6, 10, or 14) determines the number of elements in each block, and the order of energy levels for subshells create the pattern of blocks. These blocks also usually correspond to the value of/for the **outermost electron** of the atom. This has important consequences for the physical and chemical properties of the elements. Elements with orbitals that are not filled are generally less stable, there fore they are more likely to lose or attract electrons, making them chemically active. Elements with complete orbitals are generally content to remain that way (less chemically active) unless enticed to do otherwise by particularly strong elements or conditions.

Skill 14.2   The beginning teacher compares and contrasts characteristics of ionic and covalent bonds.

An **ionic bond** occurs **between a metal and a nonmetal**. In an ionic bond, the metal "gives" an electron to the nonmetal. A **covalent bond is favored between nonmetals**. In a covalent bond both atoms attract electrons and share electrons between them. A **metallic bond is favored between metals**. In a metallic bond, atoms lose electrons to a matrix of free electrons surrounding them. Many bonds have some characteristics of more than one of the above basic bond types.

An **ionic bond** describes the electrostatic forces that exist between **particles of opposite charge**. Elements that form an ionic bond with each other have a large difference in their electronegativity. Anions and cations pack together into a crystal **lattice** as shown to the right for NaCl. Ionic compounds are also known as **salts**.

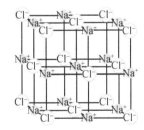

Nonmetals typically react with other nonmetals to form **covalent bonds**. A covalent bond is formed between two atoms by **sharing a pair of electrons**. The simplest covalent bond is between the two single electrons of hydrogen atoms. Covalent bonds may be represented by an electron pair (a pair of dots) or a line as shown below. The shared pair of electrons provides each H atom with two electrons in its valence shell (the $1s$ orbital), so both have the stable electron configuration of helium.

$$H\cdot \ + \ \cdot H \longrightarrow \begin{array}{c} H\!:\!H \\ H\!-\!\!-\!H \end{array}$$

Chlorine molecules have 7 electrons in their valence shell and share a pair of electrons so both have the stable electron configuration of argon.

$$:\!\ddot{C}l\cdot \ + \ \cdot\ddot{C}l\!: \longrightarrow \begin{array}{c} :\!\ddot{C}l\!:\!\ddot{C}l\!: \\ Cl\!-\!\!-\!Cl \end{array}$$

In the previous two examples, a single pair of electrons was shared, and the resulting bond is referred to as a **single bond**. When two electron pairs are shared, two lines are drawn, representing a **double bond**, and three shared pairs of electrons represents a **triple bond** as shown below for CO_2 and N_2. The remaining electrons are in **unshared pairs**.

$$\ddot{O}\!:\!:\!C\!:\!:\!\ddot{O} \qquad :\!N\!:\!:\!:\!N\!:$$

$$O\!=\!\!=\!C\!=\!\!=\!O \qquad N\!\equiv\!N$$

Skill 14.3   The beginning teacher applies the "octet" rule to construct Lewis structures.

Lewis dot structures are a method for keeping track of each atom's valence electrons in a molecule. Drawing Lewis structures is a three-step process:

1) Add the number of valence shell electrons for each atom. If the compound is an anion, add the charge of the ion to the total electron count because anions have "extra" electrons. If the compound is a cation, subtract the charge of the ion.
2) Write the symbols for each atom showing how the atoms connect to each other.
3) Draw a single bond (one pair of electron dots or a line) between each pair of connected atoms. Place the remaining electrons around the atoms as unshared pairs. If every atom has an octet of electrons except H atoms with two electrons, the Lewis structure is complete. Shared electrons count towards both atoms. If there are too few electron pairs to do this, draw multiple bonds (two or three pairs of electron dots between the atoms) until an octet is around each atom (except H atoms with two). If there are two many electron pairs to complete the octets with single bonds then the octet rule Is broken for this compound.

Example: Draw the Lewis structure of HCN.

Solution:

1) From their locations in the main group of the periodic table, we know that each atom contributes the following number of electrons: H—1, C—4, N—5. Because it is a neutral compound, the molecule will have a total of 10 valence electrons.
2) The atoms are connected with C at the center and will be drawn as: H   C   N. Having H as the central atom is impossible because H has one valence electron and will always only have a single bond to one other atom. If N were the central atom then the formula would probably be written as HNC.
3) Connecting the atoms with 10 electrons in single bonds gives the structure to the right. H has two electrons to fill its valence subshells, but C and N only have six each. A triple bond between these atoms fulfills the octet rule for C and N and is the correct Lewis structure.

Skill 14.4   The beginning teacher identifies and describes the arrangement of atoms in molecules, ionic crystals, polymers, and metallic substances.

An **element** is a substance that can not be broken down into other substances. Today, scientists have identified 109 elements: 89 are found in nature and 20 are synthetic.

An **atom** is the smallest particle of the element that has the properties of that element. All of the atoms of a particular element are the same. The atoms of each element are different from the atoms of the other elements.

A **molecule** is the smallest particle of substance that can exist independently and has all of the properties of that substance. A molecule of most elements is made up of one atom. However, oxygen, hydrogen, nitrogen, and chlorine molecules are made of two atoms each.

A **solid** has a definite volume and definite shape. The kinetic model for a solid is a collection of molecules attracted to each other with sufficient strength to essentially lock them in place. Each molecule may vibrate, but it has an average position relative to its neighbors. If these positions form an ordered pattern, the solid is called **crystalline**.

Polymers are substances whose molecules have high molar masses and are composed of a large number of repeating units called monomers. For example, polyethylene is many ethylene molecules put together, much like you would link paper clips together to make a long chain.

Example: $-[CH_2CH_2CH_2CH_2CH_2CH_2CH_2CH_2]_n$

Metals are characterized by having metallic bonding. Metallic bonds occur when the bonding is between two metals. Metallic properties, such as low ionization energies, conductivity, and malleability, suggest that metals possess strong forces of attraction between atoms, but still have electrons that are able to move freely in all directions throughout the metal. This creates a "sea of electrons" model where electrons are quickly and easily transferred between metal atoms. In this model, the outer shell electrons are free to move. The metallic bond is the force of attraction that results from the moving electrons and the positive nuclei left behind. The strength of metal bonds usually results in regular structures and high melting and boiling points.

Skill 14.5 **The beginning teacher understands the influence of bonding forces on the physical and chemical properties of ionic and covalent substances.**

Intermolecular forces are electromagnetic forces that act between molecules or between widely separated regions of a macromolecule. All types of intermolecular forces are based on the attraction of a positive charge to a negative charge. The magnitude of this force (U) is determined by the distance between charges (d) and the strengths of the two charges (Q1 and Q2). This relationship is expressed by Coulomb's Law, where k is a proportionality constant:

$$U = k(Q1Q2 / d)$$

Intermolecular forces can be electrostatic or electrodynamic interactions. These forces differ in terms of charge strength. Listed in order of decreasing strength, these interactions include Ion-ion interactions, hydrogen bonding, dipole-dipole interactions and London dispersion (Van der Waals) forces.

The strongest intermolecular force is ion-ion attraction, the intermolecular force found in ionic compounds (salts). These bonds form when the difference in electronegativity between two atoms is large enough that one atom is able to steal an electron from the other molecule. The two molecules are then oppositely charged and attracted to one another. Table salt (NaCl) is a common example of an ionic compound.

The second strongest type of intermolecular forces is hydrogen bonding. Hydrogen bonds occur between an electronegative atom and a hydrogen atom bonded to another electronegative atom. Hydrogen bonding can be seen in the compound ethanol (C_2H_6O).

Dipole-dipole interactions are weaker than ionic and hydrogen bonds. This type of interaction takes place between two molecules with permanent dipoles, which are spatially oriented areas of positive or negative charge within the molecule. Dipole-dipole interactions are similar to ionic interactions, but weaker because only partial charges are involved. This type of interaction is seen in the compound hydrochloric acid (HCl).

London dispersion forces are the weakest intermolecular forces, and involve the attraction between temporarily induced dipoles. Such polarization is usually induced by the presence of a polar molecule. These are the weakest intermolecular forces because they occur spontaneously and are easily broken. London dispersion forces are seen between molecules of the halogens, such as chlorine gas (Cl_2).

The **boiling point** of a substance is the temperature at which the majority of the substance can change from liquid to gas form at a given pressure. Boiling is a bulk process, meaning that at the boiling point of a substance, molecules anywhere in the liquid may be vaporized, resulting in the formation of vapor bubbles. Vaporization requires the input of heat, which enables the molecules of a substance to obtain enough energy to overcome intermolecular forces and change from the liquid to gas state. The stronger the forces of intermolecular attraction between molecules of a substance, the higher its boiling point. Ionic compounds, therefore, demonstrate extremely high boiling points because of the large amount of heat required to break the intermolecular forces of attraction between the charged ions. On the opposite end of the spectrum are substances demonstrating London dispersion forces. These substances, such as 02, have very low boiling points, and will commonly be found in gas form.

Vapor pressure is the pressure of a vapor in equilibrium with its non-vapor phases. This equilibrium results from the tendency of all solids and liquids to evaporate to a gaseous form, and the tendency of all gases to condense back. The vapor pressure of a particular substance at a given temperature is the partial pressure at which the gas of that substance is in dynamic equilibrium with its liquid or solid forms. When comparing two substances at any given temperature, the substance with the stronger intermolecular forces will have the lowest vapor pressure. As explained above, the stronger the intermolecular forces of a substance, the more energy required to convert this substance from liquid to gas form. Substances with ionic or hydrogen bonding will therefore have lower vapor pressures than substances with dipole-dipole interactions or Van der Waals forces.

Solubility refers to the ability for a given substance, the solute, to dissolve in a solvent. It is measured in terms of the maximum amount of solute dissolved in a solvent at equilibrium. The resulting solution is called a saturated solution of miscible components. The general rule of solubility is "like dissolves like." Meaning that polar solutes will dissolve in polar solvents, and non-polar solutes will dissolve in non-polar solvents. For this reason, ionic solutes such as sodium chloride (NaCl) will generally dissolve in polar solvents but not in non-polar solvents. Using NaCL dissolved in water as an example, the positive ion Na+ is attracted the partially negatively charged atom in the water molecule OH-, and the negative ion of the solute Cl- is attracted to the partially positively charged atom on the solvent molecule H+. Many ionic compounds are easily dissolved in water because of the ease at which hydrogen bonds are formed between ionic molecules and water molecules.

In respect to substances demonstrating dipole-dipole and London dispersion forces, the higher the polarity of these substances (be it permanent or induced), the higher their solubility in polar solvents, and the lower their solubility in non-polar solvents.

Skill 14.6   The beginning teacher identifies and describes intermolecular and intramolecular forces.

Intramolecular Forces

Intramolecular forces are the forces that hold together the atoms of a molecule. They can be divided into three groupings: Ionic, Covalent, and Metallic.

A **covalent bond** is formed when two atoms share electrons. Recall that atoms whose outer shells are not filled with electrons are unstable. When they are unstable, they readily combine with other unstable atoms. By combining and sharing electrons, they act as a single unit. Covalent bonding happens among nonmetals. Covalent bonds are always polar when between two non-identical atoms. **Covalent compounds** are compounds whose atoms are joined by covalent bonds. Table sugar, methane, and ammonia are examples of covalent compounds.

An **ionic bond** is a bond formed by the transfer of electrons. It happens when metals and nonmetals bond. Before chlorine and sodium combine, the sodium has one valence electron and chlorine has seven. Neither valence shell is filled, but the chlorine's valence shell is almost full. During the reaction, the sodium gives one valence electron to the chlorine atom. Both atoms then have filled shells and are stable. Something else has happened during the bonding. Before the bonding, both atoms were neutral. When one electron was transferred, it upset the balance of protons and electrons in each atom. The chlorine atom took on one extra electron and the sodium atom released one atom. The atoms have now become ions. **Ions** are atoms with an unequal number of protons and electrons. To determine whether the ion is positive or negative, compare the number of protons (+charge) to the electrons (-charge). If there are more electrons the ion will be negative. If there are more protons, the ion will be positive. Compounds that result from the transfer of metal atoms to nonmetal atoms are called **ionic compounds.** Sodium chloride (table salt), sodium hydroxide (drain cleaner), and potassium chloride (salt substitute) are examples of ionic compounds.

Metallic bonds occur when the bonding is between two metals. Metallic properties, such as low ionization energies, conductivity, and malleability, suggest that metals possess strong forces of attraction between atoms, but still have electrons that are able to move freely in all directions throughout the metal. This creates a "sea of electrons" model where electrons are quickly and easily transferred between metal atoms. In this model, the outer shell electrons are free to move. The metallic bond is the force of attraction that results from the moving electrons and the positive nuclei left behind. The strength of metal bonds usually results in regular structures and high melting and boiling points.

Intermolecular Forces

Intermolecular forces are a class of attractions between molecules of a substance that are weaker than covalent bonds. The strength of intermolecular forces determines the physical properties of a substance such as melting point and boiling point. The types of intermolecular forces are hydrogen bonding, dipole-dipole forces, ion-dipole forces, and London dispersion forces.

Hydrogen bonding is the strongest type of intermolecular attraction. Hydrogen atoms of polar bonds (e.g., H-F, H-O, and H-N) experience an attractive force toward electronegative atoms that have an unshared pair of electrons, usually an F, O, or N atom. Because hydrogen atoms have no inner core of electrons, when bonded with a strongly electronegative atom, the side of the atom facing away from the bond is a virtually naked nucleus with a positive charge. Thus, the positive charge interacts strongly with electronegative atoms of nearby molecules.

$$^-N - H^+ \text{-----} \ ^-F - H^+$$

Hydrogen Bond

Hydrogen bonding is responsible for many of the unique properties of water. Because each water molecule contains an electronegative oxygen atom bonded with two hydrogen atoms, the potential for intermolecular hydrogen bonding is great (each water molecule can participate in four hydrogen bonds). Extensive hydrogen bonding creates the highly structured nature of water. For example, frozen water (ice) is less dense than liquid water and water has a high heat capacity and specific heat.

Ion-dipole forces involve the interaction between a charged ion and a polar molecule (i.e. a dipole). Positively charged cations interact with the negative end of a dipole. Negatively charged anions interact with the positive end of a dipole. Ion-dipole forces are important interactions in solutions of ionic substances in polar solvents.

Dipole-dipole forces exist between neutral, polar molecules. Partial positive ends of polar molecules interact with partial negative ends of other polar molecules. Dipole-dipole forces are weaker than ion-dipole forces and polar molecules must be close together for such forces to have a significant effect.

London dispersion forces exist between neutral, non-polar molecules. As electrons orbit around atomic nuclei, the distribution of electrons may not be symmetrical at any given instance. Thus, even the atoms of non-polar molecules experience transient positive and negative dipoles. Because of electron repulsion, these transient dipoles can induce similar dipoles in neighboring molecules. When atoms are close together, London dispersion forces are a significant factor. Scientists use the term **van der Waals forces** to describe dipole and dispersion forces as a group.

Skill 14.7   The beginning teacher uses intermolecular forces to explain the physical properties of a given substance (e.g., melting point, crystal structure).

The impact of intermolecular forces on substances is best understood by imagining ourselves shrinking down to the size of molecules and picturing what happens when we stick more strongly to molecules nearby. It will take more energy (higher temperatures) to pull us away from our neighbors.

If two substances are being compared, the material with the **greater intermolecular attractive forces** (i.e. the stronger intermolecular bond) will have the following properties relative to the other substance:

For solids:
Higher melting point
Higher enthalpy of fusion
Greater hardness
Organized (crystalline) structure
Lower vapor pressure

For liquids:
Higher boiling point
Higher critical temperature
Higher critical pressure
Higher enthalpy of vaporization
Higher viscosity
Higher surface tension
Lower vapor pressure

Intermolecular attractive forces have the opposite effect from temperature.

Skill 14.8   The beginning teacher applies the concepts of electronegativity, electron affinity, and oxidation state to analyze chemical bonds.

Electronegativity measures the ability of an atom to attract electrons in a chemical bond. The most metallic elements have the lowest electronegativity. The most nonmetallic have the highest electronegativity.

In a reaction with a metal, the most reactive chemicals are the **most electronegative elements** or compounds containing those elements. In a reaction with a nonmetal, the most reactive chemicals are the **least electronegative elements** or compounds containing them. The reactivity of elements may be described by a **reactivity series**: an ordered list with chemicals that react strongly at one end and nonreactive chemicals at the other. The following reactivity series is for metals reacting with oxygen.

Metal	K	Na	Ca	Mg	Al	Zn	Fe	Pb	Cu	Hg	Ag	Au
Reaction with O_2	Burns violently		Burns rapidly					Oxidizes slowly			No reaction	

Copper, silver, and gold (group 11) are known as the **noble metals** because they rarely react.

The term **valence** is often used to describe the number of atoms that may react to form a compound with a given atom by sharing, removing, or losing **valence electrons**. A more useful term is **oxidation number**. The **oxidation number of an ion is its charge**. The oxidation number of an atom sharing its electrons is **the charge it would have if the bonding were ionic**. There are four rules for determining oxidation number:

1) The oxidation number of an element (i.e., a Cl atom in Cl_2) is zero because the electrons in the bond are shared equally.

2) In a compound, the more electronegative atoms are assigned negative oxidation numbers and the less electronegative atoms are assigned positive oxidation numbers equal to the number of shared electron-pair bonds. For example, hydrogen may only have an oxidation number of −1 when bonded to a less electronegative element or +1 when bonded to a more electronegative element. Oxygen almost always has an oxidation number of −2. Fluorine always has an oxidation number of −1 (except in F_2).

3) The oxidation numbers in a compound must add up to zero, and the sum of oxidation numbers in a polyatomic ion must equal the overall charge of the ion.

Skill 14.9   The beginning teacher evaluates energy changes in the formation and dissociation of chemical bonds.

Chemical energy is the energy stored in substances due to the arrangement of atoms within the substance. When atoms are rearranged during chemical reactions, energy is either released or consumed. It is the energy released from chemical reactions that fuels our economy and powers our bodies. Most of the electricity produced on the planet comes from chemical energy released by the burning of petroleum, coal, and natural gas. ATP is the molecule used by our bodies to carry chemical energy form cell to cell.

The energy in molecules is located in the **bonds between the atoms**. To break these bonds requires energy. Once broken apart, the atoms, ions, or molecules rearrange themselves to form new substances, making new bonds. Making new bonds releases energy.

If during a chemical reaction, **more energy is needed to break the reactant bonds than is released when the products form new bonds,** the reaction is **endothermic** and heat is absorbed. The environment becomes colder.

On the other hand, if **more energy is released when the products form new bonds than is needed to break the reactant bonds,** the reaction is **exothermic** and the excess energy is released to the environment as heat. The temperature of the environment goes up.

Bond energies

The total energy absorbed or released in the reaction can be determined by using **heats of formation** or **bond energies**. The total energy change of the reaction is equal to the total energy of all of the bonds of the products minus the total energy of all of the bonds of the reactants.

Propane (C_3H_8) is a common fuel used in heating homes and backyard grills. When burned, the combustion reaction shown below takes place and excess energy is released and used for heating or cooking:

$$C_3H_8 \ (g) + 5O_2 \ (g) \rightarrow 3CO_2 \ (g) + 4H_2O \ (l)$$

The total energy of the products is found from the bonds in the carbon dioxide molecules and the water molecules:

$$3 \ O = C = O \ + \ 4 \ H \diagup^{O}\diagdown H$$

or 6 C=O bonds and 8 H–O bonds.

A table of bond energies gives the following information:

C=O   743 kJ/mol
H–O   463 kJ/mol

For these molecules there would be:

$$(6 \times -743 \text{ kJ/mol}) + (8 \times -463 \text{ kJ/mol}) = -8162 \text{ kJ}$$

energy released when these molecules form. Negative values are used to indicate energy released for this exothermic process of bond formation.

The reactants are these:

or 2 C–C bonds, 8 C–H bonds, and 5 O=O bonds.

These bonds require the following energy to break:

C–C   348 kJ/mol
C–H   412 kJ/mol
O=O   498 kJ/mol

The total energy required for the reactants would be:

$$(2 \times 348 \text{ kJ}) + (8 \times 412 \text{ kJ}) + (5 \times 498 \text{ kJ}) = 6482 \text{ kJ}$$

energy required. Positive values are used to indicate energy required for the endothermic process of bond destruction.

The total energy change that occurs during the combustion of propane is found from the sum of the energy released by the formation of the product bonds and the energy required to break the reactant bonds:

$$-8162 \text{ kJ} + 6482 \text{ kJ} = -1680 \text{ kJ}$$

energy released for every mole of propane that burns.

Heat of reaction

When a chemical reaction takes place, the enthalpies of the products will differ from the enthalpies of the reactants. There is an energy change for the reaction ΔH_{rxn}, determined by **the sum of the products minus the sum of the reactants**:

$$\Delta H_{rxn} = H_{product\ 1} + H_{product\ 2} + \cdots \quad H_{reactant\ 1} \quad H_{reactant\ 2} \quad \cdots$$

The enthalpy change for a reaction is commonly called the **heat of reaction**.

If the enthalpies of the products are greater than the enthalpies of the reactants then ΔH_{rxn} **is positive** and the reaction is **endothermic**. Endothermic reactions **absorb heat** from their surroundings. The simplest endothermic reactions break chemical bonds.

If the enthalpies of the products are less than the enthalpies of the reactants then ΔH_{rxn} **is negative** and the reaction is **exothermic**. Exothermic reactions **release heat** into their surroundings. The simplest exothermic reactions form new chemical bonds.

The heat absorbed or released by a chemical reaction often has the impact of changing the temperature of the reaction vessel and of the chemicals themselves. The measurement of these heat effects is known as **calorimetry**.

The enthalpy change of a reaction ΔH_{rxn} **is equal in magnitude but has the opposite sign to the enthalpy change for the reverse reaction**. If a series of reactions lead back to the initial reactants then the net energy change for the entire process is zero.

When a reaction is composed of steps, the **total enthalpy change will be the sum of the changes for each step**. Even if a reaction in reality contains no steps, we may still write any number of reactions in series that lead from the reactants to the products and their sum will be the heat of the overall reaction of interest. The ability to add together these enthalpies to form ultimate products from initial reactants is known as **Hess' Law**. It is used to determine one heat of reaction from others:

$$\Delta H_{net\ rxn} = H_{rxn\ 1} + H_{rxn\ 2} + \cdots$$

A **standard** thermodynamic value occurs with all components at 25° C and 100 kPa. This *thermodynamic standard state* is slightly different from the *standard temperature and pressure* (STP) often used for gas law problems (0° C and 1 atm = 101.325 kPa). Standard thermodynamic values of common chemicals are listed in tables.

The **heat of formation** ΔH_f of a chemical is the heat taken up (positive) or emitted (negative) when elements react to form the chemical. It is also called the enthalpy of formation. The **standard heat of formation $\Delta H_f°$** is the heat of formation with all reactants and products at 25° C and 100 kPa.

Elements in their **most stable form** are assigned a value of $\Delta H_f° = 0$ kJ/mol. Different forms of an element in the same phase of matter are known as **allotropes**.

Example: The heat of formation for carbon as a gas is:

$$\Delta H_f^{\circ} \text{ for } C(g) = 718.4 \ \frac{kJ}{mol}$$

C in the solid phase exists in three allotropes. A C_{60} *buckyball* (above right) contains C atoms linked with aromatic bonds and arranged in the shape of a soccer ball. C_{60} was discovered in 1985. *Diamond* (middle right) contains single C–C bonds in a three-dimensional network. The most stable form at 25° C is *graphite* (below right). Graphite is composed of C atoms with aromatic bonds in sheets.

$$\Delta H_i^{\circ} \quad _{\circ\circ} \text{ buckminsterfullerene or buckyball}) = 38.0 \ \frac{kJ}{mol}$$

$$\Delta H_i^{\circ} \quad _{\infty} \text{ diamond}) = 1.88 \ \frac{kJ}{mol}$$

$$\Delta H_i^{\circ} \quad _{\infty} \text{ graphite}) = 0 \ \frac{kJ}{mol}$$

Heat of combustion ΔH_c (also called enthalpy of combustion) is the heat of reaction when a chemical **burns in O_2** to form completely oxidized products such as **CO_2 and H_2O**. It is also the heat of reaction for **nutritional molecules that are metabolized** in the body. The standard heat of combustion $\Delta H_c°$ takes place at 25° C and 100 kPa. **Combustion is always exothermic**, so the negative sign for values of ΔH_c is often omitted. If a combustion reaction is used in Hess' Law, the value must be negative.

Skill 14.10   The beginning teacher understands the relationship between chemical bonding and molecular geometry.

Resonance

O_2 contains a total of 12 valence electrons and the following Lewis structure:

Ozone (O_3) has a total of 18 valence electrons, and two Lewis structures are equally possible for this molecule:

Equivalent Lewis structures are called **resonance forms**. A double-headed arrow is used to indicate resonance. The actual molecule does not have a double bond on one side and a single bond on the other. The **molecular structure is in an average state between the resonance forms**.

Hybridized atomic orbitals

Electron shell structures are built up by considering different energy levels for different subshells to explain spectroscopic data about individual atoms. However, when Lewis dot structures are drawn or molecular geometries are determined, all valence electrons are treated identically to explain the bonding between atoms regardless of whether the electrons once belonged to the s or the p subshell of their atom. Reconciling these views of the individual and the bonded atom requires a theory known as hybridization.

Hybridization describes the pre-bonding **promotion of one or more electrons** from a lower energy subshell to a higher energy subshell followed by a **combination** of the orbitals into degenerate **hybrid orbitals**.

Hybridization occurs for atoms with a valence electron configuration of ns^2, ns^2np^1, or ns^2p^2. For period 2, this corresponds with Be, B, C, and N in the NH_3^+ ion.

An atom joined to its neighbor by **multiple covalent bonds** is prepared for bonding by hybridization with incomplete combination. Electrons that remain in p orbitals can contribute additional bonds between the same two atoms.

Molecular Orbital Theory

The electron configurations of isolated atoms are found in atomic orbitals, the configurations of atoms about to bond are represented by atomic and hybridized orbitals, and **the electron configurations of molecules are represented by molecular orbitals**. Molecular orbital theory is an advanced topic, but it may be simplified to representing the **bonds between atoms as overlapping electron density shapes from atomic orbitals**. There are two typical locations for molecular orbitals.

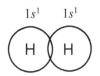

The **bonding sigma orbital** (σ) surrounds a **line drawn between the two atoms** in a bond. At least one electron pair in every bond is in a bonding σ orbital. Sigma bonds get their name from *s* orbitals because the spherical electron density shapes of two *s* orbitals overlap to form a σ orbital. A drawing of this overlap and the resulting molecular orbital is shown to the right for H_2. Hybrid or *p* atomic orbitals also form σ orbitals when they overlap such that the axis between the bonded atoms runs through the center of the combined electron density.

The **bonding pi orbital** (π) follows regions **separate from a line drawn between the two atoms** in a bond. Two overlapping *p* orbitals will form π □□ bonds to contain the additional shared electrons in molecules with double or triple bonds. π bonds prevent atoms from rotating about the central axis between them.

Molecules with double bonds next to each other and aromatic molecules based on benzene contain **more than two π□ orbitals on adjacent atoms**. The bonds, as well as the entire molecules, are described as being **conjugated**. Electrons in these molecules are free to move from one bond to the next **on the same molecule** and so are **delocalized**. Delocalized electrons are found throughout the entire substance in materials with metallic bonds.

Benzene (C_6H_6) has the following resonance forms:

Each carbon atom in benzene bonds to three atoms, so their electrons are in three sp^2 orbitals and one p orbital. Aromatic molecules are often drawn with a circle in the center of their benzene to show delocalized π electrons.

Electron Pairs

Molecular geometry is predicted using the valence-shell electron-pair repulsion or **VSEPR** model. VSEPR uses the fact that **electron pairs around the central atom of a molecule repel each other**. Imagine you are one of two pairs of electrons in bonds around a central atom (like the bonds in BeH_2 in the following table). You want to be as far away from the other electron pair as possible, so you will be on one side of the atom and the other pair will be on the other side. There is a straight line (or a 180° angle) between you to the other electron pair on the other side of the nucleus. In general, electron pairs lie at the **largest possible angles** from each other.

Electron pairs	Geometrical arrangement		Predicted bond angles	Example
2 H—Be—H	:—X—:	Linear	180°	
F B 3 F F	(X)	Trigonal planar	120°	
H C H H H	(X)	Tetrahedral	109.5°	
F F—P—F F F	(X)	Trigonal bipyramidal	120° and 90°	
F F S F F F	(X)	Octahedral	90°	

X represents a generic central atom. Lone pair electrons on F are not shown in the example molecules.

Unshared Electron Pairs

The **shape of a molecule is given by the locations of its atoms**. Outer atoms are connected to central atoms by shared electrons, but unshared electrons also have an important impact on molecular shape. Unshared electrons may determine the angles between atoms. Molecular shapes in the following table take into account total and unshared electron pairs.

Electron pairs	Molecular shape				
	All shared pairs	1 unshared pair	2 unshared pairs	3 unshared pairs	4 unshared pairs
2	A—X—A Linear				
3	Trigonal planar	Bent			
4	Tetrahedral	Trigonal pyramidal	Bent		
5	Trigonal bipyramidal	Seesaw or sawhorse	T-shaped	Linear	
6	Octahedral	Square pyramidal	Square planar	T-shaped	Linear

X represents a generic central atom bonded to atoms labeled A.

Altered Bond Angles

Unpaired electrons also have a stronger impact on molecular shape. The shared electron pairs are each attracted partially to the central atom and partially to the other atom in the bond, but the unpaired electrons are different. They are attracted to the central atom, but there is nothing on their other side, so they are free to expand toward the central atom. That expansion means that they take up more room than the other electron pairs, and the others are all squeezed a little closer together. Multiple bonds have a similar effect because more space is required for more electrons. In general, **unshared electron pairs and multiple bonds decrease the angles between the remaining bonds**.

Summary

To use VSEPR to predict molecular geometry, perform the following steps:

1) Write out Lewis dot structures.

2) Use the Lewis structure to determine the number of unshared electron pairs and bonds around each central atom, counting multiple bonds as one.

3) The second table (previous page) of this skill gives the arrangement of total and unshared electron pairs to account for electron repulsions around each central atom.

4) For multiple bonds or unshared electron pairs, decrease the angles slightly between the remaining bonds around the central atom.

5) Combine the results from the previous two steps to determine the shape of the entire molecule.

http://www.shef.ac.uk/chemistry/vsepr/ provides good explanations and diagrams of molecular geometries using VSEPR.

http://cowtownproductions.com/cowtown/genchem/09_16T.htm provides some practice for determining molecular shape.

Competency 0015 **The teacher understands and interprets chemical equations and chemical reactions.**

Skill 15.1 **The beginning teacher identifies elements, common ions, and compounds using scientific nomenclature.**

The identity of an **element** depends on the **number of protons** in the nucleus of the atom. This value is called the **atomic number** and it is sometimes written as a subscript before the symbol for the corresponding element. Atoms and ions of a given element that differ in number of neutrons have a different mass and are called **isotopes**. A nucleus with a specified number of protons and neutrons is called a **nuclide**, and a nuclear particle, either a proton or neutron, may be called a **nucleon**. The total number of nucleons is called the **mass number** and may be written as a superscript before the atomic symbol.

$$^{14}_{6}C$$

represents an atom of carbon with 6 protons and 8 neutrons.

The **number of neutrons** may be found by **subtracting the atomic number from the mass number**. For example, uranium-235 has 235 – 92 = 143 neutrons because it has 235 nucleons and 92 protons.

Different isotopes have different natural abundances and nuclear properties, but an atom's chemical properties are almost entirely due to the electrons that surround the nucleus.

Ions are atoms with an unequal number of protons and electrons. To determine whether the ion is positive or negative, compare the number of protons (+charge) to the electrons (-charge). If there are more electrons the ion will be negative (called an anion). If there are more protons, the ion will be positive (called a cation). Some common ions include H^+, K^+, $CO3^{2-}$, and $NO3^-$.

A **compound** is made of two or more elements that have been chemically combined. Atoms join together when elements are chemically combined. The result is that the elements lose their individual identities when they are joined. The compound that they become has different properties.

Skill 15.2 **The beginning teacher uses and interprets symbols, formulas, and equations in describing interactions of matter and energy in chemical reactions.**

A **chemical symbol** is an abbreviation or short representation of the name of a chemical element. Natural elements have symbols of one or two letters, and are displayed in the periodic table according to recurring chemical property trends. For example, the chemical symbol for carbon is C.

A **chemical formula** is a symbolic expression of the atoms that constitute a chemical compound. The chemical formula of a molecular compound identifies each constituent element using its chemical symbol. Subscripts after each chemical symbol are used to indicate how many atoms of a particular element are found in a discrete molecule of the chemical compound. For example, the chemical formula of the compound carbon dioxide is written as follows:

$$CO_2$$

The subscript 2 indicates that one molecule of carbon dioxide consists of one atom of carbon and two atoms of oxygen.

A **chemical equation** is a symbolic representation that expresses the net change that occurs as the result of a chemical reaction. In a chemical equation, reactant entities are displayed as chemical formulas on the left hand side of the equation, and product entities are similarly displayed on the right hand side. For example, the chemical equation for the reaction of hydrogen gas (H_2) with oxygen gas (O_2) to form water is written as follows:

$$2H_2 + O_2 \rightarrow 2H_2O$$

The '+' sign is read as 'reacts with,' while the '$\rightarrow$' is read as 'produces.' The '+' sign indicates that a chemical change is taking place. The '$\rightarrow$' sign indicates that the chemical reaction produces a new substance different from the initial reactants. Chemical equations may sometimes a symbol with arrows pointing in both directions. This is used to indicate a state of equilibrium, with the reaction flowing in both directions.

The numbers in front of each individual chemical formula are called coefficients or stoichiometric numbers (the number '1' is usually omitted). According to the law of conservation of mass, atoms are neither created nor destroyed during a chemical reaction. Thus, the same collection of atoms present before the reaction must be present after the reaction, however the arrangement of the atoms will differ. For this reason, a chemical equation must be balanced, meaning the equation must have an equal number of atoms of each element on each side of the arrow. A balanced chemical equation describes the proportionate quantities of reactants and products. For example, in the chemical equation:

$$2H_2 + O_2 \rightarrow 2H_2O$$

The first number in a set such as 2H2 indicates how many molecules (or moles) of the substance there are. Therefore, $2H_2$ represents 2 molecules (or moles) of H_2, each containing 2 atoms of hydrogen. The entire chemical equation indicates that two molecules of hydrogen gas react with one molecule of oxygen gas to produce two molecules of water.

Chemical equation coefficients

For the general equation $2A + 3B \rightarrow C + 2D$

The ratio of molecules is $2 : 3 : 1 : 2$

The ratio of moles is $2 : 3 : 1 : 2$

Physical states of matter

The physical state of each chemical may also be indicated in a chemical equation. The symbols (g), (l), and (s) represent the states of gas, liquid and solid, respectively. For example, the chemical equation

$$2H_2\ (g) + O_2\ (g) \rightarrow 2H_2O(l)$$

Indicates that hydrogen gas and oxygen gas react to produce the liquid form of water.

The symbol (aq) signifies that the ions of a reaction are in aqueous solution, and thus are hydrated, or attached to water molecules.

Ionic Compounds

Ionic compounds used in reactions are usually dissociated in aqueous solution, creating various species capable of reacting. For ionic compounds, the superscripts '+' and '-' are placed after a chemical symbol or formula to indicate the species' net charge in their dissociated state. For example, the formula NO_3^- represents a nitrate ion with a net charge of negative one.

The "Total Ionic Equation" represents all ions present in solution. For example, in the reaction

$$AgNO_3(aq) + NaCl(aq) \rightarrow AgCl(s) + NaNO_3(aq)$$

The total ionic equation would read

$$Ag^+ + NO_3^-\ + Na^+ + Cl^- \rightarrow Ag^+ + Cl^-\ + Na^+ + NO_3^-$$

When the ions Ag^+ and Cl^- are brought together, they combine to form an insoluble precipitate of silver chloride. Therefore these ions provide the driving force for the reaction. The "Net Ionic Equation" represents only those species participating in the reaction. For example, for the same reaction, the net ionic equation would read:

$$Ag^+\ (aq) + Cl^-\ (aq) \rightarrow AgCl(s)$$

From this equation it can be determined that the ions NO_3^- and Cl^- are not directly involved in this reaction, and that the net change of the reaction is the removal of the silver and chloride ions from the solution to form an insoluble solid. This equation also indicates that the reaction took place in solution and produced an insoluble solid, known as a precipitate.

Types of reactions indicated by chemical equations

All chemical reactions can be placed into one of six categories. By knowing the compounds involved in each reaction, the products and their states of matter can be predicted.

1) Combustion: oxygen combines with another compound to form water and carbon dioxide. These reactions are exothermic (producing heat). For example, the burning of napthalene:

$$C_{10}H_8 + 12\ O_2 \rightarrow 10\ CO_2 + 4\ H_2O$$

2) Synthesis: two or more simple compounds combine to form a more complex compound. General form $A + B \rightarrow AB$
For example, the synthesis of iron II sulfide from iron and sulfur:

$$8\ Fe + S_8 \rightarrow 8\ FeS$$

3) Decomposition: a complex molecule breaks down to make simpler molecules. General form: $AB \rightarrow A + B$
For example, the electrolysis of water to make oxygen and hydrogen gas:

$$2\ H_2O \rightarrow 2\ H_2 + O_2$$

4) Single displacement: one element trades places with another element in a compound. General form: $A + BC \rightarrow AC + B$
For example, magnesium replaces hydrogen in water to make magnesium hydroxide and hydrogen gas:

$$Mg + 2\ H_2O \rightarrow Mg\ (OH)_2 + H_2$$

5) Double displacement: anions and cations of two different molecules switch places, forming two entirely different compounds. General form:

$$AB + CD \text{ ---> } AD + CB$$

For example, reaction of lead (II) nitrate with potassium iodide to form lead (II) iodide and potassium nitrate:

$$Pb\ (NO_3)_2 + 2\ KI \rightarrow PbI_2 + 2\ KNO_3$$

6) Acid-base: a special kind of displacement reaction. The H^+ ion of the acid reacts with the OH^- ion in the base, causing the formation of water. Generally, the product of this reaction is some ionic salt and water: HA + BOH ---> H_2O + BA For example, the reaction between hydrobromic acid (HBr) and sodium hydroxide:

$$HBr + NaOH \rightarrow NaBr + H_2O$$

Skill 15.3   The beginning teacher understands mass relationships involving percent composition, empirical formulas, and molecular formulas.

The **percent composition** of a substance is the **percentage by mass of each element**. Chemical composition is used to verify the purity of a compound in the lab. An impurity will make the actual composition vary from the expected one.

To determine percent composition from a formula, follow these steps:

1) Write down the **number of atoms each element contributes** to the formula.

2) Multiply these values by the molecular weight of the corresponding element to determine the **grams of each element in one mole** of the formula.

3) Add the values from step 2 to obtain the **formula mass**.

4) Divide each value from step 2 by the formula mass from step 3 and multiply by 100% to obtain the **percent composition of each element**.

Example: What is the chemical composition of ammonium carbonate $(NH_4)_2CO_3$?

Solution:

1) $(NH_4)_2CO_3$ contains 2 N, 8 H, 1 C, and 3 O atoms.

2) $\dfrac{2 \text{ mol N}}{\text{mol } (NH_4)CO_3} \times \dfrac{14.0 \text{ g N}}{\text{mol N}} = 28.0 \text{ g N/mol } (NH_4)CO_3$

$$8(1.0) = 8.0 \text{ g H/mol } (NH_4)CO_3$$
$$1(12.0) = 12.0 \text{ g C/mol } (NH_4)CO_3$$
$$3(16.0) = 48.0 \text{ g O/mol } (NH_4)CO_3$$

3) Sum is $\overline{96.0 \text{ g } (NH_4)CO_3/\text{mol } (NH_4)CO_3}$

4)

$\%N = \dfrac{28.0 \text{ g N/mol } (NH_4)_2CO_3}{96.0 \text{ g } (NH_4)_2CO_3/\text{mol } (NH_4)_2CO_3} = 0.292 \text{ g N/g } (NH_4)_2CO_3 \times 100\% = 29.2\%$

$\%H = \dfrac{8.0}{96.0} \times 100\% = 8.3\%$ $\%C = \dfrac{12.0}{96.0} \times 100\% = 12.5\%$ $\%O = \dfrac{48.0}{96.0} \times 100\% = 50.0\%$

If we know the chemical composition of a compound, we can calculate an **empirical formula** for it. An empirical formula is the **simplest formula** using the smallest set of integers to express the **ratio of atoms** present in a molecule.

To determine an empirical formula from a percent composition, following these steps:

1) Change the "%" sign to grams for a basis of 100 g of the compound.

2) Determine the moles of each element in 100 g of the compound.

3) Divide the values from step 1 by the smallest value to obtain ratios.

4) Multiply by an integer if necessary to get a whole-number ratio.

Example: What is the empirical formula of a compound with a composition of 63.9% Cl, 32.5% C, and 3.6% H?

Solution:

1) We will use a basis of 100 g of the compound containing 63.9 g Cl, 32.5 g C, and 3.6 g H.

2) In 100 g, there are: $63.9 \text{ g Cl} \times \dfrac{\text{mol Cl}}{35.45 \text{ g Cl}} = 1.802 \text{ mol Cl}$

$$32.5/12.01 = 2.706 \text{ mol C}$$
$$3.6/1.01 = 3.56 \text{ mol H}$$

3) Dividing these values by the smallest yields:

$$\frac{2.706 \text{ mol C}}{1.802 \text{ mol Cl}} = 1.502 \text{ mol C/mol Cl}$$

$$\frac{3.56 \text{ mol H}}{1.802 \text{ mol Cl}} = 1.97 \text{ mol H/mol Cl}$$

Therefore, the elements are present in a ratio of C:H:Cl=1.5:2:1

4) Multiply the entire ratio by 2 because you cannot have a fraction of an atom. This corresponds to a ratio of 3:4:2 for an empirical formula of $C_3H_4Cl_2$.

The **molecular formula** describing the **actual number of atoms in the molecule** might actually be $C_3H_4Cl_2$ or it might be $C_6H_8Cl_4$ or some other multiple that maintains a 3:4:2 ratio.

Skill 15.4   The beginning teacher interprets and balances chemical equations using conservation of mass and charge.

A properly written chemical equation must contain properly written formulas and must be **balanced**. Chemical equations are written to describe a certain number of moles of reactants becoming a certain number of moles of products. The number of moles of each compound is indicated by its **stoichiometric coefficient**.

Example: In the reaction:

$$2H_2(g) + O_2(g) \rightarrow 2H_2O(l)$$

hydrogen has a stoichiometric coefficient of two, oxygen has a coefficient of one, and water has a coefficient of two because 2 moles of hydrogen react with 1 mole of oxygen to form two moles of water.

In a balanced equation, the stoichiometric coefficients are chosen so that the equation contains an **equal number of each type of atom on each side**. In our example, there are four H atoms and two O atoms on both sides. Therefore, the equation is balanced with respect to atoms.

Balancing equations is a four-step process.

1) Write an **unbalanced equation**.

2) Determine the **number of each type of atom on each side** of the equation to find out if the equation is already balanced. If not, continue with Step 3.

3) Assume that **the molecule with the most atoms** has a stoichiometric coefficient of one, and determine the other stoichiometric coefficients required to create the **same number of atoms on each side** of the equation.

4) Multiply all the stoichiometric coefficients by a whole number if necessary to eliminate fractional coefficients.

Example: Balance the chemical equation describing the combustion of methanol in oxygen to produce only carbon dioxide and water.

Solution:

1) The structural formula of methanol is CH_3OH, so its molecular formula is CH_4O. The formula for carbon dioxide is CO_2. Therefore the unbalanced equation is:

$$CH_4O + O_2 \rightarrow CO_2 + H_2O$$

2) On the left there are 1 C, 4 H, and 3 O atoms. On the right, there are 1 C, 2 H, and 3 O atoms. The equation is close to being balanced but there is still work to do.

3) Assuming that CH_4O has a stoichiometric coefficient of one means that the left side has 1 C and 4 H that are currently missing on the right. Therefore the stoichiometric coefficient of CO_2 will be 1 to balance C and the stoichiometric coefficient of H_2O will be 2 to balance H. Now we have:

$$CH_4O + ?O_2 \rightarrow CO_2 + 2H_2O$$

and only oxygen remains unbalanced. There are 4O on the right, and one of these is accounted for by methanol, leaving 3 O to be accounted for by O_2. This gives a stoichiometric coefficient of 3/2 and a balanced equation:

$$CH_4O + \frac{3}{2}O_2 \rightarrow CO_2 + 2H_2O$$

4) Whole-number coefficients are achieved by multiplying by two:

$$2CH_4O + 3O_2 \rightarrow 2CO_2 + 4H_2O$$

Reactions among ions in aqueous solution may be represented in three ways. When solutions of hydrochloric acid and sodium hydroxide are mixed, a reaction occurs and heat is produced. The **molecular equation** for this reaction is:

$$HCl(aq) + NaOH(aq) \rightarrow H_2O(l) + NaCl(aq)$$

It is called a molecular equation because the **complete chemical formulas** of reactants and products are shown. But in reality, both HCl and NaOH are strong electrolytes and exist in solution as ions. This is represented by a **complete ionic equation** that shows all the dissolved ions:

$$H^+(aq) + Cl^-(aq) + Na^+(aq) + OH^-(aq) \rightarrow H_2O(l) + Na^+(aq) + Cl^-(aq)$$

Because $Na^+(aq)$ and $Cl^-(aq)$ appear as both reactants and products, they play no role in the reaction. Ions that appear in identical chemical forms on both sides of an ionic equation are called **spectator ions** because they aren't part of the action. When spectator ions are removed from a complete ionic equation, the result is a **net ionic equation** that shows the actual changes that occur to the chemicals when these two solutions are mixed together:

$$H^+(aq) + OH^-(aq) \rightarrow H_2O(l)$$

An additional requirement for **redox** reaction is that the equation contains an **equal charge on each side**. In the example above, the positive charge on the H^+ ion cancels out the negative charge on the OH^- ion giving an overall neutral charge for both sides of the equation. Redox reactions may be divided into half-reactions which either gain or lose electrons.

Skill 15.5 **The beginning teacher understands mass relationships in chemical equations and solves problems involving moles, limiting reagents, and reaction yield.**

To convert mass to moles:

1. First determine the molar mass (molecular weight) of the substance by adding the masses for each element in the substance x number of atoms present:

Example: Determine the molar mass of $CuSO_4$.

Solution: 1 mole of Cu = 63.5 g + 1 mol of S = 32 g + 4 mol O = 4 x 16 or 48 g = 143.5 g/mol

2. Determine the number of moles present using the molar mass conversion: 1 mol = molar mass of substance.

Example: If you have 315 g of $CuSO_4$, how many moles is that?

Solution: 315 g x 1 mol/143.5 g = 2.20 mol $CuSO_4$

Moles to grams conversions are just the reverse of the process above.

To convert mass of a reactant to mass of a product or vice versa, use a three-step process:

1) Convert grams of the given compound to moles using molecular weight.

2) Obtain the number of moles of the second compound from the number of moles of the first compound using their stoichiometric coefficients from the balanced reaction equation.

3) Convert moles of the second compound to grams using molecular weight.

These steps are often combined in one series of multiplications, which may be described as **"grams to moles to moles to grams."**

Example: What mass of oxygen is required to consume 95.0 g of ethane in the following reaction?

$$2C_2H_6 + 7O_2 \rightarrow 4CO_2 + 6H_2O$$

Solution:

$$95.0 \text{ g } C_2H_6 \times \underbrace{\frac{1 \text{ mol } C_2H_6}{30.1 \text{ g } C_2H_6}}_{\text{step 1}} \times \underbrace{\frac{7 \text{ mol } O_2}{2 \text{ mol } C_2H_6}}_{\text{step 2}} \times \underbrace{\frac{32.0 \text{ g } O_2}{1 \text{ mol } O_2}}_{\text{step 3}} = 359 \text{ g } O_2$$

Gases

The progress of reactions that produce or consume a gas may be described by measuring gas volume instead of mass. The best way to solve these problems is to use the ideal gas equation to interconvert volume and number of moles:

$$n = \frac{PV}{RT} \quad \text{and} \quad V = \frac{nRT}{P}.$$

If a volume is given, the steps are "**volume to moles to moles to grams.**" If a mass is given, the steps will be "**grams to moles to moles to volume.**"
Example: What volume of oxygen in liters is generated at 40° C and 1 atm by the decomposition of 280 g of potassium chlorate in the following reaction?

$$2KClO_3 \rightarrow 2KCl + 3O_2(g)$$

Solution: We are given a mass and asked for a volume, so the steps in the solution will be "grams to moles to moles to volume." Solving first for moles:

$$280 \text{ g } KClO_3 \times \frac{1 \text{ mol } KClO_3}{122.548 \text{ g } KClO_3} \times \frac{3 \text{ mol } O_2}{2 \text{ mol } KClO_3} = 3.427 \text{ mol } O_2$$

then for volume:

$$V = \frac{nRT}{P} = \frac{(3.427 \text{ mol } O_2)\left(0.08206 \frac{\text{L-atm}}{\text{mol-K}}\right)(273.15 + 40)\text{K}}{(1 \text{ atm})} = 88.06 \text{ L } O_2$$

Solutions

In solution stoichiometry problems, the moles of solute for each solution must first be determined. This is done using the molarity definition. Once the moles of solute are determined, the problem becomes a mole-mole stoichiometry problem or a limiting reactant problem.

Example: How much of a 0.50 M $Pb(NO_3)_2$ solution is required to completely react with 25 g of KI?

$$Pb(NO_3)_2 \text{ (aq)} + 2 \text{ KI (s)} \rightarrow PbI_2 \text{ (s)} + 2 \text{ KNO}_3 \text{ (aq)}$$

Solution:

1. Find the moles of KI reacting:

   25 g KI x 1 mol KI/166 g/mol = 0.15 mol

2. Use the mole ratio from the balanced equation:

   0.15 mol KI x 1 mol $Pb(NO_3)_2$/2 mol KI = 0.075 mol $Pb(NO_3)_2$

   needed to react.

3. Use molarity to determine the volume of $Pb(NO_3)_2$ required.
   M = mol solute/L solution, or L solution = mol solute/M

   0.075 mol/0.50 M = 0.15 L or 150 mL

The **limiting reagent** of a reaction is the **reactant that runs out first**. This reactant **determines the amount of products formed**, and any **other reactants remain unconverted** to product and are called **excess reagents**.

Example: Consider the reaction $3H_2 + N_2 \rightarrow 2NH_3$ and suppose that 3 mol H2 and 3 mol N2 are available for this reaction. What is the limiting reagent?

Solution: The equation tells us that 3 mol H2 will react with one mol N2 to produce 2 mol NH3. This means that H2 is the limiting reagent because when it is completely used up 2 mol N2 will still remain.

The limiting reagent may be determined by **dividing the number of moles of each reactant by its stoichiometric coefficient.** This determines the moles of reactant if each reactant were limiting. The **lowest result** will indicate the actual limiting reagent. Remember to use moles and not grams for these calculations.

Example: 50.0 g Al and 400 g Br2 react according the following equation:

$$2Al + 3Br_2 \rightarrow 2AlBr_3$$

until the limiting reagent is completely consumed. Find the limiting reagent, the mass of AlBr3 formed, and the excess reagent remaining after the limiting reagent is consumed.

Solution: First convert both reactants to moles:

$$50.0 \text{ g Al} \times \frac{1 \text{ mol Al}}{26.982 \text{ g Al}} = 1.85\textit{3} \text{ mol Al} \text{ and } 400. \text{ g Br}_2 \times \frac{1 \text{ mol Br}_2}{159.808 \text{ g Br}_2} = 2.50\textit{3} \text{ mol Br}_2.$$

The final digits in the intermediate results above are italicized because they are insignificant. Dividing by stoichiometric coefficients gives:

$$1.85\textit{3} \text{ mol Al} \times \frac{\text{mol reaction}}{2 \text{ mol Al}} = 0.926\textit{5} \text{ mol reaction if Al is limiting}$$

$$2.50\textit{3} \text{ mol Br}_2 \times \frac{\text{mol reaction}}{3 \text{ mol Br}_2} = 0.834\textit{3} \text{ mol reaction if Br}_2 \text{ is limiting.}$$

Br2 is the lower value and is the limiting reagent.

The reaction is expected to produce:

$$2.50\textit{3} \text{ mol Br}_2 \times \frac{2 \text{ mol AlBr}_3}{3 \text{ mol Br}_2} \times \frac{266.694 \text{ g AlBr}_3}{\text{mol AlBr}_3} = 445 \text{ g AlBr}_3$$

The reaction is expected to consume:

$$2.50\textit{3} \text{ mol Br}_2 \times \frac{2 \text{ mol Al}}{3 \text{ mol Br}_2} \times \frac{26.982 \text{ g Al}}{\text{mol Al}} = 45.0 \text{ g Al}$$

50.0 g Al – 45.0 g Al = 5.0 g Al which will remain.

Skill 15.6 **The beginning teacher identifies factors (e.g., temperature, pressure, concentration, catalysts) that influence the rate of a chemical reaction and describes their effects.**

The rate of most simple reactions **increases with temperature** because a **greater fraction of molecules have the kinetic energy** required to overcome the reaction's activation energy. The chart below shows the effect of temperature on the distribution of kinetic energies in a sample of molecules. These curves are called **Maxwell-Boltzmann distributions**. The shaded areas represent the fraction of molecules containing sufficient kinetic energy for a reaction to occur. This area is larger at a higher temperature; so more molecules are above the activation energy and more molecules react per second.

This area is larger at a higher temperature; so more molecules are above the activation energy and more molecules react per second.

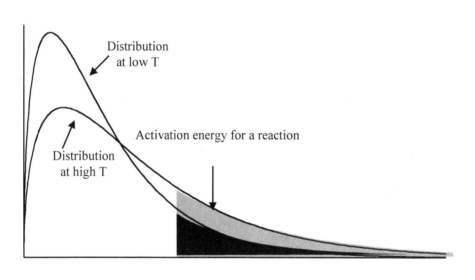

Kinetic molecular theory may be applied to reaction rates in addition to physical constants like pressure. **Reaction rates increase with reactant concentration** because more reactant molecules are present and more are likely to collide with one another in a certain volume at higher concentrations. The nature of these relationships determines the rate law for the reaction. For ideal gases, the concentration of a reactant is its molar density, and this varies with pressure and temperature as discussed in.

Kinetic molecular theory also predicts that **reaction rate constants (values for k) increase with temperature** because of two reasons:

1. More reactant molecules will collide with each other per second.
2. These collisions will each occur at a higher energy that is more likely to overcome the activation energy of the reaction.

A **catalyst** is a material that increases the rate of a chemical reaction without changing itself permanently in the process. Catalysts provide an alternate reaction mechanism for the reaction to proceed in the forward and in the reverse direction. Therefore, **catalysts have no impact on the chemical equilibrium** of a reaction. They will not make a less favorable reaction more favorable.

Catalysts reduce the activation energy of a reaction. This is the amount of energy needed for the reaction to begin. Molecules with such low energies that they would have taken a long time to react will react more rapidly if a catalyst is present.

The impact of a catalyst may also be represented on an energy diagram. **A catalyst increases the rate of both the forward and reverse reactions by lowering the activation energy** for the reaction. Catalysts provide a different activated complex for the reaction at a lower energy state.

Biological catalysts are called **enzymes.**

Skill 15.7   The beginning teacher understands principles of chemical equilibrium and solves problems involving equilibrium constants.

Many reactions occur with the reactants going completely to products and then the reaction is over (A + B → AB). However, a lot of reactions start with reactants going to products (A + B → AB) and then some of the products break down into reactants (A + B ← AB) while more reactants become products until equilibrium of the reaction is attained and maintained. Equilibrium is when the amount of reactants becoming products is equal to the amount of products becoming reactants (A + B ↔ AB). According to Le Châtelier's Principle if a stress is applied to a system in a dynamic equilibrium, the system changes to relieve the stress. Stresses that disturb equilibrium are as follows.

1. Change in concentration – if a reactant's concentration is increased, the equilibrium is displaced to the right ($\rightarrow$) meaning that the reactants are used up faster, more products are formed, and the new equilibrium has a lower concentration of reactants. Conversely, an increase in a product's concentration displaces the reaction equilibrium to the left ($\leftarrow$), favoring the reactants.
2. Change in pressure – this only applies to gases where an increase in pressure displaces the reaction equilibrium to the right ($\rightarrow$).
3. Change in temperature – addition of heat favors the endothermic reaction; however, a rise in temperature increases the rate of any reaction.

Reaction Rates and Rate Laws

In a reaction that goes to completion (one directional, not equilibrium), the reaction rate depends only on the concentrations of reactants [ ] and is called the rate law. The proportionality constant, k, called the rate constant, and n, called the order of the reactant, must both be determined experimentally.

For the reaction $2\,NO_2(g) \rightarrow 2\,NO(g) + O_2(g)$ the rate law is Rate = $k[NO_2]^2$

For reactions that reach equilibrium in a closed system, the K_{eq} is applicable. Given the generalized equilibrium equation: $wA + xB \leftrightarrow yC + zD$ where the lowercase letters represent the coefficients and the capitalized letters represent the reactants (A, B) and the products (C, D), the equilibrium constant, K_{eq}, would be

$$K_{eq} = \frac{[C]^y[D]^z}{[A]^w[B]^x}$$

The square brackets indicate concentrations, usually expressed in molarity.

For the reaction $2\,N_2(g) + 3\,H_2(g) \leftrightarrow 2\,NH_3(g)$

$$K_{eq} = \frac{[NH_3]^2}{[H_2]^3\,[N_2]^2}$$

> This reaction is second degree with regard to ammonia, second degree with regard to nitrogen, and third degree with regard to hydrogen, making it seventh degree overall.

If K_{eq} is greater than one, the products are favored at equilibrium and if K_{eq} is less than one, the reactants are favored at equilibrium. K_{eq} is also called K_c, or the concentration constant, when based upon the concentrations of the reactants and products. This number is a constant for a particular reaction at a particular temperature. If the equation is a system where all the reactants and products are gases, the K_{eq} is based upon partial pressures rather than concentrations so it is a K_p.

The equilibrium constant, K_{eq}, becomes a solubility product constant, K_{sp}, for saturated solutions. It is derived from $K_{sp} = K_{eq}[A]^a[B]^b$ where A and B are reactants and a and b are their respective coefficients.

For a reaction in which all the reactants and all the products are in the same phase (known as a homogeneous reaction), the K_{eq} includes all of the products and all the reactants as shown. However, if the reaction is heterogeneous (having a combination of gases, solids, liquids, and aqueous solutions), the equilibrium expression should only contain those things that are gases, in aqueous solution, or liquids that are not H_2O.

Example problem 1: A mixture at equilibrium at 827°C contains 0.552 mol CO_2, 0.552 mol H_2, 0.448 mol CO, and 0.448 mol H_2O. What is the value of K_{eq}?

$$CO_2(g) + H_2(g) \leftrightarrows CO(g) + H_2O(g)$$

Solution: The equation is balanced, so all the coefficients are 1.

$$K_{eq} = [CO] [H_2O] / [CO_2] [H_2]$$
$$K_{eq} = (0.448)(0.448) / (0.552)(0.552)$$
$$K_{eq} = 0.2007 / 0.3047$$
$$K_{eq} = 0.659$$

Example problem 2: Dinitrogen tetroxide (N_2O_4), a colorless gas, and nitrogen dioxide (NO_2), a dark brown gas, exist in equilibrium with each other. A liter of a gas mixture at 100°C at equilibrium contains 0.0045 mol of dinitrogen tetroxide. Its equilibrium constant is 0.20. What is the concentration of nitrogen dioxide?

Solution: The reaction is: $N_2O_4(g) \leftrightarrows NO_2(g)$, but it has to be balanced:
$$N_2O_4(g) \leftrightarrows 2 NO_2(g)$$
$$K_{eq} = [NO_2]^2 / [N_2O_4]$$
Substitute what you know: $0.20 = [NO_2]^2 / (0.0045)$
Solve: $(0.20)(0.0045) = [NO_2]^2$
$$9.0 \times 10^{-4} = [NO_2]^2$$
Take the square root of both sides: $0.030 = [NO_2]$

Skill 15.8   The beginning teacher identifies the chemical properties of a variety of common household chemicals (e.g., baking soda, bleach, ammonia) in order to predict the potential for chemical reactivity.

Chemical concepts often involve events taking place on scales that are too small for us to see. But the application of those concepts is all around us when we work and play, cook and clean, and eat and drink.

Relating chemistry to everyday activities often requires other content in this text in combination with **strong common sense reasoning**. There are some things that many people believe they know about everyday activities that aren't true.

For example, many people believe that cooks add salt when they boil water to decrease the amount of time it takes for the water to boil, but this is *false*. In reality, adding salt increases the boiling point of water and so water will take *more* time to boil. However, once the water is boiling, the fact that it is at a higher temperature means food will take less time to cook.

Boiling point elevation is a colligative property because more salt molecules at the liquid-vapor interface means fewer water molecules there, shifting:

$$H_2O\ (l) \leftrightarrow H_2O\ (g)$$

to the left according to Le Chatelier's Principle. Therefore the vapor pressure at 100° C will decrease below 1 atm, and a higher temperature along with more time will be required for boiling. However, all of **this knowledge will go to waste if you rely on a mistaken belief** instead of reasoning through the situation.

A common example of an everyday neutralization reaction is the use of **antacids**. These chemicals are bases that neutralize excess gastric acid in the stomach and provide increased buffering capacity. Gastric acid is mostly HCl.

An everyday application of the thermochemistry of reactions is in the field of **nutrition**. The energy value of food is measured in "**nutritional calories**," a unit equal to 4814 Joules. We inhale oxygen to convert organic molecules (our fuel) to carbon dioxide and water just as a flame uses oxygen to complete the same reaction, obtaining the same **heat of combustion**.

Baking soda is a **base** that is combined with acids in cooking (such as buttermilk, vinegar, sour cream, or yogurt) to create CO_2 bubbles. These bubbles cause baked goods to rise. Bleach and ammonia are other examples of household bases used for cleaning.

Competency 0016   **The teacher understands types and properties of solutions.**

Skill 16.1   **The beginning teacher analyzes factors that affect solubility (e.g., temperature, pressure, polarity of solvents and solutes).**

Solubility is defined as the amount of substance (referred to as solute) that will dissolve into another substance, called the solvent. The amount that will dissolve can vary according to the conditions, most notably temperature. The process is called solvation. To have a clear understanding of solubility curves and the interpretation of solubility curves, we need to take a close look at basic terms like solubility, solubility curve, saturated solution etc.

The **solubility** is often (though not always) measured as the mass of salt which would saturate 100 grams of water at a particular temperature.
The **solubility curve** shows how the solubility of a salt like sodium chloride or potassium nitrate varies with temperature.
A solution is **saturated** if it won't dissolve any more of the salt at that particular temperature.

A **solubility curve** tells us the solubility of a substance at a particular temperature. One way to look at it is to see what happens if the temperature is decreased at a given concentration. For example, take a near boiling solution of potassium nitrate in water. This solution has 100g of potassium nitrate and 100g of water. Let the solution cool. From examining a curve (the data), we conclude that at 57 degrees C, all the potassium nitrate dissolves in water. The solution at this point is saturated. Even if we slightly lower the temperature, some potassium nitrate will be insoluble. The lower the temperature, the less solubility of potassium nitrate in water, since water will not be able to dissolve the salt. We find crystals of potassium nitrate. At this point, there are two phases, a solution and some solid potassium nitrate. At 57 degrees C and above, there is only one phase, a solution of potassium nitrate. The solubility curve represents the boundary between these two different conditions.

Finally, a solubility curves indicates the different phases of a solution due to the change in temperature.

1. At one particular temperature, a solution is said to be saturated, because all the solute is dissolved completed. Above that temperature, we can see a homogeneous solution.

2. Below that particular temperature, there are two phase evident - one is the solution phase, the other is the solid phase due to the undissolved solute.

3. A solubility curve is the indicator of a solution due to the change in temperature.

Skill 16.2   The beginning teacher identifies characteristics of saturated, unsaturated, and supersaturated solutions.

Equilibrium occurs when no additional solute will dissolve because the rates of crystallization and solution are equal. A solution at equilibrium with undissolved solute is a **saturated** solution. The amount of solute required to form a saturated solution in a given amount of solvent is called the **solubility** of that solute. If less solute is present, the solution is called **unsaturated**. It is also possible to have more solute than the equilibrium amount, resulting in a solution that is termed **supersaturated**.

Pairs of liquids that mix in all proportions are called **miscible**. Liquids that don't mix are called **immiscible**.

Skill 16.3   The beginning teacher determines the molarity, molality, normality, and percent composition of aqueous solutions.

The **molarity** (abbreviated M) of a solute in solution is defined as the number of moles of solute in a liter of solution.

$$\text{Molarity} = \frac{\text{moles solute}}{\text{volume of solution in liters}}$$

Molarity is the most frequently used concentration unit in chemical reactions because it reflects the number of solute moles available. By using Avogadro's number, the number of molecules in a flask (a difficult image to conceptualize in the lab) is expressed in terms of the volume of liquid in the flask (a straightforward image to visualize and actually manipulate). Molarity is useful for dilutions because the moles of solute remain unchanged if more solvent is added to the solution:

$$\left(\text{Initial molarity}\right)\left(\text{Initial volume}\right) = \left(\text{molarity after dilution}\right)\left(\text{final volume}\right)$$

or

$$M_{initial}V_{initial} = M_{final}V_{final}$$

The **molality** (abbreviated m) of a solution is defined as the number of moles of a solute in a kilogram of solvent.

$$\text{Molality} = \frac{\text{moles solute}}{\text{mass of solvent in kilograms}}$$

Molality is a useful measure of concentration in situations where solution density (and thus, volume) is changing and we don't care about the impact of this change. The molarity of a solution will change with temperature because the liquid will expand or contract. Molality will remain constant. Because water typically has a density of one kilogram per liter, the molality and molarity of aqueous solutions at room temperature have roughly the same numerical value.

The **normality** (abbreviated N) of a solution is defined as the number of **equivalents** of a solute per liter of solution.

$$\text{Normality} = \frac{\text{equivalents solute}}{\text{volume of solution in liters}}$$

An equivalent is defined according to the type of reaction being examined, but the number of equivalents of solute is always a whole number multiple of the number of moles of solute, and so the normality of a solute is always a whole-number multiple of its molarity. An equivalent is defined so that one equivalent of one reagent will react with one equivalent of another reagent. For acid-base reactions, an equivalent of an acid is the quantity that supplies 1 mol of H^+ and an equivalent of a base is the quantity reacting with 1 mol of H^+. For example, one mole of H_2SO_4 in an acid-base reaction supplies two moles of H+. The mass of one equivalent of H_2SO_4 is half of the mass of one mole of H_2SO_4, and its normality is twice its molarity. In a redox reaction (see competency 9), an equivalent is the quantity of substance that gains or loses 1 mol of electrons.

Weight percentage is frequently used to represent every component of a solution (possibly including the solvent) as a portion of the whole in terms of mass.

$$\text{Weight percentage of a component} = \frac{\text{mass of component in solution}}{\text{total mass of solution}} \times 100\%$$

A **Mole fraction** is used to represent a component in a solution as a portion of the entire number of moles present. If you were able to pick out a molecule at random from a solution, the mole fraction of a component represents the probability that the molecule you picked would be that particular component. Mole fractions for all components must sum to one, and mole fractions are just numbers with no units.

$$\text{Mole fraction of a component} = \frac{\text{moles of component}}{\text{total moles of all components}}$$

Skill 16.4   The beginning teacher analyzes precipitation reactions and derives net ionic equations.

Particles in solution are free to move about and collide with each other, vastly increasing the likelihood that a reaction will occur compared with particles in a solid phase. Aqueous solutions may react to produce an insoluble substance that will fall out of solution as a solid or gas **precipitate** in a **precipitation reaction**. Aqueous solution may also react to form **additional water** or a different chemical in aqueous solution.

Solubility rules for ionic compounds

Given a cation and anion in aqueous solution, we can determine if a precipitate will form according to some common **solubility rules**.

1) Salts with NH_4^+ or with a cation from group 1 of the periodic table are soluble in water.
2) Nitrates (NO_3^-), acetates ($C_2H_3O_2^-$), chlorates (ClO_3^-), and perchlorates are soluble.
3) Cl^-, Br^-, and I^- salts are soluble except with Ag^+, Hg_2^{2+}, and Pb^{2+}.
4) Sulfates (SO_4^{2-}) are soluble except with Ca^{2+}, Ba^{2+}, Ag^+, Hg_2^{2+}, and Pb^{2+}.
5) Hydroxides (OH^-) are <u>insoluble</u> except with cations from rule 1 and with Ca^{2+}, Sr^{2+}, and Ba^{2+}.
6) Sulfides (S^{2-}), sulfites (SO_3^{2-}), phosphates (PO_4^{3-}), and carbonates (CO_3^{2-}) are insoluble except with cations from rule 1.

Skill 16.5   The beginning teacher understands the colligative properties of solutions (e.g., vapor pressure lowering, osmotic pressure changes, boiling-point elevation, freezing-point depression).

A **colligative** property is a physical property of a solution that **depends on the number of solute particles present in solution** and usually not on the identity of the solutes involved. Colligative properties may be predicted by imagining ourselves shrinking down to the size of molecules in a solution and visualizing the impact of an increasing number of generic solute particles around us.

Vapor pressure lowering, boiling point elevation, freezing point lowering

After a nonvolatile solute is added to a liquid solvent, only a fraction of the molecules at a liquid-gas interface are now volatile and capable of escaping into the gas phase. The vapor consists of essentially pure solvent that is able to condense freely. This imbalance drives equilibrium away from the vapor phase and into the liquid phase and **lowers the vapor pressure** by an amount proportional to the solute particles present.

It follows from a lowered vapor pressure that a higher temperature is required for a vapor pressure equal to the external pressure over the liquid. Thus **the boiling point is raised** by an amount proportional to the solute particles present.

Solute particles in a liquid solvent are not normally soluble in the solid phase of that solvent. When solvent crystals freeze, they typically align themselves with each other at first and keep the solute out. This means that only a fraction of the molecules in the liquid at the liquid-solid interface are capable of freezing while the solid phase consists of essentially pure solvent that is able to melt freely. This imbalance drives equilibrium away from the solid phase and into the liquid phase and **lowers the freezing point** by an amount proportional to the solute particles present.

Boiling point elevation and freezing point depression are both caused by a lower fraction of solvent molecules in the liquid phase than in the other phase. For pure water at 1 atm there is equilibrium at the normal boiling and freezing points. For water with a high solute concentration, equilibrium is not present.

Osmotic pressure

A **semipermeable membrane** is a material that permits some particles to pass through it but not others. The diagram shows a membrane that permits solvent but not solute to pass through it. When a semipermeable membrane separates a dilute solution from a concentrated solution, the solvent flows from the dilute to the concentrated solution (i.e., from higher solvent to lower solvent concentration) in a process called **osmosis** until equilibrium is achieved.

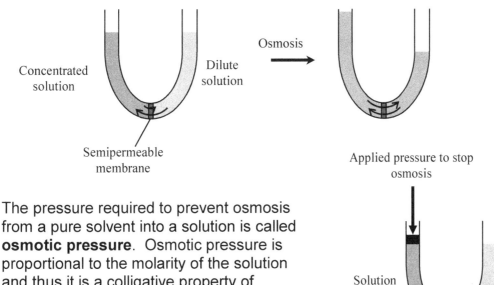

The pressure required to prevent osmosis from a pure solvent into a solution is called **osmotic pressure**. Osmotic pressure is proportional to the molarity of the solution and thus it is a colligative property of solutions, and the osmotic pressure of a pure solvent is zero.

Skill 16.6   The beginning teacher understands the properties of electrolytes and explains the relationship between concentration and electrical conductivity.

All NaCl is present in solution as ions. Compounds that are completely ionized in water are called **strong electrolytes** because these solutions easily conduct electricity. Most salts are strong electrolytes. Other compounds (including many acids and bases) may dissolve in water without completely ionizing. These are referred to as **weak electrolytes** and their state of ionization is at equilibrium with the larger molecule. Those compounds that dissolve with no ionization (e.g., glucose, $C_6H_{12}O_6$) are called **nonelectrolytes**.

Skill 16.7   The beginning teacher understands methods for measuring and comparing the rates of reaction in solutions of varying concentration.

The **reaction rate** of chemical reaction is the amount of a reactant reacted or the amount of a product formed per unit time. Reaction rate is measured by monitoring a property of reacting mixture that changes as the reaction takes place. This property must be related to the quantity or concentration of a product or reactant. To measure reaction rate, change in one of the following reaction properties may be recorded:

1. Change in reactant or product concentration
2. Change in reactant mass
3. Change in mass of a precipitate
4. Change in volume of gas release
5. Change in pressure
6. Change in color (spectroscopic measurement)
7. Change in temperature
8. Change in pH

The recorded change can be plotted on a graph, and from the graph, the average rate or instantaneous rate of reaction may be obtained through graphical method or computer data analysis.

For example, for the general reaction A + B → C + D, the following graph demonstrates the decrease in concentration of the reactant A over time. The rate of reaction at any given instant (the instantaneous rate) can be obtained by calculating the slope of the curve. The average rate of reaction is calculated by dividing the change in concentration during a definite time interval by the amount of time in the interval.

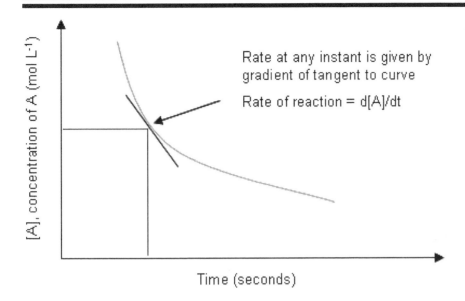

Under certain conditions, the rate of reaction may be a function of solution concentration. In this case, reaction rate is equal to the change in concentration per unit time: either the decrease of concentration per unit time of a reactant or the increase of concentration per unit time of a product. When measured as change in concentration per unit time, rate of reaction is expressed in moles / Liters-seconds or molarity / second (mol/Ls or M/s, respectively).

Increasing the concentration of the reactants normally increases the frequency of collisions between the two reactants, thus increasing the rate of reaction. The differing rates of reaction of solutions of varying concentrations may be compared by creating graphs similar to that shown above for each solution.

For example, zinc and hydrochloric acid react to form zinc chloride and hydrogen gas. In the lab, zinc granules react fairly slowly with dilute hydrochloric acid, but much faster if the acid is concentrated. To compare the effect of the concentration of hydrochloric acid on this reaction, solutions of varying acid concentration should be reacted with constant amounts of zinc. The formation of hydrogen gas should be recorded for each reaction, and plotted versus time. The average rate of reaction rate for each solution can then be calculated using the methods listed above. The graphs will provide the means to calculate instantaneous rates of reaction, as well as a visual comparison of reaction rate. These plots will demonstrate increasingly steeper slopes (and thus increasingly higher reaction rates) as concentration of hydrochloric acid increases.

Skill 16.8   **The beginning teacher analyzes models to explain the structural properties of water and evaluates the significance of water as a solvent in living organisms and the environment.**

Water is necessary for life. Its properties are due to its molecular structure and it is an important solvent in biological compounds. Water is a polar substance. This means it is formed by covalent bonds that make it electrically lopsided.

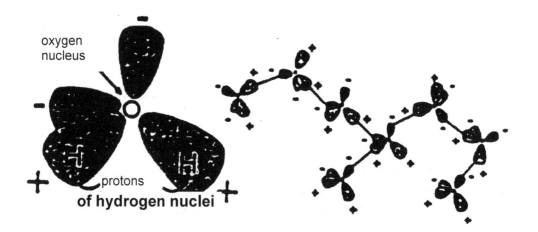

A water molecule showing polarity created by covalent bonds.

Hydrogen bonding between water molecules.

Water molecules are attracted to other water molecules due to this electrical attraction and allows for two important properties: **adhesion** and **cohesion**.

Adhesion is when water sticks to other substances like the xylem of a stem that aids the water in traveling up the stem to the leaves.

Cohesion is the ability of water molecules to stick to each other by hydrogen bonds. This allows for surface tension on a body of water or capillarity, which allows water to move through vessels. Surface tension is how difficult it is to stretch or break the surface of a liquid.   Cohesion allows water to move against gravity.

There are several other important properties of water. Water is a good solvent. An aqueous solution is one in which water is the solvent. It provides a medium for chemical reactions to occur. Water has a high specific heat of 1 calorie per gram per degree Celsius, allowing it to cool and warm slowly, allowing organisms to adapt to temperature changes. Water has a high boiling point it is a good coolant. Its ability to evaporate stabilizes the environment and allows organisms to maintain body temperature. Water has a high freezing point and a lower density as a solid than as a liquid. Water is most dense at four degrees centigrade. This allows ice to   float on top of water so a whole body of water does not freeze during the winter. In this way, animals may survive the winter.

Competency 0017   **The teacher understands energy transformations that occur in physical and chemical processes.**

Skill 17.1   **The beginning teacher analyzes the energy transformations that occur in phase transitions.**

Phase changes occur when the relative importance of kinetic energy and intermolecular forces is altered sufficiently for a substance to change its state.

The transition from gas to liquid is called **condensation** and from liquid to gas is called **vaporization**. The transition from liquid to solid is called **freezing** and from solid to liquid is called **melting**. The transition from gas to solid is called **deposition** and from solid to gas is called **sublimation**.

Heat removed from a substance during condensation, freezing, or deposition permits new intermolecular bonds to form, and heat added to a substance during vaporization, melting, or sublimation breaks intermolecular bonds. During these phase transitions, this **latent heat** is removed or added with **no change in the temperature** of the substance because the heat is not being used to alter the speed of the molecules or the kinetic energy when they strike each other or the container walls. Latent heat alters intermolecular bonds.

Skill 17.2   **The beginning teacher solves problems in calorimetry (e.g., determining the specific heat of a substance, finding the standard enthalpy of formation and reaction of substances).**

A substance's molar **heat capacity** is the heat required to **change the temperature of one mole of the substance by one degree**. Heat capacity has units of joules per mol-kelvin or joules per mol-°C. The two units are interchangeable because we are only concerned with differences between one temperature and another. A Kelvin degree and a Celsius are the same size.

The **specific heat** of a substance (also called specific heat capacity) is the heat required to **change the temperature of one gram or kilogram by one degree**. Specific heat has units of joules per mole-gram or joules per mole-kilogram.

A substance's **enthalpy of fusion** (ΔH_{fusion}) is the heat required to **change one mole from a solid to a liquid** by freezing. This is also the heat released from the substance when it changes from a liquid to a solid (melts)\

A substance's **enthalpy of vaporization** ($\Delta H_{vaporization}$) is the heat required to **change one mole of a substance from a liquid to a gas** or the heat released by condensation.

A substance's **enthalpy of sublimation** ($\Delta H_{sublimation}$) is the heat required to change one mole directly from a solid to a gas by sublimation or the heat released by deposition.

These three values are also called "heats" or "latent heats" of fusion, vaporization, and sublimation. They have units of joules per mole, and are negative values when heat is released.

$$\text{Solid} \xrightarrow[\text{melting}]{\Delta H_{fusion}} \text{Liquid} \xrightarrow[\text{vaporization}]{\Delta H_{vaporization}} \text{Gas} \qquad \text{Solid} \xrightarrow[\text{sublimation}]{\Delta H_{sublimation}} \text{Gas}$$

$$\text{Gas} \xrightarrow[\text{condensation}]{-\Delta H_{vaporization}} \text{Liquid} \xrightarrow[\text{freezing}]{-\Delta H_{fusion}} \text{Solid} \qquad \text{Gas} \xrightarrow[\text{deposition}]{-\Delta H_{sublimation}} \text{Solid}$$

Skill 17.3   **The beginning teacher applies the law of conservation of energy to analyze and evaluate energy exchanges that occur in exothermic and endothermic reactions.**

The principle of conservation states that certain measurable properties of an isolated system remain constant despite changes in the system. Two important principles of conservation are the conservation of mass and charge.

The principle of conservation of mass states that the total mass of a system is constant. Examples of conservation in mass in nature include the burning of wood, rusting of iron, and phase changes of matter. When wood burns, the total mass of the products, such as soot, ash, and gases, equals the mass of the wood and the oxygen that reacts with it. When iron reacts with oxygen, rust forms. The total mass of the iron-rust complex does not change. Finally, when matter changes phase, mass remains constant. Thus, when a glacier melts due to atmospheric warming, the mass of liquid water formed is equal to the mass of the glacier.

The principle of conservation of charge states that the total electrical charge of a closed system is constant. Thus, in chemical reactions and interactions of charged objects, the total charge does not change. Chemical reactions and the interaction of charged molecules are essential and common processes in living organisms and systems.

Because the products and reactants must remain or be manipulated, but not lost, the difference in energy is conceptualized through either an endothermic or exothermic reaction (see next skill).

Skill 17.4   The beginning teacher understands thermodynamic relationships among spontaneous reactions, entropy, enthalpy, temperature, and Gibbs free energy.

When a chemical reaction takes place, the enthalpies of the products will differ from the enthalpies of the reactants. There is an energy change for the reaction ΔH_{rxn}, determined by **the sum of the products minus the sum of the reactants**:

$$\Delta H_{rxn} = H_{product\ 1} + H_{product\ 2} + \dots \quad H_{reactant\ 1} \quad H_{reactant\ 2} \quad \dots$$

The enthalpy change for a reaction is commonly called the **heat of reaction**.

If the enthalpies of the products are greater than the enthalpies of the reactants then ΔH_{rxn} **is positive** and the reaction is **endothermic**. Endothermic reactions **absorb heat** from their surroundings. The simplest endothermic reactions break chemical bonds.

If the enthalpies of the products are less than the enthalpies of the reactants then ΔH_{rxn} **is negative** and the reaction is **exothermic**. Exothermic reactions **release heat** into their surroundings. The simplest exothermic reactions form new chemical bonds.

The heat absorbed or released by a chemical reaction often has the impact of changing the temperature of the reaction vessel and of the chemicals themselves. The measurement of these heat effects is known as **calorimetry**.

The enthalpy change of a reaction ΔH_{rxn} **is equal in magnitude but has the opposite sign to the enthalpy change for the reverse reaction**. If a series of reactions lead back to the initial reactants then the net energy change for the entire process is zero.

When a reaction is composed of substeps, the **total enthalpy change will be the sum of the changes for each step**. Even if a reaction in reality contains no substeps, we may still write any number of reactions in series that lead from the same reactants to the same products and their sum will be the heat of the reaction of interest. The ability to add together these enthalpies to form ultimate products from initial reactants is known as **Hess's Law**. It is used to determine one heat of reaction from others:

$$\Delta H_{net\ rxn} = H_{rxn\ 1} + H_{rxn\ 2} + \dots$$

It is generally the case that exothermic reactions are more likely to occur spontaneously than endothermic reactions. Molecules usually seek the lowest possible energy state. However, entropy also plays a critical role in determining whether a reaction occurs.

Gases are of greater entropy than liquids, liquids are of greater entropy than solids, and matter in the same state increases in entropy with temperature.

Entropy is also an extensive property of matter. **A greater number of moles will have a larger entropy.**

If two different chemicals are at the same temperature, in the same state of matter, and they have the same number of molecules, their entropy difference will depend mostly on the number of ways the atoms within the two chemicals can rotate, vibrate, and flex. Most of the time, **the more complex molecule will have the greater entropy** because there are more energetic and spatial states in which it may exist.

At zero Kelvin (0 K), there is no energy available for a chemical to sample different states. The **absolute entropy**, S, of a pure crystalline solid at 0 K is zero. Absolute entropy may be measured and calculated for different substances at different temperatures.

The **entropy change of a reaction**, ΔS, is given by the sum of the absolute entropies of all the products multiplied by their stoichiometric coefficients minus the sum of all the products multiplied by their stoichiometric coefficients:

For the reaction: $aA + bB \rightleftharpoons pP \quad qQ$

$$\Delta S = pS(P) + qS(Q) - aS(A) - bS(B)$$

A reaction with a negative ΔH and a positive ΔS causes a decrease in energy and an increase in entropy. **These reactions will always occur spontaneously.** A reaction with a positive ΔH and a negative ΔS causes an increase in energy and a decrease in entropy. These reactions never occur to an appreciable extent because the reverse reaction takes place spontaneously.

Whether reactions with the remaining two possible combinations (ΔH and ΔS both positive or both negative) occur depends on the temperature. If $\Delta H - T\Delta S$ (known as the **Gibbs Free Energy** is negative, the reaction will take place. If it is positive, the reaction will not occur to an appreciable extent. If $\Delta H - T\Delta S = 0$ exactly, then at equilibrium there will be 50% reactants and 50% products. A spontaneous reaction is called *exergonic*. A non-spontaneous reaction is known as *endergonic*. These terms are used much less often than *exothermic* and *endothermic*.

Competency 0018   **The teacher understands nuclear fission, nuclear fusion, and nuclear reactions.**

Skill 18.1   **The beginning teacher uses models to explain radioactivity and radioactive decay (i.e., alpha, beta, gamma).**

Isotopes are called radioisotopes when they have unstable nuclei that are radioactive. **Alpha particles** (α) are positively charged particles ($^+2$) emitted from a radioactive nucleus. They consist of two protons and two neutrons and are identical to the nucleus of a helium atom ($^4_2 He$).

Example: $^{226}_{88} Ra \rightarrow {}^4_2 He + {}^{222}_{86} Rn + 4.87\ MeV$

When an atom loses an alpha particle, the Z number (atomic number) is lower by two, so you would move back two spaces on the periodic table to find what the new element is. The new element has an A number (atomic mass number) that is four less than the original element. The energy released is the difference between the mass of the radium (226.02536 u) and the sum of the masses of the radon (222.01753 u) and the helium (4.00260). This is 0.00523 u, or 4.87 MeV.

One electron mass = 0.0005486 u = 0.511 MeV / (number of particles)^2

Because alpha particles are large and heavy, paper or clothing or even dead skin cells shield people from their effects.

Beta rays (β) are negatively charged (-1) and fast moving because they are actually electrons. They are written as an electron $^0_{-1} e$ (along with a proton) which is emitted from the nucleus as a neutron decays. Carbon-14 decays by emitting a beta particle.

Example: $^{14}_6 C \rightarrow {}^{14}_7 N + {}^0_{-1} e$

The Z number (atomic number) actually adds one since its total must be the same on both the left and the right of the arrow and the electron on the right adds a negative one. The A (atomic mass) number is unchanged. The Z determines what the element is, so look for it on the periodic table to determine the product. The electrons are at various energies ranging from 0 to 1.2 MeV. Alpha particles from each radioactive species have specific energies. Metal foil or wood is needed to shield from its effects.

Gamma rays (γ) are high energy electromagnetic waves. They are the same kind of radiation as visible light but of much shorter wavelength and higher frequency. Gamma rays have no mass or charge, so the Z (atomic) and A (atomic mass) numbers are not affected. Radioactive atoms often emit gamma rays along with either alpha or beta particles. Gamma rays from a specific radioactive species have their own specific energies. Protection from gamma radiation requires lead or concrete.

Example 1 *(with an alpha)*: $^{226}_{88}Ra \rightarrow {}^{222}_{86}Rn + {}^{4}_{2}He + \gamma$
Example 2 *(with a beta)*: $^{234}_{90}Th \rightarrow {}^{234}_{91}Pa + {}^{0}_{-1}e + \gamma$

A **positron** is a particle with the mass of an electron but a positive charge ($^{0}_{+1}e$). It may be emitted as a proton changes to a neutron.

Skill 18.2 **The beginning teacher interprets and balances equations for nuclear reactions.**

Nuclear equations are balanced by equating the sum of mass numbers and the sum of atomic numbers on both sides of a reaction equation.

Example: Balance the following nuclear transmutation:

$$^{14}_{6}C \rightarrow {}^{14}_{7}N + \underline{\hspace{2cm}}$$

Solution: The sum of the mass numbers on both the left and right side of the arrow must be the same:

Left side	Right side
14	14

They are already the same so the particle emitted during decay has a mass of 0.

The sum of the charge must be the same on the left side and right side of the arrow:

Left side	Right side
6	7

The right side has one too many positive charges to balance the 6 positive charges on the left side. Adding -1 to the right side will make it balance with 6 positive charges, so the charge of the particle emitted during decay is -1.

A particle with a mass of 0 and a -1 charge is an electron, $_{-1}^{0}e$, which should be placed in the equation to complete it:

$$_{6}^{14}C \rightarrow {}_{7}^{14}N + {}_{-1}^{0}e$$

Example: Complete the following nuclear transmutation equation:

$$_{90}^{234}Th \rightarrow {}_{-1}^{0}e + \underline{\hspace{2cm}}$$

Solution: Again, the sum of the mass numbers on each side of the arrow must be the same as well as the sum of the charges on each side.

Left side	Right side
234	0

A mass of 234 is needed on the right side to equal the left side.

For the charge:

Left side	Right side
90	-1

A 91 charge is needed on the right side to equal the left side. The particle that forms from the decay of this isotope is $_{91}^{234}Pa$ and should be inserted to complete the transmutation equation:

$$_{90}^{234}Th \rightarrow {}_{-1}^{0}e + {}_{91}^{234}Pa$$

Skill 18.3   **The beginning teacher compares and contrasts fission and fusion reactions (e.g., relative energy released in the reactions, mass distribution of products).**

Transmutation is the conversion of an atom of one element to an atom of another element such as occurs in alpha and beta radiation. It also occurs when high-energy particles (such as protons, neutrons, or alpha particles) bombard the nucleus of an atom. All the elements in the periodic table with atomic numbers above 92, called the transuranium elements, are radioactive elements that have been synthesized in nuclear reactors and nuclear accelerators.

Example: $_{92}^{238}U + {}_{0}^{1}n \rightarrow {}_{92}^{239}U \rightarrow {}_{-1}^{0}e + {}_{93}^{239}Np \rightarrow {}_{94}^{239}Pu + {}_{-1}^{0}e$

Nuclear fission is the splitting of a nucleus into smaller fragments by bombardment with neutrons. Fission releases enormous amounts of energy. Controlled fission is the source of the energy in nuclear power plants.

Example: $^{235}_{92}U + {}^{1}_{0}n \rightarrow {}^{145}_{56}Ba + {}^{88}_{36}Kr + 3\ {}^{1}_{0}n + 200$ MeV

In **nuclear fusion** hydrogen nuclei fuse together to make helium nuclei. Fusion releases even more energy than fission.

Example: $^{2}_{1}H + {}^{3}_{1}H \rightarrow {}^{4}_{2}He + {}^{1}_{0}n + 17.6$ MeV energy

The energy released in a nuclear reaction such as this is calculated by subtracting the mass of the reaction products from the mass of the interacting particles. The hydrogen bomb is an example of a fusion device.

Skill 18.4   The beginning teacher knows how to use the half-life of radioactive elements to solve real-world problems (e.g., carbon dating, radioactive tracers).

Every radioisotope has its own characteristic rate of decay. The half-life of an isotope is the time it takes for half the atoms of the radioactive material in a given sample to decay. The most accurate method of absolute dating, **Radiometric Dating** measures the decay of naturally occurring radioactive isotopes. These isotopes are great timekeepers because their rate of decay is constant. Elements decay because of the inherent structure of the nucleus of the atoms. Neutrons hold the positively charged protons together. However, the positive protons attempt to repel each other. In some heavy elements, the protons repel each other to such a degree that the proton tears itself apart (decays) and by losing protons, becomes another element. The decay starts the moment an isotope crystallizes in a rock unit, and chemicals, weathering, environment, or temperature does not affect the rate of decay.

The radioactive decay causes the (mother) element to change into an (daughter) element. The Mother-Daughter relationship of produced nuclides during the series of isotope decay is the basis for radiometric dating. Although many isotopes are used in radiometric dating, the most widely known method is referred to as **Carbon-14 dating**. Carbon-14 is unstable and decays, decomposes and transmutes to Carbon-12. The dating process compares the ratio of Carbon-14 to Carbon-12 in an object. Since the decay occurs at a known rate, it is very predictable and can be used as a clock standard. However, Carbon-14 decays quickly and can only be used to date organic compounds less than 40,000 years old.

Knowing the Half-Life of the isotopes is the key factor in the radiometric dating process. If we know the half-life, we can compare the ratio of isotopes found in the object, and count backwards to get an accurate date. The most common element checked is the ratio of Uranium to Lead. Example: 1 gram of 238Uranium. After 100 million years, you have 0.013g of 206Pb (lead) and 0.989 of 238U. After 4.5 bilion years, you have 0.433g 206Pb and .500g of 238U. Therefore, the half-life of 238U is roughly 4.5 billion years.

Note: Only Carbon-14 can be used to date organic compounds. The other isotopes are not found in organic compounds.

Radiometric Isotopes Commonly Used in Absolute Dating

Mother Isotope	Daughter Isotope	Half-life (in years)	Dating Range (in years)
40K (Potassium)	10Ar (Aragon)	1.3 billion	>10 million
87 Rb (Rubidium)	87St (Strontium)	47 billion	>100 million
235U (Uranium)	407U (Uranium)	700 million	>1 million
14C (Carbon)	206 Pb (Lead)	5,730	>750<40,000

Skill 18.5   The beginning teacher understands stable and unstable isotopes.

A stable electron arrangement is exemplified by an atom that has all of its electrons in the lowest possible energy levels. An arrangement where electron levels are incomplete results in increased activity- reactions will likely occur due to its instability.

Atoms and ions of a given element that differ in number of neutrons have a different mass and are called isotopes.

Some nuclei are unstable and emit particles and electromagnetic radiation. These emissions from the nucleus are known as radioactivity, the unstable isotopes are known as radioisotopes, and the nuclear reactions that spontaneously alter them are known as radioactive decay. The electron is assigned an atomic number of -1 to account for the conversion during radioactive decay of a neutron to a proton and an emitted electron called a beta particle:

$$_0^1n \rightarrow {}_1^1p + {}_{-1}^0e$$

Sulfur-35 is an isotope that decays by beta emission:

$$^{35}_{16}S \rightarrow {}^{35}_{17}Cl + {}^{0}_{-1}e$$

In most cases nuclear reactions result in a nuclear transmutation from one element to another.

Skill 18.6 **The beginning teacher knows various issues associated with using nuclear energy (e.g., medical, commercial, environmental).**

The continued use of nuclear reactors to generate power is a major source of contention. On the one hand, our technologically and energy dependent civilization demands ever increasing amounts of energy in the face of an ever shrinking fossil fuel supply, and admittedly, if operated correctly, nuclear power plants do not pollute the air or the water supply.

On the other hand, nuclear reactors potentially endanger our lives through accidental release of radioactivity to the air or groundwater, proliferation of weapons grade nuclear material, and safe disposal of radioactive and toxic byproducts.

Burying the radioactive wastes is an expensive and short-term solution. It also is becoming problematic to find suitable locations. The ground swell of public opinion against burial can be summed up by the acronym NIMBY, not in my backyard. The power supplied is nice, but few people welcome a radioactive waste disposal site in close proximity to their homes.

We are running out of places to store the approximately 200 tons of radioactive waste produced daily in the United States.

Most of the waste is being buried deep underground, especially in the barren desert regions bordering the mountains of the southwestern states. Other waste is being encased in concrete and lead containers and dumped in the deeper parts of the oceans. Each of these solutions presents technological difficulties and hazards.

Competency 0019   **The teacher understands oxidation and reduction reactions.**

Skill 19.1   **The beginning teacher determines the oxidation state of ions and atoms in compounds.**

The term **valence** is often used to describe the number of atoms that may react to form a compound with a given atom by sharing, removing, or losing **valence electrons**. A more useful term is **oxidation number**. The **oxidation number of an ion is its charge**. The oxidation number of an atom sharing its electrons is **the charge it would have if the bonding were ionic**. There are four rules for determining oxidation number:

1) The oxidation number of an element (i.e., a Cl atom in Cl_2) is zero because the electrons in the bond are shared equally.
2) In a compound, the more electronegative atoms are assigned negative oxidation numbers and the less electronegative atoms are assigned positive oxidation numbers equal to the number of shared electron-pair bonds. For example, hydrogen may only have an oxidation number of −1 when bonded to a less electronegative element or +1 when bonded to a more electronegative element. Oxygen almost always has an oxidation number of −2. Fluorine always has an oxidation number of −1 (except in F_2).
3) The oxidation numbers in a compound must add up to zero, and the sum of oxidation numbers in a polyatomic ion must equal the overall charge of the ion.

Skill 19.2   **The beginning teacher identifies and balances oxidation and reduction reactions.**

Redox is shorthand for *reduction* and *oxidation*. **Reduction** is the **gain of an electron** by a molecule, atom, or ion. **Oxidation** is the **loss of an electron** by a molecule, atom, or ion. These two processes always occur together. Electrons lost by one substance are gained by another. In a redox process, the **oxidation numbers** of atoms are altered. Reduction decreases the oxidation number of an atom. Oxidation increases the oxidation number.

The easiest redox processes to identify are those involving monatomic ions with altered charges. For example, the reaction

$$Zn(s) + Cu^{2+}(aq) \rightarrow Zn^{2+}(aq) + Cu(s)$$

is a redox process because electrons are transferred from Zn to Cu.

However, many redox reactions involve the transfer of electrons from one molecular compound to another. In these cases, **oxidation numbers must be determined** as follows.

Oxidation numbers, sometimes called oxidation states, are signed numbers assigned to atoms in molecules and ions. They allow us to keep track of the electrons associated with each atom. Oxidation numbers are frequently used to write chemical formulas, to help us predict properties of compounds, and to help balance equations in which electrons are transferred. Knowledge of the oxidative state of an atom gives us an idea about its positive or negative character. In themselves, oxidation numbers have no physical meaning; they are used to simplify tasks that are more difficult to accomplish without them.

1. Free elements are assigned an oxidation state of 0.

   e.g. Al, Na, Fe, H_2, O_2, N_2, Cl_2 etc have zero oxidation states.

2. The oxidation state for any simple one-atom ion is equal to its charge.

   e.g. the oxidation state of Na^+ is +1, Be^{2+}, +2, and of F^-, -1.

3. The alkali metals (Li, Na, K, Rb, Cs and Fr) in compounds are always assigned an oxidation state of +1.

   e.g. in LiOH (Li, +1), in Na_2SO_4(Na, +1).

4. Fluorine in compounds is always assigned an oxidation state of -1.

   e.g. in HF_2^-, BF_2^-.

5. The alkaline earth metals (Be, Mg, Ca, Sr, Ba, and Ra) and also Zn and Cd in compounds are always assigned an oxidation state of +2. Similarly, Al and Ga are always +3.

   e.g. in $CaSO_4$(Ca, +2), $AlCl_3$ (Al, +3).

6. Hydrogen in compounds is assigned an oxidation state of +1. Exception - Hydrides, e.g. LiH (H=-1).

   e.g. in H_2SO_4 (H, +1).

7. Oxygen in compounds is assigned an oxidation state of -2. Exception - Peroxide, e.g. H_2O_2 (O = -1).

   e.g. in H_3PO_4 (O, -2).

8. The sum of the oxidation states of all the atoms in a species must be equal to net charge on the species.

   e.g. Net Charge of $HClO_4$ = 0, i.e. $[+1(H)+7(Cl)-2*4(O)] = 0$

   Net Charge of CrO_4^{2-}=-2,

   To solve Cr's oxidation state: $x - 4*2(O) = -2$, $x = +6$, so the oxidation state of Cr is +6.

For example, the reaction

$$H_2 + F_2 \rightarrow 2HF$$

is a redox process because the oxidation numbers of atoms are altered. The oxidation numbers of elements are always zero, and oxidation numbers in a compound are never zero. Fluorine is the more electronegative element, so in HF it has an oxidation number of –1 and hydrogen has an oxidation number of +1. This is a redox process where electrons are transferred from H_2 to F_2 to create HF.

In the reaction

$$HCl + NaOH \rightarrow NaCl + H_2O,$$

the H-atoms on both sides of the reaction have an oxidation number of +1, the atom of Cl has an oxidation number of –1, the Na-atom has an oxidation number of +1, and the atom of O has an oxidation number of –2. **This is not a redox process because oxidation numbers remain unchanged** by the reaction.

An **oxidizing agent** (also called an oxidant or oxidizer) has the ability to oxidize other substances by removing electrons from them. The **oxidizing agent is reduced** in the process. A **reducing agent** (also called a reductive agent, reductant or reducer) is a substance that has the ability to reduce other substances by transferring electrons to them. The **reducing agent is oxidized** in the process.

Redox reactions may always be written as **two half-reactions**, a **reduction half-reaction** with **electrons as a reactant** and an **oxidation half-reaction** with **electrons as a product**.

For example, the redox reactions:

$$Zn(s) + Cu^{2+}(aq) \rightarrow Zn^{2+}(aq) + Cu(s) \quad \text{and} \quad H_2 + F_2 \rightarrow 2HF$$

may be written in terms of the half-reactions:

$$\begin{array}{ll} 2e^- + Cu^{2+}(aq) \rightarrow Cu(s) & 2e^- + F_2 \rightarrow 2F^- \\ \text{and} & \\ Zn(s) \rightarrow Zn^{2+}(aq) + 2e^-. & H_2 \rightarrow 2H^+ + 2e^-. \end{array}$$

An additional (non-redox) reaction, $2F^- + 2H^+ \rightarrow 2HF$, achieves the final products for the second reaction.

Determining whether a chemical equation is balanced requires an additional step for redox reactions because there must be a **charge balance.** For example, the equation:

$$Sn^{2+} + Fe^{3+} \rightarrow Sn^{4+} + Fe^{2+}$$

contains one Sn and one Fe on each side but it is not balanced because the sum of charges on the left side of the equation is +5 and the sum on the right side is +6. One electron is gained in the reduction half-reaction ($Fe^{3+} + e^- \rightarrow Fe^{2+}$), but two are lost in the oxidation half-reaction ($Sn^{2+} \rightarrow Sn^{4+} + 2e^-$).

The equation:

$$Sn^{2+} + 2Fe^{3+} \rightarrow Sn^{4+} + 2Fe^{2+}$$

is properly balanced because both sides contain the same sum of charges (+8) and electrons cancel from the half-reactions:

$$2Fe^{3+} + 2e^- \rightarrow 2Fe^{2+}$$
$$Sn^{2+} \rightarrow Sn^{4+} + 2e^-.$$

Oxidation Number Method

Redox reactions must be balanced to observe the Law of Conservation of Mass. This process is a little more complicated than balancing other reactions because the number of electrons lost must equal the number of electrons gained. Balancing redox reactions, then, conserves not only mass but also charge or electrons. It can be accomplished by slightly varying our balancing process.

$$Cr_2O_3(s) + Al\,(s) \longrightarrow Cr\,(s) + Al_2O_{3\,(s)}$$

Assign oxidation numbers to identify which atoms are losing and gaining electrons.

$$Cr_2O_3(s) + Al\,(s) \longrightarrow Cr\,(s) + Al_2O_{3\,(s)}$$
$$3+\ \ 2-\qquad\ \ 0\qquad\quad 0\qquad\ \ 3+\ \ 2-$$

Identify those atoms gaining and losing electrons:

$$Cr^{3+} \longrightarrow Cr^0 \quad \text{gained 3 electrons : reduction}$$

$$Al^0 \longrightarrow Al^{3+} \quad \text{lost 3 electrons: oxidation}$$

Balance the atoms and electrons:

$$Cr_2O_3(s) \longrightarrow 2Cr\ (s)\ +\ 6\ electrons$$

$$2Al\ (s)\ +\ 6\ electrons \longrightarrow Al_2O_3\ (s)$$

Balance the half reactions by adding missing elements. Ignore elements whose oxidation number does not change. Add H_2O for oxygen and H^+ for hydrogen.

$$Cr_2O_3(s) \longrightarrow 2Cr\ (s)\ +\ 6\ electrons\ +\ \mathbf{3\ H_2O}$$

Need 3 oxygen atoms on product side. This requires $6H^+$ on the reactant side.

$$Cr_2O_3(s) + \mathbf{6\ H^+} \longrightarrow 2Cr\ (s)\ +\ 6\ electrons\ \mathbf{+\ 3\ H_2O}$$

AND

$$2Al\ (s)\ +\ 6\ electrons\ ^+\ \mathbf{3\ H_2O} \longrightarrow Al_2O_{3\ (s)}\ ^+\ \mathbf{6\ H^+}$$

Need 3 oxygen atoms on reactant side. This requires $6H^+$ on the product side.

Put the two half reactions together and add the species. Cancel out the species that occur in both the reactants and products.

$$Cr_2O_3(s) + 6\ H^+\ ^+\ 2Al\ (s)\ +\ 6\ electrons\ ^+\ 3\ H_2O \longrightarrow 2Cr\ (s)\ +\ 6\ electrons\ +\ 3\ H_2O + Al_2O_{3\ (s)}\ ^+\ 6\ H^+$$

The balanced equation is:

$$Cr_2O_3(s) + 2Al\ (s) \longrightarrow 2Cr\ (s)\ +\ Al_2O_{3\ (s)}$$

Skill 19.3 **The beginning teacher uses reduction potentials to determine whether a redox reaction will occur spontaneously.**

The standard potential of an oxidation half-reaction $E°_{va}$ **is equal in magnitude but has the opposite sign to the potential of the reverse reduction reaction**. Standard half-cell potentials are **tabulated as reduction potentials**. These are sometimes referred to as **standard electrode potentials $E°$**. Therefore,

$$E°_{cell} \quad E°(\text{cathode}) \quad E°(\text{anode}.$$

Example: Given $E°=0.34$ V for $Cu^{2+}(aq)+2e^-\square Cu(s)$ and
$E°=-0.76$ V for $Zn^{2+}(aq)+2e^-\square Zn(s)$, what is the standard cell potential
of the $Zn(s)+Cu^{2+}(aq) \rightarrow Zn^{2+}(aq)+Cu(s)$ system ?

Solution: $E°_{cell} \quad E°(\text{cathode}) \quad E°(\text{anode})$

$= E°\ _{\backslash}Cu^{2+}(aq) \quad 2e^- \quad Cu(s)_, \quad E°\ _{\backslash}Zn^{2+}(aq) \quad 2e^- \quad Zn(s))$

$= 0.34 \text{ V} - (-0.76 \text{ V}) = 1.10 \text{ V}.$

When the value of $E°$ is positive, the reaction is spontaneous. If the $E°$ value is negative, an outside energy source is necessary for the reaction to occur. In the above example, the $E°$ is a positive 1.10 V, therefore this reaction is spontaneous.

Skill 19.4 **The beginning teacher explains the operation and applications of electrochemical cells.**

Electrolytic cells use electricity to force non-spontaneous redox reactions to occur. **Electrochemical cells generate electricity** by permitting spontaneous redox reactions to occur. An electrode is a piece of conducting metal that is used to make contact with a nonmetallic material. One electrode is an **anode**. An **oxidation reaction occurs at the anode**, so electrons are removed from a substance there. The other electrode is a **cathode**. A **reduction reaction occurs at the cathode**, so electrons are added to a substance there. Electrons flow from anode to cathode outside either device.

Electrolysis is a chemical process **driven by a battery** or another source of electromotive force. This source pulls electrons out of the chemical process at the anode and forces electrons in the cathode. The result is a **negatively charged cathode and a positively charged anode**.

Electrolysis of pure water forms O_2 bubbles at the anode by the oxidation half-reaction:

$$2H_2O(l) \rightarrow 4H^+(aq) + O_2(g) + 4e^-$$

and forms H_2 bubbles at the cathode by the reduction half-reaction:

$$2H_2O(l) + 2e^- \rightarrow H_2(g) + 2OH^-(aq).$$

The net redox reaction is:

$$2H_2O(l) \rightarrow 2H_2(g) + O_2(g).$$

Neither electrode took part in the reaction described above. An electrode that is only used to contact the reaction and deliver or remove electrons is called an **inert electrode**. An electrode that takes part in the reaction is called an **active electrode**.

An **electrochemical cell** separates the half-reactions of a redox process into two compartments or half-cells.

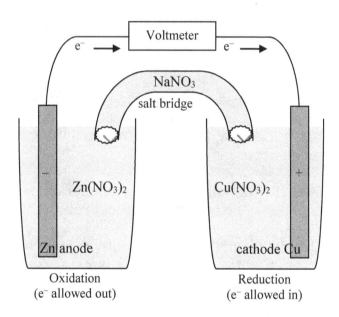

Skill 19.5   The beginning teacher analyzes applications of oxidation and reduction reactions from everyday life (e.g., combustion, rusting, electroplating, batteries).

A **chemical change** is a chemical reaction. It **converts one substance into another** because atoms are rearranged to form a different compound. Paper undergoes a chemical change when you burn it. You no longer have paper. A chemical change to a pure substance alters its properties.

Iron Nail Iron Nail: Chemical Change - iron oxide (rust) is present

Electroplating is the process of **depositing dissolved metal cations** in a smooth even coat onto an object used as an active electrode. Electroplating is used to protect metal surfaces or for decoration. For example, to electroplate a copper surface with nickel, a nickel rod is used for the anode and the copper object is used for the cathode. $NiCl_2(aq)$ or another substance with free nickel ions is used in the electrolytic cell. $Ni(s) \rightarrow Ni^{2+}(aq) + 2e^-$ occurs at the anode and $Ni^{2+}(aq) + 2e^- \xrightarrow{\text{onto Cu}} Ni(s)$ occurs at the cathode.

A **battery** consists of one or more electrochemical cells connected together. Electron transfer from the oxidation to the reduction reaction may only take place through an external circuit.

Electrochemical systems provide a **source of electromotive force**. This force is also called or *voltage* or *cell potential* and is measured in **volts**. Electrons are allowed to leave the chemical process at the anode and permitted to enter at the cathode. The result is a **negatively charged anode and a positively charged cathode**.

Electrical neutrality is maintained in the half-cells by **ions migrating** through a **salt bridge**. A salt bridge in the simplest cells is an inverted U-tube filled with a non-reacting electrolyte and plugged at both ends with a material like cotton or glass wool that permits ion migration but prevents the electrolyte from falling out. To maintain electrical neutrality in both compartments, positive ions migrate through the salt bridge from the anode half-cell to the cathode half-cell and negative ions migrate in the opposite direction.

The reducing and oxidizing agents in a standard electrochemical cell are depleted with time. In a **rechargeable battery** (e.g., lead storage batteries in cars) the direction of the spontaneous redox reaction is reversed and **reactants are regenerated** when electrical energy is added into the system. A **fuel cell** has the same components as a standard electrochemical cell except that **reactants are continuously supplied**.

Competency 0020   **The teacher understands acids, bases, and their reactions.**

Skill 20.1   The beginning teacher identifies the general properties of, and relationships among, acids, bases, and salts.

It was recognized centuries ago that many substances could be divided into two general categories. Acids have a sour taste (as in lemon juice), dissolve many metals, and turn litmus paper red. Bases have a bitter taste (as in soaps), feel slippery, and turn litmus paper blue. In general, acids give up protons (H+), while bases accept protons.

The chemical reaction between an acid and a base is called neutralization. The products of a neutralization reaction are a salt and water, for example:

$$H_2SO_4 + 2NaOH \text{ yields } Na_2SO_4 + 2H_2O$$

Litmus paper is an example of an acid-base indicator, a substance that changes color when added to an acid or a base.

Skill 20.2   The beginning teacher identifies acids and bases using models of Arrhenius, Bronsted-Lowrey, and Lewis.

Arrhenius, a Swedish chemist, defined acids as compounds that contain hydrogen, and defined bases as compounds that dissolve in water and release OH ions. His proposals had limitations. In 1923, a Danish chemist named **Johannes Bronsted** and an Englishman named **Thomas Lowry** refined the theory of Arrhenius. According to these chemists, an acid is a substance that donates a proton (this is a hydrogen ion because hydrogen atoms have no neutrons) and bases are substances capable of splitting off or taking up hydrogen ions. Traditionally, a base contains OH ions. But according to Bronsted and Lowry, $NaHCO_3$ is also a base because it is capable of accepting hydrogen ions, which the Arrhenius theory couldn't explain.

Both acids and bases are related to the concentration of hydrogen ions present. As the concentration of the hydrogen ions increases, the pH value goes down and the acidity of a substance is increased.

The opposite is true for bases. As the hydrogen ion concentration decreases, the pH value goes up and the basicity of a substance is increased. Very strong acids have a pH of 1 or below. Very strong bases have pH values exceeding 12 or more. Milk is a mild acid and HCl is a strong acid.

There is an inverse relationship between the pH value and the hydrogen ion concentration. The higher the hydrogen ion concentration, lower the pH number and greater the acidity, which means the substance is a strong base.

The lower the hydrogen ion concentration, the higher the pH value and the strength of the base is greater. Egg whites are weak bases and NaOH is a strong base.

Skill 20.3 The beginning teacher differentiates between strong and weak acids and bases.

Acid dissociation constant, acidity constant, or the acid ionization constant, (Ka), is a specific type of equilibrium constant that indicates the extent of dissociation of ions from an acid. The acidity of a substance and its Ka value are directly proportional. A larger Ka (smaller pKa) means a stronger acid. Using the values of Ka, the strength of acids can be determined easily.

The basicity constant, Kb, is the capability of a substance to accept hydrogens. The value of Kb and the strength of bases are directly proportional. The higher the value of Kb (pKb), the stronger the base.

Strong acids and bases are strong electrolytes, and weak acids and bases are weak electrolytes, so strong acids and bases completely dissociate in water, but weak acids and bases do not.

Skill 20.4 The beginning teacher applies the relationship between hydronium ion concentration and pH for acids and bases.

The concentration of H+ (aq) ions is often expressed in terms of pH. The pH of a solution is the negative base-10 logarithm of the hydrogen-ion molarity:

$$pH = -\log[H+] = \log (1/[H+])$$

A ten-fold increase in [H+] decreases the pH by one unit. [H+] may be found from pH using the expression:

$$[H+] = 10-pH$$

Because [H+] = 10-7 M for pure water, the pH of a neutral solution is 7. In an acidic solution, [H+] > 10-7 M and pH < 7. In a basic solution, [H+] < 10-7 M and pH > 7.

Example: An aqueous solution has an H+ ion concentration of 4.0×10^{-9}. Is the solution acidic or basic? What is the pH of the solution?

Solution: The solution is basic because [H+] < 10^{-7} M.

$$pH = -log[H+] = -log\ 4 \times 10^{-9} = 8.4$$

The negative base-10 log is a convenient way of representing other small numbers used in chemistry by placing the letter "p" before the symbol. Values of Ka are often represented as pKa, with pKa = -logKa.

Calculating pH and H+ concentration

The pH and [H+] of a solution containing a strong acid or strong base may be found using stoichiometry alone for a strong acid, and stoichiometry together with Kw for a base.

Example: What is the pH of a solution of 0.020 M Ca(OH)2?

Solution: Ca(OH)2 is a strong base, so it completely dissociates:

$$Ca(OH)_2(aq) \rightarrow Ca^{2+}(aq) + 2OH^-(aq)$$

The stoichiometry of the dissociation may be used to determine [OH⁻]:

$$\frac{0.020\ mol\ Ca(OH)_2}{L} \times \frac{2\ mol\ OH^-}{1\ mol\ Ca(OH)_2} = \frac{0.040\ mol\ OH^-}{L} = 0.040\ M\ OH^-$$

Using the ion-product constant of water, we may find [H⁺]:

$$K_w = 1.0 \times 10^{-14} = [H^+][OH^-] = [H^+](0.040)$$

Rearranging to solve for [H⁺]:

$$[H^+] = \frac{1.0 \times 10^{-14}}{0.040} = 2.5 \times 10^{-13}\ M$$

Finally, we determine the pH of the solution from its hydrogen ion concentration:

$$pH = -log[H^+] = -log(2.5 \times 10^{-13}) = 12.6$$

The pH and [H+] of a solution containing a weak acid or weak base may be found using Ka or Kb (together with Kw for a base). If more than 5% of the electrolyte is ionized, the quadratic equation should be used. A review of the quadratic equation in the context of chemical equilibria may be found at http://www.chem.tamu.edu/class/fyp/mathrev/mr-quadr.html.

Skill 20.5   The beginning teacher understands and analyzes acid-base equilibria and buffers.

A buffer solution is a solution that resists a change in pH after addition of small amounts of an acid or a base. Buffer solutions require the presence of an acid to neutralize an added base and also the presence of a base to neutralize an added acid. These two components present in the buffer also must not neutralize each other.

A conjugate acid-base pair is present in buffers to fulfill these requirements. Buffers are prepared by mixing together a weak acid or base and a salt of the acid or base that provides the conjugate.

Consider the buffer solution prepared by mixing together acetic acid ($HC_2H_3O_2$) and sodium acetate ($C_2H_3O_2^-$) and containing Na^+ as a spectator ion. The equilibrium reaction for this acid/conjugate base pair is:

$$HC_2H_3O_2 \text{ produces } C_2H_3O_2^- + H^+$$

If H+ ions from a strong acid are added to this buffer solution, Le Chatelier's principle predicts that the reaction will shift to the left and much of this H^+ will be consumed to create more $HC_2H_3O_2$ from $C_2H_3O_2^-$. If a strong base that consumes H^+ is added to this buffer solution, Le Chatelier's principle predicts that the reaction will shift to the right and much of the consumed H^+ will be replaced by the dissociation of $HC_2H_3O_2$. The net effect is that buffer solutions prevent large changes in pH that occur when an acid or base is added to pure water or to an unbuffered solution.

The amount of acid or base that a buffer solution can neutralize before large pH changes begins to occur is called its buffering capacity. Blood and seawater both contain several conjugate acid-base pairs to buffer the solution's pH and decrease the impact of acids and bases on living things.

Skill 20.6   The beginning teacher analyzes and applies the principles of acid-base titration.

In a typical acid-base **titration, an acid-base indicator** (such as *phenolphthalein*) or a **pH meter** is used to monitor the course of a **neutralization reaction**. The usual goal of titration is to **determine an unknown concentration** of an acid (or base) by neutralizing it with a known concentration of base (or acid).

The reagent of known concentration is usually used as the **titrant**. The titrant is poured into a **buret** (also spelled *burette*) until it is nearly full, and an initial buret reading is taken. Buret numbering is close to zero when nearly full. A known volume of the solution of unknown concentration is added to a flask and placed under the buret. The indicator is added or the pH meter probe is inserted. The initial state of a titration experiment is shown to the right above.

The buret stopcock is opened and titrant is slowly added until the solution permanently changes color or the pH rapidly changes. This is the titration **endpoint**, and a final buret reading is made. The final state of a titration experiment is shown to the right below. The endpoint occurs when the number of **acid and base equivalents in the flask are identical**:

$$N_{acid} = N_{base}. \text{ Therefore, } C_{acid}V_{acid} = C_{base}V_{base}.$$

The endpoint is also known as the titration **equivalence point**.

Titration data typically consist of:

$$V_{inital} \Rightarrow \text{Initial buret volume} \quad V_{final} \Rightarrow \text{Final buret volume}$$
$$C_{known} \Rightarrow \text{Concentration of known solution}$$
$$V_{unknown} \Rightarrow \text{Volume of unknown solution.}$$

Skill 20.7   The beginning teacher analyzes neutralization reactions based on the principles of solution concentration and stoichiometry.

Units of molarity may be used for concentration unless a mole of either solution yields more than one acid or base equivalent. In that case, concentration must be expressed using normality.

Example: A 20.0 mL sample of an HCl solution is titrated with 0.200 M NaOH. The initial buret volume is 1.8 mL and the final buret volume at the titration endpoint is 29.1 mL. What is the molarity of the HCl sample?

Solution: Calculate the moles of the known substance added to the flask:

$$0.200 \frac{mol}{L} \times \frac{1\,L}{1000\,mL} \times (29.1\,mL - 1.8\,mL) = 0.00546\ mol\ NaOH$$

At the endpoint, this much of the base will neutralize 0.00546 mol HCl. Therefore, this amount of HCl must have been present in the sample before the titration:

$$\frac{0.00546\ mol\ HCl}{0.0200\ L} = 0.273\ M\ HCl$$

A **titration curve** is a plot of a solution's **pH charted against the volume of an added acid or base**. Titration curves are obtained if a pH meter is used to monitor the titration instead of an indicator. At the equivalence point, the titration curve is nearly vertical. This is the point where the most rapid change in pH occurs. In addition to determining the equivalence point, the **shape of titration curves** may be interpreted to determine **acid/base strength.**

The pH at the equivalence point of a titration is the **pH of the salt solution obtained when the amount of acid is equal to the amount of base**. For a strong acid and a strong base, the equivalence point occurs at the neutral pH of 7. For example, an equimolar solution of HCl and NaOH will contain NaCl (*aq*) at its equivalence point.

The salt solution at **the equivalence point of a titration involving a weak acid or base will not be at neutral pH**. For example, an equimolar solution of NaOH and hypochlorous acid HClO at the equivalence point of a titration will be a base because it is indistinguishable from a solution of sodium hypochlorite. A pure solution of NaClO (*aq*) will be a base because the ClO^- ion is the conjugate base of HClO, and it consumes H^+(*aq*) in the reaction $ClO^- + H^+ \leftrightarrow HClO$.

In a similar fashion, an equimolar solution of HCl and NH_3 will be an acid because a solution of NH_4Cl (*aq*) is an acid. It generates H^+ (*aq*) in the reaction $NH_4^+ \leftrightarrow NH_3 + H^+$.

Skill 20.8 **The beginning teacher describes the effects of acids and bases in the real world (e.g., acid precipitation, physiological buffering).**

Some minerals have a distinctive reaction when exposed to acids. For example: Any mineral with calcium carbonate ($CaCO_3$) will fizz when diluted hydrochloric acid (HCl) is dropped on it. Water and water vapor may combine with other elements and gases to form acids. Water (H_2O) and carbon dioxide (CO_2) can chemically combine to become Carbonic Acid (H_2CO_3). Sulfur Dioxide (SO_2) particles can chemically combine with water (H_2O) to form Sulfuric Acid (H_2SO_4). Generally found in combination with solution, *acids* cause the majority of chemical weathering. This causes erosion of natural land formations, collapse of caves, and also damage to manmade structures (statues, buildings, etc.)

Acid precipitation affects water quality, in some cases disrupting the environment and the organisms that reside there.

The human body exists is a state of homeostasis due to small changes in the body which eventually return to equilibrium and are healthy occurrences. A major physiological buffer in blood is the carbonic acid/bicarbonate pair. If a base were added to blood, the base would be neutralized by the following reaction:

$$H_2CO_3 + OH^- \leftrightarrow HCO_3^- + H_2O$$

If an acid were added to blood, it would be neutralized in this way:

$$HCO_3^- + H^+ \leftrightarrow H_2CO_3$$

DOMAIN IV.   CELL STRUCTURE AND PROCESSES

Competency 0021   **The teacher understands the structure and function of biomolecules.**

Skill 21.1   **The beginning teacher identifies the chemical elements necessary for life and understands how these elements combine to form biologically important compounds.**

All materials of life are ultimately derived from relatively simple elements and compounds. Once they are assimilated by a living organism, these materials form the building blocks of complex compounds. Many of these complex compounds are later broken down by that organism or one that ate it into simple elemental forms again. This cycle involves the elements of carbon, oxygen, hydrogen and nitrogen and a great variety of minerals including phosphorus and sulfur.

The carbon atom can enter into thousands of different combinations within one organism and then, within others as the materials are passed on. Because carbon has the ability to form four covalent bonds, it can form long chains or branched chains and it can bond to a wide variety of other atoms. The study of compounds containing carbon is called organic chemistry since all living things (animal or plant) are comprised of carbon compounds.

All forms of life require oxygen and hydrogen for a variety of processes. Water, two hydrogen ions and one oxygen ion, is critical to life. The major inorganic source of oxygen in organic compounds is carbon dioxide (CO_2). Atmospheric oxygen, O_2, is 20% of the atmosphere and is necessary for animals to breathe.

Following carbon, hydrogen, and oxygen, the most common element in materials of life is nitrogen, which is a constituent of all proteins. No animals and only a few plants can utilize the nitrogen in the atmosphere; however, plants can utilize ammonia (NH_3), nitrates (NO_3), or various nitrites (NO_2) in making proteins. Animals then eat the plants and utilize the plant's proteins.

Most living cells also need macronutrients, which include calcium, phosphorus, chlorine, sulfur, potassium, sodium, magnesium, iodine, and iron. Phosphorus is obtained through phosphates (PO_4) and sulfur is obtained through digestion of sulfates (SO_4), which can be in combination with various metal elements such as magnesium or iron.

Skill 21.2   The beginning teacher relates the physical and chemical properties of water and carbon to the significance of these properties in basic life processes.

Water (H_20) is significantly different from its immediate Hydrogen compound cousins. **Compounds** are substances that contain two or more elements in a fixed proportion. Generally, the heavier molecules have higher boiling and freezing states based upon molecular weight.

A group of atoms held together by chemical bonds is called a **molecule**. The bonds form when the small, negatively charged electrons found near the outside of an atom are shared or transferred between the atoms. The bonds formed by the shared pair of electrons are known as **covalent bonds**.

Most substances tend to adopt a solid or gaseous form. Water is different. It wants to be a liquid. A water molecule forms when covalent bonds are established between two hydrogen atoms and one oxygen atom. However, unlike the other hydrogen compounds, water has its two hydrogen molecules on one side of the atom. It's a polar molecule.

The carbon atom can enter into thousands of different combinations within one organism and then within others as the materials are passed on. Because carbon has the ability to form four covalent bonds, it can form long chains or branched chains and it can bond to a wide variety of other atoms. The study of compounds containing carbon is called organic chemistry since all living things (animal or plant) are comprised of carbon compounds. The molecular formula for carbon dioxide, CO_2, shows us that Carbon is all around us. It is in the air, water, and every living thing. It is also found in many items that are no longer living, such as the needles and leaves you walk on in a forest path. These items will decay, the carbon will be consumed, and then enter one of many cycles within the environment. Thus the materials are always renewed and accessible to organisms higher up on the food chain.

Monomers are the simplest unit of structure. **Monomers** can be combined to form **polymers**, or long chains, making a large variety of molecules possible. Monomers combine through the process of condensation reaction (also called dehydration synthesis). In this process, one molecule of water is removed between each of the adjoining molecules. In order to break apart the molecules in a polymer, water molecules are added between monomers, thus breaking the bonds between them. This is called hydrolysis.

Skill 21.3   The beginning teacher analyzes how a molecule's biological function is related to its shape (e.g., enzymes, tRNA, DNA, receptors, neurotransmitters, lipids).

Lipids are compo_e⌐ of glycerol (an alcohol) and three fatty acids. Lipids are **hydrophobic** (water fearing) and will not mix with water. There are three important families of lipids. These are fats, phospholipids and steroids. **Fats** consist of glycerol (alcohol) and three fatty acids. Fatty acids are long carbon skeletons. The nonpolar carbon-hydrogen bonds in the tails of fatty acids are why they are hydrophobic. Fats are solids at room temperature and come from animal sources (butter, lard). **Phospholipids** are a vital component in cell membranes. In a phospholipid, one or two fatty acids are replaced by a phosphate group linked to a nitrogen group. They consist of a **polar** (charged) head that is hydrophilic or water loving and a **nonpolar** (uncharged) tail which is hydrophobic or water fearing. This allows the membrane to orient itself with the polar heads facing the interstitial fluid found outside the cell and the internal fluid of the cell. **Steroids** are insoluble and are composed of a carbon skeleton consisting of four inter-connected rings. An important steroid is cholesterol, which is the precursor from which other steroids are synthesized. Hormones, including cortisone, testosterone, estrogen, and progesterone, are steroids. Their insolubility keeps them from dissolving in body fluids.

Proteins compose about fifty percent of the dry weight of animals and bacteria. Proteins function in structure and aid in support (connective tissue, hair, feathers, quills), storage of amino acids (albumin in eggs, casein in milk), transport of substances (hemoglobin), hormonal to coordinate body activities (insulin), membrane receptor proteins, contraction (muscles, cilia, flagella), body defense (antibodies), and as enzymes to speed up chemical reactions.

All proteins are made of twenty **amino acids**. An amino acid contains an amino group and an acid group. The radical group varies and defines the amino acid. Amino acids form through condensation reactions with the removal of water. The bond that is formed between two amino acids is called a peptide bond. Polymers of amino acids are called polypeptide chains. An analogy can be drawn between the twenty amino acids and the alphabet. Millions of words can be formed using an alphabet of only twenty-six letters. This diversity is also possible using only twenty amino acids. This results in the formation of many different proteins, whose structure defines the function.

Nucleic acids consist of DNA (deoxyribonucleic acid) and RNA (ribonucleic acid). Nucleic acids contain the instructions for the amino acid sequence of proteins and the instructions for replicating. The monomer of nucleic acids is called a nucleotide. A nucleotide consists of a 5 carbon sugar, (deoxyribose in DNA, ribose in RNA), a phosphate group, and a nitrogenous base. The base sequence codes for the instructions. There are five bases: adenine, thymine, cytosine, guanine, and uracil. Uracil is found only in RNA and replaces the thymine.

Proteins are synthesized through the processes of transcription and translation. Three major classes of RNA are needed to carry out these processes. The first is **messenger RNA (mRNA)**, which contains information for translation. **Ribosomal RNA (rRNA)** is a structural component of the ribosome and **transfer RNA (tRNA)** carries amino acids to the ribosome for protein synthesis.

Enzymes act as biological catalysts to speed up reactions. Enzymes are the most diverse of all types of proteins. They are not used up in a reaction and are recyclable. Each enzyme is specific for a single reaction. Enzymes act on a substrate. The substrate is the material to be broken down or put back together. Most enzymes end in the suffix -ase (lipase, amylase). The prefix is the substrate being acted on (lipids, sugars).

$$\text{Substrate} \xrightarrow{\text{Enzyme}} \text{Product}$$

The active site is the region of the enzyme that binds to the substrate. There are two theories for how the active site functions. The **lock and key theory** states that the shape of the enzyme is specific because it fits into the substrate like a key fits into a lock. It aids in holding molecules close together so reactions can easily occur. The **Induced fit theory** states that an enzyme can stretch and bend to fit the substrate. This is the most accepted theory.

Receptors are proteins that bind to a specific molecule, such as a neurotransmitter, hormone, or other substance, and initiates the cellular response to that molecule. It is their exact fit that allows for the initiation of physiological changes that lead to the biological actions of said molecules.

Neurotransmitters are chemical messengers. The most common of which is acetylcholine. Acetylcholine controls muscle contraction and heartbeat. A group of neurotransmitters, the catecholamines, includes epinephrine and norepinephrine. Epinephrine (adrenaline) and norepinephrine are also hormones. They are produced in response to stress. They have profound effects on the cardiovascular and respiratory systems. These hormones/neurotransmitters can be used to increase the rate and stroke volume of the heart, thus increasing the rate of oxygen to the blood cells.

Skill 21.4   The beginning teacher understands the importance of chemical reactions in the synthesis and degradation of biomolecules.

Cellular respiration is the metabolic pathway in which food (glucose, etc.) is broken down to produce energy in the form of ATP. Both plants and animals utilize respiration to create energy for metabolism. In respiration, energy is released by the transfer of electrons in a process know as an **oxidation-reduction (redox)** reaction. The oxidation phase of this reaction is the loss of an electron and the reduction phase is the gain of an electron. Redox reactions are important for the stages of respiration.

Glycolysis is the first step in respiration. It occurs in the cytoplasm of the cell and does not require oxygen. Each of the ten stages of glycolysis is catalyzed by a specific enzyme. Beginning with pyruvate, which was the end product of glycolysis, the following steps occur before entering the **Krebs cycle**.

1.   Pyruvic acid is changed to acetyl-CoA (coenzyme A). This is a three carbon pyruvic acid molecule which has lost one molecule of carbon dioxide (CO_2) to become a two carbon acetyl group. Pyruvic acid loses a hydrogen to NAD^+, which is reduced to NADH.

2.   Acetyl CoA enters the Krebs cycle. For each molecule of glucose it started with, two molecules of Acetyl CoA enter the Krebs cycle (one for each molecule of pyruvic acid formed in glycolysis).

The **Krebs cycle** (also known as the citric acid cycle) occurs in four major steps. First, the two-carbon acetyl CoA combines with a four-carbon molecule to form a six-carbon molecule of citric acid. Next, two carbons are lost as carbon dioxide (CO_2) and a four-carbon molecule is formed to become available to join with CoA to form citric acid again. Since we started with two molecules of CoA, two turns of the Krebs cycle are necessary to process the original molecule of glucose. In the third step, eight hydrogen atoms are released and picked up by FAD and NAD (vitamins and electron carriers).

Lastly, for each molecule of CoA (remember there were two to start with) you get:

3 molecules of NADH x 2 cycles
1 molecule of $FADH_2$ x 2 cycles
1 molecule of ATP x 2 cycles

Therefore, this completes the breakdown of glucose.

At this point, a total of four molecules of ATP have been made; two from glycolysis and one from each of the two turns of the Krebs cycle. Six molecules of carbon dioxide have been released; two prior to entering the Krebs cycle, and two for each of the two turns of the Krebs cycle. Twelve carrier molecules have been made; ten NADH and two $FADH_2$. These carrier molecules will carry electrons to the electron transport chain. ATP is made by substrate level phosphorylation in the Krebs cycle. Notice that the Krebs cycle in itself does not produce much ATP, but functions mostly in the transfer of electrons to be used in the electron transport chain where the most ATP is made.

In the **Electron Transport Chain,** NADH transfers electrons from glycolysis and the Kreb's cycle to the first molecule in the chain of molecules embedded in the inner membrane of the mitochondrion. Most of the molecules in the electron transport chain are proteins. Nonprotein molecules are also part of the chain and are essential for the catalytic functions of certain enzymes. The electron transport chain does not make ATP directly. Instead, it breaks up a large free energy drop into a more manageable amount. The chain uses electrons to pump H^+ across the mitochondrion membrane. The H^+ gradient is used to form ATP synthesis in a process called **chemiosmosis** (oxidative phosphorylation). ATP synthetase and energy generated by the movement of hydrogen ions coming off of NADH and $FADH_2$ builds ATP from ADP on the inner membrane of the mitochondria. Each NADH yields three molecules of ATP (10 x 3) and each FADH2 yields two molecules of ATP (2 x 2). Thus, the electron transport chain and oxidative phosphorylation produces 34 ATP.

So, the net gain from the whole process of respiration is 36 molecules of ATP:

    Glycolysis - 4 ATP made, 2 ATP spent = net gain of 2 ATP
    Acetyl CoA- 2 ATP used
    Krebs cycle - 1 ATP made for each turn of the cycle = net gain of 2 ATP
    Electron transport chain - 34 ATP gained

Photosynthesis is an anabolic process that stores energy in the form of a three carbon sugar. We will use glucose as an example for this section. Photosynthesis is done only by organisms that contain chloroplasts (plants, some bacteria, some protists). The **chloroplast** is the site of photosynthesis. It is similar to the mitochondria due to the increased surface area of the thylakoid membrane. It also contains a fluid called stroma between the stacks of thylakoids. The thylakoid membrane contains pigments (chlorophyll) that are capable of capturing light energy.

Photosynthesis reverses the electron flow. Water is split by the chloroplast into hydrogen and oxygen. The oxygen is given off as a waste product as carbon dioxide is reduced to sugar (glucose). This requires the input of energy, which comes from the sun.

Photosynthesis occurs in two stages: the light reactions and the Calvin cycle (dark reactions). The conversion of solar energy to chemical energy occurs in the light reactions. Electrons are transferred by the absorption of light by chlorophyll and cause the water to split, releasing oxygen as a waste product. The chemical energy that is created in the light reaction is in the form of NADPH. ATP is also produced by a process called photophosphorylation. These forms of energy are produced in the thylakoids and are used in the Calvin cycle to produce sugar.

The second stage of photosynthesis is the **Calvin cycle**. Carbon dioxide in the air is incorporated into organic molecules already in the chloroplast. The NADPH produced in the light reaction is used as reducing power for the reduction of the carbon to carbohydrate. ATP from the light reaction is also needed to convert carbon dioxide to carbohydrate (sugar). The process of photosynthesis is made possible by the presense of the sun. The formula for photosynthesis is:

$$CO_2 + H_2O + \text{energy (from sunlight)} \rightarrow C_6H_{12}O_6 + O_2$$

Chemical digestion of food in humans occurs as a series of exothermic reactions. Mechanically speaking, the teeth and saliva begin digestion by breaking food down into smaller pieces and lubricating it so it can be swallowed. In the stomach, food is broken down by enzymes. The food enters the small intestine, where most nutrient absorption occurs. Additional enzymes are produced as necessary. This series of chemical reactions functions to digest food, consume nutrients, reabsorb water and produce vitamin K.

Skill 21.5 **The beginning teacher identifies and compares the structures and functions of different types of biomolecules, including carbohydrates, lipids, proteins, and nucleic acids.**

Carbohydrates contain a ratio of two hydrogen atoms for each carbon and oxygen $(CH_2O)_n$. Carbohydrates include sugars and starches. They function in the release of energy. **Monosaccharides** are the simplest sugars and include glucose, fructose, and galactose. They are major nutrients for cells. In cellular respiration, the cells extract the energy in glucose molecules. **Disaccharides** are made by joining two monosaccharides by condensation to form a glycosidic linkage (covalent bond between two monosaccharides). Maltose is formed from the combination of two glucose molecules, lactose is formed from joining glucose and galactose, and sucrose is formed from the combination of glucose and fructose. **Polysaccharides** consist of many monomers joined. They are storage material hydrolyzed as needed to provide sugar for cells or building material for structures protecting the cell. Examples of polysaccharides include starch, glycogen, cellulose and chitin.

Lipids are composed of glycerol (an alcohol) and three fatty acids. Lipids are **hydrophobic** (water fearing) and will not mix with water. There are three important families of lipids, fats, phospholipids and steroids.

Fats consist of glycerol (alcohol) and three fatty acids. Fatty acids are long carbon skeletons. The nonpolar carbon-hydrogen bonds in the tails of fatty acids are why they are hydrophobic. Fats are solids at room temperature and come from animal sources (butter, lard).

Phospholipids are a vital component in cell membranes. In a phospholipid, one or two fatty acids are replaced by a phosphate group linked to a nitrogen group. They consist of a **polar** (charged) head that is hydrophilic or water loving and a **nonpolar** (uncharged) tail which is hydrophobic or water fearing. This allows the membrane to orient itself with the polar heads facing the interstitial fluid found outside the cell and the internal fluid of the cell.

Steroids are insoluble and are composed of a carbon skeleton consisting of four inter-connected rings. An important steroid is cholesterol, which is the precursor from which other steroids are synthesized. Hormones, including cortisone, testosterone, estrogen, and progesterone, are steroids. Their insolubility keeps them from dissolving in body fluids.

Proteins compose about fifty percent of the dry weight of animals and bacteria. Proteins function in structure and aid in support (connective tissue, hair, feathers, quills), storage of amino acids (albumin in eggs, casein in milk), transport of substances (hemoglobin), hormonal to coordinate body activities (insulin), membrane receptor proteins, contraction (muscles, cilia, flagella), body defense (antibodies), and as enzymes to speed up chemical reactions.

All proteins are made of twenty **amino acids**. An amino acid contains an amino group and an acid group. The radical group varies and defines the amino acid. Amino acids form through condensation reactions with the removal of water. The bond that is formed between two amino acids is called a peptide bond. Polymers of amino acids are called polypeptide chains. An analogy can be drawn between the twenty amino acids and the alphabet. Millions of words can be formed using an alphabet of only twenty-six letters. This diversity is also possible using only twenty amino acids. This results in the formation of many different proteins, whose structure defines the function.

There are four levels of protein structure primary, secondary, tertiary, and quaternary. **Primary structure** is the protein's unique sequence of amino acids. A slight change in primary structure can affect a protein's conformation and its ability to function. **Secondary structure** is the coils and folds of polypeptide chains. The coils and folds are the result of hydrogen bonds along the polypeptide backbone. The secondary structure is either in the form of an alpha helix or a pleated sheet. The alpha helix is a coil held together by hydrogen bonds. A pleated sheet is the polypeptide chain folding back and forth. The hydrogen bonds between parallel regions hold it together. **Tertiary structure** is formed by bonding between the side chains of the amino acids. Disulfide bridges are created when two sulfhydryl groups on the amino acids bond together to form a strong covalent bond. **Quaternary structure** is the overall structure of the protein from the aggregation of two or more polypeptide chains. An example of this is hemoglobin. Hemoglobin consists of two kinds of polypeptide chains.

Nucleic acids consist of DNA (deoxyribonucleic acid) and RNA (ribonucleic acid). Nucleic acids contain the instructions for the amino acid sequence of proteins and the instructions for replicating. The monomer of nucleic acids is called a nucleotide. A nucleotide consists of a 5 carbon sugar, (deoxyribose in DNA, ribose in RNA), a phosphate group, and a nitrogenous base. The base sequence codes for the instructions. There are five bases: adenine, thymine, cytosine, guanine, and uracil. Uracil is found only in RNA and replaces the thymine.

Skill 21.6   The beginning teacher explains how enzymes function in synthesis and degradation of biomolecules (e.g., DNA, food).

Enzymes are critical in the duplication of DNA. DNA replication begins with a partial unwinding of the double helix. This unwinding action is accomplished by an enzyme known as DNA helicase. As the two DNA strands separate and the bases are exposed, the enzyme DNA polymerase moves into position at the point where synthesis will begin. The starting point for DNA polymerase is a short segment of RNA known as an RNA primer. The primer is "laid down" complementary to the DNA template by an enzyme known as RNA polymerase or Primase. The DNA polymerase then adds nucleotides one by one in an exactly complementary manner, A to T and G to C. These enzymes ensure that the DNA will be replicated properly.

Chemical digestion of food in humans occurs as a series of exothermic reactions. Mechanically speaking, the teeth and saliva begin digestion by breaking food down into smaller pieces and lubricating it so it can be swallowed. The lips, cheeks, and tongue form a bolus or ball of food. It is carried down the pharynx by the process of peristalsis (wave-like contractions) and enters the stomach through the sphincter, which closes to keep food from going back up. In the stomach, pepsinogen and hydrochloric acid form pepsin, the enzyme that hydrolyzes proteins. The food is broken down further by this chemical action and is churned into acid chyme. The pyloric sphincter muscle opens to allow the food to enter the small intestine. Most nutrient absorption occurs in the small intestine. Its large surface area, accomplished by its length and protrusions called villi and microvilli, allow for a great absorptive surface into the bloodstream. Chyme is neutralized after coming from the acidic stomach to allow the enzymes found there to function. Accessory organs function in the production of necessary enzymes and bile. The pancreas makes many enzymes to break down food in the small intestine. The liver makes bile, which breaks down and emulsifies fatty acids. Any food left after the trip through the small intestine enters the large intestine.

Competency 0022   **The teacher understands that cells are the basic structures of living things and have specialized parts that perform specific functions.**

Skill 22.1   **The beginning teacher differentiates among viruses, prokaryotic cells, and eukaryotic cells (e.g., structure and function).**

The cell is the basic unit of all living things. There are three types of cells. They are prokaryotes, eukaryotes, and archaea. Archaea have some similarities with prokaryotes, but are as distantly related to prokaryotes as prokaryotes are to eukaryotes.

PROKARYOTES

Prokaryotes consist only of bacteria and cyanobacteria (formerly known as blue-green algae). The classification of prokaryotes is in the diagram below.

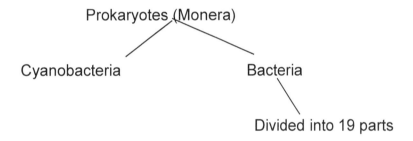

These cells have no defined nucleus or nuclear membrane. The DNA, RNA, and ribosomes float freely within the cell. The cytoplasm has a single chromosome condensed to form a **nucleoid**. Prokaryotes have a thick cell wall made up of amino sugars (glycoproteins). This is for protection, to give the cell shape, and to keep the cell from bursting. It is the **cell wall** of bacteria that is targeted by the antibiotic penicillin. Penicillin works by disrupting the cell wall, thus killing the cell.

The cell wall surrounds the **cell membrane** (plasma membrane). The cell membrane consists of a lipid bilayer that controls the passage of molecules in and out of the cell. Some prokaryotes have a capsule made of polysaccharides that surrounds the cell wall for extra protection from higher organisms.

Many bacterial cells have appendages used for movement called **flagella**. Some cells also have **pili**, which are a protein strand used for attachment of the bacteria. Pili may also be used for sexual conjugation (where the DNA from one bacterial cell is transferred to another bacterial cell).

Prokaryotes are the most numerous and widespread organisms on earth. Bacteria were most likely the first cells and date back in the fossil record to 3.5 billion years ago. Their ability to adapt to the environment allows them to thrive in a wide variety of habitats.

EUKARYOTES

Eukaryotic cells are found in protists, fungi, plants, and animals. Most eukaryotic cells are larger than prokaryotic cells. They contain many organelles, which are membrane bound areas for specific functions. Their cytoplasm contains a cytoskeleton which provides a protein framework for the cell. The cytoplasm also supports the organelles and contains the ions and molecules necessary for cell function. The cytoplasm is contained by the plasma membrane. The plasma membrane allows molecules to pass in and out of the cell. The membrane can bud inward to engulf outside material in a process called endocytosis. Exocytosis is a secretory mechanism, the reverse of endocytosis.

The most significant differentiation between prokaryotes and eukaryotes is that eukaryotes have a **nucleus**. The nucleus is the brain of the cell that contains all of the cell's genetic information.

ARCHAEA

There are three kinds of organisms with archaea cells: **methanogens** are obligate anaerobes that produce methane, **halobacteria** can live only in concentrated brine solutions, and **thermoacidophiles** can only live in acidic hot springs.

VIRUSES

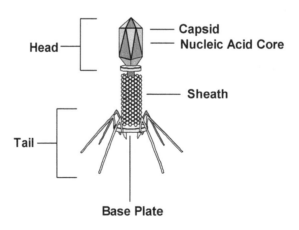

Bacteriophage

All viruses have a head or protein capsid that contains genetic material. This material is encoded in the nucleic acid and can be DNA, RNA, or even a limited number of enzymes. Some viruses also have a protein tail region. The tail aids in binding to the surface of the host cell and penetrating the surface of the host in order to introduce the virus's genetic material. Although **viruses** are not classified as living things, they greatly affect other living things by disrupting cell activity. They are considered to be obligate parasites because they rely on the host for their own reproduction. A bacteriophage is a virus that infects a bacterium. Animal viruses are classified by the type of nucleic acid, presence of RNA replicase, and presence of a protein coat.

There are two types of viral reproductive cycles:

1. **Lytic cycle** - the virus enters the host cell and makes copies of its nucleic acids and protein coats and reassembles. It then lyses or breaks out of the host cell and infects other nearby cells, repeating the process. The host cell is destroyed upon virus release.
2. **Lysogenic cycle** - the virus may remain dormant within the cells until something initiates it to break out of the cell. The host cell is not destroyed upon virus release. Herpes is an example of a lysogenic virus.

Other examples of viruses and their structures:

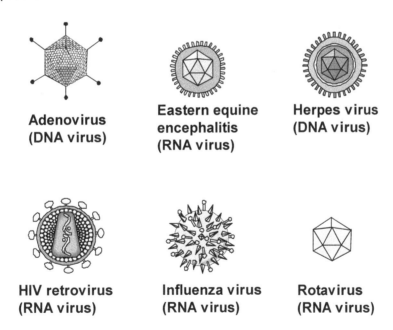

Adenovirus (DNA virus)

Eastern equine encephalitis (RNA virus)

Herpes virus (DNA virus)

HIV retrovirus (RNA virus)

Influenza virus (RNA virus)

Rotavirus (RNA virus)

Skill 22.2 **The beginning teacher describes the basic components of prokaryotic and eukaryotic cells (e.g., cell membrane, cell wall, ribosomes, nucleus, mitochondrion, chloroplast), the functions, and the interrelationships of these components.**

The most significant differentiation between prokaryotes and eukaryotes is that eukaryotes have a **nucleus**. The nucleus is the brain of the cell that contains all of the cell's genetic information. The chromosomes consist of chromatin, which is a complex of DNA and proteins. The chromosomes are tightly coiled to conserve space while providing a large surface area. The nucleus is the site of transcription of the DNA into RNA. The **nucleolus** is where ribosomes are made. There is at least one of these dark-staining bodies inside the nucleus of most eukaryotes. The nuclear envelope is two membranes separated by a narrow space. The envelope contains many pores that let RNA out of the nucleus.

Ribosomes are the site for protein synthesis. Ribosomes may be free floating in the cytoplasm or attached to the endoplasmic reticulum. There may be up to a half a million ribosomes in a cell, depending on how much protein is made by the cell.

The **endoplasmic reticulum** (ER) is folded and provides a large surface area. It is the "roadway" of the cell and allows for transport of materials through and out of the cell. There are two types of ER. Smooth endoplasmic reticulum contains no ribosomes on their surface. This is the site of lipid synthesis. Rough endoplasmic reticulum have ribosomes on their surfaces. They aid in the synthesis of proteins that are membrane bound or destined for secretion.

Many of the products made in the ER proceed on to the Golgi apparatus. The **Golgi apparatus** functions to sort, modify, and package molecules that are made in the other parts of the cell (like the ER). These molecules are either sent out of the cell or to other organelles within the cell. The Golgi apparatus is a stacked structure to increase the surface area.

Lysosomes are found mainly in animal cells. These contain digestive enzymes that break down food, substances not needed, viruses, damaged cell components and eventually the cell itself. It is believed that lysomomes are responsible for the aging process.

Mitochondria are large organelles that are the site of cellular respiration, where ATP is made to supply energy to the cell. Muscle cells have many mitochondria because they use a great deal of energy. Mitochondria have their own DNA, RNA, and ribosomes and are capable of reproducing by binary fission if there is a greater demand for additional energy. Mitochondria have two membranes: a smooth outer membrane and a folded inner membrane. The folds inside the mitochondria are called cristae. They provide a large surface area for cellular respiration to occur.

Plastids are found only in photosynthetic organisms. They are similar to the mitochondira due to the double membrane structure. They also have their own DNA, RNA, and ribosomes and can reproduce if the need for the increased capture of sunlight becomes necessary. There are several types of plastids.

Chloroplasts are the sight of photosynthesis. The stroma is the chloroplast's inner membrane space. The stoma encloses sacs called thylakoids that contain the photosynthetic pigment chlorophyll. The chlorophyll traps sunlight inside the thylakoid to generate ATP which is used in the stroma to produce carbohydrates and other products. The **chromoplasts** make and store yellow and orange pigments. They provide color to leaves, flowers, and fruits. The **amyloplasts** store starch and are used as a food reserve. They are abundant in roots like potatoes.

The Endosymbiotic Theory states that mitochondria and chloroplasts were once free living and possibly evolved from prokaryotic cells. At some point in our evolutionary history, they entered the eukaryotic cell and maintained a symbiotic relationship with the cell, with both the cell and organelle benefiting from the relationship. The fact that they both have their own DNA, RNA, ribosomes, and are capable of reproduction helps to confirm this theory.

Found in plant cells only, the **cell wall** is composed of cellulose and fibers. It is thick enough for support and protection, yet porous enough to allow water and dissolved substances to enter. **Vacuoles** are found mostly in plant cells. They hold stored food and pigments. Their large size allows them to fill with water in order to provide turgor pressure. Lack of turgor pressure causes a plant to wilt.

The **cytoskeleton**, found in both animal and plant cells, is composed of protein filaments attached to the plasma membrane and organelles. They provide a framework for the cell and aid in cell movement. They constantly change shape and move about. Three types of fibers make up the cytoskeleton.

1. **Microtubules** – the largest of the three, they make up cilia and flagella for locomotion. Some examples are sperm cells, cilia that line the fallopian tubes and tracheal cilia. Centrioles are also composed of microtubules. They aid in cell division to form the spindle fibers that pull the cell apart into two new cells. Centrioles are not found in the cells of higher plants.

2. **Intermediate filaments** – intermediate in size, they are smaller than microtubules but larger than microfilaments. They help the cell to keep its shape.

3. **Microfilaments** – smallest of the three, they are made of actin and small amounts of myosin (like in muscle tissue). They function in cell movement like cytoplasmic streaming, endocytosis, and ameboid movement. This structure pinches the two cells apart after cell division, forming two new cells.

Generalized Animal Cell

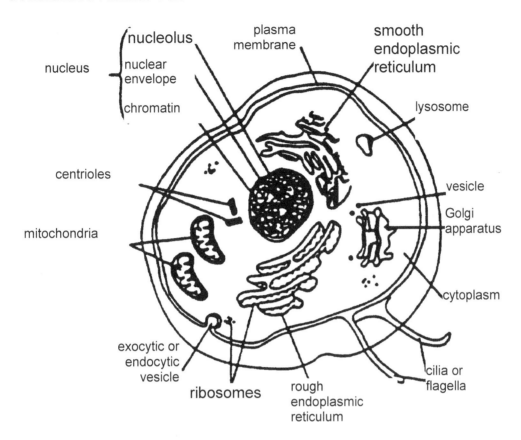

Skill 22.3 **The beginning teacher identifies differences in cell structure and function in different types of organisms (e.g., differences in plant and animal cells).**

Eukaryotic cells are found in protists, fungi, plants, and animals. Most eukaryotic cells are larger than prokaryotic cells. They contain many organelles, which are membrane bound areas for specific functions. Their cytoplasm contains a cytoskeleton that provides a protein framework for the cell. The cytoplasm also supports the organelles and contains the ions and molecules necessary for cell function. The cytoplasm is contained by the plasma membrane. The plasma membrane allows molecules to pass in and out of the cell. The membrane can bud inward to engulf outside material in a process called endocytosis. Exocytosis is a secretory mechanism, the reverse of endocytosis.

Eukaryote cells have a **nucleus**. The nucleus is the brain of the cell that contains all of the cell's genetic information. The chromosomes consist of chromatin, which is a complex of DNA and proteins. The chromosomes are tightly coiled to conserve space while providing a large surface area. The nucleus is the site of transcription of the DNA into RNA. The **nucleolus** is where ribosomes are made. There is at least one of these dark-staining bodies inside the nucleus of most eukaryotes. The nuclear envelope is two membranes separated by a narrow space. The envelope contains many pores that let RNA out of the nucleus.

Only animal cells contain Lysosomes and Mitochondria. **Lysosomes** contain digestive enzymes that break down food, substances not needed, viruses, damaged cell components and eventually the cell itself. It is believed that lysomomes are responsible for the aging process. **Mitochondria** are large organelles that are the site of cellular respiration, where ATP is made to supply energy to the cell. Muscle cells have many mitochondria because they use a great deal of energy.

Plastids are found only in photosynthetic organisms. They are similar to the mitochondira due to the double membrane structure. They also have their own DNA, RNA, and ribosomes and can reproduce if the need for the increased capture of sunlight becomes necessary. There are several types of plastids. **Chloroplasts** are the sight of photosynthesis. The **chromoplasts** make and store yellow and orange pigments. They provide color to leaves, flowers, and fruits. The **amyloplasts** store starch and are used as a food reserve. They are abundant in roots like potatoes.

Found in plant cells only, the **cell wall** is composed of cellulose and fibers. It is thick enough for support and protection, yet porous enough to allow water and dissolved substances to enter. **Vacuoles** are found mostly in plant cells. They hold stored food and pigments. Their large size allows them to fill with water in order to provide turgor pressure. Lack of turgor pressure causes a plant to wilt.

The **cytoskeleton**, found in both animal and plant cells, is composed of protein filaments attached to the plasma membrane and organelles. They provide a framework for the cell and aid in cell movement. They constantly change shape and move about.

Skill 22.4   The beginning teacher analyzes specialization of structure and function in different types of cells in living organisms (e.g., skin, nerve, and muscle cells in animals; root, stem, and leaf cells in plants).

Mitochondria, subcellular organelles present in eukaryotic cells, provide energy for cell functions. Much of the energy-generating activity takes place in the mitochondrial membrane. To maximize this activity, the mitochondrial membrane has many folds to pack a relatively large amount of membrane into a small space.

The cardiovascular system of animals has many specialized structures that help achieve the function of delivering blood to all parts of the body. The heart has four chambers for the delivery and reception of blood. The blood vessels vary in size to accommodate the necessary volume of blood. For example, vessels near the heart are large to accommodate large amounts of blood and vessels in the extremities are very small to limit the amount of blood delivered.

Animals use muscles to convert the chemical energy of ATP into mechanical work. A muscle is composed of bundles of specialized cells capable of creating movement through a combination of contraction and relaxation. Muscle fibers are grouped according to where they are found (skeletal muscle, smooth muscle, and cardiac muscle). A skeletal muscle fiber is not a single cell, but is commonly thought of as the unit of a muscle and is composed of myofibrils. Smooth muscle, including the human heart, is composed of individual cells each containing thick (myosin) and thin (actin) filaments that slide against each other to produce contraction of the cell.

All cells exhibit a voltage difference across the cell membrane. Nerve cells and muscle cells are excitable. Their cell membrane can produce electrochemical impulses and conduct them along the membrane. The nerve cell may be divided into three main parts: the cell body or soma, short processes called the dendrites, and a single long nerve fiber, the axon. The body of a nerve cell is similar to that of other cells in that it includes the nucleus, mitochondria, endoplasmic reticulum, ribosomes, and other organelles. The dendrites receive impulses from other cells and transfer them to the cell body. The effect of these impulses may be excitatory or inhibitory. The long nerve fiber, the axon, transfers the signal from the cell body to another nerve or to a muscle cell.

The guard cells control the stomata (openings for gas exchange) found in the epidermis of the leaf. These plant cells are regulated by the environmental conditions of light, CO_2 concentration and water availability. When the guard cells are activated, potassium pumps actively transport K+ (potassium) into the guard cells, resulting in a high concentration of K+ in the cells. As a result, water enters the cells by osmosis. This causes the guard cells to swell. When the stoma is open CO_2 can diffuse into the leaf and enter the Calvin Cycle. The oxygen produced in photosynthesis diffuses out of the open stoma. Water vapor also escapes from the stoma by the process of transpiration.

Finally, the structure of the skeletal systems of different animals varies based on the animal's method of movement. For example, honeycombed structure of bird bones provides a lightweight skeleton of great strength to accommodate flight. The bones of the human skeletal system are dense, strong, and aligned in such a way as to allow walking on two legs in an upright position.

Competency 0023   **The teacher understands how cells carry out life processes.**

Skill 23.1   **The beginning teacher analyzes how cells maintain homeostasis (e.g., the effects of concentration gradients, rate of movement, and surface area/volume ratio).**

All living organisms respond and adapt to their environments. Homeostasis is the result of regulatory mechanisms that help maintain an organism's internal environment within tolerable limits. It is important to recognize that homeostasis is not an independent process in and of itself. Instead, homeostasis is the combined result of many smaller changes throughout multiple parts of an organism. These small changes and cycles result in the overall state of constancy, which ensures survival.

For example, cell transport allows a cell to be balanced with its external environment. Molecules and fluid will always, according to the laws of physics, move from areas of more density/viscosity, towards areas of less density/viscosity. When given the option, fluids will leak, however cell membranes keep this in check. Cell membranes are selectively permeable, which is the key to transport. Not all molecules may pass through easily. Some molecules require energy or carrier molecules and may only cross when needed.

In humans and mammals, the skeletal system acts as a buffer in maintaining calcium homeostasis by absorbing or releasing calcium as needed. The muscular system contributes to homeostasis in two ways. First, muscle contraction produces heat as a by-product. This heat helps maintain the body's internal temperature. Second, the muscular system (in coordination with the skeletal system) allows organisms to move to environments that are more favorable from a homeostatic perspective.

The circulatory system plays a vital role in homeostasis. The circulatory system delivers nutrients and removes waste from all the body's tissue by pumping blood through blood vessels. Constriction and dilation of blood vessels near the skin help maintain body temperature. The entire function of the immune system is homeostatic in nature. The immune system protects the body's internal environment from invading microorganisms, viruses, and cancerous cells.

There are three homeostatic systems to regulate these differences. **Osmoregulation** deals with maintenance of the appropriate level of water and salts in body fluids for optimum cellular functions. **Excretion** is the elimination of metabolic waste products from the body including excess water.

Thermoregulation maintains the internal, or core, body temperature of the organism within a tolerable range for metabolic and cellular processes.

Skill 23.2   The beginning teacher understands processes by which cells transport water, nutrients, and wastes across cell membranes (e.g., osmosis, diffusion, transport systems).

In order to understand cellular transport, it is important to know about the structure of the cell membrane. All organisms contain cell membranes because they regulate the flow of materials into and out of the cell. The current model for the cell membrane is the Fluid Mosaic Model because of the ability of lipids and proteins to move and change places, giving the membrane fluidity.

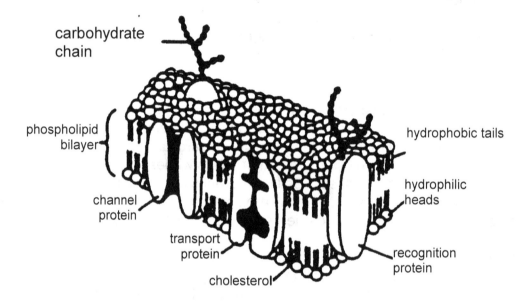

Cell membranes have the following characteristics:

1.   They are made of phospholipids which have polar, charged heads with a phosphate group which is hydrophilic (water loving) and two nonpolar lipid tails which are hydrophobic (water fearing). This allows the membrane to orient itself with the polar heads facing the fluid inside and outside the cell and the hydrophobic lipid tails sandwiched in between. Each individual phospholipid is called a micelle.

2.   They contain proteins embedded inside (integral proteins) and proteins on the surface (peripheral proteins). These proteins may act as channels for transport, may contain enzymes, may act as receptor sites, may act to stick cells together or may attach to the cytoskeleton to give the cell shape.

3.   They contain cholesterol, which alters the fluidity of the membrane.

4.   They contain oligosaccharides (small carbohydrate polymers) on the outside of the membrane. These act as markers that help distinguish one cell from another.

5.   They contain receptors made of glycoproteins that can attach to certain molecules, like hormones.

Passive transport does not require energy and moves the material with the concentration gradient (high to low). Small molecules may pass through the membrane in this manner. Two examples of passive transport include diffusion and osmosis. **Diffusion** is the ability of molecules to move from areas of high concentration to areas of low concentration.   It normally involves small uncharged particles like oxygen. **Osmosis** is simply the diffusion of water across a semi-permeable membrane. Osmosis may cause cells to swell or shrink, depending on the internal and external environments. The following terms are used in relation of the cell to the environment.

Isotonic - water concentration is equal inside and outside the cell. Net movement in either direction is basically equal.

Hypertonic - "hyper" refers to the amount of dissolved particles. The more particles in a solution, the lower its water concentration. Therefore, when a cell is hypertonic to its environment, there is more water outside the cell than inside. Water will move into the cell and the cell will swell. If the environment is hypertonic to the cell, there is more water inside the cell. Water will move out of the cell and the cell will shrink.

Hypotonic - "hypo" again refers to the amount of dissolved particles. The less particles in a solution, the higher its water concentration. When a cell is hypotonic to its environment, there is more water inside the cell than outside. Water will move out of the cell and the cell will shrink. If the environment is hypotonic to the cell, there is more water outside the cell than inside. Water will move into the cell and the cell will swell.

The **facilitated diffusion** mechanism does not require energy, but does require a carrier protein. An example would be insulin, which is needed to carry glucose into the cell.

Skill 23.3   The beginning teacher analyzes energy flow in the processes of photosynthesis and cellular respiration.

Cellular respiration is the metabolic pathway in which food (glucose, etc.) is broken down to produce energy in the form of ATP. Both plants and animals utilize respiration to create energy for metabolism. In respiration, energy is released by the transfer of electrons in a process know as an **oxidation-reduction (redox)** reaction. The oxidation phase of this reaction is the loss of an electron and the reduction phase is the gain of an electron. Redox reactions are important for the stages of respiration.

Glycolysis is the first step in respiration. It occurs in the cytoplasm of the cell and does not require oxygen. Each of the ten stages of glycolysis is catalyzed by a specific enzyme. The following is a summary of those stages.

In the first stage the reactant is glucose. For energy to be released from glucose, it must be converted to a reactive compound. This conversion occurs through the phosphorylation of a molecule of glucose by the use of two molecules of ATP. This is an investment of energy by the cell. The six carbon product, called fructose -1,6- bisphosphate, breaks into two 3-carbon molecules of sugar. A phosphate group is added to each sugar molecule and hydrogen atoms are removed. Hydrogen is picked up by NAD$^+$ (a vitamin). Since there are two sugar molecules, two molecules of NADH are formed. The reduction (adding of hydrogen) of NAD allows the potential of energy transfer. As the phosphate bonds are broken, ATP is made. Two ATP molecules are generated as each original 3 carbon sugar molecule is converted to pyruvic acid (pyruvate). A total of four ATP molecules are made in the four stages. Since two molecules of ATP were needed to start the reaction in stage 1, there is a net gain of two ATP molecules at the end of glycolysis. This accounts for only two percent of the total energy in a molecule of glucose.

Beginning with pyruvate, which was the end product of glycolysis, the following steps occur before entering the **Krebs cycle**.

1.   Pyruvic acid is changed to acetyl-CoA (coenzyme A). This is a three carbon pyruvic acid molecule which has lost one molecule of carbon dioxide (CO_2) to become a two carbon acetyl group. Pyruvic acid loses a hydrogen to NAD$^+$ which is reduced to NADH.

2.   Acetyl CoA enters the Krebs cycle. For each molecule of glucose it started with, two molecules of Acetyl CoA enter the Krebs cycle (one for each molecule of pyruvic acid formed in glycolysis).

The **Krebs cycle** (also known as the citric acid cycle), occurs in four major steps. First, the two-carbon acetyl CoA combines with a four-carbon molecule to form a six-carbon molecule of citric acid. Next, two carbons are lost as carbon dioxide (CO_2) and a four-carbon molecule is formed to become available to join with CoA to form citric acid again. Since we started with two molecules of CoA, two turns of the Krebs cycle are necessary to process the original molecule of glucose. In the third step, eight hydrogen atoms are released and picked up by FAD and NAD (vitamins and electron carriers).

Lastly, for each molecule of CoA (remember there were two to start with) you get:

3 molecules of NADH x 2 cycles
1 molecule of $FADH_2$ x 2 cycles
1 molecule of ATP x 2 cycles

Therefore, this completes the breakdown of glucose. At this point, a total of four molecules of ATP have been made; two from glycolysis and one from each of the two turns of the Krebs cycle. Six molecules of carbon dioxide have been released; two prior to entering the Krebs cycle, and two for each of the two turns of the Krebs cycle. Twelve carrier molecules have been made; ten NADH and two $FADH_2$. These carrier molecules will carry electrons to the electron transport chain. ATP is made by substrate level phosphorylation in the Krebs cycle. Notice that the Krebs cycle in itself does not produce much ATP, but functions mostly in the transfer of electrons to be used in the electron transport chain where the most ATP is made.

In the **Electron Transport Chain,** NADH transfers electrons from glycolysis and the Kreb's cycle to the first molecule in the chain of molecules embedded in the inner membrane of the mitochondrion. Most of the molecules in the electron transport chain are proteins. Nonprotein molecules are also part of the chain and are essential for the catalytic functions of certain enzymes. The electron transport chain does not make ATP directly. Instead, it breaks up a large free energy drop into a more manageable amount. The chain uses electrons to pump H^+ across the mitochondrion membrane. The H^+ gradient is used to form ATP synthesis in a process called **chemiosmosis** (oxidative phosphorylation). ATP synthetase and energy generated by the movement of hydrogen ions coming off of NADH and $FADH_2$ builds ATP from ADP on the inner membrane of the mitochondria. Each NADH yields three molecules of ATP (10 x 3) and each FADH2 yields two molecules of ATP (2 x 2). Thus, the electron transport chain and oxidative phosphorylation produces 34 ATP.

So, the net gain from the whole process of respiration is 36 molecules of ATP:

Glycolysis - 4 ATP made, 2 ATP spent = net gain of 2 ATP
Acetyl CoA- 2 ATP used
Krebs cycle - 1 ATP made for each turn of the cycle = net gain of 2 ATP
Electron transport chain - 34 ATP gained

Photosynthesis is an anabolic process that stores energy in the form of a three carbon sugar. We will use glucose as an example for this section.

Photosynthesis is done only by organisms that contain chloroplasts The **chloroplast** is the site of photosynthesis. It is similar to the mitochondria due to the increased surface area of the thylakoid membrane. It also contains a fluid called stroma between the stacks of thylakoids. The thylakoid membrane contains pigments (chlorophyll) that are capable of capturing light energy.

Photosynthesis reverses the electron flow. Water is split by the chloroplast into hydrogen and oxygen. The oxygen is given off as a waste product as carbon dioxide is reduced to sugar (glucose). This requires the input of energy, which comes from the sun.

Photosynthesis occurs in two stages: the light reactions and the Calvin cycle (dark reactions). The conversion of solar energy to chemical energy occurs in the light reactions. Electrons are transferred by the absorption of light by chlorophyll and cause the water to split, releasing oxygen as a waste product. The chemical energy that is created in the light reaction is in the form of NADPH. ATP is also produced by a process called photophosphorylation. These forms of energy are produced in the thylakoids and are used in the Calvin cycle to produce sugar.

The second stage of photosynthesis is the **Calvin cycle**. Carbon dioxide in the air is incorporated into organic molecules already in the chloroplast. The NADPH produced in the light reaction is used as reducing power for the reduction of the carbon to carbohydrate. ATP from the light reaction is also needed to convert carbon dioxide to carbohydrate (sugar).

The process of photosynthesis is made possible by the presence of the sun. Visible light ranges in wavelengths of 750 nanometers (red light) to 380 nanometers (violet light). As wavelength decreases, the amount of energy available increases. Light is carried as photons, which is a fixed quantity of energy. Light is reflected (what we see), transmitted, or absorbed (what the plant uses). The plant's pigments capture light of specific wavelengths. Remember that the light that is reflected is what we see as color. Plant pigments include:

> Chlorophyll *a* - reflects green/blue light; absorbs red light
> Chlorophyll *b* - reflects yellow/green light; absorbs red light
> Carotenoids - reflects yellow/orange; absorbs violet/blue

The pigments absorb photons. The energy from the light excites electrons in the chlorophyll that jump to orbitals with more potential energy and reach an "excited" or unstable state.

The formula for photosynthesis is:

$$\textbf{CO}_2 + \textbf{H}_2\textbf{O} + \textbf{energy (from sunlight)} \rightarrow \textbf{C}_6\textbf{H}_{12}\textbf{O}_6 + \textbf{O}_2$$

The high energy electrons are trapped by primary electron acceptors which are located on the thylakoid membrane. These electron acceptors and the pigments form reaction centers called photosystems that are capable of capturing light energy. Photosystems contain a reaction-center chlorophyll that releases an electron to the primary electron acceptor. This transfer is the first step of the light reactions. There are two photosystems, named according to their date of discovery, not their order of occurrence.

Photosystem I is composed of a pair of chlorophyll *a* molecules. Photosystem I is also called P700 because it absorbs light of 700 nanometers. Photosystem I makes ATP whose energy is needed to build glucose.

Photosystem II - this is also called P680 because it absorbs light of 680 nanometers. Photosystem II produces ATP + $NADPH_2$ and the waste gas oxygen.

Both photosystems are bound to the **thylakoid membrane**, close to the electron acceptors.

The production of ATP is termed **photophosphorylation** due to the use of light. Photosystem I uses cyclic photophosphorylation because the pathway occurs in a cycle. It can also use noncyclic photophosphorylation which starts with light and ends with glucose. Photosystem II uses noncyclic photophosphorylation only.

Below is a diagram of the relationship between cellular respiration and photosynthesis.

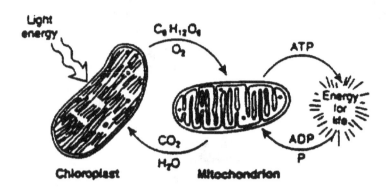

Skill 23.4   **The beginning teacher compares and contrasts anaerobic and aerobic respiration and their products.**

Glycolysis generates ATP with oxygen (aerobic) or without oxygen (anaerobic). Aerobic respiration has already been discussed. Anaerobic respiration can occur by fermentation. ATP can be generated by fermentation by substrate level phosphorylation if there is enough NAD^+ present to accept electrons during oxidation. In anaerobic respiration, NAD^+ is regenerated by transferring electrons to pyruvate. There are two common types of fermentation.

In **alcoholic fermentation**, pyruvate is converted to ethanol in two steps. In the first step, carbon dioxide is released from the pyruvate. In the second step, ethanol is produced by the reduction of acetaldehyde by NADH. This results in the regeneration of NAD^+ for glycolysis. Alcohol fermentation is carried out by yeast and some bacteria.

Pyruvate is reduced to form lactate as a waste product by NADH in the process of **lactic acid fermentation.** Animal cells and some bacteria that do not use oxygen utilize lactic acid fermentation to make ATP. Lactic acid forms when pyruvic acid accepts hydrogen from NADH. A buildup of lactic acid is what causes muscle soreness following exercise.

Energy remains stored in the lactic acid or alcohol until needed. This is not an efficient type of respiration. When oxygen is present, aerobic respiration occurs after glycolysis.

Both aerobic and anaerobic pathways oxidize glucose to pyruvate by glycolysis and both pathways have NAD^+ as the oxidizing agent. A substantial difference between the two pathways is that in fermentation, an organic molecule such as pyruvate or acetaldehyde is the final electron acceptor. In respiration, the final electron acceptor is oxygen. Another key difference is that respiration yields much more energy from a sugar molecule than fermentation does. Respiration can produce up to 18 times more ATP than fermentation.

Competency 0024   **The teacher understands how specialized cells, tissues, organs, organ systems, and organisms grow and develop.**

Skill 24.1   **The beginning teacher understands factors (e.g., hormones, cell size) that regulate the cell cycle and the effects of unregulated cell growth.**

The purpose of cell division is to provide growth and repair in body (somatic) cells and to replenish or create sex cells for reproduction. There are two forms of cell division. **Mitosis** is the division of somatic cells and **meiosis** is the division of sex cells (eggs and sperm).

Mitosis is divided into two parts: the **mitotic (M) phase** and **interphase**. In the mitotic phase, mitosis and cytokinesis divide the nucleus and cytoplasm, respectively. This phase is the shortest phase of the cell cycle. Interphase is the stage where the cell grows and copies the chromosomes in preparation for the mitotic phase. Interphase occurs in three stages of growth: **G1** (growth) period is when the cell is growing and metabolizing, the **S** period (synthesis) is where new DNA is being made and the **G2** phase (growth) is where new proteins and organelles are being made to prepare for cell division.

The mitotic phase is a continuum of change, although it is described as occurring in five stages: prophase, prometaphase, metaphase, anaphase, and telophase. During **prophase**, the cell proceeds through the following steps continuously, without stopping. The chromatin condenses to become visible chromosomes. The nucleolus disappears and the nuclear membrane breaks apart. Mitotic spindles form that will eventually pull the chromosomes apart. They are composed of microtubules. The cytoskeleton breaks down and the spindles are pushed to the poles or opposite ends of the cell by the action of centrioles. During **prometaphase**, the nuclear membrane fragments and allows the spindle microtubules to interact with the chromosomes. Kinetochore fibers attach to the chromosomes at the centromere region. (Sometimes prometaphase is grouped with metaphase). When the centrosomes are at opposite ends of the cell, the division is in **metaphase**. The centromeres of all the chromosomes are aligned with one another. During **anaphase**, the centromeres split in half and homologous chromosomes separate. The chromosomes are pulled to the poles of the cell, with identical sets at either end. The last stage of mitosis is **telophase**. Here, two nuclei form with a full set of DNA that is identical to the parent cell. The nucleoli become visible and the nuclear membrane reassembles. A cell plate is seen in plant cells, whereas a cleavage furrow is formed in animal cells. The cell is pinched into two cells. Cytokinesis, or division of the cytoplasm and organelles, occurs.

Meiosis is similar to mitosis, but there are two consecutive cell divisions, meiosis I and meiosis II in order to reduce the chromosome number by one half. This way, when the sperm and egg join during fertilization, the haploid number is reached. Similar to mitosis, meiosis is preceded by an interphase during which the chromosome replicates. The steps of meiosis are as follows:

1. **Prophase I** – the replicated chromosomes condense and pair with homologues in a process called synapsis. This forms a tetrad. Crossing over, the exchange of genetic material between homologues to further increase diversity, occurs during prophase I.
2. **Metaphase I** – the homologous pairs attach to spindle fibers after lining up in the middle of the cell.
3. **Anaphase I** – the sister chromatids remain joined and move to the poles of the cell.
4. **Telophase I** – the homologous chromosome pairs continue to separate. Each pole now has a haploid chromosome set. Telophase I occurs simultaneously with cytokinesis. In animal cells, cleavage furrows form and cell plate appear in plant cells.
5. **Prophase II** – a spindle apparatus forms and the chromosomes condense.
6. **Metaphase II** – sister chromatids line up in center of cell. The centromeres divide and the sister chromatids begin to separate.
7. **Anaphase II** – the separated chromosomes move to opposite ends of the cell.
8. **Telophase II** – cytokinesis occurs, resulting in four haploid daughter cells.

The restriction point occurs late in the G_1 phase of the cell cycle. This is when the decision for the cell to divide is made. If all the internal and external cell systems are working properly, the cell proceeds to replicate. Cells may also decide not to proceed past the restriction point. This nondividing cell state is called the G_0 phase. Many specialized cells remain in this state.

The density of cells also regulates cell division. Density-dependent inhibition is when the cells crowd one another and consume all the nutrients, therefore halting cell division. Cancer cells do not respond to density-dependent inhibition. They divide excessively and invade other tissues. As long as there are nutrients, cancer cells are "immortal."

Skill 24.2   The beginning teacher analyzes the role of cell differentiation in the development of tissues, organs, organ systems, and living organisms.

Differentiation is the process in which cells become specialized in structure and function. The fate of the cell is usually maintained through many subsequent generations. Gene regulatory proteins can generate many cell types during development. Scientists believe that these proteins are passed down to the next generation of cells to ensure the specialized expression of the genes occurs.

Stem cells are not terminally differentiated. It can divide for as long as the animal is alive. When the stem cell divides, its daughter cells can either remain a stem cell or can go forth with terminal differentiation. There are many types of stem cells. They are specialized for different classes of terminally differentiated cells.

Embryonic stem cells give rise to all the tissues and cell types in the body. In culture, these cells have led to the creation of animal tissue that can replace damaged tissues. It is hopeful that with continued research, embryonic stem cells can be cultured to replace muscles, tissues, and organs of individuals whose own are damaged.

Skill 24.3   The beginning teacher analyzes factors (e.g., genetics, disease, nutrition, exposure to toxic chemicals) affecting cell differentiation and the growth and development of organisms.

There are many, many factors that affect how an organism develops and how its tissues differentiate. Even when they are fully formed and mature, organisms continue to grow and change. Below are several important factors affecting growth and development.

Genetics
Genetics is perhaps the single most important factor in determining the growth and development of an individual organism. Genes code for the proteins that determine all the traits of a creature. Though other factors have an influence, the genes provide the road map for the differentiation of tissues and the development of the organism.

Hormones and growth factors
These molecules trigger the growth and differentiation of cells during an embryo's development, the growth of organs and tissues, and an individual's maturation. It is critical that they be present in the correct place, at the correct time, and in the correct concentration. Thus, if there are errors in their production, important pre-cursors are absent, or they (or similar molecules) are introduced artificially, the individual's development will be altered.

Nutrition

Access to the proper nutrients, including food, water and select inorganic compounds, is important for all organisms. These items provide important precursors for synthesis reactions and the energy for metabolic activities. Lack of nutrients is particularly likely to reduce the growth of organisms.

Gravity

This factor is especially important to the development of plants, which rely on gravity to trigger the downward growth of roots and upward growth of stems. Gravity is also an important factor in the development and maintenance of the muscular and skeletal systems in animals.

Sunlight

Like gravity, sunlight is especially important to the growth of plants, since they rely on it to manufacture the energy they require for all functions. Not only is it important to their development, mature plants will bend toward sunlight to maximize their exposure. Access to sunlight is also important to animals, many of which need to synthesize important factors (i.e., vitamin D).

Disease and parasites

There are a very wide range of diseases and parasites that can disrupt growth and development through a variety of mechanisms. It may be as simple as diverting resources from the organism's essential functions, thus retarding growth. Diseases may also alter the operation of certain tissues or organs, thereby disturbing various processes of the individual. This in turn can alter growth patterns or upset development, given proper timing.

Pollutants, drugs, and other artificial chemicals

Much like diseases, these chemicals can interfere with or imitate growth factors and enzymes. They can also disrupt important signaling pathways or destroy cells and tissues. Thus, these substances can be extremely damaging. Moreover, if exposure to these compounds occurs during development, they can prevent the proper differentiation of cells and deform the individual.

Skill 24.4   The beginning teacher identifies the different levels of organization in multicellular organisms and relates the parts to each other and to the whole.

Life has defining properties. Some of the more important processes and properties associated with life are as follows:

- Order – an organism's complex organization
- Reproduction – life only comes from life (biogenesis)
- Energy utilization – organisms use/make energy to do many kinds of work
- Growth and development – DNA directed growth and development
- Adaptation to the environment – occurs by homeostasis (ability to maintain a certain status), response to stimuli, and evolution.

Life is highly organized. The organization of living systems builds on levels from small to increasingly more large and complex. All aspects, whether it is a cell or an ecosystem, have the same requirements to sustain life. Life is organized from simple to complex in the following way:

Atoms→molecules→organelles→cells→tissues→organs→organ systems→organism

DOMAIN V.   **HEREDITY AND EVOLUTION OF LIFE**

Competency 0025   **The teacher understands the structures and functions of nucleic acids in the mechanisms of genetics.**

Skill 25.1   **The beginning teacher relates the structure of DNA (e.g., bases, sugars, phosphates) to the nature, function, and relationships of genes, chromatin, and chromosomes.**

Genes are sections of DNA strands that code for the formation of cellular products (e.g. RNA, proteins). DNA is the molecule that encodes genetic information. A DNA molecule is a long, double strand of nitrogenous base pairs linked by hydrogen bonding to form a twisting helix. The four nitrogenous bases found in DNA are adenine (A), thymine (T), guanine (G), and cytosine (C). A specialized protein "reads" the base sequence of genes in units of three and translates the code into amino acids or RNA molecules.

Genes have very complex structures, with many unique regions serving different functions. For example, a typical prokaryotic gene has the following regions:

- Recognition region (approximately 50 base pairs in length) – the region of the gene recognized by the RNA polymerase (the protein that transcribes DNA to RNA) for initial binding
- Transcription initiation site – the base sequence where the RNA polymerase begins transcription
- 5' untranslated region – the bases at the starting end of the gene that the cell does not translate into protein or RNA
- Translation initiation site – the base sequence that the ribosomes recognize and bind to initiate translation
- Coding region – the sequence of bases that determine the function of the gene
- Translation stop site – the sequence of bases that instructs the ribosome to stop translation
- 3' untranslated region – the bases at the end of the gene that the cell does not translate into protein or RNA
- Transcription stop site – the base sequence that instructs the RNA polymerase to stop transcription

Eukaryotic genes are similar in structure and are more complex. The main difference between eukaryotic and prokaryotic genes is that the coding region of eukaryotic genes contains both exons (actual coding regions) and introns (non-coding regions).

The central function of genes is to direct the synthesis of cellular material such as protein and RNA. In addition, genes store genetic information allowing organisms to pass genetic traits on to their offspring.

Cells read the base sequence of genes three at a time. A three base sequence, called a codon, codes for a specific amino acid that specialized proteins attach to the growing polypeptide chain. Four bases taken three at a time produces 64 possible combinations, more than enough to code for the 20 amino acids. Thus, an amino acid may have from one to six triplet codons that code for it. In addition, three of the codons are stop codons that cause termination of transcription rather than coding for an amino acid.

The genetic code has several important characteristics. First, the code is unambiguous as each codon specifies only one amino acid. Second, the code is redundant as more than one codon may code for a single amino acid. Third, in most cases the third base in a codon plays only a minor role in amino acid recognition and coding. For example, the four codons for alanine all start with GC (GCC, GCA, GCT, and GCG). Fourth, in general codons with similar sequences code for amino acids with similar chemical properties. Finally, the AUG codon that codes for methionine is also a transcription start codon.

It is also important to note that different organisms show different statistical preferences for the use of triplet codons and amino acids. This characteristic is important when attempting to transfer genes between species.

Skill 25.2   **The beginning teacher relates the structures of DNA and RNA to the processes of replication, transcription, translation, and genetic regulation.**

Replication

DNA replicates semi-conservatively. This means the two original strands are conserved and serve as a template for the new strand.

In DNA replication, the first step is to separate the two strands. As they separate, they need to unwind the supercoils to reduce tension. An enzyme called **helicase** unwinds the DNA as the replication fork proceeds and **topoisomerases** relieve the tension by nicking one strand and letting the supercoil relax. Once the strands have been separated, they need to be stabilized. Single stranded binding proteins (SSBs) bind to the single strands until the DNA is replicated.

An RNA polymerase called primase adds ribonucleotides to the DNA template to initiate DNA synthesis. This short RNA-DNA hybrid is called a **primer**. Once the DNA is single stranded, **DNA polymerases** add nucleotides in the 5' → 3' direction.

As DNA synthesis proceeds along the replication fork, it becomes obvious that replication is semi-discontinuous; meaning one strand is synthesized in the direction the replication fork is moving and the other is synthesizing in the opposite direction. The strand that is continuously synthesized is the **leading strand** and the discontinuously synthesized strand is the **lagging strand**. As the replication fork proceeds, new primer is added to the lagging strand and it is synthesized discontinuously in fragments called **Okazaki fragments**.

The RNA primers that remain need to be removed and replaced with deoxyribonucleotides. DNA polymerase has 5' → 3' polymerase activity and has 3' → 5' exonuclease activity. This enzyme binds to the nick between the Okazaki fragment and the RNA primer. It removes the primer and adds deoxyribonucleotides in the 5' → 3' direction. The nick still remains until **DNA ligase** seals it with the final product being a double stranded segment of DNA.

Once the double stranded segment is replicated, there is a proofreading system by DNA replication enzymes. In eukaryotes, DNA polymerases have 3' → 5' exonuclease activity—they move backwards and remove nucleotides where the enzyme recognizes an error, then it adds the correct nucleotide in the 5' → 3' direction. In E. coli, DNA polymerase II synthesizes DNA during repair of DNA damage.

Transcription

Proteins are synthesized through the processes of transcription and translation. Three major classes of RNA are needed to carry out these processes. The first is **messenger RNA (mRNA)**, which contains information for translation. **Ribosomal RNA (rRNA)** is a structural component of the ribosome and **transfer RNA (tRNA)** carries amino acids to the ribosome for protein synthesis.

Transcription is similar in prokaryotes and eukaryotes. During transcription, the DNA molecule is copied into an RNA molecule (mRNA). Transcription occurs through the steps of initiation, elongation, and termination. Transcription also occurs for rRNA and tRNA, but the focus here is on mRNA.

Initiation begins at the promoter of the double stranded DNA molecule. The promoter is a specific region of DNA that directs the **RNA polymerase** to bind to the DNA. The double stranded DNA opens up and RNA polymerase begins transcription in the 5' → 3' direction by pairing ribonucleotides to the deoxyribonucleotides as follows to get a complementary mRNA segment:

Deoxyribonucleotide		Ribonucleotide
A	→	U
G	→	C

Elongation is the synthesis on the mRNA strand in the 5' → 3' direction. The new mRNA rapidly separates from the DNA template and the complementary DNA strands pair together again.

Termination of transcription occurs at the end of a gene. Cleavage occurs at specific sites on the mRNA. This process is aided by termination factors.

In eukaryotes, mRNA goes through **posttranscriptional processing** before going on to translation. There are three basic steps of processing:

1. 5' capping is attaching a base with a methyl attached to it that protects 5' end from degradation and serves as the site where ribosome binds to mRNA for translation.
2. 3' polyadenylation is when about 100-300 adenines are added to the free 3' end of mRNA resulting in a poly-A-tail.
3. Introns (non-coding) are removed and the coding exons are spliced together to form the mature mRNA.

Translation

Translation is the process in which the mRNA sequence becomes a polypeptide. The mRNA sequence determines the amino acid sequence of a protein by following a pattern called the genetic code. The **genetic code** consists of triplet nucleotide combinations called **amino acids**. There are 20 amino acids mRNA codes for. Amino acids are the building blocks of protein. They are attached together by peptide bonds to form a polypeptide chain. There are 64 triplet combinations called codons. Three codons are termination codons and the remaining 61 code for amino acids.

Ribosomes are the site of translation. They contain rRNA and many proteins. Translation occurs in three steps: initiation, elongation, and termination. Initiation occurs when the methylated tRNA binds to the ribosome to form a complex. This complex then binds to the 5' cap of the mRNA. In elongation, tRNAs carry the amino acid to the ribosome and place it in order according to the mRNA sequence. tRNA is very specific – it only accepts one of the 20 amino acids that corresponds to the anticodon. The anticodon is complementary to the codon. For example, using the codon sequence below:

the mRNA reads   A U G / G A G / C A U / G C U
the anticodons are UA C / C U C / G U A / C G A

Termination occurs when the ribosome reaches any one of the stop codons UAA, UAG, or UGA. The newly formed polypeptide then undergoes posttranslational modification to alter or remove portions of the polypeptide.

Skill 25.3 The beginning teacher compares and contrasts the organization and control of the genome in viruses, prokaryotic cells, and eukaryotic cells.

Viruses are considered to be obligate parasites because they rely on the host for their own reproduction. Viruses are composed of a protein coat and a nucleic acid, either DNA or RNA. A bacteriophage is a virus that infects a bacterium. Animal viruses are classified by the type of nucleic acid, presence of RNA replicase, and presence of a protein coat. There are two types of viral reproductive cycles:

1. **Lytic cycle** - the virus enters the host cell and makes copies of its nucleic acids and protein coats and reassembles. It then lyses or breaks out of the host cell and infects other nearby cells, repeating the process.
2. **Lysogenic cycle** - the virus may remain dormant within the cells until something initiates it to break out of the cell. Herpes is an example of a lysogenic virus.

Prokaryotic cells have no defined nucleus or nuclear membrane. The DNA, RNA, and ribosomes float freely within the cell. The cytoplasm has a single chromosome condensed to form a **nucleoid**. Prokaryotes have a thick cell wall made up of amino sugars (glycoproteins). This is for protection, to give the cell shape, and to keep the cell from bursting. It is the **cell wall** of bacteria that is targeted by the antibiotic penicillin. Penicillin works by disrupting the cell wall, thus killing the cell.

The most significant differentiation between prokaryotes and eukaryotes is that **eukaryotes have a nucleus**. The nucleus is the brain of the cell that contains all of the cell's genetic information. The chromosomes consist of chromatin, which is a complex of DNA and proteins. The chromosomes are tightly coiled to conserve space while providing a large surface area. The nucleus is the site of transcription of the DNA into RNA. The **nucleolus** is where ribosomes are made. There is at least one of these dark-staining bodies inside the nucleus of most eukaryotes. The nuclear envelope is two membranes separated by a narrow space. The envelope contains many pores that let RNA out of the nucleus.

Skill 25.4   The beginning teacher understands the types, biological significance, and causes of mutations.

Inheritable changes in DNA are called mutations. **Mutations** may be errors in replication or a spontaneous rearrangement of one or more segments by factors like radioactivity, drugs, or chemicals. The severity of the change is not as critical as where the change occurs. DNA contains large segments of non-coding areas called introns. The important coding areas are called exons. If an error occurs on an intron, there is no effect. If the error occurs on an exon, it may be minor to lethal depending on the severity of the mistake. Mutations may occur on somatic or sex cells. Usually the mutations on sex cells are more dangerous since they contain the basis of all information for the developing offspring. But mutations are not always bad. They are the basis of evolution and if they make a more favorable variation that enhances the organism's survival, then they are beneficial. But mutations may also lead to abnormalities and birth defects and even death. There are several types of mutations.

A **point mutation** is a mutation involving a single nucleotide or a few adjacent nucleotides. Let's suppose a normal sequence was as follows:

Normal:	A B C D E F
Duplication - one gene is repeated	A B C **C** D E F
Inversion - a segment of the sequence is flipped around	A **E D C B** F
Deletion - a gene is left out	A B C E F (D is lost)
Insertion or Translocation - a segment from another place on the DNA is stuck in the wrong place	A B C **R S** D E F
Breakage - a piece is lost	A B C (DEF is lost)

Deletion and insertion mutations that shift the reading frame are **frame shift mutations**. A **silent mutation** makes no change in the amino acid sequence, therefore it does not alter the protein function. A **missense mutation** results in an alteration in the amino acid sequence.

A mutation's effect on protein function depends on which amino acid is involved and how many are involved. The structure of a protein usually determines its function. A mutation that does not alter the structure will probably have little or no effect on the protein's function. However, a mutation that does alter the structure of a protein can severely affect protein activity is called **loss-of-function mutation**. Sickle-cell anemia and cystic fibrosis are examples of loss-of-function mutations.

Sickle-cell anemia is characterized by weakness, heart failure, joint and muscular impairment, fatigue, abdominal pain and dysfunction, impaired mental function, and eventual death. The mutation that causes this genetic disorder is a point mutation in the sixth amino acid. A normal hemoglobin molecule has glutamic acid as the sixth amino acid and the sickle-cell hemoglobin has valine at the sixth position. This causes the chemical properties of hemoglobin to change. The hemoglobin of a sickle-cell person has a lower affinity for oxygen, and that causes red blood cells to have a sickle shape. The sickle shape of the red blood cell does not allow the cells to pass through capillaries well, forming clogs.

Cystic fibrosis is the most common genetic disorder of people with European ancestry. This disorder affects the exocrine system. A fibrous cyst is formed on the pancreas that blocks the pancreatic ducts. This causes sweat glands to release high levels of salt. A thick mucous is secreted from mucous glands that accumulates in the lungs. This accumulation of mucous causes bacterial infections and possibly death. Cystic fibrosis cannot be cured but can be treated for a short while. Most children with the disorder die before adulthood. Scientists identified a protein that transports chloride ions across cell membranes. Those with cystic fibrosis have a mutation in the gene coding for the protein. The majority of the mutant alleles have a deletion of the three nucleotides coding for phenylalanine at position 508. The other people with the disorder have mutant alleles caused by substitution, deletion, and frameshift mutations.

Skill 25.5   The beginning teacher identifies methods and applications of genetic identification and manipulation (e.g., production of recombinant DNA, cloning, PCR).

Genetic engineering has made enormous contributions to medicine. Genetic engineering has opened the door to DNA technology. The use of DNA probes and polymerase chain reaction (PCR) has enabled scientists to identify and detect elusive pathogens. Diagnosis of genetic disease is now possible before the onset of symptoms.

Genetic engineering has allowed for the treatment of some genetic disorders. **Gene therapy** is the introduction of a normal allele to the somatic cells to replace the defective allele. The medical field has had success in treating patients with a single enzyme deficiency disease. Gene therapy has allowed doctors and scientists to introduce a normal allele that would provide the missing enzyme.

Insulin and mammalian growth hormones have been produced in bacteria by gene- splicing techniques. Insulin treatment helps control diabetes for millions of people who suffer from the disease. The insulin produced in genetically engineered bacteria is chemically identical to that made in the pancreas. Human grown hormone (HGH) has been genetically engineered for treatment of dwarfism caused by insufficient amounts of HGH. HGH is being further researched for treatment of broken bones and severe burns.

Biotechnology has advanced the techniques used to create vaccines. Genetic engineering allows for the modification of a pathogen in order to attenuate it for vaccine use. In fact, vaccines created by a pathogen attenuated by gene-splicing may be safer than using the traditional mutants.

Forensic scientists regularly use DNA technology to solve crimes. DNA testing can determine a person's guilt or innocence. A suspect's DNA fingerprint is compared to the DNA found at the crime scene. If the fingerprints match, guilt can then be established.

In its simplest form, genetic engineering requires enzymes to cut DNA, a vector, and a host organism for the recombinant DNA. A **restriction enzyme** is a bacterial enzyme that cuts foreign DNA in specific locations. The restriction fragment that results can be inserted into a bacterial plasmid **(vector)**. Other vectors that may be used include viruses and bacteriophage. The splicing of restriction fragments into a plasmid results in a recombinant plasmid. This recombinant plasmid can now be placed in a host cell, usually a bacterial cell, and replicate.

The use of recombinant DNA provides a means to transplant genes among species. This opens the door for cloning specific genes of interest. Hybridization can be used to find a gene of interest. A probe is a molecule complementary in sequence to the gene of interest. The probe, once it has bonded to the gene, can be detected by labeling with a radioactive isotope or a fluorescent tag.

Gel electrophoresis is another method for analyzing DNA. Electrophoresis separates DNA or protein by size or electrical charge. The DNA runs towards the positive charge as it separates the DNA fragments by size. The gel is treated with a DNA-binding dye that fluoresces under ultraviolet light. A picture of the gel can be taken and used for analysis.

One of the most widely used genetic engineering techniques is **polymerase chain reaction (PCR)**. PCR is a technique in which a piece of DNA can be amplified into billions of copies within a few hours. This process requires primer to specify the segment to be copied, and an enzyme (usually taq polymerase) to amplify the DNA. PCR has allowed scientists to perform several procedures on the smallest amount of DNA.

Skill 25.6 The beginning teacher analyzes human karyotypes in order to identify chromosomal disorders and sex.

A **karyotype** is a photograph of the chromosomes from a single cell arranged in a standard format- in pairs, ordered by size and position of centromere for chromosomes of the same size- known as an idiogram (see picture below). Chromosomes are positioned so that the short arm of the chromosome is on top, and the long arm is on the bottom. The chromosomes of a karyotype are chemically labeled with a dye (stained) to make them visible. The pattern of individual chromosomes revealed by staining is called banding. Differently stained regions and sub-regions of these chromosomes may be given numerical designations from proximal to distal on the chromosome arms.

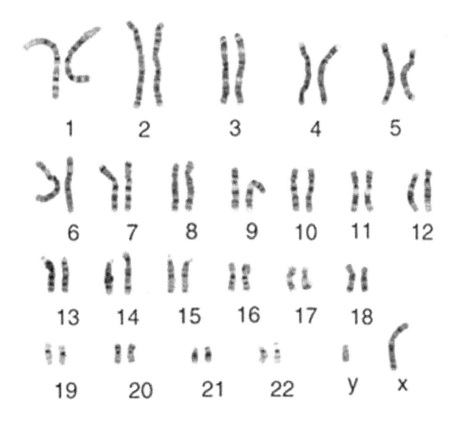

diagram courtesy of
http://www.biotechnologyonline.gov.au/images/contentpages/karyotype.jpg

Normal, diploid organisms possess two identical copies of autosomal chromosomes. Normal human karyotypes contain 22 pairs of autosomal chromosomes and one pair of sex chromosomes. Normal karyotypes for women contain two X chromosomes and are denoted 46,XX. Normal karyotypes for men have both an X and a Y chromosome and are denoted 46,XY.

Karyotypes are used to determine chromosomal abnormalities, as well as an individual's sex, through evaluation of the size, shape, and number of chromosomes in a sample of body cells. Extra, missing, or abnormal positions of chromosome pieces will indicate problems with a person's growth, development and/or body functions. Some individuals may demonstrate karyotypes with added or missing sex chromosomes. Such numerical abnormalities, also known as aneuploidy, often occur as a result of nondisjunction during meiosis in the formation of a gamete. Trisomies - three copies of a chromosome present instead of the usual two - are common numerical abnormalities.

Examples of numerical abnormalities:

- 47,XYY - indicates that a particular human male possesses 47 chromosomes instead of the normal 46, and that the extra chromosome is a Y chromosome. Males possessing an extra Y chromosome demonstrate an aneuploidy of the sex chromosomes, but maintain a normal phenotype.

- 47,XXY - indicates males with an extra X on sex chromosome 23. This disorder is known as Klinefelter's syndrome. Affected individuals demonstrate abnormal testicular development and reduced fertility. Klinefelter"s syndrome is the most common male chromosomal disease.

- 47,XXX - indicates triple X syndrome in the human female. Females with this condition are not at any increased risk for medical problems.

- 45, X – indicates Turner syndrome resulting from a single X chromosome. In Turner syndrome, female sexual characteristics are present but generally underdeveloped.

- Edward's syndrome is caused by trisomy of chromosome 18.

- Down syndrome is caused by trisomy of chromosome 21.

Chromosome abnormalities seen in karyotype photographs can also be structural. These abnormalities may include translocations, inversions, large-scale deletions or duplications. Structural abnormalities often arise from errors in homologous recombination.

Disorders that arise from loss of a piece of chromosome include:

- Cri du chat (cry of the cat) – caused by a truncated short arm on chromosome 5. This name comes from the babies' distinctive cry, caused by abnormal formation of the larynx.

- Angelman syndrome – caused by a missing segment of chromosome 15. This is a neuro-genetic disorder that causes intellectual and developmental delay, speech impediment, sleep disturbance, unstable gait, seizures, hand flapping movements and frequent laughter/smiling.

- Williams Syndrome – caused by a small deletion on the long arm of chromosome 7. The deleted region includes the elastin gene, creating disorders of the circulatory system (vascular disorders).

Competency 0026   **The teacher understands the continuity and variations of traits from one generation to the next.**

Skill 26.1   **The beginning teacher applies the laws of probability to determine genotypic and phenotypic frequencies in Mendelian inheritance (e.g., using Punnett squares, pedigree charts).**

Gregor Mendel is recognized as the father of genetics. His work in the late 1800s is the basis of our knowledge of genetics. Although unaware of the presence of DNA or genes, Mendel realized there were factors (now known as **genes**) that were transferred from parents to their offspring. Mendel worked with pea plants and fertilized the plants himself, keeping track of subsequent generations which led to the Mendelian laws of genetics. Mendel found that two "factors" governed each trait, one from each parent. Traits or characteristics came in several forms, known as **alleles**. For example, the trait of flower color had white alleles (*pp*) and purple alleles (*PP*). Mendel formed two laws: the law of segregation and the law of independent assortment.

The **law of segregation** states that only one of the two possible alleles from each parent is passed on to the offspring. If the two alleles differ, then one is fully expressed in the organism's appearance (the dominant allele) and the other has no noticeable effect on appearance (the recessive allele). The two alleles for each trait segregate into different gametes. A Punnet square can be used to show the law of segregation. In a Punnet square, one parent's genes are put at the top of the box and the other parent's on the side. Genes combine in the squares just like numbers are added in addition tables. This Punnet square shows the result of the cross of two F_1 hybrids.

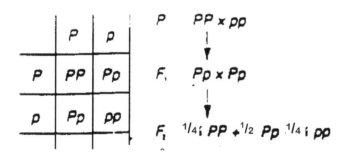

This cross results in a 1:2:1 ratio of F_2 offspring. Here, the P is the dominant allele and the p is the recessive allele. The F_1 cross produces three offspring with the dominant allele expressed (two PP and Pp) and one offspring with the recessive allele expressed (pp). Some other important terms to know:

> **Homozygous** – having a pair of identical alleles. For example, PP and pp are homozygous pairs.
> **Heterozygous** – having two different alleles. For example, Pp is a heterozygous pair.
> **Phenotype** – the organism's physical appearance.
> **Genotype** – the organism's genetic makeup. For example, PP and Pp have the same phenotype (purple in color), but different genotypes.

The **law of independent assortment** states that alleles sort independently of each other. The law of segregation applies for a monohybrid crosses (only one character, in this case flower color, is experimented with). In a dihybrid cross, two characters are being explored. Two of the seven characters Mendel studied were seed shape and color. Yellow is the dominant seed color (Y) and green is the recessive color (y). The dominant seed shape is round (R) and the recessive shape is wrinkled (r). A cross between a plant with yellow round seeds ($YYRR$) and a plant with green wrinkled seeds ($yyrr$) produces an F_1 generation with the genotype $YyRr$. The production of F_2 offspring results in a 9:3:3:1 phenotypic ratio.

F_2

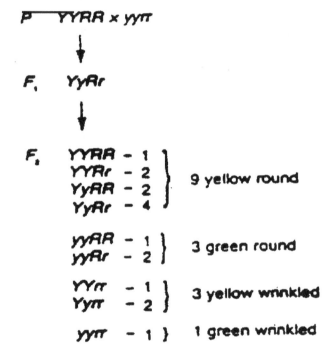

	YR	Yr	yR	yr
YR	YYRR	YYRr	YyRR	YyRr
Yr	YYRr	YYrr	YyRr	Yyrr
yR	YyRR	YyRr	yyRR	yyRr
yr	YyRr	Yyrr	yyRr	yyrr

P   YYRR x yyrr

↓

F_1 YyRr

↓

F_2
YYRR – 1 ⎫
YYRr – 2 ⎬ 9 yellow round
YyRR – 2 ⎪
YyRr – 4 ⎭

yyRR – 1 ⎫
yyRr – 2 ⎬ 3 green round

YYrr – 1 ⎫
Yyrr – 2 ⎬ 3 yellow wrinkled

yyrr – 1 } 1 green wrinkled

A family pedigree is a collection of a family's history for a particular trait. As you work your way through the pedigree of interest, the Mendelian inheritance theories are applied. In tracing a trait, the generations are mapped in a pedigree chart, similar to a family tree but with the alleles present. In a case where both parent have a particular trait and one of two children also express this trait, then the trait is due to a dominant allele. In contrast, if both parents do not express a trait and one of their children do, that trait is due to a recessive allele.

Skill 26.2 The beginning teacher compares the processes of meiosis and mitosis (in plants and animals) and describes their roles in sexual and asexual reproduction.

In sexual reproduction, Meiosis and fertilization are responsible for genetic diversity. There are several mechanisms that contribute to genetic variation in sexual reproductive organisms. Independent assortment of chromosomes and crossing over (as discussed in the following skill) increase genetic diversity. Another factor is **random fertilization**. Each parent has about 8 million possible chromosome combinations. This allows for over 60 trillion diploid combinations.

Alternation of generations refers to the life cycle of some plants and algae consisting of haploid and diploid phases. In the diploid, or sporophyte, phase each cell of the organism has two complete sets of chromosomes. In the haploid, or gametophyte, phase each cell of the organism has only one set of chromosomes. The haploid plant produces gametes by mitosis that combine to form the diploid sporophyte. The diploid sporophyte produces spores by meiosis that develop into haploid gametophytes.

In primitive plants like bryophytes (e.g. mosses), both the gametophyte and sporophyte plants are conspicuous and the gametophyte phase is actually the dominant plant observed. This contrasts greatly with less primitive plants, gymnosperms and angiosperms, in which the sporophyte plant is dominant. The gametophyte stage of gymnosperms and angiosperms consists of a few cells nourished by the sporophyte. In other words, the gametophyte is not a free-living organism and the plants observed in nature are the haploid generation.

Many types of algae (e.g. red, green, and brown algae) exhibit isomorphic alternation of generations. In isomorphic alternation of generations, the gametophyte and sporophyte generations are identical. Conversely, some algae and all plants exhibit heteromorphic isolation of generations, in which the sporophyte and gametophyte generations are structurally different.

Skill 26.3 **The beginning teacher recognizes factors influencing the transmission of genes from one generation to the next (e.g., linkage, position of genes on a chromosome, crossing over, independent assortment).**

A chromosome is, in its basic state, a long strand of DNA located in the nucleus of every cell. Chromosomes are the blueprint of their host organism. Each species has a defined number of chromosomes, with a haploid number in non-sex cells and a diploid number (or twice as many) in sex cells (gametes). The significance of haploid and diploid will be discussed elsewhere in this text.

Each chromosome contains a very large number of genes, with alleles, or two different versions, of the same gene. These variants of the same gene help to explain Mendel's observations of phenotype; when recombined the alternative genes introduce the different genotypes that are possible through reproduction.

At the metaphase I stage of meiosis, each homologous pair of chromosomes is situated along the metaphase plate. The orientation of the homologous pair is random and independent of the other pairs of metaphase I. This results in an **independent assortment** of maternal and paternal chromosomes. Based on this information, it seems as though each chromosome in a gamete would be of only maternal or paternal origin. A process called crossing over prevents this from happening.

Linkage describes the phenomenon where genes that are found on the same chromosome usually appear together unless crossing over has occurred in meiosis (example - blue eyes and blonde hair).

Crossing over occurs during prophase I. At this point, nonsister chromatids cross and exchange corresponding segments. Crossing over results in the combination of DNA from both parents, allowing for greater genetic variation in sexual life cycles.

Skill 26.4 **The beginning teacher understands how the genotype of an organism influences the expression of traits in its phenotype (e.g., dominant and recessive traits; monogenic, polygenic, and polytypic inheritance; genetic disorders).**

Based on Mendelian genetics, the more complex hereditary pattern of **dominance** was discovered. In Mendel's law of segregation, the F_1 generation have either purple or white flowers. This is an example of **complete dominance**. **Incomplete dominance** is when the F_1 generation results in an appearance somewhere between the two parents. For example, red flowers are crossed with white flowers, resulting in an F_1 generation with pink flowers. The red and white traits are still carried by the F_1 generation, resulting in an F_2 generation with a phenotypic ration of 1:2:1. In **codominance,** the genes may form new phenotypes. The ABO blood grouping is an example of codominance. A and B are of equal strength and O is recessive. Therefore, type A blood may have the genotypes of AA or AO, type B blood may have the genotypes of BB or BO, type AB blood has the genotype A and B, and type O blood has two recessive O genes.

Thousands of genetic disorders are the result of inheriting a recessive trait. These disorders range from nonlethal traits (such as albinism) to life-threatening (such as cystic fibrosis). Most people with recessive disorders are born to parents with normal phenotypes. The mating of heterozygous parents would result in an offspring genotypic ratio of 1:2:1; thus 1 out of 4 offspring would express this recessive trait. The heterozygous parents are called carriers because they do not express the trait phenotypically but pass the trait on to their offspring.

Lethal alleles - these are usually recessive due to the early death of the offspring. If a 2:1 ratio of alleles is found in offspring, a lethal gene combination is usually the reason. Some examples of lethal alleles include sickle cell anemia, tay-sachs, and cystic fibrosis. Usually the coding for an important protein is affected.

Inborn errors of metabolism - these occur when the protein affected is an enzyme. Examples include PKU (phenylketonuria) and albanism.

Polygenic characters - many alleles code for a phenotype. There may be as many as twenty genes that code for skin color. This is why there is such a variety of skin tones. Another example is height. A couple of medium height may have very tall offspring.

Sex linked traits - the Y chromosome, found only in males (XY), carries very little genetic information, whereas the X chromosome found in females (XX) carries very important information. Since men have no second X chromosome to dominate over a recessive gene, the recessive trait is expressed more often in men. Women need the recessive gene on both X chromosomes to show the trait. Examples of sex linked traits include hemophilia and color-blindness.

Sex influenced traits - traits that are influenced by the sex hormones. Male pattern baldness is an example of a sex influenced trait. Testosterone influences the expression of the gene. Mostly men loose their hair due to this condition.

Skill 26.5 The beginning teacher analyzes the effects of environmental factors (e.g., light, nutrition, moisture, temperature) on the expression of traits in the phenotype of an organism.

Environmental factors can influence the structure and expression of genes. For instance, viruses can insert their DNA into the host's genome changing the composition of the host DNA. In addition, mutagenic agents found in the environment cause mutations in DNA and carcinogenic agents promote cancer, often by causing DNA mutations.

Many viruses can insert their DNA into the host genome causing mutations. Many times viral insertion of DNA does not harm the host DNA because of the location of the insertion. Some insertions, however, can have grave consequences for the host. Oncogenes are genes that increase the malignancy of tumor cells. Some viruses carry oncogenes that, when inserted into the host genome, become active and promote cancerous growth. In addition, insertion of other viral DNA into the host genome can stimulate expression of host proto-oncogenes, genes that normally promote cell division. For example, insertion of a strong viral promoter in front of a host proto-oncogene may stimulate expression of the gene and lead to uncontrolled cell growth (i.e. cancer).

In addition to viruses, physical and chemical agents found in the environment can damage gene structure. Mutagenic agents cause mutations in DNA. Examples of mutagenic agents are x-rays, uv light, and ethidium bromide. Carcinogenic agents are any substances that promote cancer. Carcinogens are often, but not always, mutagens. Examples of agents carcinogenic to humans are asbestos, uv light, x-rays, and benzene.

Competency 0027   **The teacher understands the theory of biological evolution.**

Skill 27.1   **The beginning teacher understands stability and change in populations (e.g., Hardy-Weinberg equilibrium) and analyzes factors leading to genetic variation and evolution in populations (e.g., mutation, gene flow, genetic drift, recombination, nonrandom mating, natural selection).**

Evolution currently is defined as a change in genotype over time. Gene frequencies shift and change from generation to generation. Populations evolve, not individuals. The **Hardy-Weinberg** theory of gene equilibrium is a mathematical prediction to show shifting gene patterns. Let's use the letter "*A*" to represent the dominant condition of normal skin pigment. "*a*" would represent the recessive condition of albinism. In a population, there are three possible genotypes; *AA, Aa* and *aa*. *AA* and *Aa* would have normal skin pigment and only *aa* would be albinos. According to the Hardy-Weinberg law, there are five requirements to keep a gene frequency stable, leading to no evolution:

1. There is no mutation in the population.
2. There are no selection pressures; one gene is not more desirable in the environment.
3. There is no mating preference; mating is random.
4. The population is isolated; there is no immigration or emigration.
5. The population is large (mathematical probability is more correct with a large sample).

The above conditions are extremely difficult to meet. If these five conditions are not met, then gene frequency can shift, leading to evolution. Let's say in a population, 75% of the population has normal skin pigment (*AA* and *Aa*) and 25% are albino (*aa*). Using the following formula, we can determine the frequency of the *A* allele and the "*a*" allele in a population.

This can be used over generations to determine if evolution is occurring. The formula is $1 = p^2 + 2pq + q^2$; where 1 is the total population. p^2 is the number of *AA* individuals, $2pq$ is the number of *Aa* individuals, and q^2 is the number of *aa* individuals.

Since you cannot tell by looking if an individual is *AA* or *Aa*, you must use the *aa* individuals to find that frequency first. As stated above *aa* was 25% of the population. Since $aa = q^2$, we can determine the value of q (or *a*) by finding the square root of 0.25, which is 0.5. Therefore, 0.5 of the population has the "*a*" gene. In order to find the value for p, use the following formula: $1 = p + q$. This would make the value of $p = 0.5$.

The gene pool is all the alleles at all gene loci in all individuals of a population. The Hardy-Weinberg theorem describes the gene pool in a non-evolving population. It states that the frequencies of alleles and genotypes in a population's gene pool are random unless acted on by something other than sexual recombination.

Now, to find the number of *AA*, plug it into the first formula;

$$AA = p^2 = 0.5 \times 0.5 = 0.25$$
$$Aa = 2pq = 2(0.5 \times 0.5) = 0.5$$
$$aa = q^2 = 0.5 \times 0.5 = 0.25$$

Any problem you may have with Hardy Weinberg will have an obvious squared number. The square of that number will be the frequency of the recessive gene, and you can figure anything else out knowing the formula and the frequency of *q*!

When frequencies vary from the Hardy Weinberg equilibrium, the population is said to be evolving. The change to the gene pool is on such a small scale that it is called microevolution. Certain factors increase the chances of variability in a population, thus leading to evolution. Items that increase variability include mutations, sexual reproduction, immigration, large population, and variation in geographic local. Changes that decrease variation would be natural selection, emigration, small population, and random mating.

Genetic drift is one of the main mechanisms of evolution. Genetic drift refers to the chance deviation in the frequency of alleles (traits) resulting from the randomness of zygote formation and selection. Because only a small percentage of all possible zygotes become mature adults, parents do not necessarily pass all of their alleles on to their offspring. Genetic drift is particularly important in small populations because chance deviations in allelic frequency can quickly alter the genotypic make-up of the population. In extreme cases, certain alleles may completely disappear from the gene pool. Genetic drift is particularly influential when environmental events and conditions produce small, isolated populations. The loss of traits associated with genetic drift in small populations can decrease genetic diversity.

Convergent evolution describes the process of organisms developing similar characteristics while evolving in different locations or ecosystems. Such organisms do not descend from a common ancestor, but develop similar characteristics because they react and adapt to environmental pressures in the same way. Thus, convergent evolution reduces biological diversity by making distinct species more like each other.

Punctuated equilibrium is the model of evolution that states that organismal forms diverge, and species form, rapidly over relatively short periods. Between the times of rapid speciation, the characteristics of species are relatively stable. Punctuationalists use fossil records to support their claim. Punctuated equilibrium affects the diversity of organisms in two ways. First, during the period of rapid change and speciation, the diversity of organisms increases dramatically. Second, during the intervening periods, the diversity of organisms remains nearly unchanged.

Patterns of selection are the effects of selection on phenotypes. The four main patterns of selection are stabilizing, disruptive, directional, and balancing. Stabilizing selection is the selection against extreme values of a trait and selection for the average or intermediate values. Conversely, disruptive selection favors individuals at both extremes of the distribution of a characteristic or trait while directional selection progressively favors one extreme of a characteristic distribution. Finally, balancing selection maintains multiple alleles in a population, often by favoring heterozygote individuals. Balancing selection is the only pattern of selection that increases genetic diversity. Stabilizing, disruptive, and directional selection all decrease diversity by eliminating unfavorable characteristics from the population.

Skill 27.2 The beginning teacher analyzes the effects of natural selection on adaptations and diversity in populations and species.

Natural selection is based on the survival of certain traits in a population through the course of time. The phrase "survival of the fittest" is often associated with natural selection. Fitness is the contribution an individual makes to the gene pool of the next generation.

Natural selection acts on phenotypes. An organism's phenotype is constantly exposed to its environment. Based on an organism's phenotype, selection indirectly adapts a population to its environment by maintaining favorable genotypes in the gene pool.

There are three modes of natural selection. Stabilizing selection favors the more common phenotypes, directional selection shifts the frequency of phenotypes in one direction, and diversifying selection occurs when individuals on both extremes of the phenotypic range are favored.

Sexual selection leads to the secondary sex characteristics between male and females. Animals that use mating behaviors may be successful or unsuccessful. An animal that lacks attractive plumage or has a weak mating call will not attract the female, thereby eventually limiting that gene in the gene pool. Mechanical isolation, where sex organs do not fit the female, has an obvious disadvantage.

Skill 27.3   The beginning teacher understands the role of intraspecific and interspecific competition in evolutionary change.

Competition is one of the many factors that affect the structure of ecologic communities. Competition among members of the same species is known as intraspecific competition, while competition between individuals of different species is known as interspecific competition. Both types of competition occur when there is limited availability of resources within a habitat. Such resources include food, water and territory. According to evolutionary theory, competition within and between species for resources plays a critical role in natural selection, causing individual organisms and species less suited for competition to either adapt or die out.

Interspecific competition: Mechanisms

There are two general mechanisms of interspecfic competition: interference competition and exploitative competition. Interference competition is the direct interaction between individuals, such as fighting over limited resources. While this type of competition is typically detrimental to both species, one species usually holds an advantage (such as larger size) over the other species, resulting in a greater loss for the poorer competitor. Exploitative competition is a more indirect form of competition in which one species reduces or more efficiently uses a limiting resource, thereby depleting its availability for other species. The effects of both types of interspecific competition may influence the evolution of a species as it adapts to avoid competition.

Consequences

The competitive exclusion principle states that two species that use the same resource in the same way in the same space and time cannot coexist and must diverge from each other over time in order for the two species to coexist. In the case of interspecific competition, the superior competitor is that which more efficiently obtains or uses a limiting resource. The inferior competitor will decline in population over time, as it is gradually excluded from the area and replaced by the superior competitor. Competitive exclusion may lead to niche differentiation – the development of different patterns of resource use. This process allows for the coexistence of two species that once occupied the same ecological niche. For example, the seven species of Anolis lizard that inhabit the tropical rainforest are similar enough to have descended from a common ancestor and continue to share the food resource of insects. However, speciation occurred within this ancestral species of lizard to reduce competition and produce new, distinct species, which were able to occupy different sections of the rainforest. For example, some species are floor dwelling, while others live only in braches. If niche differentiation does not occur under the pressure of interspecific competition, local extinction of the inferior species may occur.

Intraspecific competition

Intraspecific competition plays a role in evolutionary change through its affect on a population's carrying capacity. Once populations reach high densities, density dependent inhibition is exhibited through intraspecific competition. As resources become limited, the population size can no longer increase within the defined region. Competition between members of the same species may lead certain populations to move to new regions, eventually resulting in speciation. Additionally, natural selection will favor individuals better suited for interspecific competition. For example, when a tree population becomes dense within a defined area, higher growing trees will obtain more sunlight and thus contribute more to the population's gene pool. Over time, the taller trees' higher fitness will increase the general tree height of the entire population.

Skill 27.4 **The beginning teacher compares and contrasts the different effects of selection (e.g., directional, stabilizing, diversifying) on a variable characteristic.**

Natural selection is based on the survival of certain traits in a population through the course of time. The phrase, "survival of the fittest," is often associated with natural selection, as fitness is the contribution an individual makes to the gene pool of the next generation. Natural selection acts on the phenotype of an organism, which is constantly exposed to its environment. Based on an organism's phenotype, selection indirectly adapts a population to its environment by maintaining favorable genotypes in the gene pool.

Directional selection (positive selection) shifts the frequency of phenotypes in one direction. Directional selection occurs when natural selection favors a single allele, and thereby increases the frequency of the advantageous allele within a population until it becomes fixed. The frequency of the advantageous allele will increase under directional selection independently of its dominance relative to other alleles (i.e. even if the advantageous allele is recessive).

Example: The peppered moth

Throughout the evolution of the peppered moth, the moth color phenotype significantly shifted from a lighter to a darker shade. This change in color can be attributed to directional selection, which continuously selected against lighter color moths as human industrialization increasingly blackened the moth's environment and favored the darker shade trait.

Stabilizing selection favors the more common phenotypes, and removes deleterious mutations from a population. Also referred to as purifying selection, this type of natural selection selects against extreme values of a trait, thereby decreasing genetic diversity as the population stabilizes on a particular trait value. This is the most common mechanism of action for natural selection.

Example: Human birth weight

Babies of low birth weight demonstrate low fitness. These babies lose heat and contract infectious disease more easily than do those of average birth weight. Babies of large birth weight are more difficult to deliver through the pelvis than are babies of average weight. The high fitness of average-sized babies demonstrates the effects of stabilizing selection.

Diversifying selection (disruptive selection) favors multiple alleles that may lie at extremes of a population's allele distribution. Under diversifying selection, individuals at the extremes demonstrate higher fitness and thereby produce more offspring than those in the center. These two extreme contributions to the gene pool produce two peaks in the distribution of a particular trait. Therefore, under diversifying selection, two or more divergent phenotypes in an environment may be favored simultaneously.

Example: Beak size of the Galapagos finches

During his trip to the Galapagos Islands, Darwin observed that the finch species of two different islands were similar enough to have descended from a single ancestor, however they demonstrated significantly different beak size. One island was home to large-beaked finches, the other island home to small-beaked finches. This variation in trait can be attributed to diversifying selection that simultaneously benefited two extreme traits. On one island, large seeds served as the finches' available food source. On the other island, mostly small seeds were available to eat. The variation in beak size was adaptively related to differing seed sizes. Birds possessing the medium beak trait could not retrieve small seeds nor could they carry or utilize the large seeds, and were thus selected against, eventually removing this trait from the finch population.

Skill 27.5 **The beginning teacher analyzes processes that contribute to speciation (e.g., natural selection, founder effect, reproductive isolation).**

The most commonly used species concept is the **Biological Species Concept (BSC)**. This states that a species is a reproductive community of populations that occupy a specific niche in nature. It focuses on reproductive isolation of populations as the primary criterion for recognition of species status. The biological species concept does not apply to organisms that are completely asexual in their reproduction, fossil organisms, or distinctive populations that hybridize.

Reproductive isolation is caused by any factor that impedes two species from producing viable, fertile hybrids. Reproductive barriers can be categorized as **prezygotic** (premating) or **postzygotic** (postmating).

The prezygotic barriers are as follows:

1. Habitat isolation – species occupy different habitats in the same territory.
2. Temporal isolation – populations reaching sexual maturity/flowering at different times of the year.
3. Ethological isolation – behavioral differences that reduce or prevent interbreeding between individuals of different species (including pheromones and other attractants).
4. Mechanical isolation – structural differences that make gamete transfer difficult or impossible.
5. Gametic isolation – male and female gametes do not attract each other; no fertilization.

The postzygotic barriers are as follows:

1. Hybrid inviability – hybrids die before sexual maturity.
2. Hybrid sterility – disrupts gamete formation; no normal sex cells.
3. Hybrid breakdown – reduces viability or fertility in progeny of the F_2 backcross.

Geographical isolation can also lead to the origin of species. **Allopatric speciation** is speciation without geographic overlap. It is the accumulation of genetic differences through division of a species' range, either through a physical barrier separating the population or through expansion by dispersal such that gene flow is cut. In **sympatric speciation**, new species arise within the range of parent populations. Populations are sympatric if their geographical range overlaps. This usually involves the rapid accumulation of genetic differences (usually chromosomal rearrangements) that prevent interbreeding with adjacent populations.

Skill 27.6 **The beginning teacher analyzes the development of isolating mechanisms that discourage hybridization between species (e.g., species' recognition marks, behavioral displays, ecological separation, seasonal breeding).**

Reproductive isolating mechanisms discourage hybridization between two species whose ranges overlap. These barriers to gene flow often lead to speciation – the evolution of a new species – because when a population becomes reproductively isolated from other members of the species, differences in the gene pools of the two populations accumulate that decrease the likelihood that members of the two groups will successfully mate and produce viable offspring. The majority of reproductive isolating mechanisms are prezygotic barriers, which prevent fertilization between members of different species from occurring.

Seasonal breeding (temporal isolation) is a prezygotic barrier that occurs when two species reproduce at different times of the day, season or year. Gene flow cannot occur between two such species because the species are not receptive to reproduction at the same time. For example, closely related species of fireflies often live in the same habitat but mate at different times of the night.

Ecological separation (habitat isolation) is another prezygotic barrier that separates two species whose ranges overlap but live in different habitats. Potential mates from the two species do not encounter each other because of geographic or ecological barriers. For example, during the bird-breeding season of eastern North America, five different species of flycatcher birds can be found within the same general area. However, because these species prefer different habitats, gene flow between distinct species does not occur. Some species prefer different types of habitat to others, such as open woods to farmlands. Where other species prefer to inhabit different types of trees, such as alder to beech trees, or willowy thickets to conifer woods.

Distinct **behavioral displays** may lead to behavioral isolation, which prevents reproduction between two similar species that possess their own characteristic courtship behaviors. For example, wood and leopard frogs exhibit behavioral isolation because the males of each species have vocalizations that only attract females of their species.

Recognition marks are used for intra-species recognition - recognition of a member of the same species by a different member of that species. All methods of intra-species recognition are based on the senses and prevent gene flow between species by enabling organisms to selectively mate with only members of the same species. Recognition may have a chemical signature, such as a smell, a distinctive shape or perhaps a distinct sound. For example, the displayed colors and patterns of butterfly wings allow differing species to select only mates of the same species.

Competency 0028   **The teacher understands evidence for evolutionary change during Earth's history.**

Skill 28.1   **The beginning teacher analyzes how fossils, DNA sequences, anatomical similarities, physiological similarities, and embryology provide evidence of change in populations and species.**

Palaeontology is the study of past life based on fossil records and their relation to different geologic time periods. When organisms die, they often decompose quickly or are consumed by scavengers, leaving no evidence of their existence. However, occasionally some organisms are preserved. The remains or traces of the organisms from a past geological age embedded in rocks by natural processes are called fossils. They are very important for the understanding the evolutionary history of life on earth as they provide evidence of evolution and detailed information on the ancestry of organisms.

From the horizontal layers of sedimentary rocks (these are formed by silt or mud on top of each other) called strata and each layer consists fossils. The oldest layer is the one at the bottom of the pile and the fossils found in this layer are the oldest and this is how the paleaontologists determine the relative ages of these fossils.

Some organisms appear in some layers only indicating that thy lived only during that period and became extinct. A succession of animals and plants can also be seen in fossil records, which supports the theory that organisms ten to progressively increase in complexity.

According to fossil records, some modern species of plants and animals are found to be almost identical to the species that lived in ancient geological ages. They are existing species of ancient lineage that have remained unchanged morphologically and may be physiologically as well. Hence they re called "living fossils". Some examples of living fossils are tuatara, nautilus, horseshoe crab, gingko and metasequoia.

Comparative anatomical studies reveal that some structural features are basically similar – e.g., flowers generally have sepals, petals, stigma, style and ovary but the size, color, number of petals, sepals etc., may differ from species to species.

The degree of resemblance between two organisms indicates how closely they are related in evolution.

- Groups with little in common are supposed to have diverged from a common ancestor much earlier in geological history than groups which have more in common
- To decide how closely two organisms are, anatomists look for the structures which may serve different purpose in the adult, but are basically similar (homologous)
- In cases where similar structures serve different functions in adults, it is important to trace their origin and embryonic development

When a group of organisms share a homologous structure, which is specialized, to perform a variety of functions in order to adapt to different environmental conditions are called adaptive radiation. The gradual spreading of organisms with adaptive radiation is known as divergent evolution. Examples of divergent evolution are – pentadactyl limb and insect mouthparts

Under similar environmental conditions, fundamentally different structures in different groups of organisms may undergo modifications to serve similar functions. This is called convergent evolution. The structures, which have no close phylogenetic links but showing adaptation to perform the same functions, are called analogous. Examples are – wings of bats, bird and insects, jointed legs of insects and vertebrates, eyes of vertebrates and cephalopods.

Vestigial organs: Organs that are smaller and simpler in structure than corresponding parts in the ancestral species are called vestigial organs. They are usually degenerated or underdeveloped. These were functional in ancestral species but no have become non functional, e.g., vestigial hind limbs of whales, vestigial leaves of some xerophytes, vestigial wings of flightless birds like ostriches, etc.

Comparative embryology shows how embryos start off looking the same. As they develop their similarities slowly decrease until they take the form of their particular class. Example: Adult vertebrates are diverse, yet their embryos are quite similar at very early stages. Fishlike structures still form in early embryos of reptiles, birds and mammals. In fish embryos, a two-chambered heart, some veins, and parts of arteries develop and persist in adult fishes. The same structures form early in human embryos but do not persist as in adults.

All organisms make use of DNA and/or RNA. ATP is the metabolic currency. Genetic code is same for almost every organism. A piece of RNA in a bacterium cell codes for the same protein as in a human cell. Comparison of the DNA sequence allows organisms to be grouped by sequence similarity, and the resulting phylogenetic trees are typically consistent with traditional taxonomy, and are often used to strengthen or correct taxonomic classifications. DNA sequence comparison is considered strong enough to b used to correct erroneous assumptions in the phylogenetic tree in cases where other evidence is missing. The sequence of the 168rRNA gene, a vital gene encoding a part of the ribosome was used to find the broad phylogenetic relationships between all life.

Skill 28.2   The beginning teacher understands the relationship between environmental change, mutations, and adaptations of an organism over many generations.

Anatomical structures and physiological processes that evolve over geological time to increase the overall reproductive success of an organism in its environment are known as biological adaptations. Such evolutionary changes occur through natural selection, the process by which individual organisms with favorable traits survive to reproduce more frequently than those with unfavorable traits. The heritable component of such favorable traits is passed down to offspring during reproduction, increasing the frequency of the favorable trait in a population over many generations.

Adaptations increase long-term reproductive success by making an organism better suited for survival under particular environmental conditions and pressures. These biological changes can increase an organism's ability to obtain air, water, food and nutrients, to cope with environmental variables and to defend themselves. The term adaptation may apply to changes in biological processes that, for example, enable on organism to produce venom or to regulate body temperature, and also to structural adaptations, such as an organisms' skin color and shape. Adaptations can occur in behavioral traits and survival mechanisms as well.

One well-known structural change that demonstrates the concept of adaptation is the development of the primate and human opposable thumb, the first digit of the hand that can be moved around to touch other digits and to grasp objects. The history of the opposable thumb is one of complexly linked structural and behavioral adaptations in response to environmental stressors.

Early apes first appearing in the Tertiary Period were mostly tree dwelling organisms that foraged for food and avoided predators high above the ground. The apes' need to quickly and effectively navigate among branches led to the eventual development of the opposable thumb through the process of natural selection, as apes with more separated thumbs demonstrated higher survival and reproductive rates. This structural adaptation made the ape better suited for its environment, increasing dexterity while climbing trees, moving through the canopy, gathering food and gripping tools such as sticks and branches.

Following the development of the opposable thumb in primates, populations of early human ancestors began to appear in a savannah environment with fewer trees and more open spaces. The need to cross such expanses and to utilize tools led to the development of bipedalism in certain primates and hominids. Bipedalism was both a structural adaptation in the physical changes that occurred in the skull, spine and other parts of the body to accommodate upright walking, as well as a behavioral adaptation that led primates and hominids to walk on only two feet. Freeing of the hands for tool use led, in turn, to other adaptations, and evolutionists attribute the gradual increase in brain size and expansion of motor skills in hominids largely to appearance of the opposable thumb. Thus, the developments of many of the most important adaptations of primates and humans demonstrate closely connected evolutionary histories.

Skill 28.3 The beginning teacher identifies major developments in the evolutionary history of life (e.g., backbones, vascular tissue, colonization of the land).

The first vertebrate-fish-appeared in the Paleozoic Era and eventually dominated the marine environment. To be classified as a vertebrate (chordate), the animal must have an internal skeleton and a single nerve cord or vertical column.

Classes of Fish

Agnatha: Jawless fish. Although very abundant in the early Paleozoic, only a few genera survive today. Some modern examples are the Lamprey and Hag Fish.

Placodermy: Jawed fish. Although armored, they had bad fins and were not good swimmers.

Acanthodii: Jawed fish. With only primitive fins and no armor, they went extinct in the Permian.

Chondrichtyhyes: Jawed fish. This includes sharks and other fish that have cartilage instead of bones. With paired, flexible fins, this type of fish first appeared in the Silurian and is still around today.

Osteichthyes: Jawed fish. This type of fish has bones and modem fin structure. It first appeared in the Devonian and is still around today. Osteichthyes marks the start of the move into fresh water from an oceanic environment.

The evolutionary path of fish leads to land organisms. The path moves away from heavy armor to better jaws and fin structure. By the end of the Devonian, sharks and bony fish dominated. However, some fish started to develop a modest air breathing capability.

Dipnoi: Nostril breathing lungfish. Able to breathe in either water or on the surface, they are still around today.

Crossopterygian: Lung breathing fish. A very important step in the transition to land animals, the Crossopterygian is the ancestor of the amphibians.

The rise of the amphibians in the late Devonian period required many transitions to make living on land possible. These adaptations included the following:

- Eye coverings and tear ducts to keep eyes moist.
- Ears to hear both prey and predators.
- A more efficient lung and circulatory system.
- Improved, three chambered heart.
- Strong skeleton (organisms are no longer buoyant out of the water).
- Rigid framework (a backbone and ribs to support weight and legs).
- Reproduction that does not require a water based environment.

Skill 28.4   The beginning teacher understands theories regarding the causes of extinction of species and the pace and mode of evolutionary change (e.g., punctuated equilibrium, mass extinctions, adaptive radiation).

Although Darwin believed the origin of species was gradual, he was bewildered by the gaps in fossil records of living organisms. **Punctuated equilibrium** is the model of evolution that states that organismal form diverges and species form rapidly over relatively short periods of geological history, and then progress through long stages of stasis with little or no change. Punctuationalists use fossil records to support their claim. It is probable that both theories are correct, depending on the particular lineage studied.

Mass extinctions have occurred multiple times throughout Earth's history and have been disastrous for many species. However, those that survive then have the chance to truly flourish and subsequently diversify.

Theory A: Extraterrestrial: A massive asteroid/meteor strike in Mexico's Yucatan Peninsula wreaked havoc with the environment. The dust and debris cloud raised by this collision covered the atmosphere blocking the incoming solar energy, which in turn, caused a steady cooling of the environment. A considerable amount of scientific evidence is cited to support this theory.

Theory B: Sea Level Change: Extinction occurred because the change of habitat caused by sea level change caused a collapse of life in the sea. This had a domino effect that disrupted the entire ecosystem and gradually caused the demise of land animals.

Theory C: Natural Climate Change: Naturally occurring climate change at the end of the Mesozoic causes the climate to go from very warm to very cool. Caused the collapse of the food chain.

Theory D: Arctic Ocean Water Dump: Plate tectonics abruptly opened the largely confined Arctic Ocean waters into the warm waters. The very cold water destroyed the habitats and changed the temperature of the air, thereby destroying the environment needed by the creatures.

Theory E: Worldwide Volcanism: Massive volcanism threw dust and debris in the atmosphere, causing a cooling which destroyed the food chain.

DOMAIN VI.	DIVERSITY OF LIFE

Competency 0029   **The teacher understands similarities and differences between living organisms and how taxonomic systems are used to organize and interpret the diversity of life**

Skill 29.1   **The beginning teacher compares and contrasts structural and physiological adaptations of plants and animals living in various aquatic and terrestrial environments (e.g., freshwater and marine; forest and plain; desert and tundra).**

Freshwater plant and animal adaptations

Freshwater animals need to osmoregulate the water entering their bodies as freshwater is hypotonic to the tissue fluid of the animals. Structural adaptations include heavy scales that secrete mucus to impede water passing into the body. Furthermore, the kidneys of freshwater animals are adapted to filter out extreme amounts of excess water. The gill cells of these animals actively transport salt from the water to the body as it is lost.

Freshwater and marine plants have similar adaptations for water. The plants have a waxy cuticle and often have air spaces in the leaves to help them float. In addition, a plant living in water often has many stomata on the upper epidermis of the plant, and lacks stomata on the lower epidermis.

Marine plant and animal adaptations

Seawater is isotonic to the tissue fluid of marine animals. Therefore marine animals tend to lose water from their bodies and they have to drink large amounts of seawater to avoid dehydration. They excrete a large amount of excess salt through their gills. Most of the marine animals excrete very little urine.

Marine plants have similar adaptations to freshwater plants, however they also have mechanisms to attach to a rock or the substrate and have the ability to stabilize sediment.

Desert plant and animal adaptations

Many desert animals are crepuscular, meaning they only move during dusk and dawn in order to avoid the high temperatures of the day. Many desert animals burrow or are nocturnal to avoid high temperatures. Animals in the desert are able to retain water from the plants and animals they consume without having to have an extra source of water supply.

There are two major adaptations of plants in the desert. Xerophytes are plants that have no leaves. Without leaves, the plant is able to store great amounts of water and lose very little via transpiration. Phreatophytes are plants that are able to grow very long roots. These roots are sometimes long enough to enter the water table.

Tundra plant and animal adaptations

Animals in the tundra must be able to withstand extremely cold temperatures. Therefore, many of the animals in the tundra are stocky and have short arms and legs in an effort to maintain a core body temperature. The animals also have a thick fur. Tundra animals are typically able to gain a fat layer quickly in the spring that is used to heat the animal and provide it with energy throughout the winter months.

Tundra plants are often perennials that live several years gathering nutrients before seed production. The plants are very heat efficient, many retaining old leaves to protect from the cold. The old leaves also act as a source of nutrients for the plant.

Temperate forest plant and animal adaptations

Temperate forest animals will migrate or hibernate for the winter. Many of the temperate forest animals have a system for food storage for the winter months when food is scarce.

Plant adaptations in a temperate forest include having broad leaves for photosynthesis. Many of these plants will lose their leaves in the winter in order to conserve energy.

Grassland plant and animal adaptations

Animals in the grasslands are adapted to dry and windy conditions. Many burrow to get out of the wind and dust storms. The animals are typically grazing animals or predators of the grazers. The grazing animals are adapted to run fast to avoid predators.

Grassland plants often have very colorful blossoms in order to attract insects for pollination. They also have extensive root systems ito gain the nutrients they require for life.

Skill 29.2   The beginning teacher understands the relationship between environmental changes in aquatic and terrestrial ecosystems and adaptive changes in organisms inhabiting these ecosystems.

The **non-vascular plants** represent a grade of evolution characterized by several primitive features for plants. These include: lack of roots, lack of conducting tissues, rely on absorption of water that falls on the plant or they live in a zone of high humidity, and a lack of leaves or have microphylls (in ferns). Groups included are the liverworts, hornworts, and mosses. Each is recognized as a separate division.

The characteristics of **vascular plants** are: synthesis of lignin to give rigidity and strength to cell walls for growing upright, evolution of tracheid cells for water transport and sieve cells for nutrient transport, and the use of underground stems (rhizomes) as a structure from which adventitious roots originate. There are two kinds of vascular plants: non-seeded and seeded. The non-seeded vascular plants divisions include Division Lycophyta – club moses, Division Sphenophyta – horsetails, and Division Pterophyta – ferns. The seeded vascular plants differ from the non-seeded plants by their method of reproduction, which will be discussed later.

The vascular seed plants are divided into two groups, the gymnosperms and the angiosperms. **Gymnosperms** were the first plants to evolve with the use of seeds for reproduction that made them less dependent on water to assist in reproduction. Their seeds and the pollen from the male are carried by the wind. Gymnosperms have cones that protect the seeds. Gymnosperm divisions include Division Cycadophyta – cycads, Division Ginkgophyta – ginkgo, Division Gnetophyta – gnetophytes, and Division Coniferophyta – conifers.

Angiosperms are the largest group in the plant kingdom. They are the flowering plants and produce true seeds for reproduction. They arose about seventy million years ago when the dinosaurs were disappearing. The land was drying up and the plants' ability to produce seeds that could remain dormant until conditions became acceptable allowed for their success. They also have more advanced vascular tissue and larger leaves for increased photosynthesis. Angiosperms consist of only one division, the Anthrophyta. Angiosperms are divided into monocots and dicots. Monocots have one cotelydon (seed leaf) and parallel veins on their leaves. Their flower petals are in multiples of threes. Dicots have two cotelydons and branching veins on their leaves. Flower petals are in multiples of fours or fives.

In aquatic environments, the inhabitants can be greatly affected by changes in conductivity, oxygen levels and pH.

Conductivity

The conductivity of the water is affected by the presence of dissolved inorganic molecules. The cations sodium, magnesium, calcium, iron, and aluminum affect the conductivity of the water as do the anions chloride nitrate, sulfate and phosphate. The higher the temperature of the water, the higher the conductivity. Most aquatic organisms can withstand conductivity between 0.150 mS/cm (millisiemens/centimeter) and 0.50 mS/cm. A conductivity beyond this range will have adverse effects on the aquatic life. Surrounding some industrial areas, the conductivity of the water can reach as high as 10 mS/cm, killing all of the aquatic life in the area.

Dissolved oxygen

Oxygen enters the water through photosynthesis in aquatic plants and through contact with the atmosphere. The amount of dissolved oxygen in the water varies with the season due to the photosynthesis that takes place in the aquatic plants. However, cold water has the ability to hold more dissolved gases than warm water. Therefore, warm water can become more easily saturated with oxygen because it called hold less dissolved oxygen. In the summer, aquatic organisms begin to suffer at levels below 7mg/L dissolved oxygen with production impairment. Four mg/L is the acute mortality level for many organisms.

pH

pH is the measure of the amount of hydrogen ions dissolved in water. A change in 1 pH unit is a 10 fold change in Hydrogen ion concentration. Most freshwater environments have a pH of between 6 and 8. As acidity increases, the negative effect on the organisms increases. Water that has a pH of 5 becomes invaded with plankton and moss. Small fish begin to disappear. At a pH of 4.5, all fish are killed. Alkaline water has a similar effect on aquatic organisms. Fish in water with a pH of 9.6 start to see damage to gills, eyes, and skin. At higher pH levels, fish begin to die and algae can bloom.

Skill 29.3   The beginning teacher explains the uses and limitations of classification schemes.

Phentics is a form of numerical taxonomy where the organisms are classified according to their similarities. The characteristics of a group of organisms are measured and calculated. A coefficient of a 1 is an exact match; a coefficient of 0 is an absolute dissimilarity. This form of classification is rarely used as it has a very high tendency to group unrelated organisms together. Homologous (the similarity in development and ancestry) and analogous (the similarity in function and appearance) are not distinguished in phentics.

Cladistics is the most widely used type of classification system. The Classification in cladistics is based on the way in which evolutionary lines branch from one another. It is used to relate one species to another. New species are classified as they evolve from older similar species. Cladistics does not recognize hybridization as a method of species development.

Evolutionary taxonomy, also called classical taxonomy, is a mixture of phenetics and cladistics. The evolution and the morphology of the organism are used to classify. Evolutionary taxonomy is subjective in how much evolution links and how many similarities should be used to classify the organism.

Skill 29.4   The beginning teacher relates taxonomic classification to evolutionary history and knows how to distinguish between traits that are taxonomically useful (e.g., homologous traits) and those that are not (e.g., convergent traits).

It is believed that there are probably over ten million different species of living things. Of these, 1.5 million have been named and classified. Systems of classification show similarities and also assist scientists with a world-wide system of organization.

Several different morphological criteria are used to classify organisms:

1. **Ancestral characters** - characteristics that are unchanged after evolution (ie: 5 digits on the hand of an ape).

2. **Derived characters** - characteristics that have evolved more recently (ie: the absence of a tail on an ape).

3. **Conservative characters** - traits that change slowly.

4. **Homologous characters** - characteristics with the same genetic basis but used for a different function. (ie: wing of a bat, arm of a human. The bone structure is the same, but the limbs are used for different purposes).

5. **Analogous characters** – structures that differ, but used for similar purposes (ie- the wing of a bird and the wing of a butterfly).

6. **Convergent evolution** - development of similar adaptations by organisms that are unrelated.

Biological characteristics are also used to classify organisms. Protein comparison, DNA comparison, and analysis of fossilized DNA are powerful comparative methods used to measure evolutionary relationships between species. Taxonomists consider the organism's life history, biochemical (DNA) makeup, behavior, and how the organisms are distributed geographically. The fossil record is also used to show evolutionary relationships.

Skill 29.5   The beginning teacher analyzes relationships among organisms to develop a model of a hierarchical classification system and knows how to classify aquatic and terrestrial organisms at several taxonomic levels (e.g., species, phylum/division, kingdom) using dichotomous keys.

Carolus Linnaeus is termed the father of taxonomy. **Taxonomy** is the science of classification. Linnaeus based his system on morphology (study of structure). Later on, evolutionary relationships (phylogeny) were also used to sort and group species. The modern classification system uses binomial nomenclature. This consists of a two word name for every species. The genus is the first part of the name and the species is the second part. Notice in the levels explained below that Homo sapiens is the scientific name for humans. Starting with the kingdom, the groups get smaller and more alike as one moves down the levels in the classification of humans:

Kingdom: Animalia, Phylum: Chordata, Subphylum: Vertebrata, Class: Mammalia, Order: Primate, Family: Hominidae, Genus: Homo, Species: sapiens

Species are defined by the ability to successfully reproduce with members of their own kind.

Dichotomous Key

A dichotomous key is a biological tool for identifying unknown organisms to some taxonomic level. It is constructed of a series of couplets, each consisting of two statements describing characteristics of a particular organism or group of organisms. A choice between the statements is made that bet fits the organism in question. The statements typically begin with broad characteristics and become narrower as more choices are needed.

Example: A – Numerical key

    1. Seeds round – soybeans
    1   Seeds oblong – 2
    2. Seeds white – northern beans
    2. Seeds black – black beans

    B – Alphabetical key

    A. Seeds oblong – B
    B. Seeds white – northern beans
    B. Seeds black – black beans

Skill 29.6   **The beginning teacher identifies distinguishing characteristics of kingdoms, including monerans (i.e., eubacteria, archaebacteria), protists, fungi, plants, and animals.**

The traditional classification of living things is the five-kingdom system. The five kingdoms are Monera, Protista, Fungi, Plantae, and Animalia. The following is a comparison of the cellular characteristics of members of the five kingdoms.

Kingdom Monera

Members of the Kingdom Monera are single-celled, prokaryotic organisms. Like all prokaryotes, Monerans lack nuclei and other membrane bound organelles, but do contain circular chromosomes and ribosomes. Most Monerans possess a cell wall made of peptidoglycan, a combination of sugars and proteins. Some Monerans also possess capsules and external motility devices (e.g. pili or flagella). The Kingdom Monera includes both eubacteria and archaebacteria. Though archaebacteria are structurally similar to eubacteria in many ways, there are key differences, like cell wall structure (archae lack peptidoglycan).

Kingdom Protista

Protists are eukaryotic, usually single-celled organisms (though some protists are multicellular). The Kingdom Protista is very diverse, containing members with characteristics of plants, animals, and fungi. All protists possess nuclei and some types of protists possess multiple nuclei. Most protists contain many mitochondria for energy production, and photosynthetic protists contain specialized structures called plastids where photosynthesis occurs. Motile protists possess external cilia or flagella. Finally, many protists have cell walls that do not contain cellulose.

Kingdom Fungi

Fungi are eukaryotic organisms that are mostly multicellular (single-celled yeast are the exception). Fungi possess cell walls composed of chitin. Fungal organelles are similar to animal organelles. Fungi are non-photosynthetic and possess neither chloroplasts nor plastids. Many fungal cells, like animal cells, possess centrioles. Fungi are also non-motile and release exoenzymes into the environment to dissolve food.

Kingdom Plantae

Plants are eukaryotic, multicellular, and have square-shaped cells. Plant cells possess rigid cell walls composed mostly of cellulose. Plant cells also contain chloroplasts and plastids for photosynthesis. Plant cells generally do not possess centrioles. Another distinguishing characteristic of plant cells is the presence of a large, central vacuole that occupies 50-90% of the cell interior. The vacuole stores acids, sugars, and wastes. Because of the presence of the vacuole, the cytoplasm is limited to a very small part of the cell.

Kingdom Animalia

Animals are eukaryotic, multicellular, and motile. Animal cells do not possess cell walls or plastids, but do possess a complex system of organelles. Most animal cells also possess centrioles, microtubule structures that play an important role in spindle formation during replication.

The three-domain system of classification, introduced by Carl Woese in 1990, emphasizes the separation of the two types of prokaryotes. The following is a comparison of the cellular characteristics of members of the three domains of living organisms: Eukarya, Bacteria, and Archaea.

Domain Eukarya

The Eukarya domain includes all members of the protist, fungi, plant, and animal kingdoms. Eukaryotic cells possess a membrane bound nucleus and other membranous organelles (e.g. mitochondria, Golgi, ribosomes). The chromosomes of Eukarya are linear and usually complexed with histones (protein spools). The cell membranes of eukaryotes consist of glycerol-ester lipids and sterols. The ribosomes of eukaryotes are 80 Svedburg (S) units in size. Finally, the cell walls of those eukaryotes that have them (i.e. plants, algae, fungi) are polysaccharide in nature.

Domain Bacteria

Prokaryotic members of the Kingdom Monera not classified as Archaea, are members of the Bacteria domain. Bacteria lack a defined nucleus and other membranous organelles. The ribosomes of bacteria measure 70 S units in size. The chromosome of Bacteria is usually a single, circular molecule that is not complexed with histones. The cell membranes of Bacteria lack sterols and consist of glycerol-ester lipids. Finally, most Bacteria possess a cell wall made of peptidoglycan.

Domain Archaea

Members of the Archaea domain are prokaryotic and similar to bacteria in most aspects of cell structure and metabolism. However, transcription and translation in Archaea are similar to the processes of eukaryotes, not bacteria. In addition, the cell membranes of Archaea consist of glycerol-ether lipids in contrast to the glycerol-ester lipids of eukaryotic and bacterial membranes. Finally, the cell walls of Archaea are not made of peptidoglycan, but consist of other polysaccharides, protein, and glycoprotein.

Competency 0030   **The teacher understands that, at all levels of nature, living systems are found within other living systems, each with its own boundaries and limits.**

Skill 30.1   **The beginning teacher identifies the basic requirements (e.g., nutrients, oxygen, water, carbon dioxide) necessary for various organisms to carry out life functions.**

All organisms are adapted to life in their unique habitat. The habitat includes all the components of their physical environment and is a necessity for the species' survival. Below are several key components of a complete habitat that all organisms require.

Food and water

Because all biochemical reactions take place in aqueous environments, all organisms must have access to clean water, even if only infrequently. Organisms also require two types of food: a source of energy (fixed carbon) and a source of nutrients. Autotrophs can fix carbon for themselves, but must have access to certain inorganic precursors. These organisms must also be able to obtain other nutrients, such as nitrogen, from their environment. Hetertrophs, on the other hand, must consume other organisms for both energy and nutrients. The species these organisms use as a food source must be present in their habitat.

Sunlight and air

This need is closely related to that for food and water because almost all species derive some needed nutrients from the sun and atmosphere. Plants require carbon dioxide to photosynthesize and oxygen is required for cellular respiration. Sunlight is also necessary for photosynthesis and is used by many animals to synthesize essential nutrients (i.e. vitamin D).

Shelter and space

The need for shelter and space vary greatly between species. Many plants do not need shelter, per se, but must have adequate soil to spread their roots and acquire nutrients. Certain invasive species can threaten native plants by out-competing them for space. Other types of plants and many animals also require protection from environmental hazards. These locations may facilitate reproduction (for instance, nesting sites) or provide seasonal shelter (for examples, dens and caves used by hibernating species).

Skill 30.2   The beginning teacher compares how various organisms obtain, transform, transport, release, eliminate, and store energy and matter.

Obtaining nutrients

Every living organism has a purpose and must make a living in order to avoid extinction. Organisms try to survive for a specific purpose, be it reproduction, or to advance a colony so that it may reproduce. In order to survive organisms must be able to obtain several basic needs. They must be able to obtain energy and avoid being used as energy, to obtain and conserve water, and to find a space in which they can survive the extremes of abiotic factors.

Organisms obtain food in a variety of methods depending largely on the organism and the environment. Some single-celled organisms obtain food by crawling toward prey, engulfing it and digesting it internally, while others make their own food by using energy from the sun in the same manner that plants do. Plants are able to obtain their food using the sunlight through the process of photosynthesis. The food web demonstrates how animals obtain food, having to catch and digest prey in order to maintain the nutrients and energy to survive. It is important to recognize that the only manner for organisms to obtain food is by taking the energy from another organism. All organisms require a subsystem from which to gain and use energy.

Chemoautotrophs- These organisms are able to obtain energy via the oxidation of inorganic molecules (i.e., hydrogen gas and hydrogen sufide) or methane. This process is known as chemosynthesis. Most chemoautotrophs are bacteria or archaea that thrive in oxygen-poor environments, such as deep sea vents.

Photoautotrophs- Instead of obtaining energy from simple inorganic compounds like the chemoautotrophs, organisms of this type receive energy from sunlight. They employ the process of photosynthesis to create sugar from light, carbon dioxide and water. Most higher plants and algae as well as some bacteria and protists are photoautotrophs.

Heterotrophs- Any organism that requires organic molecules as its source of energy is a heterotroph. These organisms are consumers in the food chain and must obtain nutrition from autotrophs or other heterotrophs. All animals are heterotrophs, as are some fungi and bacteria.

All organisms obtain water either from a water source or from the digestion of other organisms in the same manner they obtain food. Aside from pools of water, lakes, streams, rivers, oceans, etc., organisms must find another source for water. Plants rely on soil for most of the water they absorb. Other organisms which cannot obtain water from a water source must attempt to obtain sufficient water from the food which they consume.

Obtaining space is a matter of survival of the fittest and the ability of organisms to co-exist in the same space. As environmental factors change organisms are often forced to look for new space. They are successful if they are not prey to the predators in the new space and can also obtain the water and food they need to survive.

Storing nutrients

Vacuoles are one of the most common storage compartments used by simple organisms and plants. Though we commonly think of vacuoles as simply the organelle employed by plant cells to maintain turgor pressure, they actually have a variety of functions. For example, in budding yeast cells, vacuoles are used as storage compartments for amino acids. When the yeast cells are deprived of food, proteins are consumed within the vacuoles. This process is known as autophagy. Additionally, protists and macrophages use vacuoles to hold food when they engage in phagocytosis (the cellular intake of large molecules or other cells).

Plants have evolved various methods to store excess food. While some store extra glucose, many plants store starch in their roots and stems. Seeds are often "packaged" with additional stored food in the form of both sugar and starch. Many common examples of such plant "storage devices" are exploited as food by humans. For instance, carrots are large roots packed with the plant's extra food. Most fruits, nuts, and edible seeds also contain many calories intended to nurture the next generation of plants.

In many animals, adipose (fat) tissue is used to store extra metabolic energy for long periods. Excess calories are metabolized by the liver into fat. This, along with dietary fat, is stored by adipocytes. When this energy is needed by the body, the stored fat can supply be broken down to supply fatty acids and glycerol. Glycerol can be converted to glucose and used as a source of energy for many cells in the body, while fatty acids are especially needed by the heart and skeletal muscle. The storage and use of this fat is under the control of several hormones including insulin, glucagons, and epinephrine.

Transport of nutrients

Complex, multi-cellular organisms must have systems to distribute nutrients to all their various tissues. The following describes these systems in plants and animals.

Plants

Most of the large, complex plants are termed vascular plants because they possess specialized tissues to transport water. Vascular plants include ferns, clubmosses, horsetails, all flowering plants, conifers and gymnosperms. Remember that plants synthesize glucose through photosynthesis in their leaves and obtain water and certain nutrients (nitrogen, phosphorus) through their roots. Thus, the vascular system in plants consists of xylem and phloem. The xylem carries water and inorganic solutes up from the roots, while the phloem carries the organic solutes (mostly sugars) from the leaves to the rest of the plant. Note that there are certain simple plants, such as mosses, liverworts, and hornworts that are nonvascular. These plants must rely on diffusion alone to distribute water and nutrients. Therefore, the size that these plants may grow to is limited.

Animals

The equivalent of plants' xylem/phloem system in animals is the circulatory system. As in plants, the very simplest animals are nonvascular. Flatworms, for instance, lack circulatory systems. Their mouths lead directly to highly branched digestive systems. Nutrients, water, and gas simply diffuse from the digestive system into all the cells in the flatworm. Relying on diffusion alone to transport nutrients, of course, limits the size and complexity of organisms.

The circulatory system in any animal serves to deliver gases (oxygen) as well as nutrients from the digestive system to all the tissues of the body. Certain animals, including mollusks and arthropods, possess open circulatory systems. The circulatory fluid, called hemolymph, in these animals is rather like a combination of the blood and interstitial fluid present in higher species. The heart pumps the hemolymph into a fairly large, open cavity called the hemocoel. In the hemocoel, the hemolymph directly bathes all the animal's tissues and delivers nutrients. The hemolymph is composed of water, electrolytes, and organic compounds (carbohydrates, proteins, etc).

Higher species have closed circulatory systems, in which blood is always contained within arteries, capillaries, and veins. In these systems, the blood passes through tiny capillaries in the lungs and small intestines and absorbs oxygen and nutrients, respectively. The blood is pumped to all the tissues of the body, where the oxygen and nutrients diffuse out through more tiny capillaries. In general, arteries take oxygen and nutrients to the tissues, while veins return the blood to the heart. The various species have developed closed circulatory systems of varying complexity. Fish, for example have only a two chambered heart, while amphibians have three chambered hearts. Birds and mammals, however, have 4 chambered hearts, allowing complete separation between blood being pumped to and from the body and blood pumped to and from the lungs. To extract nutrients from their food and use these nutrients to carry on biological processes, all organisms engage in metabolism. Metabolism is simply defined as the biochemical modification of compounds by living organisms. Metabolism encompasses both anabolism, the synthesis of organic molecules and catabolism, the breakdown of organic molecules. Sequential, tightly regulated steps of specialized structures and enzymes are typically required in all metabolic pathways.

Using nutrients

As described above, autotrophs obtain the bulk of their food via either photosynthesis or chemosynthesis, which are anabolic processes. The organisms may also absorb some additional simple nutrients from the environment, such as the water and nitrogen plants take up through their roots. Heterotrophs, on the other hand, typically obtain complex organic nutrients by consuming autotrophs or other heterotrophs. Digestion is the first metabolic process these organisms must undertake to obtain nutrients. During this catabolic process, substances are chemically and mechanically broken down to liberate the simpler nutrients that can serve as energy or raw materials for the organism's catabolic pathways. Important processes include carbohydrate metabolism, fatty acid metabolism, and protein metabolism.

Once an organism has obtained these simple building blocks it can use them in a variety of anabolic pathways that allow synthesis of proteins, hormones, fat, starches, and the like. These components, in turn, are processed into cells and tissues that allow the organisms to perform all their specific biological processes. Additionally, the energy in glucose is converted to ATP, which supplies the power necessary for many of these biological processes as well as mobility of the entire organism (where applicable).

Skill 30.3 **The beginning teacher analyzes characteristics, functions, and relationships of systems in animals including humans (e.g., digestive, circulatory, nervous, endocrine, reproductive, integumentary, skeletal, respiratory, muscular, excretory, immune systems).**

HUMAN MUSCULAR SYSTEM

The muscular system's function is for movement. There are three types of muscle tissue. **Skeletal muscle** is voluntary. These muscles are attached to bones and are responsible for their movement. Skeletal muscle consists of long fibers and is striated due to the repeating patterns of the myofilaments (made of the proteins actin and myosin) that make up the fibers.

Cardiac muscle is found in the heart. Cardiac muscle is striated like skeletal muscle, but differs in that plasma membrane of the cardiac muscle causes the muscle to beat even when away from the heart. The action potentials of cardiac and skeletal muscles also differ.

Smooth muscle is involuntary. It is found in organs and enable functions such as digestion and respiration. Unlike skeletal and cardiac muscle, smooth muscle is not striated. Smooth muscle has less myosin and does not generate as much tension as the striated muscles.

A nerve impulse strikes a muscle fiber. This causes calcium ions to flood the sarcomere. Calcium ions allow ATP to expend energy. The myosin fibers creep along the actin, causing the muscle to contract. Once the nerve impulse has passed, calcium is pumped out and the contraction ends.

HUMAN SKELETAL SYSTEM

The axial skeleton consists of the bones of the skull and vertebrae. The appendicular skeleton consists of the bones of the legs, arms and tail, and shoulder girdle. Bone is a connective tissue. Parts of the bone include compact bone which gives strength, spongy bone which contains red marrow to make blood cells, yellow marrow in the center of long bones to store fat cells, and the periosteum which is the protective covering on the outside of the bone.

A joint is defined as a place where two bones meet. Joints enable movement. Ligaments attach bone to bone. Tendons attach bone to muscle. Joints allow great flexibility in movement. There are three types of joints:

1. Ball and socket – allows for rotation movement. An example is the joint between the shoulder and the humerus. This joint allows humans to move their arms and legs in many different ways.
2. Hinge – movement is restricted to a single plane. An example is the joint between the humerus and the ulna.
3. Pivot – allows for the rotation of the forearm at the elbow and the hands at the wrist.

HUMAN INTEGUMENTARY SYSTEM

The skin consists of two distinct layers. The epidermis is the thinner outer layer and the dermis is the thicker inner layer. Layers of tightly packed epithelial cells make up the epidermis. The tight packaging of the epithelial cells supports the skin's function as a protective barrier against infection.

The top layer of the epidermis consists of dead skin cells and is filled with keratin, a waterproofing protein. The dermis layer consists of connective tissue. It contains blood vessels, hair follicles, sweat glands, and sebaceous glands. An oily secretion called sebum, produced by the sebaceous gland, is released to the outer epidermis through the hair follicles. Sebum maintains the pH of the skin between 3 and 5, which inhibits most microorganism growth.

The skin also plays a role in thermoregulation. Increased body temperature causes skin blood vessels to dilate, resulting in heat radiating from the skin's surface. The sweat glands are also activated, increasing evaporative cooling. Decreased body temperature causes skin blood vessels to constrict. This results in blood from the skin diverting to deeper tissues and reduces heat loss from the surface of the skin.

HUMAN RESPIRATORY AND EXCRETORY SYSTEMS

The lungs are the respiratory surface of the human respiratory system. A dense net of capillaries contained just beneath the epithelium form the respiratory surface. The surface area of the epithelium is about $100m^2$ in humans. Based on the surface area, the volume of air inhaled and exhaled is the tidal volume. This is normally about 500mL in adults. Vital capacity is the maximum volume the lungs can inhale and exhale. This is usually around 3400mL.

The kidneys are the primary organ in the excretory system. The pair of kidneys in humans are about 10cm long each. They receive about 20% of the blood pumped with each heartbeat despite their small size. The function of the excretory system is to rid the body of nitrogenous wastes in the form of urea.

The respiratory system functions in the gas exchange of oxygen and carbon dioxide waste. It delivers oxygen to the bloodstream and picks up carbon dioxide for release out of the body. Air enters the mouth and nose, where it is warmed, moistened and filtered of dust and particles. Cilia in the trachea trap unwanted material in mucus, which can be expelled. The trachea splits into two bronchial tubes and the bronchial tubes divide into smaller and smaller bronchioles in the lungs. The internal surface of the lung is composed of alveoli, which are thin walled air sacs. These allow for a large surface area for gas exchange. The alveoli are lined with capillaries. Oxygen diffuses into the bloodstream and carbon dioxide diffuses out of the capillaries to be exhaled out of the lungs due to partial pressure. The oxygenated blood is carried to the heart and delivered to all parts of the body by hemoglobin, a protein consisting of iron.

The thoracic cavity holds the lungs. The diaphragm muscle below the lungs is an adaptation that makes inhalation possible. As the volume of the thoracic cavity increases, the diaphragm muscle flattens out and inhalation occurs. When the diaphragm relaxes, exhalation occurs.

The functional unit of excretion is the nephron, which makes up the kidneys. The structures of the excretory system and the nephron are as follows:

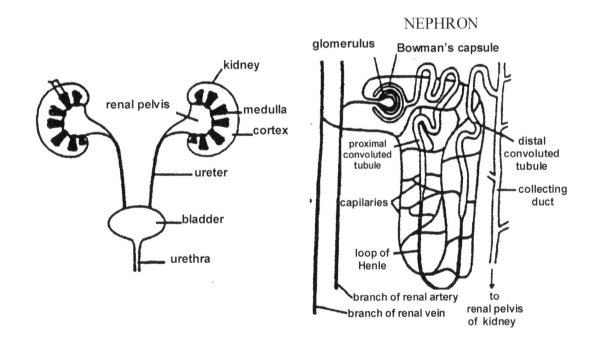

The Bowman's capsule contains the glomerulus, a tightly packed group of capillaries in the nephron. The glomerulus is under high pressure. Water, urea, salts, and other fluids leak out due to pressure into the Bowman's capsule. This fluid waste (filtrate) passes through the three regions of the nephron: the proximal convulated tubule, the loop of Henle, and the distal tubule. In the proximal convoluted tubule, unwanted molecules are secreted into the filtrate. In the loop of Henle, salt is actively pumped out of the tube and much water is lost due to the hyperosmosity of the inner part (medulla) of the kidney. As the fluid enters the distal tubule, more water is reabsorbed. Urine forms in the collecting duct that leads to the ureter then to the bladder where it is stored. Urine is passed from the bladder through the urethra. The amount of water reabsorbed back into the body is dependent upon how much water or fluids an individual has consumed. Urine can be very dilute or very concentrated if dehydration is present.

HUMAN CIRCULATORY AND IMMUNE SYSTEMS

The function of the closed circulatory system (cardiovascular system) is to carry oxygenated blood and nutrients to all cells of the body and return carbon dioxide waste to be expelled from the lungs. The heart, blood vessels, and blood make up the cardiovascular system. The structure of the heart is shown below.

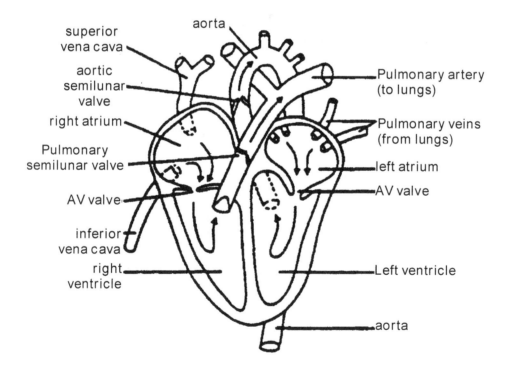

The atria are the chambers that receive blood returning to the heart and the ventricles are the chambers that pump blood out of the heart. There are four valves, two atrioventricular (AV) valves and two semilunar valves. The AV valves are located between each atrium and ventricle. The contraction of the ventricles closes the AV valve to keep blood from flowing back into the atria. The semilunar valves are located where the aorta leaves the left ventricle and the pulmonary artery leaves the right ventricle. The semilunar valves are opened by ventricular contraction to allow blood to be pumped out into the arteries and closed by the relaxation of the ventricles.

The cardiac output is the volume of blood per minute that the left ventricle pumps. This output depends on the heart rate and stroke volume. The **heart rate** is the number of times the heart beats per minute and the **stroke volume** is the amount of blood pumped by the left ventricle each time it contracts. Humans have an average cardiac output of about 5.25 L/min. Heavy exercise can increase cardiac output up to five times. Epinephrine and increased body temperature also increase heart rate and thus the cardiac output.

Cardiac muscle can contract without any signal from the nervous system. It is the sinoatrial node that is the pacemaker of the heart. It is located on the wall of the right atrium and generates electrical impulses that make the cardiac muscle cells contract in unison. The atrioventricular node shortly delays the electrical impulse to ensure the atria empty before the ventricles contract.

There are three kinds of blood vessels in the circulatory system: arteries, capillaries, and veins. **Arteries** carry oxygenated blood away from the heart to organs in the body. Arteries branch off to form smaller arterioles in the organs. The arterioles form tiny **capillaries** that reach every tissue. At their downstream end, capillaries combine to form larger venules. Venules combine to form larger **veins** that return blood to the heart. Arteries and veins are distinguished by the direction in which they carry blood.

Blood vessels are lined by endothelium. In veins and arteries, the endothelium is surrounded by a layer of smooth muscle and an outer layer of elastic connective tissue. Capillaries only consist of the thin endothelium layer and its basement membrane that allows nutrients to be absorbed.

Blood flow velocity decreases as it reaches the capillaries. The capillaries have the smallest diameter of the blood vessels, but this is not why the velocity decreases. The artery conveys blood to such a large amount of capillaries that the blood flow velocity actually decelerates as it enters the capillaries. Blood pressure is the hydrostatic force that blood exerts against the wall of a vessel. Blood pressure is greater in arteries. It is the force that conveys blood from the heart through the arteries and capillaries.

Blood is a connective tissue consisting of the liquid plasma and several kinds of cells. Approximately 60% of the blood is plasma. It contains water salts called electrolytes, nutrients, waste, and proteins. The electrolytes maintain pH of about 7.4. The proteins contribute to blood viscosity and helps maintain pH. Some of the proteins are immunoglobulins are the antibodies that help fend off infection. Another group of proteins are clotting factors.

The lymphatic system is responsible for returning lost fluid and proteins to the blood. Fluid enters lymph capillaries. This lymph fluid is filtered in the lymph nodes filled with white blood cells that fight off infection.

The two classes of cells in blood are red blood cells and white blood cells. **Red blood cells (erythrocytes)** are the most numerous. They contain hemoglobin which carries oxygen.

White blood cells (leukocytes) are larger than red blood cells. They are phagocytic and can engulf invaders. White blood cells are not confined to the blood vessels and can enter the interstitial fluid between cells. There are five types of white blood cells: monocytes, neutophils, basophils, eosinophils, and lymphocytes.

A third cellular element found in blood is platelets. **Platelets** are made in the bone marrow and assist in blood clotting. The neurotransmitter that initiates blood vessel constriction following an injury is called serotonin. A material called prothrombin is converted to thrombin with the help of thromboplastin. The thrombin is then used to convert fibrinogen to fibrin, which traps red blood cells to form a scab and stop blood flow.

HUMAN IMMUNE SYSTEM

The immune system is responsible for defending the body against foreign invaders. There are two defense mechanisms: non specific and specific.

The **non-specific** immune mechanism has two lines of defenses. The first line of defense is the physical barriers of the body. These include the skin and mucous membranes. The skin prevents the penetration of bacteria and viruses as long as there are no abrasions on the skin. Mucous membranes form a protective barrier around the digestive, respiratory, and genitourinary tracts. Also, the pH of the skin and mucous membranes inhibit the growth of many microbes. Mucous secretions (tears and saliva) wash away many microbes and contain lysozyme that kills many microbes.

The second line of defense includes white blood cells and the inflammatory response. **Phagocytosis** is the ingestion of foreign particles. Neutrophils make up about seventy percent of all white blood cells. Monocytes mature to become macrophages, which are the largest phagocytic cells. Eosinophils are also phagocytic. Natural killer cells destroy the body's own infected cells instead of the invading the microbe directly.

The other second line of defense is the inflammatory response. The blood supply to the injured area is increased, causing redness and heat. Swelling also typically occurs with inflammation. Histamine is released by basophils and mast cells when the cells are injured. This triggers the inflammatory response.

The **specific** immune mechanism recognizes specific foreign material and responds by destroying the invader. These mechanisms are specific and diverse. They are able to recognize individual pathogens. An **antigen** is any foreign particle that elicits an immune response. An **antibody** is manufactured by the body and recognizes and latches onto antigens, hopefully destroying them. They also have recognition of foreign material versus the self. Memory of the invaders provides immunity upon further exposure.

Immunity is the body's ability to recognize and destroy an antigen before it causes harm. Active immunity develops after recovery from an infectious disease (i.e. chicken pox) or after a vaccination (mumps, measles, rubella). Passive immunity may be passed from one individual to another and is not permanent. A good example is the immunities passed from mother to nursing child. A baby's immune system is not well developed and the passive immunity they receive through nursing keeps them healthier.

There are two main responses made by the body after exposure to an antigen:

1. **Humoral response** - free antigens activate this response and B cells (a lymphocyte from bone marrow) give rise to plasma cells that secrete antibodies and memory cells that will recognize future exposures to the same antigen. The antibodies defend against extracellular pathogens by binding to the antigen and making them an easy target for phagocytes to engulf and destroy. Antibodies are in a class of proteins called immunoglobulins. There are five major classes of immunoglobulins (Ig) involved in the humoral response: IgM, IgG, IgA, IgD, and IgE.

2. **Cell mediated response** - cells that have been infected activate T cells (a lymphocyte from the thymus). These activated T cells defend against pathogens in the cells or cancer cells by binding to the infected cell and destroying them along with the antigen. T cell receptors on the T helper cells recognize antigens bound to the body's own cells. T helper cells release IL-2 which stimulates other lymphocytes (cytotoxic T cells and B cells). Cytotoxic T cells kill infected host cells by recognizing specific antigens.

Vaccines are antigens given in very small amounts. They stimulate both humoral and cell mediated responses and memory cells recognize future exposure to the antigen so antibodies can be produced much faster.

HUMAN DIGESTIVE SYSTEM

The function of the digestive system is to break food down into nutrients and absorb it into the blood stream where it can be delivered to all cells of the body for use in cellular respiration.

Essential nutrients are those nutrients that the body needs but cannot make. There are four groups of essential nutrients: essential amino acids, essential fatty acids, vitamins, and minerals.

There are about eight essential amino acids that humans need. A lack of these amino acids results in protein deficiency. There are only a few essential fatty acids.

Vitamins are organic molecules essential for a nutritionally adequate diet. Thirteen vitamins essential to humans have been identified. There are two groups of vitamins: water soluble (includes the vitamin B complex and vitamin C) and water insoluble (vitamins A, D and K). Vitamin deficiencies can cause severe problems.

Unlike vitamins, minerals are inorganic molecules. Calcium is needed for bone construction and maintenance. Iron is important in cellular respiration and is a big component of hemoglobin.

Carbohydrates, fats, and proteins are fuel for the generation of ATP. Water is necessary to keep the body hydrated. The importance of water was discussed in previous sections.

The teeth and saliva begin digestion by breaking food down into smaller pieces and lubricating it so it can be swallowed. The lips, cheeks, and tongue form a bolus or ball of food. It is carried down the pharynx by the process of peristalsis (wave-like contractions) and enters the stomach through the sphincter, which closes to keep food from going back up. In the stomach, pepsinogen and hydrochloric acid form pepsin, the enzyme that hydrolyzes proteins. The food is broken down further by this chemical action and is churned into acid chyme. The pyloric sphincter muscle opens to allow the food to enter the small intestine. Most nutrient absorption occurs in the small intestine. Its large surface area, accomplished by its length and protrusions called villi and microvilli, allow for a great absorptive surface into the bloodstream. Chyme is neutralized after coming from the acidic stomach to allow the enzymes found there to function. Accessory organs function in the production of necessary enzymes and bile. The pancreas makes many enzymes to break down food in the small intestine. The liver makes bile, which breaks down and emulsifies fatty acids. Any food left after the trip through the small intestine enters the large intestine. The large intestine functions to reabsorb water and produce vitamin K. The feces, or remaining waste, are passed out through the anus.

HUMAN NERVOUS SYSTEM

The central nervous system (CNS) consists of the brain and spinal cord. The CNS is responsible for the body's response to environmental stimulation. The spinal cord is located inside the spine. It sends out motor commands for movement in response to stimuli. The brain is where responses to more complex stimuli occurs. The meninges are the connective tissues that protect the CNS. The CNS contains fluid filled spaces called ventricles. These ventricles are filled when cerebrospinal fluid which is formed in the brain. This fluid cushions the brain and circulates nutrients, white blood cells, and hormones. The CNS's response to stimuli is a reflex. The reflex is an unconscious, automatic response.

The peripheral nervous system (PNS) consists of the nerves that connect the CNS to the rest of the body. The sensory division brings information to the CNS from sensory receptors and the motor division sends signals from the CNS to effector cells. The motor division consists of somatic nervous system and the autonomic nervous system. The somatic nervous system is controlled consciously in response to external stimuli. The autonomic nervous system is unconsciously controlled by the hypothalamus of the brain to regulate the internal environment. This system is responsible for the movement of smooth and cardiac muscles as well as the muscles for other organ systems.

The **neuron** is the basic unit of the nervous system. It consists of an axon, which carries impulses away from the cell body to the tip of the neuron; the dendrite, which carries impulses toward the cell body; and the cell body, which contains the nucleus. Synapses are spaces between neurons. Chemicals called neurotransmitters are found close to the synapse. The myelin sheath, composed of Schwann cells, cover the neurons and provide insulation.

Nerve action depends on depolarization and an imbalance of electrical charges across the neuron. A polarized nerve has a positive charge outside the neuron. A depolarized nerve has a negative charge outside the neuron.

Neurotransmitters turn off the sodium pump which results in depolarization of the membrane. This wave of depolarization (as it moves from neuron to neuron) carries an electrical impulse. This is actually a wave of opening and closing gates that allows for the flow of ions across the synapse. Nerves have an action potential. There is a threshold of the level of chemicals that must be met or exceeded in order for muscles to respond. This is called the "all or none" response.

HUMAN ENDOCRINE SYSTEM

The function of the endocrine system is to manufacture proteins called hormones. **Hormones** are released into the bloodstream and are carried to a target tissue where they stimulate an action. There are two classes of hormones. Steroid hormones come from cholesterol and include the sex hormones. Peptide hormones are derived from amino acids. Hormones are specific and fit receptors on the target tissue cell surface. The receptor activates an enzyme that converts ATP to cyclic AMP. Cyclic AMP (cAMP) is a second messenger from the cell membrane to the nucleus. The genes found in the nucleus turn on or off to cause a specific response.

Hormones are secreted by endocrine cells, which make up endocrine glands. The major endocrine glands and their hormones are as follows:

Hypothalamus – located in the lower brain; signals the pituitary gland.
Pituitary gland – located at the base of the hypothalamus; releases growth hormones and antidiuretic hormone (retention of water in kidneys).
Thyroid gland – located on the trachea; lowers blood calcium levels (calcitonin) and maintains metabolic processes (thyroxine).
Gonads – located in the testes of the male and the ovaries of the female; testes release androgens to support sperm formation and ovaries release estrogens to stimulate uterine lining growth and progesterone to promote uterine lining growth.
Pancreas – secretes insulin to lower blood glucose levels and glucagon to Raise blood glucose levels.

HUMAN REPRODUCTIVE SYSTEM

Hormones regulate sexual maturation in humans. Humans cannot reproduce until about the puberty age of 8-14, depending on the individual. The hypothalamus begins secreting hormones that help mature the reproductive system and development of the secondary sex characteristics. Reproductive maturity in girls occurs with her first menstruation and occurs in boys with the first ejaculation of viable sperm.

Hormones also regulate reproduction. In males, the primary sex hormones are the androgens, testosterone being the most important. The androgens are produced in the testes and are responsible for the primary and secondary sex characteristics of the male. Female hormone patterns are cyclic and complex. Most women have a reproductive cycle length of about 28 days. The menstrual cycle is specific to the changes in the uterus. The ovarian cycle results in ovulation and occurs in parallel with the menstrual cycle. This parallelism is regulated by hormones. Five hormones participate in this regulation, most notably estrogen and progesterone. Estrogen and progesterone play an important role in the signaling to the uterus and the development and maintenance of the endometruim. Estrogens are also responsible for the secondary sex characteristics of females.

Skill 30.4   The beginning teacher analyzes characteristics, functions, and relationships of systems in plants (e.g., transport, control, reproductive, nutritional, structural systems).

CLASSIFICATION OF PLANTS

The **non-vascular plants** represent a grade of evolution characterized by several primitive features for plants: lack of roots, lack of conducting tissues, rely on absorption of water that falls on the plant or they live in a zone of high humidity, and a lack of leaves or have microphylls (in ferns). Groups included are the liverworts, hornworts, and mosses. Each is recognized as a separate division.

The characteristics of **vascular plants** are as follows: synthesis of lignin to give rigidity and strength to cell walls for growing upright, evolution of tracheid cells for water transport and sieve cells for nutrient transport, and the use of underground stems (rhizomes) as a structure from which adventitious roots originate. There are two kinds of vascular plants: non-seeded and seeded. The non-seeded vascular plants divisions include Division Lycophyta – club moses, Division Sphenophyta – horsetails, and Division Pterophyta – ferns. The seeded vascular plants differ from the non-seeded plants by their method of reproduction.

REPRODUCTION IN PLANTS

Reproduction by plants is accomplished through alternation of generations. Simply stated, a haploid stage in the plants life history alternates with a diploid stage. The diploid sporophyte divides by meiosis to reduce the chromosome number to the haploid gametophyte generation. The haploid gametophytes undergo mitosis to produce gametes (sperm and eggs). Then, the haploid gametes fertilize to return to the diploid sporophyte stage.

The non-vascular plants need water to reproduce. The vascular non-seeded plants reproduce with spores and also need water to reproduce. Gymnosperms use seeds for reproduction and do not require water.

Angiosperms are the most numerous and are therefore the main focus of reproduction in this section. The sporophyte is the dominant phase in reproduction. Angiosperm reproductive structures are the flowers.

The male gametophytes are pollen grains and the female gametophytes are embryo sacs that are inside of the ovules. The male pollen grains are formed in the anthers at the tips of the stamens. The female ovules are enclosed by the ovaries. Therefore, the stamen is the reproductive organ of the male and the carpel is the reproductive organ of the female.

In a process called **pollination**, the pollen grains are released from the anthers and carried by animals and the wind and land on the carpels. The sperm is released to fertilize the eggs. Angiosperms reproduce through a method of double fertilization. An ovum is fertilized by two sperm. One sperm produces the new plant and the other forms the food supply for the developing plant (endosperm). The ovule develops into a seed and the ovary develops into a fruit. The fruit is then carried by wind or animals and the seeds are dispersed to form new plants.

The development of the egg to form a plant occurs in three stages: growth; morphogenesis, the development of form, and cellular differentiation, the acquisition of a cell's specific structure and function.

TRANSPORT IN PLANTS

Roots absorb water and minerals and exchange gases in the soil. The xylem transports water and minerals, called xylem sap, upwards. This is pulled upwards in a process called **transpiration**. Transpiration is the evaporation of water from leaves. Gases are exchanged through the leaves and photosynthesis occurs. The sugar produced by photosynthesis goes down the phloem in the phloem sap. This sap is transported to the roots and other non-photosynthetic parts of the plant.

ADAPTIVE STRUCTURES OF PLANTS

Plants require adaptations that allow them to absorb light for photosynthesis. Since they are unable to move about, they must evolve methods to allow them to successfully reproduce. As time passed, the plants moved from a water environment to the land. Advantages of life on land included more available light and a higher concentration of carbon dioxide. Originally, there were no predators and less competition for space on land. Plants had to evolve methods of support, reproduction, respiration, and conservation of water once they moved to land. Reproduction by plants is accomplished through alternation of generations. Simply stated, a haploid stage in the plants life history alternates with a diploid stage. A division of labor among plant tissues evolved in order to get water and minerals from the earth as described in the previous section. A wax cuticle is produced to prevent the loss of water. Leaves enabled plants to capture light and carbon dioxide for photosynthesis. Stomata provide openings on the underside of leaves for oxygen to move in or out of the plant and for carbon dioxide to move in. A method of anchorage (roots) evolved. The polymer lignin evolved to give tremendous strength to plants.

Skill 30.5   The beginning teacher identifies methods of reproduction, growth, and development of various plants and animals.

Reproduction in plants is as discussed in the previous skill. Reproduction in animals, particularly humans, will be discussed here.

Gametogenesis is the production of the sperm and egg cells. **Spermatogenesis** begins at puberty in the male. One spermatogonia, the diploid precursor of sperm, produces four sperm. The sperm mature in the seminiferous tubules located in the testes. **Oogenesis**, the production of egg cells (ova), is usually complete by the birth of a female. Egg cells are not released until menstruation begins at puberty. Meiosis forms one ovum with all the cytoplasm and three polar bodies that are reabsorbed by the body. The ovum are stored in the ovaries and released each month from puberty to menopause.

Sperm are stored in the seminiferous tubules in the testes where they mature. Mature sperm are found in the epididymis located on top of the testes. After ejaculation, the sperm travels up the **vas deferens** where they mix with semen made in the prostate and seminal vesicles and travel out the urethra.

Ovulation releases the egg into the fallopian tubes that are ciliated to move the egg along. Fertilization of the egg by the sperm normally occurs in the fallopian tube. If pregnancy does not occur, the egg passes through the uterus and is expelled through the vagina during menstruation. Levels of progesterone and estrogen stimulate menstruation and are affected by the implantation of a fertilized egg so menstruation will not occur.

There are many methods of contraception (birth control) that affect different stages of fertilization. Chemical contraception (birth control pills) prevents ovulation by synthetic estrogen and progesterone. Several barrier methods of contraception are available. Male and female condoms block semen from contacting the egg. Sterilization is another method of birth control. Tubil ligation in women prevents eggs from entering the uterus. A vasectomy in men involves the cutting of the vas deferens. This prevents the sperm from entering the urethra. The most effective method of birth control is abstinence. Worldwide programs have been established to promote abstinence especially amongst teenagers.

If fertilization occurs, the zygote begins dividing apprximately 24 hours later. The resulting cells from a blastocyst and implants in about two to three days in the uterus. Implantation promotes secretion of human chorionic gonadotrophin (HCG). This is what is detected in pregnancy tests. The HCG keeps the level of progesterone elevated to maintain the uterine lining in order to feed the developing embryo until the umbilical cord forms.

Organogenesis, the development of the body organs, occurs during the first trimester of fetal development. The heart begins to beat and all the major structures are present at this time. The fetus grows very rapidly during the second trimester of pregnancy. The fetus is about 30 cm long and is very active at this stage. During the third and last trimester, fetal activity may decrease as the fetus grows. Labor is initiated by oxytocin, which causes labor contractions and dilation of the cervix. Prolactin and oxytocin cause the production of milk.

Animal tissue becomes specialized during development. The ectoderm (outer layer) becomes the epidermis or skin. The mesoderm (middle layer) becomes muscles and other organs beside the gut. The endoderm (inner layer) becomes the gut, also called the archenteron.

Sponges are the simplest animals and lack true tissue. They exhibit no symmetry.

Diploblastic animals have only two germ layers: the ectoderm and endoderm. They have no true digestive system. Diploblastic animals include the Cnideria (jellyfish). They exhibit radial symmetry.

Triploblastic animals have all three germ layers. Triploblastic animals can be further divided into:

Acoelomates - have no defined body cavity. An example is the flatworm (Platyhelminthe), which must absorb food from a host's digestive system.

Pseudocoelomates - have a body cavity but it is not lined by tissue from the mesoderm. An example is the roundworm (Nematoda).

Coelomates - have a true fluid filled body cavity called a coelom derived from the mesoderm. Coelomates can further be divided into **protostomes** and **deuterostomes**. In the development of protostomes, the first opening becomes the mouth and the second opening becomes the anus. The mesoderm splits to form the coelom. In the development of deuterostomes, the mouth develops from the second opening and the anus from the first opening. The mesoderm hollows out to become the coelom. Protostomes include animals in phylums Mollusca, Annelida and Arthropoda. Deuterostomes include animals in phylums Ehinodermata and Vertebrata.

Development is defined as a change in form. Animals go through several stages of development after fertilization of the egg cell:

Cleavage - the first divisions of the fertilized egg. Cleavage continues until the egg becomes a blastula.
Blastula - the blastula is a hollow ball of undifferentiated cells.
Gastrulation - this is the time of tissue differentiation into the separate germ layers, the endoderm, mesoderm and ectoderm.
Neuralation - development of the nervous system.
Organogenesis - the development of the various organs of the body.

Competency 0031   **The teacher understands the processes by which organisms maintain homeostasis.**

Skill 31.1   **The beginning teacher explains the importance of maintaining a stable internal environment.**

Homeostasis is a requirement for regular bodily function. It maintains life by ensuring that life within the body is within specified limits. This includes many areas such as body fluids, temperature, salinity, acidity, ion concentration, nutrients, and waste. Adjustments are made via many small transitions. Homeostasis is not the reason for these ongoing unconscious adjustments. It should be thought of instead as the result of many normal processes in concert.

Skill 31.2   **The beginning teacher describes the relationships among internal feedback mechanisms in maintaining homeostasis.**

Feedback loops in human systems serve to regulate bodily functions in relation to environmental conditions. Positive feedback loops enhance the body's response to external stimuli and promote processes that involve rapid deviation from the initial state. For example, positive feedback loops function in stress response and the regulation of growth and development. Negative feedback loops help maintain stability in spite of environmental changes and function in homeostasis. For example, negative feedback loops function in the regulation of blood glucose levels and the maintenance of body temperature.

Feedback loops regulate the secretion of classical vertebrate hormones in humans. The pituitary gland and hypothalamus respond to varying levels of hormones by increasing or decreasing production and secretion. High levels of a hormone cause down-regulation of the production and secretion pathways, while low levels of a hormone cause up-regulation of the production and secretion pathways.

"Fight or flight" refers to the human body's response to stress or danger. Briefly, as a response to an environmental stressor, the hypothalamus releases a hormone that acts on the pituitary gland, triggering the release of another hormone, adrenocorticotropin (ACTH), into the bloodstream. ACTH then signals the adrenal glands to release the hormones cortisol, epinephrine, and norepinephrine. These three hormones act to ready the body to respond to a threat by increasing blood pressure and heart rate, speeding reaction time, diverting blood to the muscles, and releasing glucose for use by the muscles and brain. The stress-response hormones also down-regulate growth, development, and other non-essential functions. Finally, cortisol completes the "fight or flight" feedback loop by acting on the hypothalamus to stop hormonal production after the threat has passed.

Skill 31.3   The beginning teacher identifies anatomical structures and physiological processes in a variety of organisms that function to maintain homeostasis in the face of changing environmental conditions.

Homeostasis is the maintenance of the internal environment within tolerable limits that enable an organism's life systems to function properly.

Physiological Processes

Internal processes that maintain biological homeostasis are responsible for reacting to and compensating for bodily changes in order to maintain a state of equilibrium. Internal homeostatic control mechanisms consist of at least three interdependent parts:

1. The **receptor** is the sensing component that monitors and responds to changes in the environment. Upon sensing a stimulus, the receptor sends information to the control center.
2. The **control center** is responsible for setting the range at which a biological variable is maintained. Based on the information received from the receptor, the control center determines an appropriate response.
3. The **effector** provides the control center's response to the stimulus by affecting the receptor. The effector may either depress the receptor's response to the stimulus through negative feedback, or enhance its response to the stimulus through positive feedback.

Negative feedback mechanisms reduce or suppress the original stimulus, thus reversing the direction of the biological change. Most homeostatic control mechanisms maintain tolerable biological conditions within a set and narrow range using a negative feedback loop. Such mechanisms include thermoregulation, osmoregulation and glucoregulation.

Positive feedback mechanisms accelerate or enhance the output created by a stimulus that has already been activated. Positive feedback mechanisms push biological conditions out of normal range through a series of cascading events that build to increase the effect of the stimulus. Examples of positive feedback within the body are rare. One such example is the continuous enhancement of release of oxytocin to intensify contractions during childbirth. Biological conditions and levels maintained by homeostasis include:

- Blood pH - controlled by both nervous and endocrine system
- Water potential - controlled by the endocrine system, kidneys and ADH
- Oxygen and CO_2 concentrations - controlled by the nervous system, ventilation rate, etc.
- Blood glucose - controlled by the endocrine system, glucagon and insulin
- Body temperature - controlled by the nervous and endocrine systems

Anatomical Structures

Pancreas

The pancreas contributes to the maintenance of biological homeostasis through its role in blood sugar regulation. The pancreas is capable of releasing two different types of hormones into the blood stream that target the liver: Glycagon, the hormone that signals the liver to convert stored glycogen to glucose for bodily use, and insulin, the hormone needed for carbohydrate metabolism. The receptors of the pancreas are responsible for monitoring glucose levels in the blood. When these receptors detect high glucose levels, the pancreas responds by releasing less glucagon and more insulin. When glucose levels are low, the pancreas releases more glucagon and less insulin.

Kidneys

The kidney is responsible for maintaining osmolarity - the measure of the concentration of substances such as sodium, chloride, potassium, urea, glucose, and other ions in human blood. Maintaining body fluids at a constant osmolarity involves regulating the volume of water contained within the body. The volume of water excreted by the kidney is controlled by the anti-diuretic hormone (ADH or vasopressin). When body fluid level falls below normal, the subsequent increase in osmolarity is detected by osmoreceptors in the hypothalamus, which releases ADH causing the kidneys to recover the maximum amount of fluid possible from the urine. When body fluid levels are above normal, the hypothalamus will stop producing ADH, and the kidneys will allow the body to excrete more fluid. The kidneys also affect homeostasis through the maintenance of the body's salt balance. If there is insufficient salt within the body (insufficient Na+), the kidney initiates the renin-angiotensin-aldosterone pathway. Through this pathway, the kidney retains more Na+ from the urine.

Structures involved in temperature regulation

The skin and the hypothalamus possess thermoreceptors. The skin is responsible for sensing external environmental temperature, and the hypothalamus is responsible for sensing internal temperature. A cold external stimulus is relayed to the cerebrum and hypothalamus. The cerebrum elicits a behavioral response, such as putting on more clothing. The hypothalamus releases thyroid releasing hormone (TRH) that causes the pituitary gland to release thyroid stimulating hormone (TSH). TSH causes the thyroid to produce thyroxin, which causes vasoconstriction, reduced sweating, hair follicle raising, shivering and increased metabolic rate. A warm external stimulus leads to the following changes through the same hormone pathway: increased sweating, vasodilation, skin hair lowering and reduced metabolic rate.

Skill 31.4   The beginning teacher analyzes the importance of nutrition, environmental conditions, and physical exercise on health in humans and other organisms.

While genetics plays an important role in health, human behaviors can greatly affect short- and long-term health both positively and negatively. Behaviors that negatively affect health include smoking, excessive alcohol consumption, substance abuse, and poor eating habits. Behaviors that positively affect health include good nutrition and regular exercise.

A healthy diet and regular exercise are the cornerstones of a healthy lifestyle. A diet rich in whole grains, fruits, vegetables, polyunsaturated fats, and lean protein and low in saturated fat and sugar, can positively affect overall health. Such diets can reduce cholesterol levels, lower blood pressure, and help manage body weight. Conversely, diets high in saturated fat and sugar can contribute to weight gain, heart disease, strokes, and cancer.

Finally, regular exercise has both short- and long-term health benefits. Exercise increases physical fitness, improving energy levels, overall body function, and mental well-being. Long-term, exercise helps protect against chronic diseases, maintains healthy bones and muscles, helps maintain a healthy body weight, and strengthens the body's immune system.

Skill 31.5   The beginning teacher analyzes the role of viruses and microorganisms in maintaining or disrupting homeostasis in different organisms (e.g., the role of bacteria in digestion, diseases of plants and animals).

Although bacteria and fungi may cause disease, they are also beneficial for use as medicines and food. Penicillin is derived from a fungus that is capable of destroying the cell wall of bacteria. Most antibiotics work in this way. Some antibiotics can interfere with bacterial DNA replication or can disrupt the bacterial ribosome without affecting the host cells. Viral diseases have been fought through the use of vaccination, where a small amount of the virus is introduced so the immune system is able to recognize it upon later infection. Antibodies are more quickly manufactured when the host has had prior exposure.

The human stomach is lined with healthy bacteria that aid in digestion. Healthy bacteria also line the human mouth and vagina. In these instances it is the absence of bacteria that causes illness. In an effort to maintain a healthy diet, many people consume probiotics, such as yogurt, that are rich in bacterial cultures.

The majority of prokaryotes decompose material for use by the environment and other organisms. The eukaryotic fungi are the most important decomposers in the biosphere. They break down organic material to be used by other living organisms.

Competency 0032   **The teacher understands the relationship between biology and behavior.**

Skill 32.1   **The beginning teacher understands how the behavior of organisms, including humans, responds to internal and external stimuli.**

Response to stimuli is one of the key characteristics of any living thing. Any detectable change in the internal or external environment (the stimulus) may trigger a response in an organism. Just like physical characteristics, organsisms' responses to stimuli are adaptations that allow them to better survive. While these responses may be more noticeable in animals that can move quickly, all organisms are actually capable of responding to changes.

Single celled organisms

These organisms are able to respond to basic stimuli such as the presence of light, heat, or food. Changes in the environment are typically sensed via cell surface receptors. These organisms may respond to such stimuli by making changes in internal biochemical pathways or initiating reproduction or phagocytosis. Those capable of simple motility, using flagella for instance, may respond by moving toward food or away from heat.

Plants

Plants typically do not possess sensory organs and so individual cells recognize stimuli through a variety of pathways. When many cells respond to stimuli together, a response becomes apparent. Logically then, the responses of plants occur on a rather longer timescale that those of animals. Plants are capable of responding to a few basic stimuli including light, water and gravity. Some common examples include the way plants turn and grow toward the sun, the sprouting of seeds when exposed to warmth and moisture, and the growth of roots in the direction of gravity.

Animals

Lower members of the animal kingdom have responses similar to those seen in single celled organisms. However, higher animals have developed complex systems to detect and respond to stimuli. The nervous system, sensory organs (eyes, ears, skin, etc), and muscle tissue all allow animals to sense and quickly respond to changes in their environment.

As in other organisms, many responses to stimuli in animals are involuntary. For example, pupils dilate in response to the reduction of light. Such reactions are typically called reflexes. However, many animals are also capable of voluntary response. In many animal species, voluntary reactions are instinctual. For instance, a zebra's response to a lion is a *voluntary* one, but, *instinctually*, it will flee quickly as soon as the lion's presence is sensed. Complex responses, which may or may not be instinctual, are typically termed behavior. An example is the annual migration of birds when seasons change. Even more complex social behavior is seen in animals that live in large groups.

Skill 32.2 **The beginning teacher recognizes that behavior in many animals is determined by a combination of genetic and learned factors.**

Animal behavior is responsible for courtship leading to mating, communication between species, territoriality, and aggression between animals and dominance within a group. Behaviors may include body posture, mating calls, display of feathers or fur, coloration or bearing of teeth and claws.

Innate behaviors are inborn or instinctual. An environmental stimulus such as the length of day or temperature results in a behavior. Hibernation among some animals is an innate behavior. **Learned behavior** is modified due to past experience.

Skill 32.3 **The beginning teacher identifies adaptive advantages of innate and learned patterns of behavior.**

Like so many factors affecting behavior, evolutionary history also does affect behavior. Ecology influences the evolutionary behavior. There are two factors that have profound influence on the behavior of animals – one is the phylogenetic characters and the other is the adaptive significance.

The factors that prevent certain groups of animals from doing certain things, for example, flying, are called phylogenetic constraints. Mammals can't fly, where as birds can. The fact that birds fly and mammals can't fly is no coincidence. The evolutionary history of these characters has helped the birds to fully develop their ability to fly. At the same time, if the birds are not threatened by predators, there is every chance that these same birds may gradually lose their ability to fly. This is evident in New Zealand, where there were no mammals, until the Europeans settled there. There used to be a higher proportion of flightless birds residing there.

Finally, all behavior is subject to natural selection as with the other traits of an animal. This emphasizes the fact that animals that are well adapted sire many offspring compared to those not so organized in their behavioral adaptation.

Evolutionary Stable strategy (ESS) is another driving force in the evolution of behavior. There are two factors that influence animal behavior – one is the optimal behavior, giving maximum benefit to the animal, and the other is the behavior adapted by the population of which it is a member.

It is important to bear in mind that evolution is not only driven by the physical environment of the animal, but also the interaction between other individuals.

Skill 32.4   The beginning teacher explains mediating factors in innate (e.g., imprinting, hormonal system) and learned (e.g., classical conditioning, play) behavior.

Innate behavior

Innate behaviors are "hard wired" into the central nervous system. A stimulus triggers a response in the central nervous system. Withdraw reflexes, such as when you pull back from a hot object, are innate behaviors. Instinctual behavior is also a form of innate behavior. Behaviors such as nesting, grooming, and foraging are all forms of innate behavior. Hormonal systems are also a form of innate behavior. Organisms will mate when the amount of estrogen or testosterone in their blood is enough to send mating signals. These mating signals may be indicated by pheromones or by a physical response in the organism (i.e. swelling of hindquarters in baboons).

Learned behavior

Learned behavior relies on the experience of the organism. **Classical conditioning** pairs a neutral stimulus with an unconditional stimulus in order to get a response. After linking the neutral stimulus and the unconditional stimulus several times, the organism learns that one equals the other. Therefore, if you take away the unconditional stimulus but keep the neutral stimulus, the response will be the same as if the unconditional stimulus remained.

Behavior scientists have found it difficult to explain play behavior. **Play** is a learned behavior that stems from interactions with other animals.

Imprinting is also a learned behavior. In imprinting, an animal, having no prior knowledge of its parents, will learn to follow another species making reasonable sounds of reasonable volume as its own parent.

Skill 32.5   The beginning teacher understands concepts linking behavior and natural selection (e.g., kin selection, courtship behavior, altruism).

Altruism seems counterintuitive to natural selection. In altruism, an organism appears to act in a way that benefits others over itself. "Survival of the fittest" does not seem to apply in these situations. Altruistic behavior is often seen in more complex social groups. An example of altruistic behavior was observed by Watson and Stokes in the study of the mating habits of wild turkey. They observed that there were several groups of male turkeys that had an internal hierarchy. These groups fought for dominance in their mating ritual, spreading their wings, gobbling, and engaging in other **courtship behaviors**. Once the group gained dominance over the other groups, the leader of this group was the one who mated most frequently with the females. It seemed like the other members of the group were altruistically assisting the leader to mate. However, upon closer study, it was found the members of the group were all brothers. This phenomenon is related to **kin selection**, the gene propagation of related individuals. By assisting the dominate turkey in the group mate, the other turkeys are perpetuating their own genes, and thereby "surviving" their clan.

Similar altruistic behaviors can be seen by other animals in nesting behavior. There are certain birds that produce several nests with many eggs. These eggs are more than can be tended to by just the parents. Therefore, siblings of the parents often help raise the young, thereby increasing the chances that the young and therefore their genes survive.

DOMAIN VII.   LIFE AND ENVIRONMENTAL SYSTEMS

Competency 0033   **The teacher understands the relationships between abiotic and biotic factors of terrestrial and aquatic ecosystems, habitats, and biomes, including the flow of matter and energy.**

Skill 33.1   **The beginning teacher analyzes types, sources, and flow of energy through different trophic levels (e.g., producers, consumers, decomposers) and between organisms and the physical environment in aquatic and terrestrial ecosystems.**

Trophic levels are based on the feeding relationships that determine energy flow and chemical cycling.

Autotrophs are the primary producers of the ecosystem. **Producers** mainly consist of plants. **Primary consumers** are the next trophic level. The primary consumers are the herbivores that eat plants or algae. **Secondary consumers** are the carnivores that eat the primary consumers. **Tertiary consumers** eat the secondary consumer. These trophic levels may go higher depending on the ecosystem. **Decomposers** are consumers that feed off animal waste and dead organisms. This pathway of food transfer is known as the food chain.

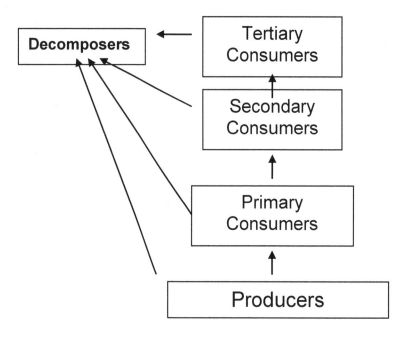

Most food chains are more elaborate, becoming food webs.

Skill 33.2 **The beginning teacher analyzes the flow of energy and the cycling of matter through biogeochemical cycles (e.g., carbon, water, oxygen, nitrogen, phosphorus) in aquatic and terrestrial ecosystems.**

Biogeochemical cycles are nutrient cycles that involve both biotic and abiotic factors.

Water cycle - 2% of all the available water is fixed and unavailable in ice or the bodies of organisms. Available water includes surface water (lakes, ocean, rivers) and ground water (aquifers, wells) 96% of all available water is from ground water. The water cycle is driven by solar energy. Water is recycled through the processes of evaporation and precipitation. The water present now is the water that has been here since our atmosphere formed.

Carbon cycle - Ten percent of all available carbon in the air (from carbon dioxide gas) is fixed by photosynthesis. Plants fix carbon in the form of glucose, animals eat the plants and are able to obtain their source of carbon. When animals release carbon dioxide through respiration, the plants again have a source of carbon to fix again.

Nitrogen cycle - Eighty percent of the atmosphere is in the form of nitrogen gas. Nitrogen must be fixed and taken out of the gaseous form to be incorporated into an organism. Only a few genera of bacteria have the correct enzymes to break the triple bond between nitrogen atoms in a process called nitrogen fixation. These bacteria live within the roots of legumes (peas, beans, alfalfa) and add nitrogen to the soil so it may be taken up by the plant. Nitrogen is necessary to make amino acids and the nitrogenous bases of DNA.

Phosphorus cycle - Phosphorus exists as a mineral and is not found in the atmosphere. Fungi and plant roots have a structure called mycorrhizae that are able to fix insoluble phosphates into useable phosphorus. Urine and decayed matter return phosphorus to the earth where it can be fixed in the plant. Phosphorus is needed for the backbone of DNA and for ATP manufacturing.

Skill 33.3   The beginning teacher understands the concept of limiting factors (e.g., light intensity, temperature, mineral availability) and the effects that they have on the productivity and complexity of different ecosystems (e.g., tropical forest vs. taiga, continental shelf vs. deep ocean).

A limiting factor is the component of a biological process that determines how quickly or slowly the process proceeds. Photosynthesis is the main biological process determining the rate of ecosystem productivity, the rate at which an ecosystem creates biomass. Thus, in evaluating the productivity of an ecosystem, potential limiting factors are light intensity, gas concentrations, and mineral availability. The Law of the Minimum states that the required factor in a given process that is most scarce controls the rate of the process.

One potential limiting factor of ecosystem productivity is light intensity because photosynthesis requires light energy. Light intensity can limit productivity in two ways. First, too little light limits the rate of photosynthesis because the required energy is not available. Second, too much light can damage the photosynthetic system of plants and microorganisms thus slowing the rate of photosynthesis. Decreased photosynthesis equals decreased productivity.

Another potential limiting factor of ecosystem productivity is gas concentrations. Photosynthesis requires carbon dioxide. Thus, increased concentration of carbon dioxide often results in increased productivity. While carbon dioxide is often not the ultimate limiting factor of productivity, increased concentration can indirectly increase rates of photosynthesis in several ways. First, increased carbon dioxide concentration often increases the rate of nitrogen fixation (available nitrogen is another limiting factor of productivity). Second, increased carbon dioxide concentration can decrease the pH of rain, improving the water source of photosynthetic organisms.

Finally, mineral availability also limits ecosystem productivity. Plants require adequate amounts of nitrogen and phosphorus to build many cellular structures. The availability of the inorganic minerals phosphorus and nitrogen often is the main limiting factor of plant biomass production. In other words, in a natural environment phosphorus and nitrogen availability most often limits ecosystem productivity, rather than carbon dioxide concentration or light intensity.

Skill 33.4 **The beginning teacher explains the relationship among abiotic characteristics of different biomes and the adaptations, variations, tolerances, and roles of indigenous plants and animals in these biomes.**

Abiotic and biotic factors play a role in succession. **Biotic factors** are living things in an ecosystem; plants, animals, bacteria, fungi, etc. **Abiotic factors** are non-living aspects of an ecosystem (soil quality, rainfall, temperature, etc).

Abiotic factors affect succession by way of the species that colonize the area. Certain species will or will not survive depending on the weather, climate, or soil makeup. Biotic factors such as inhibition of one species due to another may occur. This may be due to some form of competition between the species.

Biomes are communities and ecosystems that are typical of broad geographic regions. Specific biomes include:

Marine - covers 75% of the Earth. This biome is organized by the depth of the water. The intertidal zone is from the tide line to the edge of the water. The littoral zone is from the water's edge to the open sea. It includes coral reef habitats and is the most densely populated area of the marine biome. The open sea zone is divided into the epipelagic zone and the pelagic zone. The epipelagic zone receives more sunlight and has a larger number of species. The ocean floor is called the benthic zone and is populated with bottom feeders.

Freshwater - closely linked to terrestrial biomes. Lakes, rivers, streams, and swamplands are examples of freshwater biomes.

Tropical Forest - temperature is constant (25 degrees C), the length of daylight is about 24 hours, and located around the area of the equator. In a tropical rainforest, rainfall exceeds 200 cm. per year and has abundant, diverse species of plants and animals. A tropical dry forest gets scarce rainfall and a tropical deciduous forest has wet and dry seasons.

Savanna - temperatures range from 0 - 25 degrees C depending on the location. Rainfall is from 90 to 150 cm per year. It is grassland with scattered individual trees. Plants include shrubs and grasses. The savanna is a transitional biome between the rain forest and the desert. Located in central South America, southern Africa, and parts of Australia.

Desert - temperatures range from 10 - 38 degrees C in hot deserts. Rainfall is under 25 cm per year. Plant species include xerophytes and succulents. Lizards, snakes, and small mammals are common animals. Hot deserts are located in northern Africa, southwestern United States, and the Middle East. Cold deserts are located in the Rocky Mountain region of the United States and much of central Asia.

Temperate Deciduous Forest - temperature ranges from -24 to 38 degrees C. Rainfall is between 65 to 150 cm per year. Deciduous trees are common, as well as deer, bear and squirrels. This biome is located in most of eastern United States, middle Europe, and eastern Asia.

Taiga - coniferous forest; temperatures range from -24 to 22 degrees C. Rainfall is between 35 to 40 cm per year. Taiga is located very north and very south of the equator, getting close to the poles. Plant life includes conifers and plants that can withstand harsh winters. Animals include weasels, mink, and moose. This is the largest terrestrial biome.

Tundra - temperatures range from -28 to 15 degrees C. Rainfall is limited, ranging from 10 to 15 cm per year. The tundra is located even further north and south of the taiga, closer to the poles. Common plants include lichens and mosses. Animals include polar bears and musk ox.

Polar or Permafrost - temperature ranges from -40 to 0 degrees C. It rarely gets above freezing. Rainfall is below 10 cm per year. Most water is bound up as ice. Life is limited.

Chaparral - mild, rainy winters and hot, long, dry summers. Trees do not grow as well here. Spiny shrubs dominate. Regions include the Mediterranean, the California coastline, and southwestern Australia.

Temperate grasslands - similar to savannas, but have cold winters. Regions include parts of Russia, Europe, and the prairie land of central United States.

Competency 0034   **The teacher understands the interdependence and interactions of living things in terrestrial and aquatic ecosystems.**

Skill 34.1   **The beginning teacher understands the concepts of ecosystem, biome, community, habitat, and niche.**

Once an organism is complete, it interacts within its environment, creating another level of organization. Two organisms together (in the case of sexual reproduction) create a **mating pair** and a mating pair reproduces to proliferate the **species**. A **population** is a group of the same species in a specific area. A **community** is a group of populations residing in the same area. Communities that are ecologically similar in regards to temperature, rainfall, and inhabitants are called **biomes**. All of the world's biomes are collectively known as the **biosphere**.

The term **niche** describes the relational position of a species or population in an ecosystem. Niche includes how a population responds to the abundance of its resources and enemies (e.g., by growing when resources are abundant and predators, parasites and pathogens are scarce). Niche also indicates the life history of an organism, habitat and place in the food chain. According to the competitive exclusion principle, no two species can occupy the same niche in the same environment for a long time.

The full range of environmental conditions (biological and physical) under which an organism can exist describes its fundamental niche. Because of the pressure from superior competitors, organisms are driven to occupy a niche much narrower than their previous niche. This is known as the 'realized niche'

Skill 34.2   **The beginning teacher analyzes interactions of organisms, including humans, in the production and consumption of energy (e.g., food chains, food webs, food pyramids) in aquatic and terrestrial ecosystems.**

Energy is lost as the trophic levels progress from producer to tertiary consumer. The amount of energy that is transferred between trophic levels is called the ecological efficiency. The visual of this energy flow is represented in a **pyramid of productivity**.

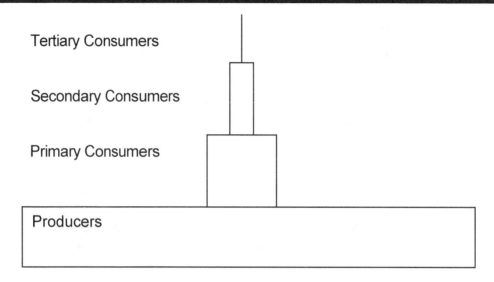

The **biomass pyramid** represents the total dry weight of organisms in each trophic level. A **pyramid of numbers** is a representation of the population size of each trophic level. The producers, being the most populous, are on the bottom of this pyramid with the tertiary consumers on the top with the fewest numbers.

The ultimate source of energy for most ecosystems is solar radiation. Primary producers are usually the organisms in an ecosystem that can convert light energy into chemical energy. Most primary producers are photosynthetic. Photosynthetic primary producers include algae, plants, and many species of bacteria. All other organisms in an ecosystem depend on primary producers to provide energy.

The main primary producers in terrestrial ecosystems are plants. In limnetic (deep-water) zone lake and pond ecosystems and open ocean ecosystems, algae and photosynthetic bacteria are the most important primary producers. In littoral (shallow water, near-shore) zone freshwater and ocean ecosystems, the main primary producers are aquatic plants and multicellular algae. Finally, one notable exception to the photosynthetic organism as primary producer rule are ecosystems near hot water vents on the deep-sea floor. Because solar energy is unavailable, chemoautotrophic bacteria that can oxidize hydrogen sulfide are the primary producers.

Humans are continuously searching for new places to form communities. This encroachment on the environment leads to the destruction of wildlife communities. Conservationists focus on endangered species, but the primary focus should be on protecting the entire biome. If a biome becomes extinct, the wildlife dies or invades another biome. Preservations established by the government aim at protecting small parts of biomes. While beneficial in the conservation of a few areas, the majority of the environment is still unprotected.

Skill 34.3 **The beginning teacher understands interspecific interactions in aquatic and terrestrial ecosystems (e.g., predator-prey relationships, competition, parasitism, commensalism, mutualism) and how they affect ecosystem structure.**

There are many interactions that may occur between different species living together. Predation, parasitism, competition, commensalisms, and mutualism are the different types of relationships populations have amongst each other.

Predation and **parasitism** result in a benefit for one species and a detriment for the other. Predation is when a predator eats its prey. The common conception of predation is of a carnivore consuming other animals. This is one form of predation. Although not always resulting in the death of the plant, herbivory is a form of predation. Some animals eat enough of a plant to cause death. Parasitism involves a predator that lives on or in their hosts, causing detrimental effects to the host. Insects and viruses living off and reproducing in their hosts is an example of parasitism. Many plants and animals have defenses against predators. Some plants have poisonous chemicals that will harm the predator if ingested and some animals are camouflaged so they are harder to detect.

Competition is when two or more species in a community use the same resources. Competition is usually detrimental to both populations. Competition is often difficult to find in nature because competition between two populations is not continuous. Either the weaker population will no longer exist, or one population will evolve to utilize other available resources.

Symbiosis is when two species live close together. Parasitism is one example of symbiosis described above. Another example of symbiosis is commensalisms. **Commensalism** occurs when one species benefits from the other without harmful effects. **Mutualism** is when both species benefit from the other. Species involved in mutualistic relationships must coevolve to survive. As one species evolves, the other must as well if it is to be successful in life. The grouper and a species of shrimp live in a mutualistic relationship. The shrimp feed off parasites living on the grouper; thus the shrimp are fed and the grouper stays healthy. Many microorganisms are in mutualistic relationships.

Skill 34.4 **The beginning teacher identifies indigenous plants and animals, assesses their roles in an ecosystem, and describes their relationships in different types of environments (e.g., fresh water, continental shelf, deep ocean, forest, desert, plains, tundra).**

Please refer to skill 33.4, which outlines biomes and includes examples of the plants and animals that are indigenous to each.

Skill 34.5 **The beginning teacher analyzes how the introduction, removal, or reintroduction of an organism may alter the food chain, affect existing populations, and influence natural selection in terrestrial and aquatic ecosystems.**

An environment is composed of all of the biotic and abiotic factors in a particular area. These biotic and abiotic factors are interdependent and make for a healthy environment. Changing any one of the biotic or abiotic factors can have disastrous affects.

Ecosystems are vulnerable to effects from changes in the climate, human activity, introduction of nonnative species, and changes in population size. Changes in climate can alter the ability of certain organisms to grow. For example, during drought conditions, plants that are less succulent are unable to maintain water regulation and perish. Organisms which previously fed on that particular plant must find a new food source, or they too will perish. When one organism/colony dies, its space is made available for another. For example, after a brush fire, low-lying shrubs are the first to die off. Taller, well-established trees with tough bark are most likely to survive a forest fire. In addition, once the ground cools, new plats will emerge; some identical to the previous, but some new plants may be introduced as there is now a large, open surface area for new species to take root. It is in situations like these that ecosystems are especially vulnerable to the introduction of nonnative species.

The introduction of a nonnative species can effectively wipe out an existing, or indigenous, species. Invasive species are problematic because they reproduce rapidly, spread over large areas, and have few/no natural controls, such as diseases or predators, to keep them in check. For example, Zebra muscles and three different species of rat have all arrived in America as stowaways on ships. Zebra muscles are now established in all the Great Lakes, most of the large, navigable rivers of the eastern United States, and in many lakes in the Great Lakes region. The presence of mussels in the Great Lakes and Hudson River has reduced the biomass of phytoplankton significantly since their accidental introduction in 1980. These nonnative muscles are consuming the phytoplankton on which native species previously fed, and the non-native species are reproducing faster than the native species. Therefore, not only are native muscles affected, but the local food web is affected by a decrease in its beginning nourishment.

As populations increase in size they naturally consume more resources and excrete more waste. These paradoxical behaviors are a drain to an ecosystem. Sometimes an ecosystem can recover from these changes, but sometimes the damage is too severe. This has never been more true than with the human species.

Skill 34.6   The beginning teacher evaluates the importance of biodiversity in an ecosystem and identifies changes that may occur if biodiversity is increased or reduced in an ecosystem.

Biological diversity is the extraordinary variety of living things and ecological communities interacting with each other throughout the world. Maintaining biological diversity is important for many reasons. First, we derive many consumer products used by humans from living organisms in nature. Second, the stability and habitability of the environment depends on the varied contributions of many different organisms. Finally, the cultural traditions of human populations depend on the diversity of the natural-world.

Many pharmacological products of importance to human health have their origins in nature. For example, scientists first harvested aspirin, a derivative of salicylic acid from the bark of willow trees. In addition, nature is also the source of many medicines including antibiotics, anti-malarial drugs, and cancer fighting compounds. However, scientists have yet to study the potential medicinal properties of many plant species, including the majority of rain forest plants. Thus, losing such plants to extinction may result in the loss of promising treatments for human diseases.

The basic stability of ecosystems depends on the interaction and contributions of a wide variety of species. For example, all living organisms require nitrogen to live. Only a select few species of microorganisms can convert atmospheric nitrogen into a form that is usable by most other organisms (nitrogen fixation). Thus, humans and all other organisms depend on the existence of the nitrogen-fixing microbes. In addition, the cycling of carbon, oxygen, and water depends on the contributions of many different types of plants, animals, and microorganisms. Finally, the existence and functioning of a diverse range of species creates healthy, stable ecosystems. Stable ecosystems are more adaptable and less susceptible to extreme events like floods and droughts.

Aside from its scientific value, biological diversity greatly affects human culture and cultural diversity. Human life and culture is tied to natural resources. For example, the availability of certain types of fish defines the culture of many coastal human populations. The disappearance of fish populations because of environmental disruptions changes the entire way of life of a group of people. The loss of cultural diversity, like the loss of biological diversity, diminishes the very fabric of the world population.

Skill 34.7   **The beginning teacher understands types and processes of ecosystem change over time in terrestrial and aquatic ecosystems (e.g., equilibrium, cyclical change, succession) and the effects of human activity on ecosystem change.**

Succession is an orderly process of replacing a community that has been damaged or has begun where no life previously existed. Primary succession occurs where life never existed before, as in a flooded area or a new volcanic island. Secondary succession takes place in communities that were once flourishing but disturbed by some source, either man or nature, but not totally stripped. A climax community is a community that is established and flourishing.

Constancy and change describe the observable properties of natural organisms and events. Constancy refers to a lack of change, and change obviously means something is altered. Scientists use different systems of measurement to observe change and constancy. For example, the freezing and melting points of given substances and the speed of sound are constant. Growth, decay, and erosion are all examples of natural change.

Since its formation some 4.6 billion years ago, Earth has experienced drastic **climate changes**, such as the periods of reduced temperatures known as the Ice Ages. Ice Ages generally result in mass glaciation, which is the expansion of polar and continental ice sheets, as well as mountain glaciers. In reference to the last million years, an Ice Age is a period of colder temperatures during which extensive ice sheets are found over the North American and Eurasian continents.

Thus far, the Earth has experienced four major ice ages. The earliest ice age is believed to have occurred around 2.7 to 2.3 billion years ago during the early Proterozoic Eon. Another ice age occurred during the Crogenian period from 800 to 600 million years ago (mya). A minor ice age occurred from 460 to 430 mya during the Late Ordovician Period. And finally, the Karoo Ice Age lasted from 350 to 260 mya, when extensive polar ice caps appeared at intervals during the Carboniferous and early Permian Periods.

Earth is currently experiencing an Ice Age that began 40 mya with growth of an ice sheet in Antarctica. Around 3 mya, this Ice Age intensified as sheets began to spread in the Northern Hemisphere. Since this time, Earth has experienced cycles of glaciation on 40,000 to 100,000-year time scales. In between ice ages and during times of warmer temperatures within ice ages, extended periods of temperate and/or tropical temperatures may exist. These times are known as interglacial periods. We are currently experiencing an interglacial period during which the Earth's icecaps have decreased by 40 % over the past 40 years.

Skill 34.8 **The beginning teacher explains the significance of plants in different types of terrestrial and aquatic ecosystems.**

Terrestrial plants

Terrestrial plants are significant in many ways. First of all, they provide a food source for animals. As they decompose, they replenish the soil with nutrients. They also act as a ground cover habitat for small animals. Terrestrial plants also are able to prevent soil loss from wind, water, and ice.

Aquatic plants

Aquatic plants (primarily algae) are the largest producers of oxygen in the atmosphere. Aquatic plants act as a carbon dioxide sink. They secure the soil from moving with the tides. Aquatic plants also provide habitat and a food source for aquatic animals.

Competency 0035 **The teacher understands the relationship between carrying capacity and changes in populations and ecosystems.**

Skill 35.1 **The beginning teacher identifies basic characteristics of populations in an ecosystem (e.g., age pyramid, density, patterns of distribution).**

A **population** is a group of individuals of one species that live in the same general area. Many factors can affect the population size and its growth rate. **Population density** is the number of individuals per unit area or volume. The spacing pattern of individuals in an area is dispersion. Dispersion patterns can be clumped, with individuals grouped in patches; uniformed, where individuals are approximately equidistant from each other; or random. Population size can depend on the total amount of life a habitat can support. This is the **carrying capacity** of the environment. Once the habitat runs out of food, water, shelter, or space, the carrying capacity decreases, and then stabilizes.

Limiting factors can affect population growth. As a population increases, the competition for resources is more intense, and the growth rate declines. This is a **density-dependent** growth factor. The carrying capacity can be determined by the density-dependent factor. **Density-independent factors** affect the individuals regardless of population size. The weather and climate are good examples. Too hot or too cold temperatures may kill many individuals from a population that has not reached its carrying capacity.

Skill 35.2 **The beginning teacher compares concepts of population dynamics, including exponential growth, logistic (i.e., limited) growth, and cycling (e.g., boom-and-bust cycles).**

Zero population growth rate occurs when the birth and death rates are equal in a population. Exponential growth rate occurs when there is and abundance of resources and the growth rate is at its maximum, called the intrinsic rate of increase. This relationship can be understood in a growth curve.

An exponentially growing population starts off with a little change, then rapidly increases.

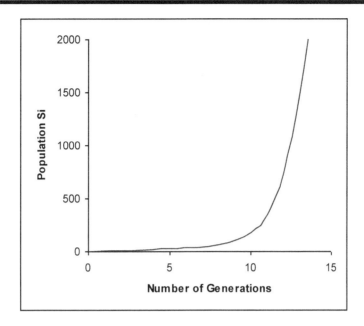

Logistic population growth incorporates the carrying capacity into the growth rate. As a population reaches the carrying capacity, the growth rate begins to slow down and level off.

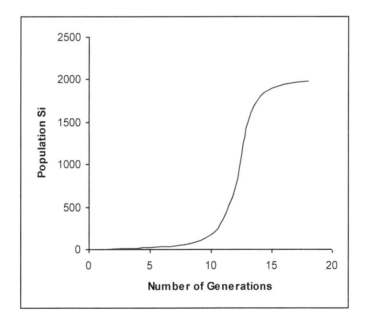

Many populations follow this model of population growth. Humans, however, are an exponentially growing population. Eventually, the carrying capacity of the Earth will be reached, and the growth rate will level off. How and when this will occur remains a mystery.

Skill 35.3   The beginning teacher relates carrying capacity to population dynamics, including human population growth.

Population density is the number of individuals per unit area or volume. The spacing pattern of individuals in an area is dispersion. Dispersion patterns can be clumped, with individuals grouped in patches; uniformed, where individuals are approximately equidistant from each other; or random.

The human population has been growing exponentially for centuries. People are living longer and healthier lives than ever before. Better health care and nutrition practices have helped in the survival of the population. Therefore, humans are an exponentially growing population. Eventually, the carrying capacity of the Earth will be reached, and the growth rate will level off.

Human activity affects parts of the nutrient cycles by removing nutrients from one part of the biosphere and adding them to another. This results in nutrient depletion in one area and nutrient excess in another. This affects water systems, crops, wildlife, and humans.

Humans are responsible for the depletion of the ozone layer. This depletion is due to chemicals used for refrigeration and aerosols. The consequences of ozone depletion will be severe. Ozone protects the Earth from the majority of UV radiation. An increase of UV will promote skin cancer and unknown effects on wildlife and plants.

Skill 35.4   The beginning teacher analyzes the impact of density-dependent and density-independent factors (e.g., geographic locales, natural events, diseases, birth and death rates) on populations.

Population density is the number of individuals per unit area or volume. The spacing pattern of individuals in an area is dispersion. Dispersion patterns can be clumped, with individuals grouped in patches; uniformed, where individuals are approximately equidistant from each other; or random.

Population densities are usually estimated based on a few representative plots. Aggregation of a population in a relatively small geographic area can have detrimental effects to the environment. Food, water, and other resources will be rapidly consumed, resulting in an unstable environment. A low population density is less harmful to the environment. The use of natural resources will be more widespread, allowing for the environment to recover and continue growth.

Population density changes to reflect the rates of birth, immigration, emigration, and death. When birth rates are high, population density increases. Conversely, when death rates are high, density decreases, and when birth and death rates are even, the population has reached equilibrium. The same system is true for immigration and emigration. Immigration swells population density, emigration decreases it, and when the two are balanced the population is level. More consumers in any one area utilize resources, so it stands true that birth and immigration both drain supply, where as emigration and death allow natural resources to replenish themselves.

Skill 35.5   The beginning teacher compares r- and K-selected reproductive strategies (e.g., survivorship curves).

The **r- selected reproductive strategy** stands for rapid selected. Those that have an r-selected strategy mature very quickly and are short lived. Most of these organisms die before they are able to reproduce. Because of this, the organisms that do survive reproduce in great numbers to ensure that some will survive. These organisms, typically pests, are opportunistic and invest very little in their young.

The **K-selected reproductive strategy** occurs in organisms that mature slowly. These organisms have long lives and low juvenile mortality. These organisms have only a few offspring at a time and care for their young. They compete for resources and their population stabilizes near the carrying capacity of the ecosystem.

Survivorship curves compare the percent of the possible life span to the number of survivors to that age in a log scale. There are three types of curves. Type 1 has a high survival rate of young. Many die in old age. This is typical of an organism with a K-selected reproductive strategy, such as elephants. The type 2 curve depicts organisms that have a constant death rate throughout the lifespan of the organism. The type 3 curve depicts a high infant mortality rate with little of the population surviving to old age. The type 3 curve represents organisms with the r-selected reproductive strategy, such as fruit flies.

DOMAIN VIII.   **EARTH'S HISTORY AND THE STRUCTURE AND FUNCTION OF EARTH SYSTEMS**

Competency 0036   **The teacher understands structure and function of the geosphere.**

Skill 36.1   **The beginning teacher analyzes the internal structure and composition of Earth and methods used to investigate Earth's interior (e.g., seismic waves, chemical composition of rocks).**

The interior of the Earth is divided in to three chemically distinct layers. Starting from the middle and moving towards the surface, these are the core, the mantle, and the crust. Much of what we know about the inner structure of the Earth has been inferred from various data. Subsequently, there is still some uncertainty about the composition and conditions in the Earth's interior.

Core

The outer core of the Earth begins about 3000 km beneath the surface and is a liquid, though far more viscous than that of the mantle. Even deeper, approximately 5000 beneath the surface, is the solid inner core. The inner core has a radius of about 1200 km. Temperatures in the core exceed 4000°C. Scientists agree that the core is extremely dense. This conclusion is based on the fact that the Earth is known to have an average density of 5515 kg/m^3 even though the material close to the surface has an average density of only 3000 kg/m^3. Therefore a denser core must exist. Additionally, it is hypothesized that when the Earth was forming, the densest material sank to the middle of the planet. Thus, it is not surprising that the core is about 80% iron. In fact, there is some speculation that the entire inner core is a single iron crystal, while the outer core is a mix of liquid iron and nickel.

Mantle

The Earth's mantle begins about 35 km beneath the surface and stretches all the way to 3000 km beneath the surface, where the outer core begins. Since the mantle stretches so far into the Earth's center, its temperature varies widely; near the boundary with the crust it is approximately 1000°C, while near the outer core it may reach nearly 4000°C. Within the mantle there are silicate rocks, which are rich in iron and magnesium. The silicate rocks exists as solids, but the high heat means they are ductile enough to "flow" over long time scales. In general, the mantle is semi-solid/plastic and the viscosity varies as pressures and temperatures change at varying depths.

Crust

It is not clear how long the Earth has actually had a solid crust; most of the rocks are less than 100 million years, though some are 4.4 billion years old. The crust of the earth is the outermost layer and continues down for between 5 and 70 km beneath the surface. Thin areas generally exist under ocean basins (oceanic crust) and thicker crust underlies the continents (continental crust). Oceanic crust is composed largely of iron magnesium silicate rocks, while continental crust is less dense and consists mainly of sodium potassium aluminum silicate rocks. The crust is the least dense layer of the Earth and so is rich in those materials that "floated" during Earth's formation. Additionally, some heavier elements that bound to lighter materials are present in the crust.

Although no one has ever drilled through the crust, geologists know the composition of the Earth through study of seismic shock waves. The composition and density the materials in the Earth cause sound waves to either slow down or speed up. By measuring the speed of the seismic wave, scientists are able to determine the approximate location and composition of the material. Upon observing the following graph, the P and S waves are visible and are defined.

Skill 36.2   The beginning teacher classifies rocks according to how they are formed as described by the rock cycle (e.g., igneous, sedimentary, metamorphic) and identifies the economic significance of rocks and minerals.

There are three major subdivisions of rocks: sedimentary, metamorphic and igneous.

Igneous rock is also known as basalt. Igneous rock is formed when either sedimentary or metamorphic rock buried deep underground succumbs to heat and pressure and is melted into magma. When the magma cools and hardens the remaining material is igneous rock.

Sedimentary rock is formed when exposed igneous or metamorphic rock erodes away and collects in water. Over time, the eroded particles are fused together by pressure, resulting in sedimentary rock. An example of sedimentary rock is sandstone.

Metamorphic rock is commonly called marble. Metamorphic rock is formed when either sedimentary or basalt rock buried deep in the Earth is surrounded by heat and pressure. These extreme conditions cause the rock to change; hence the new rock is called metamorphic rock.

Minerals are described by their chemical composition, which, within specific limits, can widely vary. These variable compositions consist of end members within a specific group/family/class, and the variability is reflected by the percentage of elements within a specific mineral. The minerals themselves are divided into families and then further subdivided into groups. Mineral classifications within each of the groups reflect both chemical composition and crystalline structure.

Mineral Families include the Native elements (i.e. gold,), Sulfides, Oxides, Halides, Carbonates, and Silicates. Orebites are economically important ore minerals. Minerals such as iron, copper, gold, silver, zinc, lead, and calcium are extracted from base ores through a variety of processes.

Skill 36.3 **The beginning teacher uses physical properties (e.g., density, hardness, streak, cleavage) to identify common minerals and understands processes affecting rock and mineral formation (e.g., temperature, pressure, rate of cooling).**

Primary Identifying Properties

Crystal Habit: the shape of the mineral. Some minerals possess distinctive shapes.

Cleavage: how the mineral breaks under pressure.
Most minerals have a tendency to break in a preferred direction along smooth surfaces. Where the atoms connect, it forms a weak point. In example, Mica *is* resistant to breaking but peels quite easily.

Not all minerals have cleavage. Instead, some have fractures.

Example: They shatter like glass.

Hardness: how hard the mineral is. Hardness is based upon the arrangement of atoms within the crystalline structure. Hardness is graded from 1 to 10, using Mohs Scale of Hardness.

Mohs Scale of Hardness

1. Talc
2. Gypsum
3. Calcite
4. Fluorite
5. Apattte
6. Orthoclase (Feldspar)
7. Quartz
8. Topaz
9. Corundum
10. Diamond

General classification is acceptable based on the scratch test.

Soft: Able to be scratched with a fingernail.
Hard: Able to scratch glass with the mineral.
Medium: not able to be scratched with a fingernail, nor able to scratch glass with the mineral.

Specific Gravity: tile ratio of the mineral's weight to wanter. Because the weight of the mineral is based upon the arrangement of the atoms, minerals will vary in specific gravity. (e.g., water = 1, but rock = 2.65.)

Color: the color of the mineral in solid form. Although some minerals, such as Sulfur, are distinctly colored-always some shade of yellow-it's relatively common to find color variations within the same mineral. As a result, identifying minerals using color as the sole basis for identification can easily lead to misidentification.

Streak: the color of the mineral in powdered form. Some minerals leave a distinctive color streak when the mineral is scratched across a Streak Plate (a piece of unglazed porcelain.)

Additional (Secondary) Identifying Properties

Luster: the surface appearance of the mineral.
Examples of luster are: Pearly, Waxy, Shiny, Dull, Earthy, Glassy.

Magnetism: inherent magnetic qualities.
Example: Magtletite=yes, Quartz=no.

Fluorescence: Soine minerals glow under a black light.
Example: Lapis Lazuli.

Reaction to Acid: Some minerals have a distinctive reaction when exposed to acids.

For example: Any mineral with calcium carbonate ($CaCO_3$) will fizz when diluted hydrochloric acid (HCl) is dropped on it.

Striations: distinctive marks on the surface of the mineral. These marks are usually parallel lines on the mineral surface. In example, Feldspar is often heavily striated.

Taste: Some minerals have a distinctive taste.
Example: Halite (NaCl) (more commonly known as salt.)

Conditions of Formation

Pressure: Rock stays solid longer if it is under pressure.

Presence of Water: Dependent on the pressure, the presence of water can delay or accelerate the melt process.

Slow cooling: forms very large crystals of minerals in the rock. Very large grains are prominent in the rock.

> **Example**: Granite.

Quick Cooling: This allows less time for the crystal to cool and form. It results in smaller—sometimes microscopic-crystals.

> **Example**: Basalt.

Squelching (Instant Cooling): The cooling occurs almost instantaneously when lava flows into the ocean or is thrown into the air by an eruption. No crystals form and the rocks usually have a glassy appearance.

> **Example**: Obsidian.

Skill 36.4   **The beginning teacher identifies different types of landforms and topographic features on the surface of Earth, including the ocean floor (e.g., faults, volcanoes, mid-ocean ridges, deltas).**

Fault: a break in a plane of rock along which one side relative to another is displaced. A fault represents a weakened area of lithospheric crustal material. There is a displacement of the rock materials involved. Faults can move in different directions. There are four main types of faults: Normal, Reverse, Transform and Overthrust.

Normal Fault: The hanging-wall moves downward in relation to the footwall.

Reverse (Thrust) Fault: The hanging-wall moves upward in relation to the footwall.

Transform (Lateral) Fault: No vertical displacement, only lateral movement. Also sometimes called a Creeping Fault.

Overthrust Fault: Both lateral and upward displacement. One place of rock essentially rides over the top of another plane of rock.

Creep (Aseismic Slip): is the small, continuous ground movement that, in many cases, causes little or no damage.

Volcanoes are built where magma, the molten liquid, or semi plastic Earth material located beneath the Earth's crust rises and erupts. Magma is produced at Hot Spots, Spreading Centers, and Subduction Zones and varies in composition according to where it is produced. Warm rock material rises through cracks in the ground according to its viscosity.

There are four major features are found on the sea floor: Continental Margins, Ocean Floor, Ridges, and Trenches.

Continental Margins: where the shore and water meet. There are three types of continental margins: the Continental Shelf, Continental Slope, and Continental Rise.

Continental Shelf: the low slope of land immediately offshore in the ocean. Contains sediment carried off the continents. The sediment buildups the continental shelf to variable widths, and can be cut by canyons known as Submarine Canyons.

Continental Slope: the point where the sediment tumbles into the deep ocean. Much steeper slope than the continental shelf, it extends from the edge of the shelf to the deep ocean floor. Material is tumbled down the slope by Turbidity Currents. However, the most prominent feature is underwater avalanches. Sediment is in the area is very fine and unstable, and it falls off and moves very rapidly. In effect, parts of the continental shelf fall down to the ocean bottom.

Continental Rise: the mound of sediment at the bottom of the continental slope. Formed from the material tumbled off the continental shelf by the turbidity currents.

The Ocean Floor

The ocean floor starts at the end of the continental rise and has an extensive Abyssal Plain. It is a flat, featureless landscape, broken only by ridges or trenches. Covered with deep deposits of sediment, the ocean floor is the flattest topography on Earth.

Ridges

There are two types of ridges, mid-ocean and aseismic.

Mid-Ocean: Characterized by great length and steep slopes, this is the site of sea floor spreading.

Aseismic Ridge: Formed by hot spots, islands, sea mounts, and guyots.

Sea Mount: a volcano that never reached the surface. A sea mount is a pointy topped undersea mountain, usually formed by a hot spot as part of a ridge or chain.

Guyot: a flat-topped undersea mountain. Originally the mountain was above the surface but either erosion and or subsidence of sea floor bulging when the tectonic plate moved off a hot spot, caused it to sink beneath the ocean surface. There is a chain of aseismic guyots linking Midway Island to Hawaii.

Trenches: The deepest parts of the ocean. They break the abysmal plain, have steep slopes, and are found at the sites of subduction zones.

Skill 36.5	**The beginning teacher identifies the types, characteristics, and uses of Earth's renewable and nonrenewable resources including marine resources (e.g., ores, minerals, soil, fossil fuels).**

Resources are elements, compounds, minerals, and rocks that are concentrated in such a way that they can be extracted for profit. Mineral reclamation, development, and use in the United States is a several billion dollar industry. Approximately 5% of the Gross Domestic Product (GDP) in the United States is the development and use of Earth resources. Everything we use or consume most likely contains some sort of mineral or fossil resource. Glass is made from sand. Furniture uses metal ores. Fertilizers for farming use minerals. Without the use of Earth's resources, the technological progress that we have made in the past 500 years would not have been possible.

The two categories of natural resources are renewable and nonrenewable. Renewable resources are unlimited because they can be replaced as they are used. Examples of renewable resources are oxygen, wood, fresh water, and biomass. Nonrenewable resources are present in finite amounts or are used faster than they can be replaced in nature. Examples of nonrenewable resources are petroleum, coal, and natural gas.

Skill 36.6 **The beginning teacher identifies sources and reservoirs for matter and energy (e.g., carbon, nitrogen, water, solar radiation, radioactive decay).**

A chemical reservoir is a place where elements and chemical compounds are held for a long period of time.

Carbon reservoir

The four major reservoirs for carbon are the atmosphere, the terrestrial biosphere, the oceans, and sediments. In the atmosphere, carbon exists primarily as carbon dioxide. In the terrestrial biosphere, carbon is found in living organisms, freshwater systems, and in the soil as decaying organisms. The ocean reservoir for carbon includes dissolved carbon from weathering of rocks, marine organisms, and tests or shells of marine organisms ($CaCO_3$). The sediment reservoir for carbon includes fossil fuels and limestone.

Nitrogen reservoir

The chemical reservoirs for nitrogen include the atmosphere, ocean, terrestrial biomass, and soil. The atmosphere is the largest reservoir for nitrogen. Nitrogen exists as N_2, N_2O, and fixed nitrogen in the atmosphere. Lightning fixes nitrogen in the atmosphere. In the oceans, nitrogen is found in dissolved minerals, in living organisms, and in sediments. The soil reservoir for nitrogen includes organic material, ammonium, and decaying matter. Nitrogen also exists to a large extent in living tissue.

Water reservoir

Water exists everywhere. The largest chemical reservoir for water is the oceans. Although the majority of the earth is covered in water, only a small proportion is accessible for human use.

Oxygen reservoir

Oxygen is found in the lithosphere, biosphere, and atmosphere. Oxygen in the lithosphere exists in minerals, primarily silicates such as quartz. Oxygen exists as a chemical compound in the cells of living organisms in the biosphere. The atmosphere reservoir for oxygen occurs mainly through the photosynthesis exchange of oxygen. Photolysis, the breakdown of water and nitrites into their component parts via UV radiation, also releases oxygen into the atmosphere.

Solar radiation

Sunlight is also important to most organisms. Organisms on land compete for sunlight, but sunlight does not reach into the lowest depths of the ocean. Organisms in these regions must find another means of producing food.

Skill 36.7   The beginning teacher analyzes the cycling and transformation of matter and energy through the geosphere (e.g., mantle convection).

It is not the case that the Earth's layers exist as separate entities, with little interaction between them. For instance, it is generally believed that swirling of the iron-rich liquid in the outer core results in the Earth's magnetic field, which is readily apparent on the surface. Heat also moves out from the core to the mantle and crust. The core still retains heat from the formation of the Earth and additional heat is generated by the decay of radioactive isotopes. While most of the heat in our atmosphere comes from sun, radiant heat from the core does warm oceans and other large bodies of water.

There is also a great deal of interaction between the mantle and the crust. The slow convection of rocks in the mantle is responsible for the shifting of tectonic plates on the crust. Matter can also move between the layers as occurs during the rock cycle. Within the rock cycle, igneous rocks are formed when magma escapes from the mantle as lava during volcanic eruption. Rocks may also be forced back into the mantle, where the high heat and pressure recreate them as metamorphic rocks.

Skill 36.8   The beginning teacher relates the principles of conservation of mass and energy to processes that occur in the geosphere (e.g., the melting of rock).

The Zeroth Law of Thermodynamics: If object A is in thermal equilibrium with object C, and object B is separately in thermal equilibrium with object C, then objects A and B will be in thermal equilibrium if they are placed in thermal contact.

This law explains why objected of the same temperature do not spontaneously change temperature. In particular, if two rocks have the same temperature, no heat will flow between them when they are placed in thermal contact.

If a third rock is added to the mix, heat will flow according to the second law of thermodynamics until equilibrium is restored. When that point is reached, the first law again applies. No heat flow, no energy transferred.

The First Law of Thermodynamics (The Law of Conservation of Energy): In a closed system, the total amount of energy always stays the same. It can change from one form to another, but the total amount of energy never changes.

What this law states is that in a closed system—one that isn't affected by any outside influences—the total energy available can change between forms without any loss.

However, the Earth is not a closed system. Although the base premise of the law still holds true, that total energy is conserved, the corollary to this law is: that any conversion of energy from one form to another results in some of the energy changing into heat.

This is why mass and energy are conserved. Specifically, throughout the formation process of the rock cycle, the amount of material remains the same. During the weathering process of the rock cycle, the amount of material remains the same. In the sedimentation process of the rock cycle, the amount of material remains the same. Lastly, throughout the reformation process of the rock cycle, the amount of material remains the same.

Competency 0037 **The teacher understands processes of plate tectonics, weathering, erosion, and deposition that change Earth's surface.**

Skill 37.1 **The beginning teacher understands how the theory of plate tectonics explains the movement and structure of Earth's crustal plates (e.g., sea-floor spreading, subduction).**

As the Earth's core produces intense heat, the heat rises through the layers. The heating, rising, cooling, and sinking of the molten, semi-plastic material in the asthenosphere, sets up **convection cells** that are constantly in motion.

When the rising material is "churned" upward by the motion of the convection cells, it hits the bottom of the llithospheric plates, where most of the material moves sideways, cools, and then sinks downward toward the core. However, some of it squeezes upward through cracks in the lithosphere. This material is referred to as Magma.

How far upward the magma moves is generally dependent on the temperature and density of the magma, as well as the size of the crack.

The laws of physics and chemistry tell us that pressure increases when a substance is forced into a confined space. As the magma moves upward, the increasing pressure can cause "ripping" effect that enlarges the crack, pushing the lithospheric materials apart.

The overall effect of the pressure-induced movement is to create a spider web of disjointed lithospheric plates called Tectonic Plates. Rigid, hard and brittle, the plates are extremely large and they essentially, "float" on the semi-plastic molten material of the asthenosphere.

The ocean floor is constantly being pushed apart at boundaries, causing **Sea Floor Spreading**. This results in the creation of huge oceanic plates. A **Subduction Zone** is a long, narrow belt where a lithospheric plate dives into the asthenosphere. The rate of subduction is relatively equal to the rate of formation of new oceanic lithospheric material at divergent boundary spreading centers. In effect, the ocean floor recycles itself.

An everyday example of convection cells is easily seen in a pot of boiling water. As the water heats, bubbles form and rise to the surface. On a rapid boil, you can clearly detect the heating, rising, cooling and sinking motions, the basic pattern of a convection cell.

Skill 37.2   The beginning teacher understands evidence for plate movement (e.g., magnetic reversals, distribution of earthquakes, GPS measurements).

Shape of the Continents: When graphically displayed, the continents look like they should largely fit together in a "jigsaw" puzzle fashion.

Paleomagnetism: As igneous rock cools; iron minerals within the rock will align much like a compass, to the magnetic pole. Scientific research has shown that the magnetic pole periodically—hundreds of thousands of years—reverses polarity. Research also shows that the bands of rocks on either side of a spreading center are mirror images of each other with regards to magnetic polarity, and that the alignment of minerals indicate a periodic shift in polarity. The reversals in polarity can be visualized as alternating "stripes" of magnetic oceanic materials.

Age of the Rock: Besides being mirror images magnetically, dating research done on rocks on either side of a spreading center also indicate a mirroring of age. The age of the rock on either side of a spreading center are mirror images and get progressively older as you move away from the center. The youngest rock is always found directly at the spreading center. In comparison to continental rock materials, the youngest rock is found on the ocean floor, consistent with the tectonic theory of cyclic spreading and subduction. Overall, oceanic material is roughly 200 million years old, while most continental material is significantly older, with age measured in billions of years.

Climatology: This is one of the most compelling arguments supporting plate movement. Cold Areas show evidence of once having been hot and visa-versa. In example, Coal needs a hot and humid climate to form. It doesn't form in the areas of extreme cold. Although Antarctica is extremely cold, it has huge coal deposits. This indicates that at one time in the past, Antarctica physically must have been much closer to the equator.

Evidence of Identical Rock Units: Rock units can be traced across ocean basins. Many rocks are distinctive in feature, composition, etc. Identical rocks units have been found on multiple continents, usually along the edges of where the plates once apparently joined.

Topographic Evidence: Topographic features can be traced across ocean basins. Some glacial deposits, stream channels, and mountain ranges terminate on one continent near the water's edge, and resume on another continent in relatively the same position.

Fossil Evidence: Limited range fossils that couldn't swim or fly are found on either side of an ocean basin.

Skill 37.3 **The beginning teacher describes the historical development of the theory of plate tectonics (e.g., Wegener's continental drift hypothesis).**

In 1906 a young meteorology student in Germany, Alfred Wegener, became intrigued by how the shape of the continents seem to have at one time fit together. In 1910 he began a lifelong pursuit of supporting evidence for what eventually became known as his theory of **Continental Drift.**

Over the ensuing years of his research efforts, Wegener became convinced that the landmasses had—at one point in history—been connected, forming a giant supercontinent that he later dubbed Pangea. As his research progressed, he collected data and offered evidence of this theory, most of which is still included in the proofs offered for modern tectonic theory.

Plate Tectonic Theory: The Earth's surface is composed of Lithospheric plates that "float" atop the Asthenosphere and are in constant motion.

Citing paleoclimatology, the fit of the shape of the continents and fossil and rock evidence, Wegener further subdivided Pangea into two giant areas he called Laurasia and Gondwanaland. Within these areas he placed the continents of North America and Eurasia, (Laurasia), and South America, India, Africa, Australia, and Antarctica (Gondwanaland).

Not surprisingly, his controversial theory of moveable continents was not readily accepted. Although Wegener believed the continents had moved, he initially concentrated his efforts on supporting the possibility of movement and made no attempt to explain "how" of movement.

For the mainline scientists of the time, this inability to explain "how" became the all-consuming barrier to acceptance. Finally, under severe academic criticism, a frustrated Wegener proposed two ill-thought-out mechanisms to explain the movement, both of which were readily disproved by physicists.

His credibility shattered, Wegener sought solace in his love of exploration; a love that eventually cost him is life. Wegener disappeared in a blinding snowstorm during a later year expedition to Greenland in 1930, and his frozen body was recovered the following summer.

Over the next 20 years or so, Wegener's theory of Continental Drift was largely ignored by science. However, as progress in scientific technology advanced, scientists were faced with a perplexing dilemma; new evidence collected did not fit the old model of an immovable Earth. Starting inn the late 1950's and early 1960's, some scientists began to reexamine Wegener's impressive collection of data, and much to their surprise, they discovered that Wegener's old data and the new data they had collected, both supported the theory of Continental Drift. Advances in technology had made possible a reasonable explanation of the "how."

Modern geology owes much to Alfred Wegener's initial postulations. The advent of new technologies has made it possible for science to verify most of his observations, and additional, new data has expanded Wegener's original concept into the widely accepted, modern theory of tectonics.

Skill 37.4   The beginning teacher analyzes the effects of plate movement, including faulting, folding, mineral formation, earthquakes, and volcanic activity.

Plate tectonic movement results from the motion induced in the lithosphere by the rise and fall of convection cell material in the asthenosphere.

Plate Boundaries: the points at which the edges of the tectonic plates abut.

Three motions characterize interactions at the plate boundaries: separation, collision, or lateral movement. Those motions directly correlate with the categorizations of plate boundaries: Divergent, Convergent, and Transform.

The geologic and geographic effects that result from the motion depend on the location of the boundaries and the types of material involved.

Divergent Boundary: The plates are separating and moving away from each other.

Ocean/Ocean Boundaries: The materials involved are composed of heavy and dense, but very thin, dark colored oceanic lithospheric material, usually Basalt.

As the magma rises, the ocean floor begins to dome upward. The upward pressure eventually forces an underwater rip in the center of the dome and the magma erupts. The erupted materials cool rapidly and build upward, forming Mid-Ocean Ridges, which are fairly common and found all over the globe.

Example: The Mid-Atlantic Ridge.

Continental/Continental Boundaries: The materials involved are composed of less dense, but very thick, lighter colored continental lithospheric material, usually Granite.

The same principles of force and motion present in divergent ocean/ocean boundaries apply to divergent continental/continental boundaries. However, as the erupted material eventually cools, a **Rift Valley** forms between the adjoining volcanic peaks. In many places around the world, these valleys play an important agricultural role because of the rich volcanic soil.

Example: East African Rift Zone.

Actually, there is not a great difference between divergent ocean/ocean, and continental/continental boundaries, except that one takes place underwater to form mid-ocean ridges and the other forms volcanic mountains with rift valleys.

Convergent Boundary: The plates are moving toward, and collide with each other.

Ocean/Ocean Boundaries: These plates are forced together by the spreading of the ocean floor. Tremendous frictional forces are created as the plates collide and some of the oceanic material builds upward, while other oceanic material bends downward.

The leading edges of the boundaries meet around 700 km downward. The forces involved push some material upward through the lithosphere to become a volcano. The built up materials may eventually break the ocean surface to become volcanic islands. This effect is actually so widespread that the islands form groupings of volcanic islands called Volcanic Arcs.

Example: The Philippines, Japan, and Guam.

The Volcanism is of the explosive type and the quick release of fantastic strain and pressure causes devastating **Deep Focus Earthquakes**. Fantastic strain and pressures cause the devastating deep focus earthquakes.

Example: Volcanism: The 1993 Mt. Pinatubo eruption in the Philippines.
Example: Earthquake: The Easter, 1964, Alaskan earthquake measured 9.2 on Richter scale.

Although some material is pushed upward, other oceanic material bends downward forming deep trenches and the leading edges of this plate will subduct back into the asthenosphere.

Example: The Mariana Trench.

Subduction Zone: A long, narrow belt where a lithospheric plate dives into the asthenosphere.

The rate of subduction is relatively equal to the rate of formation of new oceanic lithospheric material at divergent boundary spreading centers. In effect, the ocean floor recycles itself.

Ocean/Continental Boundaries: The colliding plates produce effects relatively similar to ocean/ocean collisions, but the difference in density between the materials involved causes the oceanic plate to subduct under the continental plate.

Subduction forces the continental materials upward, creating a line of on-shore volcanic mountains along the subduction zone.

Continental/Continental Boundaries: Both edges are too light to subduct. Instead, one will over ride the other, causing an uplift of material.

Example: The Himalaya Mountains were created when the Indian plate was jammed under the Asian plate. This not only built mountains but also caused devastating earthquakes in China.

Transform Boundary: The plates move laterally to each other. As the plates grind sideways, intense frictional forces are created as the lithospheric materials try to oppose the movement.

A transform boundary may be found in any location where plates abut. They may be composed of any type of lithospheric material (oceanic or continental), and they produce extreme seismic effects when the pressure between moving boundaries is released. This sudden release of pressure creates widespread destruction along the fault lines.

Examples: The 7.1 magnitude 1989 San Francisco (Loma Prieta), or the 6.8 magnitude 1994 Los Angeles (Northside) or the 7.9 magnitude 2003 (Colema) Mexico, earthquakes.

The cycling of Earth's materials through areas of upwelling and subduction cause mineral formation and/or surfacing. Specifically, **magma**: the molten liquid, or semi plastic Earth material located beneath the Earth's crust, is produced at Hot Spots, Spreading Centers, and Subduction Zones and varies in composition according to where it is produced.

Hot Spot and Spreading Center: The magma is produced in the asthenosphere and comes up mantle plume. This magma is pure magma, dense and silica poor. However overall, the material is very runny and fluid.

Subduction Zone: The magma is impure because ocean sediment is sucked down and mixed with the magma. The silica rich, water saturated magma is thicker because of the addition of ocean sediment.

Skill 37.5 **The beginning teacher knows the processes (e.g., freezing/thawing, chemical reactions) and products of weathering (e.g., soils, karst features) and compares and contrasts chemical and mechanical weathering.**

Weathering: the physical and chemical breakdown and alteration of rocks and minerals at or near the Earth's surface.

Classifying Weathering

Mechanical (also called Physical Weathering): where rock is broken into smaller pieces with no change in chemical or mineralogical composition. The resulting material still resembles the original material.

Example: Rock pieces breaking off a boulder.
The pieces still resemble the original material, but on a smaller scale.

Chemical Weathering: where a chemical or mineralogical change occurs in the rock and the resulting material no longer resembles the original material.

Example: Granite (Gneiss/Schist) eventually weathers into separate sand, silt, and clay particles.

Weathering is typically caused by a combination of chemical and mechanical processes.

Factors Influencing Weathering

Composition: Due to their composition, some rocks weather easier and will show more effects.

Rock Structure: Does it have cracks? Is it fractured? Water and other elements get in the cracks.

Climate: The more water, the greater the weathering effect. Additionally, the higher the temperature or the more the temperature varies, the greater the weathering effect.

Topography: This factor determines the amount of surface area exposed to weathering. Smaller rocks are affected more because collectively, they have less mass and more surface area than a boulder.

Vegetation: Important weathering agent. Depending on the type of vegetation, it can either hinder or accelerate the weathering process. Although vegetation may leave less surface area exposed, the vegetation's root structures can produce a biological effect that accelerates the process.

Types of Mechanical Weathering

Frost Wedging: This occurs when rock gets a crack in it, water collects, and then freezes. Over time, as this cycle repeats itself, the expanding water gradually pushes the rock apart.

Salt Crystal Growth: In a process similar to frost wedging, as the water evaporates, it leaves salt crystals behind. Eventually, these crystals build up an push the rock apart. This is a very small-scale effect and takes considerably longer than frost wedging to affect the rock material.

Abrasion: This is a key factor in mechanical weathering. The motion of the landscape materials produces significant weathering effects, scouring, chipping, or wearing away pieces of material.

Abrasive agents include wind blown sand, water movement, and the materials in landslides bashing into each other.

Biological Activity: This is a two-fold weathering agent.

> **Plants:** Seeds will sometimes land in a crack in a rock and begin to grow in the cracks. The root structure eventually acts as a wedge, pushing the rock apart.

> **Animal:** As animals burrow, the displaced material has an abrasive effect on the surrounding rock. because of the limited number of burrowing animals, plant activity has a much greater weathering effect.

Pressure Release (Exfoliation): Rock expands when compressive forces are removed, and bits of the rock break off during expansion. This can result in massive rock formations with rounded edges.

Example: Half-Dome in Yosemite National Park.

Thermal Expansion and Contraction: Minerals within a rock will expand or contract due to changes in temperature. Dependent on the minerals in the rock, this expansion and contraction occurs at different rates and to different magnitudes. Essentially, the rock internally tears itself apart. The rock may look solid but when placed under pressure, easily crumbles.

Climate is a key factor in mechanical weathering.

Types of Chemical Weathering

Oxidation (Rust): Oxygen atoms become incorporated into the formula of a mineral in a rock and the mineral becomes unstable and breaks off in flakes.

> **Example**: Iron oxide (FeO_2) changes to iron trioxide (FeO_3) due to the oxygen chemically imparted to the mineral.

Solution: Due to their inherent composition, some minerals found in rocks easily dissolve into solution when exposed to a liquid.

> **Example**: Halite (Rock Salt) completely dissolves in water.

Acids: Water and water vapor may combine with other elements and gases to form acids. Water (H_2O) and carbon dioxide (CO_2) can chemically combine to become Carbonic Acid (H_2CO_3). Sulfur Dioxide (SO_2) particles can chemically combine with water (H_2O) to form Sulfuric Acid (H_2SO_4).

Biological Activity: Plant roots growing in the cracks of rocks not only cause mechanical wedging, but also secrete acids that cause chemical weathering.

Generally found in combination with solution, *acids* cause the majority of chemical weathering.

Results of weathering

Sediment: fragments of broken rock produced by the weathering process.

Soils form when sediments undergo the process of leeching, accumulation, and addition of organic matter.

Karst topography is a specific type of rock formation with distinctive surface shapes. These structures are formed when mildly acidic water dissolves bedrock (such as limestone or dolostone). The water is made acidic by carbonic acid that forms when water combines with carbon monoxide in the atmosphere. This water then dissolves surface rock and causes fractures. These fractures enlarge over time and as large gaps are formed, underground drainage systems develop which allow even more water to flow in and dissolve the rock. Complex underground drainage systems and caves are important features of karst topography.

Over thousands of years, karsification of a landscape will eventually form features of varied size. Giant spikes, "limestone pavements", and other striking features commonly form on the surface. Sinkholes, springs, and shafts are common below the surface. In the United States, large visible surface structures and complex underground caves formed by karst topography can be found in Missouri and Arkansas.

Skill 37.6   The beginning teacher identifies the causes (e.g., wind, water, gravity, glaciers) and effects of erosion and deposition (e.g., removal of topsoil, sedimentation).

Wind is very effective in transporting sediments in areas of little vegetation. For example, the haze over the Grand Canyon is actually sand from Monument Valley, over 50 miles away. Sand dunes are essentially piles of wind-blown micro-rock.

Pebbles in mountain pools and streambeds are pieces of the mountain broken off and carried to another location by water movement. Surface run-off is water that flows over land before reaching a river, lake, or ocean. Run-off occurs when precipitation falls faster than the soil can absorb it and/or when the soil becomes saturated with precipitation. Certain human activities have increased run-off by making surfaces increasingly impervious to precipitation. Water is prevented from flowing in the ground by pavement and buildings in urban areas and by heavily tilled farmland in rural areas. Instead of renewing the ground water supplies, this precipitation is channeled directly to streams and other bodies of water. Not only does this reduce ground water supplies, it can trigger increased erosion, siltation, and flooding. The increased rate of erosion is particularly damaging to agricultural endeavors, since fertile topsoil is carried away at a higher rate.

Streams change the landscape by eroding, transporting, and depositing the landscape material. Erosion and deposition are controlled by the velocity of the stream. Whenever the velocity slows, deposition happens. This sometimes results in the formation of deltas.

Glacier: a large, long-lasting mass of ice formed on the land that moves due to gravity. A glacier forms as the result of snow accumulating, compacting, and crystallizing over a period of years. A glacier acts like a giant bulldozer, moving most everything in its path, big or small. As the glacier moves forward due to basal sliding, the underlying topography is severely abraded because of the immense pressure on the rock base due to the weight of the glacier. The key factor in the glacial erosion process is the meltwater. It causes frost wedging, which initiates the erosional sequences. As the glacier moves forward on the meltwater, some of the water seeps into cracks and freezes. This frost wedging causes a further widening and weakening of the rock material. The glacier plucks the fragments out of the cracks and pushes them along the base. These fragments act as a scouring pad, and as they increase in size and amount, they increase the abrasion on the topography. The grinding motion due to the glacial weight increases as the mass moves forward, picking up more fragments and causing striations in the underlying rock. Glaciers can move rock fragments varying in size from pebbles to entire boulders. Fine fragments are referred to as rock flour. Boulder sized rock units moved to other locations are called eratics.

Competency 0038   **The teacher understands the formation and history of Earth.**

Skill 38.1   **The beginning teacher knows the historical development of scientific theories relating to the origin and development of Earth (e.g., Hutton's uniformitarianism).**

James Hutton, a Scottish gentleman farmer, medical doctor, and amateur geologist, first postulated in 1785, the primary principle upon which modem geology is based; the **Principle of Uniformitarianism**. Hutton's observations led him to conceptualize that there is a uniformity of geoloeic processes, past and present. In essence, the Principle of Uniformitarianism states that the geologic processes that are happening today also happened in the past, and that the present is the key to the past.

Hutton's simple but profound concept provided science with a dynamic tool with which to view the past. Suddenly, when viewed in light of Hutton's principle, logical explanations were available for a wide variety of questions that had stymied geologists. By implication, the corollary to the principle of Uniformitarianism is that, because the processes that modified our planet in the past continue to work at the slow pace of today, an immense period of time must pass in order for the processes to accomplish the task. Thus by extension, Hutton's observations also introduced the concept of Geologic Time. For example, the period of time required to raise a mountain thousands of feet above the surface and then wear it down again had to have taken place over a truly impressive period of time, on the order of hundreds of thousands of human lifetimes.

Skill 38.2   **The beginning teacher understands how Earth's geosphere, hydrosphere, and atmosphere have changed over time and analyzes the significance of these changes (e.g., formation of oxygen in the atmosphere).**

Earth's **initial atmosphere** was composed of primarily hydrogen and smaller amounts of helium. However, most of the hydrogen and helium escaped into space very shortly after the earth was formed, approximately 4.6 billion years ago.

A **second atmosphere** formed during the first 500 million years of Earth's history, as the gasses trapped within the planet were out- gassed during volcanic eruptions. This atmosphere was composed of carbon dioxide (CO_2), Nitrogen (N), and water vapor (H_2O), with smaller amounts of methane (CH_4), ammonia (NH_3), hydrogen (H), and carbon monoxide (CO). However, only trace quantities of oxygen were present.

At around 3.5 billion years, Earth's **third atmosphere** began to form as the first life forms- simple, unicellular bacteria- appeared. As the primitive life forms evolved, they gradually developed the ability to conduct photosynthesis. **Photosynthsis** is the ability to combine Carbon dioxide and water in the presence of sunlight to for glucose and oxygen. The oldest evidence of life (3.4-3.5 billion years ago) is found in the Proterozoic Eon. All life during that period was protozoan, a microbial life form.

The organisms used the glucose for food and released the oxygen into the atmosphere. as the early life forms thrived and multiplied over the next 3 billion years, they gradually released increasingly greater quantities of oxygen into the atmosphere. At around 2.5 billion years ago, the **Oxygen Revolution** took place, marking the point at which sufficient oxygen had accumulated to prompt an explosive evolutionary step in life formation. More complicated- but still unicellular- organisms began to appear. At around 570 million years ago the atmosphere reached the present day ration of approximately 78% nitrogen and 21 % oxygen. This shift marked another turning point in evolution as the oxygen level has reached a point to sustain more evolved life forms, and multicellular plants and animals made their first appearance.

Water began to collect on the surface of the Earth around 4.6 billion years ago as the interstellar gas, dust, debris, and water slowly accreted under the increasing force of gravity to create the Earth's basic form. In addition to shaping basic form, gravitational collapse of the stellar material also caused the planet to grow hotter. The internal heat generated by the decay of radioactive elements further increased this heat.

Our planet's earliest history was quite violent. Besides being repeatedly struck by meteorites, the Earth's birthing process produced frequent eruptions that caused water- primarily in the form of water vapor from gaseous hydrous minerals- to rise to the surface. The solar system contributed additional water as the Earth acquired its basic form. Comets- primarily composed of water and other light, hydrous materials- bombarded the Earth's surface, and their melting added to the water volume. The primordial seas were initially very acidic, but as the hydrologic cycle of evaporation and precipitation took hold, soluble minerals dissolved and were carried to the seas, gradually easing the degree of acidity. The exchange of minerals though the hydrologic cycle further modified the water's chemistry. Sodium, being extremely soluble, remained in the water longer than the other common elements, and the percentage of sodium in the Earth's oceans has not varied appreciably foe at least 600 million years.

Skill 38.3 **The beginning teacher understands the organization of the geologic time scale and methods of relative (e.g., superposition, fossils) and absolute (e.g., radiometric, dendrochronology) dating.**

There are two basic concepts involoved in measuring time: relative and absolute time. Although both concepts are used in the Earth Sciences, absolute time provides the most accurate concept of describing the passage of time.

Relative time- making a comparison of the order of one object relative to the other. **Example**: This object is older than that object.

Absolute time- the exact age of an object. **Example**: This object is xxx years old.

In Earth Science, time is measured using Relative and Absolute Dating techniques.

Relative Dating

As the name implies, this technique involves a comparison of rock assemblages, through application of the principle laws of geology, which are as follows:

Principle of Uniformitarianism: Processes that are happening today also happened in the past.

Principle of Cross-Cutting Relations: A rock is younger than any rock it cuts across.

Principle of Original Horizontality: Rock units are originally laid down flat. Something happened to cause them to change orientation.

Principle of Super Position: The rock on the bottom is older than the rock on top.

Principle of Biologic Succession: Fossils correspond to particular periods of time.

Fossils appear and disappear periodically, providing a geologic time yardstick.

Absolute Dating

Definition: Assigning time in years before present to a rock or fossil assembelage. Four methods are used in absolute dating: Dendrochronology, Varves, Radiometric Dating, and Fission Tracking Dating.

Dendrochronology: tree ring dating. Accuracy range restricted to past 6,000 years. This was an early technique used in absolute dating. By measuring the width of the tree rings and counting the number of rings, a scientist could make an approximation of the climatology of the area and how old the tree was when it died.

Varves: sea bands in a lake. Maximum dating range limited to the past 20,000 years. Both Dendrochronology and Varves are relatively inaccurate, and are poor methods of absolute dating, and neither method is used much anymore.

Radiometric Dating: The **most accurate** method of absolute dating, this technique measures the decay of naturally occurring radioactive isotopes. These isotopes are great timekeepers because their rate of decay is constant. Elements decay because of the inherent structure of the nucleus of the atoms. Neutrons hold the positively charged protons together. However, the positive protons attempt to repel each other. In some heavy elements, the protons repel each other to such a degree that the proton tears itself apart (decays) and by losing protons, becomes another element. The decay starts the moment an isotope crystallizes in a rock unit, and chemicals, weathering, environment, or temperature does not affect the rate of decay.

The radioactive decay causes the (mother) element to change into an (daughter) element. The Mother-Daughter relationship of produced nuclides during the series of isotope decay is the basis for radiometric dating. Although many isotopes are used in radiometric dating, the most widely known method is referred to as **Carbon-14 dating**. Carbon-14 is unstable and decays, decomposes and transmutes to Carbon-12. The dating process compares the ratio of Carbon-14 to Carbon-12 in an object. Since the decay occurs at a known rate, it is very predictable and can be used as a clock standard. However, Carbon-14 decays quickly and can only be used to date organic compounds less than 40,000 years old.

Knowing the Half-Life of the isotopes is the key factor in the radiometric dating process. If we know the half-life, we can compare the ratio of isotopes found in the object, and count backwards to get an accurate date. The most common element checked is the ratio of Uranium to Lead. Only Carbon-14 can be used to date organic compounds. The other isotopes are not found in organic compounds.

Fission Tracking Dating

Fission tracking dating is a new alternative method that doesn't rely on mother-daughter techniques. Instead, it is based on counting the scars caused by the collision of atoms. There is a gap in the radiometric-dating scheme between 1 mya to 50 ya. Fission tracking fills in this gap. However, because the method is relatively new, it is controversial and not completely accepted by all scientists.

Dating Non-organics

Radioactive isotope dating is a relatively new invention. Prior to its invention, geologists relied upon relative dating methods. Radioactive isotopes are good for dating rock units because they are common in igneous rocks, some metamorphic rocks, and occasionally in sedimentary rocks such as sandstone. However, the presence of the isotope in sandstone can tell us how old the material is, but not when it was laid down. To determine the age of the sandstone, scientists try to absolute date layers above and below the sandstone.

Thus, dating sandstone uses a combination of absolute and relative dating methods. You can only tell if the lay down occurred between two dates, not the absolute date of the event. Fossils found in the sandstone are often not directly dated. Instead, the rock units surrounding it are dated. Earth Scientists examine the layers above and below the fossil to get an approximate range of how old the fossil must have been when it was laid down in the rock layers.

Chronostratagraphic Unit: rock units that correspond to a geologic or geochronologic event.

Skill 38.4   The beginning teacher identifies important events in the history of Earth (e.g., formation of major mountain chains, breakup of continents, appearance of life, appearance of multicellular organisms) and locates these events on the geologic time scale.

In the Earth Sciences, when you talk about time, you must think in terms of huge expanses of time.

Geological Time Scale: the calendar/clock of events in geology based on the appearance and disappearance of fossil assemblages.

The scale is divided into time units that are given distinctive names and approximate start and stop dates. These dates are based upon a reexamination of previously discovered fossils, using absolute dating techniques.

Eons: The largest scale division
Eras: Divided into sub categories based on profound differences in fossil life.

Periods: Smaller divisions within eras based on less profound differences in the fossil record.

Epochs: Sub-categories within some periods that are specific to the types of fossils found within.

Pre-Cambrian Time: Comprised of the Hadean, Archean, and Proterozoic Eons, 87% of all geologic time is considered Pre-Cambrian.

Major Geological Time Scale Divisions

Eon, Era, Period, or Epoch	Time Start (mya)
Hadean Eon	4600
Archean Eon	3800
Early Era	3800
Middle Era	3400
Late Era	3000
Proerozoic Eon	2500
Paleo-proterozoic Era	2500
Meso-proterozoic Era	1600
Neo-proterozoic Era	1000
Phanerozoic Eon	570
Paleozoic Era	570
Cambrian Period	570
Ordovician Period	505
Silurian Period	438
Devonian Period	408
Carboniferous Period, includes the:	360
Mississippian Period	360
Pennsylvanian Period	320
Permian Period	286
Mesozoic Era	245
Triassic Period	245
Jurassic Period	208
Cretaceous Period	144
Cenozoic Era	66
Tertiary Period, comprised of:	66
Paleogene Period	66
Paleocene Epoch	66
Eocene Epoch	58
Oligocene Epoch	37
Neogene Period	24
Miocene Epoch	24
Pliocene Epoch	5
Quarternary Period	2
Pleistocene Epoch	2
Holocene Epoch	10,000 years

Life began in the oceans of the Archean Eon. The oldest fossil found is approximately 3.4 - 3.5 billion years old. Archean Eon is defined as 3.8 to 2.5 billion years ago.

The early Earth was very hot, with a warm, toxic ocean by our present day standards. Totally devoid of Oxygen, it was composed of Hydrogen Sulfide, Methane, Ammonia, and Carbon Dioxide. Life began in the ocean. Simple logic proves this contention. There wasn't an ozone (O_3) layer because there wasn't any oxygen (O_2) to be altered into ozone. Without ozone, Ultra-Violet (UV) radiation from the Sun scrambles the DNA in a cell. Therefore, by logical extension, no life existed because the earliest single cell organism couldn't handle the uv rays.

This logic caused research scientists Miller & Urey to investigate the theory of life form development in a primordial oceanic environment. They simulated the primordial ocean atmosphere in laboratory tests, and although they didn't create life, they did create amino acids, which are the building blocks of life. Proteins form Amino Acids that are able to form complex organic molecules.

Between 4.6 and 3.6 billion years ago, something occurred that still isn't scientifically clear. We transition from an uninhabitable Earth, to the appearance of simple, single-celled bacteria. Around 2.5 billion years ago, the bacteria developed the ability of photosynthesis. This process released oxygen as a by-product and there was a massive release of oxygen as the bacteria multiplied. This massive release is called the **Oxygen Revolution** and it concurrently marks the beginning of the Proterozoic Eon.

Early Proterozoic Eon

Formation of Red Beds: The Animike Group- banded iron formations-form. These Red Beds are important because they herald the appearance of significant amounts of oxygen on the Earth. The red color is produced by rust. The rust indicates the presence of oxygen acting upon the ferrous material present in the ocean, and eventually, on the land. The presence of significant amounts of oxygen allows ozone to form, which in turn, screens out the harmful ultra-violet (UV) rays. This makes life possible outside of the protective confines of the ocean.

Stromatolites: Blue-Green algae. Stromatolites are Cyano Bacteria. Cyano bacteria produce oxygen by photosynthesis. At around 1.9 billon years ago there is an abundance of primitive bacteria, which begin to diversify. We know of this diversity through the discovery of the Gunflint Chert, an assemblage of many different types of bacterial fossils.

Middle Proterozoic Eon

Development of Eukaryotic fossils (fossils other than bacteria).

Late Proterozoic Eon

First evidence of multi-cellular organisms- **Edicaran Fauna**- at 1.0 billion years ago. Cells are organized into tissues and tissues are organized into organs. However, the early Edicaran Fauna didn't grow exterior cells. Three basic types of Edicaran Fauna:

Circular or discordal: Jellyfish looking in appearance.
Frond life forms.
Elongate forms: Worm like in appearance.

The Edicaran Fauna is three times larger than the fossils in the Gunflint Chert and gradually develops greater detail, Including growing hard and exterior shells. The very end of the Proterozoic Eon- approximately 540 million years ago- there is an abundance of shelled organisms. The first appearance of multi-cellular shelled organisms was approximately 4 billion years after the Earth's formation.

The Phanerozoic Eon

The Phanerozoic Eon: 570 million years ago (mya) to present time, is divided into 3 Eras, the Paleozoic, the Mesozoic, and the Cenozoic. Because of the extent of life form diversity that occurred during this time frame, each era is addressed separately in regard to its respective evolutionary patterns.

Pealeozoic Era

The Paleozoic Era: 570 to 245 million years ago (mya), is divided into 7 Periods:
Cambrian: 570 to 505 mya.
Ordovician: 505 to 438 mya.
Silurian: 438 to 408 mya.
Devonian: 408 to 360 mya
Mississippian: 360 to 320 mya.
Pennsylvanian: 320 to 286 mya.
Permian: 286 to 245 mya.

The Paleozoic Era was a time of great evolutionary change and begins with the development of the organisms' ability to secrete hard parts (calcium phosphate and calcium carbonate shells).

A key find in paleontology was the "Burgess Shale" formation. This formahon was a depository of very well preserved Cambrian Age fossils.

The Burgess Shale Formation provides a snapshot of life in the Cambrian Age. It shows the great abundance of life forms during the time period, and the gradual development of capabilities and characteristics.

Paleozoic Era Invertebrates included Arthropods, Brachiopods, Bryozoans, Archaeocyathids, Porifera (Sponges), Cnidarians, Molluscs, Bivalves, Gastropods, Cephalopods, Echinoderms, Graptolites and Conodots.

The first vertebrate-fish-appeared in the Paleozoic Era and eventually dominated the marine environment. To be classified as a vertebrate (chordate), the animal must have an internal skeleton and a single nerve cord or vertical column.

Evolution of Paleozoic Era Plant Life

Stromatolites: Algael Plants. Cyno-bacterical forms, Stromatolites are common at the beginning of the Cambrian Age.

Receptaculids: Very abundant, Lime secreting algae.

Evolution in the Late Paleozoic Era:

Geological changes in the Paleozoic environment spurred great evolutionary changes. Massive deformations caused by orogenies created lots of erosion. The tons of sediment carried into the waters choked many species of the Brachiopods out of existence. As the landscape changed the habitats shrunk, forcing a higher degree of competition among species.

The byword for the late Paleozoic is "evolve or die." The changes created a tendency in evolution toward greater mobility. Most surviving organisms evolved from sessile to motile creatures. Mobility is the key to survival in the late Paleozoic. In example, slow moving and with a weak shell, Trilobites did not successfully evolve and consequently, they went extinct.

Other offensive and defensive mechanisms also improved. Brachiopods developed spines and heavy shells around the same time that sharks developed broad, flat, teeth, which improved their food gathering techniques.

The evolutionary path of fish leads to land organisms. The path moves away from heavy armor to better jaws and fin structure. By the end of the Devonian, sharks and bony fish dominate. However, some fish are starting to develop a modest air breathing capability.

Dipnoi: Nostril breathing lungfish. Able to breathe in either water or on the surface, they are still around today.

Crossopterygian: Lung breathing fish. A very important step in the transition to land animals, the Crossopterygian is the ancestor of the amphibians.

Transition to Amphibian

The first land animal is the amphibian **Icthyostegides**. Appears in the late Devonian. Although primarily a land animal, the Icthyostegides-as all amphibians are-was still dependent on the water to keep its skin moist and to reproduce.

By the Mississippian and Pennsylvanian periods, the amphibians dominate, having become extremely abundant and diversified with many species, including carnivorous predators.

As the landmass of Pangea forms, land dries up and the swamps disappear. The climate turns cooler and drier, which is not good news for the amphibians.

By the end of the Permian Period, almost all amphibians have disappeared. The climactic changes caused by the formation of Pangea causes 90% of all species on Earth to go extinct. Although they once dominated, most amphibians do go extinct. The only remaining amphibians today are the frog, salamander, toad, and newt.

The end of the Paleozoic Era marks the beginning of the rise of the reptiles.

As is the nature of evolution, changes to reproductive, defensive, offensive, and dietary systems allowed the reptiles to become the dominant species. In comparison, reptiles enjoyed significant evolutionary advantages over the amphibians.

The 1st true reptiles appear in the Pennsylvanian Epoch. They are Pelecosaurs (finned backed dinosaurs). However, the Therapsids, another type of reptile also appears. Therapsids are mammal like reptiles. The Therapsids were essentially a more advanced class of reptile, in that their legs were under their bodies, they had a different skull attachment scheme which gave them greater flexibility of movement and range, and they had mammal like dentition, a variety of differently shaped teeth.

The Mesozoic Era: The Age of Reptiles

The climate is changing throughout the Mesozoic. It starts as cool and dry because of the formation of Pangea. However, as Pangea breaks up, the climate warms throughout the Mesozoic, and it is very warm by the Cretaceous Period. Tropical conditions extend to 70 degrees north and south latitude.

At the end of the Cretaceous, there is a rapid cooling and, about 80 million years ago, there is a rapid decline in the temperature of the ocean water. This decline was caused by the sudden abundance of Cocolithophores: microscopic algae with calcium carbonate ($CaCO_3$) shells. They flourished in such abundance that they caused a "Reverse Greenhouse Effect." They absorbed the carbon from the atmosphere, forcing a cooling of temperature.

As the supercontinent of Pangea breaks up, massive orogenies occur in North America, salt domes and petrified forests form, and the Atlantic Ocean opens up. Europe and North America under go transgression and regression events as Africa, India, and North America move northward. Additionally, Australia & Antarctica are connected, and South America splits off from Africa and North America.

The mass extinction in the late Permian period of the Paleozoic leaves only 10% of all life forms. Nature responds to the open habitats by causing accelerated evolution. New life forms and species appear to fill the void left behind by the extinctions.

The oyster becomes successful. Brachiopods almost completely disappear. A new type of coral, Scleractinian, appears. Crabs, shrimp, starfish, and sea urchins appear for the first time. Belemnites appear and evolve info the Squid. Oceanic Phytoplankton evolves and expands.

As the marine plants move ashore, the first step of evolution is developing spore bearing plants and trees. The next step is developing non-flowering seed plants, and the final stage is development of plants with flowers and enclosed seeds.

At the beginning of the Mesozoic, Conifers dominate. **Conifers** are non-flowering, seed bearing plants. In the middle cretaceous, a new form evolves: Angiosperms. **Angiosperms** are flowering plants with enclosed seeds.

Flowering plants had several advantages over the non-flowering species. Where non-flowering plants were solely dependent on the wind for pollination, the flowering species with their enclosed seed had a greater potential to reproduce far away. The flowering plants were attractive to insects and other animals, were eaten, and the seeds were deposited in the animal's waste distances away.

As the angiosperms flourished, it encouraged insect pollination and forced insect evolution. The increased competition among insects caused evolution to push to take better advantage of the new food source. The insects became more efficient eaters.

Likewise, as the angiosperms evolved and nut and fruit bearing species appeared, the plant itself became a food source and caused it to develop defenses to ward off predators. Thorns, acidic sap, spines, etc., were mechanisms to ensure the continuation of the plant species.

Vertebrate evolution during the Mesozoic Period also accelerated, as the reptiles became the dominant species. Four groups of reptiles emerged, divided, and are classified by the number and positioning of temporal openings (holes in the skull).

The first dinosaur was the Thecodont. It was the early ancestor to all dinosaurs and reptiles with the exception of the fin backed dinosaurs (Synapsids). Dinosaurs are divided by hip structure into two different orders (lizard hipped and bird hipped).

Saurischia: (Lizard Hipped Dinosaurs)

The first Saurischia were small, had short forelimbs, and bipedalism was common. This is an important trait as bipedalism promotes speed and agility. They also had a much lighter bone stmcture density in comparison to marine creatures.

Saurischia included both carnivores and herbivores. Carnivores were called Theropods. Herbivores were called Sauropods. Eventually most members of both types evolved into giants in the latter part of the Mesozoic Era.

The increasingly large size of the Sauropods was an evolutionary defense mechanism. Largeness became an intimidation defense and also served to regulate body temperature. Large size means less surface area versus weight and better retention of body heat.

Ornithiscians: (Bird Hipped Dinosaurs)

Evolving in the Triassic Period, all Ornithiscians were herbivores as their back teeth were arranged into grinding plates and they had a beak like mouth for cropping vegetation. They evolved as both quadrupeds and bipeds, and the quadrupeds had shorter front legs, giving them a tilted appearance.

Flying dinosaurs first appeared in the late Permian Period of the Paleozoic Era. The flying dinosaurs were not birds, instead, their aerodynamics were similar to the modern day flying squirrel in that they were gliders, not flyers.

Marine dinosaurs evolved from land-based dinosaurs, not marine based organisms. They had streamlined bodies, modified reproductive organs to allow for birth at sea, and paddle shaped limbs. Significantly, the marine dinosaurs did not have gills, but were air breathers with more efficient lungs. Some examples of the different types of marine dinosaurs are:

Birds evolved from the small Theropods (Carnivorous, lizard hipped dinosaurs). Unfortunately, because of the hollow bone structure of birds (less weight to permit flight), very few ancient bird fossils have been found.

Archeopteyx: the first scientifically undisputed bird. It first appears during the Jurassic period. Archeopteryx was about the size of a modem day crow or pigeon. It had a reptile like skeleton, and wings, claws, and a long tail. Significantly, it had feathers, which is the primary reason that Paleontologists agree that it was a bird. However, it did not have a keeled breastbone like modern day birds nor any evidence of flight muscles. Archeopteryx is believed to be an intermediate step between reptiles and a full bird in the modem sense.

The first true mammal dates from the Triassic Period. It was a small, rodent like creature. During the Mesozoic, the mammal went through evolutionary change, experimentation, and development. Mammals ended up with improved nervous, circulatory, reproductive systems, and developed warm-bloodedness. Mammals are differentiated in the fossil record by having just one bone in the lower jaw (in contrast to the reptiles' many smaller bones in the jaw), several ear bones, a larger skull cavity in relation to size than reptiles, and differentiated dentition.

The massive extinction at the KT Boundary (Cretaceous/Tertiary) ends the dominance of the reptiles as a wide range of life disappears.

Marine Extinctions: The extinction event claims all large marine dinosaurs and reptiles with the exception of the sea turtles. It also signals the end of significant numbers of marine invertebrates and species of plankton.

Land Extinctions: All Dinosaurs, Flying Reptiles, and many plants disappear. Only mammals, snakes, turtles, lizards, and the crocodile survive the event.

The Cenozoic Era: 66 million years ago (mya) to present, is divided into 2 Periods, 2 Sub-Periods, and 7 Epochs.

Tertiary Period: 66 to 2 mya.
Paleogene Sub-period: 66 to 24 mya.
Paleocene Epoch: 66 to 58 mya.
Eocene Epoch: 58 to 37 mya.
Oligocene Epoch: 27 to 24 mya.
Neogene Sub-period: 24 to 2 mya.
Miocene Epoch: 24 to 5 mya.
Pliocene Epoch: 5 to 2 mya.
Quaternary Period: 2 mya to present.
Pleistocene Epoch: 2 mya to 10,000 years ago.
Holocene Epoch: 10,000 years ago to present.

The mass extinction of almost all reptiles at the end of the Mesozoic Era left a void in the biosphere. Nature once again filled the gaps with an explosion in the diversity and number of mammals. From this point on to the present day, mammals became the dominant species.

Cenozoic Era Plant Life

Angiosperms-flowering, seed bearing plants - evolve and spread significantly during the Cenozoic Era. Grasses appear in the Miocene Epoch of the tertiary Period. Adapted and suited to the dry climate of the interior, they spread over the continents, becoming dominant on the steppes of Russia, the pampas of South America, the African veldt, and the great plains of the United States. The grasslands put enormous environmental pressure on the animals. The problems caused by the appearance of the grasslands spurs a large diversity in the animals as they adapt to fit the new environment.

New dentition evolved: Teeth grow continuously from roots. Continuous growth replaces worn down teeth.
Elongated face evolved: Needed to accommodate continuously growing teeth.
Improved Dentition: Teeth evolve to include complex infolding (both within the teeth and on the surface) and enameled surfaces. The combination of new structure and enamel makes the teeth wear resistant.
Animals grow taller: This allows them to be able to see over the tall grasses.
Improved foot design: Animals develop a new "Flight" mechanism. The original flat-footed design evolves into a new foot designed to facilitate running away from predators
Improved digestive system: A four chambered stomach evolves, allowing the animals to digest the tough grasses.

Cenozoic Era Life

Marine invertebrates: Massive numbers of marine phytoplankton species go extinct during the K/T boundary period. They are replaced by new species such as Coccolithores and Diatoms.

Fish: Fish continue to diversify and evolve with the result that they are widely abundant.

Sharks: They become abundant and diversify. Sharks go through a giant phase, but eventually return to modem size.

Amphibians: The few remaining amphibians remain virtually unchanged.

Reptiles: Poisonous snakes appear during the Miocene Epoch of the Tertiary Period. They developed in direct response to the corresponding rise in evolution of the mammals. The poisons are either a neuro-toxin or a hemo-toxin. Neuro-toxins affect the nervous system and kill the victim within minutes.

Example: African Puff Adder.
Hemo-toxins affect the blood and are slower acting.

Example: Diamondback Rattlesnake.

Birds: Birds had just started to appear in the late Mesozoic Era. During the Cenozoic Era, the birds underwent an explosion of evolution as they diversified and multiplied. In the Eocene Epoch, large flightless birds were abundant. Some of the species survived until the 16th and 17th centuries of modern times.

Example: The now extinct Dodo. Some of the species were predators: These birds looked similar to a modern day parrot, but were giant sized at 9ft tall, and used their powerful beaks to crush their victims.

Cenozoic Era Mammals

Characteristics of Mammals
Two hard palates (allows eating and breathing at the same time).
Warm-blooded (maintain constant body temperature).
Have mammary glands.
Lower jawbone is a single bone.
Three bones in the middle ear.
Seven neck vertebrae.
Expanded brain case inside the skull.
Differentiated dentition.
Have hair.

The evolutionary design of both carnivores and the herbivores improved during the Cenozoic.

Primates first appear in the fossil record around 48 million years ago.

Primate Characteristics
Generalized form: No special features such as hoof or trunk.
Flatter face and binocular vision.
Postorbital ridge that protects the eyes.
Opposable thumb on a grasping hand.
More upright posture.
Increased brain size.

Primates are classified as Order Primata, with two suborders: Prosimian and Anthropoid.

Prosimian. (More primitive.) The Prosimians that remain today are small, nocturnal creatures.

Anthropoid. (Apes, monkeys, and man.) The split between Prosimian and Anthropoid occurred around 33-34 million years ago. Anthropoids are divided into three groups: Cebidae, Cercopithecidae, and Hominoidea.

Evolution of Hominoidea

Although the fossil record is incomplete, the earliest of the Hominoidea appears to be the Proconsol, which appeared around 25 million years ago. This marked the transition point from monkey to hominoid. Around 12 million years ago the

Ramapithecus-the common ancestor to both man and ape-appeared. Ramapithecus lived closer to the ground, in the woodlands. Short in stature, they developed big teeth and successfully adapted to a woodland environment.

Around 10 million years ago, Orangutans appear in the fossil record. Approximately 8 to 6 million years ago, Hominids (Man), split from the Hominoids (Apes). This is the missing link. Because very few rock units have been found that date from 4 to 8 million years ago, no fossil record has been found. Scientists used DNA protein structural studies to project a biological clock of change. They counted the differences in DNA structures between chimpanzees and man to postulate a common ancestry.

First Appearance of the Hominids

Ardipithecus ramidus:

Discovered in 1994, this fossil dates from 4.4 million years ago, but because it consists only of a lower jaw, scientists cannot agree on exactly what the fossil represents. It may be and extremely advanced ape or it may be the common hominid ancestor of both extinct species of Australopithecus as well as modern humans.

Australopithecus afarensis:

Discovered in 1974, the fossil was nicknamed "Lucy." Although only a partial skeleton was found, between that and preserved footprints, we know that Lucy was bipedal and walked upright. Most fossil skeletons are found in the Far East and in the South Africa Rift Valley. However, "Lucy" was discovered south of that area.

The fossil record shows that a split occurred in the Hominid evolutionary lines. Scientists have two schools of thought about the split. The first theory holds that Australopithecus Afarensis is the common ancestor to both the Homo and Australopithecus evolutionary lines. The second theory is based on the concept that the ancestry of the two lines was distinctly separate. Paleontologists do agree that the Australopithecus occurred first. But newer evidence shows that members of both lines existed simultaneously for a period of time.

Genus Australopithecus

Australopithecus afarensis ("Lucy"):

Appeared 3.5 million years ago.
Cranial capacity: estimated to be about the size of a modem chimpanzee's. (Fossilized skull fragments only.) 3-4 ft. tall, with long arms and a ape-like jaw (jutting forward). Bipedal, afarensis lived in the grasslands. Used primitive tools. Didn't make them, just used materials, such as sticks, broken bones, rocks, etc.

Australopithecus africanus:

Appeared 3-2 million years ago. Cranial capacity: 450 cc.
Still unable to have articulated speech, primarily because of skull and neck construction.

Australopithecus robustus:

Appeared 2-1.5 million years ago. Cranial capacity: 530 cc.
Flat face and forehead. Very heavily built. Had a **sagital crest** (bony ridge on top of head). This crest is believed to be an anchor point for the muscles needed for the extremely heavy and powerful jaw. Still used, not made, primitive tools.

Australopithecus bosei:
Appeared 2-1.5 million years ago. Cranial capacity: 530 cc. Contemporary to Australopithecus robustus. Very large build but slightly smaller than robustus. Paleontologists suspect that robustus and bosei are the same species, and the differences between them are simply sexual dimorphism (one was male and the other female).

The Australopithecus Genus went extinct around 1.5 million years ago.

Genus Homo

Homo habilis:
Appeared around 2 million years ago. Cranial capacity: 680cc. Contemporary of Australopithecus robustus and bosei, but habillis was more advanced than the Australopithecus line. Face very ape-like. Scientists believe that rudimentary speech was possible, but not advanced speech due to head and shoulder physical constraints. Walked upright. Used primitive tools. Did not make them, only used natural tools. Evidence suggests that there was more meat in their diet and that they had a more modern hand and foot structure.

Homo erectus ("Peking Man and Java Man"):
Appeared around 1.5 million years ago, just as the Australopithecus line disappeared. Homo erectus is considered to be the first true species of humans. Cranial capacity: 775cc to 1300cc. He was the first of the Homo Genus to leave Africa, becoming widely dispersed in both Africa and Eurasia. Had a heavy brow ridge, but lower anatomy similar to modern man. Believed to have had speech and evidence of use of fire. Also were good hunters. Made and used more advanced tools such as Flint and chert axes and scrapers with wooden handles.

Homo sapiens (Archaic):
Appeared between 500,000 and 250,000 years ago. Cranial capacity: 1200cc. Represents a transition between Homo erectus and Homo Sapiens neanderthalensis. Scientists are not sure if this fossil represents an advanced erectus or an early neanderthalensis.

Homo sapiens neanderthalensis (Neanderthal):
Appears after 250,000 to 125,000 years ago. Cranial capacity: That of modem man, 1500 cc. Skull shape has big brow and a sloping forehead. Neanderthals were short in height, but big boned and very heavyset. Made and used specialized stone and bone tools. There is significant evidence that they buried their dead.

Homo sapiens sapiens (Cro-Magnon):
First appeared after 35,000 years ago. Cranial capacity: That of modern man, 1500 cc. Had modem human type features. Although they coexisted for a short period with neanderthalensis, Homo sapiens sapiens eventually emerged as the sole surviving species of the Homo genus. There are two main theories why Cro-Magnon outlasted the Neanderthals:

> 1. Cro-Magnon man interbred with the Neanderthals and eventually absorbed the line through genetics, or,
> 2. The Cro-Magnons were victorious in a longterm war, and simply killed off the Neanderthals.

They had the leisure time to create a very developed culture as evidenced by cave painting and sculptures. Both created and used well-developed stone and bone tools. Had well-developed food gathering and hunting skills. There is evidence that Cro-Magnon man domesticated animals around 15,000 years ago. Practiced burial of the dead, but burial included the deceased's possessions, suggesting some belief in an afterlife. Popularly personified as "Cave Man." Species disappeared 30,000 to 40,000 years ago.

Skill 38.5   The beginning teacher understands relationships between physical changes during Earth's history and biological evolution (e.g., plate movement and biogeography; meteoric impacts, global temperature changes, extinctions, adaptive radiations).

This information can be found within the extensive coverage of Earth's history, skill number 38.4.

Skill 38.6   The beginning teacher analyzes processes involved in the formation of fossils and how fossils are used to interpret the history of Earth.

Fossil: The trace or remains of any once living organism.

The preservation of fossils in the environment is not all that common an occurrence. Although there is no formally set time limit to be considered a fossil, the term is not usually applied to remains less than 100 years old. Although soft tissues can be fossilized, they are very rare. If preserved, the fossil is usually found as hard points. Bones and shells are the most fossilized parts of the organism.

Rapid burial is a major factor in fossilization. It helps to keep scavengers at bay and bacterial decay at a minimum. 99% of all fossils are found in he heat present in forming Igneous and Metamorphic rock generally obliterates organic remains.

Methods of Fossilization

Direct Fossilization: may be unaltered or petrified.

Unaltered Fossils: This method of fossilization involves **unaltered hard points**: the original shell or bone material remains unchanged. Very uncommon if it occurs, it usually is only found in fossils less than 5 million years old.

Petrifaction: This method is much more common as it involves **altered Hard Points**: the replacement, molecule by molecule, of the material in the organism.

There are two methods of pertrifacation; replacement and permineralization.

Replacement: the organism's material is replaced molecule by molecule, by rock material.Groundwater rich with silica or calcium carbonate runs over the buried material and the original material is replaced very slowly by silica. This allows fine detail in both the interior and exterior of the fossil.
Example: Petrified wood. Appears to be stone because silica or other mineral material has replaced the original wood material.

Permineralization: where mineral material is deposited in the porous spaces of the organism. Some of the original material may be left as hard minerals-usually silica-in the groundwater, which fills in the porous spaces of the organism, leaving the original shell material largely untouched. This is commonly found in bone and shell fossils. Organisms that have permineralized look like bone on the outside, but are actually rock on the inside.

Carbonization: This method is a very good way of preserving soft tissues. As sediments pile on, their weight causes compaction, flattening the organism. The pressure causes the gasses to squeeze out of the material, leaving only a thin film of carbon impressed into the surrounding rock unit. The result is like a silhouette on stone. However, it shows only the outline of the orgasm.

Mold: a void left in the surrounding material after an object's original material is gone This method occurs when an organism gets immediately buried or covered and the sediment around it hardens quickly, forming a mold. After it decays, an empty space or void in the shape of the organism is left. This method provides fine exterior detail.

Cast: a filled-in mold. This is a very commonly found method of fossilization. A cast is formed when a small hole develops in a mold and the interior of the mold gets filled in with silica, calcium carbonate, etc. The cast looks like the organism, but no original material remains. It appears to be a statue of the original organism. Geologists sometimes deliberately make a cast of a discovered mold except they use plaster of Paris rather than silica. When the mold is removed, it leaves a casting of the exterior of the organism.

Less Common Methods of Direct Fossilization

The preservation of the soft parts of an organism is a far less common situation.

Mummification: the preservation of an organism by **desiccation** (dying out of fluids). Mummification in terms of fossilization does not refer to man-made mummies such as discovered in Egypt. Instead, it refers to the natural processes that preserve an organism in an extremely hot and dry environment such as a desert. Preservation occurs because the body fluids dry up and prevent decay. The organism's skin, hair, and internal organs remain.

Freeze-Drying: the preservation of an organism by extreme cold.
As in mummification, the hair, skin, and internal organs do not decay and remain intact. However, extremely cold-rather than hot and dry-environments enable the process. Mastodons, wooly mammoths, and early humans have all been found preserved in this manner.
Example: The meat of a Wooly Mammoth found in late 1880's was edible.

Tar Pits: A rich source of fossils. Thick tar material bubbles up to the earth's surface, and when wet, it looks like a lake. Organisms get fooled, stuck, and eventually sucked down. The hydrocarbons of the tar seal the organism preventing decay and preserving some soft body parts.

Peat Bogs: More common in the northern climates, peat bogs are essentially dried out swamps and muck. Little decay takes place since the material seals the organism. Fossils found in beat bogs are generally very well preserved with skin, hair and internal organs intact.

Amber*:* tree sap that has solidified, hardened and turned to stone. Small insects trapped in the amber are extremely well preserved with no decay.

Indirect Fossilization

This method is based upon preservation of trace evidence of an organism's existence rather than preservation of the organism itself.

Trace Fossils: preserved tracks, trails, footprints, and burrowing marks.
Example: No trail track for Brontosaurus led to reclassification of the creature as Paddisaurus.

Gastroliths: stomach stones similar to the gizzard stones in a chicken, only much, much larger.

Coprolith: fossilized dung. Coproliths provide dietary clues about organisms.

Use of the Fossil Record

Geologic Range: the time interval between first and last appearance of an organism.

Endemic Fossil: a fossil that has a limited geographic area.

Cosmopolitan Fossil: a fossil that has a wide geographic extent.

Guide Fossil: a fossil that has a short geologic range and is cosmopolitan (geographically abundant.)
Used to help pinpoint time periods and correlate those periods to rock units.

Bio Zone (Also Called Assemblage Zone): a body of rock identified by the fossil groups within.
Example: An oyster zone.

Concurrent Range Zone: two fossils within different ranges that have a narrow overlap. This acts to pinpoint a narrow time period.

Paleoecology Studies:

Paleoecology: the study of ancient eco-systems- the plants and animals of the past.

Type of Environment: By studying the fossil's records, we can reconstruct what type of environment was present. A combination of fossils and sediments can often show what type of environment was present.

Competency 0039   **The teacher understands structure and function of the hydrosphere.**

Skill 39.1   **The beginning teacher identifies the components and distribution of hydrologic systems (e.g., rivers, lakes, aquifers, oceans) and compares and contrasts the chemical composition (e.g., salinity, acidity) and physical attributes (e.g., density, turbidity) of fresh, brackish, and salt water.**

The comparison of the ratio of the mass of the ocean to the overall amount of water on the Earth is impressive.

98% of the water on Earth is in the oceans (salt water).
1.9% is locked up in glaciers as land ice.
0.5% is groundwater.
0.2% is found in rivers and lakes.
0.001% is present in the atmosphere.

It's very important to realize the scope and scale of water in comparison to the Earth's size: 61% of the Northern Hemisphere surface area and 81% of the Southern Hemisphere surface area is covered by water. The average land elevation is 840 meters, while the mean sea depth is 3,800 meters.

If the Earth were completely covered by water, the land would be 2,440 meters (8,005 ft.) underwater. The total volume of water on Earth is estimated to equal in volume a cube 148 miles on each side.

Unfortunately, the majority of water is undrinkable without treatment. In every kilogram of ocean water, 965 grams is freshwater, and 35 grams is inorganic salts. This non-potable factor is what leads to the noted water shortages in over 80 countries. In actuality, the Earth isn't short of water, but short of drinkable water, which comprises less than 0.7% of the total water available.

Streams are confined to a specific area and are filled with fresh water. A **stream channel** is the result of normal or average water flow. If more water than average tries to flow through the channel, a **flood** results. Water that flows into a stream comes from many sources but is primarily due to run off. Rainwater evaporates, infiltrates, or runs off. The run off collects in the streams. The amount of run off depends on three major factors. These are topography, soil/sediment type, and vegetation.

In most situations water runs across land and into small streams that feed larger bodies of water. All of the land that acts like a funnel for water flowing into a single larger body of water is known as a watershed or drainage basin. The watershed includes the streams and rivers that bear the water and the surfaces across which the water runs. Thus, the pollution load and general state of all the land within a watershed has an effect on the health and cleanliness of the body of water to which it drains. Large land features, such as mountains, separate watersheds from one another. However, some portion of water from one watershed may enter the groundwater and ultimately flow towards another, adjacent watershed.

Not all water flows to the streams, rivers, and lakes that comprise the above ground water supply. Some water remains in the soil as ground water. Groundwater is usually at a constant temperature and free of contaminants and suspended load. Only minimal treatment is required to remove man-induced toxins and lead. Groundwater is generally chemically uniform and classified as hardwater. **Hardwater**: Water that has a high concentration of calcium, magnesium, and iron. Hardwater leaves red rings and a hard film, because of mineral deposits. Red deposits are from iron. Soap is not as sudsy in hardwater as it normally is. Hardwater can be turned into **softwater** through the use of sodium in equipment designed to exchange sodium for the calcium, magnesium, and iron. Groundwater flows and the path taken by it somewhat mirrors the topography of the area.

Groundwater and surface water interact. A spring is located where the groundwater intersects the surface. A spring is usually the headwaters of a stream. As the stream is fed by the groundwater, the groundwater is also fed by the stream. Therefore, if pumping of the groundwater occurs near a stream, the stream may be depleted. Conversely, if the stream is pumped for water, the water table will lower as the groundwater will continue to recharge the stream. The same is true for contamination plumes. Contamination will freely move between the groundwater and the stream water.

Wetlands (swamps and marshes) serve a very important purpose in the interaction between surface water and groundwater. The wetland will serve as a recharge area for the groundwater. The vegetation filters out contaminates before they enter the ground or stream. The wetland also acts as an area to moderate runoff into a stream. Sediment is able to settle in the marsh before it enters the stream. In times of drought a wetland is able to provide water to the stream and replenish the groundwater supply.

Areas where a river/stream meets the sea have brackish water- water that holds some properties of both salt and fresh water. **Estuaries** occur where fresh rivers and streams join the ocean. Like the continental shelf, the water here is well lit and shallow. Thus, estuaries are the home for many organisms that are well adapted to the fresh/saline conditions.

Skill 39.2 **The beginning teacher understands the water cycle and processes by which water moves through the water cycle (e.g., infiltration, runoff, evaporation, condensation, transpiration).**

Hydrologic Cycle: the Earth's water balance. All the water on our planet is all that there is available. It changes location and form, but new water is not produced. It simply recycles itself. The hydrologic cycle of water movement is driven by solar radiation from the Sun. The cycle of evaporation from the oceans, and precipitation over land is the methodology employed by nature to maintain the water balance at any given location. The Earth constantly cycles water. It evaporates from the sea, falls as rain, and flows over the land as it returns to the ocean. The constant circulation of water among sea, land, and the atmosphere is called the **hydrologic cycle**.

Evaporation

Water is constantly in motion on the Earth. As the water evaporates from the sea, it becomes water vapor in the atmosphere.

Although a small amount of water evaporates from the land and inland waterways, the majority of evaporation occurs over the oceans. An additional small amount of evaporated water comes from plants as they breathe using the process of **transpiration**.

Precipitation

The water vapor in the atmosphere is returned to the Earth in the form of precipitation. Precipitation includes rain, hail, snow, and sleet. The amount of precipitation varies according to location, with some areas of Earth receiving plentiful moisture, and others receiving little (the deserts). However the overall proportional balance of evaporation and precipitation remains relatively constant.

Runoff

As the moisture returns to the Earth's surface in the form of precipitation, the liquid moves across the land according to the topology, with most of the water eventually flowing back into the oceans. Thus the cycle starts over: evaporation, precipitation, and runoff.

Energy Transfers

As water moves through each stage of the hydrologic cycle, it changes state (phase) and has an accompanying energy transfer. This transfer is based upon the basic laws of physics and chemistry in that it will involve either an exothermic or endothermic reaction.

Skill 39.3 **The beginning teacher identifies the tools and procedures needed to collect and analyze quantitative data (e.g., pH, salinity, temperature, mineral content, nitrogen compounds, turbidity) from hydrologic systems.**

PH

pH meters are electrochemical devices. They measure pH by comparing the electrical properties of a solution to those of a reference electrode. They are used in laboratory liquids or aquatic environments. By measuring the pH we can assess the pH of the area.

Salinometer

A salinometer is used to measure the salinity, or dissolved salt, of an aqueous solution. Salinometers are also known as conductivity meters because electricity is passed through the water. Salt water is conducts electricity better than pure water, so the salinity of the water can be determined.

Thermometer

Temperature is measured on three scales. These are degrees Fahrenheit (F), degrees Celsius (C), and Kelvin units (K). temperature is measured using a thermometer.

Acoustic Doppler

Acoustic Doppler is used as a current profiler. High frequency pulses scatter off of moving molecules of water. As water is moving away from the Doppler, it creates a lower pitch. As water moves towards the Doppler, it creates a higher pitch. The change in pitch is proportional to the speed of the current. Through Acoustic Doppler, scientists can determine where organisms, nutrients, and heat are transported throughout the ocean. The monitoring of the heat transfer in the oceans can give scientists significant information in global climate change analysis.

Acoustic Monitoring

Scientists use the piezoelectricity of ceramics (hydrophone) to produce a small electrical current when it is subjected to a pressure change. As the ceramic is submerged, it creates small voltage signals when exposed to a wide frequency of sounds. By recording the electrical signals of the hydrophone, scientists can reproduce ocean sounds.

SONAR

SONAR stands for Sound Navigation and Ranging. SONAR uses sound waves to bounce off objects in the water. The sound waves travel away from the SONAR. When they bounce off of the object in the water, they are reflected back to the SONAR. The transducer measures the strength of the signal and the amount of time it took for the sound wave to return. By using the following equation, scientists can determine the depth to the object in the water.

Range = (speed of sound)(travel time/ 2)

Skill 39.4   **The beginning teacher knows how to use principles of fluid statics and dynamics (e.g., Archimedes' principle, turbulence, viscosity, hydrostatic pressure) to analyze hydrologic systems.**

Archimedes' principle

The law of buoyancy is named after Archimedes of Syracuse, the Greek man who first discovered it. Archimedes' principle states that **the buoyant force is equal to the weight of the displaced fluid.** The weight of the displaced fluid is directly proportional to the volume of the displaced fluid (specifically, if the surrounding fluid is of uniform density). Thus, among objects with equal masses, the one with greater volume has greater buoyancy. Suppose a rock's weight is measured as 10 newtons, when suspended by a string in a vacuum. Suppose that when the rock is lowered by the string into the water, it displaces water weighing 3 newtons. The buoyant force is 10 - 3 = 7 newtons. The density of the immersed object relative to the density of the fluid is easily calculated without measuring any volumes:

$$\text{Relative density} = \frac{\text{Weight}}{\text{Weight - Apparent Immersed Weight}}$$

The applications of Archimedes' principle are many and important:
* Submarines
* Diving Weighting System
* Naval Architecture
* Flotation
* Buoyancy Compensator, and many more.

Viscosity: the ability of a substance to flow.

Hydrostatic pressure is the pressure at any given point of a non-moving (static) fluid. The hydrostatic pressure of a liquid could be expected in a closed system, and NOT in the open ocean, rivers, etc. In open water systems you would expect **turbulence.** Turbulence is caused by surface heating and the effect of the topography on the wind movement. An increase in surface heating creates greater turbulence.

Skill 39.5   The beginning teacher identifies characteristics of a local watershed and the effects of natural events (e.g., floods, droughts) and human activities (e.g., irrigation, industrial use, municipal use) on a local watershed.

Land that acts like a funnel for water flowing into a single larger body of water is known as a watershed or drainage basin. The watershed includes the streams and rivers that bear the water and the surfaces across which the water runs. Thus, the pollution load and general state of all the land within a watershed has an effect on the health and cleanliness of the body of water to which it drains.

Both groundwater and surface water resources are derived from rainfall, though over very different timeframes. After it falls, rain may evaporate, infiltrate into soils, or run off into streams, rivers, or saltwater areas. If it evaporates or runs off into saltwater areas, it is unavailable to humans for use (for most purposes). Drinking water, agriculture, livestock water, and most industrial uses all require freshwater, which may come from groundwater or surface water.

If rainfall infiltrates into soils, whether or not it forms groundwater depends on whether enough water is present to fully saturate the soil. An area of soil that is fully saturated with groundwater is known as an **aquifer**, and the level that the groundwater rises to in the soil is known as the **water table**.

When rainfall runs off, it produces **surface water resources** in the form of streams, rivers, and lakes. These resources may be produced by rainfall or by snowmelt in the spring and summer. Surface water resources are renewable but ephemeral and dependent on the weather each year. If there is less rainfall or snowfall than normal, or if patterns of precipitation are unusual, communities that depend on these resources may need to conserve water that year or use a backup source. Most drinking water taken from surface water resources is removed from rivers near the headwaters to reduce the potential for contamination and the need for treatment. Like groundwater, competition for surface water resources is increasing among groups who wish to use it for drinking water, agriculture and livestock, hydropower, and conservation of in-water flows for habitat and protection of aquatic life.

Human development has had a very significant impact on water resources of various types, and on the surface processes that replenish water resources and make them available to various human and wildlife uses. The following are the major impacts of human development on water resources:

- **Damming** – Dams and reservoirs have been built on many rivers to provide a more consistent, year-round source of water and to provide hydropower throughout the year. Reservoirs are able to store runoff that may fall only at certain times of the year and provide water for uses such as agriculture and drinking water at times when rainfall is low. However, dams also dramatically change both upstream and downstream habitat, may reduce in-stream flows needed for fish habitat at certain times of year, and may flood downstream areas at other times of year, changing the hydrology and morphology of the river system. Dams also impede fish passage and have contributed to endangerment of fish that need upstream areas to spawn.

- **Paving and removal of natural vegetation** – Removing natural vegetation for development changes the hydrologic cycle, as less water is removed from the soil by transpiration and returned to the atmosphere. At the same time soil and natural vegetation allow slow and steady infiltration of water into the soil to replenish surface water aquifers. Paving these areas prevents replenishment of underlying aquifers and increases runoff through city storm drains to saltwater areas. Water runs off more quickly and is not filtered by the soil and vegetation, and picks up pollutants on the pavement and other hard surfaces. In addition, faster runoff leads to greater erosion in areas where the surface water leaves the pavement and comes into contact with soils. In general, the more pavement and hard surfaces there are in a watershed, the less the rainwater that falls is available for replenishment of surface and groundwater resources, and the more impacts from pollution there are in the receiving water.

- **Draining wetlands and channelizing streams and rivers** – Human development often results in alteration of the natural environment. Wetlands are drained or filled to create more developable land, and streams and rivers are channelized and diked to reduce flooding and maintain stream courses in a fixed position. In recent years it has been recognized that these activities may actually increase flooding in downstream areas, as the original wetlands and floodplains served as overflow areas when runoff was high, capturing some of the water and sediment and allowing the water to replenish aquifers. When wetlands are eliminated and rivers are channelized, during high periods of rainfall and runoff the water has nowhere to go, and more catastrophic floods can occur in downstream areas. These developments also have detrimental impacts on fish and wildlife, who need the natural features of the wetlands and rivers to support their life-cycle.

- **Pollution** – Human development increases the potential for pollution of groundwater, surface water, and sediments, reducing the quantity of freshwater that is suitable for various uses. As noted above, runoff across paved surfaces tends to pick up pollutants, both in dissolved and particulate form. This runoff is typically discharged through storm drains into nearby rivers or saltwater areas. Sediment from this discharge can accumulate on the bottom and pollute the rivers, along with discharges from industrial activities and vessel traffic. Surface water can become contaminated from stormwater, sewage, and industrial discharges, runoff from pavement and contaminated soils, pesticides and herbicides from agricultural areas, and organic pollutants from farms and feedlots. Groundwater can also become contaminated and unfit for use, particularly if it is located under an industrial area.

- **Over-use of water resources** – In many parts of the world today, there is intense competition for available water resources. Water resources in many developing countries are not adequate to meet the needs of growing populations, particularly in drought-stricken areas. Even in developed countries, many regions are faced with water resource deficits because of over-use by agriculture and rapidly growing developments in arid areas. Competition between users leads to many serious conflicts among agriculture, hydropower, urban users, fisherman, and natural resource agencies – many of which cross state, provincial, and international boundaries. These conflicts and deficits are projected to get worse in most areas as populations increase and global warming exacerbates drought, reduces snowpack, and changes weather patterns.

- **Salinization** – Salinization is another way that aquifers and surface water resources can become altered. When groundwater aquifers are permanently drawn down in coastal areas, saltwater may intrude into the aquifer from the ocean, making the water unfit for most uses. Farming can also contribute to salinization of surface water resources, particularly in areas where the soil contains natural salts. In these areas, irrigation may mobilize the salts and carry them into the groundwater, or to the surface of the soil, making the land unfit for farming. In these areas, freshwater is taken out of nearby streams or rivers for irrigation, then returned more salty than before. Once the river passes through large areas of farmland, it may be unusable for drinking water or habitat.

- **Climate change** – Development has also contributed to global warming, which may lead to climate change in most areas. As the temperature of the ocean surface and atmosphere increase, storms are expected to become more extreme and precipitation may occur less gently. Monsoons in tropical areas are already exhibiting more extreme force, and flooding is becoming more serious. Reduction of snowpack and changes in rainfall patterns may lead to less storage of water for drinking water use. Some areas may receive greater rainfall, while others may receive less and experience greater drought. While overall global supplies of freshwater may diminish, the specific effects on any one area are currently difficult to quantify.

Skill 39.6 The beginning teacher analyzes patterns of ocean circulation (e.g., upwelling, surface currents) and factors that influence these patterns (e.g., winds, heating).

Two effects largely drive the patterns of surface water circulation in the world's oceans— wind related to pressure gradients and Coriolis forces. **Winds** blow from areas of high atmospheric pressure to areas of low atmospheric pressure. While these vary daily and seasonally, there are certain high and low pressure patterns that tend to occur on a large scale, globally speaking. As winds blow across the ocean from high to low pressure areas, they move the surface water in that direction. The speed of the surface water current is about 2-3% of the wind velocity.

Pressure gradients can be caused by variations in temperature and density. Cold water will tend to flow toward warmer equatorial areas, while warmer water will tend to flow toward polar regions.

$$\text{Pressure Gradient} = gi$$

Where g = gravity and i = the slope of the pressure gradient.

The **Coriolis force** is a term for the effect that the Earth's rotation has on the wind's direction of travel. The wind is actually traveling in a straight line, but the Earth is always rotating. Therefore, to an observer on the surface of the Earth, the wind appears to travel along a curved path. Coriolis forces act in a perpendicular direction to the direction of travel, and are greater near the poles than at the equator. North of the equator, winds and associated surface currents travel in a clockwise direction, while south of the equator, winds and associated surface currents travel in a counter-clockwise direction. At the equator, winds and surface currents travel in a straight line.

$$\textbf{Coriolis Effect} = fV$$

Where f = planetary vorticity and V = wind velocity. The depth of the ocean water that is affected by wind and Coriolis forces is about 50-200 m.

As winds blow parallel to a shoreline, Coriolis forces tend to push the winds and surface waters offshore. Deep water wells up to replace the displaced surface water and brings up rich nutrients for the marine food chain. This upwelling results in good fishing areas, such as in the Indian Ocean and along the coasts of Oregon and Peru/Chile. Upwelling also mixes surface water and deep ocean water, and helps drive large-scale ocean currents.

The next figure shows major surface currents of the ocean. Note the migration of colder water toward the equator and warmer water toward the poles, and the differing rotational directions of the gyres in the north and south hemispheres. These features have a strong effect on local climate. For example, the United Kingdom is much warmer than areas of Alaska that are at the same latitude, because of the warm Gulf Stream current that passes by the United Kingdom. As noted above, upwelling greatly affects local fisheries resources.

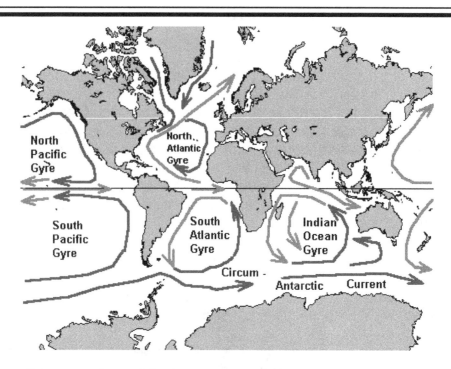

Another well-known effect of the interaction between winds and surface currents is the occurrence of El Niño and La Niña periods. In an El Niño period, trade winds along the equator weaken, and warm water is able to travel to the coast of South America. This reduces the upwelling of cold ocean water that normally occurs, and reduces fisheries resources. It also brings rain and warmer temperatures to coastal South America, and drought to Australia and the South Pacific. The effects of an El Niño period can be felt to lesser degrees in many other surrounding areas. La Niña periods, which generally follow El Niños, are characterized by colder than normal temperatures in the eastern Pacific and an increase in tropical cyclones in the Atlantic.

Skill 39.7   The beginning teacher understands the relationship between ocean depth and temperature, pressure, density, and light penetration.

Seventy percent of the Earth's surface is covered with saltwater, which is termed the hydrosphere. The mass of this saltwater is about 1.4×10^{24} grams. The ocean waters continuously circulate among different parts of the hydrosphere. There are seven major oceans: the North Atlantic Ocean, South Atlantic Ocean, North Pacific Ocean, South Pacific Ocean, Indian Ocean, Arctic Ocean, and the Antarctic Ocean.

Pure water is a combination of the elements hydrogen and oxygen. These two elements make up about 96.5% of ocean water. The remaining portion is made up of dissolved solids. The concentration of these dissolved solids determines the water's salinity.

Salinity is the number of grams of dissolved salts in 1,000 grams of sea water. The average salinity of ocean water is about 3.5%. In other words, one kilogram of sea water contains about 35 grams of salt. Sodium Chloride or salt (NaCl) is the most abundant of the dissolved salts. The dissolved salts also include smaller quantities of magnesium chloride, magnesium and calcium sulfates, and traces of several other salt elements. Salinity varies throughout the world's oceans; some areas, such as the Red Sea are considerably saltier and some, such as the Gulf of Finland, are less salty. The total salinity of the oceans varies from place to place and also varies with depth. Salinity is low near river mouths where the ocean mixes with fresh water, and salinity is high in areas of high evaporation rates.

The density of seawater is about 1020 kg·m^{-3} and the pH varies from 7.5 to 8.4. The temperature of seawater varies greatly. Certainly latitude plays an important role in this; oceans closer to the poles are nearly always colder. Patterns of wind and sun, however, can create large warming or cooling currents that influence ocean temperatures. Finally, seasonal changes play a role in ocean temperature. The high specific heat of water, however, means that these yearly changes are slow and significant effects are seen mostly in relatively shallow water (such as that near the coast).

The temperature of the ocean water varies with different latitudes and with ocean depths. The temperature of ocean water is about constant to depths of 90 meters (m). The temperature of surface water will drop rapidly from 28° C at the equator to -2° C at the Poles. The freezing point of sea water is lower than the freezing point of pure water. Pure water freezes at 0° C. The dissolved salts in the sea water keep sea water at a freezing point of -2° C. The freezing point of sea water may vary depending on its salinity in a particular location.

The ocean can be divided into three temperature zones. The surface layer consists of relatively warm water and exhibits most of the wave action present. The area where the wind and waves churn and mix the water is called the mixed layer. This is the layer where most living creatures are found due to abundant sunlight and warmth. The second layer is called the thermocline and it becomes increasingly cold as its depth increases. This change is due to the lack of energy from sunlight. The layer below the thermocline continues to the deep dark, very cold, and semi-barren ocean floor.

The various oceanic habitats are classified largely by temperature, the amount of light received, and distance from shore. Each of the oceanic environments, of course, has it's own uniquely adapted organisms.

Skill 39.8 **The beginning teacher analyzes the causes and effects of waves, tides, tidal bores, and tsunamis.**

A transfer of energy from tides, currents, or wind causes waves. Water will remain in place unless moved by the current or tide. Currents are caused by changes in water density, salinity, and pressure. Tides are primarily caused by the gravitational pull of the moon.

Waves move in an orbital pattern, causing an up and down motion. They have a forward or lateral motion only if moved by the wind, current, or tides. The depth of the waveform where the energy is felt is equal to ½ of the wavelength. Below that depth, the water remains relatively calm.

When a wave approaches the shore, the circular orbit action flattens out and becomes more elliptical. As the wavelength shortens, the wave steepens until it finally breaks, creating surf. The waves break at a distance of 1/20 of the wavelength.

The periodic rise and fall of the liquid bodies on Earth (known as tides) are the direct result of the gravitational influence of the Moon and to a much lesser extent, the Sun.

Tides are produced by the differences between gravitational forces acting on parts of an object. As shown in Netwon's Universal Law of Gravitation, the gravitational effect of two bodies is mutually constant and depends largely on the distance and mass between the objects.

The side of the Earth that faces the Moon is roughly 4,000 miles (6,400 km) closer to the moon than is the Earth's center. This has the effect of increasing the Moon's gravitational attraction on Earth's oceans and landforms. Although the effect is so small on the mass of the landforms as to be invisible, the effect on the liquid parts is greater.

The Moon's gravitational effect causes a bulge to form on both sides of the Earth. If we were able to view such subtle change from outer space, the affected waters would create an elliptical shape, compressing downward at the top and bottom of the planet and extending outward on the sides.

This double-bulge effect causes the tides to fall and rise twice a day, and the time of the high and low tides is dependent on the phase of the moon.

Yet not all locations are uniformly affected. The tidal cycle at a particular location is actually a very complicated interaction of the location's latitude, shape of the shore, etc.

Example: The Bay of Fundy has a twice-daily tide that exceeds 12 meters, while the northern coast of the Gulf of Mexico only has one tidal cycle that seldom exceeds 30 centimeters rise and fall.

Because of its distance from the Earth, the Sun's gravitational effect on tides is only half that of the Moon's.
However, when the gravitational effects of both the Sun and Moon join together during a new moon and a full moon phase, the tidal effects can be extreme.

During a new moon and a full moon, tidal effects are much more pronounced as the tidal bulges join together to produce very high and very low tides.

These pronounced types of tide are collectively known as Spring Tides. During the first and third quarters of the moon phases, the Sun's effect is negligible and consequently, the tides are lower. These are Neap Tides.

Earthquakes can trigger an underwater landslide or cause sea floor displacements that in turn, generate deep, omni-directional waves. Far out to sea these waves may be hardly noticeable. However, as they near the shoreline, the shallowing of the sea floor forces the waves upward in a "springing" type of motion. The tidal wave (tsunami) formed by the upward motion can grow to be quite immense and powerful depending on the topography of the sea floor and the magnitude of the earthquake.

Skill 39.9 The beginning teacher identifies the characteristics of different ocean zones (e.g., coastal, lighted, deep, estuaries, bays).

The ocean is commonly divided into five layers according to depth. Each layer has its own characteristics and a specific group of organisms reside there. The depth of water is key because photosynthesis requires solar energy. Therefore, the uppermost layer, where the light can penetrate, is where we can find phytoplankton. Phytoplankton are small, photosynthetic organisms which are the base of the oceanic food chain.

Epipelagic Zone – This layer extends from the surface to 200 meters (656 feet). It is in this zone that most of the visible light exists. The majority of plankton and fish are found here, as well as their predators (large fish, sharks, and rays).

Mesopelagic Zone - Extending from 200 meters (656 feet) to 1000 meters (3281 feet), the mesopelagic zone is also referred to as the twilight or midwater zone. Very little light penetrates here. Instead, most of the light observed is generated by bioluminescent creatures. A great diversity of strange fishes can be found here.

Bathypelagic Zone – This layer extends from 1000 meters (3281 feet) down to 4000 meters (13,124 feet). Here there is no penetration by solar light, so any light seen is in the form of bioluminescence. Most of the animals that live at these depths are black or red colored due to the lack of light. The water pressure at this depth is quite large, but a surprising number of creatures can be found here. Common inhabitants include fish, molluscs, jellies, and crustaceans. Sperm whales can dive down to this level in search of food.

Abyssopelagic Zone - Extending from 4000 meters (13,124 feet) to 6000 meters (19,686 feet), this zone has the least inhabitants. The water temperature is near freezing, and there is no light at all. Common organisms include invertebrates such as basket stars and squids. The name of this zone comes from the Greek meaning "no bottom", and refers to the ancient belief that the open ocean was bottomless.

Hadalpelagic Zone - This layer extends from 6000 meters (19,686 feet) to 10,000 meters (32,810 feet)- the sea floor. These areas are most often found in deep water trenches and canyons. In spite of the unimaginable pressures and cold temperatures, life can be found here. Generally, these include life forms that tolerate cool temperatures and low oxygen levels, such as starfish and tubeworms. The exception to this rule would be chemosynthetic communities living near deep-sea vents. These creatures create their own nutrients from carbon dioxide or methane released by the hot thermal vents. Chemosynthetic organisms then become prey to larger organisms. As such, chemosynthetic organisms are also primary producers and are at the bottom of the food chain, just like their photosynthetic friends, although they are at the opposite end of the ocean!

Competency 0040   **The teacher understands structure and function of the atmosphere.**

Skill 40.1   **The beginning teacher understands the composition of Earth's atmosphere.**

The Earth's atmosphere is very similar to a fluid. The atmosphere makes up only 0.25% of what we call the Earth, and like the fluids of the ocean, our atmosphere is driven by heat, primarily solar radiation. Having an atmosphere is not unique for a planet. To a degree, most of the planets in our solar system have an atmosphere, however, the presence of significant oxygen in Earth's atmosphere is unique and makes life possible on our planet.

Earth's atmosphere is composed of 78% Nitrogen, 21% Oxygen, and 1% other gasses.

Components of the Atmosphere

Water Vapor: Along with Carbon Dioxide (CO_2) and Methane, Water Vapor (H_2O) is considered a **Greenhouse** Gas: a gas that absorbs heat energy. Water Vapor is the most prevalent of the greenhouse gasses and is especially good at collecting heat energy, as evidenced by the Earth's ability to retain heat at night when solar radiation is lowest.

Dust & Aerosols: These are natural components of the atmosphere and their presence produces optical phenomena such as making the sky appear blue, rainbows, and the Northern and Southern Lights.

Pollutants: Some are man-made, including industrial waste, chemical refrigerants and hydrocarbons released from burning fossil fuels. Some are natural such as Terpene leased from trees, Saharan Dust, and CO_2 released by volcanoes.

Skill 40.2   **The beginning teacher understands the range of atmospheric conditions that organisms will tolerate (e.g., types of gases, temperature, particulate matter, moisture).**

Gases

There are numerous gases that may cause death when present in significant concentrations:

1. Hydrogen Sulfide - "sewer gas," a colorless gas with the odor of rotten eggs. Excessive exposure leads to death in confined spaces. Hydrogen sulfide causes a loss of sense of smell, inhibits the exchange of oxygen on the cellular level and causes asphyxiation.

2. Carbon monoxide - odorless, colorless gas formed by burning carbon based fuels (gas, wood). Carbon monoxide is also capable of affecting the fetus of a pregnant woman. Mild exposure to carbon monoxide may induce headaches and dizziness. Higher concentrations can cause 50% of the body's hemoglobin to be converted to carboxy-hemoglobin (HbCO), inhibiting the body's ability to transport oxygen.

3. Chlorine - toxic gas that irritates the respiratory system, normally accumulating at the bottom of poorly ventilated spaces. Causes coughing and chest pains, and may lead to death in higher concentrations.

4. Radon gas - and its solid decay products are carcinogens. Exposure to the inhaled solid radon gas decay products polonium-218 and 214 leads to the release within the lung of small bursts of energy in the form of alpha particles that can either cause double-strand DNA breaks or create free radicals that can damage DNA.

5. Other toxic gases include asbestos, bleach, diazanon (DDT), formaldehyde and kerosene.

Temperature

Human responses to the thermal environment and to internal heat production serve to maintain a narrow range of internal body temperatures of approximately 36 -38 °C (96 -100°F). The lower limit of temperature that man can endure depends on internal body temperature regulation. When core temperature falls below 35 °C (95 °F) due to external conditions, the body undergoes hypothermia, impairing normal muscular and cerebral functions and causing shivering and blood vessel constriction that leads to frostbite in extremities. At a core temperature of 32°C (89.6°F), humans experience delirium, complete confusion and extreme sleepiness. Death from extremely cold temperatures occurs at 24-26°C (75.2-78.8°F) or less due to irregular heartbeat or respiratory arrest. At 0 °C, all liquids within the body would be frozen.

The human body demonstrates signs of heat stress when core temperature climbs above 39°C (102.2°F). Between 39°C and 42°C, the following physiological reactions may occur: sweating, increased heart rate, severe vomiting, fainting, dizziness, convulsion, delirium, hallucinations, palpitations, breathlessness and drowsiness. Death may occur when core temperature reaches 43°C (109.4°F) through brain damage and cardio-respiratory shock. At 45 °C, thermal coagulation of intracellular proteins occurs. Mammalian muscle would be completely rigid at approximately 50°C.

Particulate Matter

Particulates (also referred to as aerosols or fine particles) are tiny particles of solid or liquid suspended in a gas. They range in size from less than 10 nanometres to more than 100 micrometres in diameter. The effects of inhaling particulates depend on the size of the particle, concentration of the particle and time of exposure. Larger particles are generally filtered in the nose and throat and do not cause problems. High concentrations of the fine particles of particulate matter have been found to present a serious threat to human health if they accumulate in the respiratory system. Particulate matter smaller than about 10 micrometres (PM10) may settle in the bronchi and lungs and cause health problems. Particles smaller than 2.5 micrometres (PM2.5) may penetrate into the gas-exchange regions of the lung, and may also cause plaque deposits in arteries, leading to vascular inflammation and atherosclerosis. Sources of PM2.5 include atmospheric reactions near power plants; car, truck, bus and off-road vehicle exhausts; and the burning of fuels such as wood, heating oil, coal and grass. PM2.5 is also produced by tobacco smoke, cooking, burning candles or oil lamps, and operating fireplaces and fuel-burning space heaters (e.g., kerosene heaters).

Moisture

The human body is comfortable when relative humidity ranges between 20 and 60 percent, because the body releases heat through evaporation of perspiration, heat conduction to the surrounding air and thermal radiation. High humidity decreases the evaporation of sweat from the skin and impairs the body's efforts to maintain acceptable body temperature. The combination of high humidity and temperature may inhibit the heat shed of warm blood brought to the body's surface through conduction to the air, resulting in a condition called hyperpyrexia.

Extremely dry air may also negatively affect the body. The breathing of dry air may cause asthma, bronchitis, sinusitis, nosebleeds and dehydration. Skin moisture evaporation can cause skin irritations and eye itching. Mild shocks to the body may occur when metal is touched, and the body may feel colder than the indicated atmospheric temperature.

Moisture content is important to the life cycle of amphibians, who require wetlands to reproduce. Animals and plants living in extreme areas, for example the rainforests and deserts, are also adapted to specific moisture content. In the desert, animals often forsage or hunt at night. In both the rainforests and deserts, xerophytes prosper.

Skill 40.3 **The beginning teacher identifies the layers of the atmosphere (e.g., troposphere, ionosphere, mesophere) and the characteristics of each layer.**

Layers of the Atmosphere

Troposphere: (Ground level to 11Km, 0 to 17.6 miles, or 0 to 92,928 feet.) The Troposphere varies in height according to the temperature. It is lower at the poles and higher at the equator. Because the pressure decreases, it gets colder as you go up in the Troposphere. Only very rarely do you have a mixing between the Troposphere and the next layer, the Stratosphere. All storms, weather fronts, and weather occur in the Troposphere.

Stratosphere: (11Km to 50Km, 17.6 to 80 miles, or 92,980 to 422,400 feet.) The Stratosphere is characterized by weak vertical air motion, and strong horizontal air motion. There is very little lifting or sinking air in the Stratosphere. Temperatures warm as you go up due to the presence of the Ozone layer contained within the Stratosphere.

Mesosphere: (50 to 85Km, 80 to 136 miles, or 422,400 to 718,080 feet.) It is bitterly cold in the Mesosphere.

Thermosphere: (85 to 600Km, 136 to 960 miles, or 718,000 to 5,068,800 feet.) This is the hottest portion of the atmosphere with rapid warming accompanying a rise in altitude. There are very few molecules left to block out the incoming solar radiation. The outer reaches of the Thermosphere are also sometimes referred to as the Exosphere.

Ionosphere: (Located within the upper portion of the Mesosphere at 80Km and goes into the Thermosphere). The ionosphere is an area of **free ions**: positively charged ions, produced as a result of solar radiation striking the atmosphere.

The solar wind strikes the Ionosphere at the polar dips in the Magnetosphere. The ions are excited to a higher energy state and this energy is released into the visible spectrum to form the Aurora Borealis (Northern Lights).

The Ionosphere varies with the time of day, season, and Sunspot cycles: When the Sunsets at night, less ions strike, extending radio wave communications. There is more radiation during Sunspot cycles. These hypercharge the atmosphere and can disrupt radio waves during the daytime.

<u>Ozone Laver</u> (O_3): (Contained within the Stratosphere). Ozone is essential to life on Earth and is continually formed and destroyed within the atmosphere. Only a very thin layer of ozone protects against UV (ultra violet) radiation. Ultra violet radiation scrambles the DNA codes in human cells, and can kill the cells or, at a minimum, cause cancer.

Skill 40.4   The beginning teacher recognizes that the Sun is the ultimate source of energy for the atmosphere.

The vast majority of energy on the Earth's surface is derived from sunlight. However, sunlight is attenuated by the Earth's atmosphere, so that not all this solar energy reaches the planet's surface. Specifically, about 1300 watts are delivered per square meter of Earth, but only about 1000 watts actually reach the surface.

It is easy for us to understand how sunlight warms the land and water on the surface of the Earth. We are similarly familiar with the capture of sunlight by solar cells, which then can be used for heating or electricity. However, it is important to understand that sunlight is the basis for many of our other sources of power. This is because sunlight is used to drive photosynthesis, which is the major method by which carbon is fixed by living things. The energy harnessed by plants is used to fuel all heterotrophs further up the food chain. When these life forms (plant or animal) die, they may ultimately be converted to fossil fuels. Thus the petroleum, oil, and other fossil fuels we use as a major power source all originally derived their energy from sunlight.

The sun and the energy it transfers to the Earth also influence the movement of air and water (i.e., the winds and ocean currents). This is a result of the fact that different areas of the Earth's surface receive varying amounts of energy from the sunlight. The movements of warmer and cooler masses of air or water are the source of wind and water currents. Note that this means that wind and hydrologic energy also have their origin in energy from the sun.

Finally, it is important to recognize that the Sun is a star with its own strong and ever changing magnetic field. These changes in the field are responsible for solar activity such as sunspots, solar flares, and solar wind. These changes in turn affect Earth's climate and sometimes increase or decrease the solar energy that reaches the entire Earth or certain areas. Fluctuations in the solar cycles can also lead to especially low or high temperatures. For instance, during the 17th and 18th centuries there was a period in which very few sunspots were seen. This lasted for about 70 years and coincided with the "Little Ice Age" in Europe, an era of unusually cold temperature throughout the continent. It is not only the extended period of changes in solar activity that effect climate and weather on Earth. For example, it has been observed that stratospheric winds near the equator blow in different directions, depending on changes in the solar cycle.

Skill 40.5 **The beginning teacher understands processes of energy transfer (e.g., convection, radiation, conduction, phase changes of water) within the atmosphere and at the boundaries between the atmosphere, landmasses, and oceans.**

Heat can be transferred through the processes of conduction, radiation, and convection. Conduction is the transmission of heat across something. Heat transfer always moves from a higher to a lower temperature. More dense substances usually conduct heat more readily than less dense matter. Radiation is the process of emitting energy. Energy is radiated in the form of waves or particles. Convection is the transfer of heat by currents within fluid form (liquids and gases only). Air in the atmosphere acts as a fluid for the transfer of heat energy. Convection, resulting indirectly from the energy generated by sun light, is responsible for many weather phenomena including wind and clouds.

The majority of the transfer of energy begins with the Sun. The Sun provides 17.3×10^{16} watts of energy to Earth's systems. This is 5000 times more energy than the Earth receives from its interior. Wind, rain, hail, snow, lightning, tornados and hurricanes are all results of energy transformations brought about by solar energy on the Earth. Some 34% of this is immediately reflected by the planetary albedo, as a result of clouds, snowfields, and even reflected light from water, rock or vegetation. The remaining energy from the Sun, and the energy from the interior of the Earth, drives Earth's systems.

Uneven heating of the Earth's surface causes the Earth's atmosphere to be warmed unevenly. During its ascent or descent, a parcel of air is neither heated nor cooled by radiation, conduction, phase changes of water, or mixing with its surroundings. Heating and cooling is solely accomplished by the expansion or contraction of the air in response to pressure changes. Air over the equator rises. As it rises, it moves northward, cools over the poles and sinks. When it sinks, it moves southward, warms and begins the convection current again. The Coriolis effect causes the wind to veer in each hemisphere, causing three circulation belts in each hemisphere to form.

Skill 40.6   The beginning teacher knows types, characteristics, and processes of formation of clouds (e.g., cumulus, stratus, cirrus) and precipitation (e.g., rain, snow, hail).

Cloud formation

Condensation or the removal of water above the Earth's surface results in the formation of clouds. Generally, clouds develop in any air mass that becomes saturated or has a relative humidity of 100%. Certain processes that cool the temperature of an air mass to its dew point or frost point can cause saturation. There are four processes or any combination of these processes that create saturation and cause clouds to form.

1. Orographic uplift occurs when elevated land forces air to rise.
2. Convectional lifting is the result of surface heating of air at ground level. If enough heating occurs, the air rises, expands, and cools.
3. Convergence or frontal lifting occurs when two air masses come together. One of the air masses is usually warm and moist, while the other is cool and dry.
4. Radiative cooling usually occurs at night when the sun is no longer heating the ground and the surrounding air. The ground and the air begin to cool forming fog.

Clouds are classified by their physical appearance and given special Latin names corresponding to the cloud's appearance and the altitude where they occur. Classification by appearance results in three simple categories: cirrus, stratus, and cumulus clouds. Cirrus clouds appear fibrous. Stratus clouds appear layered. Cumulus clouds appear as heaps or puffs, similar to cotton balls in a pile. Classification by altitude result in four groupings: high, middle, low, and clouds that show vertical development. Other adjectives are added to the names of the clouds to show specific characteristics.

Cloud Classifications

High Clouds: -13 °F (-25 °C) Composed almost exclusively of ice crystals
> Cirrus >23,000 ft (7,000 m). Nearly transparent, delicate silky strands (mare's tails), or patches.
> Cirrostratus >23,000 ft (7,000 m). A thin veil or sheet that partially or totally covers the sky. Nearly transparent, the sun or moon readily shines through.
> Cirrocumulus >23,000 ft (7,000 m). Small, white, rounded patches arranged in a wave or spotted mackerel pattern

Middle Clouds: 32 - -13 °F (0 - -25 °C) Composed of supercooled water droplets or a mixture of droplets and ice crystals
> Altostratus 6600 - 23,000 ft (2000 - 7000 m). Uniform white or bluish-gray layers that partially or totally obscure the sky layer
> Altocumulus 6600 - 23,000 ft (2000 - 7000 m). Roll-like puffs or patches that form into parallel bands or waves

Low Clouds: > 23 °F (-5 °C) Composed mostly of water droplets
> Stratocumulus 0-6,600 ft (0-2000 m). Large irregularly shaped puffs or rolls separated by bands of clear sky
> Stratus 0-6600 ft (0-2000 m). Uniform gray layer that stretches from horizon to horizon. Drizzle may fall from the cloud
> Nimbostratus 0-13,120 ft (0-4000 m). Thick, uniform gray layer from which precipitation (significant rain or snow) is falling

Clouds with Vertical Development: Water droplets build upward and spread laterally
> Cumulus 0-9840 ft (0-3000 m). Resemble cotton balls dotting the sky.
> Cumulonimbus 0-9840 ft (0-3000 m). Often associated with thunderstorms, these large puffy, clouds have smooth or flattened tops, and can produce heavy rain and thunder.

Precipitation

All forms of precipitation start from an interaction of water vapor and other particulate matter in the atmosphere. These particulates act as a nucleus for raindrops, as the water vapor particles attached themselves to the other airborne particles.

Because one of water's major properties is that its water particles attract other water particles, the raindrop grows as water vapor particles accrete around the nuclei.

Drizzle: any form of liquid precipitation where the drops are less than 0.02 inches in diameter.

Rain: any form of liquid precipitation where the drops are greater than 0.02 inches in diameter.

Virga: the meteorological condition where rain evaporates before touching the ground. You see it rain, but it never hits the ground.

Snow: water molecules that form into ice crystals through freezing. The shape of the snowflakes depend on the temperature at which they formed:

Needles = 0°C to -10°C.
Dendrites= -10°C to -20°C.
Plates= -20°C to -30°C.
Columns= -30°C to -40°C.

Freezing Rain: drops fall as rain but immediately depose (freeze) upon hitting an extremely cold surface such as power lines, roofs, or the ground. This is also called an **Ice Storm**.

Rime Ice: ice droplets that have tiny air bubbles trapped within the ice, producing an opaque whitish layer of granular ice.

Sleet: officially called ice pellets, these are drops of rain 5mm or less in diameter. Sleet freezes before hitting the ground and bounce when they strike a surface.

Hail: precipitation in the form of balls or lumps of ice. Hail forms when an ice pellet is transported through a cloud that contains varied concentrations of super cooled water droplets. The pellet may descend slowly through the entire cloud, or it may be caught in a cycle of updraft and downdraft. The ice pellet grows by accreting (adding) freezing water droplets. Eventually, weight of the hail grows too heavy to be supported by the air column and falls to the ground as a hailstone. The size of the stone depends on the amount of time spent in the cloud.

Fog: a cloud that touches the ground. Fog forms when cold air moves over a warmer surface. Fog is very common along shorelines because the specific heat of water retains heat and is consequently much warmer than the overlaying air. Fog can also form inland where the same basic conditions exist.

Skill 40.7 **The beginning teacher knows the characteristics of air masses (e.g., temperature, moisture) and how air masses form and interact (e.g., fronts).**

Parcel of Air (Air Mass): a large area of air, which assumes a characteristic temperature, pressure, and humidity from sitting over a landmass. Horizontally, the parcel has relatively uniform temperature, pressure, and humidity. Vertically, the parcel may have widely differing temperatures, pressures, and humidity. *Remember: when you think of air parcels, think in the horizontal plane.*

Front: a narrow zone of transition between air masses of different densities that is usually due to temperature contrasts. Because they are associated with temperature, fronts are usually referred to as either warm or cold.

Warm Front: a front whose movement causes the warm air (less dense) to advance, while the cold air (more dense) retreats. A warm front usually triggers a cloud development sequence of cirrus, cirrostratus, altostratus, nimbostratus, and stratus. It may result in an onset of light rain or snowfall immediately ahead of the front, which gives way as the cloud sequence forms, to steady precipitation (light to moderate), until the front passes, a time frame that may exceed 24 hours.

The gentle rains associated with a warm front are normally welcomed by farmers. However, if it is cold enough for snow to fall, the snow may significantly accumulate. If the air is unstable, cumulonimbus clouds may develop, and brief, intense thunderstorms may punctuate the otherwise gentler rain or snowfall.

Cold Front: a front whose movement causes the cold air (more dense) to displace the warm air (less dense). The results of cold front situations depend on the stability of the air. If the air is stable, nimbostratus and altostratus clouds may form, and brief showers may immediately precede the front.

If the air is unstable, there is greater uplift, cumulonimbus clouds may tower over nimbostratus and cirrus clouds are blown downstream from the cumulonimbus by the winds at high altitude. Thunderstorms may occur, accompanied by gusty surface winds and hail, as well as other, more violent weather. If the cold front moves quickly (roughly 28 mph or greater), a squall line of thunderstorms may form either right ahead of the front or up to 180 miles ahead of it.

Occluded Front: a front where a cold front has caught up to a warm front and has intermingled, usually by sliding under the warmer air. Cold fronts generally move faster than warm fronts and occasionally overrun slower moving warm fronts. The weather ahead of an occluded front is similar to that of a warm front during its advance, but switches to that of a cold front as the cold front passes through.

Stationary Front: a front that shows no overall movement. The weather produced by this front can vary widely and depends on the amount of moisture present and the relative motions of the air pockets along the front. Most of the precipitation falls on the cold side of the front.

Skill 40.8   The beginning teacher understands the types (e.g., blizzards, hurricanes, tornadoes), characteristics, and causes of severe weather.

A **Meteorological Bomb** is the term applied to rapidly dropping pressure (1mb/hr) and this drop creates a very strong pressure gradient that is often associated with stormy weather such as hurricanes or 'noreasters.

Hurricanes are produced by temperature and pressure differentials between the tropical seas and the atmosphere.

Powered by heat from the sea, they are steered by the easterly trade winds and the temperate Westerlies, as well as their own incredible energy. Hurricane development starts in June in the Atlantic, Caribbean, and Gulf of Mexico, and lasts until the end of hurricane season in late November.

Hurricanes are called by different names depending on their location. In the Indian Ocean they are called **Cyclones**. In the Atlantic, and east of the international dateline in the Pacific, they are called Hurricanes. In the western Pacific they are called **Typhoons**. Regardless of the name, a hurricane can be up to 500 miles across, last for over two weeks from inception to death, and can produce devastation on an immense scale.

Tornado: an area of extreme low pressure, with rapidly rotating winds beneath a cumulonimbus cloud. Tornadoes are normally spawned from a Super Cell Thunderstorm. They can occur when very cold air and very warm air meet, usually in the Spring.

Tornadoes represent the lowest pressure points on the Earth and move across the landscape at an average speed of 30 mph. The average size of a tornado is 100 yards, but they can be as large a mile wide. A tornado's wind speed ranges from 65 to 300 mph and has an average duration of 10 to 15 minutes, but has been known to last up to 3 hours. Tornadoes usually occur in the late afternoon (3 to 7 p.m.) in conjunction with the rear of a thunderstorm. Most tornadoes spin counter-clockwise in the northern hemisphere, and spin clockwise in the southern hemisphere. They are not dependent on the Coriolis Effect because of the way they are formed.

Worldwide, the U.S. has the most tornadoes and most of these occur in the spring. Texas has the most tornadoes, but Florida has the largest number per square mile. Tornadoes are without a doubt the most violent of all storms. Roughly 120 people each year are killed in the United States by tornadoes.

Storms that occur only in the winter are known as **blizzards** or ice storms. A blizzard is a storm with strong winds, blowing snow and frigid temperatures. An ice storm consists of falling rain that freezes when it strikes the ground, covering everything with a layer of ice.

Skill 40.9 The beginning teacher identifies the types, characteristics, and distribution of climates and the factors (e.g., latitude, maritime effect, deforestation) that affect local and global climate.

The Köppen climate system explains that the origin of the climate is based on the average monthly and yearly temperatures, location of the landmass, precipitation rates, and seasonality of the precipitation. When Köppen, a climatologist, created his classification system, he determined that one of the best indicators for climate is native plant life. He created the Köppen climate system map with native vegetation in mind.

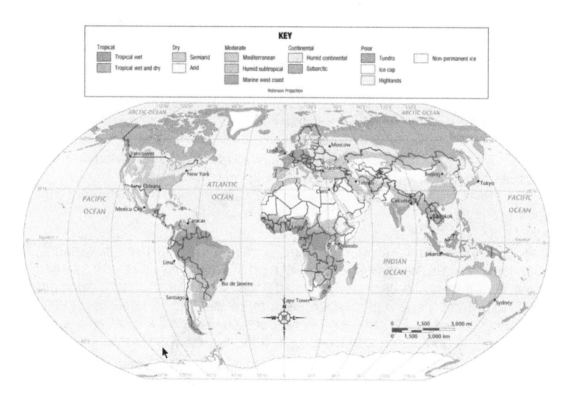

Types of Climate

1.) **Tropical/Megathermal Climate**: Characterized by a constant high temperature over 18°C or 64.4°F. There are three subcategories: tropical rain forest, tropical monsoon, and tropical Savanna. The tropical rain forest climate has more than 60 mm of rain each month of the year. There are no season changes. The tropical monsoon climate will have more than 100 mm of rain total in the year, but may have some months that fall below 60 mm of rain due to change in wind direction as the seasons change. The tropical savanna climates have a prominent dry season and have less than 100 mm of rain each year.

2.) **Arid and Semiarid Climate:** The precipitation of the region is less than the evapotranspiration of the region.

3.) **Temperate/Mesothermal Climate:** The average temperature is above 10°C for the warmest months and between -3°C and 18°C in the coldest months. There are four subcategories: Mediterranean climate, humid subtropical, maritime temperate, and maritime subarctic. The Mediterranean climate is found on the western sides of continents. It has moderate temperatures and experiences a polar front in the winter and a tropical front in the summer. Summers are usually hot and dry. The humid subtropical climate is found on the interior of the continents or on the east coast of the continents. The summers are usually very humid due to the trade winds bringing moisture to the region. The maritime temperate climate experiences a polar front all year. It is usually found on the continents between 45° and 55° latitude. The weather is usually overcast year round. Finally, the maritime subarctic climate is closer to the poles than the maritime temperate climates and is usually limited to thin strips of land or islands off the western coast of the continents.

4.) **Continental/Microthermal Climate:** Characterized by temperatures above 10°C in the summer months and below -3°C in the winter months. There are three subcategories: hot summer continental climate, warm summer continental climate, and continental subarctic climate. The hot summer continental climate occurs inland around 30° to 40° latitude. They can be affected by monsoons. The warm summer continental climate is found inland between 40° to 50° latitude in North America, and up to 60° latitude in Eastern Europe due to wind patterns. The continental subarctic climate exists inland in the 50° to 60° latitude.

5.) **Polar Climates:** Temperatures are below 10°C all year. There are two subcategories: the tundra climate and the ice cap climate. The tundra climate is dry and has an average temperature between 0° and 10°C in the warmest months. The ice cap climate has temperature below 0°C year round.

A number of factors affect the climate of a given location. These factors include latitude, elevation, topography, and proximity to large bodies of water and cold or warm ocean currents.

Latitude

Latitude is the measure of how far you are north or south of the equator. Latitude has a pronounced effect on climate because it determines how much solar energy a location receives. Locations close to the equator receive more direct sunlight and, thus, more radiant energy and heat. Locations distant from the equator (and nearer the Earth's poles) receive less direct sunlight as the sun's rays strike the Earth at an angle. Thus, locations closer to the poles receive less radiant energy and heat.

Locations between the Tropics of Capricorn and Cancer, located approximately 23 degrees south and north of the equator respectively, experience a tropical climate, typified by hot, moist weather throughout the year. The Arctic and Antarctic Circles, located at approximately 66 degrees north and south of the equator respectively, define the Polar Regions. Locations north of the Arctic Circle and south of the Antarctic Circle experience a polar climate, typified by extremely cold temperatures and varying lengths of days. Finally, the temperate zones, defined as the areas between the tropics and the Polar Regions, experience seasonal climates, typified by cold weather in the winter and warm weather in the summer.

Elevation

In general, elevation, or distance above sea level, has a clear effect on climate. When comparing two locations at the same latitude, the one with the higher elevation will have a cooler climate. As you go up a mountain, for instance, the air pressure decreases and the air gets less dense. Less dense air does not hold heat as well as more dense air does. Thus, locations at higher elevations have consistently cooler climates.

Topography

Topography, or the features of the land, can also affect a location's climate. For example, the presence or absence of mountains can greatly affect the amount and location of precipitation in a given region. Mountains typically receive a large amount of precipitation because less dense air at higher elevations cannot hold as much moisture. As air rises up a mountain precipitation is more likely to occur. Conversely, as air currents travel over a mountain and down the other side, the air heats up, becomes denser, and is able to hold more moisture. Thus, the leeward side of mountains (or side facing away from the wind) is often very dry. For example, Death Valley in California is a leeward desert caused by the aforementioned mountain effect.

Proximity to Large Bodies of Water

Large bodies of water have a pronounced affect on the climate of surrounding landmasses, by moderating temperatures and increasing precipitation. Coastal areas generally experience cooler temperatures during the summer and warmer temperatures during the winter than their inland counterparts. This moderation of temperature results from the ability of large bodies of water to absorb a large amount of solar energy. During the summer, bodies of water trap heat, keeping temperatures cooler. Conversely, during the winter, the latent heat stored in the water escapes to warm the atmosphere slightly. Finally, coastal areas generally receive more precipitation because the bodies of water serve as a direct source of moisture.

Cold or Warm Ocean Currents

There is a direct relationship between the temperature of ocean currents and the temperature of surrounding landmasses. Coastal areas near warm ocean currents experience warmer climates than coastal areas at similar latitudes near cold ocean currents. Warm ocean currents heat the air above the ocean, while cold ocean currents cool the air above the ocean. The varying atmospheric temperatures and related wind patterns act to warm or cool the related coastal regions.

Skill 40.10 The beginning teacher identifies the effects of global phenomena (e.g., jet stream, El Niño) on local weather patterns.

El Nino is a reverse of the normal weather patterns in the Pacific. A low-pressure area normally sits in the Pacific Ocean west of Hawaii and a high-pressure area normally sits off of the California coast. When an El Nino forms, these pressure areas shift eastward, causing the low-pressure area to be situated below Hawaii and the high-pressure area to move inland over California. Because of the shift in pressure areas, an El Nino affects the wind patterns (especially the jet stream and trade winds), and creates a wide variety of effects., including a direct impact on commercial fishing.

Normally, there is a shallow warm water layer over the colder, deeper waters along the coastlines. The temperature disparity causes an upwelling of rich nutrients from the lower layers of the cold water, creating a feeding zone that attracts a variety of marine life forms. In an El Nino situation, the warm water layer increases in both area coverage and depth. It extends downward, blocking the nutrient rich upwell from reaching the feeding zone. Although many species can migrate to more friendly waters, some have limited mobility and die. The fishery area can become permanently barren depending on the intensity, duration, and repetition of El Nino events. Other effects of El Nino are both direct and indirect.

Direct Effects
In the west, fires and drought.
In the east, rain, landslides, and fish migration.

Indirect Effects
Greater chance of hurricanes in Hawaii.
Lesser chance of hurricanes in Virginia because of weakened Trade Winds.
Less rain during September and October.
Coastal erosion in the western states.
Fewer storms that deposit snow in the Cascades in Washington and Oregon.
The Jet Streams are altered as the high pressure areas move.

A **La Nina** is the opposite of El Nino. However, it does not have as great effect. It causes the East to be wetter and the west to be drier. Many scientists believe that both of these conditions are caused by a change in the surface temperature of the water of the Pacific Ocean.

The rise and fall of heat at the 0°, 30°, 60°, and 90' latitudes drive convection cells by causing the pressure gradients to speed up or slow down. The **Jet Streams** are zones of very strong, moving air confined to narrow columns and mark the zones where the cold Polar air and the warmer air meet This produces the greatest pressure gradients. The Jet Streams can be either straight or dramatically dip, creating ridges and troughs on the 500-300mb pressure surface.

The flatter the isobars, the more evenly balanced the weather. The more pronounced the ridges and troughs, the more pronounced the swings in the weather.

Skill 40.11   The beginning teacher understands weather maps and the principles, procedures, and technology of weather forecasting (e.g., satellite technology, computer models).

Meteorologists use a combination of many resources to forecast weather. Satellites in space send us pictures of the atmosphere (clouds). From these images, meteorologists can learn about the amount, density, and type of clouds present. This is especially helpful when tracking storms forming over water, such as a hurricane. For radar maps, a beam of energy is sent out and then how much of that beam is reflected back and the time needed for the beam to return are measured. Those measurements are plotted to give meteorologists an idea of what is in the sky. For example, rain, snow, and sleet will reflect the energy beam back to the radar. More return energy is mapped by bright colors. This is why a television station's broadcasting map of a storm center is often red or orange. When a small amount of the energy beam is detected by the radar, we say there is low reflectivity and this is indicated by darker colors. Temperature maps are also color coded. As you might expect, a red color indicates hot, and blue indicates cold with gradients in between the two. Numerals are often superimposed over colors to add specificity. There are also maps showing wind presence/direction and storm fronts. All of these maps together help a meteorologist to predict weather. The resulting local forecast often includes a great deal of **Kentucky Windage**: experience based guesses by local meteorologists, and can vary considerably from the forecasts of the National Weather Service. The accuracy of local forecasting is dependent on the experience and expertise of the local meteorologist. Forecasting is only as good as the data collected and local intuition (experience) modifications.

Skill 40.12   The beginning teacher understands that climate changes over time (e.g., ice ages).

Climate varies over time. The diurnal cycle is how the weather has changed in the last 24 hours. Over a year, regions experience changes in seasons. Climate of a region may vary due to changes in atmospheric dust from large dust storms and volcanic eruptions. Over the course of 10 years, changes in climate may take place due to the El Niño and La Niña cycles in Earth's oceans. Climate change over the course of 100 years can be attributed to solar variability and changes within ocean temperature. Over the last 100 years, significant climate changes have been noted in some regions due to deforestation and increased carbon dioxide output. Climate variability over 1000 years can be linked to thermocline circulation in the oceans and changes in the carbon cycle. Paleoclimatology indicates that climate variation on the 100,000 year time frame can be attributed to the Milankovich cycles, solar variability, precession, and orbit eccentricity. By studying variations in climate, paleoclimatologists can determine how current changes in climate are related to long term trends. This can help scientists to further understand humanity's effect on climate change.

Over the past two to three million years, the Earth has undergone periods of glaciation where up to one-third of northern Europe and northern North America were covered in expansive sheets of snow and ice. These glaciations are collectively known as the **Ice Ages**. The last ice age period spanned the time frame of 18,000 to 10,000 years ago.

Although there is some scientific evidence that suggests even earlier periods of glaciation- up to a billion years past- the vast majority of these advance and retreat cycles took place in the Pleistocene epoch, spanning a time period of roughly two million to ten thousand years in the past.

The bulk of scientific argument generally falls within two schools of thought: causes external to the Earth, and causes exclusively internal to the Earth's processes.

During the "Great Ice Age" of the Pleistocene and Holocene Epochs, ice and snow - an estimated 40 million km^3 –covered approximately one-third of the Earth's surface. The glaciations also caused a 50 to 75 ft drop in sea level worldwide, which in turn, caused land bridges between continents to form. **Examples**: England was not an island. There was a land bridge to the European continent. Likewise, Asia and North America were connected by the Bearing Straits land bridge.

The cyclic periods of the ice ages placed great stress on the various life forms. It forced the "evolve or die" principle of evolution to be applied. As the glaciations spread southward, arctic climatic conditions spread across northern Europe and the United States. These conditions promoted gigantism among life forms, because larger sizes were better able to retain and regulate body heat.

Competency 0041   **The teacher understands the effects of natural events and human activity on Earth systems.**

Skill 41.1   **The beginning teacher analyzes issues (e.g., economic impact, environmental effects, availability) regarding the use of Earth resources (e.g., fossil fuels, renewable and nonrenewable resources).**

Humans have a tremendous impact on the world's natural resources. The world's natural water supplies are affected by human use. Waterways are major sources for recreation and freight transportation. Oil and wastes from boats and cargo ships pollute the aquatic environment. The aquatic plant and animal life is affected by this contamination. To obtain drinking water, contaminants such as parasites, pollutants and bacteria are removed from raw water through a purification process involving various screening, conditioning and chlorination steps. Most uses of water resources, such as drinking and crop irrigation, require fresh water. Only 2.5% of water on Earth is fresh water, and more than two thirds of this fresh water is frozen in glaciers and polar ice caps. Consequently, in many parts of the world, water use greatly exceeds supply. This problem is expected to increase in the future.

Plant resources also make up a large part of the world's natural resources. Plant resources are renewable and can be re-grown and restocked. Plant resources can be used by humans to make clothing, buildings and medicines, and can also be directly consumed. Forestry is the study and management of growing forests. This industry provides the wood that is essential for use as construction timber or paper. Cotton is a common plant found on farms of the Southern United States. Cotton is used to produce fabric for clothing, sheets, furniture, etc. Another example of a plant resource that is not directly consumed is straw, which is harvested for use in plant growth and farm animal care. The list of plants grown to provide food for the people of the world is extensive. Major crops include corn, potatoes, wheat, sugar, barley, peas, beans, beets, flax, lentils, sunflowers, soybeans, canola, and rice. These crops may have alternate uses as well. For example, corn is used to manufacture cornstarch, ethanol fuel, high fructose corn syrup, ink, biodegradable plastics, chemicals used in cosmetics and pharmaceuticals, adhesives, and paper products.

Other resources used by humans are known as "non-renewable" resources. Such resources, including fossil fuels, cannot be re-made and do not naturally reform at a rate that could sustain human use. Non-renewable resources are therefore depleted and not restored. Presently, non-renewable resources provide the main source of energy for humans. Common fossil fuels used by humans are coal, petroleum and natural gas, which all form from the remains of dead plants and animals through natural processes after millions of years. Because of their high carbon content, when burnt these substances generate high amounts of energy as well as carbon dioxide, which is released back into the atmosphere increasing global warming. To create electricity, energy from the burning of fossil fuels is harnessed to power a rotary engine called a turbine. Implementation of the use of fossil fuels as an energy source provided for large-scale industrial development.

Mineral resources are concentrations of naturally occurring inorganic elements and compounds located in the Earth's crust that are extracted through mining for human use. Minerals have a definite chemical composition and are stable over a range of temperatures and pressures. Construction and manufacturing rely heavily on metals and industrial mineral resources. These metals may include iron, bronze, lead, zinc, nickel, copper, tin, etc. Other industrial minerals are divided into two categories: bulk rocks and ore minerals. Bulk rocks, including limestone, clay, shale and sandstone, are used as aggregate in construction, in ceramics or in concrete. Common ore minerals include calcite, barite and gypsum. Energy from some minerals can be utilized to produce electricity fuel and industrial materials. Mineral resources are also used as fertilizers and pesticides in the industrial context.

Skill 41.2   The beginning teacher analyzes the effects of natural events (e.g., fires, hurricanes, volcanic eruptions) and human activity (e.g., mining, fishing, reforestation, ocean dumping, municipal development) on aquatic and terrestrial ecosystems.

An important topic in science is the effect of natural disasters and events on society and the effect human activity has on inducing such events. Naturally occurring geological, weather, and environmental events can greatly affect the lives of humans. In addition, the activities of humans can induce such events that would not normally occur.

Nature-induced hazards include floods, landslides, avalanches, volcanic eruptions, wildfires, earthquakes, hurricanes, tornadoes, droughts, and disease. Such events often occur naturally, because of changing weather patterns or geological conditions. Property damage, resource destruction, and the loss of human life are the possible outcomes of natural hazards. Thus, natural hazards are often extremely costly on both an economic and personal level.

While many nature-induced hazards occur naturally, human activity can often stimulate such events. For example, destructive land use practices such as mining can induce landslides or avalanches if not properly planned and monitored. In addition, human activities can cause other hazards including global warming and waste contamination. Global warming is an increase in the Earth's average temperature resulting, at least in part, from the burning of fuels by humans. Global warming is hazardous because it disrupts the Earth's environmental balance and can negatively affect weather patterns. Ecological and weather pattern changes can promote the natural disasters listed above. Finally, improper hazardous waste disposal by humans can contaminate the environment. One important effect of hazardous waste contamination is the stimulation of disease in human populations. Thus, hazardous waste contamination negatively affects both the environment and the people that live in it.

One of the most significant effects of human activity on the coastline is the building of **structures** that affect coastal morphology. In many areas, sand would normally be transported along a beach due to wave action, and beaches and sandbars would shift with time and major weather events. However, homeowners and businesses frequently build in these areas, as they are desirable locations. This creates a need to control and retain the beach. It is becoming increasingly clear that it is difficult or impossible to do so over the long-term. The photo below shows how jetties and groins retain sand behind them, but deplete sand in areas beyond. A jetty that protects one person's beach may destroy another further along.

Seawalls placed along shorelines are intended to protect property from erosion, but reflect wave energy back. This increased wave energy increases erosion of beaches in front of the seawall and may eventually cause undermining of the structure.

Mining is the process by which minerals are extracted from the Earth. These minerals may often include coal, limestone, gold, silver, and many other metals. Mining causes serious disturbance of land and ecosystems. Mine reclamation is the process by which mined land is restored to a useful state, such as a productive ecosystem or industrial or municipal land. Mine reclamation has become a regular part of modern mining industry, and improves water and air quality in abandoned mine areas. Reclaimed sites may function as pasture, hayland, recreational areas, wild life habitat and wetlands.

Mine reclamation techniques stabilize land surfaces against water and wind erosion using material placement and capping. The final step in mine reclamation is often the replacement of topsoil and its revegetation with suitable plant species. Revegetation techniques include hydroseeding, a process commonly used for large-scale or hillside properties in which grass seed is sown in a stream of water aimed at the ground, as well as native seed drilling techniques, through which seeds can be sown in well-spaced rows at specific depths. Tree planting is another important part of mine reclamation. Trees are generally planted in low densities to allow for natural propagation. Tree seeds can be pelletalized to prevent excessive movement by the wind. This method proves particularly effective on rocky, barren slopes.

In 1972, the **Marine Protection, Research and Sanctuaries Act** was issued to "prevent or strictly limit the dumping into ocean waters of any material that would adversely affect human health, welfare, or amenities, or the marine environment, ecological systems, or economic potentialities." Prior to this act, the dumping of industrial, nuclear, and other waste products into the ocean was common practice. For example, a 1970 Report to the President from the Council on Environmental Quality concluded that 38 million tons of dredged material (34% of which was polluted) 4.5 million tons of industrial waste, 4.5 million tons of sewage sludge containing heavy metals, and 0.5 million tons of construction and demolition debris was disposed in ocean waters in 1968.

Currently, illegal ocean dumping is widespread. The majority of material dumped at sea is generated by dredging and amounts to hundreds of millions of tons a year. Approximately 10% of this material contains pollutants from shipping, industrial and municipal discharges and land run off. These pollutants include heavy metals, such as cadmium, mercury and chromium, hydrocarbons, such as oil, pesticides and nutrients such as nitrogen and phosphorous.

Ocean dumping may result in the rapid and substantial degradation of marine water quality and ecosystems. Toxic materials disposed of at sea may cause acute or chronic toxic effects on marine organisms, and potentially contaminate human food sources. Dumping may also cause drastic decreases in ocean water oxygen concentrations, resulting in dead zones. When one habitat or species is affected by ocean pollution, the survival of organisms that rely on that niche is compromised as well, resulting in massive loss of life and even extinction. For example, sea turtles, manatees, fish, shrimp and crabs rely on sea grass for survival. This plant is particularly sensitive to pollution, and its numbers are decreasing drastically. Loss of sea grass affects the survival of animals such as sea lions, which in turn causes sea urchins, the sea lion's prey, to increase in number, upsetting the delicate ecosystem that is the ocean.

Skill 41.3 **The beginning teacher demonstrates an understanding of factors affecting the quality, use, and conservation of water (e.g., floods, droughts, agriculture, dams).**

FLOOD

A **stream channel** is the result of normal or average water flow. If more water than average tries to flow through the channel, a **flood** results.

Water that flows into a stream comes from many sources but is primarily due to run off. Rainwater evaporates, infiltrates, or runs off. The run off collects in the streams. The amount of run off depends on three major factors.

- Topography: The steeper the topography, the greater the run off. A lower topography encourages infiltration.

- Soil/Sediment type: A porous material encourages infiltration, a non-porous material encourages run off.

- Vegetation: Acts as a barrier to slow or stop water, allowing infiltration to occur.

Flood Terms

Stage: the elevation of the water's surface.

Flood Stage: the elevation where the stream will exceed the height of the bank.

Crest: the maximum elevation of the water's surface during a flood event.

Upstream Flood: a flood that occurs closer to the stream head, usually in an area with steeper topography. These floods are usually localized and quickly move out of upstream and move downstream which is better able to handle excess water.

Downstream Flood: a type of flood that occurs downstream, it affects a wider area and is slower to recede. Major flood events are usually downstream floods.

Yearly Flood: the stage to which the stream can be expected to rise due to spring melt or large rainstorms.

DROUGHT

A drought is a period of time of abnormal dryness. Drought is caused by atmospheric flow. In times of normal precipitation, water vapor rises with a low pressure system, condenses, forms clouds, and precipitation occurs. In times of drought, however, areas of high pressure stall allowing the water vapor to stay close to the surface. If the water vapor does not rise, it cannot condense to form clouds and thus precipitation is low. High pressure systems stall because of upper atmospheric conditions and the jet stream. La Niña, a cooling of the water in the Pacific, can also cause drought. If the water in the Pacific is cooler, less air rises over the Pacific. The water vapor does not rise, therefore clouds and precipitation do not form. Periods of drought do not have to be periods of time with complete lack of precipitation. Times of minimal precipitation cause drought as well. If the input of precipitation in the system is less than the amount of water going out through plant and human use, drought occurs.

WATER AND AGRICULTURE

Another important environmental aspect of the effect of human activity on run-off is the additional contribution to water pollution. As the run-off flows across land, it picks up and carries particulates and soil contaminants. The pollutants, including pesticides and fertilizers used agriculturally, then accumulate in the body of water to which the run-off flows. Increased run-off means even more pollutants in the water supply and that even more fertilizer and pesticides must be applied to grow crops efficiently. Better agricultural techniques to prevent soil depletion, reclamation of waterways, and banning use of chemicals damaging to the atmosphere are examples of ongoing initiatives to ensure resources for future generations.

Skill 41.4   The beginning teacher evaluates methods of land use and understands issues in land-use management (e.g., development of barrier islands).

One of the big issues of late has been land use management. Natural disasters and pollution issues have made it necessary to create better plans for managing land. Planning for land use can include the following:

1.) Safety of humans and property
2.) Water quality protection
3.) Protection of ecosystems
4.) Increasing recreation and access to an area
5.) Delineation of landslide prone areas and floodplains
6.) Identification of water pollution and soil pollution problems

By addressing these and other issues, environmental problems, loss of life, and loss of property can be averted.

Barrier Islands: Barrier Islands make up 80% of the U.S. East Coast. Natural examples include Spits, Baymouth Bars, and Tomboloes. Man made structures also exist to protect certain coastal areas. Unfortunately, this often has the unwanted effect of damaging areas further downstream.

Skill 41.5 The beginning teacher identifies the sources (e.g., burning of fossil fuels, industrial production of heavy metals, release of chlorofluorocarbons) and effects of pollution (e.g., mercury contamination of fish, acid rain, lead poisoning, ozone depletion).

Global environment is posing a huge challenge to governments of all countries. Our technological and scientific advances have drastically affected our environment. Many governments are trying to face this challenge by using technology and also by passing laws to stop some undesirable practices that are polluting our planet.

The governments of some nations (including the U.S.) are taking this problem very seriously. They are concerned with multiple things: to allow industrial growth while restoring the environment and ensuring the health of humans. In order to understand this problem, we need to look at some of the contemporary issues like - CFCs as coolants, ozone depletion, insecticides for protecting crops, and pollution events.

CFCs as coolants

Chlorofluorocarbons (CFCs) are a family within the group called haloalkanes (also known as halogenoalkanes). This group of chemical compounds consists of alkanes (such as methane or ethane), with one or more halogens (chlorine or fluorine) linked, making them a type of organic halides. They are known under many chemical names and are widely used as fire extinguishers, propellants, and solvents. Some haloalkanes have negative effects on the environment such as ozone depletion. Use of certain chloroalkanes has been phased out by the IPPC directive on greenhouse gases in 1994 and by the Volatile Organic Compounds (VOC) directive of the EU (European Union) in 1997.

Burning of fossil fuels

Pollution also affects our air. The uncontrolled burning of fossil fuel hydrocarbons and high-sulfur content coals pose severe health risks, especially to the very young and very old. Smog alerts are routine in many of the major metropolitan areas, and in Mexico City, air pollution is reaching a critical level.

Acid Rain

Sulfur Compounds are naturally released through volcano eruptions. The man-made sources are primarily from the combustion of coal and oil products. When released, the sulfur combines with the atmosphere and changes to an oxidizer, Sulfur Dioxide (SO_2). Further chemical modifications transform this into Sulfate, and when combined with water, it changes to Sulfuric Acid ($SO4$). This acid precipitation is popularly known as Acid Rain. The solution to the problem is to use low sulfur content coal. Since the EPA mandated its use, there has been an 11% drop in the amount of acid rain.

Ozone depletion

The ozone layer (ozonosphere layer) is part of the earth's atmosphere, which contains relatively high concentrations of ozone. The ozone layer was first discovered in 1913 by two French physicists- Charles Fabry and Henry Buisson. About 90% of the ozone in our atmosphere is contained in the stratosphere, the region from about 10 to 50 km above the earth's surface. The remaining 10% of the ozone is contained in the troposphere, the lowest part of our atmosphere. Although the concentration of ozone in the ozone layer is very small, it is vitally important to life because it absorbs biologically harmful ultraviolet radiation (UV) emitted from the sun. Depletion of the ozone layer allows more of the harmful UV to reach the earth and causing increased genetic damage to living things.

Lead poisoning

Metal substances are the byproducts of a variety of manufacturing processes. Some sources are sandblasting, leaded gasoline, and leaded paint.

Example: Since the EPA banned the use of lead in gasoline and paint there has been a major drop in the lead accumulation problem in the environment. The major problem with the metals is that almost all of them are carcinogenic, and because the metals accumulate in the fatty tissues of the body, they also cause a long-term problems with nervous system disruption.

Insecticides

An insecticide is a pesticide used against insects in all developmental forms. Insecticides are widely used in agriculture, households, businesses, and even in medicine. Insecticides are one of the factors behind the increase in the agricultural productivity of the 20th century. It is very important to balance agricultural needs with safety concerns because the insecticides have the potential to significantly alter the ecosystems by entering the food chain.

Skill 41.6   The beginning teacher recognizes that Earth is composed of interacting systems and that regional changes in the environment may have global effects (e.g., weather changes due to reforestation, global warming).

While the hydrosphere, lithosphere, and atmosphere can be described and considered separately, they are actually constantly interacting with one another. Energy and matter flows freely between these different spheres.   For instance, in the water cycle, water beneath the Earth's surface and in rocks (in the lithosphere) is exchanged with vapor in the atmosphere and liquid water in lakes and the ocean (the hydrosphere). Similarly, significant events in one sphere almost always have effects in the other spheres. The recent increase in greenhouse gases provides an example of this ripple effect. Additional greenhouse gases produced by human activities were released into the atmosphere where they built up and caused widening holes in certain areas of the atmosphere and global warming. These increasing temperatures have had many effects on the hydrosphere: rising sea levels, increasing water temperature, and climate changes. These lead to even more changes in the lithosphere such as glacier retreat and alterations in the patterns of water-rock interaction (run-off, erosion, etc).

Skill 41.7   The beginning teacher demonstrates an understanding of how individuals, communities, and governments can conserve, protect, and restore habitats and ecosystems.

Stewardship is the responsible management of resources entrusted to one. Because human presence and activity has such a drastic impact on the environment, humans are the stewards of the Earth. In other words, it is the responsibility of humans to balance their needs as a population with the needs of the environment and all of the Earth's living creatures and resources. Stewardship requires the regulation of human activity to prevent, reduce, and mitigate environmental degradation. An important aspect of stewardship is the preservation of resources and ecosystems for future generations of humans. Finally, the concept of stewardship often, but not necessarily, draws from religious, theological, or spiritual thought and principles.

Strategies for the management of renewable resources focus on balancing the immediate demand for resources with long-term sustainability. In addition, renewable resource management attempts to optimize the quality of the resources. For example, scientists may attempt to manage the amount of timber harvested from a forest, balancing the human need for wood with the future viability of the forest as a source of wood. Scientists attempt to increase timber production by fertilizing, manipulating trees genetically, and managing pests and density. Similar strategies exist for the management and optimization of water sources, air quality, and other plants and animals.

The main concerns in nonrenewable resource management are conservation, allocation, and environmental mitigation. Policy makers, corporations, and governments must determine how to use and distribute scare resources. Decision makers must balance the immediate demand for resources with the need for resources in the future. This determination is often the cause of conflict and disagreement. Finally, scientists attempt to minimize and mitigate the environmental damage caused by resource extraction. Scientists devise methods of harvesting and using resources that do not unnecessarily impact the environment.   After the extraction of resources from a location, scientists devise plans and methods to restore the environment to as close to its original state as possible.

Recycling is the reprocessing of materials into new products. Recycling prevents useful material resources being wasted, reduces the consumption of raw materials and reduces energy usage, and hence greenhouse gas emissions, compared to virgin production.

DOMAIN IX.	COMPONENTS AND PROPERTIES OF THE SOLAR SYSTEM AND THE UNIVERSE

Competency 0042   **The teacher understands the implications of Earth's placement and orientation in the solar system.**

Skill 42.1   **The beginning teacher analyzes the relationship between Earth's placement in the solar system and the conditions on Earth that enable organisms to survive.**

Most cosmologists believe that the Earth is the indirect result of a supernova. The thin cloud (planetary nebula) of gas and dust from which the Sun and its planets are formed, was struck by the shock wave and remnant matter from an exploded star(s) outside of our galaxy. Following the birth of a proto-sun, its gravitational mass pulled heavier, denser elements inward from the clouds of cosmic material surrounding it. These elements eventually coalesced through the process of Accretion: *the clumping together of small particles into large masses,* into the planets of our solar system. The period of accretion lasted approximately 50 to 70 million years, ceasing when the proto-sun experienced nuclear fusion to become the Sun. The violence associated with this nuclear reaction swept through the inner planets, clearing the system of particles, ending the period of rapid accretion. The closest planets Mercury, Venus, and Mars, received too much heat and consequently, did not develop the planetary characteristics to support life, as we know it. The farthest planets did not receive enough heat to sufficiently coalesce the gasses into solid form. Earth was the only planet in the perfect position to develop the conditions necessary to maintain life.

Earth is unique among all the planets of the solar system for the extent of water present. Over 70% of the planet is composed of water. The presence of the water makes possible the protective atmosphere and more important, life forms. This planet is the only known location of life in the universe.

Skill 42.2   **The beginning teacher demonstrates an understanding of the Sun's effects (e.g., gravitational, electromagnetic, solar wind, solar flares) on Earth.**

Solar wind strikes the Ionosphere at the polar dips in the Magnetosphere. The ions are excited to a higher energy state and this energy is released into the visible spectrum to form the Aurora Borealis (Northern Lights).

The Sun's **gravitational force** keeps Earth in it's position within the solar system and effects, although to a lesser extent than the moon, Earth's tides.

A **sunspot** is a region on the Sun's surface (the photosphere) that is characterized by a lower temperature than its surroundings. The lower temperatures of these areas are caused by intense magnetic activity, which inhibits convection. The surface of the Sun is approximately 5800 K. Sunspots, however, usually demonstrate temperatures around 4000–4500 K. For this reason, sunspots are clearly visible as dark spots on the Sun's surface.

The number of sunspots rises and falls in a periodic manner, with a cycle of approximately 11 years. The 11-year sunspot cycle is related to the 22-year cycle for the reversal of the Sun's magnetic field. During this period, the Sun's magnetic field rotates 360 degrees, causing its poles to switch. The periods of time during which the Sun demonstrates the largest and smallest numbers of sunspots are known as the solar maxima and minima, respectively. The most recent solar maximum was observed in 2001. The Sun began a new cycle with a solar minimum in 2007.

It has recently been determined that areas of the Sun's surface surrounding sunspots increase in brightness as sunspots form. For this reason, sunspot maxima generally correspond to periods of higher solar radiation and solar activity, including increased solar winds, aurorae, magnetic storms, flares, prominences and non-thermal radio, x-ray and UV emission. Studies estimate that the Sun's radiant energy varies by up to 0.2% between extremes of the sunspot cycle. Because of increased solar irradiation, more energy is delivered to the Earth's atmosphere, and global temperatures may rise. In fact, the combined effects of sunspot-induced changes in solar irradiance and increases in greenhouse gases may best account for the observed rise in global temperatures over the past century.

At solar minima, less energy from the Sun arrives at the Earth's atmosphere. Because the normal sunspot cycle lasts only 11 years, the Earth's climate is not seriously affected at every solar minimum. However, solar minima that continue for decades, such as the Sporer, Maunder, and Dalton Minimas, can produce serious cooling effects on Earth. These minima occurred during a period of time known as the "Little Ice Age" (1645-1710). During this time, Europe was struck by famine as record low temperatures were reported. During an earlier Maunder Minimum (1400-1510), a Viking settlement in Greenland was reportedly decimated due to complete failure of crops.

The sunspots also cause **solar flares** that can accelerate to velocities of 900 km/hr, sending shock waves through the solar atmosphere. The particles emitted by these flares can disrupt radio communications on Earth and cause the northern lights as the highly charged particles strike the Earth's magnetosphere.

Skill 42.3 **The beginning teacher understands the effects of Earth's rotation, revolution, and tilt of axis on its environment (e.g., day/night length, seasons).**

Seasonal change on Earth is caused by the orbit and axial tilt of the planet in relation to the Sun's Ecliptic: the rotational path of the Sun. These factors combine to vary the degree of insolation at a particular location and thereby change the seasons.

Equinox and Solstice

There are four key points on the Ecliptic. The Equinoxes and the Solstices.

Winter Solstice (December 21) = Shortest day of the year in the northern hemisphere.

Summer Solstice (June 21) = Longest day of the year in the northern hemisphere.

Vernal Equinox (March 21) = Marks beginning of spring.

Autumnal Equinox (Sept 21) = Marks beginning of autumn (Fall)

These dates will vary slightly in relation to leap years.

During the summer solstice, insolation is at a maximum in the northern hemisphere, and at a minimum in the southern hemisphere.

Because of the tilt and curvature of the Earth, in order to get the sun directly overhead, you must be between 23.5°N Latitude and 23.5°S Latitude. This is between the Tropic of Cancer and the Tropic of Capricorn.

Another result is that during the summer months in the northern hemisphere, the far northern latitudes receive 24 hours of daylight. This situation is reversed during the winter months, when you have 24 hours of darkness.

Skill 42.4 **The beginning teacher identifies the effects of the Moon and Sun on tides.**

The periodic rise and fall of the liquid bodies on Earth are the direct result of the gravitational influence of the Moon and to a much lesser extent, the Sun.

Tides are produced by the differences between gravitational forces acting on parts of an object. As shown in Netwon's Universal Law of Gravitation, the gravitational effect of two bodies is mutually constant and depends largely on the distance and mass between the objects.

The side of the Earth that faces the Moon is roughly 4,000 miles (6,400 km) closer to the moon than is the Earth's center. This has the effect of increasing the Moon's gravitational attraction on Earth's oceans and landforms. Although the effect is so small on the mass of the landforms as to be invisible, the effect on the liquid parts is greater.

The Moon's gravitational effect causes a bulge to form on both sides of the Earth. If we were able to view such subtle change from outer space, the affected waters would create an elliptical shape, compressing downward at the top and bottom of the planet and extending outward on the sides.

This double-bulge effect causes the tides to fall and rise twice a day, and the time of the high and low tides is dependent on the phase of the moon.

Yet not all locations are uniformly affected. The tidal cycle at a particular location is actually a very complicated interaction of the location's latitude, shape of the shore, etc.

Example: The Bay of Fundy has a twice-daily tide that exceeds 12 meters, while the northern coast of the Gulf of Mexico only has one tidal cycle that seldom exceeds 30 centimeters rise and fall.

Because of its distance from the Earth, the Sun's gravitational effect on tides is only half that of the Moon's.

However, when the gravitational effects of both the Sun and Moon join together during a new moon and a full moon phase, the tidal effects can be extreme.

During a new moon and a full moon, tidal effects are much more pronounced as the tidal bulges join together to produce very high and very low tides.

These pronounced types of tide are collectively known as Spring Tides. During the first and third quarters of the moon phases, the Sun's effect is negligible and consequently, the tides are lower. These are Neap Tides.

Skill 42.5 **The beginning teacher analyzes information about lunar phases and lunar and solar eclipses to model the Earth, Moon, and Sun system.**

Eclipse: a phenomenon that occurs when a stellar body is shadowed by another and as a result, is rendered invisible.

The Earth, Moon, and Sun must be in perfect alignment with each other to result in either a Lunar or Solar eclipse.

There are two types of eclipses: Lunar and Solar.

Lunar Eclipse: The shadow of the Earth darkens the Moon. The Moon is in the Earth's shadow.

Solar Eclipse: The Moon is between the Sun and the Earth. The Earth is in the Moon's shadow.

Both types of eclipses have two forms: partial and full.

A total eclipse can only be seen in the equatorial regions. Most total eclipses are spaced 6 months apart. They normally are 2 to 10 minutes in duration.

A partial eclipse occurs when the moon does not completely enter the Earth's shadow.

The Sun never moves in between the Earth and the Moon. The orbits of the Earth and Moon cause them to move in and out of the shadow areas.

Forms of solar eclipse: Annular (Partial) and Total (Full).

Annular: a type of solar eclipse in which the darkest part of the shadow (the Umbra) doesn't touch the Earth.

Total: a type of solar eclipse in which the darkest part of the shadow (the Umbra) does touch the Earth.

Umbra: the central region of the shadow caused by an eclipse. No light hits in this region. This is typically associated with total eclipses.

Penumbra: the lighter outer edges of the shadow created during an eclipse. Some light hits in these regions. This is typically associated with annular (partial) eclipses.

The appearance of the Sun changes during a total and annular eclipse.

Annular: The moon appears as a small, dark spot in the center of the Sun.
Total: The moon covers most of the Sun, usually only showing a flaming Corona around the edges.

Competency 0043   **The teacher understands the role of the sun in the solar system and the characteristics of planets and other objects that orbit the sun.**

Skill 43.1   **The beginning teacher knows the approximate size, mass, motion, temperature, structure, and composition of the Sun.**

Located at an average distance of 1.00 AU (1.495979×10^8 km) from the Earth, the Sun's diameter of 1.4 million kilometers is over 54 times the diameter of Earth, and at 1.989×10^{30} kg, its mass is roughly 330,000 times greater than Earth's.

In fact, scientists estimate that the Sun contains approximately 99.8% of all the mass in our solar system. Its not surprising then that the Sun's gravitational effect is so strong as to capture and hold the planets of our solar system in orbits around it.

The Sun is intensely hot. At the center, it has a 140,000-kilometer diameter Core composed of hydrogen (92%) and helium (7.8%) that provide the fuel for the Sun's nuclear reaction (fusion). At approximately 15 million °C, the core gives off a tremendous amount of energy.

However, the density of the Sun precludes the direct release of all this energy into space. Instead, it is slowly absorbed and re-emitted by the various layers of the Sun.

The first layer above the core is the very thick Radiative Layer. The energy produced in the core warms this layer to an average temperature of 3 million °C. On top of the radiative layer is the Convective Layer, where as the name implies, energy is transferred via convection. This layer has an average temperature of 8,000 °C.

The Sun's atmosphere comprises its visible layers. The atmosphere is made up of three layers. The first layer is the Photosphere: the inner layer of the Sun's atmosphere that forms the Sun's visible surface. The photosphere is a very thin layer, only 400 kilometers deep and its average temperature is around 5,500 °C.

The photosphere's many small (1,000 kilometer in diameter), bright areas referred to as Granules: the tops of rising columns of hot gas. The dark granules represent sinking columns of cooler gasses.

Larger dark spots called Sunspots also appear regularly on the Sun's surface. These spots vary in size from small to 150,000 kilometers in diameter and may last from hours to months.

The sunspots also cause solar flares that can accelerate to velocities of 900 km/hr, sending shock waves through the solar atmosphere. The particles emitted by these flares can disrupt radio communications on Earth and cause the northern lights as the highly charged particles strike the Earth's magnetosphere.

The second layer of the atmosphere is the Chromosphere: a 2,500-kilometer thick layer of turbulent gases. The temperature in the chromosphere increases to 100,000 degrees Celsius. Spicules: jets of heated gasses shoot upward from the chromosphere, reaching average proportions of 7,000 kilometers wide by 7,000 kilometers tall.

The third and final layer of the Sun's atmosphere is called the Corona: a very thin layer of gas that merges with outer space. The Corona's temperature is approximately 2 million degrees Celsius, and it heated by twisted magnetic fields that carry energy up to it.

These energy particles move very fast, generating high temperatures. Prominences: red, flaming jets of gas that rise from the corona, can travel as far as 1 million kilometers outward into space. Electrons are stripped off of atoms and they and the reduced nuclei fly off into space, creating the Solar Wind. This wind surrounds the Earth and even reaches to the farthest regions of the solar system.

Skill 43.2   The beginning teacher compares and contrasts conditions essential to life on Earth (e.g., temperature, water, mass, gases) to conditions on other planets.

Earth is the third planet outward from the Sun. It is primarily composed of ferric and silicate materials. As the Earth is already detailed in other parts of this book, the information presented in this section will be brief. The Earth has an extremely dense core surrounded by layers of lesser density materials. The outer surface of the planet rides on a semi-molten layer that periodically renews itself through volcanism and subduction zones. The atmosphere is composed of nitrogen and oxygen.

The Earth's axis currently points at the Star Polaris. This eventually will change just as it has done in the past. This change in axial direction is called **precession.** In 30,000 BC, the axial pole pointed to the Star Thuban. In 14,000 AD, the axial pole will point to the Star Vega.

Earth is unique among all the planets of the solar system for the extent of water present. Over 70% of the planet is composed of water. The presence of the water makes possible the protective atmosphere and more important, life forms. This planet is the only known location of life in the universe. To become a watery planet, specific criterion must be met:

- An ocean world must move in a nearly circular orbit around a stable star and the distance of the planet from the star must be just right to provide a temperature environment in which water is liquid.
- A watery planet's sun must not be a double or multiple star, or the orbital year would have irregular periods of intense heat and cold.
- The materials that accreted to form the planet must include both water and substances capable of forming a solid crust. Likewise, volcanoes or steaming vents are needed to vent water vapor to the surface.
- The planet must have enough mass, density, and gravity to create and keep an atmosphere, preventing the oceans from drifting off in space.

Earth is also the only known planet to meet the additional conditions needed to support life.

- Earth's gravity is strong enough to retain an ocean, but not strong enough to crush the life forms that came from it.
- The planet has a magnetic field provided by the iron core that deflects radiation that would otherwise harm the genetic instructions of the organisms.
- The single moon causes relatively gentle tides that encourage life forms to leave the sea and reside on land.
- The atmosphere is relatively clear so that sunlight penetrates to the surface, but moist enough to form rains and winds that drive the ocean currents.
- The upper atmosphere contains Ozone (O_3), which protects against the most harmful ultraviolet (UV) rays.

Skill 43.3   The beginning teacher compares and contrasts the planets in terms of orbit, mass, size, composition, rotation, atmosphere, moons, and geologic activity.

Our solar system consists of the Sun, planets, comets, meteors, and asteroids. The planets are ordered in the following way: Mercury, Venus, Earth, Mars (with Asteroid Belt), Jupiter, Saturn, Uranus, and Neptune. Pluto has historically been considered the ninth planet. Recently, scientists have created new requirements for the definition of a planet, and it is possible that Pluto will be considered only a celestial body. A common memory aid for remembering the order of the planets is My Very Educated Mother Just Served Us Nine Pies.

The Inner Planets

MERCURY	
Average Distance from the Sun	0.387 AU (5.79×10^7 km)
Density	5.44 g/cm^3
Diameter (equatorial)	4878 km (0.38 of Earth)
Mass	3.31×10^{23} kg (0.055 of Earth)
Atmosphere	None (Trace gasses only of H, He, Na, K)
Axial Rotation Period Solar Revolution Period	58.6 days 87.9 days
Axial Tilt	0°
Surface Temp	-173°C to 330°C
Moons	None
Composition	Silicate & Iron rocks

VENUS	
Average Distance from the Sun	0.723 AU (1.082×10^8 km)
Density	5.3 g/cm^3
Diameter (equatorial)	12,104 km (0.95 of Earth)
Mass	4.87×10^{24} kg (0.82 of Earth)
Atmosphere	Runaway Greenhouse effect 96.5% CO_2, 3.5% N.
Axial Rotation Period Solar Revolution Period	243.01 days 224.68 days
Axial Tilt	177° (Makes the planet appear as if it was rotating clockwise)
Surface Temp	472°C
Moons	None
Composition	Unknown, crustal materials believed to be similar to Earth

EARTH	
Average Distance from the Sun	1.00 AU (1.495×10^8 km)
Density	5.497 g/cm^3
Diameter (equatorial)	12,756 km
Mass	5.976×10^{24} kg
Atmosphere	78% Nitrogen, 21% Oxygen
Axial Rotation Period Solar Revolution Period	24.00 hours 365.26 days
Axial Tilt	23.5°
Surface Temp	-50°C to 50°C
Moons	1 The Moon

MARS	
Average Distance from the Sun	1.523 AU (2.279 x 10^8 km)
Density	3.94 g/cm^3
Diameter (equatorial)	6796 km (0.53 of Earth)
Mass	0.6424 x 10^{24} kg (0.1075 of Earth)
Atmosphere	95% CO_2
Axial Rotation Period	24.61 hours
Solar Revolution Period	686.9 days
Axial Tilt	23° 59'
Surface Temp	-140°C to 20°C
Moons	2 (*Deimos* and *Phobos*) (Panic and Fear). They may actually be captured asteroids because of irregular shape.
Composition	Identical to Earth's

The Outer Planets

JUPITER	
Average Distance from the Sun	5.202 AU (7.783 x 10^8 km)
Density	1.34 g/cm^3
Diameter (equatorial)	142,900 km (11.20 of Earth)
Mass	1.899 x 10^{27} kg (317.83 of Earth)
Atmosphere	Hydrogen, Helium, and Ammonia
Axial Rotation Period	9.83 hours
Solar Revolution Period	11.867 years
Axial Tilt	3.5°
Surface Temp	29,727 °C at surface -120°C in atmosphere
Moons	47, of which only 4 are significant. These are the Galilean Moons: *Io, Europa, Ganymede, and Callisto*.
Composition	No surface, gaseous atmosphere

SATURN	
Average Distance from the Sun	9.538 AU (14.27 x 10^8 km)
Density	0.69 g/cm^3
Diameter (equatorial)	120,660 km (9.42 of Earth)
Mass	5.69 x 10^{26} kg (95.17 of Earth)
Atmosphere	Hydrogen and Helium
Axial Rotation Period Solar Revolution Period	10.65 hours 29.461 years
Axial Tilt	26° 24'
Surface Temp	Unknown at surface -180° in atmosphere
Moons	17 total of which *Titan* is the largest and most significant.
Composition	No surface, gaseous atmosphere

URANUS	
Average Distance from the Sun	9.538 AU (14.27 x 10^8 km)
Density	1.29 g/cm^3
Diameter (equatorial)	51,118 km (4.01 of Earth)
Mass	8.69 x 10^{25} kg (14.54 of Earth)
Atmosphere	Hydrogen, Helium, and Methane
Axial Rotation Period Solar Revolution Period	17.23 hours 84.013 years
Axial Tilt	97° 55'
Surface Temp	Unknown at surface -220° in atmosphere
Moons	15 total of which *Oberon* is the largest at 1,500 km diameter.
Composition	Unknown, frozen gasses

NEPTUNE	
Average Distance from the Sun	30.061 AU (44.971 x 10^8 km)
Density	1.66 g/cm^3
Diameter (equatorial)	49,500 km (3.88 of Earth)
Mass	10.30 x 10^{26} kg (17.23 of Earth)
Atmosphere	Hydrogen, Helium, and Methane
Axial Rotation Period	16.05 hours
Solar Revolution Period	164.793 years
Axial Tilt	28° 48'
Surface Temp	Unknown at surface -216°C in atmosphere
Moons	8 total, 2 of significance, *Triton* and *Nereid*.
Composition	Unknown, mostly ice

PLUTO	
Average Distance from the Sun	39.44 AU (59.00 x 10^8 km)
Density	2.0 g/cm^3
Diameter (equatorial)	2,300 km (0.19 of Earth)
Mass	1.2 x 10^{22} kg (0.002 of Earth)
Atmosphere	Nitrogen and Methane
Axial Rotation Period	9.3 days
Solar Revolution Period	247.7 years
Axial Tilt	122°
Surface Temp	-230°C
Moons	1 *Charon*
Composition	Frozen nitrogen & rock

Skill 43.4   The beginning teacher identifies objects other than planets that orbit the sun (e.g., asteroids, comets) and analyzes their characteristics (e.g., mass, size, composition, trajectory, origin).

Comets: small icy bodies that orbit the Sun and produce a glowing tail of gas and dust as the comet nears the Sun. Comets are not planets.

Asteroids: small, rocky worlds that orbit the Sun. Asteroids are sometimes called the minor planets.

Meteoroids: a meteor in space. Meteoroids often are asteroid fragments, but they do not have a specific orbit. Meteoroids can become either meteors, or meteorites depending on whether they burn up or make it through the atmosphere.

Meteors: small fragments of rock debris that turn incandescent and burn up upon entering the Earth's atmosphere.

Meteorites: meteor fragments that do not burn up in the atmosphere and actually strike a planet.

Our solar system contains an asteroid belt located between Mars and Jupiter. The asteroid belt is composed of over 2,000 rocky bodies circling the Sun. The largest of these asteroids is over 1,000 km but the smallest are mere particles. The composition of the asteroids is similar to meteorites that have struck the Earth.

Skill 43.5 The beginning teacher relates gravitational force to the motion and interactions of objects within the solar system (e.g., Sun, planets, moons, comets, meteors).

The mass of any celestial object may be determined by using Newton's laws of motion and his law of gravity.

For example, to determine the mass of the Sun, use the following formula:

$$M = \frac{4\pi^2}{G} = \frac{a^3}{P^2}$$

where M = the mass of the Sun, G = a constant measured in laboratory experiments, a = the distance of a celestial body in orbit around the Sun from the Sun, and P = the period of the body's orbit.

In our solar system, measurable objects range in mass from the largest, the Sun, to the smallest, a near-Earth asteroid. (This does not take into account, objects with a mass less than 10^{21} kg.)

The surface temperature of an object depends largely upon its proximity to the Sun. One exception to this, however, is Venus, which is hotter than Mercury because of its cloud layer that holds heat to the planet's surface. The surface temperatures of the planets range from more than 400 degrees on Mercury and Venus to below -200 degrees on the distant planets.

Most minor bodies in the solar system do not have any atmosphere and, therefore, can easily radiate the heat from the Sun. In the case of any celestial object, whether a side is warm or cold depends upon whether it faces the sun or not and the time of rotation. The longer rotation takes, the colder the side facing away from the sun will become, and vice versa.

If the density of an object is less than 1.5 grams per cc, then the object is almost exclusively made of frozen water, ammonia, carbon dioxide, or methane. If the density is less than 1.0, the object must be made of mostly gas. In our solar system, there is only one object with that low a density -- Saturn. If the density is greater than 3.0 grams per cc, then the object is almost exclusively made of rocks; and if the density exceeds 5.0 grams per cc, then there must be a nickel-iron core. Densities between 1.5 and 3.0 indicate a rocky-ice mixture.
The density of planets correlates with their distance from the Sun. The inner planets (Mercury-Mars) are known as the terrestrial planets because they are rocky, and the outer planets (Jupiter and outward) are known as the icy or Jovian (gaslike) planets.

In order for two bodies to interact gravitationally, they must have significant mass. Gravitational force is defined as the force of attraction between all masses in the universe. Every object exerts gravitational force on every other object. This force depends on the masses of the objects and the distance between them. The gravitational force between any two masses is given by Newton's law of universal gravitation, which states that the force is inversely proportional to the square of the distance between the masses. Near the surface of the Earth, the acceleration of an object due to gravity is independent of the mass of the object and therefore constant. When two bodies in the solar system interact gravitationally, they orbit about a fixed point (the center of mass of the two bodies). This point lies on an imaginary line between the bodies, joining them such that the distances to each body multiplied by each body's mass are equal. The orbits of these bodies will vary slightly over time because of the gravitational interactions.

Skill 43.6 The beginning teacher understands theories of the formation of the solar system.

Most cosmologists believe that the Earth is the indirect result of a supernova. The thin cloud (planetary nebula) of gas and dust from which the Sun and its planets are formed, was struck by the shock wave and remnant matter from an exploded star(s) outside of our galaxy. In fact, the stars manufactured every chemical element heavier than hydrogen.

The turbulence caused by the shock wave caused our solar system to begin forming as is absorbed some of the heavy atoms flung outward in the supernova. In fact, our solar system is composed mostly of matter assembled from a star or stars that disappeared billions of years ago.

Around five billion years ago our planetary nebulae spun faster as it condensed and material near the center contracted inward forming a proto-sun. As more materials came together, mass and consequently gravitational attraction increased, pulling in more mass. This cycle continued until the mass reach the point that nuclear fusion occurred and the Sun was born.

Concurrently, the proto-sun's gravitational mass pulled heavier, denser elements inward from the clouds of cosmic material surrounding it. These elements eventually coalesced through the process of **accretion**: the clumping together of small particles into large masses, into the planets of our solar system.

The period of accretion lasted approximately 50 to 70 million years, ceasing when the proto-sun experienced nuclear fusion to become the Sun. The violence associated with this nuclear reaction swept through the inner planets, clearing the system of particles, ending the period of rapid accretion.

Competency 0044 **The teacher understands composition, history, and properties of the universe.**

Skill 44.1 **The beginning teacher describes how nuclear fusion produces energy in stars, such as the Sun.**

All stars derive their energy through the thermonuclear fusion of light elements into heavy elements. The minimum temperature required for the fusion of hydgrogen is 5 million degrees. Elements with more protons in their nuclei require higher temperatures. For instance, to fuse Carbon requires a temperature of about 1 billion degrees.

A star that is composed of mostly hydrogen is a young star. As a star gets older its hydrogen is consumed and tremendous energy and light is released through fusion. This is a three-step process: (1) two hydrogen nuclei (protons) fuse to form a heavy hydrogen called deuterium and release an electron and 4.04 MeV energy, (2) the deuterium fuses with another hydrogen nucleus (proton) to form a helium-3 and release a neutron and 3.28 MeV energy, and (3) and the helium-3 fuses with another helium-3 to form a helium-4 and release two hydrogens and 10.28 MeV energy.

In stars with central temperatures greater than 600-700 million degrees, carbon fusion is thought to take over the dominant role rather than hydrogen fusion. Carbon fusions can produce magnesium, sodium, neon, or helium. Some of the reactions release energy and alpha particles or protons.

Skill 44.2 **The beginning teacher identifies different types of stars, their characteristics and motions (e.g., temperature, age, relative size, composition, and radial velocity) and understands the use of spectral analysis to determine these characteristics.**

A star is a ball of hot, glowing gas that is hot enough and dense enough to trigger nuclear reactions, which fuel the star. In comparing the mass, light production, and size of the Sun to other stars, astronomers find that the Sun is a perfectly ordinary star. It behaves exactly the way they would expect a star of its size to behave. The main difference between the Sun and other stars is that the Sun is much closer to Earth.

Most stars have masses similar to that of the Sun. The majority of stars' masses are between 0.3 to 3.0 times the mass of the Sun. Theoretical calculations indicate that in order to trigger nuclear reactions and to create its own energy—that is, to become a star—a body must have a mass greater than 7 percent of the mass of the Sun. Astronomical bodies that are less massive than this become planets or objects called brown dwarfs. The largest accurately determined stellar mass is of a star called V382 Cygni and is 27 times that of the Sun.

The range of brightness among stars is much larger than the range of mass. Astronomers measure the brightness of a star by measuring its <u>magnitude</u> and luminosity. Magnitude allows astronomers to rank how bright, comparatively, different stars appear to humans. Because of the way our eyes detect light, a lamp ten times more luminous than a second lamp will appear less than ten times brighter to human eyes. This discrepancy affects the magnitude scale, as does the tradition of giving brighter stars lower magnitudes. The lower a star's magnitude, the brighter it is. Stars with negative magnitudes are the brightest of all.

Magnitude is given in terms of absolute and apparent values. Absolute magnitude is a measurement of how bright a star would appear if viewed from a set distance away. Astronomers also measure a star's brightness in terms of its luminosity. A star's absolute luminosity or intrinsic brightness is the total amount of energy radiated by the star per second. Luminosity is often expressed in units of watts.

Stars are not all alike. Their energy outputs vary from 111,000th of the energy to 100,000 times the energy, of Earth's sun. The laws of physics tell us that the more energy an object has, the hotter it is. They also relate color to temperature. Therefore, by observing the color of a star, we get information about its temperature. This is done by using the Hertzsprung-Russell diagram.

Skill 44.3　The beginning teacher describes stages in the life cycle of stars using the Hertzsprung-Russell diagram.

In 1913 American astronomer Henry Norris Russell and Danish astronomer Ejnar Hertzsprung theorized that the energy emitted by a star is directly related to the star's color. Their supporting graph is now known as the **Hertzsprung-Russell Diagram (H-R Diagram):** a graph that shows the relationship between a star's color, temperature, and mass.

On a H-R Diagram the majority (90%) of the stars plotted form a diagonal line called the **Main Sequence**: the region of the H-R Diagram running from top left to bottom right. Hot, blue stars are at the top left; cooler, red stars are at the bottom right. The middle of main sequence contains yellow stars, like the Sun.

Star mass is also shown on the H-R diagram, increasing from the bottom to the top of the main sequence.

The stars at the bottom right have masses about one-tenth of that of Earth's sun, and the masses increase until you reach the top left where there are stars with masses ten times greater than that of the Sun.

The truly large stars are called **Supergiant Stars**: exceptionally massive and luminous stars 10 to 1,000 times brighter than the Sun. The smallest stars are called **Dwarf Stars**: dying stars that have collapsed in size. Although small in size, dwarf stars are extremely dense. Although Supergiants are extremely large, they may be less dense than the Earth's outer atmosphere.

We can also use the H-R Diagram to illustrate the life cycle of stars. Stars form in **Planetary Nebulae**: cold clouds of dust and gas within a galaxy, and go through different stages of development in a specific sequence. This theory of star development is called the **Condensation Theory**.

Sequence of Development

In the initial stage, the diffuse area of the nebula begins to shrink under the influence of its own weak gravity. The cloud-like spheres condense into a knot of gasses called a **Protostar**. The original diameter of the protostar is many times greater than the diameter of our solar system, but gravitational forces cause it to continue to contract. This compression raises the internal temperature of the protostar.

When the protostar reaches a temperature of around 10 million °C (18 million °F), nuclear fusion starts, which stops the contraction of the protostar and changes its status to a star. It's the fusion of atoms, not combustion, which causes the star to shine.

A star's life cycle depends on its initial mass. Red stars have a small mass. Yellow stars have a medium mass. Blue stars have a large mass. Large mass stars consume their hydrogen at a faster rate and have a short life cycle in comparison to small mass stars that consume their hydrogen at a much slower rate. All stars eventually convert a large percentage of their hydrogen to heavier atoms and begin to die. However, just as their mass determines the length of their life, it also determines the pattern they follow in the last stages of their existence.

Lower Main Sequence Stars

When small and medium mass stars (such as the Sun) consume all of their hydrogen, their inner cores begin to cool. The stars begin to consume the heavier elements produced fusion (carbon and oxygen) and the star's shell tremendously expands outward, causing the star to become a **Giant Star**: large, cool extremely luminous stars 10 to 100 times the diameter of the Sun.

Example: In roughly 4.6 billion years from now our Sun will become a giant star. As it expands, its outer layers will reach halfway to Venus.

The dying Giant gives off thermal pulses approximately every 200,000 years, throwing off concentric shells of light gasses enriched with heavy elements. As it enters its last phases of the life cycle its depleted inner core begins to contract, and the Giant becomes a **White Dwarf Star**: a small, slowly cooling, extremely dense star, no larger than 10,000 km in diameter.

The final phase of a lower main sequence star life cycle can take two paths: most main sequence white dwarfs after a few billion years completely burn out to become **Black Dwarfs**: cold, dead stars. However, if a White Dwarf is part of a **Binary Star**: two suns in the same solar system, instead of slowly cooling to become a Black Dwarf, it may capture hydrogen from its companion star. If this happens, the temperature of the White Dwarf soars and when it reaches approximately 10 million °C, a nuclear explosion occurs, creating a **Nova**: a sudden brightening of a lower main sequence star to approximately 10,000 times its normal luminosity; caused by the explosion of the star. A nova reaches its maximum brightness in a short time (one or two days) and then gradually dims as the gasses and cosmic dust cool.

Upper Main Sequence Stars

The initial sequence of the high mass, upper main sequence stars is identical to the lower mass stars, Planetary Nebulae to Protostar. However, if the protostar accretes enough material, it forms as a **Blue Star**. When a Blue Star has consumed all of its hydrogen it, too, expands outward, but on a much larger scale then experienced by a lower mass star. It becomes a **Supergiant Star**: an exceptionally bright star, 10 to 1,000 times the diameter of the Sun.

The Supergiant's now depleted core cannot support such a vast weight and collapses inward, causing its temperature to soar. When it reaches roughly 599 million °C, it implodes and then explodes, creating a **Supernova**: the massive explosion of an upper main sequence Supergiant star caused by the detonation of carbon within the star.

A supernova releases more energy than Earth's sun will produce in its entire life cycle. The luminosity of a supernova is as bright as 500 million Suns. For example: Chinese astronomers in 1054 recorded the sudden appearance of a new star in what is now known as the Taurus Constellation. Bright enough to be seen during daytime for over a month, it remained visible for over 2 years.

The explosive release of energy in a supernova is so great (1,028 megatons of TNT) as to literally blow the atomic nuclei of the carbon to bits. The shattered mass is accelerated outward at nearly the speed of light (300,000 km/sec. or 186,000 mph). 90 percent of the shattered mass scatters into space, becoming planetary nebulae from which the life cycle may begin anew.

Skill 44.4   The beginning teacher compares and contrasts characteristics of different types of galaxies.

A **galaxy** is a large group (billions) of stars held together by mutual gravitation attraction.

If you look into the night sky you may see a ribbon of star packed so densely together that it appears to be a starlight cloud. You are looking at **the Milky Way Galaxy**, the galaxy in which our solar system is located. This ribbon of brilliance in the night is actually a collection of over 180 billion stars and a huge volume of interstellar dust and gasses.

You may also notice that there are groups of stars that appear closer together. These are **Globular Clusters**: a tightly grouped, high concentration of stars.

These spherically arranged masses of stars are believed to be the oldest stars in the galaxy, approximately 10-20 billion years old. Each of the clusters contains between 10,000 to 1,000,000 individual stars and virtually no interstellar dust.

Although not the prevalent form, a spherical arrangement of stars is not uncommon. The Milky Way Galaxy is a **Spiral Galaxy**: a grouping of stars arranged in a thin disk, spiraling geometric pattern, which has a central pivot point (nucleus) and arms radiating outward on which stars rotate around the nucleus, somewhat suggestive of the shape of a pinwheel. It is approximately 100,000 light-years in diameter and 2,000 light-years thick at the center, decreasing to 1,000 light-years at the edges.

Our Sun is located on one of the arms of the galaxy, roughly 30,000 light-years from the center of the galaxy, midway between the upper and lower edges.

The Sun rotates around the center of the galaxy at a speed of 250 km/s, and makes one full rotation every 200 million years. This rotational pattern means that in the estimated 4.6 billion years of Earth's existence, our Sun has completed 23 rotations.

Other Galaxies

In the late 1700's early astronomers studied hazy objects in the sky that weren't stars. However, it wasn't until the 1850's that telescopes became powerful enough to discern that the hazy objects had a spiraling structure.
Almost a hundred years would pass before their identity was solved. In 1924, American astronomer Edwin Hubble determined that the objects were farther away than previously thought. This meant that for us to even see them, that they must have a greater luminosity than a single star. The conclusion was obvious; the objects were other galaxies, each composed of billions of stars.

Our galaxy is but one of billions of galaxies in the universe. Although most of the other galaxies cannot be seen with the naked eye, one galaxy that is visible (besides the Milky Way), is called a **Nebulae**: an often-glowing cloud of interstellar dust and gasses that because of reflected light, appears similar to a cloud or hazy star.

Some nebulae are hot enough to emit light; others are cooler and absorb light. In many cases, a particular nebula represents the remnants of a failed star system such as the Crab Nebula that is the remains of supernova in 1054 A.D.

Galactic Shapes

Galaxies are named for their shapes as observed from Earth.

Spiral Galaxy: As the name implies, the arrangement of the stars forms a spherical pattern. Spiral galaxies usually contain a great deal of interstellar gasses and dust.

Irregular Galaxy: There is no discernable pattern in the arrangement of the stars. Like a spiral galaxy, irregular galaxies tend to have a large volume of interstellar gasses and dust.

Barred Galaxy: The shape of this type of galaxy suggests a straight center core of stars joined by two or more relatively straight arms. About 30% of all galaxies are barred.

Elliptical Galaxy: The pattern of this type of galaxy centers on an elliptical shaped central mass of stars, with other stars above or below the center, giving the entire mass an overall ovoid appearance. They contain virtually no dust or gasses and rotate very slowly if at all. Most galaxies are elliptical.

The distance from the Earth to the other galaxies varies. The two closest galaxies, the *Large*, and *Small Magellanic Cloud,* are approximately 170,000 light-years distant. As vast a distance as that may seem, it pales in comparison to the distance to the *Great Spiral Galaxy* two million light-years away.

Skill 44.5   The beginning teacher interprets data to make inferences about the formation of stars and galaxies.

Please see skill number 44.3 for information about how to use the Hertzsprung-Russell diagram to infer a star's age and stage of its life cycle.

Skill 44.6 **The beginning teacher identifies types, characteristics, and significance of other deep-space objects in the universe (e.g., pulsars, nebulae, black holes).**

Nebulae: an often-glowing cloud of interstellar dust and gasses that, because of reflected light, appears similar to a cloud or hazy star. This is where stars and galaxies form.

Following a supernova explosion, the core of the star, is blown inward, becoming a **Neutron Star**: a very small - 10 km diameter-core of a collapsed Supergiant star that rotates at a high speed (60,000 rpm) and has a strong magnetic field (1012 Gauss).

A neutron star may capture gas from space, a companion star, or a nearby star and become a **Pulsar**: a neutron star that emits a sweeping beam of ionized-gas radiation. As the pulsar rotates, the beams of light sweep into space similar to a beacon from a lighthouse. Since first discovered in 1967, over 350 pulsars have been catalogued.

The alternate product of a supernova is a **Black Hole**: a volume of space from which all forms of radiation cannot escape. Black Holes are created when a Supergiant star with a mass roughly 3 times that of the Sun implodes. The inner core of the star is compacted by the supernova into a Singularity: an object of zero radius and infinite density. A singularity is difficult to picture. Zero radiuses imply objects with size less than an electron, but also possessing a density that precludes the escape of all radiation including light. Although a singularity has yet to be detected, theoretically, they exist in and cause the effects exhibited by Black Holes.

Quasar: a very distant interstellar object less than one-light year in diameter that emits an extremely large quantity of energy in the form of electromagnetic radio waves. Quasars have puzzled astronomers for decades but it was until the mid 1960's that astronomers made an astonishing discovery that started to unravel the mystery. These perplexing objects emitted energy primarily as radio waves rather the visible light, as is the case in most stars. Further investigations into the next decade revealed that these quasi-stellar objects (hence, quasars) actually were twin lobed, radio sources.

Actually only 3 percent of the 8,000 quasars so far discovered are actively emitting, but the modern theory about their origin suggests that they actually represent still active galaxies, billions of light-years distant from Earth.

Quasars show a tremendous Red Shift indicating that they are moving away from Earth. If so, their brilliance gives some indication of the energy involved, 10 to 100 times more than most galaxies.

Skill 44.7 **The beginning teacher interprets empirical data and scientific theories regarding the estimated age, origin, and evolution of the universe (e.g., big bang, inflation).**

How and when the universe formed has puzzled humans for millennia. Although many theories have been offered, no one knows for sure how or when it was created. The early models of the universe were primarily products of philosophical musings as combined with religious and social tenets, and observable phenomenon.

Scientific Models of the Universe

As civilizations continued to advance so did our understanding of the physical processes affecting the universe. The early scientific models still blended elements of philosophy and religious thought with measurable data, but as our technological base improved, models reflected less and less of those influences to the point that today, it's a commonly accepted practice to totally discount them in modeling the universe.

The Steady State Theory

Steady State Theory: a scientific theory that held that the universe was static and that it did not evolve, having always maintained a balance of the same general properties through replacement of dying stars and galaxies by new stars and galaxies. This theory was simultaneously both a popular and controversial explanation of the universe during its heydays in the 1950's and 1960's.

However, all astronomers did not accept the concept of a static universe, and they proposed an alternate theory centered on non-static, expanding universe. Steady state supporter, American astronomer Fred Hoyle sarcastically dubbed this theory the "Big Bang".

The controversy between supporters and opponents of the steady state theory continued until the late 1960's when detection of primordial background radiation dealt a decisive blow to the steady state theory. In a static state the background radiation should be uniform, however, since it clearly was not, this indicated that something had occurred to cause it to "clump" together. The logical explanation was a massive explosion that disordered the radiation.

The "Big Bang" Theory

Big Bang Theory: a theory that proposes that all the mass and energy of the universe was originally concentrated at a single geometric point and for unknown reasons, experienced a massive explosion that scattered the matter throughout the universe.

The concept of a massive explosion is supported by the distribution of background radiation and the measurable fact that the galaxies are moving away from each other at great speed.

The Universe originated around 15 billion years ago with the "Big Bang," and continued to expand for the first 10 billion years. The universe was originally unimaginably hot, but around 1 million years after the Big Bang, it cooled enough to allow for the formation of atoms from the energy and particles.

Most of these atoms were hydrogen and they comprise the most abundant form of matter in the universe. Around a billion years after the Big Bang, the matter had cooled enough to begin congealing into the first of the stars and galaxies.

Cosmic microwave background radiation (CMBR) is the oldest light we can see. It is a snapshot of how the universe looked in its early beginnings. First discovered in 1964, CMBR is composed of photons which we can see because of the atoms that formed when the universe cooled to 3000 K. Prior to that, after the Big Bang, the universe was so hot that the photons were scattered all over the universe, making the universe opaque. The atoms caused the photons to scatter less and the universe to become transparent to radiation. Since cooling to 3000K, the universe has continued to expand and cool.

COBE, launched in 1989, was the first mission to explore slight fluctuations in the background. WMAP, launched in 2001, took a clearer picture of the universe, providing evidence to support the Big Bang Theory and add details to the early conditions of the universe. Based upon this more recent data, scientists believe the universe is about 13.7 billion years old and that there was a period of rapid expansion right after the Big Bang. They have also learned that there were early variations in the density of matter resulting in the formation of the galaxies, the geometry of the universe is flat, and the universe will continue to expand forever.

Skill 44.8 **The beginning teacher describes the role of supernovas on the chemical composition of the universe (e.g., origin of carbon on Earth).**

Most cosmologists believe that the Earth is the indirect result of a supernova. The thin cloud (planetary nebula) of gas and dust from which the Sun and its planets are formed, was struck by the shock wave and remnant matter from an exploded star(s) outside of our galaxy. In fact, the stars manufactured every chemical element heavier than hydrogen. Carbon, nitrogen, and oxygen are three of the most abundant elements in the universe. All are vital for human life. It is believed that these elements were either thrown into space upon the death of stars via explosions, or were placed on Earth through meteorite impacts.

Competency 0045   **The teacher understands the history and methods of astronomy.**

Skill 45.1   **The beginning teacher recognizes that all of science including current theories of the origin and evolution of the universe are based on the assumption that the fundamental laws of nature do not change over space and time.**

A **hypothesis** is an educated guess based upon observations and/or research. A **theory** is a hypothesis that has been supported by repeated testing. A law is a **theory** that has stood the test of time and is agreed upon by scientists to be true. Laws are fundamental in that they do not change. In particular to Earth science is a law of geology, the **Principle of Uniformitarianism**, which states that processes that are happening today also happened in the past. Also pivotal are the laws of **thermodynamics**, the laws of **planetary motion** by Kepler, Newton's laws of **gravity**, and the laws of **conservation of mass and charge**. Knowing that these laws are constant allows scientists to make certain assumption when conducting research and inferring results from data.

Skill 45.2   **The beginning teacher describes the historical origins of the perceived *patterns of constellations* and their role in navigation.**

Constellation: a region of the night sky in which a group of stellar objects form a discernible pattern; usually named after mythological gods, animals, objects, or people.

The stars visible in the night sky have always fascinated humans. Ancient humans were very dependent on stars, assigning a mystic aspect to them that influenced political and social decisions of the period. Names were assigned to the stellar patterns to produce a sense of order and purpose to the cosmos. The majority of the constellation names are based on Greek Mythology.

Example: Orion, Taurus, and Pegasus. However, because the patterns appear slightly different depending on the viewer's geographic location, different names are assigned to the constellations by different cultures.

Example: In the Chinese culture Taurus the Bull is the Snake, and Aquarius is the Tiger.

The ancient observers believed that the Sun changed places with the stars to create nighttime. These visible stars formed the basis of the Zodiac Constellations: the first constellations to be named by early astronomers. The scholars who studied the Zodiac Constellations were **Astrologers**: people who studied the stellar objects in the Zodiac Constellations in order to predict the future. Besides the original twelve constellations comprising the Zodiac

Constellation, modern astronomy has found and named an additional 76 others for a total of 88 constellations. Consequently, this divides the sky into 88 sections.

Locating the Stars

The positions of the stars are referenced in relation to the Earth and are described in terms of the celestial coordinates of Right Ascension and Declination.

The declination and right ascension is described in reference to the **Celestial Sphere/Globe Model.** You can picture this model as having the Earth centered in the middle of a sphere. The outer framework of the sphere rotates clockwise (east to west) in relation to the Earth. The north and south poles of the Earth correspond to the north and south celestial poles. The Earth's equator corresponds to the celestial equator. **Right Ascension** is roughly analogous to lines of Longitude and is measured eastward from the vernal equinox. **Declination** is roughly analogous to lines of Latitude and is measured in relation to the celestial equator: positive to the north, and negative to the south.

Right Ascension and Declination are measured in units of degrees and time. 1 sec = 1/3600 of a degree.

Example: 15° 12' 5" Right Ascension. The sky shifts 15° every hour. That's why photo-telescopes must move with the stars.

Skill 45.3   The beginning teacher describes the historical development and significance of the law of universal gravitation and planetary motion, the big bang theory of the origin of the universe, and the theory of special relativity.

The earliest recorded instances of possible explanation all had mystical-religious foundations, which is not surprising, given that the early civilizations had a deep belief in gods.

Just as civilizations differ according to culture, so do the explanations of how, when, and why the universe was created. However, a sense of balance was a common thread of the explanations.

By whatever names ascribed (i.e. good versus evil, Ying and Yang, etc.), balance provided a sense of order and symmetry out of the inexplicable chaos of what was visible in the world.

Most of the civilizations found comfort in a **Creationist Theory**: the belief that a powerful deity or deities created and controlled all things. However, at various stages of development, most religions largely abandoned polytheism, the belief in more than one god, in exchange for a single, all-powerful God. This was particularly true in the western civilizations as Christianity eventually displaced paganism (naturalism) and animism as the dominant system of belief.

Early Models of the Universe

The early models of the universe were primarily products of philosophical musings as combined with religious and social tenets, and observable phenomenon.

Geocentric Model: the original model of universal object arrangement in which the universe was Earth centered and all other stellar objects rotated around the Earth. The Sun followed a track around the outer edge of the rotational sphere. The ancient Greeks later modified this model into the Greek Celestial Model (Aristolian Model).

Greek Celestial Model (Aristolian Model): The ancient Greek model was also geocentric. The Earth is still at the center of the universe but the planets, Sun, and stars all are on different spheres orbiting around the Earth. God (heaven) is on the outermost sphere. This model was widely accepted because it was based on the philosophical teachings of Aristotle.

Ptolemaic Model: The Alexandrian Greek Astronomer Ptolemy, observing the planetary motions in 140 A.D., realized that reality didn't fit the Greek model well. He modified the Greek Celestial model to fit his observations while still retaining a geocentric orientation. Ptolemy's model had the moon orbiting around the Sun in an Epicyclic motion. An **epicycle is a retrograde**: backward motion, in which and object spins or moves clockwise.

Early Dissension to the Geocentric

Aristarchus (260 B.C): 400 Years prior to Ptolemy, the Greek Mathematician Aristarchus proposed the first recorded reference to a Heliocentric: sun centered, universe. He based his conclusion on the study of perfect geometry. His calculations showed that the motions of the observable stellar objects could not be possible if they were geocentric. However, his postulation of heliocentricity was vehemently suppressed by the astronomers of the day. The conclusion would have meant that if the Earth weren't at the center, then it would make the Earth less perfect. This ran completely counter to the deeply entrenched and accepted philosophical thought about God, Earth, and the Heavens.

The Heliocentric Model

Nicolaus Copernicus (1507 A.D.)- Based solely on his extensive planetary observations, Polish monk Nicolaus Copernicus, in his paper *"Revolutions of the Heavenly Spheres,"* triggered *an* earth-shaking revision of human thought by publicly proposing that the universe is heliocentric, not geocentric. He also claimed that the Earth's axis was tilted in relation to the Sun, using retrograde motion, only in a different way.

Copernicus knew that his theory would be highly controversial and out of fear of excommunication by church authorities, he didn't publish his paper until near the end of his life. As he expected, his paper raised a storm of argument between scholars and the church authorities. The debate between Copernicus' supporters and detractors grew so heated as to lead to bloodshed on several occasions. Clearly, this new concept was not to be forgotten as was in the case of Aristarchus.

Tycho Brahe (1572 A.D.)- Spurred on by the growing interest in science, Danish nobleman Tycho Brahe rejected a career as a lawyer and politician, and devoted his life to astronomy and mathematics. In 1572, Tycho, as he is usually referred as, observed a brilliant new star in the sky and like other classically trained astronomers of the day, he was puzzled by its appearance. This new star did not fit into the Aristolian scheme of the heavens, which held that the starry regions were perfectly complete. This meant that the star must be between the moon and the Earth. However, by measuring the parallax of motion, his calculations showed that the star must be further away, challenging the Ptolemaic concepts.

His conclusions were published in a small book *"De Stella Nova (the New Star)"* in 1573 and attracted the attention of the King of Denmark, who offered him funds to build a planetary observatory on the Danish isle of Hveen. Tyco's greatest contribution to astronomy was not theoretical. Instead, his true value to the science lay in his observations.

For over 20 years Tycho constructed new and highly improved existing instruments and studied the motion of over 700 stellar objects, collecting the most the most complete data sets of astronomical observations since the early Egyptian times. Amazingly he did this with the naked eye, as the telescope wasn't invented until almost a hundred years after his death. Tycho hired several mathematicians and astronomers to assist him in collecting and compiling the data. Among these individuals was Johannes Kepler, who would continue Brahe's work following Tycho's death in 1610.

Johannes Kepler (1600 A.D.)- In collating Tycho Brahe's data sets, Johannes Kepler discovered that the data wouldn't fully support the Copernican model. In an effort to try and make the data fit, he postulated what is now known as **Kepler's Laws of Planetary Motion**.

The significance of Kepler's Laws is that it overthrew the ancient concept of uniform circular motion, which was a major support for the geocentric arguments. Although Kepler postulated three laws of planetary motion, he was never able to explain *why* the planets move along their elliptical orbits, only that they did.

Galileo Galilei (1633 A.D.)- One of the truly brilliant minds of his time, Galileo Galilei was an Italian astronomer and inventor who built his first telescope in 1609. Contrary to popular myth, Galileo didn't invent the telescope but used existing plans and gradually improved upon the design.

The major significance of Galileo's observations is that they totally disproved the geocentric model of the universe. In doing so, Galileo totally destroyed the Aristolic vision of the universe that had been the basis of astronomical and philosophical though for over 2,000 years.

Galileo's destruction of the Aristolian theory of the universe created a large problem. If Aristotle was correct, what was the truth? People began to openly question blind belief in religious explanations and sought the answer to their questions through science.

Scientific Models of the Universe

As civilizations continued to advance so did our understanding of the physical processes affecting the universe. The early scientific models still blended elements of philosophy and religious thought with measurable data, but as our technological base improved, models reflected less and less of those influences to the point that today, it's a commonly accepted practice to totally discount them in modeling the universe.

Steady State Theory: a scientific theory that held that the universe was static and that it did not evolve, having always maintained a balance of the same general properties through replacement of dying stars and galaxies by new stars and galaxies. This theory was simultaneously both a popular and controversial explanation of the universe during its heydays in the 1950's and 1960's.

However, all astronomers did not accept the concept of a static universe, and they proposed an alternate theory centered on non-static, expanding universe. Steady state supporter, American astronomer Fred Hoyle sarcastically dubbed this theory the "Big Bang".

The controversy between supporters and opponents of the steady state theory continued until the late 1960's when detection of primordial background radiation dealt a decisive blow to the steady state theory. In a static state the background radiation should be uniform, however, since it clearly was not, this indicated that something had occurred to cause it to "clump" together. The logical explanation was a massive explosion that disordered the radiation.

Big Bang Theory: a theory that proposes that all the mass and energy of the universe was originally concentrated at a single geometric point and for unknown reasons, experienced a massive explosion that scattered the matter throughout the universe.

The concept of a massive explosion is supported by the distribution of background radiation and the measurable fact that the galaxies are moving away from each other at great speed.

The Universe originated around 15 billion years ago with the "Big Bang," and continued to expand for the first 10 billion years. The universe was originally unimaginably hot, but around 1 million years after the Big Bang, it cooled enough to allow for the formation of atoms from the energy and particles.

Most of these atoms were hydrogen and they comprise the most abundant form of matter in the universe. Around a billion years after the Big Bang, the matter had cooled enough to begin congealing into the first of the stars and galaxies.

Skill 45.4 The beginning teacher recognizes and explains the patterns of movement of the Sun, Moon, planets, and stars in the sky.

When we look at the night sky we see stars in different locations depending on the time of night and the time of year. The reason we observe this phenomenon is because the Earth spins, causing the stars to rise and set, just as the Sun and Moon do. If you were to chart your sky one night, and do it again the next, the stars would appear to be in the same position, but the moon would appear to have moved. This is because the Earth spun around exactly once, causing the stars to appear the same. In addition to rising and setting, however, the Sun and the Moon have an additional motion across the sky.

It takes about 27 days for the Moon to orbit the Earth one time. This is why, when you charted your night sky on two consecutive days, the moon appeared to be in a different position. It had not yet completed its orbit around the Earth. What would happen if you looked for the same stars you had previously charted a month later? They would probably be found in a slightly different part of the sky then they were before. This is due to the Earth's motion around the Sun. The Earth orbits the Sun in one full calendar year. During that year one can see many different groups of stars in the sky. These groups are known as constellations.

The Earth is moving not just around the Sun, but also on its own axis. The Earth is inclined at an angle of 23.5 degrees to the plane of its orbit. The direction of the inclination (with respect to the stars) does not change as the Earth moves around the Sun, causing the Earth to sometimes be tilted towards the Sun and sometimes tilted away from it. The Earth's spin on its axis makes the Sun appear to move across the sky. Because the Earth is facing the Sun at a different angle each day, the "path" the Sun makes in the sky is different each day of the year. Only on the equinoxes (Sept/Mar 21st) does the Sunrise/set at due East/West. At the solstices (Dec/June 21st) the position is its furthest South/North of East/West. This causes the seasons.

The position of Moonrise and Moonset, like that of Sunrise and Sunset, varies as the Earth goes around the Sun, but also with the phases of the Moon. This is because the phase of the Moon depends on the relative positions of the Sun, Moon and Earth. For example, when the Moon is Full it is opposite the Earth from the Sun, so when the Sun sets, the Moon must rise and vice versa.

Skill 45.5 The beginning teacher demonstrates the use of units of measurement in astronomy (e.g., light year, astronomical units).

Measurement Units in Astronomy

Astronomical distances represent mind-boggling amounts of distance. Because our standard units of distance measurement (i.e. kilometers) would result in so large of a number as to become almost incomprehensible, physicists use different units of measurement to reference the vast distances involved in astronomy.

Within our solar system, the standard unit of distance measurement is the **AU (Astronomical Unit)**. The **AU** is the mean distance between the Sun to the Earth. 1 AU = 1.495979×10^{ll}m. Outside of our solar system, the standard unit of distance measurement is the **Parsec.** 1 Parsec = 206,265 AU or 3.26 Light Years (LY).

Light year (LY): the distance light travels in one year. As the speed of light is 3.00×10^8 m/sec, one light year represents a distance of 9.5×10^{12} km, or 63,000 AU.

Measuring the Distance to the Stars

The distances are measured using a shift in viewpoint. This is called the **Parallax**: an apparent change in the position of an object due to a change in the location of the observer. In astronomy, parallax is measured in seconds of arc. 1 second of arc = 1/3600 of a degree.

The concept of measuring distances by parallax is based on the mathematical discipline of trigonometry.

Example: Photos of the distant stars are taken at different times, usually 6 months apart. The apparent shift in position that the star has moved in comparison to the previous photo is the parallax.

By measuring the angles, we can use trigonometric functions of sine, cosine, and tangent to determine a distance to the object. The smaller the parallax is, the greater the distance to the star.

Skill 45.6 **The beginning teacher explains how various technologies (e.g., Earth- and space-based telescopes, deep-space probes, artificial satellites) are used in advancing knowledge about the universe.**

Telescopes are one of the oldest technologies used to gain information about space. Most telescopes are optical, though spectrum telescopes for gathering all types of electromagnetic radiation also exist. Optical telescopes have been used for hundreds of years to observe bodies and phenomena in outer space. As technology has allowed telescopes to be launched into outer space, even more detailed information has been obtained. Particularly, these telescopes have allowed observation unhindered by the interference of the Earth's atmosphere. The Hubble telescope, which is in orbit around Earth, is one famous optical telescope that has been utilized in this manner. The Chandra X-ray observatory is another famous telescope, though it collects X-rays. These and other telescopes have gleaned much information about distant bodies in outer space.

Some of earliest forays into true space exploration were unmanned missions involving space probes. The probes are controlled remotely from Earth and have been shot into outer space and immediately returned, placed into orbit around our planet, and sent to and past the other planets in our solar system. The first was the USSR's Sputnik I in October of 1957. It was the first man-made object ever launched into space. This was the beginning of the "space race" between the USSR and USA. The USA's first successful launch of a space probe occurred with Vanguard I in December of 1957. A few early, unmanned missions were space probes carrying animals, such as the Soviet dog Laika that became the first animal in orbit in November of 1957. Animals are included only for research purposes in current missions. Space probes are still used for certain applications where risk, cost, or duration makes manned missions impractical. The Voyager probes are among the most famous probes. They were launched to take advantage of the favorable planetary alignment in the late 1970s. They returned data and fascinating pictures from Jupiter and Saturn as well as information from beyond our solar system. It is hoped that, as technology continues to improve, space probes will be allow us to investigate space even farther away from Earth.

Skill 45.7   **The beginning teacher understands how mathematical models, computer simulations, and data collected by the space and other science programs have contributed to scientific knowledge about Earth, the solar system, and the universe.**

One of the primary means of learning more about the planetary bodies of the solar system is through space exploration. Beginning in the 1960's when the first probes journeyed toward Earth's Moon, a planned sequence of spacecraft has visited some of the planetary objects in our solar system. Unmanned missions are carried out if they are deemed too dangerous for humans to undertake. Sputnik was the first unmanned mission. It was a Russian mission launched on Oct. 4, 1957, during the Cold War. The Americans were driven to compete and ramp up their space program.

Mariner 10- This American mission was the first to use the gravitational pull of one planet to reach another planet.

Deep Space 1- This American mission tested twelve advanced technologies to benefit future space travel.

Magellan- The Magellan mission is so called because the American Magellan took pictures of and collected information on Venus. Magellan was followed by:

Mars Exploration Rover, Mars Pathfinder, and Sputnik 1

Sputnik 2 - sent the first life, a dog named Laika, into orbit around Earth.

Voyager 1 / Voyager 2

Throughout history there have been many manned missions including many "firsts" such as first animal, man on moon, women in space, preventable catastrophe, and first fatal catastrophe. As of 2007, the manned missions have been contained to orbiting around the Earth and landing on the Moon. With new knowledge of propulsion it would be possible to reach Mars with a manned mission. Previously, unmanned missions have used land rovers to collect over 17,000 photo images and collect rock and soil samples.

Aside from actually entering outer space, much study about the solar system and universe can be controlled from Earth. Many of the telescopes used by astronomers are Earth-based, located in observatories around the world. However, only radio waves, visible light, and some infrared radiation can penetrate our atmosphere to reach the Earth's surface. Therefore, scientists have launched telescopes into space, where the instruments can collect other types of electromagnetic waves. Space probes are also able to gather information from distant parts of the solar system.

In addition to telescopes, scientists construct **mathematical models** and **computer simulations** to form a scientific account of events in the universe. These models and simulations are built using evidence from many sources, including the information gathered through telescopes and space probes.

A **geosynchronous orbit** is an orbit around the Earth that has an orbital period matching the Earth's sidereal rotation period. This means that for an observer at a fixed location on Earth, a satellite placed in a geosynchronous orbit returns to exactly the same place in the sky at exactly the same time each day, making measurements easy and predictable.

Polar Orbiting satellites follow an orbit from pole to pole. The Earth rotates underneath the satellite and gives a view of different areas. In effect, it produces slices of the Earth.

Satellites: The National Weather Service heavily depends on its network of weather satellites (i.e. GOES Satellite), to provide a wide-area coverage of the Earth. These satellites primary provide infrared, water vapor, and photographic data and are used to track the formation, development and motion of major meteorological events such as hurricanes and tropical storms.

The most accurate method to measure global temperature is to use space satellite technology. Since 1979, the GOES Satellite has collected temperature readings. Instead of sampling only the cities, the GOES samples all areas in blocks of data, including the oceans. Data taken during the period of 1979-1998 showed no net warming. However, from a scientific method point of view, this is not a long enough period of sampling to be fully conclusive.

The **GOES Satellite** is a key source of weather information. GOES is a geostationary satellite that primarily scans the Atlantic Ocean & U.S. East Coast.

Satellites have improved our ability to communicate and transmit radio and television signals. Navigational abilities have been greatly improved through the use of satellite signals. Sonar uses sound waves to locate objects, especially underwater. The sound waves bounce off the object and are picked up to assist in location. Seismographs record vibrations in the Earth and allow us to measure earthquake activity.

DOMAIN X.	SCIENCE LEARNING, INSTRUCTION, AND ASSESSMENT

Competency 0046 **The teacher understands research based theoretical and practical knowledge about teaching science, how students learn science, and the role of scientific inquiry in science instruction.**

Skill 46.1 **The beginning teacher knows research-based theories about how students develop scientific understanding and how developmental characteristics, prior knowledge, experience, and attitudes of students influence science learning.**

Learning styles refers to the ways in which individuals learn best. Physical settings, instructional arrangements, materials available, techniques, and individual preferences are all factors in the teacher's choice of instructional strategies and materials. Information about the student's preference can be done through a direct interview or through a checklist where the student rates his preferences.

Physical Settings

A. **Noise**: Students vary in the degree of quiet that they need and the amount of background noise or talking that they can tolerate without getting distracted or frustrated.

B. **Temperature and Lighting**: Students also vary in their preference for lighter or darker areas of the room, tolerance for coolness or heat, and ability to see the chalkboard, screen, or other areas of the room.

C. **Physical Factors**: This refers to the student's need for workspace and preference for type of work area, such as desk, table, or learning center. Proximity factors such as closeness to other students, the teacher or high traffic areas such as doorways or pencil sharpeners, may help the student to feel secure and stay on task, or may serve as distractions, depending on the individual.

Instructional Arrangements
Some students work well in large groups; others prefer small groups or one-to-one instruction with the teacher, aide or volunteer. Instructional arrangements also involve peer-tutoring situations with the student as tutor or tutee. The teacher also needs to consider how well the student works independently with seatwork.

Instructional Techniques

Consideration of the following factors will affect the teacher's choice of instructional techniques, as well as selecting optimal times to schedule certain types of assignments. Some of these factors are listed below:

- How much time the student needs to complete work
- Time of day the student works best
- How student functions under timed conditions
- How much teacher demonstration and attention is needed for the task
- The student's willingness to approach new tasks
- Student's willingness to give up
- Student's preference for verbal or written instruction
- Student's frustration tolerance when faced with difficulty
- Number of prompts, cues, and attention needed for the student to maintain expected behavior

Material and Textbook Preferences

Students vary in their ability to respond and learn with different techniques of lesson presentation. They likewise vary in their preference and ability to learn with different types of materials. Depending on the student's preference and success, the teacher can choose from among these types of instructional materials:

- Self-correcting materials
- Worksheets wit or without visual cues
- Worksheets with a reduced number of items or lots of writing space
- Manipulative materials
- Flash cards, commercial or student-prepared
- Computers
- Commercial materials
- Teacher-made materials
- Games, board or card
- Student-made instructional materials

Learning Styles

Students also display preferences for certain learning styles and these differences are also factors in the teacher's choice of presentation and materials.

A) **Visual:** Students who are visual may enjoy working with and remember best from books, films, pictures, pictures, modeling, overheads, demonstrating and writing.

B) **Auditory:** Students who are auditory may enjoy working with and remember best from hearing records of tapes, auditory directions, listening to people, radio, read-aloud stories, and lectures.

C) **Tactile:** Indicators are drawing, tracing, manipulating and working with materials such as clay or paints.

Kinesthetic: Indicators include learning through writing, experiments, operating machines, such as typewriters or calculators, motor activities and games, and taking pictures.

Experience: Various factors influence or affect understanding of science. The most important aspect is to lay the foundation at an early stage. Whatever students are taught has to be correct and contextualized. When an activity is done, it has to be explained. Prior knowledge is absolutely important for a correct understanding of science. The students must have positive experiences in science learning. Good attitude is important for learning. This applies to science as well. Some students have a strong opinion that science is difficult and not interesting. It falls upon the teacher to be creative and make science interesting.

Skill 46.2 **The beginning teacher understands the importance of respecting student diversity by planning activities that are inclusive and selecting and adapting science curricula, content, instructional materials, and activities to meet the interests, knowledge, understanding, abilities, and experiences of all students, including English Language Learners.**

Teaching students of diverse backgrounds is very challenging and must be handled very carefully since the teacher must be politically correct, when handling such students. Apart from that, from a humanitarian point of view, the teacher needs to be compassionate and empathetic, since it is a challenge to settle in a different country and call it home.

The lesson plans must reflect the teachers understanding and respect towards the diverse students.
Incorporating the different cultural practices into the lessons and connecting them with science is helpful. For example, studying the contributions to science made

by the Latino scientists, the African American scientists, the Native American scientists, the Asian scientists etc. In February, we can study about famous scientists of African American origin. Same thing goes with other cultures. When this is done, the students feel very happy and appreciate the effort and thought of their teacher, who took time to recognize their heritage.

Decorating the classroom using ethnic material would be interesting and also creates an atmosphere of being at home. Incorporating the cultural and linking them to science needs a little bit of time and ingenuity, which will go a long way in establishing good relationships with students and their families.

Skill 46.3   The beginning teacher knows how to plan and implement strategies to encourage student self-motivation and engagement in their own learning (e.g., linking inquiry-based investigations to students' prior knowledge, focusing inquiry-based instruction on issues relevant to students, developing instructional materials using situations from students' daily lives, fostering collaboration among students).

Two important things in teaching science are theory: explaining the lesson and answering why, how, when, what and which (out of these five why and how are the most important/useful to gain knowledge) and practical exploration, which is actively doing something/experimenting. Both need to be balanced and only then can a student understand science properly. Students are motivated when they are encouraged to ask questions and given opportunities to contribute to their own learning as well.

Linking of ideas is very important because the students' prior knowledge is taken into consideration. Basing on the prior knowledge of the students, the next step of instruction has to be planned. When students have not got the knowledge they are expected to have for their grade level, some thing must be done to remedy the situation for the student's benefit.

Inquiry based instruction is popular because the students have questions and they must be answered. They need to be encouraged to ask questions and create opportunities to find answers for those questions. The best way to find answers for some of their questions is to let them investigate, experiment and find for themselves the answers to their questions.

Another aspect of importance is that whatever is being taught in the science curriculum must have some practical relevance to their lives. Science has to be contextualized. If the learning to connected to everyday life, it motivates the students because they can relate to it. Because biology is the study of living things, we can easily apply the knowledge of biology to daily life and personal decision-making. For example, biology greatly influences the health decisions humans make everyday. What foods to eat, when and how to exercise, and how often to bathe are just three of the many decisions we make everyday that are based on our knowledge of biology. Other areas of daily life where biology affects decision-making are parenting, interpersonal relationships, family planning, and consumer spending.

Skill 46.4   The beginning teacher knows how to use a variety of instructional strategies to ensure all students comprehend content-related texts, including how to locate, retrieve, and retain information from a range of texts and technologies.

The word strategy means a careful plan or method. Instructional strategies are plans / methods used in teaching students. Educators use a variety of instructional strategies. The success of teaching lies in using a variety of strategies to keep the students interested. Let's examine some of the instructional strategies employed by educators.

Lecture
This is an activity in which the teacher presents the information and knowledge orally through a series of organized and structured explanations. In this strategy, the student involvement is least. Lectures can be both formal and informal. In formal lectures, the student interaction is non-existent but the informal lectures, student there is an increase of 20% in student retention of information.

There are ways to make the lecture method more interesting and beneficial to the students.

1. Feedback lecture - lecture lasts only for 10 minutes and then the students are divided into study groups and discuss what was lectured and also they have an opportunity to study the notes before the lecture.

2. Guided lecture - lasts for 20 minutes followed by discussion in small groups.

3. Responsive lecture - Devotes one class /week to answer open ended questions and student generated questions.

4. Demonstration lecture - Demonstrating a lab/activity in the middle of the lecture.

5. Pause procedure lecture - after every 5-6 minutes of lecture, the students are 2 minutes to compare notes with their peers and will fill in any missing information.

6. Think / Write / Discuss lecture - This method starts with a critical thinking question and during the lecture, students are questioned about the topic and at the end students are questioned again to find out how much they understood.

Mnmonic strategy
Mnemonic strategies are memory aids that provide a very systematic approach for organizing and remembering facts that have no apparent link or connection of their own.

Re Quest
Re Quest is a strategy that fosters active, rather than passive, reading of a text. This strategy provides a structure for the students to ask questions about the learning. Both teacher and student ask each other questions about what they are doing in terms of lesson.

Reciprocal teaching
This is an instructional activity in the form of interactive dialogue between the teacher and the students regarding the segments of the text. The dialogue involves four strategies

1. Summarizing
2. 2. Question generating
3. Clarifying and
4. Predicting.

The teacher guides the students in all the above steps.

The most versatile computer helps us in locating information and retrieving it. It is important for the students to be familiar with various websites that give academic information. It is also equally important for the students to locate the information in books and journals. Students need to be introduced to various journals in their core subjects, which also provide latest pieces of research.

For retaining information, there are strategies to improve memory and to retain it. Some of the strategies discussed above provide information on memory and retention of knowledge.

Skill 46.5 **The beginning teacher understands the science teacher's role in developing the total school program by planning and implementing science instruction that incorporates school wide objectives and the statewide curriculum as defined in the Texas Essential Knowledge and Skills (TEKS).**

Science needs to be contextualized in order for the students to relate to it. It is much easier for the students to be interested in it when it is connected to their everyday lives. The role of the science teacher is to facilitate this by planning and introducing school wide science programs. These programs are across the board and are group learning activities, though they seem simply like fun activities.

The following are some ideas that could be used as school wide science programs.

1. Butterfly garden: Butterflies are attractive and most of the students would be interested in them. Their beauty and movement are worth observing and the fact that come from caterpillars is another interesting fact. A committee consisting of student representatives from all grade levels must be formed. Initial planning includes money to carry out this project; a willing group of students across the school; a small area to grow plants that would attract butterflies to lay eggs; and monitoring progress daily, observing and recording. This project lasts a few months. Another way to do this project would be to separate the students into a number of groups that could pool their observations and come up with a more authentic set of observations.

2. Weather station: This is another great idea for involving the whole school. A group of students across the board can measure and record the rainfall in a year.

3. Preserving natural resources: In this example students are made aware of the implications of using natural resources meaningfully and economically. For instance, preserving forests starts with using paper economically, though we can afford to buy plenty of it. Awards should be instituted to reward students who are aware of conservation and practice it.

A science teacher should also take advantage of natural phenomena such as hurricanes, volcanic eruptions, and tornadoes and teach the students about their causes. Students can track hurricane pathways and monitor volcanic eruptions.

Skill 46.6 **The beginning teacher knows how to design and manage the learning environment (e.g., individual, small-group, whole-class settings) to focus and support student inquiries and to provide the time, space, and resources for all students to participate in field, laboratory, experimental, and non-experimental scientific investigation.**

Learning environment is a very important factor in teaching any discipline. Ideally, the learning environment has to be designed in such a way that most of the students are motivated to learn. When we talk about learning environment, we are talking about the learning environment for the regular students. There is always a small number of students who are disruptive and interfere with the learning of other students, and these students have to be handled in a different manner depending on their individual needs. It is the responsibility of the teacher to make the environment in the classroom suitable for various types of learning - individual, pairs, small groups, whole class setting.

The physical environment, such as the arrangement of furniture, has to be taken care of depending on the activity, e.g., if the teacher has planned collaborative pairs for learning, the tables have to be moved around to achieve that. This should be done before the lesson or activity starts.

Next comes the actual learning activity. Individual teaching should be the method for exceptional students and those who need more attention than the regular student. A few minutes of explaining the lesson or the task on hand will be very helpful. In the case of pair share or collaborative pairs, a small assignment could be given and a time frame set, at the end of which students will share as a class what they have learned. This is very good if an exceptional student and a bright student are paired. A small group is very productive since there are many things involved in that situation, such as sharing information, waiting for one's turn, listening to other's ideas, views, and suggestions, and taking responsibility for doing a job in the group (writing/presenting/drawing etc.) which also teach basic manners. Teaching as a class involves traditional and modern methods such as lecture, lecture/demonstration, pause and lecture, etc. The same applies for experimental, field and nonexperimental work.

Today's learning, especially science, is largely inquiry-based. Sometimes it becomes part of teaching to encourage the students to ask questions. Sufficient time must be given to students to ask these questions.

As a teacher, one must be a good manager of not only the classroom but also of time, resources, and space. The teacher needs to plan how much time should be given to exceptional students, bright students, regular students, and disruptive students. The exceptional and the disruptive students must get more of the teacher's time. Next will be the regular and last the bright students, since they are a few steps ahead of the rest. If they finish work quickly, however, bright students need to be engaged, so some extra work must be available. In terms of space the same things apply. Resources must be shared equally as far as possible, since everybody has the right to have equal opportunity. However, there must be modification of resources suitable for the exceptional students, if required.

One thing is most important - a teacher must use logic and be able to think laterally since all the answers are not in books. The best teaching is part original thinking and part innovation and ingenuity.

Skill 46.7   The beginning teacher understands the rationale for using active learning and inquiry methods in science instruction and how to model scientific attitudes such as curiosity, openness to new ideas, and skepticism.

Learning can be broadly divided into two kinds - active and passive. Active learning involves, as the name indicates, a learning atmosphere full of action whereas in passive learning students are taught in a nonstimulating and inactive atmosphere. Active learning involves and draws students into it, thereby interesting them to the point of participating and purposely engaging in learning.

It is crucial that students are actively engaged, not entertained. They should be taught the answers for "How" and "Why" questions and encouraged to be inquisitive and interested.

Active learning is conceptualized as follows:

A Model of Active Learning

Experience of	Dialogue with
Doing	Self
Observing	Others

This model suggests that all learning activities involve some kind of experience or some kind of dialogue. The two main kinds of dialogue are "Dialogue with self" and "Dialogue with others". The two main kinds of experience are "Observing" and "Doing".

Dialogue with self: This is what happens when a learner thinks reflectively about a topic. They ask themselves a number of things about the topic.

Dialogue with others: When the students are listening to a book being read by another student or when the teacher is teaching, a partial dialogue takes place because the dialogue is only one sided. When they are listening to an adult and when there is an exchange of ideas back and forth, it is said to be a dialogue with others.

Observing: This is a most important skill in science. This occurs when a learner is carefully watching or observing someone else doing an activity or experiment. This is a good experience, although it is not quite like doing it for themselves.

Doing: This refers to any activity where a learner actually does something, giving the learner a firsthand experience that is very valuable.

Inquiry is invaluable to teaching in general and to teaching science, especially. The steps involved in scientific inquiry are discussed in the following section.

The scientific attitude is to be curious, open to new ideas, and skeptical. In science, there is always new research, new discoveries, and new theories proposed. Sometimes, old theories are disproved. To view these changes rationally, one must have such openness, curiosity, and skepticism. (Skepticism is a Greek word, meaning a method of obtaining knowledge through systematic doubt and continual testing. A scientific skeptic is one who refuses to accept certain types of claims without subjecting them to a systematic investigation.)

The students may not have these attitudes inherently, but it is the responsibility of the teacher to encourage, nurture, and practice these attitudes so that their students will have a good role model.

Skill 46.8   **The beginning teacher knows principles and procedures for designing and conducting an inquiry-based scientific investigation (e.g., making observations; generating questions; researching and reviewing current knowledge in light of existing evidence; choosing tools to gather and analyze evidence; proposing answers, explanations, and predictions; communicating and defending results).**

Science investigations in the classroom environment are very important because they are something a student can do by himself/herself with assistance from the teacher. Through such "active learning," the student gains experience and knowledge.

Scientific investigations are carried out by the method generally known as the Scientific Method. The Scientific Method is composed of a series of steps to solve a problem. We use this method in order to eliminate, to the extent possible, our preconceived ideas, prejudices, and bias. When students are explained the purpose of the method, they will be able to appreciate it better. The Scientific Method is an inquiry-based method. It consists of the following steps:

Problem / Question: In order to investigate, we must have a problem or question to begin with. A problem or question may come from observing, one of the most important skills in science, or from theory. The problem needs to be communicated in clear terms and in simple language, so that anybody reading it will be able to understand it.

Research / Gathering information

There are number of resources available to students - websites, scientific journals, magazines, books, and people who are knowledgeable and experienced, which may help them research what is already known about the topic.

Formulating a hypothesis

This is also known as making an educated guess. An informed guess is made regarding a possible solution to the problem, which will be tested as part of the experiment.

Experimental design

Conducting an experiment is very exciting and interesting, but designing the experiment well is a challenging task. It is important that students understand this. They should not rush to do an experiment, but must have a clear understanding of the different elements of an experiment: identifying the control/standard, determining the constants, and deciding on the independent and dependent variables. Involving students in the experimental design rather than having it pre-determined will greatly increase their understanding and appreciation of the experiment.

An ideal experiment at the high school level should not last more than 12-14 days.

Collection of data

Through conducting an experiment, we acquire data. The data should be organized and visually presented, in tabular form and/or graphically.

Analysis of the data

The data should be analyzed to test the hypothesis and identify interesting patterns. Numbers are important, but they are typically not as useful or enlightening as patterns in the data.

Drawing conclusions

In the conclusion the investigator attempts to provide plausible answers to the initial question, determine whether the hypothesis was correct, summarize any trends or patterns observed, and make suggestions regarding subsequent research.

Communication

Oral and written communication skills are a necessity for anybody pursuing research. Effective oral communication is needed to present the research in front of the classroom or school. Written communication is needed to present a report on the research. It should be made clear to students that, in this age of communication, those who cannot communicate effectively will be left behind. Accordingly, the evaluation system should make provision for communication skills and activities.

Defending results

Defending results is as important as conducting an experiment. One can honestly defend one's own results only if the results are reliable, and experiments must be well-controlled and repeated at least twice to be considered reliable. It must be emphasized to the students that honesty and integrity are the foundation for any type of investigation.

Skill 46.9 **The beginning teacher knows how to assist students with generating, refining, focusing, and testing scientific questions and hypotheses.**

Scientific questions are very important because they are the starting point for learning. Students need to be encouraged, provoked and challenged to ask questions. The questions need not necessarily make sense at the beginning, but as the time goes by, these questions begin to make lot of sense.

The teacher must realize that questioning is an important tool in teaching and it can be an effective in learning as well. It must be mentioned here that not all students are curious and inquisitive. Not all parents encourage their children to ask questions. In such cases the teacher needs to show lot of patience in encouraging the students to be inquisitive and curious. This takes time and with time, this could be achieved to a large extent.

The next step in this process of teaching students to question is **refining** questions. The next step is **focusing**. The questions need to be focused on the topic under discussion or investigation.

The last step in this is **testing scientific questions and hypotheses.** All questions can not be tested. Some questions can answered by research. Like the question that was cited above regarding the moon, can not be tested, but on the other hand, can be answered by research. A wealth of information could be discovered and most of the questions will be answered.

Skill 46.10   The beginning teacher knows strategies for assisting students in learning to identify, refine, and focus scientific ideas and questions guiding an inquiry-based scientific investigation; to develop, analyze, and evaluate different explanations for a given scientific result; and to identify potential sources of error in an inquiry-based scientific investigation.

The first task is to encourage the students to ask **questions**. They need to learn to frame questions. There are a few ways in which the students can be encouraged to ask questions.

1. Brainstorming the topic under study
2. Discussing it in the class and inviting students to ask questions
3. By letting students discuss in small groups and come up with questions - this is extremely useful to students who are introverts and shy by nature.

By now the students have learned to ask questions. These questions may not be completely relevant to the topic under discussion, but still the students have a set of questions. It is the responsibility of the teacher to take these questions and **refine** them to "How" and "Why" type of open ended questions. Many time s the students may end up asking closed end questions. e.g. Who landed on the moon? This sort of closed ended questions are not really knowledge generating questions. They are not thought provoking questions. The teacher can modify this question to "what did the missions to moon accomplish?" With this type of question, a lot of discussion will be generated - who landed on the moon first, the weather of moon, the moon's rock samples etc. The questions need to be **focused** on the topic under discussion or investigation. Focusing is important because it is very easy to be carried away and to be side tracked. The students need to be made aware of being able to focus on a topic understand and not to deviating from it, however tempting it may be.

There are many ways in which errors could creep in measurements. Errors in measurements could occur because:

1.   Improper use of instruments used for measuring – weighing etc.
2.   Parallax error – not positioning the eyes during reading of measurements
3.   Not using same instruments and methods of measurement during an experiment
4.   Not using the same source of materials, resulting in the content of a certain compound used for experimentation

When erroneous results are used for interpreting data, the conclusions are not reliable. An experiment is valid only when all the constants like time, place, method of measurement etc. are strictly controlled.

Skill 46.11 **The beginning teacher understands how to implement inquiry strategies designed to promote the use of higher-level thinking skills, logical reasoning, and scientific problem solving in order to move students from concrete to more abstract understanding.**

Inquiry learning provides opportunities for students to experience and acquire thought processes through which they can gather information about the world. This requires a higher level of interaction among the learner, the teacher, the area of study, available resources, and the learning environment. Students become actively involved in the learning process as they:

1. Act upon their curiosity and interests
2. Develop questions that are relevant
3. Think their way through controversies or dilemmas
4. Analyze problems
5. Develop, clarify, and test hypotheses
6. Draw conclusions
7. Find possible solutions

The most important element in inquiry-based learning is questioning. Students must ask relevant questions and develop ways to search for answers and generate explanations. High order thinking is encouraged.

Below are some **inquiry strategies.**

1. Deductive inquiry: The main goal of this strategy is moving the student from a generalized principle to specific instances. The process of testing general assumptions, applying them, and exploring the relationships between specific elements is stressed. The teacher coordinates the information and presents important principles, themes, or hypotheses. Students are actively engaged in testing generalizations, gathering information, and applying it to specific examples.

2. Inductive inquiry: The information-seeking process of the inductive inquiry method helps students to establish facts, determine relevant questions, and develop ways to pursue these questions and build explanations. Students are encouraged to develop and support their own hypotheses. Through inductive inquiry, students experience the thought processes that require them to move from specific facts and observations to inferences.

3. Interactive instruction: This strategy relies heavily on discussion and sharing among participants. Students develop social skills, learning from teacher and peers. They also learn organizational skills. Examples are debates, brainstorming, discussion, laboratory groups, etc.

4. <u>Direct instruction strategy</u>: This is highly teacher-oriented and is among the most commonly used strategies. It is effective for providing information or developing step-by-step skills. Examples are lecture, demonstrations, explicit teaching, etc.

5. <u>Indirect instruction</u>: This is mainly student-centered. Direct and indirect instruction strategies can compliment each other. Indirect instruction seeks a high level of student involvement such as observing, investigating, drawing inferences from data, or forming hypotheses. In this strategy, the role of the teacher shifts from that of teacher/lecturer to that of facilitator, supporter, and resource person. Examples are problem solving, inquiry, concept formation, etc.

6. <u>Independent study</u>: Independent study refers to the range of instructional methods that are purposely provided to foster the development of individual student initiative, self reliance, and self improvement. Examples are research projects, homework, etc.

The above mentioned strategies promote higher-level thinking skills such as problem solving, synthesizing (hypothesizing), designing (identifying the problem), analyzing (analyzing data in an experiment), and connecting (logical thinking).

Skill 46.12   The beginning teacher knows how to sequence learning activities in a way that uncovers common misconceptions, allows students to build upon their prior knowledge, and challenges them to expand their understanding of science.

Critical thinking and reasoning are two important skills that the students should be encouraged to use to discover facts – for example, that heat is a form of energy. Here, the students have to be challenged to use their critical thinking skills to reason that heat can cause change – for example, causing water to boil – and so it is not a thing but a form of energy, since only energy can cause change.

It is particularly important in science that each lesson builds upon prior knowledge. For example, if students do not understand the concept of cells, they won't understand the progression from cells to tissue, to organs, to systems.

There are many common misconceptions about science. The following are a few scientific misconceptions that are or have been common in the past:

* The Earth is the center of the solar system.
* The Earth is the largest object in the solar system
* Rain comes from the holes in the clouds
* Acquired characters can be inherited
* The eye receives upright images
* Energy is a thing
* Heat is not energy

Competency 0047   **The teacher knows how to monitor and assess science learning in laboratory, field, and classroom settings.**

Skill 47.1   **The beginning teacher knows how to use formal and informal assessments of student performance and products (e.g., projects, laboratory and field journals, rubrics, portfolios, student profiles, checklists) to evaluate student participation in and understanding of inquiry-based scientific investigations.**

It is vital for teachers to track students' performances through a variety of methods. Teachers should be able to asses students on a daily basis using informal assessments such as monitoring during work time, class discussions, and note taking. Often these assessments are a great way to determine whether or not students are "on track" learning selected objectives. Generally teachers can assess students just by class discussion and often this is a great time to give participation points, especially to those students who have special needs and participate well in class but may struggle with alternative assignments. More formal assessments are necessary to ensure students are fully understanding selected objectives. Regular grading using selected performance skills is necessary, however teachers should develop personal ways of grading using a variety of assessment tools. For example, students could keep a "Science Journal" and track progress of ongoing assignments, projects, and labs. Another great tool for observing and evaluating students is the use of rubrics and checklists. Student profiles and checklists are a great way to quickly determine if students are meeting selected objectives. These are useful during monitoring time for teachers. It is easy for a teacher to check off students who are meeting objectives using a checklist while monitoring students' work done in class. See example below:

Student Name	Objective #1	Objective #2	On task
Joe Student	X	X	X
Jon Student		X	X

Checklists provide an easy way for teachers to track students and quickly see who is behind or needs a lesson or objective reviewed.

Skill 47.2   **The beginning teacher understands the relationship between assessment and instruction in the science curriculum (e.g., designing assessments to match learning objectives, using assessment results to inform instructional practice).**

All children enrolled in our educational system will experience testing throughout their schooling, whether it is preschool sensory screenings, teacher-made quizzes, or annual standardized assessments. Assessment is continuous, and occurs on a regular basis. There are a variety of assessment instruments: standardized, criterion-referenced, curriculum-based, and teacher-made. Teachers in the field should possess sufficient knowledge to be able to determine quantitative dimensions such as the validity and reliability of tests, to recognize sound test content, and to choose appropriate tests for specific purposes. Continuous assessment allows the teacher to direct, and sometimes redirect, resources appropriately.

Skill 47.3   **The beginning teacher knows the importance of monitoring and assessing students' understanding of science concepts and skills on an ongoing basis by using a variety of appropriate assessment methods (e.g., performance assessment, self-assessment, peer assessment, formal/informal assessment).**

Much of science is based on past research. Because the concepts build upon one another it is vital that the student understands all previous concepts. For instance, a child who does not sufficiently grasp the difference between chemical and physical properties will be unable to make the leap towards understanding chemical reactions, nor would s/he then understand the law of conservation of matter. For this reason, assessment should occur regularly. Where a student or students is/are not proficient, the subject matter should be covered again to enhance understanding.

Skill 47.4   **The beginning teacher understands the purposes, characteristics, and uses of various types of assessment in science, including formative and summative assessments, and the importance of limiting the use of an assessment to its intended purpose.**

Formative assessment is the sum of all activities undertaken by teachers and by their students that provide information. That information can be considered feedback, and the teacher should modify the teaching and learning activities in response.

Teachers are responsible for assessment. They are required to give a report on each student's progress to both parents and administrators, as well as above and beyond regular administrators (often state mandates require a report as well). These reports inform parents, other teachers, officials, and also serve accountability purposes. In addition, other teachers are informed in regards to placement and teaching skills necessary for students to be successful. Teachers must take on multiple roles and must use formative assessment to help support and enhance student learning. The teacher ultimately decides the future for most students and must make summative judgments about a student's achievement at a specific point in time for purposes of placement, grading, accountability, and informing parents and future teachers about student performance. Teachers have special skills and observe students on a daily basis therefore giving them the power to use their perspective and knowledge to make recommendations for students in the future. Teachers are able to observe and assess over a period of time. This assessment may conflict with other performances and a teacher may be able to make better recommendations for students. Teachers must also remember that assessment-based judgments must be adjusted and reexamined over long periods of time to insure that conclusions are accurate.

Summative assessments are typically used to evaluate instructional programs and services. Typically these take place at the end of each school year. The overall goal of summative assessments is to make a judgment of student competency after an instructional phase is complete, in an attempt to see what has been learned or mastered by the students. Summative evaluations are used to determine if students have mastered specific competencies and to identify instructional areas that need additional attention. Some formative and summative assessments that are common in K-12 schools are listed below:

Formative Assessments	Summative Assessments
Anecdotal records	Final Exams
Quizzes and essays	State wide tests
Diagnostic tests	National tests
Lab reports	Entrance exams (SAT & ACT)

Skill 47.5   The beginning teacher understands strategies for assessing students' prior knowledge and misconceptions about science and how to use these assessments to develop effective ways to address these misconceptions.

Some strategies to uncover and dispel misconceptions include:

1. Planning appropriate activities, so that the students will see for themselves where there are misconceptions.

2. Web search is a very useful tool to dispel misconceptions. Students need to be guided in how to look for answers on the Web, and if necessary the teacher should explain scientific literature to help the students understand it.

3. Science journals are a great source of information. Recent research is highly beneficial for the senior science students.

4. Critical thinking and reasoning are two important skills that the students should be encouraged to use to discover facts – for example, that heat is a form of energy. Here, the students have to be challenged to use their critical thinking skills to reason that heat can cause change – for example, causing water to boil – and so it is not a thing but a form of energy, since only energy can cause change.

Skill 47.6   The beginning teacher understands characteristics of assessments, such as reliability, validity, and the absence of bias in order to evaluate assessment instruments and their results.

Assessments should be reliable, valid, and free from bias. The Miriam Webster dictionary gives the following definition for reliability: the extent to which an experiment, test, or measuring procedure yields the same results on repeated trials. The test should therefore be a strong indicator of the student's performance.   The same source defines validity as follows: well-grounded or justifiable: being at once relevant and meaningful; appropriate to the end in view: effective. Based upon this definition, the assessment used should be applicable to the testing area.

It is always important to limit bias, both in the laboratory setting and when considering students. We know that experiments can be biased. Scientific research can be biased in the choice of what data to consider, in the reporting or recording of the data, and/or in how the data are interpreted. The scientist's emphasis may be influenced by his/her nationality, sex, ethnic origin, age, or political convictions. For example, when studying a group of animals, male scientists may focus on the social behavior of the males and typically male characteristics.

Objectivity may not be easily attained. However, one precaution that may be taken to guard against undetected bias is to post grades by number- not name. When in the classroom, remember that some students are strongly right brained, while others are strongly left brained, and their learning styles differ. Teach to accommodate ALL styles, so that every student has the chance to succeed. Some teachers will average grades, to give students a boost, particularly if they see good effort on students' behalf (for example, completed homework, attendance, and behavior). In a science classroom it may be appropriate to walk around during lab, not just to watch for safety, but also to interject questions. This discussion time could give the teacher an idea of what the student understands, especially for those who are not great at test taking. Lastly, develop useful and fair test questions, and record these as facts that can be reviewed. Upon review there should be no room for subjectivity (bias).

Skill 47.7 **The beginning teacher understands the role of assessment as a learning experience for students and strategies for engaging students in meaningful self-assessment.**

The National Academy of Science says the following about developing self-directed learners:

"Students need the opportunity to evaluate and reflect on their own scientific understanding and ability. Before students can do this, they need to understand the goals for learning science. The ability to self-assess understanding is an essential tool for self-directed learning. Through self-reflection, students clarify ideas of what they are supposed to learn. They begin to internalize the expectation that they can learn science. Developing self-assessment skills is an ongoing process throughout a student's school career, becoming increasingly more sophisticated and self-initiated as a student progresses.

Conversations among a teacher and students about assessment tasks and the teacher's evaluation of performance provide students with necessary information to assess their own work. In concert with opportunities to apply it to individual work and to the work of peers, that information contributes to the development of students' self-assessment skills. By developing these skills, students become able to take responsibility for their own learning.
Teachers have communicated their assessment practices, their standards for performance, and criteria for evaluation to students when students are able to:

* Select a piece of their own work to provide evidence of understanding of a scientific concept, principle, or law--or their ability to conduct scientific inquiry.
* Explain orally, in writing, or through illustration how a work sample provides evidence of understanding.
* Critique a sample of their own work using the teacher's standards and criteria for quality.
* Critique the work of other students in constructive ways.

Involving students in the assessment process increases the responsibilities of the teacher. Teachers of science are the representatives of the scientific community in their classrooms; they represent a culture and a way of thinking that might be quite unfamiliar to students. As representatives, teachers are expected to model reflection, fostering a learning environment where students review each others' work, offer suggestions, and challenge mistakes in investigative processes, faulty reasoning, or poorly supported conclusions.

A teacher's formal and informal evaluations of student work should exemplify scientific practice in making judgments. The standards for judging the significance, soundness, and creativity of work in professional scientific work are complex, but they are not arbitrary. In the work of classroom learning and investigation, teachers represent the standards of practice of the scientific community. When teachers treat students as serious learners and serve as coaches rather than judges, students come to understand and apply standards of good scientific practice."

Skill 47.8 **The beginning teacher recognizes the importance of selecting assessment instruments and methods that provide all students with adequate opportunities to demonstrate their achievements.**

Some assessment methods can be both formal and informal tools. For example, observation may incorporate structured observation instruments as well as other informal observation procedures, including professional judgment. When evaluating a child's developmental level, a professional may use a formal adaptive rating scale while simultaneously using professional judgment to assess the child's motivation and behavior during the evaluation process.

Curriculum-Based Assessment—Assessment of an individual's performance of objectives of a curriculum, such as a reading, math, or science program. The individual's performance is measured in terms of what objectives were mastered. This type of testing be verbal, written, or demonstration based. Its general structure may include such factors as how much time to complete, amount to complete, and group or individual testing. The level of response may be multiple choice, essay, or recall of facts.

Momentary time sampling—This is a technique used for measuring behaviors of a group of individuals or several behaviors from the same individual. Time samples are usually brief, and may be conducted at fixed or variable intervals. The advantage of using variable intervals is increased reliability, as the students will not be able to predict when the time sample will be taken.

Multiple Baseline Design—This may be used to test the effectiveness of an intervention in a skill performance or to determine if the intervention accounted for the observed changes in a target behavior. First, the initial baseline data is collected, followed by the data during the intervention period. To get the second baseline, the intervention is removed for a period of time and data is collected again. The intervention is then reapplied, and data collected on the target behavior. An example of a multiple baseline design might be ignoring a child who calls out in class without raising his hand. Initially, the baseline could involve counting the number of times the child calls out before applying interventions. During the time the teacher ignores the child's call-outs, data is collected. For the second baseline, the teacher would resume the response to the child's call-outs in the way she did before ignoring. The child's call-outs would probably increase again, if ignoring actually accounted for the decrease. If the teacher reapplies the ignoring strategy, the child's call-outs would probably decrease again.

Group Tests And Individual Tests

The obvious distinction between a group test and in individual test is that individual tests must be administered to only one person at a time, whereas group tests are administered to several people simultaneously, or can be administered individually. However, there are several other subtle differences.

When administering an individual test, the tester has the opportunity to observe the individual's responses and to determine how such things as problem solving are accomplished. Within limits, the tester is able to control the pace and tempo of the testing session, and to rephrase and probe responses in order to elicit the individual's best performance. If the child becomes tired, the examiner can break between sub tests of end the test; if he loses his place on the test, the tester can help him to regain it; if he dawdles or loses interest, the tester can encourage or redirect him. If the child lacks self-confidence, the examiner can reinforce his efforts. In short, individual tests allow the examiner to encourage best efforts, and to observe how a student uses his skills to answer questions. Thus, individual tests provide for the gathering of both quantitative and qualitative information. On the other hand, with a group test, the examiner may provide oral directions for younger children, but beyond the fourth grade, directions are usually written. The children write or mark their own responses, and the examiner monitors the progress of several students at the same time. He cannot rephrase questions, or probe or prompt responses. Even when a group test is administered to only one child, qualitative information is very difficult, if not impossible, to obtain.

The choice between group and individual testing should be primarily determined by purpose and efficiency. When testing for program evaluation, screening, and some types of program planning (such as tracking), group tests are appropriate. Individual tests could be used but are impractical in terms of time and expense. Special consideration may need to be given if there are any motivational, personalities, linguistic, or physically disabling factors that might impair the examinee's performance on group tests.

Skill 47.9 The beginning teacher recognizes the importance of clarifying teacher expectations by sharing evaluation criteria and assessment results with students.

Effective teachers:
- offer students a safe and supportive learning environment, including clearly expressed and reasonable expectations for behavior;
- create learning environments that encourage self-advocacy and developmentally appropriate independence; and
- offer learning environments that promote active participation in independent or group activities.

Such an environment is an excellent foundation for building rapport and trust with students, and communicating a teacher's respect for and expectation that they take a measure of responsibility for their educational development. Ideally, mutual trust and respect will afford teachers opportunities to learn of and engage students' ideas, preferences and abilities.

Sample Test

1. **In which situation would a science teacher be legally liable?**
(Skill 1.1)(Average Rigor)

   A. The teacher leaves the classroom for a telephone call and a student slips and injures him/herself.
   B. A student removes his/her goggles and gets acid in his/her eye.
   C. A faulty gas line in the classroom causes a fire.
   D. A student cuts him/herself with a dissection scalpel.

2. **Which is the most desirable tool to use to heat substances in a middle school laboratory?**
(Skill 1.3)(Average Rigor)

   A. Alcohol burner.
   B. Freestanding gas burner.
   C. Bunsen burner.
   D. Hot plate.

3. **When measuring the volume of water in a graduated cylinder, where does one read the measurement?**
(Skill 1.4)(Easy Rigor)

   A. At the highest point of the liquid.
   B. At the bottom of the meniscus curve.
   C. At the closest mark to the top of the liquid
   D. At the top of the plastic safety ring.

4. **Chemicals should be stored**
(Skill 1.4)(Easy Rigor)

   A. in the principal's office.
   B. in a dark room.
   C. in an off-site research facility.
   D. according to their reactivity with other substances.

5. **Which of the following is the least ethical choice for a school laboratory activity?**
(Skill 1.4)(Rigorous)

   A. A genetics experiment tracking the fur color of mice.
   B. Dissection of a preserved fetal pig.
   C. Measurement of goldfish respiration rate at different temperatures.
   D. Pithing a frog to watch the circulatory system.

6. **In an experiment measuring the inhibition effect of different antibiotic discs on bacteria grown in Petri dishes, what are the independent and dependent variables respectively?**
    (Skill 1.5)(Rigorous)

    A. Number of bacterial colonies and the antibiotic type.
    B. Antibiotic type and the distance between antibiotic and the closest colony.
    C. Antibiotic type and the number of bacterial colonies.
    D. Presence of bacterial colonies and the antibiotic type.

7. **By discovering the structure of DNA, Watson and Crick made it possible to:**
    (Skill 2.1)(Average Rigor)

    A. Clone DNA
    B. Explain DNA's ability to replicate and control the synthesis of proteins
    C. Sequence human DNA
    D. Predict genetic mutations

8. **Koch's postulates on microbiology include all of the following except:**
    (Skill 3.1)(Easy Rigor)

    A. The same pathogen must be found in every diseased person.
    B. The pathogen must be isolated and grown in culture.
    C. The same pathogen must be isolated from the experimental animal.
    D. Antibodies that react to the pathogen must be found in every diseased person.

9. **Which of the following is not considered ethical behavior for a scientist?**
    (Skill 3.4)(Rigorous)

    A. Citing the sources before data is published.
    B. Publishing data before other scientists have had a chance to replicate results.
    C. Collaborating with other scientists from different laboratories.
    D. Publishing work with an incomplete list of citations.

10. A baseball is thrown with an initial velocity of 30 m/s at an angle of 45°. Neglecting air resistance, how far away will the ball land?
(Skill 4.2)(Rigorous)

A. 92 m
B. 78 m
C. 65 m
D. 46 m

11. A force is given by the vector 5 N x + 3 N y (where x and y are the unit vectors for the x- and y- axes, respectively). This force is applied to move a 10 kg object 5 m, in the x direction. How much work was done?
(Skill 4.3)(Rigorous)

A. 250 J
B. 400 J
C. 40 J
D. 25 J

12. The temperature of a liquid is raised at atmospheric pressure. Which liquid property increases?
(Skill 4.6)(Rigorous)

A. critical pressure
B. vapor pressure
C. surface tension
D. viscosity

13. All of the following are considered Newton's Laws except for:
(Skill 5.1)(Easy Rigor)

A. An object in motion will continue in motion unless acted upon by an outside force.
B. For every action force, there is an equal and opposite reaction force."
C. Nature abhors a vacuum.
D. Mass can be considered the ratio of force to acceleration.

14. Newton's Laws are taught in science classes because _____.
(Skill 5.1)(Average Rigor)

A. they are the correct analysis of inertia, gravity, and forces.
B. they are a close approximation to correct physics, for usual Earth conditions.
C. they accurately incorporate relativity into studies of forces.
D. Newton was a well-respected scientist in his time.

15. Which of the following is most accurate?
(Skill 5.3)(Easy Rigor)

A. Mass is always constant; Weight may vary by location.
B. Mass and Weight are both always constant.
C. Weight is always constant; Mass may vary by location.
D. Mass and Weight may both vary by location.

16. The electromagnetic radiation with the longest wave length is/are

_____.

(Skill 6.7)(Easy Rigor)

A. radio waves.
B. red light.
C. X-rays.
D. ultraviolet light.

17. In Ohm's Law (I=V/R), the V represents:
(Skill 7.2)(Average Rigor)

A. Current.
B. Amperes.
C. Potential Difference.
D. Resistance.

18. A 10 ohm resistor and a 50 ohm resistor are connected in parallel. If the current in the 10 ohm resistor is 5 amperes, the current (in amperes) running through the 50 ohm resistor is:
(Skill 7.2)(Rigorous)

A. 1
B. 50
C. 25
D. 60

19. Resistance is measured in units called _____.
(Skill 7.2)(Easy Rigor)

A. watts.
B. volts.
C. ohms.
D. current.

20. Which of the following is not a characteristic of all electrically charged objects?
(Skill 7.5)(Easy Rigor)

A. Opposites attract.
B. Like repels like.
C. Charge is conserved.
D. A magnetic charge develops.

21. A light bulb is connected in series with a rotating coil within a magnetic field. The brightness of the light may be increased by any of the following except:
(Skill 7.5)(Rigorous)

A. Rotating the coil more rapidly.
B. Adding more loops to the coil.
C. Using tighter loops for the coil.
D. Using a stronger magnetic field.

22. Energy is:
(Skill 8.1)(Easy Rigor)

A. The combination of power and work.
B. The ability to cause change in matter.
C. The transfer of power when force is applied to a body.
D. Physical force.

23. A ball rolls down a smooth hill. You may ignore air resistance. Which of the following is a true statement?
(Skill 8.2)(Rigorous)

A. The ball has more energy at the start of its descent than just before it hits the bottom of the hill, because it is higher up at the beginning.
B. The ball has less energy at the start of its descent than just before it hits the bottom of the hill, because it is moving more quickly at the end.
C. The ball has the same energy throughout its descent, because positional energy is converted to energy of motion.
D. The ball has the same energy throughout its descent, because a single object (such as a ball) cannot gain or lose energy.

24. The transfer of heat from the Earth's surface to the atmosphere is an example of
(Skill 9.1)(Easy Rigor)

A. Convection
B. Radiation
C. Conduction
D. Advection

25. The change in phase from liquid to gas is called:
(Skill 9.1)(Average Rigor)

A. Evaporation.
B. Condensation.
C. Vaporization.
D. Boiling.

26. The transfer of heat by electromagnetic waves is called _____ .
(Skill 9.1)(Average Rigor)

A. conduction.
B. convection.
C. phase change.
D. radiation.

27. A long silver bar has a temperature of 50 degrees Celsius at one end and 0 degrees Celsius at the other end. The bar will reach thermal equilibrium (barring outside influence) by the process of heat

_____.

(Skill 9.2)(Rigorous)

A. conduction.
B. convection.
C. radiation.
D. phase change.

28. What is the best explanation of the term "latent heat"?
(Skill 9.3)(Average Rigor)

A. The amount of heat it takes to change a solid to a liquid.
B. The amount of heat being radiated by an object.
C. The amount heat needed to change a substance to undergo a phase change.
D. The amount of heat it takes to change a liquid to a gas.

29. Sound waves are produced by _____ .
(Skill 10.1)(Easy Rigor)

A. pitch.
B. noise.
C. vibrations.
D. sonar.

30. Sound can be transmitted in all of the following except

_____ .

(Skill 10.1)(Average Rigor)

A. air.
B. water.
C. A diamond.
D. a vacuum.

31. The speed of light is different in different materials. This is responsible for _____ . (Skill 10.4)(Rigorous)

A. interference.
B. refraction.
C. reflection.
D. relativity.

32. A converging lens produces a real image _____. (Skill 10.4)(Rigorous)

A. always.
B. never.
C. when the object is within one focal length of the lens.
D. when the object is further than one focal length from the lens.

33. A semi-conductor allows current to flow (Skill 11.5)(Average Rigor)

A. Never
B. Always
C. As long as it stays below a maximum temperature
D. When a minimum voltage is applied

34. If the volume of a confined gas is increased, what happens to the pressure of the gas? You may assume that the gas behaves ideally, and that temperature and number of gas molecules remain constant. (Skill 12.2)(Rigorous)

A. The pressure increases.
B. The pressure decreases.
C. The pressure stays the same.
D. There is not enough information given to answer this question.

35. The elements in the modern Periodic Table are arranged _____. (Skill 12.7)(Average Rigor)

A. in numerical order by atomic number.
B. randomly.
C. in alphabetical order by chemical symbol.
D. in numerical order by atomic mass.

36. Which parts of an atom are located inside the nucleus? (Skill 12.7)(Easy Rigor)

A. electrons and neutrons.
B. protons and neutrons.
C. protons only.
D. neutrons only.

37. **Which group of metals is the most chemical active? (Skill 12.7)(Average Rigor)**

    A. Alkaline Earth Metals
    B. Transition elements
    C. Alkali Metals
    D. Metalloids

38. **Which of the following is not a property of metalloids? (Skill 12.8)(Rigorous)**

    A. Metalloids are solids at standard temperature and pressure.
    B. Metalloids can conduct electricity to a limited extent.
    C. Metalloids are found in groups 13 through 17.
    D. Metalloids all favor ionic bonding.

39. **Which of the following statements is true of all transition elements? (Skill 12.9)(Rigorous)**

    A. They are all hard solids at room temperature.
    B. They tend to form salts when reacted with Halogens.
    C. They all have a silvery appearance in their pure state.
    D. All of the Above

40. **2.00 L of an unknown gas at 1500. mm Hg and a temperature of 25.0 °C weighs 7.52 g. Assuming the ideal gas equation, what is the molecular weight of the gas? (Skill 13.1)(Rigorous)**

    760 mm Hg=1 atm
    R=0.08206 L-atm/(mol-K)

    A. 21.6 u
    B. 23.3 u
    C. 46.6 u
    D. 93.2 u

41. **The relationships between pressure and temperature and between temperature and volume are examples of: (Skill 13.3)(Average Rigor)**

    A. Indirect variations.
    B. Direct variations.
    C. Boyle's Law.
    D. Charles' Law.

42. **Which of the following occur when NaCl dissolves in water? (Skill 14.5)(Rigorous)**

    A. Heat is required to break bonds in the NaCl crystal lattice.
    B. Heat is released when hydrogen bonds in water are broken.
    C. Heat is required to form bonds of hydration.
    D. The oxygen end of the water molecule is attracted to the Cl– ion.

43. The electrons in an atom that are used to form a chemical bond are called _____.
(Skill 14.6)(Average Rigor)

A. outer shell electrons.
B. excited electrons.
C. valence electrons.
D. reactive electrons.

44. The chemical equation for water formation is: 2H2 + $O_2 \rightarrow 2H_2O$. Which of the following is an incorrect interpretation of this equation?
(Skill 14.9)(Rigorous)

A. Two moles of hydrogen gas and one mole of oxygen gas combine to make two moles of water.
B. Two grams of hydrogen gas and one gram of oxygen gas combine to make two grams of water.
C. Two molecules of hydrogen gas and one molecule of oxygen gas combine to make two molecules of water.
D. Four atoms of hydrogen (combined as a diatomic gas) and two atoms of oxygen (combined as a diatomic gas) combine to make two molecules of water.

45. Catalysts assist reactions by _____.
(Skill 15.6)(Easy Rigor)

A. lowering effective activation energy.
B. maintaining precise pH levels.
C. keeping systems at equilibrium.
D. adjusting reaction speed.

46. Which of the following is a correct definition for 'chemical equilibrium'?
(Skill 15.7)(Average Rigor)

A. Chemical equilibrium is when the forward and backward reaction rates are equal. The reaction may continue to proceed forward and backward.
B. Chemical equilibrium is when the forward and backward reaction rates are equal, and equal to zero. The reaction does not continue.
C. Chemical equilibrium is when there are equal quantities of reactants and products.
D. Chemical equilibrium is when acids and bases neutralize each other fully.

47. 15 g of formaldehyde (CH_2O) are dissolved in 100. g of water. Calculate the weight percentage and mole fraction of formaldehyde in the solution.
(Skill 16.3)(Rigorous)

   A. 13%, 0.090
   B. 15%, 0.090
   C. 13%, 0.083
   D. 15%, 0.083

48. ^3_1H decays with a half-life of 12 years. 3.0 g of pure ^3_1H were placed in a sealed container 24 years ago. How many grams of ^3_1H remain?
(Skill 16.4)(Rigorous)

   A. 0.38 g
   B. 0.75 g
   C. 1.5 g
   D. 3.0 g

49. A seltzer tablet changing into bubbles is an example of:
(Skill 17.1)(Average Rigor)

   A. A physical change.
   B. A chemical change.
   C. Conversion.
   D. Diffusion.

50. Which of the following is not true about phase change in matter?
(Skill 17.1)(Rigorous)

   A. Solid water and liquid ice can coexist at water's freezing point.
   B. At 7 degrees Celsius, water is always in liquid phase.
   C. Matter changes phase when enough energy is gained or lost.
   D. Different phases of matter are characterized by differences in molecular motion.

51. Matter's phase (solid, liquid, or mass) is identified by its:
(Skill 17.3)(Average Rigor)

   A. Color and Size.
   B. Shape and Volume.
   C. Size and Volume.
   D. Color and Volume.

52. The Law of Conservation of Energy states that

   _____.
(Skill 17.3)(Average Rigor)

   A. There must be the same number of products and reactants in any chemical equation.
   B. Mass and energy can be interchanged.
   C. Energy is neither created nor destroyed, but may change form.
   D. One form energy must remain intact (or conserved) in all reactions

53. What part of an atom has to change to create another isotope of an element? (Skill 18.2)(Average Rigor)

A. The number of Electrons.
B. The number of Neutrons.
C. The arrangement of the electrons.
D. The number of Protons.

54. Write a balanced nuclear equation for the emission of an alpha particle by polonium-209. (Skill 18.2)(Rigorous)

A. $^{209}_{84}Po \rightarrow {}^{205}_{81}Pb + {}^{4}_{2}He$
B. $^{209}_{84}Po \rightarrow {}^{205}_{82}Bi + {}^{4}_{2}He$
C. $^{209}_{84}Po \rightarrow {}^{209}_{85}At + {}^{0}_{-1}e$
D. $^{209}_{84}Po \rightarrow {}^{205}_{82}Pb + {}^{4}_{2}He$

55. Write a balanced nuclear equation for the decay of calcium-45 to scandium-45. (Skill 18.2)(Rigorous)

A. $^{45}_{20}Ca \rightarrow {}^{41}_{18}Sc + {}^{4}_{2}He$
B. $^{45}_{20}Ca + {}^{0}_{1}e \rightarrow {}^{45}_{21}Sc$
C. $^{45}_{20}Ca \rightarrow {}^{45}_{21}Sc + {}^{0}_{-1}e$
D. $^{45}_{20}Ca + {}^{0}_{1}p \rightarrow {}^{45}_{21}Sc$

56. The result of radioactive decay is? (Skill 18.4)(Average Rigor)

A. parent element
B. daughter element
C. half-life
D. an unstable atom

57. Which reaction is **not** a redox process? (Skill 19.2)(Rigorous)

A. Combustion of octane:
$2C_8H_{18} + 25O_2 \rightarrow 16CO_2 + 18H_2O$
B. Depletion of a lithium battery:
$Li + MnO_2 \rightarrow LiMnO_2$
C. Corrosion of aluminum by acid:
$2Al + 6HCl \rightarrow 2AlCl_3 + 3H_2$
D. Taking an antacid for heartburn:
$CaCO_3 + 2HCl \rightarrow CaCl_2$
$+H_2CO_3 \rightarrow CaCl_2 + CO_2 + H_2O$

58. Which statement about acids and bases is **not** true? (Skill 20.2)(Average Rigor)

A. All strong acids ionize in water.
B. All Lewis acids accept an electron pair.
C. All Brønsted bases use OH⁻ as a proton acceptor
D. All Arrhenius acids form H⁺ ions in water.

59. Amino acids are carried to the ribosome in protein synthesis by _____. (Skill 21.3)(Average Rigor)

A. transfer RNA (tRNA).
B. transport enzymes.
C. ribosomal RNA (rRNA).
D. cytoskeletal transport proteins.

60. **Which of the following features is/are found in eukaryotic cells but not in prokaryotic cells?**
(Skill 22.1)(Easy Rigor)

A. Nucleus
B. Mitochondria
C. Cytoskeleton
D. Vacuoles

61. **What cell organelle contains the cell's stored food?**
(Skill 22.2)(Easy Rigor)

A. Vacuoles.
B. Golgi Apparatus.
C. Ribosomes.
D. Lysosomes.

62. **Which of the following is not a necessary characteristic of living things?**
(Skill 23.1)(Average Rigor)

A. Movement.
B. Reduction of local entropy.
C. Ability to cause change in local energy form.
D. Reproduction.

63. **Which of the following hormones is least involved in the process of osmoregulation?**
(Skill 23.1)(Average Rigor)

A. Antidiuretic Hormone.
B. Melatonin.
C. Calcitonin.
D. Glucagon

64. **What is necessary for ion diffusion to occur spontaneously? (diffusion realtes to the movement of particles)**
(Skill 23.2)(Rigorous)

A. Carrier proteins.
B. Energy from an outside source.
C. A concentration gradient.
D. Activation Energy

65. **A product of anaerobic respiration in animals is _____.**
(Skill 23.4)(Easy Rigor)

A. carbon dioxide.
B. lactic acid.
C. oxygen.
D. sodium chloride

66. **Which process(es) result(s) in a haploid chromosome number?**
(Skill 24.1)(Easy Rigor)

A. Mitosis.
B. Meiosis.
C. Both mitosis and meiosis.
D. Neither mitosis nor meiosis.

67. Cancer cells divide extensively and invade other tissues. This continuous cell division is due to
(Skill 24.1)(Rigorous)

A. density dependent inhibition
B. density independent inhibition
C. chromosome replication
D. growth factors

68. A virus that can remain dormant until a certain environmental condition causes its rapid increase is said to be
(Skill 25.3)(Average Rigor)

A. lytic
B. benign
C. saprophytic
D. lysogenic

69. The two strands of a DNA molecule are held together by what kind of bond?
(Skill 25.4)(Average Rigor)

A. Polar-covalent
B. Ionic
C. Non-polar Covalent
D. Hydrogen

70. Electrophoresis uses electrical charges of molecules to separate them according to their:
(Skill 25.5)(Average Rigor)

A. Polarization.
B. Size.
C. Type.
D. Shape.

71. Klinefelter Syndrome is a condition in which a person is born with two X chromosomes and one Y chromosome. What process during meiosis would cause this to happen?
(Skill 25.6)(Rigorous)

A. Inversion
B. Translocation
C. Non-disjunction
D. Arrangement failure

72. In the Law of Dominance:
(Skill 26.1)(Average Rigor)

A. Only one of the two possible alleles from each parent is passed on to the offspring.
B. Alleles sort independently of each other.
C. One trait may cover up the allele of the other trait.
D. Flowers have white alleles and purple alleles.

73. A white flower is crossed with a red flower. Which of the following is a sign of incomplete dominance?
(Skill 26.1)(Easy Rigor)

A. Pink flowers.
B. Red flowers.
C. White flowers.
D. No flowers.

74. A child has type O blood. Her father has type A blood, and her mother has type B blood. What are the genotypes of the father and mother, respectively?
(Skill 26.1)(Average Rigor)

A. AO and BO.
B. AA and AB.
C. OO and BO.
D. AO and BB.

75. A monohybrid cross has four possible gene combinations. How many gene combinations are possible in a dihybrid cross?
(Skill 26.1)(Rigorous)

A. Eight.
B. Sixteen.
C. Thirty-Two.
D. Sixty-Four.

76. An Arabic horse's purebred bloodline makes it a good example of:
(Skill 26.2)(Rigorous)

A. A homozygous animal.
B. A heterozygous animal.
C. Codominance.
D. A Poly-genic Character.

77. Which of the following is not characteristic of Gymnosperms?
(Skill 26.2)(Rigorous)

A. They are less dependent on water to assist in reproduction than other plant groups.
B. Gymnosperms have cones that protect their seeds.
C. Gymnosperms reproduce asexually.
D. Gymnosperm seeds and pollen are easily carried by the wind.

78. A carrier of a genetic disorder is heterozygous for a disorder that is recessive in nature. Hemophilia is a sex-linked disorder. This means that:
(Skill 26.4)(Rigorous)

A. Only females can be carriers
B. Only males can be carriers.
C. Both males and females can be carriers.
D. Neither females nor males can be carriers.

79. An animal choosing its mate because of attractive plumage or a strong mating call is an example of:
(Skill 27.2)(Average Rigor)

A. Sexual Selection.
B. Natural Selection.
C. Peer Selection.
D. Linkage

80. **Which of the following is not considered to be a cause of evolution? (Skill 27.3)(Average Rigor)**

    A. Sexual Reproduction.
    B. Immigration.
    C. Large Populations.
    D. Random Mating.

81. **Which of the following is not one of the principles of Darwin's Theory of Natural Selection? (Skill 27.4)(Rigorous)**

    A. More individuals are produced than will survive.
    B. The Individuals in a certain species vary from generation to generation.
    C. Only the fittest members of a species survive.
    D. Some genes allow for better survival of an animal.

82. **Which of the following is the best example of an explanation of the theory of evolution? (Skill 27.4)(Average Rigor)**

    A. Giraffes need to reach higher for leaves to eat, so their necks stretch. The giraffe babies are then born with longer necks. Eventually, there are more long-necked giraffes in the population.
    B. Giraffes with longer necks are able to reach more leaves, so they eat more and have more babies than other giraffes. Eventually, there are more long-necked giraffes in the population.
    C. Giraffes want to reach higher for leaves to eat, so they release enzymes into their bloodstream, which in turn causes fetal development of longer-necked giraffes. Eventually, there are more long-necked giraffes in the population.
    D. Giraffes with long necks are more attractive to other giraffes, so they get the best mating partners and have more babies. Eventually, there are more long-necked giraffes in the population.

83. **What is the principle driving force for evolution of antibiotic resistant bacteria?**
(Skill 27.4)(Average Rigor)

A. Mutation
B. Reproduction method
C. Population size
D. Emigration

84. **A duck's webbed feet are examples of _____ .**
(Skill 28.1)(Average Rigor)

A. mimicry.
B. structural adaptation.
C. protective resemblance.
D. protective coloration.

85. **Laboratory researchers have classified fungi as distinct from plants because the cell walls of fungi _____ .**
(Skill 29.6)(Easy Rigor)

A. contain chitin.
B. contain yeast.
C. are more solid.
D. are less solid.

86. **Which of the following is found in the least abundance in organic molecules?**
(Skill 30.2)(Average Rigor)

A. Phosphorous.
B. Potassium
C. Argon.
D. Oxygen.

87. **Which is the correct statement regarding the human nervous system and the human endocrine system?**
(Skill 30.3)(Rigorous)

A. the nervous system maintains homeostasis whereas the endocrine system does not
B. endocrine glands produce neurotransmitters whereas nerves produce hormones
C. nerve signals travel on neurons whereas hormones travel through the blood
D. the nervous system involves chemical transmission whereas the endocrine system does not

88. **Multiple Sclerosis is an autoimmune disease that prevents nerves that are being attacked from being properly insulated, thus preventing normal propagation of the nerve signal. Which part of the nervous system is the most likely target of the body's immune system in this disease?**
(Skill 30.3)(Rigorous)

A. Axon
B. Synapse
C. Dendrite
D. Myelin

89. Which part of a plant is responsible for transporting water.
(Skill 8.4)(Easy Rigor)

A. Phloem
B. Xylem
C. Stomata
D. Cortex

90. Characteristics of coelomates include:
(Skill 30.5)(Average Rigor)

I. no true digestive system
II. two germ layers
III. true fluid filled cavity
IV. three germ layers

A. I
B. II and IV
C. IV
D. III and IV

91. After sea turtles are hatched on the beach, they start the journey to the ocean. This is due to:
(Skill 32.2)(Easy Rigor)

A. innate behavior
B. territoriality
C. the tide
D. learned behavior

92. What makes up the largest abiotic portion of the Nitrogen Cycle?
(Skill 33.2)(Rigorous)

A. Nitrogen Fixing Bacteria.
B. Nitrates.
C. Decomposers.
D. Atmosphere.

93. What are the most significant and prevalent elements in the biosphere? (The Biosphere contains all Biomes)
(Skill 33.4)(Rigorous)

A. Carbon, Hydrogen, Oxygen, Nitrogen, Phosphorus.
B. Carbon, Hydrogen, Sodium, Iron, Calcium.
C. Carbon, Oxygen, Sulfur, Manganese, Iron.
D. Carbon, Hydrogen, Oxygen, Nickel, Sodium, Nitrogen.

94. Which one of the following biomes makes up the greatest percentage of the biosphere?
(Skill 33.4)(Easy Rigor)

A. Desert
B. Tropical Raine Forest
C. Marine
D. Temperate Deciduous Forest

95. A wrasse (fish) cleans the teeth of other fish by eating away plaque. This is an example of _____ between the fish.
(Skill 34.3)(Average Rigor)

A. parasitism.
B. symbiosis (mutualism).
C. competition.
D. predation.

96. **In commensalism:**
(Skill 34.3)(Average Rigor)

   A. Two species occupy a simlar place; one species benefits from the other and one species is harmed by the other.
   B. Two species occupy a similar place and neither is harmed or benefits.
   C. Two species occupy the similar place and both species benefit.
   D. Two species occupy the same habitat and one preys upon the other.

97. **The theory of 'sea floor spreading' explains**

   _____.
   (Skill 36.4)(Rigorous)

   A. the shapes of the continents.
   B. how continents collide.
   C. how continents move apart.
   D. how continents sink to become part of the ocean floor.

98. **Which of the following statements about radiant energy is not true?**
(Skill 36.7)(Rigorous)

   A. The energy change of an electron transition is directly proportional to the wavelength of the emitted or absorbed photon.
   B. The energy of an electron in a hydrogen atom depends only on the principle quantum number.
   C. The frequency of photons striking a metal determines whether the photoelectric effect will occur.
   D. The frequency of a wave of electromagnetic radiation is inversely proportional to its wavelength

99. **Fossils are usually found in _____ rock.**
(Skill 38.3)(Average Rigor)

   A. igneous.
   B. sedimentary.
   C. metamorphic.
   D. cumulus.

100. **Which of the following is the longest (largest) unit of geological time?**
(Skill 38.4)(Easy Rigor)

   A. Solar Year.
   B. Epoch.
   C. Period.
   D. Era.

101. **The salinity of ocean water is closest to _____ . (Skill 39.1)(Average Rigor)**

A. 0.035 %
B. 0.5 %
C. 3.5 %
D. 15 %

102. **What is the source for most of the United States' drinking water? (Skill 39.1)(Average Rigor)**

A. Desalinated ocean water.
B. Surface water (lakes, streams, mountain runoff).
C. Rainfall into municipal reservoirs.
D. Groundwater.

103. **Contamination may enter groundwater by _____. (Skill 39.1)(Average Rigor)**

A. air pollution
B. leaking septic tanks
C. photochemical processes
D. Sewage Treatment plants

104. **What is the most accurate description of the Water Cycle? (Skill 39.2)(Rigorous)**

A. Rain comes from clouds, filling the ocean. The water then evaporates and becomes clouds again.
B. Water circulates from rivers into groundwater and back, while water vapor circulates in the atmosphere.
C. Water is conserved except for chemical or nuclear reactions, and any drop of water could circulate through clouds, rain, ground-water, and surface-water.
D. Weather systems cause chemical reactions to break water into its atoms.

105. **The process of Transpiration requires which of the following? (Skill 39.2)(Rigorous)**

A. Xylem
B. Stomata
C. Roots
D. Capillary action

106. **The Doppler Effect is associated most closely with which property of waves? (Skill 39.3)(Rigorous)**

A. amplitude.
B. wavelength.
C. frequency.
D. intensity.

107. **Which of the following terms does not describe a way that the human race has had a negative impact on the biosphere?**
(Skill 39.5)(Rigorous)

A. Biological magnification
B. Pollution
C. Carrying Capacity
D. Simplifcation of the food web

108. **Surface ocean currents are caused by which of the following?**
(Skill 39.6)(Average Rigor)

A. temperature.
B. density changes in water.
C. wind.
D. tidal forces.

109. **Which of the following is not a way in which alcohol, drugs, or tobacco affect the normal processes of the human body?**
(Skill 40.2)(Rigorous)

A. Absorption of nutrients
B. Interference with physical and mental development
C. Damaging developing organs
D. Boosting the immune system

110. **Which of the following causes the aurora borealis?**
(Skill 40.3)(Rigorous)

A. gases escaping from earth
B. particles from the sun
C. particles from the moon
D. electromagnetic discharges from the North pole.

111. **Which is a form of precipitation?**
(Skill 40.6)(Easy Rigor)

A. snow
B. frost
C. fog
D. All of the above

112. **Which layer of the atmosphere would you expect most weather to occur?**
(Skill 41.5)(Rigorous)

A. Troposphere
B. Thermosphere
C. Mesosphere
D. Stratosphere

113. **Which of the following is the most accurate definition of a non-renewable resource?**
(Skill 41.7)(Rigorous)

A. A nonrenewable resource is never replaced once used.
B. A nonrenewable resource is replaced on a timescale that is very long relative to human life-spans.
C. A nonrenewable resource is a resource that can only be manufactured by humans.
D. A nonrenewable resource is a species that has already become extinct.

114. **"Neap Tides" are especially weak tides that occur when the Sun and Moon are in a perpendicular arrangement to the Earth, and "Spring Tides" are especially strong tides that occur when the Sun and Moon are in line. At which combination of lunar phases do these tides occur (respectively)?**
(Skill 42.4)(Rigorous)

A. Half Moon and Full Moon
B. Quarter Moon and New Moon
C. Gibbous Moon and Quarter Moon
D. Full Moon and New Moon

115. **Earth is the only planet known to have life. This is because Earth:**
(Skill 43.1)(Average Rigor)

A. is far enough from the Sun to be too hot.
B. is close enough to the Sun to receive its warmth.
C. has water.
D. all of the above.

116. **A star's brightness is referred to as**
(Skill 44.2)(Easy Rigor)

A. magnitude
B. mass
C. apparent magnitude
D. Intensity

117. **Which of the following is the best explanation of the fundamental concept of Uniformitarianism?**
(Skill 45.1)(Rigorous)

A. The types and varieties of life between will see a uniform progression over time.
B. The physical, chemical and biological laws that operate in the geologic past operate in the same way today.
C. Debris from catastrophic events (i.e. volcanoes, and meteorites) will be evenly distributed over the effected area.
D. The frequency and intensity of major geologic events will remain consistent over long periods of time.

118. **Which of the following units is not a measure of distance?**
(Skill 45.5)(Average Rigor)

A. AU (astronomical unit).
B. Light year.
C. Parsec.
D. Lunar year.

119. **A telescope that collects light by using a concave mirror and can produce small images is called a**

_____.

(Skill 45.6)(Rigorous)

A. radioactive telescope
B. reflecting telescope
C. refracting telescope
D. optical telescope

120. **Many times science teachers are faced with the dilemma of not having enough funds to perform all the wonderful science laboratory exercises that they find. Which of these items might help with this problem?**
(Skill 46.1)(Average Rigor)

A. Getting supplies at hardware and grocery stores.
B. Applying for Grant Money.
C. Use of School Gardens or natural areas.
D. All of the above.

121. **Which type of student activity is most likely to expose a student's misconceptions about science?**
(Skill 46.1)(Average Rigor)

A. Multiple-Choice and fill-in-the-blank worksheets.
B. Laboratory activities, where the lab is laid out step by step with no active thought on the part of the student.
C. Teacher- lead demonstrations.
D. Laboratories in which the students are forced to critically consider the steps taken and the results.

122. **Which of the following is not an appropriate aspect of scientific attitude?**
(Skill 46.7)(Average Rigor)

A. Scientific Curiousity.
B. Scientific Open-mindedness.
C. Scientific Conformity.
D. Scientific Skepticism.

123. Which is the correct order
of methodology?
(Skill 46.8)(Rigorous)

1. collecting data
2. planning a controlled
experiment
3. drawing a conclusion
4. hypothesizing a result
5. re-visiting a hypothesis
to answer a question

A. 1,2,3,4,5
B. 4,2,1,3,5
C. 4,5,1,3,2
D. 1,3,4,5,2

124. The control group of an
experiment is:
(Skill 46.8)(Average Rigor)

A. An extra group in which all
experimental conditions
are the same and the
variable being tested is
unchanged.
B. A group of authorities in
charge of an experiment.
C. The group of experimental
participants who are given
experimental drugs.
D. A group of subjects that is
isolated from all aspects of
the experiment.

125. What is the scientific
method?
(Skill 46.8)(Average Rigor)

A. It is the process of doing
an experiment and writing
a laboratory report.
B. It is the process of using
open inquiry and
repeatable results to
establish theories.
C. It is the process of
reinforcing scientific
principles by confirming
results.
D. It is the process of
recording data and
observations.

Answer Key

1.	A	45.	A	89.	B
2.	D	46.	A	90.	D
3.	B	47.	C	91.	A
4.	D	48.	B	92.	D
5.	D	49.	B	93.	A
6.	B	50.	B	94.	C
7.	B	51.	B	95.	B
8.	D	52.	C	96.	B
9.	D	53.	B	97.	C
10.	A	54.	D	98.	A
11.	D	55.	C	99.	B
12.	B	56.	B	100.	D
13.	C	57.	D	101.	C
14.	B	58.	C	102.	D
15.	A	59.	A	103.	B
16.	A	60.	D	104.	C
17.	C	61.	A	105.	C
18.	A	62.	B	106.	C
19.	C	63.	C	107.	C
20.	D	64.	A	108.	C
21.	C	65.	B	109.	D
22.	B	66.	B	110.	A
23.	C	67.	B	111.	A
24.	C	68.	D	112.	A
25.	A	69.	D	113.	B
26.	D	70.	B	114.	B
27.	A	71.	C	115.	D
28.	C	72.	C	116.	A
29.	C	73.	A	117.	B
30.	D	74.	A	118.	D
31.	B	75.	B	119.	B
32.	D	76.	A	120.	D
33.	D	77.	C	121.	D
34.	B	78.	A	122.	C
35.	A	79.	A	123.	B
36.	B	80.	D	124.	A
37.	C	81.	C	125.	B
38.	D	82.	B		
39.	B	83.	C		
40.	C	84.	B		
41.	B	85.	A		
42.	A	86.	C		
43.	C	87.	C		
44.	B	88.	D		

Rigor Table

Easy Rigor 20%	Average Rigor 40%	Rigorous 40%
3, 4, 8, 13, 15, 16, 19, 20 22, 24, 29, 36, 45, 60, 61, 65, 66, 73, 85, 89, 91, 94 100, 111, 116	1, 2, 7, 14, 17, 25, 26, 28, 30, 33, 35, 37, 41, 43, 46, 49, 51, 52, 53, 56, 58, 59, 62, 63, 68, 69, 70, 72, 74, 79, 80, 82, 83, 84, 86, 90, 95, 96, 99, 101, 102, 103, 108, 115, 118, 120, 121, 122, 124, 125	5, 6, 9, 10, 11, 12, 18, 21, 23, 27, 31, 32, 34, 38, 39, 40, 42, 44, 47, 48, 50, 54, 55, 57, 64, 67, 71, 75, 76, 77, 78, 81, 87, 88, 92, 93, 97, 98, 104, 105, 106, 107, 109, 110, 112, 113, 114, 117, 119, 123

Rationales with Sample Questions

1. **In which situation would a science teacher be legally liable?**
   (Skill 1.1)(Average Rigor)

   A. The teacher leaves the classroom for a telephone call and a student slips and injures him/herself.
   B. A student removes his/her goggles and gets acid in his/her eye.
   C. A faulty gas line in the classroom causes a fire.
   D. A student cuts him/herself with a dissection scalpel.

Answer: A. The teacher leaves the classroom for a telephone call and a student slips and injures him/herself.

Teachers are required to exercise a "reasonable duty of care" for their students. Accidents may happen (e.g. (D)), or students may make poor decisions (e.g. (B)), or facilities may break down (e.g. (C)). However, the teacher has the responsibility to be present and to do his/her best to create a safe and effective learning environment. Therefore, the answer is (A).

2. **Which is the most desirable tool to use to heat substances in a middle school laboratory?**
   (Skill 1.3)(Average Rigor)

   A. Alcohol burner.
   B. Freestanding gas burner.
   C. Bunsen burner.
   D. Hot plate.

Answer: D. Hot plate.

Due to safety considerations, the use of open flame should be minimized, so a hot plate is the best choice. Any kind of burner may be used with proper precautions, but it is difficult to maintain a completely safe middle school environment. Therefore, the best answer is (D).

3. **When measuring the volume of water in a graduated cylinder, where does one read the measurement?**
   (Skill 1.4)(Easy Rigor)

   A. At the highest point of the liquid.
   B. At the bottom of the meniscus curve.
   C. At the closest mark to the top of the liquid
   D. At the top of the plastic safety ring.

Answer: B. At the bottom of the meniscus curve.

To measure water in glass, you must look at the top surface at eye-level, and ascertain the location of the bottom of the meniscus (the curved surface at the top of the water). The meniscus forms because water molecules adhere to the sides of the glass, which is a slightly stronger force than their cohesion to each other. This leads to a U-shaped top of the liquid column, the bottom of which gives the most accurate volume measurement. (Other liquids have different forces, e.g. mercury in glass, which has a convex meniscus.) This is consistent only with answer (B).

4. **Chemicals should be stored**
   (Skill 1.4)(Easy Rigor)

   A. in the principal's office.
   B. in a dark room.
   C. in an off-site research facility.
   D. according to their reactivity with other substances.

Answer: D. According to their reactivity with other substances.

Chemicals should be stored with other chemicals of similar properties (e.g. acids with other acids), to reduce the potential for either hazardous reactions in the store-room, or mistakes in reagent use. Certainly, chemicals should not be stored in anyone's office, and the light intensity of the room is not very important because light-sensitive chemicals are usually stored in dark containers. In fact, good lighting is desirable in a store-room, so that labels can be read easily. Chemicals may be stored off-site, but that makes their use inconvenient. Therefore, the best answer is (D).

5. **Which of the following is the least ethical choice for a school laboratory activity?**
   (Skill 1.4)(Rigorous)

   A. A genetics experiment tracking the fur color of mice.
   B. Dissection of a preserved fetal pig.
   C. Measurement of goldfish respiration rate at different temperatures.
   D. Pithing a frog to watch the circulatory system.

Answer: D. Pithing a frog to watch the circulatory system.

Scientific and societal ethics make choosing experiments in today's science classroom difficult. It is possible to ethically perform choices (A), (B), or (C), if due care is taken. (Note that students will need significant assistance and maturity to perform these experiments.) However, modern practice precludes pithing animals (causing partial brain death while allowing some systems to function), as inhumane. Therefore, the answer to this question is (D).

6. **In an experiment measuring the inhibition effect of different antibiotic discs on bacteria grown in Petri dishes, what are the independent and dependent variables respectively?**
   (Skill 1.5)(Rigorous)

   A. Number of bacterial colonies and the antibiotic type.
   B. Antibiotic type and the distance between antibiotic and the closest colony.
   C. Antibiotic type and the number of bacterial colonies.
   D. Presence of bacterial colonies and the antibiotic type.

Answer: B. Antibiotic type and the distance between antibiotic and the closest colony.

To answer this question, recall that the independent variable in an experiment is the entity that is changed by the scientist, in order to observe the effects the dependent variable. In this experiment, antibiotic used is purposely changed so it is the independent variable. Answers A and D list antibiotic type as the dependent variable and thus cannot be the answer, leaving answers B and C as the only two viable choices. The best answer is B, because it measures at what concentration of the antibiotic the bacteria are able to grow at, (as you move from the source of the antibiotic the concentration decreases). Answer C is not as effective because it could be interpreted that that a plate that shows a large number of colonies a greater distance from the antibiotic is a less effective antibiotic than a plate a smaller number of colonies in close proximity to the antibiotic disc, which is reverse of the actually result.

7. **By discovering the structure of DNA, Watson and Crick made it possible to:**
   (Skill 2.1)(Average Rigor)

   A. Clone DNA
   B. Explain DNA's ability to replicate and control the synthesis of proteins
   C. Sequence human DNA
   D. Predict genetic mutations

Answer: B. Explain DNA's ability to replicate and control the synthesis of proteins.

While more recent discoveries have made it possible to sequence the human genome, clone DNA, and predict genetic mutations, it was Watson and Crick's discovery of DNA's structure that made it possible for scientists to understand and therefore explain DNA's ability to replicate and control the synthesis of proteins. Thus, the correct answer is (B).

8. **Koch's postulates on microbiology include all of the following except:**
   (Skill 3.1)(Easy Rigor)

   A. The same pathogen must be found in every diseased person.
   B. The pathogen must be isolated and grown in culture.
   C. The same pathogen must be isolated from the experimental animal.
   D. Antibodies that react to the pathogen must be found in every diseased person.

Answer: D. Antibodies that react to the pathogen must be found in every diseased person.

Koch postulated that the same pathogen must be found in every diseased person, this pathogen must be isolated and grown in a culture, the disease must be induced in experimental animals from the same pathogen, and that this pathogen must then be isolated from the experimental animal. Koch's postulates do not mention antibodies being found. Thus, the answer is (D).

9. **Which of the following is not considered ethical behavior for a scientist?**
   (Skill 3.4)(Rigorous)

   A. Citing the sources before data is published.
   B. Publishing data before other scientists have had a chance to replicate results.
   C. Collaborating with other scientists from different laboratories.
   D. Publishing work with an incomplete list of citations.

Answer: D. Publishing work with an incomplete list of citations.

One of the most important ethical principles for scientists is to cite all sources of data and analysis when publishing work. It is reasonable to use unpublished data (A), as long as the source is cited. Most science is published before other scientists replicate it (B), and frequently scientists collaborate with each other, in the same or different laboratories (C). These are all ethical choices. However, publishing work without the appropriate citations, is unethical. Therefore, the answer is (D).

10. **A baseball is thrown with an initial velocity of 30 m/s at an angle of 45°. Neglecting air resistance, how far away will the ball land? (Skill 4.2)(Rigorous)**

   A. 92 m
   B. 78 m
   C. 65 m
   D. 46 m

Answer: A. 92 m

To answer this question, recall the equations for projectile motion:
$y = \frac{1}{2} a t^2 + v_{0y} t + y_0$
$x = v_{0x} t + x_0$
where x and y are horizontal and vertical position, respectively; t is time; a is acceleration due to gravity; v_{0x} and v_{0y} are initial horizontal and vertical velocity, respectively; x_0 and y_0 are initial horizontal and vertical position, respectively.
For our case:
x_0 and y_0 can be set to zero
both v_{0x} and v_{0y} are (using trigonometry) = $(\sqrt{2} / 2)$ 30 m/s
$a = -9.81$ m/s^2

We then use the vertical motion equation to find the time aloft (setting y equal to zero to find the solution for t):
$0 = \frac{1}{2} (-9.81 \text{ m/s}^2) t^2 + (\sqrt{2} / 2)$ 30 m/s t
Then solving, we find:
t = 0 s (initial set-up) or t = 4.324 s (time to go up and down)

Using t = 4.324 s in the horizontal motion equation, we find:
$x = ((\sqrt{2} / 2)$ 30 m/s) (4.324 s)
$x = 91.71$ m

This is consistent only with answer (A).

11. A force is given by the vector 5 N x + 3 N y (where x and y are the unit vectors for the x- and y- axes, respectively). This force is applied to move a 10 kg object 5 m, in the x direction. How much work was done?
(Skill 4.3)(Rigorous)

A. 250 J
B. 400 J
C. 40 J
D. 25 J

Answer: D. 25 J

To find out how much work was done, note that work counts only the force in the direction of motion. Therefore, the only part of the vector that we use is the 5 N in the x-direction. Note, too, that the mass of the object is not relevant in this problem. We use the work equation:
Work = (Force in direction of motion) (Distance moved)
Work = (5 N) (5 m)
Work = 25 J
This is consistent only with answer (D).

12. The temperature of a liquid is raised at atmospheric pressure. Which liquid property increases?
(Skill 4.6)(Rigorous)

A. critical pressure
B. vapor pressure
C. surface tension
D. viscosity

Answer: B. vapor pressure.

The critical pressure of a liquid is its vapor pressure at the critical temperature and is always a constant value. A rising temperature increases the kinetic energy of molecules and decreases the importance of intermolecular attraction. More molecules will be free to escape to the vapor phase (vapor pressure increases), but the effect of attractions at the liquid-gas interface will fall (surface tension decreases) and molecules will flow against each other more easily (viscosity decreases).

13. **All of the following are considered Newton's Laws except for:**
    (Skill 5.1)(Easy Rigor)

    A. An object in motion will continue in motion unless acted upon by an
       outside force.
    B. For every action force, there is an equal and opposite reaction force."
    C. Nature abhors a vacuum.
    D. Mass can be considered the ratio of force to acceleration.

Answer: C. Nature abhors a vacuum.

Newton's Laws include his law of inertia (an object in motion (or at rest) will stay
in motion (or at rest) until acted upon by an outside force) (A), his law that
(Force)=(Mass)(Acceleration) (D), and his equal and opposite reaction
force law (B). Therefore, the answer to this question is (C), because "Nature
abhors a vacuum" is not one of these.

14. **Newton's Laws are taught in science classes because _____.**
    (Skill 5.1)(Average Rigor)

    A. they are the correct analysis of inertia, gravity, and forces.
    B. they are a close approximation to correct physics, for usual Earth
       conditions.
    C. they accurately incorporate relativity into studies of forces.
    D. Newton was a well-respected scientist in his time.

**Answer: B. They are a close approximation to correct physics, for usual
        Earth conditions.**

Although Newton's Laws are often taught as fully correct for inertia, gravity, and
forces, it is important to realize that Einstein's work (and that of others) has
indicated that Newton's Laws are reliable only at speeds much lower than
that of light. This is reasonable, though, for most middle- and high-school
applications. At speeds close to the speed of light, Relativity considerations must
be used. Therefore, the only correct answer is (B).

15. **Which of the following is most accurate?**
    (Skill 5.3)(Easy Rigor)

    A. Mass is always constant; Weight may vary by location.
    B. Mass and Weight are both always constant.
    C. Weight is always constant; Mass may vary by location.
    D. Mass and Weight may both vary by location.

Answer: A. Mass is always constant; Weight may vary by location.

When considering situations exclusive of nuclear reactions, mass is constant (mass, the amount of matter in a system, is conserved). Weight, on the other hand, is the force of gravity on an object, which is subject to change due to changes in the gravitational field and/or the location of the object. Thus, the best answer is (A).

16. **The electromagnetic radiation with the longest wave length is/are**

    _____.
    (Skill 6.7)(Easy Rigor)

    A. radio waves.
    B. red light.
    C. X-rays.
    D. ultraviolet light.

Answer: A. Radio waves.

As one can see on a diagram of the electromagnetic spectrum, radio waves have longer wave lengths (and smaller frequencies) than visible light, which in turn has longer wave lengths than ultraviolet or X-ray radiation. If you did not remember this sequence, you might recall that wave length is inversely proportional to frequency, and that radio waves are considered much less harmful (less energetic, i.e. lower frequency) than ultraviolet or X-ray radiation. The correct answer is therefore (A).

17. **In Ohm's Law (I=V/R), the V represents:**
    (Skill 7.2)(Average Rigor)

    A. Current.
    B. Amperes.
    C. Potential Difference.
    D. Resistance.

Answer: C. Potential Difference.

In Ohm's Law, I stands for current, which is measured in amperes. R stands for resistance, and V stands for potential difference. The answer is (C).

18. **A 10 ohm resistor and a 50 ohm resistor are connected in parallel. If the current in the 10 ohm resistor is 5 amperes, the current (in amperes) running through the 50 ohm resistor is**
    (Skill 7.2)(Rigorous)

    A. 1
    B. 50
    C. 25
    D. 60

Answer: A. 1

To answer this question, use Ohm's Law, which relates voltage to current and resistance:V = IR where V is voltage; I is current; R is resistance.We also use the fact that in a parallel circuit, the voltage is the same across the branches. Because we are given that in one branch, the current is 5 amperes and the resistance is 10 ohms, we deduce that the voltage in this circuit is their product, 50 volts (from V = IR).
We then use V = IR again, this time to find I in the second branch. Because V is 50 volts, and R is 50 ohm, we calculate that I has to be 1 ampere. This is consistent only with answer (A)

19. **Resistance is measured in units called _____.**
    (Skill 7.2)(Easy Rigor)

    A. watts.
    B. volts.
    C. ohms.
    D. current.

Answer: C. Ohms.

A watt is a unit of energy. Potential difference is measured in a unit called the volt. Current is the number of electrons per second that flow past a point in a circuit. An ohm is the unit for resistance. The correct answer is (C).

20. **Which of the following is not a characteristic of all electrically charged objects?**
    (Skill 7.5)(Easy Rigor)

    A. Opposites attract.
    B. Like repels like.
    C. Charge is conserved.
    D. A magnetic charge develops.

Answer: D. A magnetic charge develops.

All electrically charged objects share the following characteristics: Like charges repel one another. Opposite charges attract one another. Charge is conserved. While magnetic charges develop in some electrically charged objects, this does not occur in all electrically charged objects. The answer is (D).

21. **A light bulb is connected in series with a rotating coil within a magnetic field. The brightness of the light may be increased by any of the following except:**
    (Skill 7.5)(Rigorous)

    A. Rotating the coil more rapidly.
    B. Adding more loops to the coil.
    C. Using tighter loops for the coil.
    D. Using a stronger magnetic field.

Answer: C. Using tighter loops for the coil.

To answer this question, recall that the rotating coil in a magnetic field generates electric current, by Faraday's Law. Faraday's Law states that the amount of emf generated is proportional to the rate of change of magnetic flux through the loop. This increases if the coil is rotated more rapidly (A), if there are more loops (B), or if the magnetic field is stronger (D). Tighter loops would not change the amount of material in the loops, like using more loops would.

22. **Energy is:**
     (Skill 8.1)(Average Rigor)

     A. The combination of power and work.
     B. The ability to cause change in matter.
     C. The transfer of power when force is applied to a body.
     D. Physical force.

Answer: B. The ability to cause change in matter.

Physical force is one form of power. The transfer of power when force is applied to a body is work. The combination of power and work is not energy. Energy is simply the ability to cause change in matter. The answer is (B).

23. **A ball rolls down a smooth hill. You may ignore air resistance. Which of the following is a true statement?**
     (Skill 8.2)(Rigorous)

     A. The ball has more energy at the start of its descent than just before it hits the bottom of the hill, because it is higher up at the beginning.
     B. The ball has less energy at the start of its descent than just before it hits the bottom of the hill, because it is moving more quickly at the end.
     C. The ball has the same energy throughout its descent, because positional energy is converted to energy of motion.
     D. The ball has the same energy throughout its descent, because a single object (such as a ball) cannot gain or lose energy.

Answer: C. The ball has the same energy throughout its descent, because positional energy is converted to energy of motion.

The principle of Conservation of Energy states that (except in cases of nuclear reaction, when energy may be created or destroyed by conversion to mass), "Energy is neither created nor destroyed, but may be transformed." Answers (A) and (B) give you a hint in this question—it is true that the ball has more Potential Energy when it is higher, and that it has more Kinetic Energy when it is moving quickly at the bottom of its descent. However, the total sum of all kinds of energy in the ball remains constant, if we neglect 'losses' to heat/friction. Note that a single object can and does gain or lose energy when the energy is transferred to or from a different object. Conservation of Energy applies to systems, not to individual objects unless they are isolated. Therefore, the answer must be (C).

24. **The transfer of heat from the Earth's surface to the atmosphere is an example of _____.**
(Skill 9.1)(Easy Rigor)

A. Convection
B. Radiation
C. Conduction
D. Advection

Answer: C. Conduction

Radiation is the process of warming through rays or waves of energy, such as the Sun warms Earth. The Earth returns heat to the atmosphere through conduction. This is the transfer of heat through matter, such that areas of greater heat move to areas of less heat in an attempt to balance temperature.

25. **The change in phase from liquid to gas is called:**
(Skill 9.1)(Average Rigor)

A. Evaporation.
B. Condensation.
C. Vaporization.
D. Boiling.

Answer: A. Evaporation.

Condensation is the change in phase from a gas to a liquid; Vaporization is the conversion of matter to vapor- not all gases are vapors. Boiling is one method of inducing the change from a liquid to a gas; the process is evaporation. The answer is (A).

26. **The transfer of heat by electromagnetic waves is called _____.**
(Skill 9.1)(Average Rigor)

A. conduction.
B. convection.
C. phase change.
D. radiation.

Answer: D. Radiation.

Heat transfer via electromagnetic waves (which can occur even in a vacuum) is called radiation. (Heat can also be transferred by direct contact (conduction), by fluid current (convection), and by matter changing phase, but these are not relevant here.) The answer to this question is therefore (D).

27. **A long silver bar has a temperature of 50 degrees Celsius at one end and 0 degrees Celsius at the other end. The bar will reach thermal equilibrium (barring outside influence) by the process of heat _____.**
(Skill 9.2)(Rigorous)

    A. conduction.
    B. convection.
    C. radiation.
    D. phase change.

Answer: A. conduction.

Heat conduction is the process of heat transfer via solid contact. The molecules in a warmer region vibrate more rapidly, jostling neighboring molecules and accelerating them. This is the dominant heat transfer process in a solid with no outside influences. Recall, also, that convection is heat transfer by way of fluid currents; radiation is heat transfer via electromagnetic waves; phase change can account for heat transfer in the form of shifts in matter phase. The answer to this question must therefore be (A).

28. **What is the best explanation of the term "latent heat"?**
(Skill 9.3)(Average Rigor)

    A. The amount of heat it takes to change a solid to a liquid.
    B. The amount of heat being radiated by an object.
    C. The amount heat needed to change a substance to undergo a phase change.
    D. The amount of heat it takes to change a liquid to a gas.

Answer: C. The amount heat needed to change a substance to undergo a phase change.

Answer (A) is a description of the term ' heat of fusion' and answer (D) is a description of the term 'heat of vaporization', both of which a specific examples of latent heat. Answer (C) includes both of these examples by using the term 'phase change' which includes the changes from solid to liquid, and liquid to gas. Answer (B) talks about at objects giving off heat without an accompanying change in state.

29. **Sound waves are produced by _____ . (Skill 10.1)(Easy Rigor)**

    A. pitch.
    B. noise.
    C. vibrations.
    D. sonar.

Answer: C. Vibrations.

Sound waves are produced by a vibrating body. The vibrating object moves forward and compresses the air in front of it, then reverses direction so that the pressure on the air is lessened and expansion of the air molecules occurs. The vibrating air molecules move back and forth parallel to the direction of motion of the wave as they pass the energy from adjacent air molecules closer to the source to air molecules farther away from the source. Therefore, the answer is (C).

30. **Sound can be transmitted in all of the following except _____ . (Skill 10.1)(Average Rigor)**

    A. air.
    B. water.
    C. A diamond.
    D. a vacuum.

Answer: D. A vacuum.

Sound, a longitudinal wave, is transmitted by vibrations of molecules. Therefore, it can be transmitted through any gas, liquid, or solid. However, it cannot be transmitted through a vacuum, because there are no particles present to vibrate and bump into their adjacent particles to transmit the waves. This is consistent only with answer (D). (It is interesting also to note that sound is actually faster in solids and liquids than in air.)

31. **The speed of light is different in different materials. This is responsible for _____ .**
(Skill 10.4)(Rigorous)

    A. interference.
    B. refraction.
    C. reflection.
    D. relativity.

Answer: B. Refraction.

Refraction (B) is the bending of light because it hits a material at an angle wherein it has a different speed. (This is analogous to a cart rolling on a smooth road. If it hits a rough patch at an angle, the wheel on the rough patch slows down first, leading to a change in direction.) Interference (A) is when light waves interfere with each other to form brighter or dimmer patterns; reflection (C) is when light bounces off a surface; relativity (D) is a general topic related to light speed and its implications, but not specifically indicated here. Therefore, the answer is (B).

32. **A converging lens produces a real image _____.**
(Skill 10.4)(Rigorous)

    A. always.
    B. never.
    C. when the object is within one focal length of the lens.
    D. when the object is further than one focal length from the lens.

Answer: D. When the object is further than one focal length from the lens.

A converging lens produces a real image whenever the object is far enough from the lens (outside one focal length) so that the rays of light from the object can hit the lens and be focused into a real image on the other side of the lens. When the object is closer than one focal length from the lens, rays of light do not converge on the other side; they diverge. This means that only a virtual image can be formed, i.e. the theoretical place where those diverging rays would have converged if they had originated behind the object. Thus, the correct answer is (D).

33. **A semi-conductor allows current to flow**
   (Skill 11.5)(Average Rigor)

   A. Never
   B. Always
   C. As long as it stays below a maximum temperature
   D. When a minimum voltage is applied

Answer: D. When a minimum voltage is applied.

To answer this question, recall that semiconductors do not conduct as well as conductors (eliminating answer (B)), but they conduct better than insulators (eliminating answer (A)). Semiconductors can conduct better when the temperature is higher (eliminating answer (C)), and their electrons move most readily under a potential difference. Thus the answer can only be (D).

34. **If the volume of a confined gas is increased, what happens to the pressure of the gas? You may assume that the gas behaves ideally, and that temperature and number of gas molecules remain constant. (Skill 12.2)(Rigorous)**

   A. The pressure increases.
   B. The pressure decreases.
   C. The pressure stays the same.
   D. There is not enough information given to answer this question.

Answer: B. The pressure decreases.

Because we are told that the gas behaves ideally, you may assume that it follows the Ideal Gas Law, i.e. $PV = nRT$. This means that an increase in volume must be associated with a decrease in pressure (i.e. higher T means lower P), because we are also given that all the components of the right side of the equation remain constant. Therefore, the answer must be (B).

35. **The elements in the modern Periodic Table are arranged**
_____.
(Skill 12.7)(Average Rigor)

A. in numerical order by atomic number.
B. randomly.
C. in alphabetical order by chemical symbol.
D. in numerical order by atomic mass.

Answer: A. In numerical order by atomic number.

Although the first periodic tables were arranged by atomic mass, the modern table is arranged by atomic number, i.e. the number of protons in each element. (This allows the element list to be complete and unique.) The elements are not arranged either randomly or in alphabetical order. The answer to this question is therefore (A).

36. **Which parts of an atom are located inside the nucleus?**
(Skill 12.7)(Easy Rigor)

A. electrons and neutrons.
B. protons and neutrons.
C. protons only.
D. neutrons only.

Answer: B. Protons and Neutrons.

Protons and neutrons are located in the nucleus, while electrons move around outside the nucleus. This is consistent only with answer B.

37. **Which group of metals is the most chemically active?**
(Skill 12.7)(Average Rigor)

A. Alkaline Earth Metals
B. Transition elements
C. Alkali Metals
D. Metalloids

Answer: C. Alkali Metals

Answer (D) is the only answer of the four that is not considered one of the metal groups and can thus bee dismissed. From right to left on the periodic table the answers would be (C), (A), and then (B), this is also the order of decreasing chemical activity that we see. Thus the answer is (C). An impressive, yet somewhat dangerous demonstration of the Alkali metals activity can be seen by the small explosion that is created when a small amount of pure sodium is dropped into water.

38. **Which of the following is not a property of metalloids? (Skill 12.8)(Rigorous)**

   A. Metalloids are solids at standard temperature and pressure.
   B. Metalloids can conduct electricity to a limited extent.
   C. Metalloids are found in groups 13 through 17.
   D. Metalloids all favor ionic bonding.

Answer: d. Metalloids all favor ionic bonding.

Metalloids are substances that have characteristics of both metals and nonmetals, including limited conduction of electricity and solid phase at standard temperature and pressure. Metalloids are found in a 'stair-step' pattern from Boron in group 13 through Astatine in group 17. Some metalloids, e.g. Silicon, favor covalent bonding. Others, e.g. Astatine, can bond ionically. Therefore, the answer is (D). Recall that metals/nonmetals/metalloids are not strictly defined by Periodic Table group, so their bonding is unlikely to be consistent with one another.

39. **Which of the following statements is true of all transition elements? (Skill 12.9)(Rigorous)**

   A. They are all hard solids at room temperature.
   B. They tend to form salts when reacted with Halogens.
   C. They all have a silvery appearance in their pure state.
   D. All of the Above

Answer: B. They tend to form salts when reacted with Halogens.

Answer (A) is incorrect because of Mercury which has a low melting point is thus a liquid at room temperature. Answer (C) is incorrect because Copper and Gold do not have a silvery appearance in the natural states. Since answers (A) and (C) are not correct then answer (D) cannot be correct either. This leaves only answer (B).

40. **2.00 L of an unknown gas at 1500. mm Hg and a temperature of 25.0 °C weighs 7.52 g. Assuming the ideal gas equation, what is the molecular weight of the gas?**
    (Skill 13.1)(Rigorous)

    760 mm Hg=1 atm
    R=0.08206 L-atm/(mol-K)

    A. 21.6 u
    B. 23.3 u
    C. 46.6 u
    D. 93.2 u

Answer: C. 23.3 u

Pressure and temperature must be expressed in the proper units. Next the ideal gas law is used to find the number of moles of gas.

$$P = 1500 \text{ mm Hg} \times \frac{1 \text{ atm}}{760 \text{ mm Hg}} = 1.974 \text{ atm and } T = 25.0 + 273.15 = 298.15 \text{ K}$$

$$PV = nRT \implies n = \frac{PV}{RT}$$

$$n = \frac{(1.974 \text{ atm})(2.00 \text{ L})}{\left(0.08206 \frac{\text{L-atm}}{\text{mol-K}}\right)(298.15 \text{ K})} = 0.1613 \text{ mol.}$$

The molecular mass may be found from the mass of one mole.

$$\frac{7.52 \text{ g}}{0.1613 \text{ mol}} = 46.6 \frac{\text{g}}{\text{mol}} \implies 46.6 \text{ u}$$

41. **The relationships between pressure and temperature and between temperature and volume are examples of:**
    (Skill 13.3)(Average Rigor)

    A. Indirect variations.
    B. Direct variations.
    C. Boyle's Law.
    D. Charles' Law.

Answer: B. Direct variations.

Charles' Law deales strictly with the relationship between Temperature and Volume. Boyle's Law deals with the relationship between pressure and volume. These relationships are called direct variations because when one component increases, the other decreases. The answer is (B).

42. **Which of the following occur when NaCl dissolves in water?**
    (Skill 14.5)(Rigorous)

    A. Heat is required to break bonds in the NaCl crystal lattice.
    B. Heat is released when hydrogen bonds in water are broken.
    C. Heat is required to form bonds of hydration.
    D. The oxygen end of the water molecule is attracted to the Cl– ion.

Answer: A. Heat is required to break bonds in the NaCL crystal lattice.

The lattice does break apart, H-bonds in water are broken, and bonds of hydration are formed, but the first and second process require heat while the third process releases heat. The oxygen end of the water molecule has a partial negative charge and is attracted to the Na^+ ion.

43. **The electrons in an atom that are used to form a chemical bond are called _____.**
    (Skill 14.6)(Average Rigor)

    A. outer shell electrons.
    B. excited electrons.
    C. valence electrons.
    D. reactive electrons.

Answer: C. valence electrons.

Answers (A), (B), and (C) could all be used as turns to describe the electrons involved in chemical bonding, depending on the situation. However only answer (C) valence electrons is the correct answer because it the specific name given to these electron and not a description of the electrons.

44. The chemical equation for water formation is: 2H2 + O_2 → 2H₂O.
Which of the following is an incorrect interpretation of this equation?
(Skill 14.9)(Rigorous)

    A. Two moles of hydrogen gas and one mole of oxygen gas combine to make two moles of water.
    B. Two grams of hydrogen gas and one gram of oxygen gas combine to make two grams of water.
    C. Two molecules of hydrogen gas and one molecule of oxygen gas combine to make two molecules of water.
    D. Four atoms of hydrogen (combined as a diatomic gas) and two atoms of oxygen (combined as a diatomic gas) combine to make two molecules of water.

Answer: B. Two grams of hydrogen gas and one gram of oxygen gas combine to make two grams of water.

In any chemical equation, the coefficients indicate the relative proportions of molecules (or atoms), or of moles of molecules. They do not refer to mass, because chemicals combine in repeatable combinations of molar ratio (i.e. number of moles), but vary in mass per mole of material. Therefore, the answer must be the only choice that does not refer to numbers of particles, i.e. answer (B), which refers to grams, a unit of mass.

45. Catalysts assist reactions by _____ .
(Skill 15.6)(Easy Rigor)

    A. lowering effective activation energy.
    B. maintaining precise pH levels.
    C. keeping systems at equilibrium.
    D. adjusting reaction speed.

Answer: A. lowering effective activation energy.

Chemical reactions can be enhanced or accelerated by catalysts, which are present both with reactants and with products. They induce the formation of activated complexes, thereby lowering the effective activation energy—so that less energy is necessary for the reaction to begin. Although this often makes reactions faster, answer (D) is not as good a choice as the more generally applicable answer (A), which is correct.

46. **Which of the following is a correct definition for 'chemical equilibrium'?**
(Skill 15.7)(Average Rigor)

   A. Chemical equilibrium is when the forward and backward reaction rates are equal. The reaction may continue to proceed forward and backward.
   B. Chemical equilibrium is when the forward and backward reaction rates are equal, and equal to zero. The reaction does not continue.
   C. Chemical equilibrium is when there are equal quantities of reactants and products.
   D. Chemical equilibrium is when acids and bases neutralize each other fully.

Answer: A. Chemical equilibrium is when the forward and backward reaction rates are equal. The reaction may continue to proceed forward and backward.

Chemical equilibrium is defined as when the quantities of reactants and products are at a 'steady state' and are no longer shifting, but the reaction may still proceed forward and backward. The rate of forward reaction must equal the rate of backward reaction. Note that there may or may not be equal amounts of chemicals, and that this is not restricted to a completed reaction or to an acid-base reaction. Therefore, the answer is (A).

47. **15 g of formaldehyde (CH_2O) are dissolved in 100. g of water. Calculate the weight percentage and mole fraction of formaldehyde in the solution.**
(Skill 16.3)(Rigorous)

   A. 13%, 0.090
   B. 15%, 0.090
   C. 13%, 0.083
   D. 15%, 0.083

Answer: C. Remember to use the total amounts in the denominator.

$$\text{For weight percentage: } \frac{15 \text{ g } CH_2O}{(15+100) \text{ g total}} = 0.13 = 13\%.$$

For mole fraction, first convert grams of each substance to moles:

$$15 \text{ g CH}_2\text{O} \times \frac{\text{mol CH}_2\text{O}}{(12.011+2\times1.0079+15.999) \text{ g CH}_2\text{O}} = 0.4996 \text{ mol CH}_2\text{O}$$

$$100 \text{ g H}_2\text{O} \times \frac{\text{mol H}_2\text{O}}{(2\times1.0079+15.999) \text{ g H}_2\text{O}} = 5.551 \text{ mol H}_2\text{O}.$$

Again use the total amount in the denominator $\dfrac{0.4996 \text{ mol CH}_2\text{O}}{(0.4996+5.551) \text{ mol total}} = 0.083.$

48. ^3_1H decays with a half-life of 12 years. 3.0 g of pure ^3_1H were placed in a sealed container 24 years ago. How many grams of ^3_1H remain? (Skill 16.4)(Rigorous)

   A. 0.38 g
   B. 0.75 g
   C. 1.5 g
   D. 3.0 g

Answer: B. 0.75 g

Every 12 years, the amount remaining is cut in half. After 12 years, 1.5 g will remain. After another 12 years, 0.75 g will remain.

49. A seltzer tablet changing into bubbles is an example of: (Skill 17.1)(Average Rigor)

   A. A physical change.
   B. A chemical change.
   C. Conversion.
   D. Diffusion.

Answer: B. A chemical change.

A physical change is a change that does not produce a new substance. Conversion is usually used when discussing phase changes of matter. Diffusion occurs in aspects of a mixture when the concentration is equalized. A seltzer tablet changing into bubbles produces a new substance- gas- which is a characteristic of chemical changes.
The answer is (B).

50. **Which of the following is not true about phase change in matter? (Skill 17.1)(Rigorous)**

   A. Solid water and liquid ice can coexist at water's freezing point.
   B. At 7 degrees Celsius, water is always in liquid phase.
   C. Matter changes phase when enough energy is gained or lost.
   D. Different phases of matter are characterized by differences in molecular motion.

Answer: B. At 7 degrees Celsius, water is always in liquid phase.

According to the molecular theory of matter, molecular motion determines the 'phase' of the matter, and the energy in the matter determines the speed of molecular motion. Solids have vibrating molecules that are in fixed relative positions; liquids have faster molecular motion than their solid forms, and the molecules may move more freely but must still be in contact with one another; gases have even more energy and more molecular motion. (Other phases, such as plasma, are yet more energetic.) At the 'freezing point' or 'boiling point' of a substance, both relevant phases may be present. For instance, water at zero degrees Celsius may be composed of some liquid and some solid, or all liquid, or all solid. Pressure changes, in addition to temperature changes, can cause phase changes. For example, nitrogen can be liquefied under high pressure, even though its boiling temperature is very low. Therefore, the correct answer must be (B). Water may be a liquid at that temperature, but it may also be a solid, depending on ambient pressure.

51. **Matter's phase (solid, liquid, or mass) is identified by its: (Skill 17.3)(Average Rigor)**

   A. Color and Size.
   B. Shape and Volume.
   C. Size and Volume.
   D. Color and Volume.

Answer: B. Shape and Volume.

Matter's phase is not dependent on nor has anything to do with its color, and the size of matter is not a necessary component in identifying its phase, eliminating answers A, C, and D. The correct answer is (B).

52. **The Law of Conservation of Energy states that _____.**
    (Skill 17.3)(Average Rigor)

    A. There must be the same number of products and reactants in any chemical equation.
    B. Mass and energy can be interchanged.
    C. Energy is neither created nor destroyed, but may change form.
    D. One form energy must remain intact (or conserved) in all reactions

Answer: C. Energy is neither created nor destroyed, but may change form.

Answer (C) is a summary of the Law of Conservation of Energy (for non-nuclear reactions). In other words, energy can be transformed into various forms such as kinetic, potential, electric, or heat energy, but the total amount of energy remains constant. Answer (A) is untrue, as demonstrated by many synthesis and decomposition reactions. Answers (B) and (D) may be sensible, but they are not relevant in this case. Therefore, the answer is (C).

53. **What part of an atom has to change to create another isotope of an element?**
    (Skill 18.2)(Average Rigor)

    A. The number of Electrons.
    B. The number of Neutrons.
    C. The arrangement of the electrons.
    D. The number of Protons.

Answer: B. The number of Neutrons.

A change in the number of electrons (answer (A)) creates an ion. The change in the arrangement of the electrons (answer (C)), could change the reactivity of an atom temporary. A change of the number of Protons (answer (D)), will change the atom into an ion and/or isotope of another element (this usually only happens in nuclear reactions). Answer (B) is the only one that does not change the relative charge of an atom, while changing the weight of and atom, which in essence is what an isotope is.

54. **Write a balanced nuclear equation for the emission of an alpha particle by polonium-209.**
   (Skill 18.2)(Rigorous)

   A. a. $^{209}_{84}Po \rightarrow {}^{205}_{81}Pb + {}^{4}_{2}He$

   B. $^{209}_{84}Po \rightarrow {}^{205}_{82}Bi + {}^{4}_{2}He$

   C. $^{209}_{84}Po \rightarrow {}^{209}_{85}At + {}^{0}_{-1}e$

   D. $^{209}_{84}Po \rightarrow {}^{205}_{82}Pb + {}^{4}_{2}He$

Answer: D. $^{209}_{84}Po \rightarrow {}^{205}_{82}Pb + {}^{4}_{2}He$

The periodic table shows that polonium has an atomic number of 84. The emission of an alpha particle, $^{4}_{2}He$ (eliminating choice C), will leave an atom with an atomic number of 82 and a mass number of 205 (eliminating choice A). The periodic table identifies this element as lead, $^{205}_{82}Pb$, not bismuth (eliminating choice B).

55. **Write a balanced nuclear equation for the decay of calcium-45 to scandium-45.**
   (Skill 18.2)(Rigorous)

   a. $^{45}_{20}Ca \rightarrow {}^{41}_{18}Sc + {}^{4}_{2}He$

   b. $^{45}_{20}Ca + {}^{0}_{1}e \rightarrow {}^{45}_{21}Sc$

   c. $^{45}_{20}Ca \rightarrow {}^{45}_{21}Sc + {}^{0}_{-1}e$

   d. $^{45}_{20}Ca + {}^{0}_{1}p \rightarrow {}^{45}_{21}Sc$

Answer: C. $^{45}_{20}Ca \rightarrow {}^{45}_{21}Sc + {}^{0}_{-1}e$

All four choices are balanced mathematically. "A" leaves scandium-41 as a decay product, not scandium-45. "B" and "D" require the addition of particles not normally present in the atom. If these reactions do occur, they are not decay reactions because they are not spontaneous. "C" involves the common decay mechanism of beta emission.

56. The result of radioactive decay is the _____.
(Skill 18.4)(Average Rigor)

A. parent element
B. daughter element
C. half-life
D. an unstable atom

Answer: B. daughter element

Radioactive decay causes the mother element (the unstable element) to change into a daughter element (stable element). The Mother-Daughter relationship of produced nuclides during the series of isotope decay is the basis for radiometric dating. Although many isotopes are used in radiometric dating, the most widely known method is referred to as Carbon-14 dating. Knowing the half-life (how long it takes for half of the material to decay) is the key factor in the radiometric dating process.

57. Which reaction is <u>not</u> a redox process?
(Skill 19.2)(Rigorous)

A. Combustion of octane: $2C_8H_{18} + 25O_2 \rightarrow 16CO_2 + 18H_2O$
B. Depletion of a lithium battery: $Li + MnO_2 \rightarrow LiMnO_2$
C. Corrosion of aluminum by acid: $2Al + 6HCl \rightarrow 2AlCl_3 + 3H_2$
D. Taking an antacid for heartburn:
$CaCO_3 + 2HCl \rightarrow CaCl_2 + H_2CO_3 \rightarrow CaCl_2 + CO_2 + H_2O$

Answer: D. Taking an antacid for heartburn:
$CaCO_3 + 2HCl \rightarrow CaCl_2 + H_2CO_3 \rightarrow CaCl_2 + CO_2 + H_2O$

The oxidation state of atoms is altered in a redox process. During combustion (choice A), the carbon atoms are oxidized from an oxidation number of –4 to +4. Oxygen atoms are reduced from an oxidation number of 0 to –2. All batteries (choice B) generate electricity by forcing electrons from a redox process through a circuit. Li is oxidized from 0 in the metal to +1 in the $LiMnO_2$ salt. Mn is reduced from +4 in manganese(IV) oxide to +3 in lithium manganese(III) oxide salt. Corrosion (choice C) is due to oxidation. Al is oxidized from 0 to +3. H is reduced from +1 to 0. Acid-base neutralization (choice D) transfers a proton (an H atom with an oxidation state of +1) from an acid to a base. The oxidation state of all atoms remains unchanged (Ca at +2, C at +4, O at –2, H at +1, and Cl at –1), so D is correct. Note that choices C and D both involve an acid. The availability of electrons in aluminum metal favors electron transfer but the availability of CO_3^{2-} as a proton acceptor favors proton transfer.

58. **Which statement about acids and bases is not true?**
    (Skill 20.2)(Average Rigor)

    A. All strong acids ionize in water.
    B. All Lewis acids accept an electron pair.
    C. All Bronsted bases use OH⁻ as a proton acceptor
    D. All Arrhenius acids form H⁺ ions in water.

Answer: C. All Bronsted bases use OH⁻ as a proton acceptor

Choice A is the definition of a strong acid, choice B is the definition of a Lewis acid, and choice D is the definition of an Arrhenius acid. By definition, all Arrhenius bases form OH⁻ ions in water, and all Brønsted bases are proton acceptors. But not all Brønsted bases use OH⁻ as a proton acceptor. NH_3 is a Brønsted base for example.

59. **Amino acids are carried to the ribosome in protein synthesis by:**
    (Skill 21.3)(Average Rigor)

    A. transfer RNA (tRNA).
    B. transport enzymes.
    C. ribosomal RNA (rRNA).
    D. cytoskeletal transport proteins.

Answer: A. Transfer RNA (tRNA).

The job of tRNA is to carry and position amino acids to/on the ribosomes. mRNA copies DNA code and brings it to the ribosomes; rRNA is in the ribosome itself. Although there are enzymes and proteins, both attached and not attached to the cell's cytoskeleton, neither transport individual amino acids to the ribosome. Thus, the answer is (A).

60. **Which of the following features is/are found in eukaryotic cells but not in prokaryotic cells?**
    (Skill 22.1)(Easy Rigor)

    A. Nucleus
    B. Mitochondria
    C. Cytoskeleton
    D. Vacuoles

Answer: D. 1, 2 and 3

All cells contain vacules, which may serve a diverse number of purposes depending on the cell. The other three items can be found in all eukaryotic cells.

61. **What cell organelle contains the cell's stored food?**
(Skill 22.2)(Easy Rigor)

   A. Vacuoles.
   B. Golgi Apparatus.
   C. Ribosomes.
   D. Lysosomes.

Answer: A. Vacuoles.

In a cell, the sub-parts are called organelles. Of these, the vacuoles hold stored food (and water and pigments). The Golgi Apparatus sorts molecules from other parts of the cell; the ribosomes are sites of protein synthesis; the lysosomes contain digestive enzymes. This is consistent only with answer (A).

62. **Which of the following hormones is least involved in the process of osmoregulation?**
(Skill 23.1)(Average Rigor)

   A. Antidiuretic Hormone.
   B. Melatonin.
   C. Calcitonin.
   D. Glucagon

Answer: B. Melatonin.

Osmoregulation relates to the body's attempt to control the concentration of water and different soluble materials in the body. Antidiruetic Hormone (ADH) regulates the kidneys' reabsorption of water and so directly relates to the amount of water in the body. The body's failure to produce ADH can lead to a life threatening condition where an individual die of dehydration within a matter of hours. Calcitonin controls the removal of calcium from the blood. Glucagon, like insulin, controls the amount of glucose in the blood. Melatonin is involved in homostasis however it is not directly invovled in osmoregulation, rather it is involved in the regulation of body rhythms.

63. **What is necessary for ion diffusion to occur spontaneously? (diffusion realtes to the movement of particles)**
(Skill 23.2)(Rigorous)

   A. Carrier proteins.
   B. Energy from an outside source.
   C. A concentration gradient.
   D. Activation Energy

Answer: C. A concentration gradient.

Spontaneous diffusion occurs when random motion leads particles to increase entropy by equalizing concentrations. Particles tend to move into places of lower concentration. Therefore, a concentration gradient is required, and the answer is (C). No proteins (A), outside energy (B), or activation energy (which is also outside energy) (D) are required for this process.

64. **Which of the following is not a necessary characteristic of living things?**
(Skill 23.1)(Average Rigor)

   A. Movement.
   B. Reduction of local entropy.
   C. Ability to cause change in local energy form.
   D. Reproduction.

Answer: A. Movement.

There are many definitions of "life," but in all cases, a living organism reduces local entropy, changes chemical energy into other forms, and reproduces. Not all living things move, however, so the correct answer is (A).

65. A product of anaerobic respiration in animals is _____.
(Skill 23.4)(Easy Rigor)

    A. carbon dioxide.
    B. lactic acid.
    C. oxygen.
    D. sodium chloride

Answer: B. Lactic acid.

In animals, anaerobic respiration (i.e. respiration without the presence of oxygen) generates lactic acid as a byproduct. (Note that some anaerobic bacteria generate carbon dioxide from respiration of methane, and animals generate carbon dioxide in aerobic respiration.) Oxygen is not normally a by-product of respiration, though it is a product of photosynthesis, and sodium chloride is not strictly relevant in this question. Therefore, the answer must be (B). By the way, lactic acid is believed to cause muscle soreness after anaerobic weight-lifting.

66. Which process(es) result(s) in a haploid chromosome number?
(Skill 24.1)(Easy Rigor)

    A. Mitosis.
    B. Meiosis.
    C. Both mitosis and meiosis.
    D. Neither mitosis nor meiosis.

Answer: B. Meiosis.

Meiosis is the division of sex cells. The resulting chromosome number is half the number of parent cells, i.e. a 'haploid chromosome number'. Mitosis, however, is the division of other cells, in which the chromosome number is the same as the parent cell chromosome number. Therefore, the answer is (B).

67. Cancer cells divide extensively and invade other tissues. This continuous cell division is due to
(Skill 24.1)(Rigorous)

A. density dependent inhibition
B. density independent inhibition
C. chromosome replication
D. Growth factors

Answer: B. Growth Factors

Density dependent inhibition is when the cells crowd one another and consume all the nutrients; therefore halting cell division. Cancer cells, however, are density independent; meaning they can divide continuously as long as nutrients are present.

68. A virus that can remain dormant until a certain environmental condition causes its rapid increase is said to be
(Skill 25.3)(Average Rigor)

A. lytic
B. benign
C. saprophytic
D. lysogenic

Answer: D. lysogenic

Lysogenic viruses remain dormant until something initiates it to break out of the host cell.

69. The two strands of a DNA molecule are held together by what kind of bond?
(Skill 25.4)(Average Rigor)

A. Polar-covalent
B. Ionic
C. Non-polar Covalent
D. Hydrogen

Answer: D. Hydrogen

If covalent bonding (polar or non-polar) was used to join the strands of DNA together the bonds would require a great deal of energy to separate, making transcription and copying difficult. Ionic bonds are not stable enough in solution to maintain the double helix. Hydrogen bonds form between the complementary base pair in the DNA, 2 bonds for Adenine and Thymine, and 3 bonds between Cytosine and Guanine.

70. **Electrophoresis uses electrical charges of molecules to separate them according to their:**
(Skill 25.5)(Average Rigor)

   A. Polarization.
   B. Size.
   C. Type.
   D. Shape.

Answer: B. Size.

Electrophoresis uses electrical charges of molecules to separate them according to their size. The molecules, such as DNA or proteins, are pulled through a gel toward either the positive end of the gel box or the negative end of the gel box. DNA is negatively charged and moves toward the positive charge. Thus, the answer is (B).

71. **Klinefelter Syndrome is a condition in which a person is born with two X chromosomes and one Y chromosome. What process during meiosis would cause this to happen?**
(Skill 25.6)(Rigorous)

   A. Inversion
   B. Translocation
   C. Non-disjunction
   D. Arrangement failure

Answer: C. Non-disjunction

Non-disjunction describes the process by which chromosomes (or chromatids) fail to separate, and one cell (in this case gamette) recieves both copies and the other cell receives none. Inversion is a process where a gene reverses itself wit in the chromosome. Translocation can lead to some gentic disorders, because a portion of one chromosome is swapped with a portion of another chromosome. As a term arrangement failure might be a good description for a number of genetic processes (including non-disjunction) but does not have a specifc meaning itself.

72. **In the Law of Dominance:**
   (Skill 26.1)(Average Rigor)

   A. Only one of the two possible alleles from each parent is passed on to the offspring.
   B. Alleles sort independently of each other.
   C. One trait may cover up the allele of the other trait.
   D. Flowers have white alleles and purple alleles.

Answer: C. One trait may cover up the allele of the other trait.

Alleles sort independently of one another in the Law of Independent Assortment; The Law of Segregation states that only one of the two possible alleles from each parent is passed on to the offspring. The color of flower alleles has nothing to do with any particular laws of inheritance. The answer is (C). The Law of Dominance says that in a pair of alleles, one trait may cover up the allele of the other trait.

73. **A white flower is crossed with a red flower. Which of the following is a sign of incomplete dominance?**
   (Skill 26.1)(Easy Rigor)

   A. Pink flowers.
   B. Red flowers.
   C. White flowers.
   D. No flowers.

Answer: A. Pink flowers.

Incomplete dominance means that neither the red nor the white gene is strong enough to suppress the other. Therefore both are expressed, leading in this case to the formation of pink flowers. Therefore, the answer is (A).

74. **A child has type O blood. Her father has type A blood, and her mother has type B blood. What are the genotypes of the father and mother, respectively?**
   (Skill 26.1)(Average Rigor)

   A. AO and BO.
   B. AA and AB.
   C. OO and BO.
   D. AO and BB.

Answer: A. AO and BO.

Because O blood is recessive, the child must have inherited two O's—one from each of her parents. Since her father has type A blood, his genotype must be AO; likewise her mother's blood must be BO. Therefore, only answer (A) can be correct.

75. **A monohybrid cross has four possible gene combinations. How many gene combinations are possible in a dihybrid cross? (Skill 26.1)(Rigorous)**

   A. Eight.
   B. Sixteen.
   C. Thirty-Two.
   D. Sixty-Four.

Answer: B. Sixteen.

In a monohybrid cross there are two possible contributions from each parent. For example if a parents genotype is Gg then the posibile contributions is either G or g. Since each parent has two possible ways to contribute, you then multiply the 2 possibilities form 1 parent times the 2 from the other parent to get 4 combinations in a monhybrid cross. In a dihybrid cross two genes are being considered for each parent, and so more combinations are possible. If a parent's genotype was GgRr, then the they might contrigbute either GR, Gr, gR, or gr to the child. WIth each parent contributing 4 possibilities, you end up with 16 gene combinations in the cross (4 from 1 parent times 4 possibilites from the other).

76. **An Arabic horse's purebred bloodline makes it a good example of: (Skill 26.2)(Rigorous)**

   A. A homozygous animal.
   B. A heterozygous animal.
   C. Codominance.
   D. A Poly-genic Character.

Answer: A. A homozygous animal.

A heterozygous animal is a hybrid. Codominance occurs when the genes form new phenotypes. A polygenic character is when many alleles code for one phenotype. A homozygous animal is a purebred, having two of the same genes present, as in a purebred horse breed. The answer is (A).

77. **Which of the following is not characteristic of Gymnosperms?**
    (Skill 26.2)(Rigorous)

    A. They are less dependent on water to assist in reproduction than other plant groups.
    B. Gymnosperms have cones that protect their seeds.
    C. Gymnosperms reproduce asexually.
    D. Gymnosperm seeds and pollen are easily carried by the wind.

Answer: C. Gymnosperms reproduce asexually.

Gymnosperms (which means naked seeds) were the first plants to evolve with seeds. They are less dependent on water to assist in reproduction, and their seeds are transported by wind. Pollen from the male is also carried by the wind. Thus, Gymnosperms cannot be asexual, which makes (C) the correct answer.

78. **A carrier of a genetic disorder is heterozygous for a disorder that is recessive in nature. Hemophilia is a sex-linked disorder. This means that:**
    (Skill 26.4)(Rigorous)

    A. Only females can be carriers
    B. Only males can be carriers.
    C. Both males and females can be carriers.
    D. Neither females nor males can be carriers.

Answer: A. Only females can be carriers

Since Hemophilia is a sex-linked disorder the gene only appears on the X chromosome, with no counterpart on the Y chromosome. Since males are XY they cannot be heterozygous for the trait, what ever is on the single X chromosome will be expressed. Females being XX can be heterozygous. Answer (C) would describe a genetic disorder that is recessive and expressed on one of the somatic chromosomes (not sex-linked). Answer (D) would describe a genetic disorder that is dominant and expressed on any of the chromosomes. An example of answer (C) is sickle cell anemia. An example of answer (D) is Achondroplasia (the most common type of short-limbed dwarfism), in fact for this condition people that are Homozygous dominant for the gene that creates the disorder usually have severe health problems if they live past infancy, so almost all individuals with this disorder are carriers.

79. **An animal choosing its mate because of attractive plumage or a strong mating call is an example of:**
    (Skill 27.2)(Average Rigor)

    A. Sexual Selection.
    B. Natural Selection.
    C. Peer Selection.
    D. Linkage

Answer: A. Sexual Selection.

The coming together of genes determines the makeup of the gene pool. Sexual selection, the act of choosing a mate, allows animals to have some choice in the breeding of its offspring. The answer is (A).

80. **Which of the following is not considered to be a cause of evolution?**
    (Skill 27.3)(Average Rigor)

    A. Sexual Reproduction.
    B. Immigration.
    C. Large Populations.
    D. Random Mating.

Answer: D. Random Mating.

Evolution is caused by increase of the chances of variability in a population, which can be brought about by large populations, immigration, and simple sexual reproduction. Random mating actually decreases the chances of variability in a population, making the correct answer (D).

81. **Which of the following is not one of the principles of Darwin's Theory of Natural Selection?**
    (Skill 27.4)(Rigorous)

    A. More individuals are produced than will survive.
    B. The Individuals in a certain species vary from generation to generation.
    C. Only the fittest members of a species survive.
    D. Some genes allow for better survival of an animal.

Answer: C. Only the fittest members of a species survive.

Answers (A), (B) and (D) were all specifically noted by Darwin in his theory. Answer (C) is often misquoted to represent this particular theory, but was not mentioned by Darwin himself.

82. **Which of the following is the best example of an explanation of the theory of evolution?**
(Skill 27.4)(Average Rigor)

   A. Giraffes need to reach higher for leaves to eat, so their necks stretch. The giraffe babies are then born with longer necks. Eventually, there are more long-necked giraffes in the population.
   B. Giraffes with longer necks are able to reach more leaves, so they eat more and have more babies than other giraffes. Eventually, there are more long-necked giraffes in the population.
   C. Giraffes want to reach higher for leaves to eat, so they release enzymes into their bloodstream, which in turn causes fetal development of longer-necked giraffes. Eventually, there are more long-necked giraffes in the population.
   D. Giraffes with long necks are more attractive to other giraffes, so they get the best mating partners and have more babies. Eventually, there are more long-necked giraffes in the population.

Answer: B. Giraffes with longer necks are able to reach more leaves, so they eat more and have more babies than other giraffes. Eventually, there are more long-necked giraffes in the population.

Although evolution is often misunderstood, it occurs via natural selection. Organisms with a life/reproductive advantage will produce more offspring. Over many generations, this changes the proportions of the population. In any case, it is impossible for a stretched neck (A) or a fervent desire (C) to result in a biologically mutated baby. Although there are traits that are naturally selected because of mate attractiveness and fitness (D), this is not the primary situation here, so answer (B) is the best choice.

83. **What is the principle driving force for evolution of antibiotic resistant bacteria?**
    (Skill 27.4)(Average Rigor)

    A. Mutation
    B. Reproduction method
    C. Population size
    D. Emigration

Answer: C. Population size

Most bacteria reproduce asexually, thus there is not a contribution to the variiabilty of the population, thus answer (B) is not the driving force. Answer (D) emigration, or the act of moving away from an area usually occurs after a bacteria has developed a resistance and not before. Mutation, answer (A), is a critical aspect in the evolution of antibiotic resistant bacteria, however usefull mutations happen rarely and thus alone would be unlikely to develop a strain of antibiotic resistent bacteria. Only a large population size, answer (C), and the ability to quickly build that population would make it likely that a member of the colony would have devloped a useful mutation.

84. **A duck's webbed feet are examples of _____ .**
    (Skill 28.1)(Average Rigor)

    A. mimicry.
    B. structural adaptation.
    C. protective resemblance.
    D. protective coloration.

Answer: B. Structural adaptation.

Ducks (and other aquatic birds) have webbed feet, which makes them more efficient swimmers. This is most likely due to evolutionary patterns where webbed-footed-birds were more successful at feeding and reproducing, and eventually became the majority of aquatic birds. Because the structure of the duck adapted to its environment over generations, this is termed 'structural adaptation'. Mimicry, protective resemblance, and protective coloration refer to other evolutionary mechanisms for survival. The answer to this question is therefore (B).

85. **Laboratory researchers have classified fungi as distinct from plants because the cell walls of fungi _____ .**
(Skill 29.6)(Easy Rigor)

    A. contain chitin.
    B. contain yeast.
    C. are more solid.
    D. are less solid.

Answer: A. Contain chitin.

Kingdom Fungi consists of organisms that are eukaryotic, multicellular, absorptive consumers. They have a chitin cell wall, which is the only universally present feature in fungi that is never present in plants. Thus, the answer is (A).

86. **Which of the following is found in the least abundance in organic molecules?**
(Skill 30.2)(Average Rigor)

    A. Phosphorous.
    B. Potassium
    C. Argon.
    D. Oxygen.

Answer: C. Argon.

Organic molecules consist mainly of Carbon, Hydrogen, and Oxygen, with significant amounts of Nitrogen, Phosphorus, and often Sulfur. Other elements, such as Potassium, are present in much smaller quantities. Argon being a noble gas, the atoms rarely bond to any other atoms, making it extremely rare for argon to be part of an organic compound. Therefore the answer is (C).

87. **Which is the correct statement regarding the human nervous system and the human endocrine system?**
(Skill 30.3)(Rigorous)

   A. the nervous system maintains homeostasis whereas the endocrine system does not
   B. endocrine glands produce neurotransmitters whereas nerves produce hormones
   C. nerve signals travel on neurons whereas hormones travel through the blood
   D. the nervous system involves chemical transmission whereas the endocrine system does not

Answer: C. nerve signals travel on neurons whereas hormones travel through the blood

In the human nervous system, neurons carry nerve signals to and from the cell body. Endocrine glands produce hormones that are carried through the body in the bloodstream.

88. **Multiple Sclerosis is an autoimmune disease that prevents nerves that are being attacked from being properly insulated, thus preventing normal propagation of the nerve signal. Which part of the nervous system is the most likely target of the body's immune system in this disease?**
(Skill 30.3)(Rigorous)

   A. Axon
   B. Synapse
   C. Dendrite
   D. Myelin

Answer: D. Myelin

Answers (A), (B), and (C) are all part of the neuron, and although they all play a part in propagating a nerve impulse, only the myelin sheath composed of Schwann cells insulates these parts of the neuron. It is possible that in later stages of Multiple Sclerosis there will be damage to axons. This will usually only happen after the myelin sheath has been stripped away.

89. **Which part of a plant is responsible for transporting water.**
    (Skill 30.4)(Easy Rigor)

    A. Phloem
    B. Xylem
    C. Stomata
    D. Cortex

Answer: B. Xylem

The Xylem transport a plants food. A stomata is an opening on the underside of a leaf that allows for the passage of carbon dioxide, oxygen and water. The Cortex is where a plant stores food. The only answer is (B) the Xylem, which is where water is transported up the plant.

90. **Characteristics of coelomates include:**
    (Skill 30.5)(Average Rigor)

    > I. no true digestive system
    > II. two germ layers
    > III. true fluid filled cavity
    > IV. three germ layers

    A. I
    B. II and IV
    C. IV
    D. III and IV

Answer: D.

Coelomates are triplobastic animals (3 germ layers). They have a true fluid filled body cavity called a coelom.

91. **After sea turtles are hatched on the beach, they start the journey to the ocean. This is due to**
    (Skill 32.2)(Easy Rigor)

    A. innate behavior
    B. territoriality
    C. the tide
    D. learned behavior

Answer: A. innate behavior

Innate behaviors are inborn or instinctual. The baby sea turtles did not learn from their mother. They immediately knew to head towards the ocean once they hatched.

92. **What makes up the largest abiotic portion of the Nitrogen Cycle? (Skill 33.2)(Rigorous)**

    A. Nitrogen Fixing Bacteria.
    B. Nitrates.
    C. Decomposers.
    D. Atmosphere.

Answer: D. Atomsphere.

Since answers (A) and (C) are both examples of living organisms they are biotic components of the nitrogen cycle. Nitrates are one type of nitrogen compond, (making it abiotic) that can be found in soil and in living organisms, however it makes up a small portion of the avaible nitrogen. The atmosphere being 78% Nitrogen gas (an abiotic component) makes up the largest source available to the Nitrogen Cycle.

93. **What are the most significant and prevalent elements in the biosphere? (The Biosphere contains all Biomes) (Skill 33.4)(Rigorous)**

    A. Carbon, Hydrogen, Oxygen, Nitrogen, Phosphorus.
    B. Carbon, Hydrogen, Sodium, Iron, Calcium.
    C. Carbon, Oxygen, Sulfur, Manganese, Iron.
    D. Carbon, Hydrogen, Oxygen, Nickel, Sodium, Nitrogen.

Answer: A. Carbon, Hydrogen, Oxygen, Nitrogen, Phosphorus.

Organic matter (and life as we know it) is based on Carbon atoms, bonded to Hydrogen and Oxygen. Nitrogen and Phosphorus are the next most significant elements, followed by Sulfur and then trace nutrients such as Iron, Sodium, Calcium, and others. Therefore, the answer is (A). If you know that the formula for any carbohydrate contains Carbon, Hydrogen, and Oxygen, that will help you narrow the choices to (A) and (D) in any case.

94. **Which one of the following biomes makes up the greatest percentage of the biosphere? (Skill 33.4)(Easy Rigor)**

    A. Desert
    B. Tropical Raine Forest
    C. Marine
    D. Temperate Deciduous Forest

Answer: C. Marine

All land biomes, which includes answers (A), (B), and (D) make up approximately 25% of the earths surface, leaving the other 75% to the marine biome. Additionally the marine biome can range in depth from the air above the water, to several miles in depth. THis combined make answer (C) the correct answer.

95. **A wrasse (fish) cleans the teeth of other fish by eating away plaque. This is an example of _____ between the fish. (Skill 34.3)(Average Rigor)**

    A. parasitism.
    B. symbiosis (mutualism).
    C. competition.
    D. predation.

Answer: B. Symbiosis (mutualism).

When both species benefit from their interaction in their habitat, this is called 'symbiosis', or 'mutualism'. In this example, the wrasse benefits from having a source of food, and the other fish benefit by having healthier teeth. Note that 'parasitism' is when one species benefits at the expense of the other, 'competition' is when two species compete with one another for the same habitat or food, and 'predation' is when one species feeds on another. Therefore, the answer is (B).

96. **In commensalism:**
(Skill 34.3)(Average Rigor)

   A. Two species occupy a simlar place; one species benefits from the other and one species is harmed by the other.
   B. Two species occupy a similar place and neither is harmed or benefits.
   C. Two species occupy the similar place and both species benefit.
   D. Two species occupy the same habitat and one preys upon the other.

Answer: B. Two species occupy a similar place and neither is harmed or benefits.

Answer (A) best describes a parastic relationship between the two species. Mutualism (or symobiosis) describes the relationship that is seen in answer (C). Anytime that the a species can be considered a prey there is a Predation relationship between the species, this is answer (D). Leaving answer (B) as the description of commensalis.

97. **The theory of 'sea floor spreading' explains _____.**
(Skill 36.4)(Rigorous)

   A. the shapes of the continents.
   B. how continents collide.
   C. how continents move apart.
   D. how continents sink to become part of the ocean floor.

Answer: C. How continents move apart.

In the theory of 'sea floor spreading', the movement of the ocean floor causes continents to spread apart from one another. This occurs because crust plates split apart, and new material is added to the plate edges. This process pulls the continents apart, or may create new separations, and is believed to have caused the formation of the Atlantic Ocean. The answer is (C).

98. Which of the following statements about radiant energy is not true? (Skill 36.7)(Rigorous)

    A. The energy change of an electron transition is directly proportional to the wavelength of the emitted or absorbed photon.
    B. The energy of an electron in a hydrogen atom depends only on the principle quantum number.
    C. The frequency of photons striking a metal determines whether the photoelectric effect will occur.
    D. The frequency of a wave of electromagnetic radiation is inversely proportional to its wavelength

Answer: A. The energy change (ΔE) is _inversely_ proportional to the wavelength (Δ) of the photon.

This is according the equations:

$$\Delta E = \frac{hc}{\lambda}.$$

where h is Planck's constant and c is the speed of light.

Choice B is true for hydrogen. Atoms with more than one electron are more complex. The frequency of individual photons, not the number of photons determines whether the photoelectric effect occurs, so choice C is true. Choice D is true. The proportionality constant is the speed of light according to the equation:

$$v = \frac{c}{\lambda}.$$

99. Fossils are usually found in _____ rock. (Skill 38.3)(Average Rigor)

    A. igneous.
    B. sedimentary.
    C. metamorphic.
    D. cumulus.

Answer: B. Sedimentary

Fossils are formed by layers of dirt and sand settling around organisms, hardening, and taking an imprint of the organisms. When the organism decays, the hardened imprint is left behind. This is most likely to happen in rocks that form from layers of settling dirt and sand, i.e. sedimentary rock. Note that igneous rock is formed from molten rock from volcanoes (lava), while metamorphic rock can be formed from any rock under very high temperature and pressure changes. 'Cumulus' is a descriptor for clouds, not rocks. The best answer is therefore (B).

100. Which of the following is the longest (largest) unit of geological time? (Skill 38.4)(Easy Rigor)

    A. Solar Year.
    B. Epoch.
    C. Period.
    D. Era.

Answer: D. Era.

Geological time is measured by many units, but the longest unit listed here (and indeed the longest used to describe the biological development of the planet) is the Era. Eras are subdivided into Periods, which are further divided into Epochs. Therefore, the answer is (D).

101. The salinity of ocean water is closest to _____ . (Skill 39.1)(Average Rigor)

    A. 0.035 %
    B. 0.5 %
    C. 3.5 %
    D. 15 %

Answer: C. 3.5 %

Salinity, or concentration of dissolved salt, can be measured in mass ratio (i.e. mass of salt divided by mass of sea water). For Earth's oceans, the salinity is approximately 3.5 %, or 35 parts per thousand. Note that answers (A), (B) and (D) can be eliminated, because (A) and (B) are so dilute as to be hardly saline, while (D) is so concentrated that it would not support ocean life. Therefore, the answer is (C).

102. What is the source for most of the United States' drinking water? (Skill 39.1)(Average Rigor)

A. Desalinated ocean water.
B. Surface water (lakes, streams, mountain runoff).
C. Rainfall into municipal reservoirs.
D. Groundwater.

Answer: D. Groundwater.

Groundwater currently provides drinking water for 53% of the population of the United States. (Although groundwater is often less polluted than surface water, it can be contaminated and it is very hard to clean once it is polluted. If too much groundwater is used from one area, then the ground may sink or shift, or local salt water may intrude from ocean boundaries.) The other answer choices can be used for drinking water, but they are not the most widely used. Therefore, the answer is (D).

103. Contamination may enter groundwater by? (Skill 39.1)(Average Rigor)

A. air pollution
B. leaking septic tanks
C. photochemical processes
D. Sewage Treatment plants

Answer: B. leaking septic tanks

Leaking septic tanks allow contamination to slowly seep into the ground, where it is absorbed into the water table and infects the groundwater. The only other reasonable possibility is Sewage treatment plants, which isolate the waste from ground water until it has reached a state that it will not be hazardous to release into ground or surface water.

104. What is the most accurate description of the Water Cycle? (Skill 39.2)(Rigorous)

A. Rain comes from clouds, filling the ocean. The water then evaporates and becomes clouds again.
B. Water circulates from rivers into groundwater and back, while water vapor circulates in the atmosphere.
C. Water is conserved except for chemical or nuclear reactions, and any drop of water could circulate through clouds, rain, ground-water, and surface-water.
D. Weather systems cause chemical reactions to break water into its atoms.

Answer: C. Water is conserved except for chemical or nuclear reactions, and any drop of water could circulate through clouds, rain, ground-water, and surface-water.

All natural chemical cycles, including the Water Cycle, depend on the principle of Conservation of Mass. (For water, unlike for elements such as Nitrogen, chemical reactions may cause sources or sinks of water molecules.) Any drop of water may circulate through the hydrologic system, ending up in a cloud, as rain, or as surface- or ground-water. Although answers (A) and (B) describe parts of the water cycle, the most comprehensive and correct answer is (C).

105. The process of Transpiration requires which of the following?
(Skill 39.2)(Rigorous)

   1 Xylem

   2 Stomata

   3 Roots

   4 Capillary action

   A. 1 and 2
   B. 2 and 3
   C. 1,2,3, and 4
   D. 1 and 3

Answer: C. 1, 2, 3, and 4

Transpiration requires all four items to function successfully. The roots are required as the source of the water, and the Xylem is required as the tube to carry the water. The stomata allows for evaporation which creates a pressure difference between the top of the Xylem and the bottom (much the same as when you suck on a straw). Capillary action is the process by which water's cohesive nature allows it to travel up the Xylem. Capillary action is also what causes water to travel up paper when an edge is dipped into a dish of water.

106. The Doppler Effect is associated most closely with which property of waves?
(Skill 39.3)(Rigorous)

   A. amplitude.
   B. wavelength.
   C. frequency.
   D. intensity.

Answer: C. Frequency.

The Doppler Effect accounts for an apparent increase in frequency when a wave source moves toward a wave receiver or apparent decrease in frequency when a wave source moves away from a wave receiver. (Note that the receiver could also be moving toward or away from the source.) As the wave fronts are released, motion toward the receiver mimics more frequent wave fronts, while motion away from the receiver mimics less frequent wave fronts. Meanwhile, the amplitude, wavelength, and intensity of the wave are not as relevant to this process (although moving closer to a wave source makes it seem more intense). The answer to this question is therefore (C).

107. **Which of the following terms does not describe a way that the human race has had a negative impact on the biosphere? (Skill 39.5)(Rigorous)**

   A. Biological magnification
   B. Pollution
   C. Carrying Capacity
   D. Simplifcation of the food web

Answer: C. Carrying Capacity

Most people recongize the harmful effects that pollution has cause, espically air pollution and the concept of Global Warming. Pollution, and regular use of pesticides and herbicides introduce toxins in the food web, biological magnification realtes to how the concetration of these toxins increases the farther you move away from the source, so that animals at the top of the food chain, for example Bald Eagles, develop dangerous levels of toxins, and maybe responcible for declining birth rates in some species. Simplification of the food web, has to do with a small variety farming crops replacing large habitats, and thus shrinking or destroying some ecosystems. Carrying Capacity on the other hand is simply a term that relates amount of life a certain habitat can sustain, it is term independent of human action, so the answer is (C). This is not to say that the number of humans is not having an impact, we are overpopulating the planet, in doing so moving past the carrying capacity of many habitats.

108. **Surface ocean currents are caused by which of the following? (Skill 39.6)(Average Rigor)**

   A. temperature.
   B. density changes in water.
   C. wind.
   D. tidal forces.

Answer: C. wind

A current is a large mass of continuously moving oceanic water. Surface ocean currents are mainly wind-driven and occur in all of the world's oceans (example: the Gulf Stream). This is in contrast to deep ocean currents which are driven by changes in density. Surface ocean currents are classified by temperature. Tidal forces cause changes in ocean level however they do not effect surface currents.

109. **Which of the following is not a way in which alcohol, drugs, or tobacco affect the normal processes of the human body? (Skill 40.2)(Rigorous)**

    A. Absorption of nutrients
    B. Interference with physical and mental development
    C. Damaging developing organs
    D. Boosting the immune system

Answer: D. Boosting the immune system.

Depending on the substance, alcohol, drugs, and tobacco are all toxic items in the human body. They can slow down or speed up the absorption of nutrients, can have devastating affect on the development of mental and physical processes, and their effect on developing organs can cause major diseases such as bronchitis and asthma. The one thing they do not do, despite wishful thinking, is to positively effect the body by boosting the immune system.

110. **Which of the following causes the aurora borealis? (Skill 40.3)(Rigorous)**

    A. gases escaping from earth
    B. particles from the sun
    C. particles from the moon
    D. electromagnetic discharges from the North pole.

Answer: A. particles from the sun

Aurora Borealis is a phenomenon caused by particles escaping from the sun. The particles escaping from the sun include a mixture of gases, electrons and protons, and are sent out at a force that scientists call solar wind. Together, we have the Earth's magnetosphere and the solar wind squeezing the magnetosphere and charged particles everywhere in the field. When conditions are right, the build-up of pressure from the solar wind creates an electric voltage that pushes electrons into the ionosphere. Here they collide with gas atoms, causing them to release both light and more electrons.

**111. Which is a form of precipitation?
(Skill 40.6)(Easy Rigor)**

    A. snow
    B. frost
    C. fog
    D. All of the above

Answer: A. snow

Snow is a form of precipitation. Precipitation is the product of the condensation of atmospheric water vapor that falls to the Earth's surface. It occurs when the atmosphere becomes saturated with water vapor and the water condenses and falls out of solution. Frost and fog do not qualify as precipitates.

**112. Which layer of the atmosphere would you expect most weather to occur?
(Skill 41.5)(Rigorous)**

    A. Troposphere
    B. Thermosphere
    C. Mesosphere
    D. Stratosphere

Answer: A. Troposphere

The troposphere is the lowest portion of the Earth's atmosphere. It contains the highest amount of water and aerosol. Because it touches the Earth's surface features, friction builds. For all of these reasons, weather is most likely to occur in the Troposphere.

113. Which of the following is the most accurate definition of a non-renewable resource?
(Skill 41.7)(Rigorous)

A. A nonrenewable resource is never replaced once used.
B. A nonrenewable resource is replaced on a timescale that is very long relative to human life-spans.
C. A nonrenewable resource is a resource that can only be manufactured by humans.
D. A nonrenewable resource is a species that has already become extinct.

Answer: B. A nonrenewable resource is replaced on a timescale that is very long relative to human life-spans.

Renewable resources are those that are renewed, or replaced, in time for humans to use more of them. Examples include fast-growing plants, animals, or oxygen gas. (Note that while sunlight is often considered a renewable resource, it is actually a nonrenewable but extremely abundant resource.) Nonrenewable resources are those that renew themselves only on very long timescales, usually geologic timescales. Examples include minerals, metals, or fossil fuels. Therefore, the correct answer is (B).

114. "Neap Tides" are especially weak tides that occur when the Sun and Moon are in a perpendicular arrangement to the Earth, and "Spring Tides" are especially strong tides that occur when the Sun and Moon are in line. At which combination of lunar phases do these tides occur (respectively)?
(Skill 42.4)(Rigorous)

A. Half Moon and Full Moon
B. Quarter Moon and New Moon
C. Gibbous Moon and Quarter Moon
D. Full Moon and New Moon

Answer: B. Quarter Moon, and New Moon

"Spring tides" are especially strong tides that occur when the Earth, Sun and Moon are in line, allowing both the Sun and the Moon to exert gravitational force on the Earth and increase tidal bulge height. These tides occur during the full moon and the new moon. "Neap tides" occur during quarter moons, when the sun is illuminating half of the Moon's surface, (the term quarter is used to refer to the fact that the Moon has traveled 1/2 of it's way there its cycle, not the amount of the surface illuminated by the Sun.) A Gibbous Moon describes the Moon between Full and Quarter.

115. Earth is the only planet known to have life. This is because Earth:
(Skill 43.1)(Average Rigor)

    A. is far enough from the Sun to be too hot.
    B. is close enough to the Sun to receive its warmth.
    C. has water.
    D. all of the above.

Answer D: all of the above.

As the third planet way from the Sun, Earth is perfectly positioned to receive the Sun's warmth but far enough away to be protected from its extreme heat and solar flares. Earth is the only planet known to have water, which enables life.

116. A star's brightness is referred to as
(Skill 44.2)(Easy Rigor)

    A. magnitude
    B. mass
    C. apparent magnitude
    D. Intensity

Answer: A. magnitude

Magnitude is a measure of a star's brightness. The brighter the object appears, the lower the number value of its magnitude. The apparent magnitude is how bright an observer perceives the object to be. Mass has to do with how much matter can be measured, not brightness. The term intensity is not defined in reference to stars.

117. Which of the following is the best explanation of the fundamental concept of Uniformitarianism?
(Skill 45.1)(Rigorous)

A. The types and varieties of life between will see a uniform progression over time.
B. The physical, chemical and biological laws that operate in the geologic past operate in the same way today.
C. Debris from catastrophic events (i.e. volcanoes, and meteorites) will be evenly distributed over the effected area.
D. The frequency and intensity of major geologic events will remain consistent over long periods of time.

Answer: B. The physical, chemical and biological laws that operate in the geologic past operate in the same way today.

While answers (A), (C), and (D) all could represent theories that have been proposed in geology, none of them is an accurate explanation of uniformitarianism. The general idea can be expressed, by the quote, "the present is the key to the past". The forces that we can observe today have been at work over most of Earth's history.

118. Which of the following units is not a measure of distance?
(Skill 45.5)(Average Rigor)

A. AU (astronomical unit).
B. Light year.
C. Parsec.
D. Lunar year.

Answer: D. Lunar year.

Although the terminology is sometimes confusing, it is important to remember that a 'light year' (B) refers to the distance that light can travel in a year. Astronomical Units (AU) (A) also measure distance, and one AU is the distance between the sun and the earth. Parsecs (C) also measure distance, and are used in astronomical measurement- they are very large, and are usually used to measure interstellar distances. A lunar year, or any other kind of year for a planet or moon, is the time measure of that body's orbit. Therefore, the answer to this question is (D).

119. **A telescope that collects light by using a concave mirror and can produce small images is called a _____.**
(Skill 45.6)(Rigorous)

   A. radioactive telescope
   B. reflecting telescope
   C. refracting telescope
   D. optical telescope

Answer: B. reflecting telescope

Reflecting telescopes are commonly used in laboratory settings. Images are produced via the reflection of waves off of a concave mirror. The larger the image produced the more likely it is to be imperfect. Refracting telscopes use lenses to bend light to focus the image. The term optical telescope can be used to describe both reflecting and refracting telescopes.

120. **Many times science teachers are faced with the dilemna of not having enough funds to perform all the wonderful science laboratory exercises that they find. Which of these items might help with this problem?**
(Skill 46.1)(Average Rigor)

   A. Getting supplies at hardware and grocery stores.
   B. Applying for Grant Money.
   C. Use of School Gardens or natural areas.
   D. All of the above.

Answer: D. All of the above

As a teacher anything you can get to help you teach science go for it, as long as it doesn't break any laws or put anyone (you or students) in danger. Lots of common supplies can be found in your local stores. In addition to government grant moneys there are many private sources of grant money that you can pursue. Too often we try to teach about nature while sitting in the classroom, if you can get outdoors, then do so.

121. **Which type of student activity is most likely to expose a student's misconceptions about science?**
   (Skill 46.1)(Average Rigor)

   A. Multiple-Choice and fill-in-the-blank worksheets.
   B. Laboratory activities, where the lab is laid out step by step with no active thought on the part of the student.
   C. Teacher- lead demonstrations.
   D. Laboratories in which the students are forced to critically consider the steps taken and the results.

Answer: D. Laboratories in which the student are forced to critically consider the steps taken and the results.

Answer (A) is a typical retain and repeat exercise, where a student just needs to remember the answer and doesn't need to understand it. Answer (B), is often called a cookie cutter lab because everything fit to a specific plan. Students are often able to guess the right answer without understanding the process. Teacher lead demonstrations can be interesting for the students and my challenge a student's misconceptions. A student's misconceptions are often firmly routed and will require critical thought and reflection by the student for it to change, often an attempt to illuminate a student's misconception doesn't get rid of it, but gets incorporated into their inaccurate understanding of the universe. Answer (D) requires active mental participation on the behalf of the student and thus is most likely to alter their personally understanding. These types of labs are often referred to as guided discovery laboratories.

122. **Which of the following is not an appropriate aspect of scientific attitude?**
   (Skill 46.7)(Average Rigor)

   A. Scientific Curiousity.
   B. Scientific Open-mindedness.
   C. Scientific Conformity.
   D. Scientific Skepticism.

Answer: C. Scientific Conformity.

Open mindedness and curiosity are two of the backbones of science. It is important not to confuse conformity with reproduceability. Scientific Skepticism is a method of obtaining knowledge through systematic doubt and continual testing. A skeptical scientist is one who refuses to accept certain types of claims without subjecting them to a systematic investigation. This is an important skill to develop in students. Thus, the answer is (C).

123. Which is the correct order of methodology?
(Skill 46.8)(Rigorous)

1. collecting data
2. planning a controlled experiment
3. drawing a conclusion
4. hypothesizing a result
5. re-visiting a hypothesis to answer a question

A. 1,2,3,4,5
B. 4,2,1,3,5
C. 4,5,1,3,2
D. 1,3,4,5,2

Answer: B. 4,2,1,3,5

The correct methodology for the scientific method is first to make a meaningful hypothesis (educated guess), then plan and execute a controlled experiment to test that hypothesis. Using the data collected in that experiment, the scientist then draws conclusions and attempts to answer the original question related to the hypothesis. This is consistent only with answer (B).

124. The control group of an experiment is:
(Skill 46.8)(Average Rigor)

A. An extra group in which all experimental conditions are the same and the variable being tested is unchanged.
B. A group of authorities in charge of an experiment.
C. The group of experimental participants who are given experimental drugs.
D. A group of subjects that is isolated from all aspects of the experiment.

Answer: A. An extra group in which all experimental conditions are the same.

A group of authorities in charge of an experiment, while they might be in control, they are not a control group. The group of experimental participants given the experimental drugs would be the experimental group, and a group of subjects isolated from all aspects of the experiment would not be part of the experiment at all. Thus, the answer is (A).

125. What is the scientific method?
(Skill 46.8)(Average Rigor)

A. It is the process of doing an experiment and writing a laboratory report.
B. It is the process of using open inquiry and repeatable results to establish theories.
C. It is the process of reinforcing scientific principles by confirming results.
D. It is the process of recording data and observations.

Answer: B. It is the process of using open inquiry and repeatable results to establish theories.

Scientific research often includes elements from answers (A), (C), and (D), but the basic underlying principle of the scientific method is that people ask questions and do repeatable experiments to answer those questions and develop informed theories of why and how things happen. Therefore, the best answer is (B).

CPSIA information can be obtained
at www.ICGtesting.com
Printed in the USA
JSHW021403110422
24807JS00007B/384